Anonymous

Report from the Committee of Secrecy

Appointed to enquire into the causes of the war in the Carnatic, and of the British possessions in those parts

Anonymous

Report from the Committee of Secrecy
Appointed to enquire into the causes of the war in the Carnatic, and of the British possessions in those parts

ISBN/EAN: 9783337012601

Printed in Europe, USA, Canada, Australia, Japan

Cover: Foto ©Suzi / pixelio.de

More available books at **www.hansebooks.com**

APPENDIX, N° 58.

Extract of Bombay Select Committee, the 28th November, 1774.

At a Committee;

PRESENT,

The Honourable William Hornby, Esquire, President and Governor,
Daniel Draper,
John Watson, William Tayler.

The Wᵒ Peter Elwin Wrench,
Esquire, indisposed.

READ, and approved, our Proceedings under the 25th Instant, being our last Consultation.

The President acquaints the Committee, that he has desired this Meeting purposely to lay before them a Letter he received Yesterday from Mr. Robert Henshaw, who at present resides at Goa, dated the 31st Ultimo; giving an Account of the Military and Marine Force lately arrived at Goa from Portugal, and of the Intentions of the Portugueze speedily to attempt the Recovery of the Dominions they formerly possessed to the Northward of this Place, and particularly the Island of Salsette and Bassein.

This Letter being accordingly read, and taken under mature and deliberate Consideration; it is observed, that there appears no Doubt of the Portugueze Intentions against the Island of Salsette; and as surely as they attempt the Conquest of that Island with their present Force, so surely they will gain the Possession of it; which Event will not only put it out of our Power ever to acquire the Possession of it for the Honourable Company, who have so frequently expressed their ardent Wishes to obtain it, but will also be attended with infinite Prejudice to the Trade and Interest of the Honourable Company here, by reducing their Customs and Revenues in a very great Degree, as the Portugueze, by the Possession of Salsette, will become Masters of the Passes Inland, and consequently it will be entirely in their Power to obstruct our Trade, and to lay whatever Impositions they please upon it, which they were formerly so prone on every Occasion to do; and we therefore think it becomes our undoubted Duty to endeavour, to the utmost of our Power, to prevent it if possible from falling into their Hands without the least Delay, by taking it ourselves; and it is observed that a more favourable Opportunity than the present one, will probably never again offer, as by the Divisions in the Maratta Government there is now no Head in that Empire, and it will be out of the Power of either Party to send any effectual Force to obstruct our Proceedings.

The President hereupon acquaints the Committee, that agreeable to their Recommendation in the Month of March last, he has continued to temporize with the People, who made Proposals to him for the Delivery of the Island into our Hands; that they have since been frequently very pressing with him on the Subject, and that they are now equally desirous as before of giving up the Island to the Honourable Company.

The Committee taking all these Circumstances under Consideration, together with the Negociation now depending with Ragoba, as well as the Situation of Mr. Mostyn at Poonah, who is within the Power of the ministerial Party, are unanimously of Opinion, it is a Duty highly incumbent on them to prevent the Portugueze from attaining Possession of the Island of Salsette, by gaining Possession of it for the Honourable Company: Resolved, therefore, that we close with the Offers made for giving it up with the utmost Expedition, and that we pursue the speediest Means in our Power for effecting it, by sending a Body of Forces to gain Possession of it in the Manner that may be agreed on between the President and the Persons who have treated with him for that Purpose.

The President is accordingly desired to, and impowered to close immediately, on the most moderate Terms he can obtain, with the Persons who have been treating with him for the Delivery of Salsette; and every other Preparation must in Consequence be made for effecting this desirable End.

And in order that this Proceeding may not affect the Negociation depending with Ragoba, Mr. Gambier must be apprized of our Intentions, and directed to assure him, that if he will not be induced to cede the Island of Salsette to the Company, we will give it up to him (on his granting us what we may deem an Equivalent for it, and paying the Charges we shall incur by it) whenever he may be in full Possession of the Maratta Empire; our only Intention at this Time being to prevent it falling into the Hands of the Portugueze, which, from the present Situation of the Affairs of the Marattas, most undoubtedly would shortly be the Case, unless we pursue the necessary Measures to prevent it.

Mr. Mostyn must also be advised of our Intention, and of the Motives that have impelled us to it; and as we hope this Step will not be the Means of breaking that good Understanding which has till now subsisted with the Ministry at Poona, we wish him to continue there, and to endeavour to reconcile the Ministry to the Measures we are pursuing, giving them the same Assurances in case they prevail in their Contest with Ragoba, as we have directed Mr. Gambier to give to Ragoba. But should Mr. Mostyn be convinced, on his being acquainted with our Inteutions, that he can no longer remain with Safety to his Person, we then permit him to come away, though we much hope this will not be the Case, as we think his continuing at Poona will be the Means of reconciling the Ministry to the Measure, and serve to convince them of the Sincerity of our Professions.

We deem it necessary here to remark, that we have not yet heard of the Arrival at Bengal of such of the Council lately appointed by Act of Parliament as were to proceed from England, and consequently we are not restricted by that Act from undertaking this Affair; but even had we heard of their Arrival in the Form prescribed by the Act, we must think the Necessity of executing this Measure without any Delay, and it being entirely agreeable to the repeated Orders of the Honourable the Court of Directors, would fully authorize us for undertaking it without waiting for the Permission of the Governor General and Council, agreeable to a Clause in the said Act, which provides for such a Contingency.

As we shall probably be in want of some additional Force at the Presidency, in case the Matters now on Foot should be executed; it is agreed to embrace this Opportunity of reducing the Garrisons of Tellicherry and Anjengo.

Resolved, therefore, that the Military Force at the latter Place shall henceforward consist only of One Subaltern Officer, (who for the present is to be Lieutenant Brownrigg) with Three Serjeants, Three Corporals, and One Drummer, and Thirty-six private Topasses of Infantry, with One Bombardier, Two Gunners, and Two Matrosses of Artillery; the Remainder must be sent hither by the first Opportunity.

The whole Company of Europeans, with their Officers, except Ten private, now doing Duty at Tellicherry, must be withdrawn, and sent here as soon as possible, and the future Garrison of that Place must be considered as compleat without them.

Letters to the Chiefs at Tellicherry and Anjengo must be prepared, to apprize them of our Resolution. Letters also to Mr. Gambier and to Mr. Mostyn, must be wrote agreeable to our foregoing Minutes; but that to the latter must not be forwarded till Matters are so far advanced, as to put it out of the Power of the Ministry in any Degree to obstruct our Views, in case Mr. Mostyn should communicate our Intentions to them; but he must also have Time to come away before the Affair becomes public, in case he should deem it absolutely necessary to do so.

Adjourned.

Wm. Hornby,
D. Draper,
W. Tayler,

Geo. Skipp,
Sec.

APPENDIX, N° 58.

To the Honourable William Hornby, Esquire, President and Governor, &c.

Honourable Sir,

I have already publickly advised the Board of the Arrival of Don Joze Pedro de Camera, &c. and the Reason I have been so long silent to your Honour on this Subject, arose from a Desire of informing you, with some Degree of Certainty, of the Force and Intentions of the Portuguese. The Capture of the St. Anna, a Forty Gun Ship, by the Marattas, has awakened the Court of Lisbon, and spirited it up to take Satisfaction for the Insult committed on the Flag of Portugal; for this Purpose it was that the above Gentleman, a General Officer of approved Abilities in his Profession, and in whom were united the Requisites necessary to insure Success in such an important Undertaking, was appointed Governor and Captain General of India. Since his Arrival, very many Alterations and great have taken Place. In the King's Yards they work double Tides in preparing the Fleet. Gallivats that have been unemployed these Seven Years (a few only excepted, used as Luggage Boats) are fitting out with the utmost Expedition, and a Bomb Vessel is ordered to be prepared. When ready, their Force by Sea consists as follows, viz.

		Guns.			Guns.
Madre de Deos	—	70	Conceicao	—	70
St. Francis Havier	—	44	Crusario	—	36
Penha de Franca	—	30	St. Miguel	—	30
St. Antonio, Grab	—	22	Two Sloops, each	—	12

Fifteen Gallivats, mounting each One heavy Prow Gun, and from Four to Six Swivels each.

The Madre de Deos and Crusario arrived this Season from Portugal, and are to remain in India until such Period as Six Frigates of 20 Guns each are built at Demaun, which the King has ordered, and whose Iron of every Denomination came from Portugal in the Madre de Deos, together with Cordage, Canvas, &c. and Cannon compleat for the Whole. The Madre de Deos her lower Decks are 24 lbs.

Their Military Force consists of Four Regiments quite compleat; Three whereof are Infantry, and One of Artillery; viz.

	Col.	Lt.Col.	Maj.	Capt.	Lieut.	Ensi.	Privates.	Total.
Regiment of Henriques	1	1	1	7	7	7	455	479
Regiment of Britto	1	1	1	7	7	7	455	479
Regiment of	—	—	—	—	—	—	455	479
Regiment of Artillery	1	1	1	14	14	14	700	745
	3	3	3	28	28	28	2,065	2,158

I have not inserted the Officers of the Third Regiment, as it is not yet formed, the Men arriving only this and the last Season, and no one as yet appointed to the Command. The Whole is commanded by the above Henriques, who is a Brigadier General. Exclusive of the foregoing, the King has ordered a Legion to be formed of Sepoys, to be cloathed as the English, and to consist of 1,200 private Men, exclusive of Officers; to each Company, One European Captain and One Lieutenant. To this Legion is joined the Two Troops of European Horse now here, consisting of 75 private Men each. The Command of this Legion is given by his Majesty, by Special Commission, to Don Antonio Joze de Nourontia, the famous Bishop of Halicarnassus, known over India by the Title the Nizam gave him of Nabob Delour Jehung Behadur

I have given your Honour this Detail of their Naval and Military Force, previous to what I have to advise your Honour of their Intentions, that you may therefrom be enabled to judge of their Abilities to execute the Schemes they have in View.—The Recovery of the Province of the Norte, or what we call Salsette, is their primary Object; and the Capture of the Saint Anna, with the Forts of Gheriah, Sevendroog, &c. their secondary Object. My Reasons for supposing such, arise as follows: The

 Bishop

Bishop abovenamed, who, exclusive of the Command of the Sepoys, is Conseiller du Guerre, has in several Interviews I have had with him, endeavoured to draw from me my Opinion on several Questions he put to me. First Time he stated these Questions, he begged my Sentiments of a Union between us and the Portugueze against the Marattas. If I judged it feasible? If Bombay could make such a Union, without previously obtaining Orders from the Governor General at Bengal? If I judged a Proposition of this Nature would be agreeable to Bombay? and in case of a Union, did I think that Bombay would consent to the Portugueze having the Province of the Norte? —To these Points, I need not advise your Honour what Reply I made.—In a Second Interview, he renewed the Subject; I was silent; he then asked me, If it was true, the Report that prevailed here, that Bombay was on the Eve of joining one of the Parties now contending for the Maratta Government, and that in Recompence, ere the Assistance marched, the Island of Salsette was to be delivered over to us for ever? —I was about to reply, when he proceeded and said, he was well convinced, that if such was the Case, his Majesty's Troops would join the adverse Party, first protesting against the Proceedings of Bombay (mere Portugueze Bombast) for that his most Faithful Majesty still deemed Salsette Part of his Dominions, as he did the Ship Saint Anna, a Vessel of his Fleet; and that he was determined to rescue the one and the other from the Hands of those who so unjustly detained them. I have been repeatedly asked by many here (Persons I am convinced employed to pump me, as the Expression is) of the Intentions of Bombay regarding Salsette, &c. and whether I could procure any Charts of that Island, or Plan of Bassein and Tannah Forts, and if the Passage round the Island was known to us; with numberless other Questions. In short, I find from many, but especially from the Bishop of Halicarnassus, that it is determined upon, and that very speedily, the Reduction of the Province of the Norte, unless we are beforehand with them, which they much suspect, and in which Case they will protest most loudly against us; but that is all they have done hitherto, and as much as they will then do, for more they dare not do, without special and further Orders from Portugal. The Governor has also hinted as much to me, with a View, as I can but think, that it should be made known to you, in the Belief that the Knowledge of such his most Faithful Majesty's Intentions, would prevent Bombay carrying into Execution any Schemes they might entertain against the Island of Salsette. In short, it seems here no Secret the Intentions of the Portugueze; and all those who formerly had Estates on Salsette when the Property of the Portugueze, are as conscious to Appearance of once more possessing, as I am certain of my Existence.

I remain, with the greatest Esteem and Respect,
Honourable Sir,
Your most obliged and obedient Servant,
Robert Henshaw.

Goa,
31st October 1774.

List of Officers arrived at Goa from Portugal, 1774.

Artillery, viz.

Colonel.	Theodosio de Sa. Raboxa.
Lieutenant Colonel.	Gustavus Adolphus Hercules de Chermont.
Captains.	João Nunes de Figureido,
	Pedro Paulo de Foneca,
	Jozes Lopez da Souza,
	Ignacio Joquim de Castro,
	Antonio Pedro Gallego Sarmanho,
	João Baptista Viera Godinho.
First Lieutenants.	Feliciano Antonio Falcao,
	João Baptista Dias,
	Theotino Gomez,
	Antonio Fernandez,
	João Joze Baptista,
	Custodio Cæsar de Faria,
	Joze Manoel Pinto de Faria
Second Lieutenants.	Domingo Janeiro Azario,
	Lucas Joã,

Joze

	Joze Coelho de Amoral,
	Manoel Godinzho da Mira,
	Bento Alexis de Souza.
Major of the Regiment.	Antonio Joze de Sepulvara.
	Legion, viz.
	Cavalry, viz.
Lieutenant Colonel.	Antonio de Affa Castello Branco.
Major.	
Captains.	Antonio Duarte de Fonceca,
	Silverco Manoel.
Lieutenant.	Diogo James Murphy, Irish.
	Sepoys, viz.
Majors.	Joquin Vincente Godinho de Mira,
	Joze Lewis Pinti de Souza.
Captains.	Francisco Godinho de Mira,
	Lewis Mendez Tores,
	Antonio Manoel,
	Francisco Ricardo,
	Francisco Soanes.
Lieutenants.	Bernardino Joze Contento,
	João Manoel Nogazette,
	Antonio Telli de Menezes,
	Antonio Joze de Olivarez.
Infantry Captains.	John Emanuel Wade, Irish,
	Philip Manoel Franco.

Tuesday 29th November 1774. Signed the following Letters to Mr. Mostyn at Poona, and to Mr. Gambier at Surat; the latter was directly forwarded, but the former is to be detained some Days for the Reasons given in our Minutes of Yesterday.

To Thomas Mostyn, Esquire.

Sir,

We have received undoubted Intelligence that the Portugueze are fitting out a very respectable Armament at Goa, with Intention of acquiring, with the utmost Expedition, the Possession of the Dominions formerly belonging to them; and in particular the Island of Salsette. Orders from Europe, and a considerable Sea and Land Force being sent from thence, have enabled them to undertake this Expedition.

Their being in Possession of the Island of Salsette, would be of the utmost Detriment to the Trade and Interests of the Honourable Company here, by having it in their Power to obstruct the former, as they would become possessed of the Passes Inland, when they would undoubtedly lay whatever Impositions they pleased upon it, as they were formerly so prone, on every Occasion, to do. Besides, on such an Event, we could have no Hopes of ever acquiring it for the Honourable Company, who, as you well know, have long much wished to become possessed of it.

In this Situation we have esteemed it our undoubted Duty to be beforehand with the Portugueze, by acquiring Possession of it for our Honourable Employers; and have in consequence determined to embrace some Offers which have been made for facilitating this Acquisition.

We have chiefly been impelled to this Step, by a thorough Conviction that it would otherwise fall into the Hands of the Portugueze; as from the present Situation of the Affairs of the Marattas, it must be out of their Power to send such a Force as would be able to oppose them.

We still earnestly wish to remain on good Terms with the Marrattas; and hope this Step will not by any Means break that good Understanding which has so long subsisted. However, we do not absolutely direct that you should remain at Poona after the Receipt of this Letter, if you are convinced the Safety of your Person is endangered thereby; but if on the contrary no Harm can happen to yourself, we then much wish you should continue there, and direct that you endeavour to reconcile the Ministry to the Measure

Measure we have pursued, by acquainting them with our Motives for it; and by assuring them, in case their Party prevails in the present Contest, we shall then be ready to give it up (if they will not be induced to cede it to us) on their granting us what we may esteem an Equivalent, and paying the Expences we shall incur thereby.

In case you quit Poona, you will of course bring your Assistant with you; but we again tell you, we wish you may remain, in order to convince the Ministry of the Sincerity of our Professions.

We are
Your loving Friends.

Bombay Castle,
29 November 1774.

To Mr. Robert Gambier, at Surat.

Sir,

The Portugueze have this Season received a very considerable Supply of Men from Europe; their Naval Force is also put on a respectable Footing, and we have received undoubted Intelligence that they are fitting out an Armament with the utmost Expedition from Goa, with Intention of recovering the Dominions they formerly possessed to the Northward of this Place, and in particular the Island of Salsette.

As their being in Possession of Salsette would be of the utmost Detriment to the Trade and Interest of the Honourable Company in these Parts, by leaving it in their Power to obstruct our Trade, and lay whatever Impositions they please upon it, which they were formerly so prone on every Occasion to do; and as on such an Event, we could have no Hopes of ever procuring for our Honourable Employers the Possession of that Island, which they have so often expressed their Desire of attaining, we have therefore resolved, as our undoubted Duty, to acquire Possession of it for the Honourable Company.

We have in consequence determined to embrace some Offers that have been made us for facilitating the Acquisition of it; and a suitable Force will accordingly be sent in a few Days to effect it.

It is our Wish that this Step may not impede the Negociation at present depending with Ragoba; and we accordingly direct you to assure him, that no other Motives have impelled us to take this Step than to prevent it from falling into the Hands of the Portugueze, which it would most undoubtedly, as well from the Force they propose sending against it, as from the present Situation of the Affairs of the Marattas, which puts it out of their Power to send any Succours to prevent it.

This you are to explain to Ragoba; and to assure him that, provided he cannot be induced to cede it to our Honourable Employers, we will give it up to him on his granting what we may esteem an Equivalent for it, and paying the Expences that will be incurred thereby, so soon as he may be in full Possession of the Maratta Empire.

We are
Your loving Friends,

Bombay Castle,
29 November 1774.

A P P E N D I X, N° 59.

Extract of Bombay Select Committee, December the 1st, 1774.

OUR Address to the Honourable the Court of Directors, intended to be forwarded by our Honourable Masters Ship Thames, having been considered and approved, is this Day signed as follows:

Honourable Gentlemen,

By our Address of the 10th Ultimo, a Duplicate of which is inclosed, we informed you of the Proposals that had been made to us by Ragoba, through Mr. Gambier at Surat, for the Assistance of a Body of the Company's Forces against his Enemies, the ministerial

ministerial Party at Poona, in order to re-establish him in the Government of the Maratta Empire.

We also communicated our Resolution to assist him, provided such Matters were settled to our Satisfaction as we judged necessary to stipulate with him, in order that, should a Treaty take Place, it might turn out truly beneficial to the Honourable Company our Employers.

We have since received Two Letters from Mr. Gambier on the Subject, entered in our Diary under the 17th and 25th Ultimo, the last of which was accompanied by the Translate of a Treaty proposed by Ragoba; wherein, though his Offers fall far short of our Demands, he nevertheless proposed to cede a Territory to the Company near Surat, that, according to Mr. Gambier's Account, would produce an Annual Revenue of about Eight Lacks of Rupees; which, added to the Share of the Revenues the Guicawars at present receive from the Town and Purgunnahs of Broach, being near Three Lacks, which he also offered, made in the Whole about Eleven Lacks per Annum: He likewise proposed to deposit Six Lacks of Rupees in Money, and to give Security for the Payment of Half a Lack monthly, for Six Months, which was to be considered as the Expence of our Forces for that Term, which he proposed should be reckoned at a Lack and a Half of Rupees per Month, without further Account; and provided they continued with them longer than Six Months, he then proposed to make another Advance of Six Lacks, and to continue paying Half a Lack monthly as before; but he refused to cede the Island of Salsette or Bassein, which we demanded, amongst other Articles, for the Assistance we were to afford him.

Our Remarks on these Letters from Mr. Gambier are fully stated in our Minutes of the 17th and 25th Ultimo, and though we have by no Means agreed to the Terms of the Treaty as proposed by Ragoba, we have nevertheless been induced to recede in some Degree from our first Demands, as well with respect to the Sum to be previously deposited, as in regard to the Cession of the Islands of Salsette and Bassein.

As to the Deposit, our Demand was for Fifteen Lacks of Rupees, or Twenty if possible, as Security for the Expences of our Forces, and to ensure the Company from any Loss. Ragoba has rendered Six; and as Mr. Gambier has represented that he believes it to be out of Ragoba's Power, in his present Situation, to offer more, and as ample Security must be given for the monthly Payment for the Lack and a Half of Rupees for the Expences of your Forces, we have been induced so far to reduce our Demand in this Particular.

Ragoba is also very averse to the Cession of Salsette and Bassein, insomuch that insisting on those Places might probably have caused an entire Stop to be put to the depending Negociation. In Deference to the Opinion of your Honours, we much wish that he could have been prevailed upon to grant them to the Honourable Company; but we were at the same Time of Opinion, that it was by no Means for their Interest to run the Risk of oversetting the Whole on that Account, as much more material Advantages might be granted elsewhere; and we therefore determined to wave making any further Demand for those Places till a more favourable Opportunity: Those are the only Points in which we have any Ways receded from our First Demands.

The following are therefore the Terms on which we have at present offered to afford him the Honourable Company's Assistance:

That the Poona Share of the Revenue formerly annexed to the Government of Surat, from 30 Purgunnahs and 4 Cusbahs, amounting, according to the late Mr. Price's Statement entered in our Diary in the Month of May 1772, to about Twelve Lacks and a Half per Annum, be given up for ever:

That the Guicawar Share of the Broach Revenues, with any Revenues collected by the Poona Government, from the Broach Town and Purgunnah, amounting to about three Lacks per Annum, be also ceded for ever to the Company:

And that the Revenue now possessed by the Poona Government, which belonged to the Castle Governor at Surat, at the Time the Moguls were in the Fulness of their Power, be also made over to the Company, amounting to about three Lacks of Rupees.

The Whole of the foregoing amounts to about 18 Lacks and a Half of Rupees annually, which we have insisted shall be ceded for ever. There are also some other Articles of our Demands, all of which are specified in a Sketch of the Treaty we have drawn up and forwarded to Mr. Gambier, as entered under the 26th Ultimo, that in case Ragoba should embrace our Offers, no Time may be lost in entering into the necessary Engagements

gagements on that Account; and Mr. Gambier is accordingly impowered to enter into a Treaty on the Terms herein set down.

Should we obtain the Whole for the Company that is inserted in this Draft for a Treaty, or even should we be obliged to recede in some Degree from the Largeness of our present Demands, we must think we shall merit your Honours full Approbation of our Proceedings, as the Advantages that the Company will reap therefrom, will be considerable and lasting; and we think, that with the Body of Forces we propose sending to the Assistance of Ragoba, there can be little Doubt of his obtaining the full Possession of the Government of the Maratta Empire.

Thus this Matter stands at present, and we shall not fail to embrace the First Opportunity of advising you of the Result.

We have also another Affair of equal Importance at present in Agitation, owing to the Intelligence we received a few Days ago from Mr. Robert Henshaw, one of your Servants at present residing at Goa, of the Designs of the Portugueze to attempt the immediate Recovery of the Island of Salsette, and the other Places they formerly possessed to the Northward.

Mr. Henshaw's Letter is recorded under the 28th Ultimo; and being taken under the most mature Consideration, we could not entertain a Doubt of the Designs of the Portugueze, and were convinced, if they attempted the Conquest of Salsette in the present distracted Situation of the Maratta Government, with the large Force they can now command, that they would certainly make a Conquest of it, which it is our undoubted Duty if possible to prevent, by gaining immediate Possession of it for the Company; for, should the Portugueze acquire that Island, it would not only put it out of our Power ever to gain it for the Company, but would be attended with infinite Prejudice to their Trade and Interests at this Place; as by the Portugueze being in Possession of the adjacent Passes to the Inland Country, they would have it in their Power to obstruct our Trade, and to lay what Impositions they pleased upon it, which in former Times upon every Occasion they were so prone to do.

We accordingly resolved to attempt to gain it for the Honourable Company; and as the People who made Proposals to the President for delivering up the Island, as related in our Diary in the Month of March last, are still equally ready to do so now, we have impowered the President to close with their Offers on the most moderate Terms procurable; which he will do as soon as possible; and in the mean Time, every Preparation is making with that Secresy the Affair requires, or will admit of, to prevent a Disappointment, even should the Garrison at Tannah, the principal Fort, not be so ready to deliver it up, as we have Reason to conclude they will be.

For further Particulars respecting this Affair, permit us to refer you to our Diary, wherein is pointed out the Means we have pitched upon to prevent, as much as in our Power, the Negociation with Ragoba from being affected hereby; and as to Mr. Mostyn at Poona, we shall give him timely Intelligence of our Intentions, so that he may repair hither, in case he should esteem his Person in Danger by remaining at Poona till our Intentions become public.

As we may possibly be in Want of some additional Force at the Presidency, we have embraced this Opportunity of reducing the Garrisons at Tellicherry and Anjengo, and of fixing their Military Establishment much lower than before, as you will observe by our Minutes of the 28th; and we have also ordered, that all the great Guns at Anjengo, from 12 lbs. and upwards, shall be sent to the Presidency. By this Means, the Expences of both these Places will be annually much reduced; we therefore flatter ourselves, your Honours will approve of it: And as we can assure you, that in our Proceedings in general, we have no other Object in View, than what we esteem the Interest of our Honourable Employers, we trust that the Whole of our Proceedings will meet with your Honours Approbation.

We have the Hour to be, with much Respect,
Honourable Gentlemen,
Your most faithful Servants.

Bombay Castle,
1st December 1774.

APPENDIX, N° 60.

Extract of Bombay General Consultations, the 12th December 1774.

PRESENT,

The Honourable William Hornby, Esquire, President and Governor.
The W° Daniel Draper, Esquire, Robert Gordon,
Thomas Mostyn, Brice Fletcher,
William Tayler, Robert Garden.

BY Ten o'Clock this Morning, that Part of the Military Force intended to proceed by Land to Tanna, marched out of Town, commanded by Brigadier General Robert Gordon. At Seven, P. M. the Remainder of the Military Force intended to proceed to Tanna, embarked on board sundry Boats, and proceeded with the following Vessels and Gallivats to Tanna: Terrible Bomb, Adam Sheriff; Triumph Prahm, John Hall; Spy Cutter, Samuel Hardy; Otter Gallivat, Thomas Buncombe; Greyhound Gallivat, Walter Barlau; Lively's Prize Gallivat, Nathaniel Smith; Fly Gallivat, William Augustus Skynner; and Wolf Gallivat, Brice Hardy.——John Watson, Esquire, Superintendant, embarked on One of the above Vessels, and proceeded as Commander of the Marine Force to Tanna, with Instructions to the Brigadier General and himself, to consult and co-operate with each other for the Good of the Service.

At the same Time sailed out of Port, the Bombay Grab, George Emptage, to cruize.

Extract from Journal of Brigadier General Robert Gordon, on the Siege of Tanna and Reduction of the Island Salsette.

Monday, 12th December 1774.

This Day the Armament intended for the Reduction of the Island Salsette, set off from Bombay in the following Order; viz.

Marched by Land,

The General and his Staff,
Lieutenant Colonel Cockburn.

First Company of Grenadiers, 100 Private, with their Officers.
Second Company of Grenadiers, 100 Private, with their Officers.
The Two Grenadier Companies of the Second Battalion of Sepoys of 100 each, with Lieutenant Cadgu and Ensign Richardson.
Eighty Light Infantry from the Second Battalion of Sepoys, commanded by Ensigns Ormiston and Denson.
The Two Grenadier Companies of the Third Battalion of Sepoys, with their Officers, each Company 100 Private.
Two Three Pounders, with 50 Lascars, and the Proportion of Artillery Men, under Lieutenant Hallamby.
The Engineers, Captain Nelson, and Mr. Whitman.
Twenty Biggarees with Ten Chests of Ammunition.
Two European Carpenters with broad Axes.
Thirty Bhaldars with Iron Crows, &c.
Thirty Biggarees to carry Arrack.
Quarter Master and his Stores.

A P P E N D I X, N° 60.

Troops, &c. by Sea, under Colonel Egerton and Major Henry.

Captain Abington, 1st Company, 100 Private.

Lieutenant Henry,	Acting Ensign, Williams.
Ensign Jones,	Do, Do. Riddell.

Second Company 100 Private.

Lieutenant Panton, Bennet,	Ensign Newgent.

First Company, 2d Battalion, 100 Private.

Captain Farrer,	Ensign Symes.
Ensign O'Hara,	Acting Do. Brownrig.

520 Sepoys, with their Officers, under Captain Jackson.
122 Artillery Do.
150 Lascars.
70 Bhaldars and Biggarees.

An Abstract of the Above.

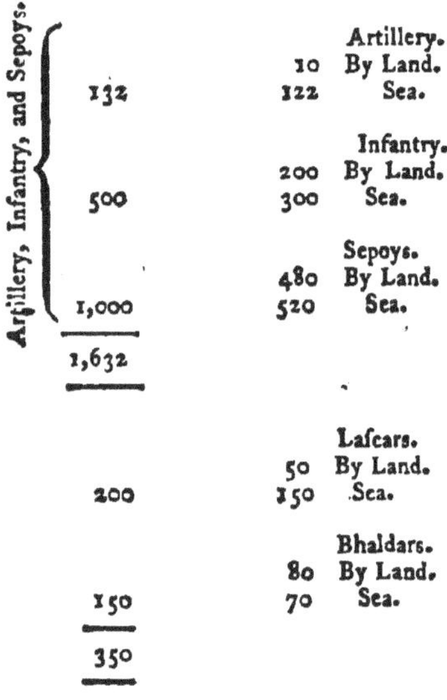

	Total	Number	
Artillery, Infantry, and Sepoys.			Artillery.
		10	By Land.
	132	122	Sea.
			Infantry.
		200	By Land.
	500	300	Sea.
			Sepoys.
		480	By Land.
	1,000	520	Sea.
	1,632		
			Lascars.
		50	By Land.
	200	150	Sea.
			Bhaldars.
		80	By Land.
	150	70	Sea.
	350		

Extract of Bombay Select Committee, the 30th December 1774.

Signed an Addrefs to the Honourable the Court of Directors, and a Letter to the Agent and Council of Buffora, which were difpatched in Duplicate per Dingey, bound to Mufcat.

Honourable Gentlemen,

By the Honourable Company's Ship Thames, which failed from hence under the 4th Inftant, to compleat her Cargo for Europe on the Coaft, we advifed your Honours from this Department of our Refolution to fend a fuitable Force to reduce the Ifland of Salfette, with the other adjacent Ifles. We alfo then apprized you at large with our Motives for fo doing; and we make no Doubt but that they will prove fufficiently fatisfactory to your Honours.

A Dingey

APPENDIX, Nº 61, 62.

A Dingey being now bound to Muscat, affords us an Opportunity to transmit to your Servants at Bussora this Address, which is solely to convey to you the pleasing Intelligence of the Reduction of the Fort of Tannah, the principal one on Salsette, which was taken by your Forces by Storm on the 28th Instant. The Fort of Versova was reduced a few Days before by Lieutenant Colonel Keating; and as there is no other Post on the Island of any Importance, the Conquest of the Whole is as good as compleated; on which happy Event we beg Leave to congratulate your Honours, assuring you it shall be our Study to make it as beneficial to you as possible. We shall shortly write you further by a Vessel we shall dispatch directly to Bussora. In the mean Time we have the Honour to remain, with much Respect,

Honourable Gentlemen,

Bombay Castle,
30th December 1774.

Your most obedient
and faithful Servants.

APPENDIX, Nº 61.

Extract of Bombay General Consultations, the 20th December 1774.

PRESENT,

The Honourable William Hornby, Esquire, President and Governor,
The Wo. Daniel Draper, Thomas Mostyn,
Brice Fletcher,
William Taylor, Robert Garden,
John Watson, Esquire, at Tanna.

Fort William. The Governor General and Council announcing their having assumed that Government.

READ a Letter from the Governor General and Council at Fort William, signifying their having taken upon them the Government of Bengal, in Virtue of the late Act of Parliament; and desiring to be furnished with the necessary Intelligence of the Company's political Concerns on this Side India.

Ordered, that a proper Letter be drawn out by the Secretary, giving them every Information that the said Act directs.

APPENDIX, Nº 62.

Extract of Fort William Secret Consultations, March 8th 1775.

PRESENT,

The Honourable Warren Hastings, Governor General, President,
Lieutenant General John Clavering,
The Honourable George Monson,
Richard Barwell, } Esquires.
Philip Francis, }

To the Honourable Warren Hastings, Esquire, Governor General, &c. Council at Fort William.

Honourable Sir, and Gentlemen,

CONFORMABLE to the Board's Address of this Date, we shall proceed to communicate to your Honour, &c. our Motives for determining at this Juncture to endeavour at acquiring Possession of the Island of Salsette, by Force of Arms, from the Marattas, the late Possessors of it, of which we particularly advised the Honourable the

Court

Court of Directors in our Address per Thames, several Days before the Receipt of your Letter of the 24th of October, wherein we were acquainted of your having taken Possession of the Government of Fort William in Virtue of the late Act of Parliament; and we flatter ourselves our Reasons for this Undertaking will appear so satisfactory and convincing to them as well as to you, that we shall be fully justified in our Proceedings. In the Commands of the Honourable Court of Directors to this Presidency, dated the 31st March 1769, an attested Copy of which we inclose for your Information, they are pleased to direct that we should be ever watchful to obtain the Island of Salsette, with the other Place therein pointed out, which they acquaint us must be the constant Objects we are always to have in View, in all our Treaties, Negociations, and Military Operations.

Again, the Honourable Company, in their Letter of the 6th April 1772, expresly direct, that Mr. Mostyn, one of our Members, should be established at Poona, for endeavouring to acquire that Island, with the other Places mentioned in their former Commands; and that they point out what they permit us to give as an Exchange.

Mr. Mostyn was accordingly fixed as Resident at the Maratta Durbar in the Year 1772, during the Life-time of Mhadarow, and about a Year before that Government fell into the Confusion it has been in since the Assassination of his Successor, Narrow Row; but he found no Probability of obtaining the Places desired by the Company, even though he was instructed to offer Broach, with its Territories (which we had just then acquired from the Nabob) in Addition to the Terms pointed out by our Honourable Employers.

Some Time after the Maratta State fell into that Confusion which at present distracts it, when in Fact there is no Head in that Empire still; we took no Step for attaining by Force of Arms the Possession of Salsette, notwithstanding the Opportunity was very favourable, and that we have Reason to conclude Salsette, with the smaller adjacent Isles, was ceded to the Crown by the Marriage Contract between King Charles the Second and the King of Portugal.

Previous however to the Receipt of your Letter to the Board, communicating the Intelligence of your Honour, &c. having taken upon you the Government of Bengal, we received Advice from Mr. Robert Henshaw, (a Gentleman in the Service then residing on some Business of the Company's at Goa) that the Portugueze had this Season received with their new Captain General, Don Joze Pedro de Camera, a very considerable Reinforcement of Men and Ships from Europe, and that their undoubted Designs were immediately to attempt at recovering from the Marattas the Possession of Salsette, Bassein, and the other Countries they formerly possessed, so far as Damman, called by them the Province of the North: An Extract of this Letter for your Information we also inclose.

We could not entertain a Doubt, from the distracted Situation of the Affairs of the Marattas, that the Portugueze, with the Force they commanded, would certainly gain Possession of Salsette, which is their favourite Object, and most probable of the other Parts of their former Possessions.

Had this Event taken Place, it would not only effectually have prevented us from ever acquiring Salsette for the Honourable Company, but the Portugueze would then again have had it in their Power to obstruct our Trade, by being in Possession of the principal Passes to the Inland Country, and to lay whatever Impositions they pleased upon it, which in former Times upon every Occasion they were so prone to do, which of course would have been of infinite Prejudice to the Trade, Revenues and Interest of the Company in these Parts, insomuch that we should in a great Measure have been subject to the Caprice of the Portugueze.

What then remained for us to do in this Emergency? Had we sat inactive Spectators of the Event, we should in our Opinions have betrayed the Interest of our Honourable Employers; had we wrote to you for Instructions and Advice, your Sentiments and Recommendations most probably must have arrived much too late to have enabled us to prevent the Execution of the Designs of the Portugueze; and though we had not any Account at this Time of your being established in your Government of Fort William, and consequently were not restricted by Law from pursuing such Measures as we judged most for the Interest of our Honourable Employers, yet as the Matter was in every Point of View of an important Nature, and we shortly expected to hear you were arrived, we should have been very glad to have submitted to your Judgment the Directions of the Measures necessary to be pursued, but we were obliged either to act at this very Juncture, or entirely to give up all Thoughts of attempting to avert the Evils with which

which we were threatened; we therefore determined, after the most mature Deliberation, in order to prevent the Mischiefs which must have ensued to the Interest of the Honourable Company, from the Portugueze being in Possession of Salsette, to attempt obtaining it for our Honourable Employers; and as some Offers had been made to the President some Months before by the Killidar of Sannah, the principal Fort on the Island, to deliver it to us for a Sum of Money, the President was impowered to close with him on the most moderate Terms; but the Killidar now excused himself from proceeding any further in the Business, alledging that the Ministry at Poonah having obtained Intelligence of the Designs of the Portugueze, had reinforced his Garrison, which put it out of his Power to deliver it up in the Manner he before wished to do: It therefore only remained for us to send such a Military and Marine Force as was judged necessary to reduce it; which was accordingly dispatched under the Command of Brigadier General Gordon, and Mr. Watson, Superintendant of our Marine; and we have the Pleasure to acquaint you that Sannah, the principal Fort on the Island, was taken by Storm on the 28th Instant, after our Army had been Fifteen Days before the Place. Versova, another Fort on Salsette, was also taken by a separate Party, under the Command of Lieutenant-Colonel Keating, and in Consequence the whole Island is now in our Possession.

The Island of Caranja also surrendered Yesterday, which compleats the Conquest we had determined to make near this Place.

The very Day after our Forces set out against Tanna, Part of the Portugueze Fleet appeared off this Port, with their Trade under its Convoy, bound to Damaun, a Settlement they still retain to the Northward of this Place; the Commander of which, so soon as he gained Intelligence of our Proceedings, delivered a small Protest, by the Directions, as he said, of the Captain-General of Goa; which shews the Necessity of the Measures we have pursued, and evidently corroborates Mr. Henshaw's Account of their Intentions; to this Protest we delivered a suitable Reply, and thus it rests between us.

The Revenues of Salsette amount to about 3,30,000 Rupees, on a moderate Calculation, and those of Caranja to about 40,000; we shall fix a suitable Civil Establishment at each of these Places, for their Government, and for the Collection of the Revenues, with a proper Military Force for their Protection.

Before we entered upon these Enterprizes, we judged it very necessary to recal Mr. Mostyn from Poona. Yet it is the farthest from our Wishes to occasion a Rupture between us and the Marattas, by the Steps we have been under the Necessity of pursuing; the President therefore, agreeable to our Resolution, will explain to the Ministerial Party at Poona, the real Motives for our Proceedings; and they shall be assured, that in case they gain the Advantage in the present Contest, by the Overthrow of Ragoba, that we shall resign the Islands to them so soon as they are in a Condition to defend them from the Portugueze, if they cannot be induced to cede them to us, provided also that they will give a suitable Equivalent or Compensation for them; for your Honour, &c. will observe, that we have been impelled to this Proceeding at this Juncture, and without your Concurrence, more from our Duty to prevent those Places from falling into the Hands of the Portugueze, than to retain them in the Company's Possession, though this last is much to be wished, as the Honourable Company are so desirous of them; and therefore, when we accommodate Matters with the Marattas, which shall be done as soon as possible, our utmost Endeavours shall be used to reconcile them to our keeping them.

The same Assurances as will be given to the Ministerial Party, will also be given to Ragoba, should he again obtain the supreme Power over the Marrattas, and we hope he may be easily satisfied; but it is necessary now to advise you of the Rise and Progress of a Negociation at present depending with him, which we shall accordingly here proceed to do.

Near Twelve Months ago, some Overtures were made by an Agent from Ragoba to Mr. Mostyn, our Resident at Poona, for the Assistance of Men and Money to re-establish his Affairs. His Demands however were so large, especially for Money, which he then much wanted, and it being our fixed Resolution by no Means to assist him with any, but on the contrary, that we should expect a considerable Sum from him, if we joined him with our Forces, as well as many Grants of Territory for our Employers, that the Matter was presently dropped.

About Four Months ago, Ragoba, by Means of an Agent he has residing at Surat, again made Proposals through the Chief of Surat, for the Assistance of a Body of Forces against his Enemies, the Ministerial Party at Poona. As we were of Opinion very material Advantages might be obtained for our Honourable Employers, by affording him some Assistance, we directed the Chief to enter upon a Negociation, and pointed out the Terms on which we might be induced to assist him with a Body of European Artillery and Infantry and Sepoys, to the Amount of about 2,500 Men; which, in Consideration of the Advantages the Company were to reap from the Alliance, we judged we might be able to spare some few Months on this Service. For this Assistance, we first demanded that a Deposit should be previously made of Fifteen, or if possible Twenty Lacks of Rupees, to answer the Expence; and, to insure the Company from any Loss, that the Islands of Salsette, Bassein, and the other small Islands adjacent to this Place, should be ceded to the Honourable Company, together with the Maratta Share of the Revenues of those Pergunnahs near to Surat, which formerly did belong to the Governor of that Town; all of which the Honourable the Court of Directors have repeatedly enjoined us to embrace every Opportunity in our Power to endeavour at obtaining: We also demanded the Share collected by the Guicavars, from the Territories of Baroche. We further ordered, that it should be stipulated, in case of a Treaty taking Place, that Ragoba should confirm all the former Treaties of this Presidency with the Marattas; that he should engage never to disturb the Tranquillity of the Company's Possessions in Bengal or the Carnatic; with some other less material Points which relate to this Place alone.

His Agent set out from Surat, to communicate our Demands to his Master, but partly owing to his Sickness, and to other Difficulties which attended his Journey, it was a considerable Time before he returned. At length however his Master's Proposals were communicated to us, which, as your Honour, &c. may suppose, at first fell far short of our Demands, and particularly Ragoba absolutely refused to cede the Islands of Salsette or Bassein, and declared it was totally out of his Power to deposit so large a Sum as was demanded.

Though we wished to obtain those Two Places, in Deference to the Opinion of our Honourable Employers; yet, as more material Advantages might be gained by a Cession of Territory near to Surat, we judged it improper to break off the Negociation on this Account, and therefore ordered that it should proceed, and from Time to Time gave the necessary Directions respecting it. At length, Ragoba's Agent agreed on the Part of his Master, to cede to the Company certain Pergunnahs near to Surat, whose annual Revenues amounted to Eighteen Lacks and Twenty-five thousand (18,25,000) Rupees, in Consideration of our assisting him with the Body of Forces we before mentioned. He also agreed to deposit Six Lacks (6,00,000) Rupees in Money, and to secure to the Company the Payment of the Sum of One and a Half Lack of Rupees per Month, for the Expence of the Force with which we were to assist him. The other Articles, such as his engaging never to disturb the Tranquillity of the Company's Possessions in Bengal, or the Carnatic, he readily consented to, as well as to confirm the Treaties with us, and the other less material Points we demanded.

Some Matters however remain still to be adjusted, relative to the Time when the Company were to be put in Possession of the Places to be ceded to them; which we insisted should be so soon as the Treaty was executed, as we were determined to proceed on the most secure Grounds, and to run no Hazards whatever, without ample Security in Hand. Agreeable to which, we instructed the Chief of Surat, that he might adjust the same on a proper Footing, which we had no Doubt he would speedily have done; but the Agent was at this Time absent from the City, collecting the Revenues of certain Districts near to Surat, for his Master, to enable him to pay the Advance of Six Lacks, (he being his Choutai in those Parts) and he was also taking Possession of the Purgunnahs that were to be delivered over to the Company; in which Business he was seized by a Party of the Ministerial Forces, and is at present confined by them. Ragoba had drawn near to Surat with his Army, which was very considerable, in order that our Forces might easily join him, as he expected the Treaty would be speedily finished; but suspecting some Treachery about this Time from a Part of his Troops, he speedily separated from them with those he could rely on, and for the present is actually retreating towards Delhi. He has however caused the Chief to be assured, that he shall speedily return, when he desired this Treaty might be concluded.

At the Time we first entered upon this Negociation, we had not heard that those Gentlemen of Your Board who have arrived from England had even left it; we therefore were not at all restricted by Law at that Time, from entering into any Engage-

ments

ments we judged beneficial to our Honourable Employers, to whom we have fully explained ourselves on the Subject, and whose Orders we were only pursuing by the Measures we had adopted; besides, if this Treaty takes Place, we shall obtain such a Revenue for the Honourable Company, as will enable this Presidency to support itself, and consequently relieve you from the Burthen of furnishing us annually with the large Sum we shall otherwise indispensably require, and therefore doubt not but it must be approved by the Company and you, Gentlemen; for it is most probable, should this Opportunity escape us, that such another will never again offer, and as it would have endangered the Whole had we put a Stop to the Treaty (after we received Intelligence of your Arrival) till your Concurrence was obtained, we therefore flatter ourselves we shall be fully justified in your Opinions for continuing the Negociation, as well as for concluding it, which we propose to take the First Opportunity in our Power of doing.

That Ragoba may take no Umbrage at the Measures regarding Salsette, our Motives for the same will be explained to him as advised in the preceding Part of this Letter; and the same Assurances will be given him in case of his Success (and with our Assistance, we can have little Doubt of his succeeding) as will be given to the ministerial Party.

As a considerable Part of our Marine Force is employed at Bussora and in the Persian Gulph, we have at present not a sufficient Marine for the Protection of our Trade on the Coast of Malabar from the Maratta Fleet, which it is most probable will attempt to make some Depredations on it. We shall therefore immediately address a Letter to the Commander in Chief of His Majesty's Squadron in India, who we conclude is now at Madras, advising him of the Situation of Affairs, and desiring him, if he cannot repair to the Coast with his whole Squadron, that he will send Two of his Ships for the Protection of the Trade on the Coast.

And as our Military Force is not sufficient to garrison our new Conquests, and for the other Service for which it may be presently wanted, we shall apply to the President and Council at Fort Saint George, desiring they will furnish us with Two Companies of European Infantry, and One compleat Battalion of Sepoys, until such Time as we may be able to return them by our own Levies being compleated.

We are, &c.

Bombay Castle, the 31st December 1774. William Hornby, &c. Council.

Extract of Fort William Secret Consultations, the 13th March 1775.

PRESENT,

The Honourable Warren Hastings, Governor General, President,
Lieutenant General John Clavering,
The Honourable George Monson,
Richard Barwell, } Esquires.
Philip Francis, }

Received from Commodore Sir Edward Hughes the following Letter and Inclosure:

Salisbury, in Madras Road, the 21st February, 1775.

Sir, and Gentlemen,

I arrived here on the 13th of this Instant; and received a Letter from the Governor and Council of Bombay, dated the 4th Ultimo, requesting me, if it should be too inconvenient for me to go there with the Squadron, to send at least Two ships thereof for the Protection of the Trade against the Maratta Fleet, which they were apprehensive would make Reprisals, in consequence of the seizing on the Island of Salsette; which, they say, they have judged it expedient to do. The Season of the Year is coming on when no Ship can act on the Coast of Malabar. I have however ordered the Captain of his Majesty's Ship the Sea Horse, when he hath landed the Company's Treasure at Bombay, and the Captain of His Majesty's Ship the Swallow, to act agreeable to the Request of the Governor and Council of Bombay, and to concert Measures with them, and occasionally with the Chiefs of the Company's Settlements on that

that Coast accordingly; but the Swallow having met with an Accident, it will detain her some Time longer before she can proceed to the Malabar Coast.

I should certainly be informed of the Motives for the seizing the Island of Salsette, or for any Act of Hostility committed by the Company's Servants; in consequence of which I may be required by them to lend the Aid of His Majesty's Ships under my Command.

I have the Honour to be, &c.

(Signed) Edward Hughes.

To Sir Edward Hughes, Knight, Commodore and Commander in Chief of His Majesty's Ships in the East Indies, at Fort Saint George.

Sir,

Our Letter of the 16th of September acknowledged the Receipt of your Favour of the 5th of August.

The Situation of Affairs here lately, rendered it very expedient for us to obtain Possession of Salsette, and of the smaller adjacent Islands from the Marattas. In consequence of which we sent such a Military and Marine Force as effected the Conquest of Salsette; Tannah, the capital Fort, being taken by Storm on the 28th Ultimo, after our Forces had been fifteen Days before the Place; and the whole Island is now in our Possession, with the other small adjacent Islands.

As it is absolutely necessary, till the Marattas may be reconciled to the Motives of our Proceedings, that the Trade up and down the Coast of Malabar should be protected by strong Convoys, lest the Maratta Fleet should attempt making Reprisals on it; and as a considerable Part of our Marine Force is at this Juncture employed in the Gulph, in so much that we have not sufficient Force for the Services required; we therefore strongly recommend to you, Sir, to proceed to this Coast with your Squadron for the Protection of the Trade; but should that be inconvenient, we then earnestly request you will send Two of the Ships under your Command for that Purpose, with Directions to the Commanders to concert the necessary Measures with us, and the Chiefs of our Settlements on the Coast, so as effectually to answer the desired End of affording the Protection it must necessarily require.

We are, &c.

(Signed) Wm. Hornby and Co.

Bombay Castle, 4th January 1775.

APPENDIX, Nº 63.

Extract of Fort William Secret Consultations, the 16th January 1775.

PRESENT,

The Honourable Warren Hastings, Governor General, President,
Lieutenant General John Clavering,
The Honourable George Monson,
Richard Barwell, } Esquires.
Philip Francis, }

READ the following Letter, this Instant arrived from Mr. Mostyn, Resident at Poona.

To the Honourable Warren Hastings, President, &c. Member of the Select Committee of Fort William.

Honourable Sir, and Sirs,

Having this Instant received a Letter from the Governor of Bombay, directing me immediately on the Receipt of it, to withdraw with the utmost Speed to the Presidency, this

this is purposely to acquaint you thereof, to prevent your addressing any further Letters to me at this Place; and inclose your Honours, &c. Duplicate of my last.

I am, &c.

(Signed) T. Mostyn.

Poona, 5th December 1774.

As the Removal of Mr. Mostyn from the Capital of the Maratta State has deprived the Board of the only Means of obtaining Intelligence in that Quarter; and as no Advice has been received of the Motives which have influenced the President and Council of Bombay to recall him in so sudden a Manner, which may render it unsafe or improper to supply his Place by any Appointment from this Presidency;

Resolved, that the following Letter be written to Bombay, and dispatched immediately in Duplicate, one Copy by Return of the Shaik Gullivat, and the other over Land.

To the Honourable William Hornby, President, &c. Council at Bombay.

Gentlemen,

We have just received Advice from Mr. Mostyn, your Resident at Poona, of your having suddenly recalled him from that Capital, with Advice to return to your Presidency with all Expedition; but as he does not mention the Reasons, we are altogether to conjecture, and must only conclude, that it proceeds from some important Consideration, of which we shall doubtless receive Advice. In the mean Time we cannot avoid expressing our Surprize at not having already received such Advice, and must impute the Delay to some Accident. As you were directed to give us regular Information of your political Proceedings, we repeat our Desire to be duly and punctually informed of every Circumstance in your political Transactions and Events, which may any Way affect the general System of the Company's Affairs committed to our especial Charge.

We are, &c.

Extract of Fort William Secret Consultations, the 30th January 1775.

PRESENT,

The Honourable Warren Hastings, Governor General, President,
Lieutenant General George Monson,
Richard Barwell, } Esquires.
Philip Francis, }

Received the Two following Letters from Fort St. George:

To the Honourable Warren Hastings, Esquire, Governor General, &c. Council.

Honourable Sir, and Sirs,

On the Third Instant we received a Letter from Mr. Mostyn, who, by Appointment from the Court of Directors, had resided for some Time past at Poona, advising, that on the 5th December, he had received Orders from the Governor and Council of Bombay to withdraw from thence, and repair to the Presidency with the utmost Speed. As he did not communicate to us the Reason for his sudden Recall, and the Gentlemen at Bombay gave us no Intimation on the Subject, we are at a Loss how to account for the same.

This Morning the President received a Letter from Captain Cook, commanding at Palamcotah, dated the 3d Instant, advising, that on the preceding Evening he received a Letter from a Gentleman at Anjengo, dated the 29th December, in which was the following Paragraph:

" A Pattamar Boat is just arrived from the Presidency, informing us that our Troops have taken the Field against the Marattas, and are now before Tanna. The Marattas have a large Fleet now looking out for our China Ships; but I make no

Doubt we ſhall ſoon hear of their being diſperſed, as there is a ſtrong one of ours fitting out at Tellicherry to go againſt them."

Although we have not received any Advices on this Subject from the Gentlemen at Bombay, neither can we aſſign the Reaſon of their engaging in Hoſtilities againſt the Marattas; yet, as the Intelligence, if true, is of the utmoſt Importance to the Company's Affairs, we have thought it proper to give your Honours, &c. the moſt early Intelligence for your Information, as that we may be favoured with your Sentiments reſpecting the Conduct to be obſerved by us, ſhould the Gentlemen at Bombay find it expedient to apply to us for Aſſiſtance, or to co-operate with them.

It is neceſſary for us to obſerve, that our Revenues and Reſources are very inadequate to our undertaking a War at any Rate; and our Situation with reſpect to the Nabob, on whom we muſt depend for Aſſiſtance, in caſe of our being obliged to take up Arms, has been fully explained to you in the Letter from the Board in their Military Department of 7 December laſt.

The Nabob has acquainted us, that by the lateſt Intelligence he learns, that Ragonut Raw, jealous of the Two Hindoſtan Chiefs, on Account of the ſame Letter he had intercepted, had ſeparated himſelf from them, and it was thought had arrived on the Banks of the Norbuddah, with about Ten thouſand Horſes, and was retiring towards the Malva Province.

We have the Honour to be, &c.
(Signed) A. Wynch,
Joſeph Smith,
A. M. Stone,
E. Stracey.

Fort Saint George,
10th Jan. 1775.

To the Honourable Warren Haſtings, Eſquire, Governor General, &c. Council.

Honourable Sir, and Sirs,

Since diſpatching our Letter of Yeſterday, private Advice is arrived from Tellicherry, which ſays, that our Troops had taken Poſſeſſion of Salſette and Baſſein; but no Particulars regarding the Capture are mentioned. The ſame Advice adds, that it ſeems the Portugueſe had determined to have poſſeſſed themſelves of thoſe Places, if we had not done it before them; that they have this Year brought on Three Frigates and Three Merchantmen, a large Quantity of warlike Stores, and are determined to repoſſeſs themſelves of ſome of the Territories they formerly enjoyed, and to put Goa on a different Footing.

We have the Honour to be, &c.
(Signed) A. Wynch,
Joſeph Smith,
A. M. Stone,
E. Stracey.

Fort Saint George,
11th Jan. 1775.

Reſolved, that a Council be ſummoned to meet To-morrow Morning in this Department, purpoſely for taking into Conſideration the above Two Letters, juſt arrived from Fort St. George.

Extract of Fort William Secret Conſultations, the 31ſt January 1775.

PRESENT,

The Honourable Warren Haſtings, Eſquire, Governor General, Preſident,
Lieutenant General John Clavering,
The Honourable George Monſon,
Richard Barwell, } Eſquires.
Philip Francis, }

Read, and approved, the Proceedings of the Council held Yeſterday.

The Board being met agreeable to the Reſolution of Yeſterday, to take into Conſideration the Letter then received, and recorded, from the Preſidency of Fort Saint George;

Ordered,

Ordered, that the Secretary dispatch a Letter immediately after Captain Downs, Commander of the Shark Galliot, to stop his Vessel in the River till further Orders.

The above Letter is accordingly sent to the Master Attendant, with Directions to dispatch it as speedily as possible after Captain Downs, if there is not certain Intelligence of his having already left the River.

The Board, after mature Consideration of the Subjects contained in the Letters from Fort St. George, are of Opinion, that the Intelligence, though not of public Authority, bears too strong Appearances of Truth for them to entertain any Doubts of it; and indeed, the Board have no other Way of accounting for the sudden and abrupt Recall of the Agent or Resident at the Maratta Court, but by attributing it to some hostile Intention formed by the President of Bombay against that Nation; the Board however forbear to make any Remarks on this extraordinary Event, until they shall receive some authentic Advice of it from the Presidency of Bombay, or until the Report shall obtain Confirmation; but they think it necessary to address the Presidency immediately on the Subject by different Conveyances.

Agreed, that a Letter be written to the President and Council of Bombay, to the following Purport:

That in the last Letter to them, the Board took Notice of Mr. Mostyn's Recall from Poona. At that Time, amongst various other Conjectures, they had Suspicions of that Presidency being engaged in Hostilities with the Marattas, for which Reason it was not thought proper to appoint another Person from this Establishment to reside at Poona; that these Suspicions have been since confirmed by the Letters from Madras, which though in Consequence of private Advices, are so circumstantial, that the Board might give Credit to them, at least to allow them to have some Foundation, and therefore repeat their Expression of Surprize at the Inattention of the President and Council of Bombay to this Government, in not sending Advice of these Particulars; and peremptorily to require that Presidency to transmit immediate Accounts of the Reality of these Facts, and if true, of their Causes; and to report constantly, by different Conveyances, their further Intentions and Events as they may occur, that this Government may be enabled to fulfil the Commands and Expectations of the British Legislature, and of the Company, by watching over and taking early Measures for securing the Interest of the Company in India: That on Intelligence of so alarming a Nature, the Board find themselves under great Uneasiness at being obliged to remain inactive, but that they must remain so till they hear from the President and Council at Bombay, who must be answerable for the Consequences of the Steps they have taken.

Extract of Fort William Secret Consultations, 3d February 1775.

PRESENT,

The Honourable Warren Hastings, Governor General, President,
Lieutenant General John Clavering,
The Honourable George Monson,
Richard Barwell, } Esquires.
Philip Francis, }

To the Honourable Warren Hastings, Esquire, Governor General, &c. Council.

Honourable Sir, and Sirs,

Inclosed are Triplicates of our Letters of the 10th and 11th Instant.

The President this Day received a Letter from Mr. Boddam at Tellicherry, dated the 31st Ultimo; an Extract of which, as also the Intelligence which accompanied it, waits on you herewith, and which it appeared necessary to communicate to you with all Expedition.

We have the Honour to be, &c.
(Signed) A. Wynch,
&c. Council.

Fort Saint George,
14 January 1775.

APPENDIX, Nº 63.

Extract of a Letter from Rawson Hart Boddam, Esquire, Chief of Tellicherry, dated the 31st December 1774, and received the 14th January 1775.

To the Honourable Alexander Wynch, Esquire, President and Governor of Fort Saint George.

Honourable Sir,

I have this Morning been favoured with your Letter of the 22d November by our returned Putterah; and, agreeable to what therein noticed, now sit down with the greatest Cheerfulness to comply with your Desire as far as lays in my Power.

The Accounts you notice to have received relative to the Force come out this Season and expected by the Portugueze, is well founded, as you will observe by the inclosed Extracts of some Advices sent me by my Correspondents, which I have long since forwarded to Mr. Hornby. They still expect another 50 or 60 Gun Ship, which sailed in Company with a Merchantman who passed this Place about Ten or Fifteen Days past, and had only 85 Men as Recruits on board for Goa. They have now Two Frigates laying to the Southward of Cochin to join this expected Ship, and convey her safely to Goa. The Intentions of this Reinforcement was to repossess themselves of the Conquests made from the Portugueze Nation, formerly by the Marattas, particularly Salsette and Bassein; but as our Troops are *now* acting against those Places, which without Doubt you have some Time been advised by the Select Committee at Bombay, was their Intentions, I hope, in a few Days, to advise you that every Success has attended the Expedition; though by a Letter received Yesterday from Mr. Hornby, per Drake Cruizer, dated the 23d Instant, he acquaints me Tannah Fort still held out, though they had destroyed all their Defences, and were preparing that Day to storm, which it was imagined would put the Place into our Hands. They had sustained the Attack of our Battery for Seven Days, the Fort being high, and the Walls thick and well built by the Portugueze.

By a small Vessel just come in, I learn that the Maratta Fleet, now cruizing betwixt Gheriah and Puttenah Gheriah, consists of Five Ships and Three Ketch Grabs, with 30 or 40 Gallivats. It is at present uncertain if Dowlal, the Governor of Gheriah, will join Ragoba's Party or not; if the contrary, our Trade will run some Risque of suffering, if the Men of War do not speedily appear on this Coast.

A true Extract.
(Signed) James Capper,
Assistant Secretary.

Extracts.

The 21 September arrived at Goa, Don Joze Pedro de Camara, as Governor and Captain General of India, with two Ships of War, one of 64 Guns, the other a large long Frigate; both to remain in India. The Government will undergo almost a total Change, as well in Religion as in Civil Matters.

Two Brigadiers and Two Lieutenant Colonels, with a suitable Number of Officers, are come out; the Infantry is to be augmented, and a Regiment of Artillery to be raised. Three of the largest Convents are taken for Barracks to accommodate them. The Artillery are to have Senior D'Cave. The Inquisition to be totally abolished; all the poor unhappy Wretches set at Liberty; and the House taken for the Viceroy's Palace. No Padres to be made for Twenty Years to come. All the Riches of the Churches taken by the King, and only a Feast allowed to be kept throughout the whole Year; the Expences of which is to be ascertained by the Viceroy. The King has also taken to himself the Advantages arising by the Tobacco Farm, and the Sale of the Annual Consignment of Portugal Snuff sent out by the Queen. Officers of Justice are come out to take Cognizance of all Matters that require Redress. A Liberty of Conscience is permitted; and the Asiatics, of whatever Denomination, are permitted to exercise their Religion and build Pagodas, &c. The Portugueze are going to put their Marine on a different Footing to what it was. Six Frigates, of 36 Guns each, to be built at Damaun with the utmost Expedition. All the Gallivats at Goa are repairing: And the Two Men of War that are arrived, have brought no Trade of any Kind, being

being full of Implements of every Kind for the above Six Frigates, with a very large Quantity of Cannon, Shot, Powder, and all Kind of Military Stores. They brought, Seamen included, One thousand effective Men; and there is hourly expected another Ship of Cunlofer, commanded by Coats, &c. and a Freight Ship; on these are coming also from 5 to 600 Military and Marines. The Bishop of Alicarnassa or Delevar Jung, has the Rank of Brigadier General. It is said they fully intend attacking the Marattas. I think they must have some Intentions of that Nature, by increasing their Military and Marine Forces so considerably. An Act of Grace has taken Place upon the Arrival of the new Viceroy; and all Delinquents pardoned and set at Liberty.

Account of the Portugueze Forces at Goa, &c.

Four Regiments of Infantry, consisting of Seven Companies of Eighty Men each Company, are — — — — —	2,240
One Regiment of Marines, consisting of Ten Companies, each Eighty Men	800
One Troop European Horse — — — —	200
Three Regiments of Natives, consisting together of — —	2,000
Sepoys — — — — —	6,000

Two Ships of Sixty-four and Seventy Guns.
Four Do. of Fifty, Forty-four, and Forty Guns.
A Grab Ship of Thirty-six Guns.
One Patack, a Frigate of Thirty-six Guns.
Fifty Minchlras and Gallivats, carrying Ten or Twelve Guns each.
Two Bartotes or Fire Ships of Fourteen Guns each.

A true Copy of the Extract.

(Signed) James Capper.

APPENDIX, N° 64.

Extract of Fort William Secret Consultations, 3d February, 1775.

PRESENT,

The Honourable Warren Hastings, Governor General, President,
Lieutenant General George Monson,
Richard Barwell, } Esquires.
Philip Francis, }

THE Governor General recommends, that a Letter be written to the Presidency of Fort Saint George, in Reply to theirs now before the Board, in Substance as follows:

To thank them for their Diligence in conveying the Intelligence to us which they had received concerning the Affairs of Bombay; and to inform them, that we have no other Advice of these Transactions; and therefore, although we cannot doubt of some Event similar to what is reported having taken Place, yet, till we obtain more precise and authentic Intelligence, we must remain undetermined as to the Measures which it may be necessary to adopt on the Occasion; to declare, however, that we cannot apprehend any Consequences from such an Event, which is likely to affect the Company's Interest in the Carnatic, or require the Intervention of that Presidency; that in this Persuasion, we can only recommend that they concert with the Nabob such general cautionary Measures as may tend to the Defence of his Possessions whenever they shall be liable to an Invasion, but neither to send any Part of their Forces into the Field, or take any other Step for his Service which may draw the Company into an Expence, without a formal Requisition from him, and an Engagement to defray the extraordinary Charge, taking Care that he appropriate a Fund for that Purpose; that this is the Plan which occurs to us at present as the most adviseable; nor do we foresee a Pro-a Probability of any Circumstances happening which should engage them in more distant Operations, or draw their Attention from their own Possessions, or those of our Ally the Nabob; that we recommend to them to keep a watchful Eye over the French and Hyder Ally, and write to us as often as any fresh Occurrences of Consequence shall come to their Knowledge.

(Signed) Warren Hastings.

The Governor further offers the following Observations to the Consideration of the Board:

Although the Conduct of the Government of Bombay may prove, as it at present seems to be, precipitate and unwarrantable, and may eventually compel us to adopt a Plan of Politics dictated by them, from a partial Consideration of their own limited Concerns, instead of waiting to receive from us their Rule of Action, formed on a System adapted to the general Interest of the Company, and of the British Nation in India; yet it does not appear likely to produce any Consequences of immediate Danger. The present interesting Distraction of the Maratta State, and its long Continuance, must have considerably exhausted both their Strength and Resources; the ministerial Party which compose the actual Government, have yet too formidable an Opponent in Ragonaut Row, the regular Chief, to engage in new Contests, especially with a Power with whom the Marattas have always shewn a Disinclination to break even in the Height of their Prosperity.

By the latest Advices Ragonaut Row, supported by Jaccoojee Mulcar and Maldajee Cinde, had retreated to the City of Ugein, the Capital of the Malavar Province; it is probable that a slight Diversion afforded to his Adversaries would invite him to return, as it would render the Contest less unequal than it has lately proved; neither is it likely that it will resent an Act of the Government of Bombay, which can only tend to favour his Cause by lessening his Credit, and disconcerting the Projects of his Enemies.

From these Reasons, it appears unlikely that the Marattas will attempt a Retaliation of the Injury which has been offered to their Nation, either on this Government or on that of Fort St. George; the Chiefs attached to the Party of Ragonaut Row, who have hitherto conducted the Affairs of the Marattas on this Side, have other Interest to provide for, and the Ministers are too weak (as has been already observed) for distant Enterprizes, or even to act with Vigour against the Presidency of Bombay.

The only Powers to whom this Event may be supposed to afford a Pretext, or an Occasion to create us Trouble, are Hyder Ally and Shabajee Boosla; the former understands his own Interest too well to quarrel with the English, from whom he can gain nothing, and with whom he may hazard all he has; and he is already sufficiently occupied by more rational Projects, the Establishment of his own Country, and the Annexation of the petty States of his Neighbourhood to his own Dominion; Shahabajee Boosla has for some Time sought the Alliance of this Government, and derives his surest Means of Independance from the Weakness of the Government to which he is legally subject.

On the Grounds thus described, the Governor has proposed the above Draft of the Letter to the Presidency of Fort Saint George; and offers it as his further Opinion, that it is unnecessary to take any immediate Measures for obviating the Consequences of the supposed Injuries offered by the Presidency of Bombay to the Maratta Government.

(Signed) Warren Hastings.

The above Two Papers having been delivered in by the Governor General, and sent in Circulation to the other Members of the Board, the Draft for a Letter to Fort Saint George was not agreed to by General Clavering, Colonel Monson, and Mr. Francis: Agreed, therefore, that it lie for Consideration.

APPENDIX, N° 65.

AGREED, That the following Letter be now written, and dispatched over Land to Bombay:

To the Honourable William Hornby, Esquire, President, &c. and Council at Bombay.

Gentlemen,

We have received your Letters of the 31st December, containing as well the general State we required of the political Situation of Affairs of your Presidency, as the particular Accounts of your late Operations at Salsette and Bassein. The First will be taken into Consideration as soon as the Hurry of other Business will permit us, and Directions in Consequence will be transmitted to you. As to the last, the Tardiness of your Advices almost precludes us from saying any Thing at present on the Subject. Our Sentiments of this Inattention will be sufficiently known to you by our Letter of the 3d February, Triplicate of which accompanies this: We must however add, that we cannot admit the Plea of your being unacquainted with the new Government having taken Place here, because we conceive that the Operations in which you were going to engage, were too interesting to the Company's Affairs at large, and too likely in their Consequences to affect this Settlement, not to have become Matter of the most early Intelligence to this Presidency under the late Administration.

We have received Advices from Fort Saint George, of the Steps they had taken in Consequence of your Application to them for Assistance. For the Reason we have already given, we suspend our Opinion on your late Measures, and the Consequence of it; but can assure you that we shall be ready to afford you such Support in your present Circumstances, as may be necessary for preventing, as far as may lie in our Power, any Injury to the Company's Affairs.

We are alarmed at the Declaration of your Intention to join Ragoba; we must disapprove of this as inconsistent with your Negociations with the ruling Party at Poona, and with the Authority of this Government. Your own Report of his Decline, and the Power of his Opponents, prove it to be a Measure of Danger; it may force us into a Rupture with Shabajee Boosla, his declared Enemy, and our Neighbour, with whom we are on Terms of Friendship. We cannot ratify your Engagements with Ragoba, without such Reasons as we cannot now foresee; we positively direct that you suspend your Negociations with him till you receive our further Instructions. We were disappointed in not receiving an Account of the Forces on your Establishment, with the general State of your political Affairs which you sent us, more especially as you informed us of your having found it necessary to require a Reinforcement from Madras; we therefore desire that you transmit us such a State by the First Opportunity.

We also desire that you will prepare and transmit to us an accurate State of the whole Revenues of your Presidency, specifying the gross Amount, Charges, and Nett Produce of each Branch.

Fort William, 8th March, 1775.

We are, &c.

APPEN-

APPENDIX, Nº 66.

Extract of Bengal Secret Consultations, the 11th May 1775.

PRESENT,

Warren Hastings, Governor General, President,
Lieutenant General John Clavering,
The Honourable George Monson,
Richard Barwell, } Esquires.
Philip Francis, }

READ, a Letter from Sir Edward Hughes, as follows:

To Warren Hastings, Esquire, Governor General, &c. Council.

Sir, and Gentlemen,

In consequence of the Accident which befel his Majesty's Sloop the Swallow, which I acquainted you with in the Letter I did myself the Honour of writing to you on the 21st February last, that Sloop could not proceed, as was intended, for the Malabar Coast, to join the Sea Horse there for the Protection of the Trade, having been in a great Measure dismantled. I have informed the Presidency of Bombay thereof, and of my Design to repair to that Coast myself, whenever the Season will admit. I am now to acquaint you, Gentlemen, that I am going with the Salisbury and Swallow to Trinconomalle, on the Island of Ceylon, as well to avoid the petty Monsoon, as to inspect the Condition of the Sloop, and to put her into proper Order again for Service, and that I mean to return to this Road about the Middle of the next Month.

I have heard of the Arrival of the Sea Horse on the Coast of Malabar, and have no Doubt but she has long since landed the Company's Treasure, and been employed agreeable to the Request of the President and Council there.

I have the Honour to be, &c.
(Signed) Edward Hughes.

To the Honourable Alexander Wynch, Esquire, President and Governor of Madras.

Honourable Sir,

Under the 7th Instant I was favoured with your Letter of the 16th January, and am happy that any Information my Address of the 31st December would give you has proved agreeable; you may in future depend, Sir, I will embrace every Opportunity of sending you any Advices that I may judge worthy your Notice.

This Morning anchored in our Road the Honourable Company's Cruizers, Revenge, and Bombay Grab, from Bombay; they left the Island the 26th Ultimo, in order to proceed down hither, to give Convoy to the laying here, but falling in a little to the Southward of Rajanoul with the Convoy under the Calcutta (Thompson) which they judged not sufficiently strong to encounter the Maratta Fleet that was cruizing betwixt them and the Residency, proceeded up again just a little to the Southward of the Island; seeing them clear from any Risk of the Enemy, then made the best of their Way (the Ships Revenge and Bombay Grab) and off Cape Dobbs fell in with the Maratta Fleet, and luckily destroyed their Admiral's Ship, mounting 40 Guns as set forth in the Narrative now enclosed for your Perusal, wrote by a Passenger in the Bombay Grab, which I now send for your Perusal. I do not hear of any further Acts of Hostility by the Presidency of Bombay; their Troops, since the getting Possession of Salsette and Caranja, except the entirely defeating and destroying a Body of Marattas that had made a Descent on Salsette in order to plunder and ravage the Country. The Packet from the Presidency which I now forward to Anjengo for your Board, I dare say fay will fully explain the Gentlemen of Bombay their further Intentions, to which I beg Leave to refer you. The Portugueze I do not hear have made any Attempts against any of the Maratta Ports; they were not prepared; and our acting so materially in the very Point they had in View, I believe has entirely disconcerted their Plans.

I beg you will believe me, with great Esteem, &c. &c.

Tellicherry,
9th February 1775.

(Signed) R. H. Boddam.

APPENDIX, Nº 67.

Extract of Bengal Secret Consultations, the 25th May 1775.

PRESENT,

The Honourable Warren Hastings, Governor General and President,
Lieutenant General John Clavering,
The Honourable John Monson,
Richard Barwell, Philip Francis, } Esquires.

GENERAL Clavering lays before the Board, the following Extract of Advices which he has received from Brigadier General Gordon, at Bombay.

Copy of Brigadier General Gordon's Letter, dated 12th February; offering his Services to command the Troops.

Honourable Sir, and Sirs,

As you have been pleased to resolve that a large Part of the Troops shall take the Field immediately, I beg Leave to offer my Services to command them. This I hope you will think from my Rank here I have a Right to.

It is true that I have desired Leave to resign, when an Opportunity, which is agreeable to me, offers for my proceeding to Europe by the Way of China; but that Zeal I have for the Service, added to the Respect which I owe to those Friends who so warmly supported my Appointment in the General Court of Proprietors, makes me wish most earnestly to render some further Services to the Honourable Company. I am therefore to request, that your Honour, &c. will permit me to take the Command of the Forces which are immediately to be employed.

I am, &c.
(Signed) Robert Gordon.

Copy of the Board's Answer, dated 14th February, in Answer to the above.

To Brigadier General Gordon.

Sir,

I am directed by the Honourable the President and Council, to acknowledge the Receipt of your Letter, tendering your Services to command the Forces now to be detached from hence; and to observe to you in Reply, that the Board, with yourself, having been of Opinion, in Consultation the 11th Instant, that the Object in View, could not be accomplished by the Time you had limited for your Stay in India, you on this Account then declined the Command; whereupon Lieutenant Colonel Keating was then appointed. As this Appointment has thus taken Place, they do not now think proper to annul it; but they shall mention your Readiness for this Service, in a suitable Manner, in their Advices to the Honourable Company.

I am Sir, &c.
(Signed) George Skipp,
Secretary.

APPENDIX, Nº 67.

Copy of Brigadier General Gordon's Letter, claiming the Command of the Troops ordered to take the Field, dated the 15th February 1775.

Honourable Sir, and Sirs,

Yesterday Evening I received Three Letters from your Secretary, dated 14th February; in the First, the Receipt of my Letter, tendering my Services to command the Forces to be detached from hence, is acknowledged; and it is signified to me in Reply, that as the Board with myself had, on the 11th Instant, been of Opinion, that the Object in View could not be accomplished by the Time I had limited for my Stay in India, that I had on that Account declined the Command, whereupon Lieutenant Colonel Keating was then appointed; and as this Appointment had then taken Place, you did not think proper to annul it.—The Second Letter contains Directions to me to order Lieutenant Colonel Keating, and the Officers who are to proceed on that Detachment, to be ready to embark on a Moment's Warning.—In the Third, your Commands respecting the Embarkation, and also ordering Captain Lieutenant Brickets to Fort Victoria, are signified to me.

In Answer to the First of these Letters, I am to observe, that I never declined the present Service, but repeatedly declared that I was always ready for the executive Part, while I remained in India; and by my subsequent Letter, that I was ready to accept of the Command, and to continue in the Service, till the present was brought to a Conclusion.

I claimed the Command as my Right, from my Rank and Appointment by the Court of Proprietors, as well as that of the Court of Directors; and I conceive, the depriving me of it to be an Act of Injustice towards me, to which the Success which has attended the Company's Arms as often as I have had the Direction of them in the Field, should not have exposed me; and I believe, this is the first Instance of a Brigadier General, who had been appointed to the Command of the Forces at any Presidency by the Vote of a General Court of Proprietors, having been refused the Command of an Army about to take the Field, to make Room for a Lieutenant Colonel of Artillery. But admitting that my having signified my Intentions of returning to Europe was a sufficient Reason for depriving me of the Command, it should then have been offered to Colonel Egerton, who is next to me in Succession, and who is ready to take it upon him.

The Appointment of a Chief Engineer, or Commandant of Artillery as such, to the Chief Command of a Body of Forces, is, I believe, almost without Example either in the King's or Company's Service. I think Lieutenant Colonel Keating is, for many Reasons, a very improper Person for the Appointment which you have given him; I therefore repeat my Protest against the Troops taking the Field under his Command; nor will I be answerable in the smallest Degree for the Consequences which may attend any of the Measures which you are about to pursue.——I come now to the Second Letter: Before I received it, the Governor had put the Names of the Officers, who are intended for the Expedition, in Orders, directing therein that they were to be in Readiness to embark at a Moment's Warning; and he had signified it, as his Command to me, by the Town Major, that Lieutenant Colonel Keating was to chuse such Men as he thought proper from amongst the Troops here to take with him; which in consequence he has done. In ordering the Officers for this Service, no Raster, no military Rule whatever, has been observed. By this Means much Injustice is done to many Officers; as, however lightly some People may think of it, I know of few greater Injuries which can be done to an Officer than depriving him of his Tour of Duty on actual Service. I mention this for the Notice of our Honourable Masters, who, I doubt not, will grant Redress to Gentlemen who have served them long, honourably, and faithfully.

Respecting the Third Letter, I was informed by Lieutenant Colonel Keating, that he had began to prepare his Stores, &c. &c. before I received it. I have therefore only to say, that your Orders, as far as depends upon me, shall be punctually complied with.

I am now to submit to your Consideration the weak State to which all the new Conquests and Subordinates will be reduced when the Troops for this Service are drawn from them, and the total Inability of the Presidency to afford them Relief, should any of them be attacked. In my Opinion, these Points merit your most serious Attention;

as,

as, should any Accident happen to the Forces who are about to take the Field (and every Army, even if ever so ably commanded, is liable to untoward Chances) I say, in such a Case, the Company's Settlements on this Side of India would be exposed to the utmost Danger. I do not think the Troops expected from Madras would, if they were arrived, be sufficient for the Purposes for which they are wanted. The new Battalions of Sepoys now find great Difficulty in getting Recruits, as no Bounty is given to encourage Men to enter into the Service. It is also to be considered, that as these Battalions take a great Part of the Duties of the Garrison, Drilling must go on very slowly, and it must be long before they can be made so fit for Service as to be depended on in any Business of Importance. However, I would recommend the using every Means to get them compleated as fast as possible; and that no Time should be lost in applying to the Supreme Council for Assistance to guard against whatever may happen, and to protect those other Territories promised to be ceded to us.

I am, &c.

(Signed) Robert Gordon.

Ordered, that the Return of the Bombay Forces, delivered in with the above, be entered after the Consultation.

It appearing from the foregoing Extract, and other private Advices received from Bombay, that the President and Council there had actually sent a considerable Force to the Assistance of Ragonaut Row, and had entered into an offensive Treaty with him to reinstate him upon the Musnud at Poona, of which they have transmitted no authentic Intelligence to this Government, by the Conveyance that has brought the above News;

Agreed, That the following Letter be written to them in Cypher, and dispatched in Duplicate; one Copy by Way of Benares, and the other by Fort Saint George.

To the Honourable William Hornby, President, &c. Council at Bombay.

Honourable Sir, and Sirs,

We have not been favoured with any Letters from you or your Select Committee, respecting the political Affairs of your Presidency, since your Letter dated the 31st December; nor have we received any authentic Advices of the late Occurrences in your Parts, but from private Letters and other Intelligence, all concurring in the same Points.

We understand that you have entered into an offensive Treaty with Ragonaut Row, and have sent a considerable Force to his Assistance, which has actually taken the Field.

This last is confirmed by Letters received by the Commander in Chief, with Returns of the Force actually sent. Embarrassed and perplexed with these Reports, the Truth of which we cannot doubt, and ignorant of the Force of your Enemies, and of the immediate Plan of your Operations, we are obliged to remain inactive in Circumstances which may possibly require our utmost Exertion for your Support and Relief.

In this Situation your Silence becomes truly astonishing; but under the Want of precise and authentic Information from yourselves, we are obliged to suspend our final Judgment of your Proceedings, and in the mean Time protest against all the Consequences of any hostile Measures taken, or offensive Engagements entered into by you without our Consent. We consider them as directly contradictory to the Provisions made in the Act of Parliament, for uniting the several Presidencies under the political Superintendance of this Government, and equally contrary to the common Principles of Prudence and Policy; since the partial Resolutions and Operations of a single Presidency may eventually involve all the Company's Settlements in a general War, without any previous Concert, or a general Plan for conducting it.

Our Letter of the 3d February last contained very explicit Orders on these Heads, and we expect that you will be full and circumstantial in your Answer to it, and in explaining the Motives for your late Conduct.

We are, &c.

A P P E N D I X, Nº 68.

Extract of Bengal Secret Consultations, the 31st May 1775.

P R E S E N T,

The Honourable Warren Hastings, Governor General, President,
Lieutenant General John Clavering,
The Honourable George Monson,
Richard Barwell, } Esquires.
Philip Francis, }

RECEIVED, the following Letter and Inclosures from the President and Council at Bombay.

Honourable Sir, and Gentlemen,

In our Address of the 31st December last, which has been already transmitted in Triplicate, we acquainted you with every Thing needful from this Department, as well with regard to the Attack of Salsette, as to the Negociation depending with Ragoba, the rightful Supreme Governor of the Maratta Empire. We have been since favoured with your Letter in your secret Departments of the 16th of January, to which our abovementioned Address, we flatter ourselves, will be considered by you as a full and satisfactory Reply.

Shortly after the Date of that Address, Ragoba with his Army arrived at Bradera, not very far from Surat; the Negociation with him was continued through the Chief of Surat, in the Manner he before acquainted you that we proposed doing, and at Length was brought so near to a Conclusion, that we had transmitted from hence a Treaty on the Terms we proposed, and had every Reason to believe that it would be directly executed; Jewels, to the Amount of Six Lacks of Rupees, were deposited by Ragoba, and the necessary Sunnuds were delivered for the several Districts and Territories the Company were to be entitled to in Virtue of the Treaty, and of the Assistance that agreeable to the Treaty we were to afford him.

Our Forces accordingly proceeded from hence to Surat, that they might be ready to proceed from thence to join his Army as soon as the Treaty was actually concluded, and we had great Reason to hope that the War between Ragoba and the Ministerial Party, through the Assistance of the Company's Forces, would speedily have been brought to an happy and glorious Issue, by which, when accomplished, the Company will become quiet Possessors of sundry Districts and Pergunnahs, whose Annual Revenue will amount to near 20 Lacks of Rupees, and by which we hope this Presidency may be enabled to maintain itself, and relieve you from the Burthen of sending us large Annual Supplies; and to add to our Satisfaction, about this Time, some material Advantages were gained by Ragoba, over the Enemy's Army.

This pleasing Prospect was however for a short Time clouded; the Ministerial Party, possibly learning that Ragoba was on the Eve of concluding a Treaty with the Company, that would most probably overset their ambitious Hopes of subduing him, corrupted, as it is supposed, a Part of his Forces, mostly Arabs, on whom he placed considerable Reliance, and where he himself was posted; they then attacked that Quarter with the Strength of their Army. Ragoba, seeing in the Midst of the Battle, that the Arabs neglected to do their Duty, and then not knowing how far the Treachery had spread, or whom in this Emergency to trust, precipitately fled from the Field, with about One thousand Horse only, towards Cambay.

The Nabob of this Place, seeing his Situation, and dreading the Power of his Enemies, refused to admit him; he then made the best of his Way towards Bownagur, where he luckily met with One of our Gallivats, embarked on board her, and on the 23d Ultimo arrived at Surat, where the Chief received and entertained him as a Friend and Ally to the Company.

Notwithstanding

Notwithstanding this alarming Step, it shortly appeared to us, (*Mr. Draper excepted, who has given his Reasons in Writing for differing with us in this Opinion, as per Copy enclosed*) that Ragoba's Affairs were not nearly in the desperate Situation there was at first Reason to fear. Two principal Chiefs, Conderow and Govind Row, with many of his great Officers, remain firm to his Interest, and have collected an Army to the Number of 25,000 Men, mostly Horse, within 40 Coss of Cambay; many others are also likely soon to join him; we therefore esteem it our indispensable Duty, not to give up the great Advantages that were to be reaped by the Company from the Treaty, when so fair an Opportunity offered of retrieving his Affairs, by sending our Forces to Cambay to join his Army. Ragoba earnestly pressed us to this Step, and we have little Doubt when a Junction is once effected, but that Success will attend their Operations. Our Forces proceeded accordingly, and arrived at Cambay the 17th Instant.

We have given Lieutenant Colonel Keating, the Commanding Officer of this Detachment, proper Instructions for his Conduct; have enjoined him to observe the utmost Prudence of Circumspection, and never to engage in Measures beyond his own Power to retrieve.

On the 6th Instant, while Ragoba was yet at Surat, he executed the Treaty to the Company; the Chief also executed one to him, which has been since ratified and confirmed by us; an attested Copy of which we transmit your Honour, &c. inclosed, for your full Information, and we hope it will meet with your entire Approbation.

From the Want of a sufficient Military Force, we were under a Necessity of stipulating, that a less Number should at first proceed than was originally intended, as your Honour, &c. will observe by the Treaty; but the President and Council at Fort St. George having with great Readiness complied with our Request for Troops from thence, and Two Companies of European Infantry being actually arrived here, and a Battalion of their Sepoys shortly expected, we therefore resolved to complete the Detachment of Two thousand Five hundred Men, the Number first proposed; and the Remainder accordingly now proceeds to Surat, from whence they will embark for Cambay to join the former Detachment. And as the different Persons that form the Ministerial Party, are reported to be very much divided amongst themselves, and that Madjee Sindy has actually deserted their Cause, and others it is expected will very shortly fall from them, we therefore have Reason to hope that Ragoba may in a short Time be able to reduce them all to their due Obedience to him.

We are, &c. &c.

(Signed) William Hornby,
President, &c. Council.

Bombay Castle, 31st March 1775.

The Seal of the Company.

Articles of Agreement and Treaty between the Honourable William Hornby, Esquire, President and Governor, &c. Council of Bombay, and of all its Dependencies, on the Part and Behalf of the Honourable United English East India Company, on the one Part, and Ragonath Row Ballajee, Peshwa, on the other Part. Dated the 6th Day of March, in the Year of our Lord 1775, on the Third Day of the Month Moherum, and Year 1189, Ijay, Mahometan Style, on the Day of the Month and Year 1180, Gentoo Style.

Article 1st. The Treaty concluded between the Government of Bombay and Padjerow Pundit Pardans, or First Minister of his Serene Highness the Sou Raja, dated July 1739 or 1140 of the Mahometan Style, and that concluded on the Part of this Government with Ballajee Budserow Pardan, dated the 12th October 1756, or of the Mahometan Style 17th of Moherum 1170, are hereby ratified and confirmed in their full Extent, according to the true and full Intent and Meaning of them, in the same full and ample

ample Manner, and in the same Light in which they have hitherto been ever understood.

Art. 2d. All other Governments subsisting between this Government of Bombay and that of the Marattas, are hereby ratified and confirmed, and after the Re-establishment of Ragoba in the Government of the Maratta Dominions, Peace and Tranquillity shall subsist uninterrupted between this Government, in Behalf of the Honourable Company, and the Maratta Government.

Art. 3d. Ragoba on his Part, and on the Part of the Maratta Government, engages from this Day forward never on any Pretence, or in any Manner, to assist the Enemies of the Honourable Company in any Part whatever of their Dominions in India; and the Honourable the Governor and Council of Bombay do in the like Manner engage never to assist the Enemies of Ragoba.

Art. 4th. The Honourable the President and Council of Bombay, in Behalf of the Honourable Company, and in Consideration of the undermentioned Grants and Cessions made by Ragoba to the Company, do hereby engage and agree as soon as possible after these Articles of Agreement and Treaty are fully ratified, executed, and confirmed on the Part of Ragoba, to assist him with a strong Body of Forces, with proper Guns and Warlike Stores, as a Field Train of Artillery, which are to join his Army, and act in Conjunction with his Forces against his Enemies, the Ministerial Party: In the said Forces shall be included no less than 700 Europeans, and the Whole shall not be less in Number than 2,500 Men, but at present only 500 Europeans, and One thousand Sepoys and Lascars, with a proper and effectual Number of Guns, will be sent, and the rest if wanted afterwards.

Art. 5th. In Consideration of such effectual Assistance on the Part of the Honourable Company, Ragoba, as Peshwa and as Supreme Governor of the whole Maratta Empire, doth hereby engage on his Part to cede and make over to the Honourable Company for ever the undermentioned Places and Territories, and he doth accordingly by these Presents make over the same to them in the most full and ample and effectual Manner, and he doth with these Presents deliver the necessary Sunnuds; granting, in the fullest Manner, all the present and future full Right and Title of the Maratta Government to them; and in case of the Loss at any Time of the Sunnuds now delivered, these Presents are at all Times to be considered as such, and of full equal Validity as any Sunnud whatever:

Bassein, and the Whole of its Dependencies, in its fullest Extent, and all Rents and Revenues thereunto belonging, together with the Fort or Forts, and every Thing belonging unto the Poona Government in it.

Salsette, the whole and entire Island, with all the Revenues of the different Places annexed to it, as collected by Anunt Row and Ramajee Punt.

Jamboseer and Orpad, } with the Whole of their Dependencies in their full Extent, together with every Thing belonging to the Poona Government in those Purgunnahs.

The Four following Islands adjacent to Bombay, with every Thing belonging to the Poona Government therein, viz. Caranje, Canary, Elephanta and Hog Island.

Art. 6th. Ragoba also engages immediately to procure from the Guicawar, a Grant to the Honourable Company for ever, with all the necessary Sunnuds, of their Share in the Revenues collected by the Guicawar in the Town and Purgunnahs of Broach.

Art. 7th. The Honourable Company to be considered as the sole Lords and Proprietors from the Day of the Signing of this Treaty, of all and every of the Places ceded by the Two last Articles, in the like Manner as the Poona Government, or the Guicawar Government were before considered; and are accordingly, from this Day forward, to exercise every Right and Authority in these Places, and to receive every Revenue which the Poona Government, or the Guicawar before exercised or received.

Art. 8th. Ragoba also engages faithfully to make good to the Company for ever, the Sum of Seventy-five thousand Rupees Annually, from his Share of the Revenues of Jalasies; which Sum is to be paid by his Pundit, in Two different Payments at stated Periods.

Art. 9th. Ragoba engages to pay in full for the Charges and Expences of the Body of Forces with which he is to be assisted, consisting of Two thousand Five hundred Men, with Guns and Ammunition, the Sum of One hundred and Fifty thousand Rupees monthly and every Month, which the Honourable Governor and Council agree

to

further Account, and is to commence the Day the Forces leave Bom-
iole Number of Forces will not at first proceed, he is only to pay a pro-
ly Sum, till the whole Force, if necessary, may be sent to join him.
y this Stipend monthly; and as Security for the same, till his Affairs
to furnish Money, which he promises to do as soon as possible, he
esents the Revenues of the following Places: viz.

emaining Share, after dedicating what is before by these Presents
urable Company,

ll its Districts,

its Districts,

its Districts.

clared, that the Revenues of these Places belong to the Honourable
r than till the Amount of the monthly Stipend that may be due for
the Company's Forces is fully discharged, when all further Demands
ces are to be relinquished; and in this Light, the Honourable the
ncil declare, they accept these Four Purgunnahs.

s it has been mutually agreed during the Course of this Negociation,
Six Lacks of Rupees should be deposited by Ragoba, with the Agent
e Company, to be accounted for at the Expiration of the Service in-
rmed against his Enemies, the Ministerial Party; and Ragoba finding
ally impossible for him to raise the Sum to be deposited, though still
do it was it in his Power, the contracting Parties have mutually
s Point as follows; that Ragoba shall immediately deposit with the
at Surat, to the full Value of Six Lacks of Rupees in Jewels, to
ourable Company's Possessions till redeemed, which must be done as
Affairs will possibly admit: All this Ragoba faithfully and firmly en-
and the Honourable Company to accept.

case of Opposition from any Person or Persons whatever, to the Com-
sion of all or any of the Places hereby firmly and effectually ceded to
th engage to pay the Expence that will be incurred by their gaining
effectual Means to put them in Possession, as well as to secure them
et Possession of all the Revenues and Places now ceded to the Honour-

ould Ragoba make Peace with his Enemies the Ministers, he firmly
ges, that the Honourable English East India Company shall be in-
r Satisfaction.

doth also engage, never to molest the Dominions of the Honourable
l.

ges not to make War, or commit any Depredations in the Carnatic,
st Treaty subsisting between the Two Governors is adhered to by the

it should happen (which God forbid) that any of the Company's
r the Ships, Vessels, or Boats of any Person or Persons trading un-
n, should be shipwrecked on any Part of the Maratta Coast, every
given by the Government and Inhabitants to save as much as possi-
le that may be saved shall be returned, all reasonable Expences being
s.

Places ceded for ever to the Company by this Treaty are to be con-
e Right and Property from the Day this Treaty is signed; and this
Day to be considered in full Force, just as if the expected Services
lished, whether Ragoba shall make Peace with his Enemies or not.

ately after the Ratification of the foregoing Articles, and after the
Amount of Six Lacks of Rupees are deposited, and the Security
ven for the Payment of the monthly Expences of the Forces so long
ith Ragoba, and till their Return, all in the Manner abovemen-
nor and Council engage that the Company's Forces, agreeable to
in the Body of this Treaty, shall proceed from Bombay to join the
and they trust, by the blessing of the Almighty, that they will
his Enemies, the Ministerial Party, and establish him at Poona in
f the Maratta Empire.

The

The foregoing Articles having been agreed to by the Honourable the President and Council of Bombay, who have empowered me to accept the same in their Behalf, I do, in Confirmation thereof, affix the Seal of the said Honourable Company, and sign my own Name thereto, in Surat, the Day and Year abovewritten; and I do engage to procure a Ratification of this Treaty under the Seal of the Honourable Company, and under the Hands and Seals of the Honourable the President and Council of Bombay, within Thirty Days from this Date.

(Signed) Robert Gambier.

We, the President and Council of Bombay aforesaid, having empowered Mr. Robert Gambier to execute a Treaty with Ragonaut Row Ballajee, Peshwa, in our Behalf, on Account of the Honourable Company, of the foregoing Tenor, which he has accordingly done, of the Date abovementioned; and the same having been signed to, ratified and confirmed by Ragonaut Row Ballajee Row; and whereas by the last Article it is covenanted and agreed that a Ratification of the said Treaty shall be transmitted by us under the Seal of the Honourable Company, and under our proper Hands and Seals, within One Month from the above Date; these therefore are to certify, that we hereby ratify and confirm the foregoing Treaty in all and every Part: In Testimony whereof we have caused the Seal of the aforesaid Honourable Company to be hereunto affixed, and do now sign the same with our Hands, and affix our proper Seals thereto this 16th Day of March, in the Year of our Lord One thousand Seven hundred and Seventy-five.

(Signed)
William Hornby,
Daniel Draper,
Thomas Mostyn,
Brice Fletcher,
Will. Taylor.

L.S.

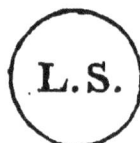

By Order of the Honourable William Hornby, Esquire, President and Governor, &c. Council, of his Majesty's Castle and Island of Bombay, and of all Forts, Factories, Territories, Forces, and Affairs of the Honourable English East India Company on the Western Side of India, and on the Coast of Persia and Arabia.

A true Copy.

(Signed) Cha. Skipp, Secretary.

To the Honourable William Hornby, President, &c. Members of the Select Committee at Bombay.

Honourable Sir, and Sirs,

I am concerned, that after concurring with you in the whole Progress of the Negociations with Ragoba, and likewise in every Measure relative to the intended Expedition for the re-establishing him in the Government at Poona, I should think myself under the Necessity of dissenting to the Resolution you came to the 7th Instant, for ordering our Troops to proceed on the Expedition, in Conjunction with Ragoba as soon as he may have ratified the Treaty, and have given us sufficient Satisfaction relative to the Payment of the monthly Allowance, for defraying the Charges of the Expedition, agreeable to the Minutes of that Day. As I conceive that in consequence of Ragoba having so lately been routed and fled from his Army to Surat, attended only by an inconsiderable Quantity of Followers, that there is a great Alteration for the worse in the State of his Affairs, to what it was about the Middle of last Month, on our Troops leaving Bombay, when, according to the Advices we then had, he was at the Head of so numerous an Army as to have lately engaged the Ministerial Troops more than once with Success; whereas from the Intelligence in general we have since received from Surat, Broach, and Cambay, the Forces of which his Army was composed are still dispersed at a considerable Distance from Cambay; and in my Opinion any large Number of them re-assembling and acting with the necessary Spirit and Firmness, is become very doubtful, especially as the Company's Credit (as to immediately raising Cash) as well as his, is now very unfortunately known to be at a low Ebb at Surat. I cannot therefore but consider

consider the Resolution your Honour, &c. came to the 7th Instant, as premature; and of course that it would have been more adviseable to have postponed it, if necessary, about Twenty Days; as I cannot but think that by so doing we might be qualified to come to a proper Determination on so very weighty an Affair, both to the Honourable Company and Ragoba, especially for the following Reasons:

1st. Because, that by the above Time we may reasonably hope to have a pretty certain Account what Number of Ragoba's Forces may be able and willing to join him, and whether he may have any tolerable Prospect of paying them, so long as our Troops may be supposed to act jointly with him.

2dly. That we may likewise, by the above Time, hope to be at a Certainty about the Squadron with the expected Reinforcement of Troops from Madras, also the expected Supply of Money from Bengal; the former of which would enable us to determine, whether it would have been best that the present small Body of the Honourable Company's Forces, under Lieutenant Colonel Keating, consisting of about 1,500 Men, should or should not proceed with Ragoba without waiting for the Reinforcement, considering the Difficulty and Risque of their effecting a Junction afterwards. And the Supply of Money would enable us to relieve the Company's pressing Necessities at Surat, without having Recourse to the pledging of Ragoba's Jewels, or lowering the present very disadvantageous Rate of Exchange with Bengal, and also put the Demands of our Troops on a Certainty of being answered; without which, I apprehend very serious Consequences may ensue.

3dly. That should Cambay then on the Whole be thought the most eligible Place for our and Ragoba's Troops assembling at, the Season might permit of it; and in the same Time Ragoba's Friends, wherever situated, could have no Doubt from the Continuance of our Forces with him at or near Surat, that they were kept in Readiness to prosecute his Cause, even though it might then be judged most adviseable, in order to be joined by the Madras Troops, to have deferred proceeding with the Expedition till after the Rains.

4thly. Because I am of Opinion, that with Ragoba's Concurrence at least, the Expedition had better be so deferred than prosecuted at this Juncture, without a very reasonable Prospect of their being able to carry him to Poona before the Rains; and in which Case the Troops might remain at or near Surat, thereby affording full Protection to that Settlement and Broach, and be very serviceable, I conclude, in recovering the Revenues of the Districts to be ceded to the Company, conformable to the 11th Article of the Treaty, particularly those on Account the Monthly Allowance; and during the Rains, I imagine good Offers might be made Ragoba and us by the Ministerial Party, for accommodating Matters, if he and we should think proper to attend to them.

These were the principal Reasons of my dissenting to your Honour, &c. abovementioned Resolution; but in case Ragoba and our Troops should be enabled to set out from Surat agreeable thereto, which in consequence of Ragoba's late Defeat appears to be rather improbable, your Honour, &c. have my best Wishes that your Expectations therein may be fully answered; being with Respect,

Signed

Bombay, 11th March 1775. Daniel Draper.

Ordered, That the Letter agreed upon, to be written in Cypher to the President and Council of Bombay at the last Consultation, be now withheld.

The Governor General begs Leave to record the following Minute upon the Subject of the above Letter.

The Intelligence conveyed in these Dispatches appears of so great Importance to the general Interests of the Company, that I think it incumbent on me to offer my particular Sentiments previous to the Deliberation of the Board upon it.

If the Measures adopted by the Presidency of Bombay had been attended with any decisive Effects, I should not have judged it necessary for this Board to pass either Censure or Approbation upon them; but on the contrary, I am sorry to declare that I see a Tendency in them to a very extensive and indefinite Scene of Troubles, in which this Government, and all the Connections of the Company in India, may be eventually involved. I think therefore it becomes incumbent on us to interfere in such a Manner as either to put a total Stop to the Operations, or to mark the Degree of our

Acquiescence in them. I must plainly declare, that I regard their Conduct in this Instance as unseasonable, impolitic, unjust, and unauthorized.

It is unseasonable, because the Treaty was formed with Ragoba at a Time in which he appears to have been totally abandoned by his former Adherents. It was impolitic, because it threw the whole Burthen of the War on the Company, without a Force at the Command of that Presidency equal to the Undertaking, without Money or certain Resources; and because it was undertaken without any Regard to the general Interest of the other Settlements of the Company in India.

It was unjust, because they had received no Injury from any Part of the Maratta State which could authorize their interfering in their mutual Dissensions, nor were under any actual Ties to assist Ragoba; on the contrary, it appears from their Letter of the 31st December, that they were in actual Treaty with those very Powers against whom they have since declared War, and had even laid the Foundation of it at the Time in which they were making them Offers of Friendship. I quote the Words of their Letter as a Proof of this, " Yet it is the furthest from our Wishes to occasion a Rup- " ture between us and the Marattas, by the Steps we have been under the Necessity of " pursuing. The President therefore, agreeable to our Resolution, will explain to the " Ministerial Party at Poona the real Motives for our Proceedings, and they shall be " assured, that in case they gain the Advantage in the present Contest, by the Over- " throw of Ragoba, that we shall resign the Islands to them so soon as they are in a " Condition to defend them from the Portugueze, if they cannot be induced to cede " them to us; provided also that they will give a suitable Equivalent or Compensation " for them."——And in the Paragraph almost immediately following, they say, " About Four Months ago Ragoba, by Means of an Agent he has residing at Surat, " again made Proposals, through the Chief of Surat, for the Assistance of a Body of " Forces against his Enemies, the Ministerial Party at Poona. As we were of Opi- " nion very material Advantages might be derived from it to our Honourable Employ- " ers, by affording them some Assistance, we directed the Chief to enter upon the Nego- " ciation; and pointed out the Terms on which we might be induced to assist him with " a Body of Europeans, Artillery and Infantry, and Sepoys, to the Amount of about " 2,500 Men, which, in Consideration of the Advantages the Company were to reap " from the Alliance, we judged we might be able to spare for some few Months on " this Service."

These opposite Negociations, which must become public to the whole World, cannot fail to destroy that Confidence which the Powers of India have hitherto placed in the Honour and good Faith of the British Government in India.

It is unauthorized, because it is expressly contrary to the Act of Parliament, which declares, it shall not be lawful for them " to make any Orders for commencing Hos- " tilities, or declaring or making War against any Indian Princes or Powers, or for " negociating or concluding any Treaties of Peace or other Treaty with any such In- " dian Princes or Powers, without the Consent and Approbation of the said Governor " General and Council first had and obtained, except in such Cases of imminent Ne- " cessity as would render it dangerous to postpone such Hostilities or Treaties until the " Orders from the Governor General and Council might arrive, and except in such " Cases where the said Presidents and Councils respectively shall have received special " Orders from the said United Company; and any President and Council of Madras, " Bombay, or Bencoolen, who shall offend in any of the Cases aforesaid, shall be " liable to be suspended from his or their Office by the said Governor General and " Council."——The Exceptions above specified will no Wise apply to the present Case; they were in no actual Danger, nor had they even the Plea of a favourable Crisis, the Advantages of which might be lost by missing the Instant Opportunity to seize it. I do not therefore hesitate to pronounce, that they have been guilty of a direct Infringement of the Act of Parliament, and the Authority of this Government founded upon it.

Having thus declared my Opinion on the Measure itself, I am compelled to add my equal Disapprobation of the Manner in which they have commenced the Prosecution of it, by the Removal of their Forces to so great a Distance, both from the Center of their own Possessions, and from the Capital of the Maratta State, which I conceive ought to have been the immediate and principal Object of such an Enterprize; they have laid the Foundation of an indefinite War, depending on a Series of unconcerted Operations, each

each liable to be frustrated by a Variety of probable Accidents, against which it does not appear that they have made any Provision.

On the Whole, I offer it as my Opinion, that we ought to protest against the Treaty formed by the Presidency of Bombay, as invalid, and against the War, as dangerous, impolitic, and unauthorized.

Although I am thus clear in my Opinion of what is past, I confess I have Doubts of the Part which this Government ought to take with respect to the future. It is impossible to conjecture *amidst such a Variety of probable Contingencies, and under our total Ignorance of their Plan of Operations,* what Turn Affairs may have taken, or what may be their actual State at the Time our Orders may arrive. It is certainly to be wished they could be replaced on the same Footing on which they were before their Engagement with Ragoba; but this is now impossible, and to withdraw abruptly after having entered into positive Engagements with one Party, and offended the other perhaps beyond the Hopes of Reconciliation, may be attended with greater Danger than prosecuting the original Design, and even with National Dishonour; I can therefore only venture to propose, that the President and Council of Bombay be peremptorily enjoined to cancel the Treaty with Ragoba, and to withdraw the Detachment immediately to their own Possessions, by whatever Means may be in their Power, unless any of the following Cases shall have occurred; viz.

1st. That they shall have obtained any decisive Advantages over the Enemy.

2d. That the Detachment shall have proceeded to such a Distance, or be in such a Situation as to make it dangerous either to retreat, or not to go on.

3d. That a Negociation shall have taken Place between Ragoba and his Opponents, in consequence of the Support afforded by this Alliance.

These I conceive to be all the Cases of Necessity which must compel them to persevere, and which I must recommend to be made Exceptions to the general Order; I can form the Idea of many others, but I dare not propose them; to multiply Exceptions, would tend to frustrate our Intentions, and I allude to these only, to shew the unfortunate Dilemma to which we are reduced, that we must either proceed with Danger, or retreat with Disgrace, and have no Option but that of the least Evil.

The Board concurring in the Opinion of the Governor General, excepting the Articles of Reservation with respect to the Recall of the Forces from their Expedition to Cambay;

The Question is put, Whether the Recall of the Troops shall be ordered without any specific Exceptions?

Mr. Francis—I agree entirely with the Governor General, in disapproving the Conduct of the Government of Bombay, and in protesting against all the Consequences which may attend it. I think that their engaging the Company's Troops in distant Inland Expeditions, especially without any determinate Object for their Operations, or Limitation of Time for their Service, ought not to receive the least Countenance or Authority from us; and that we ought to insist upon their recalling the Troops, without any Consideration but that of their safe Retreat.

Mr. Barwell—I think not.

Colonel Monson—I think they should, except of the single Consideration of the Safety of the Troops.

General Clavering—Agrees with Mr. Francis in the Whole of his Opinion above entered.

The Governor General—I think not; I should propose the Exceptions which are contained in the preceding Minute, which I have laid before the Board.

Agreed, that the Troops be ordered to be recalled without any Exception, but the single Consideration of their Safety.

General Clavering—I propose that a Paragraph be inserted in a Letter to Bombay, to acquaint the Government there, that as we have directed them to quit their Engagements with Ragoba, and to withdraw their Forces from him into their own Garrisons; and as it is not lawful for them either to negociate or conclude any Treaty of Peace, or other Treaty, with any Indian Prince or Power, without the Consent of the Governor General and Council; we will endeavour to open a Negociation with the governing Maratta Power at Poona, for the Re-establishment of a Peace with that State, upon the most advantageous Terms we can for the Government at Bombay, and the other Settlements of the Company in India. But in case we are not able to open such Negociation with the Maratta States at Poona, that we do empower them to do it, in the first Place to refer the Negociation to us; but if that should not be be found practicable, then to conclude a Treaty of Peace with the ruling Power of the Maratta State at Poona, upon the most advantageous Terms, having always in View the obtaining the Islands of Salsette, &c. of which they are in actual Possession for the Company.

Resolved, that a Negociation be accordingly opened with the Regent at Poona, that Notice thereof be given to the President and Council at Bombay, with Directions to encourage and receive any pacific Overtures which may be made them; and hold, as the first Objects, an immediate Cessation of Arms with the Marattas, and a Confirmation of the Islands of Salsette and Bassein to the Company.

Resolved, that the following Letter be written in Cypher, and dispatched in Triplicate, by different Conveyances, to Bombay.

To the Honourable William Hornby, President, &c. Council at Bombay.

Gentlemen,

We have received yours of the 31st of March, with the Copy of your Treaty with Ragoba enclosed, and the Advices of your subsequent Operations.

Our Duty imposes upon us the painful Necessity of declaring, that we totally condemn the Measures which you have adopted; that we hold the Treaty which you have entered into with Ragoba invalid; and the War which you have undertaken against the Maratta State impolitic, dangerous, unauthorized, and unjust. Both are expresly contrary to the late Act of Parliament; you have imposed on yourselves the Charge of conquering the whole Maratta Empire, for a Man who appears incapable of affording you any effectual Assistance in it. The Plan which you have formed, instead of aiming at a decisive Conquest, portends an indefinite Scene of Troubles, without an adequate Force, without Money or certain Resources to extricate you from them; nor have you the Plea either of Injury sustained from the Party which you have made your Enemy, or of any prior Obligation to defend the Man whose Cause you have espoused.

We solemnly protest against you for all the Consequences, and peremptorily require you to withdraw the Company's Forces to your own Garrisons in whatsoever State your Affairs may be, unless their Safety may be endangered by an instant Retreat. We leave the Means of effecting this to you, but shall expect your punctual Compliance with our Commands.

You have neither informed us for what Purpose the Detachment was sent to a Distance so remote from the obvious Scene of its Operations as Cambay, nor what Plan you had concerted for their subsequent Progress. You have not informed us of the Situation of the Places assigned you for Payment of the Subsidy, in whose Possession they were, from whom they were to be either peaceably surrendered, or taken by Force, nor of the Amount of the ceded Islands; all which Points we conceive to be essentially necessary for our Information.

In the dangerous Consequences which we apprehend from the State in which you had placed the Company's Affairs in your Quarter, we scarce advert to any Part of your Conduct, which respects merely the formal Line of your Duty; yet, as this Government has been charged by a solemn Act of Legislature itself, with the general Interests of the Company in India, and armed with a Controul over the other Presidencies, we cannot pass by, without Notice, the entire Disregard which you appear to have shewn to our Authority.

For the past, we content ourselves with leaving to you the Responsibility of your own Actions; but for the future, in Cases of the like Inattention on your Part, after the peremptory Injunctions which we may have found it necessary to prescribe for your Conduct, we shall deem ourselves accountable, if we neglect to exercise the Powers vested in us by the Act of Parliament, for the Support of the Authority committed to us.

In order that nothing may be omitted on our Part to extricate you from any Difficulties to which your immediately relinquishing your Engagement with Ragoba may expose you, it is our Intention to open a Negociation with the ruling Party of the Maratta State at Poona, as soon as possible. We shall advise you of the Measures we take for this Purpose; in the mean Time, we direct you to receive and encourage any

pacific

pacific Overtures that may be proposed to you, making the Instant Cessation of Arms, and a Confirmation of your Possession of the Islands of Salsette and Bassein, your First Objects; but you are not to aim at more expensive Acquisitions, or conclude any definitive Treaty without our Approbation.

We are, &c. &c.

The Governor General.—I must inform the Board, that the Person whom the Ministerial Party at Poonah have constituted the Paishwa or Prime Minister of the Maratta State in the Place of Ragoba, is an Infant, and that the Man, who I understand has the chief Conduct of their Affairs, is Suckharam Baboo.

I would recommend to the Board, that a Letter be addressed to this Person, signifying to him the Sentiments and Intention of the Board previous to the proposed Negociation; which if agreed to, I move that the following Draft be written to him to that Effect.

To Suckharam Baboo.

Understanding that the chief Administration of the Maratta State is in your Hands, I have judged it expedient to address you upon the Subject of the Transactions which have lately passed between your Government and that of the English Company at Bombay. I am informed by Letters from the Governor and Council of that Place, that they have entered into an offensive Alliance with Ragoba, and sent a large military Force to support him in his Pretensions to the Peshwaship of the Maratta State. As this is contrary to the Orders of the Company, which expresly enjoin the strictest Forbearance of every Act which may lead their Servants to become the Aggressors in any Wars and Disputes with the Powers of India, and to the Commands of the King of Great Britain my Master, by which the other Governments and Settlements of the Company are prohibited from forming Treaties, or engaging in Hostilities, without the previous Concurrence of the Governor General and Council of Bengal, Orders have therefore been sent from myself and the Council aforesaid, to the Governor and Council of Bombay, to withdraw the Forces which they have detached to the Assistance of Ragoba, and to desist from all further Acts of Hostility with any Party of the Maratta Nation, unless in Cases in which they shall be compelled to it in their own Defence; and it is my Intention to depute a proper and trusty Person to Poona, which, being the Seat of the Maratta Empire, is also contiguous to Bombay, to treat with you concerning the Points of Difference between the Government of Poona and that of Bombay, and to establish the Conditions of a future Peace and lasting Friendship between both.

I shall wait for your Answer to this Letter before I give the Deputy his Dispatches, that I may be first assured it will be agreeable to you to receive him; and in the mean Time I hope you will give Orders for the Cessation of all Hostilities on your Part with the Forces of the English Company, that no Impediment may remain to the proposed Pacification.

I have written this solely with a View to the Restoration of Peace and Friendship with your Nation, and the Preservation of good Order, and consistent with the Affairs of the English Company, which are subject to my Charge. From the Report which has been universally made to me of your Wisdom, I have the greatest Reliance on your Disposition to second with Heartiness my Endeavours, that neither you nor I may be blamed, if the Event should not prove answerable to them.

APPENDIX, N° 69.

Extract of Bengal Secret Consultations the 21st June 1775.

PRESENT,

The Honourable Warren Hastings, Esquire, Governor General, President,
Lieutenant General John Clavering,
The Honourable George Monson,
Richard Barwell, }
Philip Francis, } Esquires.

THE Board taking into Consideration the Appointment of a Person on a Deputation to the Maratta Court at Poona;

The Governor General recommends Lieutenant Colonel Dow for that Appointment.

From the Novelty and Delicacy of this Commission, he conceives it to require a Person of known and uncommon Abilities to execute it. The well-known Character of Colonel Dow will justify the Choice that he has made of him for this Trust. Added to a good Understanding, and the Advantages of a liberal Education, he possesses a very competent Knowledge of the Country Languages, and an intimate Acquaintance with the political Interest of the Company; and the Government believes that he has resided some Time at Bombay, which may have afforded him an Opportunity of informing himself of the particular State, Exigencies, and Means of that Presidency.

Mr. Francis—I agree with the Governor General in his Opinion of Colonel Dow's Merit. It was that Opinion which induced me to give my hearty Concurrence to his late Appointment of Commissary General, for which I have since had the greatest Reason to think him particularly qualified. I cannot consent to remove him so soon from an Office in which he has done, and may do, the Company the most essential Service.

Mr. Barwell acquiesces in the Governor General's Motion.

Col. Monson—I agree with the Governor General and Mr. Francis, in the acknowledged Abilities of Col. Dow; but he is now placed in an Office in which he has already acquitted himself to my full Approbation, and I think the suddenly removing him from it, may be attended with some Prejudice to the Company's Affairs in that Department. I therefore do not consent to this Appointment on the Deputation to Poona.

General Clavering—The singular Talents, Integrity, Assiduity, and Firmness, which Lieut. Col. Dow has shewn since his Appointment to the Office of Commissary General, has convinced me that it could not be filled so ably by any Man in the Company's Service. I know that he has saved the Company several Lacks of Rupees; in doing which, he has acquired much Ill Will from the Army. I therefore cannot give my Consent to his Removal, as this would in effect be; because during his long Absence it would be impossible to send a Deputy who should possess all those Requisites for that Employment which Col. Dow possesses. If the Governor General shall think a Military Man of Col. Dow's Rank proper for that Employment, I would recommend Lieut. Col. Upton to it, as I believe him very capable and intelligent.

The Governor General.—I confess that in naming a Military Man, I was guided by the intimate Persuasion, that the Choice of the Board would be confined to that Line. I think the Rank of Colonel Dow rather an Objection than a Recommendation; but I regarded only the other Qualifications which I believed him to be possessed of.

Resolved, That Lieutenant Colonel Dow be not appointed.

Mr. Francis—I agree to Lieutenant Colonel Upton's Appointment.

Mr. Barwell acquiesces.

Colonel Monson agrees to the Motion.

General Clavering agrees.

The Governor General also assents.

Agreed, That Lieutenant Colonel Upton be appointed to Poonah; and that he be allowed 1000 Rupees per Annum, besides the Pay and double Batta which will be his Due as on Service out of the Provinces.

Ordered, That the Secretary acquaint Colonel Upton of his Nomination, and direct him to repair immediately to the Presidency.

The Secretary having prepared the Instructions for the Deputy to Poona, conformably to the Orders of the Board, now produces them; and they are approved in the following Words:

Sir,

Having thought it necessary to depute you to Poona, the Capital of the Maratta State, with Powers to act on Behalf of this Government, in settling with the Peishwa, or acting Minister of that Nation, the Terms for a Restoration of Peace with the Government of Bombay; we direct that you proceed thither with all possible Dispatch, and attend to the following Instructions:

1st. On your Arrival at Poona you will deliver the Credentials herewith given you, unto Sukharam Baboo, or the Peishwa or acting Minister for the Time being; and take the First Opportunity of expressing to him the Regret of this Government for the hostile Measures which have been adopted by the President and Council at Bombay, in Concurrence with Ragoba. You will inform him that we entirely disapprove of the Treaty they have entered into with him, which was done without any Authority from us; that our only Desire is to re-establish that Peace which has been infringed by the Presidency of Bombay, and to live in Amity and Union with the Maratta Nation.

2. You will use all your Endeavours to obtain a Cession of the Islands of Salsette and Bassein to the Company, with the other conquered Islands, viz. Caringa, Canary, Elephanta, and Hog Island. You will represent the Intentions of the Portugueze to have seized these Islands, and that a Naval Force had actually arrived at Goa for this Purpose; that the Government of Bombay possessed themselves of them as soon as they were informed of this Intention, without the least Degree of Enmity to the Maratta Government, but merely to frustrate the Designs of the Portugueze, which have since proved evident in this Respect, they having formally protested against our Proceedings, and asserted an old Claim to the Possession of the above Places. It might be further urged, that the Portugueze will continue to keep a watchful Eye upon them, but their Court being at Peace with the English Nation, they would not pretend to set on Foot any Expedition against them while they remain in our Hands; and if they should be given up to the Marattas, the Portugueze would not fail to take the first Occasion of making any Attack upon them, and either overpower the Garrisons usually stationed for their Defence, or make it necessary to maintain in them such a Force in constant Pay, as the Revenues could by no Means afford to support.

3. If there is any Foundation for the Intelligence which we have lately received, and which we believe to be authentic, of some signal Advantages which have been gained by Ragonaut Row over the Ministerial Army, we apprehend you may be able to obtain the Cession of Salsette and Bassein, with the other conquered Islands, without much Difficulty; and in this Case you may also have it in your Power probably to gain more substantial Advantages to be yielded to the Company. Your next Object therefore must be to obtain a formal Surrender of the Moiety held by the Marattas of the Revenues of the Town and Purgunnah of Broach. But we must leave these, or any other Parts which you may be able to secure for the Interest and Advantage of the Company, to your Discretion; and you will propose them, or not, as you see Occasion from the Spirit of the Court, the Event of the Operations of Ragoba, and the Inclination of the Ministerial Party to a Pacification. If any Offers shall have been made before your Arrival by the Ministerial Party to the Government of Bombay, it is unnecessary to recommend to you to insist on them if they should be for the Advantage of the Company.

4. Though we do not mean to insist absolutely upon all these Concessions, if manifest Advantages should have been gained against the Company's Arms, yet we are determined on no Account to relinquish the Possession of Salsette and Bassein; therefore, should the Peishwa hold out against yielding them to the Company, you are at no Rate to agree to restore them, declaring to them, if necessary, that the Matter having been referred to the Honourable Court of Directors, it is impossible to relinquish these

these Places without their express Permission; and you are to advise us immediately of what has passed.

Although we have thought it necessary to disapprove the Measure of the Presidency of Bombay, in entering into the Treaty with Ragoba, and have ordered them to withdraw their Assistance from him, yet we think it consistent with the Honour of the Nation, and this Government, to endeavour to stipulate some Conditions for him with his Adversaries; what these should be, must depend on the Circumstances in which you may find him on your Arrival; we must therefore leave this chiefly to your Discretion, and only direct in general, that in whatever Treaty you may negociate with the Marattas, you will endeavour to include Ragoba, and obtain such Terms for him as in his actual Situation it may appear to you reasonable to expect, and which may not frustrate the immediate Objects of your Negociations.

We inclose the Translation of a Letter which the Governor General has lately written to Sukharam Baboo, on the Subject of our Intention to depute a Person to the Maratta Court; also, Copy of the Treaty entered into by the Presidency of Bombay with Ragoba, as they may serve for a Guide to you in your Negociations.

Ordered, That they be copied fair, and delivered to Lieutenant Colonel Upton on his Arrival.

APPENDIX, N° 70.

Extract of Bengal Secret Consultations, the 26th June 1775.

PRESENT;

The Honourable Warren Hastings, Esquire, Governor General, President,
Lieutenant General John Clavering,
The Honourable George Monson,
Richard Barwell, } Esquires.
Philip Francis, }

READ, a Letter from the Presidency at Bombay, as follows:

Honourable Sir, and Gentlemen,

In our Letter of the 31st Ultimo we acquainted you of the Treaty that had been entered into with Ragoba, of his Situation, and of the Steps we had pursued for fulfilling our Engagements; at the same Time we inclosed a Copy of the Treaty for your Information: A Duplicate of that Letter, of the Copy of the Treaty, and of another Paper, then inclosed, accompanies this Address.

We have now the Satisfaction to acquaint your Honours, &c. that our Forces were joined by Ragoba's Army, in Number near 40,000 Horse and Foot, at a Village about Two Miles from Cambay, on the 19th Instant, as we are just informed by Advices from the Commanding Officer of our Forces there. The Ministerial Army by the same Account is not more than Six Miles distant from the Place of their Encampment, so that we shortly expect to hear of a decisive Action, which we think can only be prevented by an Accommodation taking Place between Ragoba and the Ministerial Party; some Overtures for which have been made, though we are yet unacquainted with the Particulars; but it appears to us, that the Heads of that Party, divided as we are assured they are amongst themselves, are endeavouring to make some Terms of Advantage with their Master while they yet have it in their Power.

We before advised your Honour, &c. that Madjee Sindy had deserted the Confederate Ministers. We are now assured that he has actually entered into Engagements for assisting Ragoba, and only waits for the first favourable Opportunity to do so. Tookajee Holcar it is also asserted will never act against him, and Futty Sing it is said is entering into Engagements with him.

Thus

Thus it should seem from the Advices of Lieutenant Colonel Keating, that the grand Confederacy will be shortly greatly weakened, if not entirely dissolved. He represents, that nothing is wanting to give Life to Ragoba's Affairs but Money, for which he is it seems in very great Distress. Colonel Keating, and indeed Ragoba himself, have urged us to furnish him with a Supply of at least Five Lacks of Rupees; which Request has been denied, as out of our Power to grant him.

Beside, had it been just at that time in our Power to furnish that Sum, or any other, yet, whatever Sum of Money we could have lent, though considerable to the Company, would have gone but a little Way with so numerous an Army, towards retrieving Ragoba's Affairs, and he would probably again have been soon in the same Distress. We therefore judged it more prudent, especially as we had entirely complied with the Terms of the Treaty on our Part, to give an absolute Denial, that he might at once endeavour to find a pecuniary Supply from some other Quarter. From this, your Honour, &c. will judge that it is not yet in Ragoba's Power to bear any Part of the Expence of our Forces, which by Treaty he has engaged to do. The whole Expence of our Army therefore at present falls on the Company, which by being in the Field is of course very considerable; this Circumstance, together with many other urgent Calls for Money, induces us earnestly to request you will send us a large Supply in Specie or otherwise, as soon as possible; and we hope, that when the Matters at present depending are brought to a successful Issue, and the Company in consequence in quiet Possession of the Factories ceded to them, that we shall be enabled from the Revenues, to carry on our Employers Affairs, without being any longer a Burthen to your Presidency.—The Revenge and Bombay Grab, Two of our Cruizers, fell in with the Maratta Fleet some Time ago, in their Passage to Tellicherry, and were attacked by them; the Enemy however presently sought their Safety by Flight; One of their Vessels only escaped, who was drove on Shore and totally destroyed; it was the Commodore's Vessel, and mounted Four-and-Forty Guns.—We have been favoured with your Letter of the 3d of February, and doubt not but our Address of the 31st December would reach you shortly after, when we hope your Honour, &c. would be convinced that we have done what the Legislature required of us, in giving you every Information you could desire. We did not write you at the Time that Mr. Mastyn was ordered to quit Poona, as the Notice of your having taken on you the Government of Bengal, in virtue of the late Act of Parliament, had not then reached us, and when it did, it required some Days to compile and digest the Detail of the Company's Affairs at this Presidency, which you desired, as well as to give you a clear Idea of the important Matters we had then in Hand. At that Time the Siege of Tannah was carrying on, which also occasioned our Advices being retarded for a few Days, as we were then in daily and even hourly Expectation of being in Possession of the Fort; and we wished, together with the Motives of our Proceedings, to be able to advise you of the Success that had attended them; but it happened that our Operations at Tannah were protracted much beyond the Time we had Reason to suppose. It is not therefore at all extraordinary, that private Advices should be received before our Letter reached you; but your Honour, &c. may depend, that we shall always send you ample and timely, and we hope satisfactory Accounts of our Proceedings.

We are, &c.

(Signed) Wm Hornby, &c. Council.

Bombay Castle,
30 April 1775.

APPENDIX, N° 71.

Extract of Bengal Secret Consultations, the 5th July 1775.

The Honourable Warren Hastings, Governor General, President,
Lieutenant John Clavering,
The Honourable George Monson,
Richard Barwell, } Esquires.
Philip Francis, }

RECEIVED, the following Advices from Fort Saint George:

Honourable Sir, and Sirs,

A Packet under your Address, from the Select Committee at Bombay, was Yesterday received by the Success Grab, and forwarded over Land.

Although we doubt not but the Gentlemen at Bombay have communicated to your Honour, &c. particular Intelligence regarding their Operations, yet we have thought it necessary to transmit to you Copy of their Letter to us, and of the Papers which accompanied it.

The Intelligence mentioned in Mr. Townsend's Letter respecting Hyder Ally's Designs against the Rajah of Travenore, we believe to have but little Foundation, as the Raja is expressly included in the Treaty entered into between this Government and Hyder Ally in 1769; and we can scarce think that Hyder Ally will venture to break the Treaty by attacking the Raja.

We have the Honour to be, &c.

Fort Saint George, A. Wynch, &c. Council.
20 June 1775.

To the Honourable Alexander Wynch, Esquire, President, &c. &c. at Fort Saint George.

Honourable Sir, and Sirs,

You are advised from the Board, under the 10th April, of the Arrival here of the Two Companies of European Infantry that you had sent to our Assistance. We are now to acquaint your Honour, &c. that the Whole of the Battalion of Sepoys under the Command of Captain Kelly is also safely arrived, except about an Hundred Men that are on board the Ship Calcutta, which has been for some Days past expected from the Coast.

The Two Companies of European Infantry were sent to join our Forces at present engaged in assisting to re-establish Ragonaut Row, the Peishwa, in the Supreme Government of the Marattas. Our Forces, in Conjunction with those of the Peishwa, are in full March from Cambay, towards Poona. In Five successive Engagements which they have had with the Ministerial Army, they have always been victorious, and without any Loss to our Forces (the Advantage has always been obtained by them) except in the last, which happened on the 18th ultimo, when the Victory was more compleat than in any of the former Actions, and the Number of the Enemy killed, and their Horse very considerable indeed. Yet, owing to an Accident or Mistake, a Detachment of our Forces sustained considerable Loss, being that wherein the Madras Infantry was posted; the Loss sustained by your Infantry, was Two Commissioned Officers, and Fourteen Non-commissioned Officers and Private Men killed; and One Officer and Twenty-eight Non-commissioned Officers and Privates wounded: The Particulars of this Affair are related in a Letter from Lieutenant Colonel Keating to us; an Extract of which we now inclose for your Information.

We have lately learnt by Advices from the Resident at Onnore, that an Embassy has been sent by the Dutch at Cochin to the Nabob Hyder Ally, at Seringapatam; and that there is great Reason to suppose that a Treaty has been entered into between them, whereby

whereby the Dutch, in Consideration of Grants for the Purchase of Pepper and Sandall Wood, have engaged to assist the Nabob, by Sea and Land, in making a Conquest of the Travencore Country. A Copy of the Letter containing this Intelligence is enclosed, and should it be any ways useful, we shall be happy in having communicated it you.

The enclosed Packet, for the Chief at Anjengo, we request you will be pleased to forward.

We are, &c.
(Signed) Wm Hornby,
&c. Council.

Bombay Castle,
1st June, 1775.

A true Copy,
(Signed) Jas Capper,
Assistant Secretary.

Extract of a Letter from Lieutenant Colonel Thomas Keating, Commanding Officer of the Forces with Ragoba, to the Select Committee at Bombay; dated at Betasse Camp, 19th May, 1775.

As soon as the Enemy's Guns began firing, I rode to the Rear, and found Captain Meyers moving agreeable to Orders; when near enough, our Guns and Howitzers fired on their Army, and at their Cannon, until the former fled and the latter were silenced. Captain Meyers and several other Officers then reported to me, that Two Guns belonging to the Enemy were but a little Way from the Right of the Division engaged, and the Enemy cutting down Hedges to make Room to carry them off; on this Information I ordered the Second Company of European Grenadiers from the Head of the Line of March to join Captain Meyers' Division, and directed Captain Meyers to endeavour to possess himself of the Two Guns, ordering him to avail himself of the strong Milk Bush Inclosures and Wood, and move with the utmost Regularity to cover them; I remained with the Guns, Two 12 Pounders, One 6 and One 8 Inch Howitzer. Soon after the Division with Captain Meyers quitted their Ground, I observed them to move much too quick: I called to them to slacken their Pace, which they then did; but I since find they were soon after ordered to move on rapidly. However, they got well formed near the Guns, when the Enemy charged them from the Left with a very large Body, which I reached with Round and Case Shot, and with the Musquetry; they were soon repulsed. They charged a Second Time, and were again repulsed. At this Time Captains Meyers and Serte were killed just at the Moment a very large Body of the Enemy with Two War Elephants got into a Lane immediately in the Rear of the Division, but declared they were Ragoba's Party, and this was affirmed by one of his Officers, named Hurry Punt, and was heard by many of our People, and some of our Scindian Horse, calling to the Enemy to Advance, adding, "Now is your Time, here are the English without their Guns." These Circumstances, added to the Endeavours of the Horse and Elephants to break in on the Division, obliged them to face to the Right about, and give them a general Fire, which totally routed them: Thus were the Enemy repulsed in Front and Rear, with great Loss to them, and very little to us, when the First Company of European Grenadiers were observed by the rest of the Division to go to the Right about, and make a running March or Retreat from their Ground. This occasioned the Sepoys and Madras Infantry to follow their Example, but not further than to join the Grenadiers, though they all retreated very quick. It was something regular till they came to the Milk Bush Hedges in their now run-away Front, where the Openings were very small; there commenced their Destruction, every Man pushed were he could, without observing the least Order, though repeatedly called upon by most of their Officers. The Enemy observing their Confusion, rode amongst them Sword in Hand, and cut a great Number of them to Pieces. As soon as I observed our Men in this Disorder, I pointed all our Fire to cover their Retreat, and went to rally them. The first I met were the Grenadiers, as flying before about Fifty Horse, cutting them down without Opposition; with great Difficulty I got them to the Right about, and ordered them to fire; instead of which, they answered, "These are our Friends;" Your Friends!" said I, "see them cutting down our Sepoys under pushed Bayonets." This was the Case; they were not 15 Yards distant. The Moment I assured them it was the Enemy, in place of firing they fled shamefully, without firing a single Musket, though our Cannon

Cannon were scarce 40 Yards distant from them; nor did they halt for some Time. Then it was our Artillery made amazing Slaughter, in a few Minutes our Case Shot covered the Field with their dead Bodies. But it is a Business I cannot account for, that in Spite of every Annoyance those People always carry off their Dead; on this Occasion they lost immense Numbers by their Attention to it; not more than Nine or Ten were left behind.

As far as was in our Power we advanced upon the Enemy, and totally repulsed them, after the above shameful Retreat, in which we sustained our whole Loss, which I believe is greater than ever was known in India out of the same Number engaged. Out of 15 Officers, 6 were killed, Captains Meyer and Serte, Lieutenants Morris, Stonny, Prosser, and Anderson; and Five badly wounded, Captain Frith, Lieutenants Dawson and Young, Ensigns Denson and Turing. For the rest of the Killed and Wounded, I beg Leave to refer your Honour, &c. to the accompanying Return.

After remaining on the Field of Battle to bury our Dead, and procure Conveyance for our Wounded, we marched to this Place, which is One Coss from the Banks of the River Mahe, where we propose marching To-morrow, having persuaded the Peishwa not to remain on this Side during the Rains.

The Enemy's Loss must be very considerable indeed, though the Numbers, as yet are not mentioned from any Accounts; in general our Intelligence is exceeding bad. Three Elephants were left dead on the Field, and a great Number of Horses. At the First Tank they watered, as I am told, upwards of 500 died of their Wounds. Two Thousand good Horse would have made it as compleat a Victory as ever was made in India, but Two Hundred cannot be procured in this Army. Indeed, I impute a great deal of their backward Behaviour to their having no Pay, and scarce Provision to eat.

A true Extract.
Geo. Skipp,
Secretary,

A true Copy of the Extract.
(Signed) Jas. Capper,
Assistant Secretary,

APPENDIX, N° 72.

Extract of Bengal Secret Consultations, 10th July, 1775.

To the Honourable Warren Hastings, Esquire, Governor General, &c. &c. Fort William Select Committee.

Honourable Sir, and Gentlemen,

IN the last Address from this Department to your Honour, &c. we advised you of the Junction of our Forces with the Peishwa Army, and of the then Situation of Affairs. A Duplicate thereof is now enclosed.

Since then, nothing very decisive has taken Place. Our Forces, in Conjunction with the Peishwa of Ragoba's Army, are now on their March from Cambay towards Poona; and by this Time, as we have Reason to suppose, are near Broach. In Five successive Actions with the Ministerial Army, they have always been victorious without any Loss to our Forces, except in the last, which happened on the 18th ult. when though the Victory was much more compleat than in any of the former Actions, and the Number of the Enemy killed and wounded were very considerable indeed, with a great Number of their Horses; yet, owing to some Accident or Mistake, a Detachment of our Forces sustained considerable Loss. The Particulars of this Affair are related in a Letter from Lieutenant Colonel Keating to us, dated the 19th ult. an Extract of which is inclosed for your fuller Information. Six commissioned Officers were killed, and Five wounded on this Occasion, with about Seventy Europeans killed and wounded, and about the like Number of Sepoys.

Inclosed

APPENDIX, N° 72.

Inclosed we transmit to your Honour, &c. a Copy of a Letter from our Resident at Onnore, containing Intelligence of the Designs of Hyder Ally and of the Dutch. We have communicated the same to the Presidency of Fort Saint George, and have directed the Chief of Angengo to apprize the Rajah of Travencore of the Designs against him.

Your Favour of the 8th March came to Hand the 12th ultimo, to which we shall fully reply by the first direct Conveyance; but, agreeable to your Request, we inclose a Return of the Forces of this Presidency, and a State of its Revenues; in the last of which you will observe, is not included the Revenues of any of the Places ceded to us by Treaty, Salsette and the other Islands only excepted.

We return you Thanks for your Assurances of Assistance. At present, the most material Matter we have to desire, is a Supply of Money, which we request you will send us by Bills, or in Specie, as soon as you may be able; and in the mean Time the Chief and Council at Surat have Orders to draw upon your Honour, &c. for such Sums as they can procure; and they have lately succeeded in obtaining about Two Lacks of Rupees.

We have judged it necessary to appoint Mr. Moyston to proceed to and to reside at Ragoba's Durbar, in order, amongst other Matters, to relieve the Commanding Officer from all other Duties but the Command of the Troops. He will accordingly set out for Surat very shortly; from whence we make no Doubt but that he may easily join the Army.

As, by the Orders of the Honourable the Court of Directors, political Matters as well as those relative to military Operations, are conducted by the Select Committee, we request that your Honour, &c. in your Advices on those Subjects, will address your Letters accordingly.

Bombay Castle, 1st June, 1775.

We are, &c. &c.
(Signed) Wm. Hornby,
&c. Council.

Resolved, That the following Answer be written in Cypher, and sent to Bombay.

To the Honourable William Hornby, Esquire, President, &c. Select Committee at Bombay.

Gentlemen,

We are favoured with your Dispatches of the 1st ultimo, which contain among other, some Advices of the Operations of the Army of Ragoba, and of your Detachment with him.

We find these Accounts so incompleat and so unsatisfactory, that we are still at a Loss to form a true Idea of the State of these Affairs from them. The only Part of Colonel Keating's Correspondence, which you have communicated to us, is a broken Extract from a Letter containing a Relation of his Transactions, beginning in the Middle of an Engagement, from which we are unable to judge of his Intentions before the Battle, or of the Operations he proposed in consequence of it. We only learn, that he was arrived near the River Mage, and had persuaded Ragoba to cross it before the Rains; which appears to us rather to controvert your Information of his being in full March towards Poona. It should rather seem that he means to cross the River, in order to put his Army in Quarters during the Rains. We therefore think it necessary to require Copies of your Correspondence with Colonel Keating from the beginning of the Campaign, and that you continue to furnish us with Copies of what may pass between you in future.

We cannot avoid observing, that notwithstanding our Instructions of the 8th of March last, and the peremptory Stile in which we found it necessary to convey them, you have still thought it proper to depute Mr. Mostyn as public Minister to Ragoba's Court, without informing us of the Designs or Object of his Mission, or of the Measures which you may have taken for a Compliance with those Instructions, although it appears, that Ten Days had elapsed from the Receipt of them till the Date of your Letter now before us; neither have you informed us what Supplies you have received or expect from Ragoba for maintaining the Burthen of the War you have entered into on his Behalf. In a Word, we are still as much in the Dark as we were on the First Intelligence of your projected Campaign, notwithstanding our earnest Intreaties to be furnished with every Information that could enable us to judge what Assistance our Duty might make it incumbent upon us to afford you. We now desire, in Addition to the other Lights we have

have required from you, that you send us a Copy of your Instructions to Mr. Mostyn; and that you give Orders to him to transmit to us, by every Opportunity, successive Intelligence of the State of Affairs in Ragoba's Army while he continues there, and of all other Matters relating to his Negotiations, and the State of the present War with the Marattas, as far as may fall under his Notice.

From what we have said you will perceive that we can in no Shape approve of your late Instructions: It is painful to us to repeat Remonstrances. We shall leave you to answer for this Conduct to the Court of Directors. In the mean Time, left in the Uncertainty of which we complain, we cannot think ourselves justified in sending you the Supplies you require. We remain in Hopes, that the Letter you promise us in Answer to ours of the 8th of March, will be more explicit, and both enable us to afford you our Aid, and point out the Objects which are to be obtained by it.

We have already advised you of our Intention to open a Negociation with the ruling Party at Poona, for the Re-establishment of Peace with the Marattas. We also addressed Sukeram Baboo at the same Time on that Subject, acquainting him of our Desire to depute a Person to treat with him there. We have since appointed Lieutenant Colonel Upton to this Charge, who is now ready to set off, and will wait at Calpee on the River Jumna, for Passports from Sukeram Baboo. We inclose a Copy of such Parts of his Instructions as we think materially necessary for your Information.

Fort William, 10th July 1775. We are, &c. &c.

APPENDIX, N° 73.

Extract of Bengal Secret Consultations, the 10th July, 1775.

PRESENT,

The Honourable Warren Hastings, Governor General, President,
Lieutenant General John Clavering,
The Honourable George Monson,
Richard Barwell, } Esquires.
Philip Francis, }

GENERAL Clavering lays before the Board, the following Proposal, which was delivered to him for that Purpose by Lieutenant Colonel Upton.

Memorandums from Lieutenant Colonel Upton, for the Perusal of General Clavering, respecting the Embassage to Poona.

Route Colonel Upton prefers, by Allahabad to Calpee, and there wait Letters from Poona, and be supplied with the necessary Passes.

Reasons for giving the Preference to this Route.

Passage by Water to Calpee, which will be effected as soon as the Nana's Letters can reach that Place, and sooner than any Vessel can get out, consequently all this Time gained should the Embassage not proceed; the Inconvenience arising from this Journey to the Company or the Colonel, &c. is very immaterial. The Road from Calpee to Poona, a high Road, which the Marattas always take when coming into the upper Parts of Indostan. By Letters sent to the Nabob Assaph ul Dowlah, as soon or soon after the Departure of Colonel Upton, Passes will be easily obtained, and meet him at Allahabab or Calpee, from what few independent Rajas may possess the Country that he has to pass through. However, the Country to be passed is almost entirely in the Possession of the Marattas, or influenced by them. To strengthen this Opinion, supposed waiting till the Middle of August to go by Sea, the Uncertainty of the Passage (suppose) to Masulipatam, the waiting for every Thing necessary there, and then having to go to Poona quite as far by Land as from Calpee to Poona, through a very bad travelling Country, which Colonel Upton has in Part experienced, as well as the very tedious De-

lays

lays always found there in supplying the most trifling Wants; these Circumstances put together, shew at one View that the Time is quite gained from Calcutta to Calpee.

The Occasion is too obvious to observe the Necessity of Letters being dispatched instantly to the Nanah, in which the Name of the Minister should be mentioned.

Letters to the Nabob Assaph ul Dowlah should also be forwarded directly. Letters to Cheit Sing, will procure what Elephants and Cauffet Camels may be wanted.

The Journey from Calpee to Poona, is about Twenty-five Days. Our Ally Assaph ul Dowlah will supply the necessary Guards till met by the Nanahs.

Agreed, that this Plan for the Route of Colonel Upton, be adopted by him in his Journey to Poona, but that he be directed to wait at Calpee, for Passports from the Peishwa of the Maratta State.

Agreed, That the Governor General be requested to write to Nudjiff Cawn, desiring him to furnish Colonel Upton with Passes, and to afford him every necessary Assistance in his Way to Calpee, if he should find it requisite to apply for them; and also to write to Sukeram Baboo, for Passports through the Marattas Dominions, to be forwarded to meet Colonel Upton at Calpee.

Resolved, That the following Letter be also written to Mr. Bristow.

To Mr. John Bristow.

Sir,

We have received your Two Letters of the 20th and 21st June. Having ordered Lieutenant Colonel Upton to proceed on a Deputation to Poona, to negociate a Treaty of Peace with the Maratta State at that Capital; and as it is thought proper that he should take the Route of Allahabad, and by Calpee, we desire you will obtain from the Nabob the necessary Passports for his Safety in travelling through his Dominions, together with a Guard to conduct him as far as Calpee, and to remain with him there until the Arrival of Passports from the Peishwa at Poona, at which Time we could wish that it were at Colonel Upton's Direction, either to dismiss the Guard, or to take it on with him if he should find it necessary. You will take Care that Blanks be left in the Passports, for the Names of any Persons who may attend Colonel Upton in his Business.

Fort William, 10th July 1775.

We are, &c.

The following Letter of Dispatch is sent with the Instructions of the Board to Colonel Upton:

To Lieutenant Colonel John Upton.

Sir,

The Commander in Chief has communicated to us the Route by which you propose to perform your Journey to Poona, and your Reasons for prefering it.

As we approve of your pursuing this Route, we have directed Mr. Bristow to procure from the Nabob Assoph ul Dowlah, Passports for you, and a Guard to accompany you through his Dominions, as far as Calpee. Nudjiff Cawn has also been requested to afford his Assistance, if you should find it necessary to apply for Passes to him; and a Letter has been dispatched to the Peishwa at Poona, desiring him to send Passports to meet you at Calpee, at which Place you will wait for them. We wish you a safe Journey; and

Fort William, 10th July 1775.

We are, &c. &c.

Extract

APPENDIX, Nº 73.

Extract of Bengal Secret Consultations the 17th July, 1775.

PRESENT,

The Honourable Warren Hastings, Governor General, President,
Lieutenant General John Clavering,
The Honourable George Monson,
Richard Barwell, } Esquires.
Philip Francis, }

Read, the following Letter and Inclosures, sent in by Lieutenant Colonel Upton.

To the Honourable Governor General, &c. Council.

Gentlemen,

I was Yesterday honoured with your Letter of the 10th, and am taking every Measure to hasten my Departure, which I imagine may be by the 21st, if the Board should find it convenient to give me their ultimate Instructions by that Time.

I have taken the Liberty to inclose the Names of the Gentlemen I could wish to be permitted to take with me on this Service, and shall be happy if they are approved of by the Board, and established with their fixed Salaries whilst employed on this Service.

I have also the Honour to inclose Memorandums of what Guards, Escorts, Camp Equipage, Boats, &c. &c. appear to me necessary, which I hope may meet with your Approbation, and Order to procure.

I have made a few Remarks on my Instructions, which you will do me the Honour to observe upon in my private (or what farther) Instructions you may be pleased to give.

Fort William, I have the Honour to be, &c.
July 14, 1775. (Signed) J. Upton.

Remarks submitted to the Consideration of the Honourable the Governor General and Council, by Lieutenant Colonel Upton.

1st. Farther Advantages to be obtained for the Company, &c. Should this be practicable, of what Nature, whether Money or Territory? If the former, under what Head or Account? If Territory, where?

2d. Stipulation for Ragoba.—Is he entitled (or should it be) to possess Country? Should this be guaranteed by the Company? Should he receive any Money from the Ministerial Party, how much should be obtained for him, if possible, and how secured to him?

3d. To endeavour to get the Surrender of the Moiety of the Revenues of the Town and Purgunnah of Broach.—Is it meant then that Broach with its Purgunnah, is (if possible) to be entirely the Property of the Company, independent of any other Power?

4th. What is the Name of the present Nana, or Person in Chief, ruling the Maratta Empire, and meant to be kept in Possession thereof?

5th. Upon the Treaty's being concluded, are the Settlements of Bombay and Madras to be informed thereof by me, and immediately thereupon, or not till after I have heard from the Governor General and Council?

6th. Should I have not with me the Seal of the Company? Should it not also be affixed to my Instructions, as it may have great Weight at the Court of Poona?

7th. Sukaram Baboo has been wrote to twice.—Should not a Letter to him be given to me to use in case of Miscarriage of these Letters, (or as they may tell me, mislay or lost) again fully maintaining that he is to treat with me only? Should he have already treated with the Governor and Council of Bombay, is he to be advised of the Necessity of a Ratification of such Treaty, and this by me, on your Parts, or wait till it shall be referred to Bengal?

8th. Letters to the Governor and Council of Bombay, (to be made use of only on Necessity); they may alledge, the not fully comprehending their Letters from Bengal;

that

that they wait further Instructions that will determine the Business they are negotiating; in short, that they may delay my Business by various Pretexts — such Letter will effectually prevent it.

9th. It may be necessary to have a Letter to the Governor and Council of Fort St. George also, to make Use of only upon Necessity; acquainting them with the Nature of my Deputation, to prevent my being obstructed therein, as well as to receive any Assistance from them should it be required.

Gentlemen recommended by Lieutenant Colonel Upton, with their Appointments, to the Honourable the Governor General and Council, to proceed with him on his Embassage to Poona.

Captain Allan Macpherson, of the first Regiment,	Interpreter and Persian Translator.
Lieutenant James Paterson, of the 1st Regiment,	Secretary.
Sutton Banks, M. D.	Surgeon.
Captain Benjamin Wroe, of the 1st Regiment	A general Charge of all Guards, Camp Equipage, Elephants, Camels, Stores, &c. &c. belonging to the Honourable Company.

Extract of Bengal Secret Consultations, the 17th July, 1775.

Resolved, That the further Orders and Resolutions of the Board upon the above, be signified to Colonel Upton in the following Letters:

To Lieutenant Colonel Upton.

Sir,

Having considered the several Questions which you thought it necessary, for the Elucidation of your Instructions, to propose to us, we shall proceed to acquaint you with our Resolutions upon each.

1st. The direct Purposes of your Appointment are to negociate and conclude a Treaty of Peace between the Maratta Government and the Presidency of Bombay, and to obtain a Confirmation to that Presidency of the Islands of Salsette and Bassein for the Company; these Points you are to consider as indispensable.

If, however, from the Success of Ragoba's Forces against the Ministerial Party, you should find the latter disposed to make further Concessions for our Neutrality, we have mentioned in our former Instructions, that a Renunciation of the remaining Moiety of the Revenues of the Town and Purgunnah of Broach, is a Point which we wish to secure; for the rest, you must be guided entirely by your own Discretion, which will be actuated by the State and Objects of the Negociation which may have taken Place between the Government at Bombay and the Ministry at Poona: But we would not have you prolong the Negociations for a Day, in Hopes of obtaining any other Conditions than those which we have expressly mentioned, or required. We cannot point our Intentions herein more explicitly, as your Conduct must depend entirely upon the Circumstances and Situation of Affairs.

2dly. With respect to the Terms to be obtained from Ragoba: This likewise is an Article on which we cannot give you more particular Instructions, because, as we have already told you, it must rest wholly upon contingent Circumstances; but whatever may be settled for him by the Treaty, if it forms a Clause in it, it will of course be guaranteed to him by the Company.

3dly. The Town and Purgunnah of Broach are already possessed independent in their Government by the Company; our Orders were only intended to free the Company from any Participation of the Revenues of these Places with the Marattas.

4thly. Ragonaut Row is the Peishwa or Chief Ruler of the Maratta State; but he was obliged by the Ministerial Party at Poona to quit that Capital, and they have since proclaimed in his Stead the Son of Narrain Row, the late Peishwa, who is still an Infant. We conceive it impossible to foresee what Accommodation will take Place between the two Parties now contending for the Peishwaship, but it is most probable that

that if the Ministry prevail, the Elevation of the Son of Narrain Row will be confirmed. If the Peace is to be effected by a Negociation, the Terms of it must be left to the Parties themselves, and we shall agree to acknowledge whomsoever they shall finally resolve among themselves to establish; but in the present State of Affairs, as we cannot formally address ourselves to either of the Competitors, we have referred you to Sukaram Baboo, the ruling Minister at Poona; and in Case he should not be living at the Time of your Arrival at Poona, you will address yourself in like Manner to the Person who may be found in actual Possession of the chief Administration, delivering to him the Letters addressed to Sukaram Baboo, together with your Letter of Credence, which will contain full Powers for treating with any Person who shall be possessed of that Authority of the State.

5thly. You will advise the Bombay Presidency of your Arrival at Poona, and inform them constantly, as well as the Presidency of Fort Saint George, of all Transactions which you may think of Use for them to know.

6thly. We do not think it necessary to furnish you with a Seal. The Company's Seal will be affixed to your Credentials, which will give full and ample Validity to any Treaty which you may conclude with the Marattas.

7thly. You have been already directed not to leave Calpee till you hear from Sukaram Baboo, or obtain Passports from him. You will have a Letter for him delivered to you with your Credentials, in which he is informed, that we do not admit the Authority of any Person to conclude a Treaty on Behalf of the Company with the Maratta Government but yourself; and if any should have taken Place with the President and Council at Bombay, it is to be of no Effect until ratified by you.

8thly. The Governor and Council of Bombay have already been advised of your Appointment; a Duplicate of that Letter is inclosed, with a further Notification of the Power vested in you by the foregoing Paragraph. This Packet you will send to Bombay by the first safe Conveyance.

9thly. The Fort Saint George Presidency being informed of your Deputation, there can be no Necessity to furnish you with any Letter under their Address.

We herewith deliver to you a Cypher, which you are to keep in your own Possession, and make Use of when you find Occasion in your Advices to us and the other Presidencies.

Fort William,
the 17th July 1775.

We are, &c.

To Lieutenant Colonel Upton.

Sir,

In a separate Letter of this Date we have given you our Sentiments of Directions upon the particular Articles which you referred to our Consideration in your Paper of Remarks. We shall now reply to the other Inclosures in your Address of the 14th Instant.

We approve of your taking with you Captains Wroe and Macpherson, Lieutenant Paterson, and Doctor Banks: They are to receive the usual Pay of their respective Ranks, with full double Batta, as if on Command without the Provinces, from the 15th Instant; that is to say, the Military Officers will receive the Appointment of their Ranks in the Army, and Doctor Banks those of a full Surgeon on this Establishment.

We had previously fixed a Salary of 1,000 Rs. per Mensem, to be drawn by you, besides your Pay and double full Batta: These Allowances are to take Place from the Date of your Instructions, that is the 21st Ultimo.

APPEN-

APPENDIX, N° 74.

Extract of Bengal Secret Consultations, the 24th July, 1775.

AGREED, that the following Letters be consequently written to Bombay and to Fort Saint George; and that the former be conveyed by Means of Colonel Upton.

To the Honourable William Hornby, Esquire, President, &c. Council at Bombay.

Gentlemen,

In our last, in which a Duplicate is inclosed, we informed you of the Appointment of Lieutenant Colonel Upton, to negociate a Treaty of Peace with the Marattas.

This will be forwarded to you by him; and we think it proper to advise you, that in Case any Treaty may have been formed, or any Conditions settled by you with the Ministerial Party, they must be confirmed and ratified by Colonel Upton before we can allow them to be of any Effect, as we have given him ample Instructions and full Powers to conclude upon such Terms only as he may judge proper.

We have furnished him with a Copy of the small Cypher, No. 2, Letter B, framed in March 1755, which we have directed him to make Use of whenever he may find Occasion for it.

Fort William,
17th July 1775.

We are, &c.

To the Honourable Alexander Wynch, Esquire, President, &c. Council, at Fort Saint George.

Gentlemen,

You are already fully apprized of the Operations of the President and Council at Bombay, in Conjunction with Ragoba, against the Ministerial Party of the Maratta Government at Poona. We think it proper however to inform you, that we highly disapprove of the Conduct of that Presidency in having entered into an offensive Alliance with Ragoba, not only as we deemed it repugnant to the Intention of the Legislature of Great Britain, and to the positive Injunctions of the Company, which recommend a profound Peace with all the Powers of Hindostan; but also because, by the Treaty entered into, they engaged to assist a Man who had not the Means even to support his own Army in an extensive Conquest, which must naturally lead to an indefinite War, and perhaps to the Disgrace of the English Arms, besides throwing the Burthen of it upon them. We therefore directed them immediately to withdraw the Company's Troops into their own Garrisons, and to receive any Overtures which might be made for a Pacification or Cessation of Arms; but to suspend any Conclusions upon them until further Orders.

That nothing may be wanting on our Part to extricate the Presidency of Bombay from the Difficulties in which they were likely to be involved, and to restore a Peace between the Company and the Maratta Government, we have deputed Lieutenant Colonel Upton to proceed to Poona to conclude a Treaty of Peace with that State; and have furnished him with full Powers and Instructions for this Purpose. The Peishwa has been advised of this Deputation, and desired to forward Passports for Colonel Upton to meet him at Calpee.

Colonel Upton has received Orders to communicate to you any Transactions which he may think material enough to deserve your Notice.

Fort William,
the 17th July 1775.

We are, &c.

Resolved,

Resolved, that the following Letter of Credence be written in Persian, and delivered under the Company's Seal to Colonel Upton.

Whereas Troubles have arisen, and Hostilities actually taken Place between the Government of Bombay and the Maratta State at Poona, which is repugnant to the Commands of the Company, and to the Wishes which they have constantly manifested to maintain a perpetual Peace and Amity with that Nation; We, the Governor General and Council of Bengal, in Virtue of the Powers vested in us by the Legislature of Great Britain, and by the said Company, to direct and controul the Company's Settlements in India, relying on your Fidelity, Prudence, and Integrity, have deputed you to proceed to Poona, and to negociate and conclude with the Chiefs and Rulers of that State, a Treaty of Peace and Friendship between them and the English Company, on such Terms as shall be for the mutual Benefit, Honour, and Satisfaction of both Parties, and remove all the Cause of Enmity which at this Time may have taken Place between the Marattas and the Government of Bombay: And we hereby give you full Powers to that Effect, declaring that we will ratify and confirm whatever shall be so concluded by you, in our Names, and in our Behalf, according to the Instructions with which we have furnished you for that Purpose.

Given in Fort William this

Warren Hastings,
J. Clavering,
Geo. Monson,
Richard Barwell,
P. Francis.

Extract of Bengal Secret Consultations, 24th July, 1775.

Colonel Upton's Embassy to Poona affording a favourable Opportunity to survey the Peninsula of India, and likewise to ascertain the true Distance of Places through which he will pass, Colonel Monson proposes, That the Reverend Mr. Smith be appointed to attend Colonel Upton for this Purpose—To which the Board agree, and allow Mr. Smith to draw the Pay and Allowances of a Captain of Engineers, employed on a similar surveying Service.

APPENDIX, N° 75.

Extract of Bengal Secret Consultations, the 24th July, 1775.

PRESENT,

The Honourable Warren Hastings, Governor General, President,
Lieutenant General John Clavering,
The Honourable George Monson,
Richard Barwell, Philip Francis, } Esquires.

READ, the following Paper of Intelligence, received by the Governor General, and extracted from his Book of News.

Intelligence from the Decan, dated the 27th of Rubbee Assanie, or June.

We hear that Ragonaut Row, with the English Army, having crossed the Nurbudder, in the Neighbourhood of Broche, began his March towards Surat. Hurrajee Purkeah determined likewise to cross the Nurbudder with his Army, and had sent over his Baggage and Military Stores, there being a Space of 10 Coss between him and the Army of Ragonaut Row.

In

In the mean Time the English having embarked in Boats, suddenly appeared, and falling on the Baggage of Harrajee Purkeah, plundered it. They slew great Numbers of his Men, and very many were drowned in the River; Hurrajee fled, and took the Road to Goserant; Focajee, who had not sent his Baggage or Stores across the River, returned with them in Safety, in Company with Hurrajee.

Ragonaut Row is encamped on the Banks of the Nurbudder, and designs to pursue his Route to the Decan during the Continuance of the Rains.

Suceram Baboo is very ill, occasioned by Grief for the Death of his Son.

The People of the Decan are in the utmost Consternation.

Nizam Ally Khan and Moodajee Boosla, with One Consent have entered into a League with Ragonaut Row.

The Rains are set in very heavily in the Decan.

We are in a State of Uncertainty as to who is to be Ruler of the Decan.

It being beyond the Reach of Conjecture what Face the War with the Marattas may bear at the Period of Colonel Upton's Arrival at Poona; and the Governor General considering the Probability of Ragoba's complete Success, recommends to the Board that Colonel Upton be instructed in such Case to treat with him.

Agreed, That the following Directions be given to Lieutenant Colonel Upton on this Head; and that a Letter of Introduction, and implying the Powers vested in him to treat and conclude a Treaty in Behalf of the Company with Ragoba, be also addressed to that Prince, and given in Charge to the Colonel.

To Lieutenant Colonel Upton.

Sir,

It being uncertain how the Issue of the War now depending between Ragoba and the Ministerial Party may turn out at the Time of your Arrival at Poona, and as it is possible that Ragoba may have made himself Master of that Place, we hereby authorize you in such Case, or if you shall find so great a Superiority on his Side as to give you Reason to expect that the Operations will be entirely decisive in his Favour, to negociate and conclude a Treaty with him, instead of the present Ministry; and for this Purpose, a Letter will be delivered you, addressed to Ragoba; and as you are furnished with a Copy of his Treaty with the Bombay Presidency, by the Assistance of this and your former Instructions, you will be able to settle it upon such Terms as you may conceive will best answer our Ideas.

We are, &c.

Fort William,
24th July 1775.

To Ragonaut Row, sent by Colonel Upton, written the 31st July 1775.

It is with great Concern that we have heard of the late Distractions of the Maratta State; but as it has pleased God to crown your Arms with Success, we are in Hopes that an End will be soon put to them. The President and Council of the Company's Settlement at Bombay duly informed us of the Treaty of Alliance which they concluded with you, and of the effectual Assistance which they afforded to your Cause. That Service being now performed, we are desirous of reverting to that System of Peace and Tranquillity, which bests suits the Commercial Views of the Company. For that Reason, in Virtue of the Powers vested in us by the Legislature of Great Britain and the Company, to superintend and controul all the Political Affairs in India, we have deputed Lieutenant Colonel John Upton to conclude a new Treaty of Peace and perpetual Friendship between the Company and the Maratta Nation. He will apply to you as the Ruler of that State, and you will listen to his Proposals as if coming from us; and we have no Doubt but you will find his Terms moderate and just, as we have determined to remove every Object of Ambition, and to adhere only to such as are necessary for the Security and Peace of the Company's Possessions.

To

To Siccaram Baboo. Written the 31st July 1775.

I have already written you concerning the appointing of Colonel Upton to negociate a Treaty of Peace between the Company and the Maratta Nation. He now proceeds to Poona with full Powers for that Purpose; and I request you will cheerfully receive him; and whatever Treaty you may settle with the Colonel, will be agreed to by this Government. No Person but the Colonel is impowered to that Purpose.

APPENDIX, N° 76.

Extract of Bengal Secret Consultations, the 10th August 1775.

PRESENT,

The Honourable Warren Hastings, Esquire, Governor General, President,
Lieutenant General John Clavering,
The Honourable George Monson,
Richard Barwell, } Esquires.
Philip Francis, }

THE Secretary informs the Board, that the following Letters have been received since their last Meeting, and sent in Circulation; one from the Select Committee at Bombay.

Honourable Sir, and Sirs,

Our Letter of the 1st Instant (which had been forwarded in Duplicate) acknowledged the Receipt of your Favour, dated the 8th of March.

In that Letter we communicated to you the Progress of our Army under the Command of Lieutenant Colonel Keating; we have not since received any further Advices from him, nor have we received any Letters from you since our last; this therefore is chiefly to reply to your Letter of the 8th of March, agreeable to what we promised in our Address of the 1st Instant.

We trust, that the Reasons which have been assigned in our Letter of the 30th of April, for not sending more early Intelligence of our Designs and Operations against Salsette, will prove sufficiently satisfactory, more especially when you consider that it was, as we well knew, from the distracted State of the Maratta Government, totally out of its Power to disturb the Tranquillity of the Company's Possessions in Bengal, or those of their Allies, on Account of our Proceedings on this Side of India; and so the Event has fully proved; and provided our Operations in Support of Ragoba are crowned with that Success which we hope they will, the Treaty we have entered into fully binds Ragoba and his Successors from ever taking Part against the Company, and indeed we doubt not but that Gratitude will induce him always to be ready to act in their Behalf.

Your Honour, &c. observe, "That you are alarmed at the Declaration of our Intentions of joining Ragoba; which, you add, you must disapprove, as inconsistent with our Negociations with the Ruling Powers at Poona; and that it is a Measure which may force you into a Rupture with Sabajee Bouncello, his declared Enemy and your Neighbour, with whom you are on Terms of Friendship."

We never had any Negociations with the Ministerial Party, who we suppose you mean by the Ruling Powers; we only acquainted you on this Head, long before we concluded the Treaty with Ragoba, and at a Time that there was little Probability that it ever would be concluded, that in Case they gained the Advantage in the present Contest, that we should endeavour to reconcile them, by explaining our Motives for attacking Salsette. The Conclusion of the Treaty, and the Part we in consequence took against them, rendered any Explanation or Negociation on this Account quite

quite unnecessary, and therefore all Thoughts of a Negociation with them, independent of Ragoba, had been long dropped; and though Ragoba's Affairs have wore but an unfavourable Aspect, yet we make no Doubt but a steady Perseverance and proper Conduct will enable him, with our Assistance, to overcome his Enemies, or else to accommodate Matters favourably with them; which in the End must ensure to the Company, on a stable Footing, the great Advantages granted to them by the Treaty, a Copy of which has been long since transmitted to you.

When your Honour, &c. take this Subject under your Consideration, we request that you will particularly attend to the following Circumstances:

First. That the Part we have taken, is in the Support of the rightful Supreme Governor of the Marattas, and who had been in Possession of that Dignity; and that the Ministerial Party are his Subjects, who have rebelled against him, and most unjustly are endeavouring to dispossess him of his Seat.

2dly. That by acting in the Manner we have done, we have secured to the Company, by the most effectual Grants (which Ragoba was the only Person who had any Right to give) the Right of possessing those Places, such as Salsette, Bassein, &c. which they have repeatedly and earnestly enjoined us to procure for them; and even more, which is still further for their Benefit, the Expences that will be incurred during this War, are to be amply repaid to them, and in the End we doubt not but that such a Currency will be given to the Affairs of the Company in these Parts, and to Trade in general, as will be attended with singular Benefit to them, and to Individuals trading under their Protection; in this Light, we flatter ourselves you will view our Proceedings when the Whole comes before you.

We were and are convinced, that your Honour, &c. may be perfectly free from any Apprehensions of being forced into a Rupture with the Bouncello's on Account of our Proceedings, even had Subajee been yet alive; for, from the Death of Janojee Boncello, which happened about Three Years ago, till Subajee was killed, as he lately was by Moodajee, that Government commonly known to us by the Name of the Berar Government, was torn in Pieces by the Civil Dissensions between Sabajee and Moodajee; but since the Death of the former it has been restored to Quiet; and as Moodajee (who now governs for his Son that was adopted by the late Janojee) is a known Friend to Ragoba, he will consequently be rejoiced at the Part we have taken, instead of being disgusted at it.

Thus we hope that we have removed your Honour, &c. Objections to our entering into the Treaty with Ragoba, and that you will concur with us in Opinion, that we were and are pursuing the true Interest of our Employers; for had we not laid hold of the present Opportunity, which was so very favourable, to procure Grants of the Places that they wished to possess, it is more than probable that another such would never again have offered.

We beg Leave here to remark, that as your Honour, &c. are situated so very distant from this Presidency, it would be totally impossible for us to benefit by Circumstances as they fall out, provided we always wait for your Directions: We need produce no other Instance than the Letter before us, which is dated the 8th March, not being received here till the 21st Ultimo, and is an Answer to our Advices of the 31st December last. Had we waited for your Reply to those Advices, Ragoba would have been entirely lost, and the Advantages the Company gain by the Treaty gone, most probably for ever. The Legislature indeed has provided against this great Inconvenience in the late Act of Parliament, which we make no Doubt but you will always consider; and we assure you, that we shall take no material Step in any political Matters without your Concurrence, unless when it may be dangerous to postpone for so long a Time coming to a Determination thereon.

In the preceding Part of this Letter, we acquainted you that we had no Advices from Lieutenant Colonel Keating since the Date of those noticed in our last Address; but private Letters from the Chief of Surat mention, that the Army is arrived in the Neighbourhood of Broach, in its March towards Poona; that our Forces have had another Engagement with the Ministerial Army, in which the latter were again worsted; and that the Affairs of the Confederacy, owing to their Want of Money, and to Dissensions amongst themselves, are in a very declining Way.

The Marattas lately made an Attempt on Salsette, by landing about 3,500 Men from Bassein, but they were quickly drove off by a Detachment only from the Madras

Battalion of Sepoys, with very considerable Loss on their Side, while on ours we had only One Sepoy killed, and Two or Three wounded.

We are, &c.

Bombay Castle, (Signed) William Hornby,
24 June 1775. President, &c. Council.

From Madajee Boosla; received 20 July 1775.

The Animosity and Contention which have for these Three Years prevailed in this Family, since the Death of the Rajah of blessed Memory (Janojee Boosla) the destructive Flames of which have spread from the River the Kistnah to the Nurbudda, are well known, and no Doubt have been written to you by the News-writers. After repeated Struggles, the hostile Ranks were at length drawn up in Array of Battle on the Plain of Naugpore, against my younger Brother, Sabajee Boosla; when, notwithstanding the few Adherents of my Party, and the very inconsiderable Number of my Troops, opposed to upwards of 20,000 of his, besides Artillery, Rocket Men, and others, all well armed and accoutred, I obtained a complete and decisive Victory; of this I some Time ago did myself the Pleasure to acquaint you in my Answer to your Letter. After a Shower of Arrows and Rockets from the Lines of the Combatants, whose Lightnings darted through Clouds of Armour, dealing Destruction and Death around, 5,000 brave Fellows were laid dead in the Field, and as many wounded; the Remainder, actuated with Ambition and Glory, closed in with their Elephants, and after some Time trying the Metal of their Weapons, Victory perched upon my Banners, and the Tree of Enmity was overset in the Storm. This is all evidently owing to the Interposition of Providence; in Gratitude for which I offered up my Prayers, and have since employed myself in regulating the Affairs of the Country, in consoling and gaining the Hearts of my Friends, and rewarding the Meritorious and Loyal; and also intend shortly marching with my Army to Barar, having appointed Babojee Anunt to the Soubadary of Cuttack; he has sent his Son thither with a proper Force, who, on his Arrival, will undoubtedly write you, and transmit you this Letter. Our Friendship will now be more firmly established than ever: And as it is my Desire to maintain and preserve every Treaty and Engagement inviolate; so I hope you have the same Desire on your Part, as it will be attended with innumerable Advantages to both. After the Arrival of Beney Ram Pundit, I shall write you further Particulars.

From Madagee Boosla; received the 22d July 1775.

Your Letter, under Date the 24th of Salfor, I had the Pleasure to receive at my Encampment at Ellichpore in the Soubah of Barrar. Your friendly Disposition to maintain and preserve inviolate the Friendship and Engagements you had entered into with the deceased Rajah Janogee Boosla; the Joy you expressed at the Victory which I have by the Favour of the Almighty obtained; your Wish to unite the Interest and Affairs of the Company with those who are endowed with the Virtues of Steadiness and Bravery, and distinguished with the Favour of the Almighty; and your referring me for the Particulars of all these Matters to Benaram Pundit, have given me infinite Joy and Satisfaction. The Situation of Affairs here is this: Soon after the Victory which I obtained in the late Engagement with my younger Brother, and before my Troops had recovered of the Wounds which they had received, I had a Congress with the Nabob Nizam, who, at the Requisition of the Ministers at Poona, arrived at Berhanpore in the Zelah of Barrar, to take a Part in the War with Ragonaut Row; and although possessed of no friendly Disposition towards me, yet, as he had long been on Terms of Friendship with, and done many Acts of Favour to, my Family, I deemed it inconsistent with Gratitude to commence any Difference with him, and therefore remained pacifically inclined. The confused State of Affairs in the Decan, and the open Hostilities which have some Time subsisted between Ragonaut Row and the Ministers at Poona, are now the Subject of Discussion; and whatever we determine on, I shall write for your Information, and in the Space of a Week break up the Congress. As uniting the ambitious in Bonds of Cordiality and Friendship, is not less necessary for establishing the Peace and Prosperity of the Country, than for retrieving Affairs which have already sunk to the Brink of Ruin; whatever may be the Result of our Deliberations to that End,

End, you will not only be acquainted with from me, but from the Letters of the Nizam.—Beneram Pundit is not yet arrived; I am hourly expecting him; and as soon as I have learnt from him the State of Affairs with you, I will again give him his Dispatches. I hope that you will continually keep our Friendship in View, which will be the Means of strengthening and confirming it.

APPENDIX, N° 77.

Extract of Bengal Secret Consultations, the 10th August 1775.

PRESENT,

The Honourable Warren Hastings, Esquire, Governor General, President,
Lieutenant General John Clavering,
The Honourable George Monson,
Richard Barwell, } Esquires.
Philip Francis, }

Sir, and Gentlemen,

I Have the Honour to inclose to you a Letter from the Nabob of the Carnatic, at the Request of his Highness; and that of being with great Esteem,

(Signed) Edw. Hughes.

From the Nabob of Arcot: Received 6th August 1775.

I have from the first relied on your Friendship for the Success of my Affairs, and especially since more extensive Powers have been granted you. I have had the most sanguine Hopes that every Thing would succeed to my Wish. Since the Governor and Council of Bombay have espoused the Cause of Ragonaut Row, and assisted him in the War against the Ministers of Poona, those Ministers have repeatedly insinuated to my Vackeel Rowjee, whom I have stationed at Poona, and have also directed him to write me, that I had long made Declarations to them concerning my own Friendship and that of the English, but that the Steps lately taken by the Settlement of Bombay was in direct Contradiction thereto; that I should take upon myself the Part of a Mediator, and accommodate their Differences, which would be productive of Security to the Carnatic. When the Governor and Council of Bombay commenced Disturbances with the Marattas, with a View to some new Acquisition in that Quarter, I thought it had been a Plan of your's, and therefore said nothing upon it; but I have since learnt, that you disapprove of that Presidency's having entered into the War, and that for the Sake of Security to the Country, and promoting the Happiness and Ease of the People, you are desirous of accommodating a Peace with the Poona Ministers, and of sending some Person of Trust thither for that Purpose. You will therefore have a fine Opportunity of shewing your Attention to the Affairs of my Country, that is, for securing it in Peace, an Object much desired by the King of Great-Britain, and my Friends the Company, and attended with many Advantages to the Country, to the Company, and to Trade, since it is at Poona the Peace of this Country may easily be preserved; but should it have no Share in your Negociations, and you only attend to the Affairs of Bombay, and to the Alliance with Ragonaut Row, without Doubt the Marattas will raise Disturbances in this Country; and when we are at War on this Coast, what will a Peace signify on the other? Lord Pigot, in the Agreement under Date the 8th of Zeanda 1173, of the Hejerie, equal to the 23d of June 1760, wrote me in these Terms; viz.

As you and the Company are now united in the same Interest, all political Transactions and Negociations with the Nabob Salabat Jung Nizam Ally Cawn, and other Powers, shall be conducted with your Advice; for your Advice I esteem above all others.

And accordingly this Rule has been observed by all Governors, as they considered it best for the Company's Affairs, and for the Security of this Country. I therefore request that you will order the Person whom you have appointed to go to Poona, to take this Route, and to visit me that I may explain my Sentiments to him with respect to the Security of the Carnatic, and send a Person with him on my own Behalf, to cooperate with him in his Negociations for fulfilling your Instructions on the Subject of the Company's Affairs, and also for securing Tranquillity to the Carnatic. But should he have set out before you receive this Letter, I request you will immediately transmit him Instructions to make the Security of the Carnatic a Clause in the Treaty of Peace, and write him an Order to consult and act conjointly with the Deputy from hence in his Negociations with the Marattas; which Order transmit to me that I may send it by the Hands of the Deputy himself. By the Favour of the Almighty I shall then be perfectly at Ease from any Apprehensions of the Marattas disturbing the Peace of the Carnatic, and shall think myself indebted for it to your friendly Endeavours. This Transaction will give you lasting Credit in this Country, and do you Honour at Home with the King and the Company.

Extract of Bengal Secret Consultations, the 16th August 1775.

PRESENT,

The Honourable Warren Hastings, Esquire, Governor General, President,
Lieutenant General John Clavering,
The Honourable George Monson,
Richard Barwell, } Esquires.
Philip Francis, }

The Board now take into Consideration the Letter from the Nabob of Arcot to the Governor General, transmitted by Sir Edward Hughes, and recorded in Consultation 10th Instant.

Resolved, That proper Attention be had to the Interest of the Nabob of the Carnatic in the Treaty of Peace to be entered into with the Maratta State at Poona; and that the following Instructions on this Head be therefore sent to Lieutenant Colonel Upton.

To Lieutenant Colonel Upton.

Sir,

We think it proper to give you the following Instructions in Addition to your former, and require you to pay all due Attention to them in entering upon your Negociations at Poona.

As the Nabob of Arcot is a particular Friend and Ally of the English, and as his Interest may be affected with any Treaty you may conclude with the Maratta Government, we direct that you make the Maratta Chiefs acquainted with the Union that subsists between him and the Company, and insist on including him in the Treaty, in an express Article to the following Effect: That the Nabob Wallah Jah Bahadar, Nabob of the Carnatic, having been for a considerable Course of Years united to the English Company by the strongest Ties of Friendship and Alliance, and the Company having ever considered his Enemies as their Enemies, and his Friends as their Friends, it is agreed, that the Maratta Chiefs likewise shall hereafter regard him as their Friend, and his Enemies as their Enemies. At the same Time we are to acquaint you, that we have desired the Nabob of Arcot, if there are any particular Articles which he wishes to have stipulated for him, to state these Articles to us, assuring him, that we would take them into Consideration, and give you such further Orders respecting them as shall be compatible with the other Objects which we have in View in concluding the Treaty of Peace with the Marattas.

We have further to direct, that whatever Treaty you enter into with the Maratta State, you require that it be signed by all the Chiefs nominally and individually; and that you insist on this as a Point from which you cannot depart.

A Duplicate of this Letter will be delivered to you by the Nabob of Arcot's Vackeel at Poona, with whom you will consult upon any Thing which he may have to propose for

for his Master's Interest, and attend to his Representations as far as may be consistent with the general Tenor of your Instructions.

We inclose for your Information Copy of a Treaty which was executed between the Presidency of Bombay and the Maratta Government, on the 12th October 1756.

We are, &c. &c.

Agreed, That the Governor General be requested to write an Answer to the Letter from the Nabob of Arcot in the following Terms:

To the Nabob of Arcot.

I have received the Letter with which your Excellency honoured me through the Channel of Sir Edward Hughes, acquainting me, that the Ministers of Poona had repeatedly insinuated to your Vackeel Roujee, that the Steps lately taken by the Settlement of Bombay were in direct Contradiction to the Declarations you had long made to them concerning your own Friendship, and that of the English; and that they wished you should take upon yourself the Part of a Mediator to accommodate their Differences, which would be productive to the Security of the Carnatic. You farther acquaint me, that as you have learned that the Board here disapprove of the Proceedings of the Presidency of Bombay, and have sent a Person of Confidence thither to negociate a Treaty of Peace with the Marattas, in which you are desirous of being included, and request that the Person thus deputed may take the Route of Madras and visit you, that you might explain your Sentiments to him with respect to the Security of the Carnatic, and send a Person with him in your Behalf, to co-operate in his Negociations.

I now have the Honour to acquaint your Excellency, that the Person chosen by the Board for this Deputation, is Colonel John Upton, and that he took his Departure from hence about a Month ago, in his Way to Poonah, by the Road of Allahabad and Calpee. When the Board first took the Determination to send a Minister to Poona, they acquainted the President and Council of Fort Saint George of it, not doubting but they would communicate it to your Excellency, and that you would deliberate upon what might be necessary for you to propose for your Interests, jointly with those of the Company, in the proposed Treaty.

We did not judge it proper to instruct our Minister to take any Steps on your Behalf, knowing that there were Treaties subsisting already betwixt you and the Marattas, to the Nature of which we were Strangers; and therefore uncertain whether any Proposals which might come from this Government, would coincide with those Treaties, or your particular Views.

But on Receipt of your Excellency's Letter, Orders were sent to our Minister at Poona, a Duplicate of which I now transmit as you desire, to be delivered to him by your Vackeel, in which we have conveyed to him the positive Instructions of the Board, to make the Maratta Chiefs acquainted with the Relation which has long subsisted between your Excellency and the Company, and insist on a separate Article in the Treaty to this Effect, That the Nabob Wallah Jah Bahadar has been, during a Course of many Years, united to the Company by the strongest Ties of Friendship and Alliance; and as the Company have ever considered his Enemies as their Enemies, and his Friends as their Friends, it shall be agreed, that the Maratta Chiefs also shall regard him as their Friend, and his Enemies as their Enemies.

We have also directed him to consult with your Vackeel on every Thing regarding your Interest; but as our principal View in the present Negociation, is to restore Peace to the Presidency at Bombay, we wish not to involve that Object in any extraneous Matter, and therefore, that whatever regards the Carnatic, be also confined merely to its Peace and Tranquillity. If however your Excellency should have any Particulars to propose relating to these Objects, I beg you to communicate them to me, together with a Copy of the Treaties which may now be subsisting between you and the Maratta State, that Orders may be issued to Colonel Upton in consequence; and further, as the Interests of the Presidency of Fort Saint George are so closely connected with yours, I request, that whatever Proposals you may think fit to transmit to me, you will be pleased to deliver a Copy to the President and Council there, that this Board may have the Advantage of receiving at the same Time their Sentiments upon them.

As I understand that the Names of the principal Maratta Chiefs will be necessary to be affixed to the proposed Treaty, to give it a due Sanction; and as you have had the Opportunity of a long Intercourse with the People, to obtain a Knowledge of the Persons on whom the Administration of the State depends, I request that you will be pleased to transmit to me an exact List of their Names, it not being in my Power to procure that Information here with sufficient Exactness.

(Signed) W. H.

APPENDIX, N° 78.

Extract of Bengal Secret Consultations, the 7th September, 1775.

PRESENT,

The Honourable Warren Hastings, Governor General, President,
Lieutenant General John Clavering,
The Honourable George Monson,
Richard Barwell, } Esquires.
Philip Francis, } Esquires.

RECEIVED the following Letter from Bombay Select Committee.

Honourable Sir, and Sirs,

The War we are at present engaged in for the Support of Ragoba is of the utmost Importance to the Honourable Company, as we have already fully represented to you, and it therefore calls upon us particularly to pursue every Means in our Power to bring it to a speedy and successful Issue, for on that will depend the great Advantages that the Company are to reap by the Engagements we have entered into on their Behalf; and it is moreover a Matter of the utmost Importance to conclude the War if possible in the Course of the ensuing Season.

Our Forces in every Engagement with the Enemy have gained all the Advantage that we had Reason to hope for, so far as depended on them; but at the Time we sent the Body of Men we did to the Assistance of Ragoba, it was concluded his own Forces would be of material Service in the Course of the Campaign; the contrary however has been found to be the Case, and it has therefore frequently happened that our Army has been unable to reap every Advantage that might have been expected from its Victories over the Enemy. The Commanding Officer has therefore requested, and Ragoba earnestly solicited, that a Reinforcement may be sent against the Time that they will be able again to take the Field, which will be in the Beginning of November next; the rainy Season having obliged the Army to go into Quarters at Dubhoy, near the Banks of the Nerbuddah. For this Reinforcement, (the Necessity of sending which we are sufficiently convinced of,) Ragoba is to make over additional Advantages to the Honourable Company, exclusive of those mentioned in the Treaty.

We shall also require a Military Force for the Protection of Salsette, and the Provinces ceded to the Company, as well as to ensure the Collection of the Revenues of them for the ensuing Season.

We have made the same Statement to the Presidency of Fort Saint George, of the Services for which a large Military Force is required here, as we have now done to your Honour, &c. and we have at the same Time acquainted those Gentlemen, as we beg Leave now to do to you, that it will be totally out of our Power to furnish the whole Force that will be requisite, without the Assistance of the other Presidencies. Being convinced that we could receive a Reinforcement from Madras (as it may march by Land to Anjengo and Tellicherry) much more early than we could do from you; we have therefore earnestly requested the Governor and Council there to send by that Route

Three

Three Hundred European Rank and File, and Two complete Battalions of Sepoys, in Time for the Services that will be required of them.

Should that Presidency be unable to assist us with the whole Force that is now desired, we then earnestly request that your Honour, &c. will furnish such Part as they may be deficient in sending, or that you will be pleased to send the Whole from your Army. Should those Gentlemen be unable to send any Part of the Succours we have now required of them, in such Case, we require that they may be sent so early that we may be enabled to reap the Benefit of their Services during the whole Course of the ensuing fair Season.

The Gentlemen at Fort St. George are desired to communicate to your Honour, &c. their Resolution in Consequence of what we now write them, that you may be enabled to regulate your Determination; and we again repeat it as our earnest Wish, that the Arrival of the Forces which may be sent from your Presidency may, if possible, not be later than the ensuing Month of November.

We are well aware that we formerly wrote your Honour, &c. that the most material Assistance which you could then afford, was in furnishing us with ample Supplies of Money; at that Time we expected that Ragoba's Forces would do their Duty, but the repeated Complaints from our Commanding Officer of their Misconduct and Misbehaviour, induces us no longer to have any Reliance on them, and therefore will oblige us to make a suitable Addition to our own Army.

We again repeat our Request, that you will send us a liberal Supply of Money, exclusive of the annual one of Fifteen Lacks; and should your Forces be sent to our Assistance instead of those from Fort Saint George, it will be very convenient to us that their own Military Chest should accompany them.

Our last Address was dated the 24th Ultimo, and has already been forwarded in Duplicate.

Bombay Castle, 13th July, 1775.

We are, &c.
(Signed) William Hornby,
President and Council.

Honourable Sir, and Sirs,

We addressed you on the 13th Ultimo in Duplicate, since when we have not been favoured with any Letter from you.

The Situation of our Army in the Field is the same as we last advised, the Season of the Year not admitting of their quitting their present Cantonments; but we have the Pleasure to acquaint you that Ragoba has obtained a very material Advantage, by Futty Sing having quitted the Ministerial Party and come over to his; a Treaty has been concluded between them, by which he is to furnish the Peshwa with the same Body of Forces, and to pay the same annual Stipend, as the Guicawars always used to do; and he is moreover to pay the Peshwa, for making Peace with him, the Sum of Twenty-six Lacks of Rupees, within Sixty Days after the Treaty was executed, which is about One Month ago.

The immediate Advantages to the Company from this Event are, that Futty Sing has made over his Right and Title for ever, as well as those of his Family, to their Share in the Town and Districts of Broach, which by our Treaty Ragoba had obliged himself to obtain; Futty Sing has also given up Two Districts to the Company for ever, convenient to Surat and Broach, for their Mediation in this Business, whose annual Revenue may be about a Lack and a Half of Rupees.

Bombay Castle, 6th August, 1775.

We are, &c.
(Signed) William Hornby,
President and Council.

P. S. The inclosed Packets would have been forwarded sooner, if the Ships Stafford and Diana, by which they were transmitted, had not returned into Port on Account of the Badness of the Weather.

The Question is put, Whether we shall send or authorize the Supplies of Men and Money which the President and Council of Bombay have required in their Letter of the 13th July?

Mr.

Mr. Francis delivers the following Opinion.

The Presidency at Bombay seem now to be alarmed for the Consequence of those unwarrantable Measures in which their Union with Ragoba has involved them. It appears to me that they engaged in the present War without an Army, without Funds, without a Plan of Operations, or even a determinate Object. I say nothing of the Right or Justice of their Quarrel, since they take no Notice of it themselves. With respect to the Success which they say has constantly attended Colonel Keating's Operations, I confess I place little or no Dependance on their Accounts of them. There have been few Actions in India between European and Black Troops, in which the former have suffered more both in Loss of Men and Loss of Honour, than that of the 18th May, which yet was represented to us in the Light of a Victory. With the Knowledge of this Fact before me, I cannot give Credit to any general Assurances they may send us of the Success of our Arms; neither am I moved from my first Opinion of their Proceedings, by the Expectation of any Advantages to be granted us by Ragoba. The Lands he pretends to assign to us, might have been obtained by our own Strength without his Assistance, nor have we any other Security for the Possession of them. They have given us no exact Description of those Lands, but we know with Certainty that at present they produce nothing towards the Support of the War. Whether these, or any other expected Acquisitions, can compensate for the Losses we have already suffered, the Expence which we have and must still incur, and the Hazard to which our Army is exposed, will not, I am persuaded, be a Question in the Minds of the Court of Directors. It is well known that the Consequences of this ruinous War have not been confined to the Operations of the War itself; the Disaster which the Trade of Surat suffered by their Fleet being detained there for Want of Convoy till the Monsoon broke up, can only be attributed to our Rupture with the Marattas: This Fleet was chiefly laden with Cotton: The immediate Loss is generally computed at Twenty-five Lacks of Rupees. The Importation of Cotton into Bengal has failed considerably, and the Price of that Article has risen in Proportion, which cannot happen without the greatest Prejudice to the Manufactures of this Country. I am also assured that the Cotton Trade to China has, from the same Cause, been almost wholly lost this Season. The Court of Directors, I doubt not, will see with Indignation the Trade of India sacrificed by their Servants to the Spirit of Conquest, with as little Consideration of the true and natural Interest of a commercial Company, as of the obvious Dictates of Policy and Justice.

In my Opinion, we cannot pass a Condemnation too solemn or severe upon the whole Conduct of the Council of Bombay, with respect to their Rupture with the Marattas. They now, in effect, admit that they have little Assistance to expect from their Ally Ragoba; his own Troops will not fight, and he has no Money to pay ours.—I am against sending them any Reinforcements of Men. We may spare them a moderate Supply of Money, but not on the Principle of continuing the War. I think we should repeat and insist upon our former Orders, to recall Colonel Keating, without any Respect or Consideration whatsoever, but the Safety of the Troops under his Command. I understand that he may effect a Retreat from his present Cantonments to Broach without Difficulty, from thence I think the Army should be withdrawn as soon as possible to cover Bombay.

(Signed) P. F.

Mr. Barwell—I think both Men and Money should be sent to Bombay.

The Honourable George Monson—The Court of Directors, in their first Instructions, require us to fix our Attention to the Preservation of Peace throughout India, and that in all our Deliberations and Resolutions we should make the Safety and Prosperity of Bengal our principal Object. The Presidency of Bombay having made an Alliance with a Prince who had neither Men nor Money, and they themselves without either Men or Money determining upon a War against the most powerful State in India, without any Cause or Pretext whatsoever, appears to me both unwarrantable and impolitic.

That War was not our Measure, nor are we responsible to the Court of Directors and to our Nation for the Event of it; but if we should now think proper to assist the Presidency of Bombay with Men and Money to carry on a War which was not undertaken on Principles of Policy or Interest for the Company, I think we make ourselves responsible for all the Consequences of it: I therefore am for enforcing our former Orders to the

the Presidency of Bombay, to retract their Engagements with Ragoba, and to secure the Company's Army and present Possessions in the best Manner they shall be able; we have already sent a Person to Poona to conclude a Treaty of Peace with the Ministerial Party, and I have not the smallest Doubts but he will be able to effect it to the Honour of the Nation, and for the Security of the Company's Possessions. As the Presidency of Bombay is in Want of Cash for their immediate Demands, I would answer their Bills to a certain Amount, if they could procure them; if not, as there is no Alternative, the Specie must be sent from this Country.

General Clavering—The Principles which the present Administration established as the Object of their Conduct, were the preserving the Peace of India, as far as it could be done consistently with the Safety of the Company's Possessions. Agreeable to this Principle, we first applied ourselves to put an End to the Rohilla War. We then refused the Offers made to us, through the Government of Madras, to the Nizam, to assist him against the Marattas, with all the alluring Advantages with which the Proposal was accompanied. We no sooner heard the Government of Bombay had commenced Hostilities against the Marattas to take the Island of Salsette, than we testified our Disapprobation of it, and further signified to that Government our Commands to desist from their Engagements with Ragoba, and even at last to withdraw the Troops with which they had joined his Army. These have been the Principles which have guided our Conduct since the Commencement of our Administration; our Views in the Pursuits of this Conduct have been not less to conform to the positive Commands of the Court of Directors, directing us to preserve the Peace in India, than the declared Intentions of the Legislature, which invested us with Powers for that Purpose; the Measures we have taken to effect this, and with regard to the present Maratta War, are now carrying into Execution by the Mission of Colonel Upton to Poona; and we have Reason to hope that the Marattas seeing the Justice and Moderation of this Government, and that our Intentions are finally to put a Stop to that Spirit of Conquest, Encroachment, and Injustice, which seems hitherto to have prevailed too much in India, will listen to the Proposals that we have made them, to conclude a firm and lasting Peace with them. Till therefore they refuse to conclude a Peace, I shall object to sending any more Troops than what have been sent from the Presidency of Madras, or any Money more than what is sufficient for the Supplies of their Investment. It has been usual to send them annually about Fourteen or Fifteen Lacks: I would not therefore increase that Sum more than to make it up Twenty, with the specific Condition that it shall not be employed but for the Purpose abovementioned.

The Governor General.—I am of Opinion that the Presidency of Bombay should be furnished with Supplies both of Men and Money. The Question before us is not, whether the Presidency of Bombay have acted properly, or improperly, in their original Engagements with Ragoba? nor to support a political System. We have condemned the Measures of the Presidency of Bombay. We have unanimously passed the severest Censure upon it. The Effects of that Measure should not be considered as affecting that Presidency, but the Interests of the Company, which are involved in it, not only at Bombay, but in every Part of their Possessions. The Question therefore before us is, By what Means it will be most expedient to endeavour to extricate the Company's Affairs from the Danger which has befallen them in a War thus too precipitately undertaken?—All our private Advices concur in representing the Ministerial Party at Poona in a State of Distraction, and in Decision they appear not to have any Principle of Action, nor Leader whose Pretensions to the Government could enable him to guide their Measures, or to connect the Attachment of their People. The Overtures which have been made to the Nabob of Arcot by the Government of Poona, and their Intreaties that he will stand forth as their Intercessor to obtain a Peace with the Company, strongly confirm the above Reports, and leave every Reason to believe that the State of the Ministerial Party is yet worse than that whose Cause we have espoused. Under such Circumstances, it appears to me that nothing is wanting on the Part of this Government but a temporary, though vigorous Exertion of its Powers to maintain that Ascendant which it has acquired, and by which alone the Success of the future Negociations can be insured. If the Detachment now employed in the Support of Ragoba, should be either defeated for want of Succour, or recalled at such a Crisis to Bombay, and Ragoba abandoned to Ruin, I will venture to foretel that Colonel Upton's Negociations will be fruitless, and attended with Disgrace. On the other Hand, I will with equal Confidence risk my Credit with the Company, in foretelling that the Issue of it will be successful and

honourable

honourable if we maintain our Superiority at the Time in which it ſhall take Place, and ſhew a Reſolution to dictate, not receive, the Terms of an Accommodation. For theſe Reaſons, I am of Opinion that the effectual Support of the Preſidency of Bombay, in the War undertaken by them, will prove the ſureſt Means of reſtoring the Peace of India. We have thoſe Means in our Power, and I therefore think it our Duty to employ them.

General Clavering.—The Opinion which the Governor General has now given, appears to me ſo inconſiſtent with that which he formerly gave, for withdrawing the Company's Troops from the Aſſiſtance of Ragoba, and for ſending Colonel Upton to Poona, for negociating a Treaty, that I cannot tell how to reconcile ſuch Opinion with the Meaſure in which I underſtand he concurred with the other Members of Council. Our Letters to the Preſident and Council of Bombay, which peremptorily require that Preſidency to withdraw their Forces into their Garriſons, in whatever State they might be, without endangering their Safety by an inſtant Retreat, muſt have been received and carried into Execution before this Time, if they mean to obey the Orders of this Government: Therefore, the adopting a Plan for the Support of a War which we have not only condemned, but have directed ſhould be finiſhed by the Retreat of our Troops, appears to me a Meaſure, at preſent both ſuperfluous and incompatible with the Meaſures that we have already taken, of ſending to treat with the other Party at Poona. It would not only ſhew to the Powers of India, that we have no Syſtem of political Conduct, but would likewiſe expoſe our Negociations to the other Party to Contempt and Deriſion, and perhaps even the Perſons of the Gentlemen themſelves who are gone to negociate a Treaty, to the greateſt Danger. In our Letter to the Court of Directors of the 5th Auguſt, we have acquainted them how much we had condemned the ridiculous Project of the Council at Bombay, of undertaking the Conqueſt of the Maratta Empire with ſo ſmall a Force; we have informed them of our having given peremptory Orders for the withdrawing the Troops from the Army; what would they think of our Conduct ſhould we, inſtead of purſuing the Plan which we adopted, as we thought with ſo much Wiſdom and Propriety, if we were now to alter that Reſolution? To be conſiſtent therefore with the Principles which we have eſtabliſhed for the Rule of our Government, and the Meaſures we have already adopted, I muſt adhere to the Opinion I have already given, of only ſending a Succour of five Lacks in Addition to the 15 Lacks which has been uſually given to the Preſidency of Bombay.

Colonel Monſon.—If I can collect any Thing from the Governor General's Minute, it is, that to obtain an honourable Peace at Poona, and to maintain that Superiority which the Britiſh Troops have acquired in India, that we ſhould ſupport a Prince whoſe Right to the Government of Poona is controvertible; that we ſhould ſend a Reinforcement of Troops and Money to maintain a War, the Object of which is not defined, nor the Advantages to the Company no Way mentioned. If the Governor General is of Opinion that an honourable Treaty of Peace with the Marattas is not to be obtained but by reinforcing the preſent Army in the Field, and continuing that injudicious War, I beg Leave to ſubmit to him, whether the War could not be more deciſive (as War is his Object) if the whole Force of the Company from the three Preſidencies, ſupported by their Allies, were put in Motion againſt the Maratta State? I think ſuch a Meaſure would be deciſive, and might be advantageous to the Company, but not honourable to the Government. Many Actions may be honourable to the Arms of a State, that are diſgraceful to the Conductors of it; and I think a Meaſure of this Kind would be highly diſhonourable, as we may be underſtood to be the Aggreſſors in the Maratta War. To eſtabliſh a Peace of this Empire, a Syſtem, a Policy muſt be adopted, diametrically oppoſite to that which has for many Years been purſued. The only certain Method of introducing Tranquillity and Subordination in their Empire, is to ſupport an Authority in the Perſons who have a legal Right to govern; a contrary Maxim has been purſued; every Kind of Protection and Support has been withdrawn from the Prince of the Empire; his Poſſeſſions wreſted from him, though given him under the moſt ſacred Treaties, and ſold to his Servants and Dependents; his Servants protected and ſupported in ſubduing Nations, and extirpating Races of People, to feed his Ambition, and to gratify the Avarice of an Ambitious Prince, whoſe Object, I firmly believe, from the Declarations which I have heard he has made, was to place himſelf with the late Adminiſtration on the Throne of Hindoſtan. This ambitious Prince, whoſe Views were ſupported by the late Adminiſtration, violated the moſt ſacred Treaties, and re-

fuſed

fused to make over to his Sovereign the Countries which he had pledged himself to deliver, and which he had conquered with the Assistance of the English Arms, who he looked upon to be entirely at his Command, and to be the Instruments of his obtaining his ambitious Projects. If War is to be the Means by which the Company's Investment is to be provided, and their Civil and Military Establishments maintained, let us wage it with that Degree of Splendour and Command which our Force would give us; but not to fritter away the Honour of the Nation, the Force or Wealth of the Company, by assisting an ill-advised Undertaking; the supporting of which can be the only Means of protracting the War, which Protraction must be attended with every Advantage to the Company's Commercial Concerns, as well as to the Revenues.

The Governor-General.—In the Discussion of a Point so important to the Safety of the Company's and the National Interest in India, as that now before us, it is of little Consequence whether my Opinions, which have never had any Weight in the political Measures of the present Administration, are strictly consistent with each other or not; yet it concerns my Credit to defend them. If I truly recollect the Substance of the Minute which I originally delivered upon this Subject, or if I know my own Mind, I think nothing will be found in it to which my present Opinion is contradictory. The best Part of the Consistency of these Opinions, will be, to set them in Opposition to each other. I will therefore beg Leave to subjoin so much of my former Minute as has Relation to the Subject now before the Board.

"Although I am thus clear in my Opinion of what is past, I confess I have Doubts "of the Part which this Government ought to take with respect to the future; it is "impossible to conjecture, amidst such Variety of probable Contingencies, and under "our total Ignorance of their Plan of Operations, what Turn Affairs may have taken, "or what may be their actual State at the Time our Orders may arrive. It is certainly "to be wished they could be replaced on the same Footing on which they were before "their Engagement with Ragoba; but this is now impossible; and to draw abruptly, "after having entered into positive Engagements with one Party, and offended the "other, perhaps beyond the Hopes of Reconciliation, may be attended with greater "Danger than prosecuting the original Design, and even with national Dishonour. I "can therefore only venture to propose, that the President and Council of Bombay be "peremptorily enjoined to cancel the Treaty with Ragoba, and to withdraw the De- "tachments immediately to their own Possessions, by whatever Means may be in their "Power, unless any of the following Cases shall have occurred; viz.

"1st. That they shall have obtained any decisive Advantage over the Enemy.

"2d. That the Detachment shall have proceeded to such a Distance, or to be in such "a Situation, as to make it dangerous either to retreat or not to go on.

"3d. That a Negociation shall have taken Place between Ragoba and his Oppo- "nents, in consequence of the Support afforded by this Alliance.

"These I conceive to be all the Cases of Necessity which must compel them to per- "severe, and which I must recommend to be made Exceptions to the general Order."

In this Minute, Three Cases were submitted to the Board as Exceptions to the Orders proposed for the Recall of the Troops. The Board adopted only the Second. The First is the Ground of my present Opinion. Our Troops have obtained an Advantage over the Enemy, which, added to the Situation, I consider as decisive, provided only such timely Succours are sent them as it is in our Power to afford them.

The General has observed, that to adopt a Plan for the Support of a War which we have condemned, would be incompatible with the Measures that we have taken of sending to treat with the other Party at Poonah. I apprehend, that to treat in the Midst of a War, is no new Practice even with the most civilized Nations; in the present Case It appears to me unavoidable; Peace is not effected by the Retreat of one Party, especially if the other shall thereby become not only Masters of the Field, but enabled by it to take such Measures at their Leisure as shall preclude the other from the Possibility of renewing the War. In that Case there is no Room for a Negociation, which can only be conducted with a Probability of Success but to that Party which has some Advantages to offer, or some Dangers to threaten. By precipitately abandoning the War, we give up all, even the Dread of Retaliation of any Injuries which we may sustain by any subsequent Conduct of our Enemies. I do not conceive it to be necessary, that any Reinforcement which we might send should take the Field, if they are at Hand, and we have it in our Power to offer the Alternative of Peace on such just and honourable Conditions as the Nature of the Cause which we are engaged in may allow or re-

 quire;

quire; or of War, in Defence of our own Rights and Safety. The same End, I think, may be obtained, even though the Forces already employed shall have been withdrawn to Bombay.

Colonel Monson has ascribed Maxims to me which do not follow from any Thing which I have asserted, and Objects which I do not avow. I have never asserted, that to obtain an honourable Peace at Poona, and to maintain that Superiority which the British Troops have acquired in India, we should support a Prince whose Right to the Government of Poona is controvertible; that we should send a Reinforcemet of Troops and Money to maintain a War, the Object of which is not defined. My Opinion is, that we should maintain our Superiority for the Sake of obtaining an honourable Peace. War is not my Object; my Object is Peace, which is most likely to be obtained by being prepared for War. It does not necessarily follow, because I object to one Extreme, I must therefore have Recourse to the opposite; that because I object to an abrupt Conclusion of the War, I should therefore put the Forces of all the Three Presidencies in Motion for the Prosecution of it. The Principle which I have recommended, is a Medium between the Two Extremes, and such as I think most likely to conduce to the End aimed at by the other Members of the Board. I will in this Place frankly own, that the Opinions which I have formerly given upon this Subject, were not strictly conformable to my Judgment of the Measures which ought to have been pursued under a different Administration. I knew the general Sense of the Board, and I wished, in the Opinion I gave at the same Time, to accommodate it to their Sentiments, and to prevent the Extremities to which I feared they would lead. Perhaps if it had been in my Power to have guided the Measures of this Government, and I could have depended on the unanimous Support of the Members of it in their Execution, I might have proposed a different Plan of Action. That which appears in my Minute of the 31st May, I still think most suitable to the Times, though not to the Occasion, independently considered. The Reflections thrown out by Colonel Monson, upon the Conduct of the late Administration in their Transaction with the King and the Vizier, the Treaty of Benares, and the Rohilla War, are all foreign from the Subject of the present Question. I have repeatedly replied to them, and am weary of dwelling on an exhausted Argument.

Mr. Francis—When the Governor General recommends the sending a Reinforcement of Men to the Army under Colonel Keating, I presume he means it with an immediate View to a vigorous Prosecution of the present unjust and impolitic War, though ultimately to the Establishment of a safe and honourable Peace. On this Principle, the Reinforcement must of Necessity be very considerable, since it is plain that we have little or nothing to expect from the Assistance of Ragoba. If, in Conformity to the Governor's Opinion, such a Force as the Occasion would require were to be sent to the Coast of Malabar, I should have hoped that he would have come to the Council prepared to inform us from what Quarter it could be spared; what the general Plan of our military Operations should be; together with the precise Object and exact Limits of them: In my Opinion, such a Reinforcement as it would be necessary to send, if we sent any, is not to be safely spared from the Two Brigades remaining in those Provinces, for the Defence of which an Establishment of Three Brigades has been thought necessary. We cannot, consistently with our Engagements with the Nabob of Oude, withdraw the Brigade from his Country, and if we did, we know that his Ruin would be the Consequence. I presume it will not be thought adviseable to divide and weaken the Company's Force upon the Coast; we should thereby leave the Carnatic open to the Incursions of the Marattas, and Madras itself exposed to Insult from Hyder Ally, or perhaps from an European Enemy.

Suppose Colonel Keating to penetrate farther into the Country, we ought at least to determine what Object we are to propose to ourselves from his Success; how far he is to carry the Company's Troops from the Defence of their Possessions; or how his Retreat is to be secured in Case of any unexpected Check. These are Considerations which I think should accompany every Proposal to commence or continue a War. The Governor General's Opinion goes simply to the Continuation of a War which he himself has condemned; which, from the Distance of the Scene of Action, would not be under our Guidance; and which, having no determinate Plan, Object, or Limitation, would probably involve the Company's Affairs in endless Difficulties. I adhere therefore to the Opinion I have already given, that the War on the Malabar Coast ought not to be supported, and that the safest and most prudent Measure we can adopt, is, to withdraw our Troops from their present hazardous Situation, to the Defence of our own Possessions.

The

The Regard to Justice and Moderation which we have shewn in taking the First Step towards an humble Accommodation with the Government at Poona, will probably make the Consideration of hostile Measures against that State unnecessary.

Resolved, That the Sum to be supplied to the Bombay Presidency in the Course of this Year, commencing from 1st May last, be extended to Twenty Lacks of Rupees, including the Amount which they have already drawn for since that Period.

Agreed, That the following Letter be immediately dispatched for that Presidency.

Gentlemen,

We have just received your Letters of the 13th July and 6th August; that of the 24th June had before reached us.

The last Advices which you acknowledge the Receipt of from us, being dated the 8th March, we take this Opportunity of transmitting you, by a Sea Conveyance, Copies of all our Letters to your Presidency since that Date.

The Sense we entertain of your Engagements with Ragoba, and the Whole of your Conduct in respect to your Transactions with him, cannot more fully appear than from the Tenor of those Letters.

We are now sorry to find the Truth of our Conjectures, as to the Consequence of this Engagement, that the whole Burthen of the extensive War, undertaken by you in Support of Ragoba's Claim to the Peshwaship, has fallen upon yourselves, and that no Dependance can be placed on the Assistance of his Troops.

We have been so particularly enjoined by the Court of Directors to attend to the Preservation of Peace in general with the Country Powers throughout India, that we thought it necessary, in our Letters of the 31st May, to give you positive Orders to recall your Army from Ragoba to your own Garrisons, in whatsoever State your Affairs might be, unless the Safety of the Troops might be endangered by an instant Retreat. We hope you have acted with Conformity thereto; but if not, we now repeat those Directions, judging it more particularly requisite at this Period, as it appears that Ragoba is not able to fulfil his Part of the Treaty; and we require you to confine your Views to the Protection of the Company's Possessions, including Salsette, and the Share in the Revenues of Broach given up by Futty Sing, in the best Manner you are able. This last we have also instructed our Minister at Poona to secure, if possible, by the Treaty with that State. We cannot consequently grant our Consent to any further Reinforcement of Troops being sent to join you from this Side of India; I have therefore forbid the Council at Fort St. George to comply with your Request for 300 Europeans and Two Battalions of Sepoys. Another Reason which has Weight with us against supplying you with Troops is, that having appointed Lieutenant Colonel Upton to proceed to Poona, to negociate a Treaty of Peace with the Ministerial Party there, he will most probably arrive and open the Business of his Mission to that Court before any Reinforcement of Troops could be brought to co-operate with your Army, even supposing they should still remain in their Quarters at Dubhoy; the Junction of fresh Troops might be alarming to the Marattas, and appear contrary to good Faith, at a Time when we are treating for Peace.

We have the greatest Reason to hope that Colonel Upton will find the Ministry inclined to listen to his Proposals for an Accommodation, especially if they reflect upon the Justice and Moderation of this Government in the Part it has taken, and discover by this, that it is our Wish to promote a general Pacification. Colonel Upton will no doubt, under these Circumstances, effect an honourable Peace for the British Nation, and upon Terms of Security to the Company's Possessions in India.

We have agreed to furnish you to the Amount of 20 Lacks of Rupees in the Course of the present Year, commencing the 1st May last, in which we include the Drafts accepted from your Presidency and Surat since that Date; and we authorize you to continue drawing upon us for such Sums as you may be able to obtain at the most reasonable Exchange in your Power to that Extent.

APPENDIX, N° 78.

Translate of a Letter from Setwajee Gonkescan, Somerbatan, to Colonel Thomas Keating,

After Compliments.

As you have made a Friendship between me and Ragonaut Row Punt, I have therefore from my Sircar ceded for ever to the Company a Purgunnah called Chickly; and the Friendship must be continued, without any Alteration, according to the Agreement dated the Ninth of Jonia.

Delout Setwagee Row,
Gorkwar Someubadon.

The Copy of this Sunnud having been received in Cypher, has occasioned some Inaccuracies in the spelling of the Names.

True Copy.
(Signed) Edward Ravenscroft,
Sec.

Translate of the Copy of the Treaty between Ragonaut Bajarow Pundit Predan, on one Part, and Futty Sing and Seagee Row, Sermshere Babader, on the other Part.

That Seagee and Futty Sing, Shirmshere Bahadar, had disobeyed and joined with the Rebels; but now by the Means of Colonel Thomas Keating, who for and in Behalf of the United English East India Company have, by promising Presents, accommodated Matters with Pundit Predan, the following are the Articles of the Guicawar Proposals.

Article 1st, That Secajee and Futty Sing, Guicawar Shermshere Bahadar, do hereby agree to pay the Sum of Eight Lacks of Rupees every Year to the Sircar.

2d, That they are to attend as usual with a Troop of 3000 good Horse and Men, which Number is not to be lessened.

3d, In the late Maderow's Time they used to pay every Year Three Lacks of Rupees to Govinrow, Guicawar Senackeskel Shumshere Bahader; which Sum is settled not to be paid him in future, about which Govinrow is to make no Claim against Secajee and Futty Sing.

4th, Conderow, Guicawar Jumuth Bahader, is to be continued on the same Footing, and agreeable to the Agreement made in the Time of the late Damajee, deceased.

5th, That the Government and Revenue of the Purgunnahs of Broach have been ceded to the Honourable Company, agreeable to the Agreement made between them and Sheremuth Punt Predan, about which Secajee and Futty Sing are not to make any Dispute.

6th, The Purgunnahs Chickly and Vercow, near Surat, and Coral, near the Nubadah River, and about 15 Coss distant from Broach, which together makes Three Purgunnahs, the Guicawar have ceded to the Honourable Company for ever, on Account of the Peace they have made between the Guicawar and Sheremuth Punt Predan.

7th, That in the Court of Sheremuth Punt Predan, the Guicawars must pay a due Attention to every Thing that is reasonable, without having any Communication with its Enemies.

8th, That for the Confirmation and Compliance of the above Articles, the Honourable Company stand Security; and should the Guicawars appear any Way false, the Honourable Company is not to protect them; Ragoba is also to fulfil the above Articles without any Difference.

A true Copy.
(Signed) Edward Ravenscroft,
Sec.

APPEN-

APPENDIX, Nº 79.

Extract of Bengal Secret Consultations, the 11th September 1775.

PRESENT,

The Honourable Warren Hastings, Governor General, President,
Lieutenant General John Clavering,
The Honourable George Monson,
Richard Barwell, Esquire.
Mr. Francis, indisposed.

RECEIVED, the following Letter and Inclosures from the President and Council at Fort St. George:

Honourable Sir, and Sirs,

We have had the Honour to receive your Letter of the 17th July, communicating to us the Reasons which have induced your Honour, &c. to depute Lieutenant Colonel Upton to Poona, as well as your Sentiments on the Measures adopted by the Presidency of Bombay, in acting in Conjunction with Ragoba against the Ministerial Party of the Maratta Government.

Accompanying, your Honour, &c. will receive a Copy of a Letter which the Nabob has lately received from Savay Maudheveron Pundit Pridhawn; in consequence of which we have addressed a Letter to the Nabob, wherein we advise him in Reply to Maudheveron, to refer him to Lieutenant Colonel Upton, who on the Spot can best inform him of the favourable Intentions of the English towards his Government. And we have further requested that the Nabob will inform us if there is any Thing relative to the Safety or Prosperity of the Carnatic, which he may think may be obtained from the Maratta Government by Means of Colonel Upton's Deputation, and which he would wish us to communicate to your Honour, &c. for that Purpose.

In a Letter lately received by our President from Mr. Whitehill, Chief of Masulipatam, we are given to understand that Allyar Beg, Brother to Fazel Beg Cawn, who commands the Subah's Army, and who has extensive Influence both over his Councils and Government, is shortly expected to arrive at Masulipatam, in order to celebrate a Festival at that Place; and on this Account we think it adviseable to acquaint your Honour, &c. that we believe something of Importance to the Company may be obtained through his Means, particularly as Fazel Beg has expressed himself greatly inclined to a more intimate Connection than at present subsists between the English and the Soubah. At all Events we think a Negociation with the Soubah might be probably carried on, not only as it might affect our Northern Circars, but as it might be of immediate Consequence to the forwarding the Intention of the Deputation which your Honour, &c. have thought proper to send to Poona. The Soubah has heretofore had great Weight with the Ministerial Party of the Maratta Government, and we therefore are of Opinion that Advantages from that Quarter may be had through his Means; in this Matter, however, your Honour, &c. will be best enabled to judge. Mr. Whitehill has been directed to sound Allyar Beg with respect to the Soubah's real Intentions towards the English, and on being advised of the Result of his Enquiry, we shall not fail to communicate it to your Honour, &c. for your Information.

The accompanying Letter from the Presidency of Bombay, addressed to your Honour, &c. having been just received, we have now the Honour of forwarding it to you, together with Copy of a Letter which we have received from them, as well as of our Reply; in consequence whereby you will observe, that they request a further Reinforcement of Troops from this Establishment; and that we, in consequence of your Honour's, &c. Desire, have declined supplying them with that Succour which they required.

We are, &c.

Fort Saint George, (Signed) A. Wynch,
26th August, 1775. President and Council.

To

To the Honourable Alexander Wynch, Esq; President, &c. Council at Fort Saint George.

Honourable Sir, and Sirs,

The War we are at present engaged in for the Support of Ragoba, is of the utmost Importance to the Honourable Company, and loudly calls upon us to pursue every Means in our Power that we can think of to bring it to a speedy and successful Issue; for on that will depend the greatest Advantages that the Company are to reap by the Engagements we have entered into on their Behalf. And it is a Matter of the utmost Importance to them, to conclude the War in the Course of the ensuing Season.

Our Forces, in every Engagement with the Enemy, have gained every Advantage that we have Reason to expect; but at the Time we sent the Body of Men we did, it was concluded, that Ragoba's own Forces would be of material Service during the Campaign. The contrary, however, has been found to be the Case; and it therefore has happened, that our Army has often not been able to reap any Advantage that might have been expected from the Victories they have gained over the Enemy. The Commanding Officer has in consequence requested, and Ragoba earnestly solicited, a Reinforcement may be sent by the Time that they will be able again to take the Field, which will be in the Beginning of the Month of November next, the rainy Season having at present obliged the Army to go into Winter Quarters at Dubay, near the Banks of the Nerbedah; for this Reinforcement which Ragoba has so earnestly intreated, he is to make over additional Advantages to the Honourable Company, exclusive of those mentioned in the Treaty.

We shall also require a Military Force for the Protection of Salsette, and of the Provinces already ceded to the Company, as well as to insure the Collection of the Revenues of the ensuing Season.

We have thus stated to your Honour, &c. the Services for which a large Military Force is required, and shall now proceed to acquaint you, that it is totally out of our Power to furnish from hence the Whole that will be requisite; but satisfied as we are how much you have the Interest of the Honourable Company at Heart, and being convinced that we can receive a Reinforcement much more early from your Presidency, than from the Governor General and Council at Fort William, who have offered us Assistance, we therefore again take the Liberty to apply to you, earnestly requesting that you will supply us with Three hundred Europeans Rank and File, and Two compleat Battalions of Sepoys, which we may receive in Time for the Services that will be required of them, by your Honour, &c. ordering them to march by Land to Anjengo, from whence they will be directed to proceed to Tellicherry, at which Place Conveyances shall be ready to transport them hither; and we can assure you that your Compliance with this Request will be of very material Benefit to our honourable Employers.

The inclosed Packet for the Governor General and Council of Fort William, communicates to them the same Intelligence as we have now done to you; and we request that your Honour, &c. will acquaint them with your Resolution and Determination on the Application we now make to you; for should you be unable to assist us with the whole Force that is now desired, we have requested those Gentlemen to supply the Deficiency, or even the Whole, should you not be able to spare any Part; but at the same Time, we request that you will consider, that it is more than probable that the Succours from Bengal, should you leave it to the Governor General and Council to supply us, cannot arrive at the Scene of Action so early as the Beginning of November next, which is the Time, as we before said, that our Operations must begin.

It will be very acceptable, if the State of your Finances will enable you to supply the Force that you may detach to our Assistance with a Military Chest, as we have so many Calls for Money, that we are apprehensive our Resources may be insufficient to satisfy all the Demands upon us; more especially, as one of our most material Resources is almost shut up, namely, the Receipt of Money for the Sales of the Company's Goods; for, owing to the present Situation of the Maratta Country, Trade is at this Time almost at a Stand.

We are, &c.
(Signed) D. Draper,
&c. Council.

Bombay Castle,
13th July, 1775.

A true Copy.
(Signed) R. Sulivan,
Secretary.

To

APPENDIX, N° 79.

To the Honourable William Hornby, Esquire, President, &c. Council at Bombay.

Honourable Sir, and Sirs,

We have been favoured with Duplicate of your Letter, of the 13th Ultimo, together with a Letter addressed to the Governor General and Council, which shall be forwarded to Bengal with the utmost Expedition.

In consequence of the Aid of Troops, which in Compliance with your earnest Desire we before sent you, we informed the Governor General and Council of our having done so, and of the weighty Reasons which influenced us to such a Measure; but although they did not disapprove of our having granted you that Reinforcement at your urgent Request, yet they desire that for the future we do not detach any Part of our Forces out of our Provinces, unless for the Security of our own Possessions, without their previous Concurrence. From this therefore, your Honour, &c. will perceive, that we are not at Liberty, even if our Military Establishment could afford it, to send you that Assistance which you require; but indeed, were we left discretionally to act, our incomplete Establishment of Europeans would not admit of our making the smallest Draught from it, much less of so considerable a one as that requested by your Honour, &c. of 300 Rank and File.

Having a few Days ago received a Letter from the Governor General and Council, containing an Account of the Reasons which have induced them to depute Lieutenant Colonel Upton to Poona, we shall here furnish you with an Extract of that Part of it, which immediately relates to the Embassy, and the Powers given to Colonel Upton; viz.

We have deputed Lieutenant Colonel Upton to proceed to Poona, to conclude a Treaty of Peace with that State; I have furnished him with full Powers and Instructions for this Purpose.—The Peishwa has been advised of this Deputation, and desired to forward Passports for Colonel Upton, to meet him at Calpee.

Agreeably to your Request, we shall immediately inform the Governor General and Council, of our Determination to decline acquiescing in the Request you have made, in order, if it shall appear to them proper, that you be supplied with a Reinforcement of Military from that Establishment.

Fort Saint George,
26th August 1775.

We are, &c.
(Signed) A Wynch,
President, &c. Council.

A true Copy.
(Signed) Rd. Sulivan,
Secy.

Resolved, that the following Reply to the foregoing Letters be immediately dispatched to Fort St. George.

Gentlemen,

We have received your Letter of the 26th August, by the Ankerwyke; also that of the 12th August, with your Proceedings, which we shall take into Consideration as soon as possible.

We do not conceive it necessary to employ the Mediation of the Nizam, in effecting the proposed Treaty with the Maratta Government; and we think it is not likely that he would willingly engage in it, without some View to his own Advantage. And as it is not our Intention to solicit a Reconciliation with the Maratta State, but to propose it to them as an Act of Justice due from this Government, and as being a Duty enjoined us by the Instructions of the Court of Directors, for the Preservation of Peace throughout India, we judge it unnecessary to enter into any Negociation for this End, either with the Nizam or any other Power, and mean to rely solely on our own Influence for effecting it.

We think however it would be highly proper for you to direct the Chief at Masulipatam to inform the Nizam's Minister, Fazel Beg, should he visit that Place, that we entertain the above Sentiments; that we have already declared our entire Disapprobation of the War in which the Bombay Presidency have engaged the Company against the

Maratta

Marratta Government at Poona, and that we have sent them Orders to discontinue it. —He may also inform the Minister of our Deputation of Colonel Upton to Poona, to settle the Terms of a Treaty of Peace with the ruling Power there.

We think it would be improper to communicate to him any more than these Circumstances.

We are, &c.

APPENDIX, N° 80.

From the Nabob, dated 12th August 1775; received 13th Do. Do.

YESTERDAY, being the 11th August, at Evening, the Letter from Savay Maudheverow, a Copy of which I now inclose for your Perusal, was brought to me by two Post Camels. You will be pleased to inform me what Mode you think it adviseable to adopt in replying to it. What shall I say more?

Copy of a Letter from Savay Maudheverow Pundit Pridhawin to the Nabob; received at the Durbar 11th August 1775.

From the first Establishment of the English Factories on this Coast, we have, in Reliance on their Sincerity and Veracity, afforded them every Kind of Assistance that could tend to make their Settlements flourish, and their Trade increase; and the good Understanding between us seemed firm and prosperous, insomuch that the late Iru Mant Maudheverow, on receiving a Letter from your Highness and Mr. Bourchier, the then Governor of Madras, by the Mediation of Naugoo Row, on the Subject of the Conquest of the Maisore Country and Reidenoor, and the Chastisement of Hyder Cawn, applied himself, from a Regard to the Laws of Friendship, to succour your Highness and the English, and advanced in Person repeatedly into the Country of Maisore with that Intent. He then sent Maudeverow Sadashevah to your Highness, who staid with you for a considerable Length of Time; and notwithstanding that no Signs appeared of your sending us a Force, and that the dilatory Promise of Letters from Europe was brought up in the Matter of the Succours we require, yet, after receiving Letters from your Highness and Governor Dupre, full of friendly Expressions and Declarations of steady Adherence, he returned from thence; and though your Highness's Country was close by, did not transgress the Bounds of Amity. We had an entire Dependance on the Continuance of that good Will which was expressed in your Highness's and the said Governor's Letters from first to last.

Now however the Governor of Bombay having got Possession of Salsette by Artifice, is acting in Concert with my Uncle Ragonaut Row, in open Hostility with the Circar Army. This perhaps you have already heard. Such a Proceeding on the Part of the English, contrary to all Expectation, is highly injurious; and, considering the Conduct of my Uncle towards my Father, which must appear atrocious to all Nations, it is wonderful that the English, famed as they are for their Sincerity and Uprightness, and informed as they are of this Circumstance and the Nature of my Government, should undertake to assist him.

Your Highness frequently wrote the late Iru Mant Maudheverow, and pledged your Word to Maudheverow Sedahevah that you would be Security for the Union subsisting between us and the English. I therefore desire of your Highness, that you will speak with the Governor of Madras that he may write, and that you yourself also will write, to the Governor General and Council of Calcutta; and that they send Directions to the Governor

Governor of Bombay to desist from succouring my Uncle, and remain in the Path of ancient Friendship, which I shall esteem a Favour. For the rest may your Highness's Joy be perpetual.

A true Copy.

(Signed) Richard Sullivan,
Secretary.

APPENDIX, N° 81.

Extract of Bengal Secret Consultations, the 18th September 1775.

PRESENT,

The Honourable Warren Hastings, Governor General, President,
Lieutenant-General John Clavering,
The Honourable George Monson,
Richard Barwell, } Esquires.
Philip Francis, }

THE Governor General lays before the Board, two Letters, this Morning received from Sukaram Baboo and Ballajee Pundit, with the following Letters from the Chief of Masulipatam, and Mr. Motte.

Honourable Sir,

I have the Honour to transmit you herewith, Two Letters received this Day, the one from Sukaram Baboo, and the other from Nana Pudanviss, both addressed to you.

Masulipatam,
2d September 1775.

I am, &c.
(Signed) John Whitehill.

Sir,

I do myself the Honour to inclose Two Letters received from Poona by returned Pattamars, and Two received at the same Time, dispatched from thence by Sukaram Baboo by express Pattamars.

Benares,
9th September 1775.

I am, &c.
(Signed) T. Motte.

From Sicca Ram Baboo; dated 29th July; received 18th September.

The many Instances of your Wisdom, Prudence, and Abilities, which have come to my Knowledge, have long made me desirous of cultivating your Friendship; but there is a Time fixed for every Thing, before which it cannot take Place. I thank God that, agreeably to my most earnest Wishes, I have at this happy Time enjoyed the Pleasure of a Letter from you; and by a Perusal of its Contents, am satisfied of your Friendship and Regard.

You are therein so kind as to inform me that you have written to the Sirdars of Bombay, to recall the Forces which, contrary to the Orders of the Company, they have sent to the Assistance of Ragonaut Row, and to refrain from any Act injurious to the Government of Surmunt Row; and you desire that I will also put a Stop to all Hostilities against them by Troops of this Government. You further inform me, that it is your Intention to depute a trusty Person to me to adjust all Differences; but that you wait for my Answer, and a Discovery of my Sentiments thereon. I perfectly understand all these Particulars.

The Circumstances, my Friend, are these: Formerly the strictest Union subsisted between the Family of the Paishwa and the Bombay Sirdars, which was cemented by a great Number of Treaties; but by a sudden Change of Fortune, Narrain Row being murdered by Ragonaut Row, the Circumstances of which are well known, by the Favour of God a Son was born to the deceased Row, under whose Shadow we are protected; his Birth raised the Hopes of all Men, and he was seated on the Musnud of the Peshwaship.

During the Life-time of the late blessed Row, I and Ballajee Pundit had, under him, the Management of all Affairs of the Government; and out of Gratitude to them, we still continue to exert ourselves with the utmost Assiduity for the Service of our Master, and are satisfied therein by all the Dependants of the Peshwa, both great and small. Moreover, the Nabob Nizam ul Mulk, adhering strictly to the Rights of his ancient Friendship, shews Favour and Kindness to us.

When this Affair became public, Ragonaut Row went towards Hindostan, pursued by the Forces of the Decan; and the Bombay Sirdars, notwithstanding there had not been the least Appearance of a Breach of Friendship on the Part of this Government, in Violation of their Treaties, fraudulently seized on Salsette, belonging to this Government, and entering into an Alliance with Ragonaut Row, who was wandering about with a very few Followers, engaged in Hostilities with the Armies of the Sirkar. As the most strict Attention is paid to the Performance of Treaties in your Country, which the contracting Parties preserve inviolably to the End of their Lives, such Conduct from the Sirdars of Bombay, in Violation of their Friendship, filled me with Astonishment, and they daily enter further into this Business. It therefore becomes necessary to oppose them; and our Army, supplied with all Kinds of Necessaries, has taken the Field for that Purpose.

There has been One or Two Engagements between them, which you must have received Advices of.

I have no other Wish than to restore the Affairs of my Master, to procure Ease and Security to the People, and to preserve Harmony amongst the Families of the Nobles. This is also your Intention. Agreeable to your Promise, you will, I doubt not, direct the Recall of the Forces from the Field; but it is a Matter of the highest Importance that your Orders to the Sirdars at Bombay should be conveyed in the most positive Terms. Our mutual Interest consists in a strict Friendship being preserved between us. I have written all these Particulars for your Information, and wait for your Answer, and the Arrival of a confidential Agent from you. The sooner an Answer arrives the better.

Ballajee Pundit has also written to you, to whom it is necessary you should return an Answer.

On a separate Paper.

Several Affairs of Importance are delayed for your Concurrence. As soon as the present Affair is settled, I will instruct a Person therein, and send him to you. Let me frequently have the Pleasure to hear from you.

From Ballajee Pundit; dated 29th July.

The many Instances which I have heard of your Wisdom, Prudence, and Abilities, have long made me desirous of cultivating your Friendship; but there is a Time decreed for every Thing, till which it cannot take Place. God be thanked, that agreeable to my most earnest Wishes, Sicca Ram Pundit has at this happy Time received a Letter from you, which inspired me with the greatest Pleasure; by a Perusal of its Contents I am satisfied of your Friendship.

Sicca Ram Pundit has written you very fully, by which you will be made acquainted with every Particular.

I am in Expectation of your Answer, and the Arrival of a confidential Agent from you; the sooner they arrive the better. Several Affairs of Importance are delayed for your Concurrence. After the present Negociation is brought to a Conclusion, I will send a Person to you fully informed on these Points.

N. B. Duplicates of the same Date were received with the above Letters, together with Triplicates dated 8th of Jummadu Assani, or 6th of August.

Resolved,

Resolved, That the following Reply be sent to the foregoing Letters.

To Sicca Ram Baboo, dated 20th September 1775.

I have been favoured with your Letter of the 29th of Jummadee ul Awel, together with a Duplicate of the same Date, and Triplicate of the 8th of Jummade Assani, and was made happy by a Perusal of its Contents. You write me, that you are anxious for the Arrival of my Answer, and of a trusty Person to accommodate all the Causes of Difference between the Gentlemen at Bombay and the Maratta State. My Friend Col. Upton, who has been appointed with full Powers to treat with you, set out from hence about the latter End of Jummadee ul Awel, and will proceed directly to Poona by the Way of Calpee. As I have already expressed my firm Wish to restore the Blessings of Peace, and to establish a lasting Friendship between the Company and Maratta Nation, I have nothing else to add, but to desire, that as Colonel Upton must pass through your Country, and may meet with Obstructions, you will facilitate his Passage as much as possible, by ordering the Chiefs of the Country through which he is to pass, to afford him such Assistance as he may require. Considering me as your sincere Friend, let me frequently have the Pleasure to hear of your Health.

To Ballajee Pundit, of the same Tenor and Date.

Resolved, That the above Letters be sent to Colonel Upton, together with Copies of them, and of those just received for his Information; and that the following Letter be immediately written to him.

To Colonel Upton.

Sir,

The Governor General having received Answers from Sicca Ram Baboo and Ballajee Pundit, the Ministers of the Maratta Government at Poona, to the Letters which he wrote them concerning our Intention to depute a Person to negotiate a Treaty of Peace with that State, we enclose Translations of these Papers, together with Copies of the Replies now dispatched to them, for your Information. The original Replies, which we also enclosed, we desire you will forward by a speedy Conveyance to Poona, with a Letter from yourself addressed to Sicca Ram Baboo, requesting any Assistance that you may find you may have Occasion for in your Route to that Capital.

We think it proper to add, that it appears highly necessary you should proceed with all possible Dispatch.

We are, &c.

APPENDIX, Nº 82.

Extract of Bengal Secret Consultations, 5th October 1775.

To the Hon. Warren Hastings, Esq; Governor General, &c. Council at Fort William.

Honourable Sir, and Gentlemen,

WE addressed you in Duplicate under the 6th Instant; and have since received the Duplicate of your Letter of the 31st May, the Contents whereof give us great Concern; not only because the Interest of our Honourable Employers, we apprehend, must be very materially affected by the Measures you have thought proper to adopt for bringing about a general Pacification, and the due Weight of this Government affected in a Manner we fear scarcely to be retrieved, by the Letter of Sacram Bappo at Poona, but also because your Honour, &c. seem to think we have been guilty of a premeditated and intentional

intentional Disrespect to the Powers entrusted by the Legislature to your Government, which we take this early Opportunity to assure you was by no Means the Case; but the Negociation for the Treaty with Ragoba being begun before your Administration commenced, and as we thereby secured to the Company the Possession of Salsette, and the Right to Bassein and the Purgannahs near to Surat, all of which our Honourable Employers have repeatedly enjoined us to procure for them; and as the Revenues of these Purgunnahs can be collected without much Trouble or Expence, and is so considerable as to amount, including Salsette and Bassein, to near Twenty (20) Lacks of Rupees per Annum, which will be the Means of enabling this Presidency to support itself, without being any longer a Burthen to your's, of which the late Administration frequently complained; and it was moreover absolutely requisite for us to determine, whether we would conclude the Treaty, or absolutely reject it; for any Delay in the then Situation of Ragoba's Affairs would, we judged, have been the same as if we had determined to remain inactive; we say, for all these cogent Reasons, we thought that we were not precluded by the late Act of Parliament from pursuing the Measures we did.

Another weighty Consideration impelled us also to this Measure; we have been induced, from the Motives we fully stated to your Honour, &c. in our Address of the 31st December last, to attack and reduce Salsette, and we think that the Welfare of this Presidency entirely depended on our preventing that Island from again falling into the Hands of the Portugueze; in this Situation we are of Opinion Policy required that we should side with one of the contending Parties in the Maratta State, that it might be reconciled to our Motives for that Attack, and to our continuing in Possession of that Island; this necessarily being allowed, Justice doubtless required that we should take Part with Ragoba the Peshwa; and in Duty to our Employers we made this decisive Step as advantageous to them as possible, as we think is evident from the Treaty.

We are induced to hope for these Reasons, that your Honour, &c. will not continue to consider our Treaty as invalid, nor the War which was the Consequence of it, either unauthorized, impolitic, or unjust; that it was not dangerous, the Event of it hitherto has shewn; but even had it been so in some Degree, we flatter ourselves your Honour, &c. will admit something might have been risked for the great Probability we had of acquiring a Revenue of nearly Two hundred and Fifty thousand (250,000 £. stg.) Pounds Sterling per Annum, for the future necessary Support of this Presidency, and his by a Means that Equity as we conceive, allowing for Circumstances, cannot censure; for though we have not the Plea of Injury sustained by the Poona Party, yet it must be observed, that Party is composed of the traitorous and rebellious Subjects of Ragoba, who by his large Offers for our Assistance, his just Pretensions, and the Necessity of our taking a Part for the Reasons above assigned, induced us to espouse his Cause, and to hope for your Honour, &c. Concurrence.

We are convinced, that were you fully acquainted with the equitable and undeniable Pretensions of Ragoba to the Dignity of Peshwa, of which he has been near Two Years in Possession, (as you will please to observe on Reference to a Letter from Mr. Mostyn, Resident at the Durbar, to the late Select Committee of your Presidency, under Date 29th November 1773) and that a large Part of the Maratta Empire at present acknowledge him such, with the fair Prospect we had of shortly fixing him therein, and also of the distracted State of the Affairs of the rebellious Confederacy, without an adequate Army, or an effectual Means to procure one, together with the Detriment that must accrue to the Company, and the Disgrace to this Presidency, by the Orders you have given for annulling our Treaty, and in Consequence deserting Ragoba; we say that had your Honour, &c. been fully apprized respecting all these Points, we cannot but flatter ourselves that your Orders would have been very different, or at least they would have left us to have carried into Execution your Resolution for a general Pacification, which we are satisfied might have been done with Honour and Credit, had you not at the same Time peremptorily required us to withdraw our Forces, acquainted the Ministerial Party so expresly of your having done so, and of your Condemnation of our Conduct.

This Intelligence we received from Poona in a Letter to the President, as per Copy enclosed, and at the same Time we received a Copy of one from Governor Hastings to Saccaram Bappo; both were delivered by an Agent from that Party, who had been here some Time to solicit Peace; but the Indisposition of this Agent, and of our President afterwards, prevented his Proposals being received till after he had got this Letter; he will now make no other Overtures than, that on Condition of delivering up Ragoba and the Island of Salsette, and of relinquishing our Pretensions to Bassein, and all other Places ceded

ceded by Treaty, our Expences may be defrayed; though we are satisfied those he came with were widely different indeed: He also assures us, as well as the Letter from Poona, that Orders are gone to their Army to cease all Hostilities; which Orders the Agent declares he understands extend to Ragoba, his Officers and Adherents. In Obedience to your positive Injunctions, we have also sent Directions to our Commanding Officer to cease from all Acts of Hostility, and as soon as the Season will possibly admit, our Forces will be withdrawn into our own Garrisons.

But in order more fully than can be done by Letter at so great a Distance, to represent to your Honour, &c. the Motives for all our Proceedings, and the present Situation of Affairs, with the Danger and Discredit that must attend our Treaty being annulled, and Ragoba deserted; as well as to represent to you at large, the particular Interest of this Presidency; we have deputed to your Honour, &c. Mr. William Tayler, who from being long a Member of our Board and of the Select Committee, is sufficiently qualified to give your Honour, &c. every requisite Information: And we earnestly request that you will attend to the Representations that he may make you on the Subject in Question, and all others dependent on it; and we hope, that on further Consideration you may be induced to revoke your present Orders, to confirm our Treaty, and to permit us to carry Ragoba to Poona, in the Manner first proposed; for we can assure your Honour, &c. that with your Countenance and Support we are firmly of Opinion no ill Consequences can result therefrom, but on the contrary, that great and permanent Advantages must be secured to the Company thereby; we hope also that you will do us the Justice to believe that it is our Wish and Intention at all Times to pay the most implicit Obedience to your Authority. We would willingly take upon ourselves the Consequences of the War, for which your Honour, &c. by your Protest declare we are responsible, provided we have your Support, and are allowed to conduct it to its Issue.

For every other requisite Information, as well with regard to the Places ceded for ever by Treaty, as for those granted for the Subsidy, also for the Situation of the Purgunnahs that have since been made over to the Company by Ragoba and Futty Sing, for mediating the Reconciliation of the latter with the former, likewise for the Company's general Interest at this Presidency in its present Situation, permit us to refer your Honour, &c. to Mr. Tayler; assuring you that we remain, &c.

Bombay Castle, 23d August 1775. (Signed) Wm. Hornby, and Council.

To Madaurao Narron.

After Compliments:

By the Hands of your Servant Biccajee, I received your Letter, and understand its Contents. You write, that a Letter has been received from Governor Hastings at Bengal, in the Name of Saca am Bagwant, of which you have sent me a Copy, and that you have sent written Orders to all your Officers, charging them not to fight with or molest the English Forces. This is well. Your Servant Biccajee has assured me in your Name, that your Orders to your Officers also extend to Ragoba, his Forces, and all his Adherents, that is, that they are not to fight with or molest him, or them; this also is proper, for Ragonaut Row Peshwa is under our Protection. All is to remain just in the same Situation as at present, as your Servant assures me is your Meaning and Intention; this also is mine, and I have therefore sent the necessary Orders to the Commander of our Forces. Take Care, I desire, that your Orders are not infringed, and then mine will be exactly obeyed, till a Treaty may be concluded.

A true Copy.

(Signed) Geo. Skipp, Secretary.

Ordered, That this Letter lie for Consideration.

APPENDIX, N° 83.

To Colonel Upton.

Sir,

WE have received Advice from the President and Council at Bombay, and also learnt from Mr. Tayler, one of their Council, who has been deputed from them to this Government, that a total Cessation of Arms has taken Place between the Maratta Army and the Company's Troops, lately employed in Support of Ragoba; both Parties will consequently remain in this State of Suspence, until your Arrival at Poona. It is unnecessary therefore to say, how earnestly we repeat our Directions for your proceeding with all possible Dispatch.

Fort William,
5th October 1775.

We are, &c.

Resolved, That Mr. Tayler from Bombay be requested to meet the Board at Ten o'Clock on Monday next, that Day being set apart for his Reception.

Ordered, That Notice be sent him by the Secretary.

Bengal Secret Consultations, 9th October 1775.

Such were the great and leading Motives which induced the Government of Bombay to engage with Peishwah Ragonath Row. It seems the very Crisis wished for by the Company, an Opportunity of accomplishing the Objects they had so strenuously enjoined them ever to keep in View, with Honour, with Justice, and without the Hazard of a general War with the whole Marratta Empire, with their especial and repeated Orders on this Head before them, unrepealed by every Letter that accompanied the new Act. So far from meaning a Disregard to that Act, or to the Power with which it vests your Honour, &c. the Government of Bombay would have deemed themselves wanting, in their Conception of it, to the Spirit of the Legislature expressed in the Words, "except in such "Cases where the said President and Council respectively shall have received special Or-"ders from the said United Company," and most highly to our Employers, had they so slumbered over their Interests, as to have let pass by unregarded this Opportunity, perhaps the only one that may offer again, of establishing their Affairs in the West of India, on the Footing they have so long sought to place them. To have hesitated closing with the Peishwah, would in Effect have been the same as a plain Refusal, for in the Situation he then was, he must certainly have had Recourse to other Assistance; and from the respectable Footing in which the late Increase of their Military and total Change of Government has placed them, it would most probably have been to the Portugueze, who would gladly have cherished a Stroke of Fortune so unexpectedly co-operating, the Execution of the very Views to which all their late Expences and Arrangements have solely tended, viz. the Recovery of the Provinces of the North, the great Object of their Interest and Honour ever since the Capture of them in 1739, by Chimnajee Oppa, and which they would certainly have now obtained, had it not been for an Interference equally timely and fortunate to the Honourable Company.

Besides these, other strong Inducements were not wanting to take the Part they did; the Reduction of Salsette, without the Consent of either Party, rendered it necessary to side with one, in order to procure a Degree of Title to the Possession; and to prevent the disagreeable Alternative of either endangering the Welfare of the Settlement, by relinquishing this Conquest, or sustaining at some Period a general War with the combined Forces of the Marattas, to maintain it.

A due Attention to the Safety and Tranquillity of the Company's Possessions in the East of Hindostan, was also no small Motive in these Engagements. It was judged, that should the Success of the Confederates at Poona, end in the total Depression of Ragoba, and once give them Leisure to advert to other Objects, the very first that would strike their Attention, would be to enrich themselves by the Collection of Chout in the Name

of

of their Sircar. In this all Parties among the Marattas never fail to concur. I cannot pretend to say how far the Bengal Provinces might be engaged; but from the Vicinity of the Carnatic, there seems no Doubt of their paying it a Visit. They never want a Pretence; and the Reduction of Tanjore had given great Jealousy at Poona, particularly to the Maratta Chiefs, as the Rajah of Tanjore is related to the Rajah. The Safety and Tranquillity of the Company's Territories in the East would, for these Reasons, be secured for a longer Time, by not suffering the Ministerial Confederacy to predominate by the Treaty with the Paishwa. This great Object is for ever accomplished as far as solemn Engagements can bind; and, could Circumstances permit of a general Exertion at this Period, our Security in this Point might be still more perfect.

Indeed, by these several Motives, the Government of Bombay concluded a Treaty with the Vackeel of Ragoba: It was much to be wished that their Resources in Men and Money had been more adequate to this Undertaking; but trusting that the same Sentiments would generally prevail of the Policy and Utility of their Engagements, the Aid of the other Presidencies was not doubted. Accordingly such Troops as could possibly be spared were embarked for Surat, from whence they were to proceed to form a Junction with the Army of Ragoba, in the Manner that Circumstances on their Arrival might point out to be most expedient; the First Step proposed being to reduce Brodirah, the Capital of the Guicawars, put the Officers of Govindrow and Candahrow in Possession of the Country, and direct the March towards Poona, which could then be done with greater Safety, as we should have a Country in Alliance with us in our Rear.

Hurry Punt Furkia, a Bramin, one of the Confederates and Commander in Chief of the Army, hearing of Ragoba's Intention to secure our Aid, judged there was no Time to be lost; and therefore determined, if possible, to attack him while he had yet the Superiority; he accordingly directed his March towards Broderah, which obliged Ragoba to raise the Siege of it, and retire Northwards of the Myhie River, near Cambay. Futty Sing Guicawar joined the Confederates; and being well acquainted with the Country, led their Army, by short Routs, through Passes and Defiles, crossed Myhie, came unexpectedly on the Army of Ragoba, attacked the Center of it, where he was; a smart Action ensued between the Armies, but a Party of Arabs, whom Ragoba had got from Govind Row, declining to engage, he thought himself betrayed, quitted the Field, and narrowly escaped to Cambay, with about 1000 Horse. His General, Monackjee Phankria, retreated with the best of his Troops and valuable Effects to the Fort Copperwange, about 50 Coss from Cambay, as did Govind Row and Sanda Row.

From Cambay the Paishwa made the best of his Way to Surat, where our Army found him. The Treaty agreed on by his Vackeel was here ratified by him; and having received Advice from his General and his Allies of their safe Retreat to Copperwange, from whence they acquainted him, that they doubted not of effecting a Junction with the English Troops, could they advance to Cambay, it was therefore determined our Army should proceed there, as we could transport it by Sea, and were well assured of its perfect Security. It accordingly arrived there the 18th March; and though the Ministerial Army was at first between us and our Allies, yet by a concerted Motion the Commander in Chief having brought himself in a secure Post between the Enemy and the Paishwa's Troops, a Junction was happily formed with them on the 19th April.

The combined Army then consisted of 35,000 Horse and Foot belonging to Ragoba and Govind Row, and 2,500 English Troops. The Army of the Confederates had suffered a very material Reduction, and of their best Troops, by the Desertion of Madoojee Sindia, the Jagierdaar of Ugien, owing entirely to the impolitic Advice of the Bramins, who deeming Ragoba's Ruin certain on his late Defeat, paid no further Attention to their Northern Friends, but sent Orders to Hurry Punt Furkia to seize Madoojee Sindia, and send him to Poona to settle his Accounts. The Maratta got Intelligence of this, and knowing the Meaning was to fleece him, he decamped with about 12,000 of the best Horse in the Army, under Pretence that Troubles in his own Jaghier called him there.

As soon as possible after Junction, Colonel Keating, the Commander in Chief of our Forces, advanced towards the Enemy in order to bring them to an Engagement, but, though something superior, they studiously avoided it, and fled before us at different Times. At the Request of the Paishwa, for some particular Reasons our Army moved towards the North; but Poona being our final Object, as the Paishwa's Arrival there would bring Matters to a Conclusion, Colonel Keating was ordered not to be diverted from it by any Object so remote from his Destination, but with all Expedition possible to direct his March Southward.

Discouraged

Discouraged by the Defection of so considerable a Partizan as Sindia; by the Doubts they were in regarding their other Northern Ally, Hulcar; by the Duplicity of the Nizam's Conduct, who, notwithstanding their Cessions and Subsidies, had still declined advancing any Troops to their Assistance; by the Loss of their Ally, Shabajee Bonsola, cut off by his Brother Moodajee; by their Fears of several leading Men, who not only refused to join the Confederacy, but they judged would declare openly for Ragoba as he advanced to Poona; and knowing the utter Impossibility they were in to resist, should the Engagement of the English with Ragoba become general; from these several Motives, the Junction at Poona, it is said, directed Hurry Punt Furkia at all Events to risk an Engagement with us at any Rate; their Prospects could not be worse, and a fortunate Success might give a favourable Turn to a Negociation, which Sacaram Bapoo and Nana Furnesse were then meditating with the President and Council of Bombay.

When the Peshwa was compelled to fly on the unfortunate Surprizal of his Army, he had brought off with him about Six Lacks of Rupees in Jewels, the rest of his valuable Effects were secured in the Fort of Dhaar with his Family; these Six Lacks were insisted on as a Pledge for his Engagement with the Company. He wanted to make a Loan at Surat, but from the State of Affairs, the Shroffs did not chuse to trust him on his own Security, and the President and Council could not in Prudence engage the Credit of the Company; from this Want of Money, infinite Distress succeeded, and in Action, Advantages were lost by it, as it is well known the hired Troops of India can never be brought to engage without some Prospect of immediate Satisfaction; the Ministers know this, and were therefore more desirous to come to Action before a Turn to his Affairs relieved him from this Distress, which they were sensible would in Fact deprive him of any great Benefit from his own Troops, whatever their Number might be.

Accordingly, on the 18th of May they made Dispositions to engage:—Accounts have already been transmitted of this Action, in which the Confederates were defeated, and though by some unfortunate Accident on our Side, and the Inaction of the Paishwa's Force, it was not so complete a Victory as might have been hoped for, yet it sufficed to throw their Troops into utter Discouragement, and they never could be brought to face us again, but suffered us quietly to pursue them through defensible Passes and Defiles without Opposition, till on the 7th of June we came up with their Rear in crossing the Nerbedah, killed them several People, obliged them to sink their Cannon in the River, and many Men, Horses, and Camels, &c. were afterwards found floating down with the Tide; this was the last Time we could come to Action with them, Hurry Punt Furkia having fled with the Remainder of his Army entirely out of the Guzerat Provinces.

The Approach of the Monsoon, when it would be impossible for our Troops to march, forbad all Thoughts of advancing further Southward before the Rains; not to lose any Time, however, it was determined by the Colonel to avail himself of the remaining Part of the fair Season to reduce Dubboy, a fortified Place, situated between Broach and Broderah, where our Army could winter, and on the opening of the Season be easily joined from Broach by such Reinforcement and Supplies as might be sent from Bombay, and from thence march to reduce Broderah, should the Negociation then on Foot between Futty Sing and the Paishwa fail to secure us a friendly Country in our Rear, on the March of the Army towards Poona. The Reduction of Dubboy was effected without Loss, and with it concluded all our Military Operations that Campaign.

The Engagements of Futty Sung Guicawar with the Confederates, seems to have been solely with the View of preventing the Ravage and Destruction of his Country for ever. At the Time he joined their Army, he made distant Overtures to Ragoba; he knew that the Interests which the late Cessions gave to the English in the Welfare of Guzerat would preserve it on their Part, and his Junction with the Ministerial Army secure it on the other; as soon therefore as the Retreat of Hurry Punt Furkia confirmed his Safety in that Quarter, he began to make serious Overtures of Accommodation to Ragoba, who from the general Face of Things he judged must prevail, and in that Case his Government would be for ever lost to him. As the former Appointment of Govind Row, and his firm Attachment to Ragoba, left no Doubt of his Rival being established in the Guicawar Possession, the better to insure Success he applied for the Mediation of the English, to whom he not only gave the Confirmation of the Grants engaged by the Paishwa to be obtained from the Guicawar, but further convenient Cessions in Perpetuity to the Amount of about 1,78,000 Rupees per Annum. With Ragoba he stipulated for the usual Chout and Aid due to the Poona Durbar; and what was most convenient in his present Circumstances, the Sum of Twenty-six Lacks to be paid in Sixty Days, the Paishwa having previ-

ously

ously satisfied Govind Row; a Treaty of Peace and Alliance was finally concluded in the Month of July last.

At Sea the Marattas at first made a formidable Appearance. Induced by the Hopes of making some rich Captures, the Officer at Gheria equipped a Squadron consisting of

1 Ship	—	46 Guns	2 Gallivats of 9 Guns.
1 Ditto	—	38 Ditto	8 Ditto from 2 to 4 Guns,
1 Ditto	—	32 Ditto	besides Swivels.
2 Ditto	—	26 Ditto	
5			

This formidable Fleet in Appearance was met on the 2d of February by the Revenge and Bombay Grab, under the Command of Commodore John More; the Commodore immediately stood towards them, when their whole Fleet bore away; he however singled out the Admiral's Ship, called the Shumshur Jung, of 46 Guns, and directed the Grab, being the best Sailer, to give her Chace. The Ship stood in for the Shore, with Design it seems to run aground, but the Grab came up with her, and began engaging, which giving Time to the Commodore to come up, he kept up a very smart Fire on her for about Two Hours, when she blew up and was intirely destroyed, with the Commander, and most of her People.

Proper Convoys being given to the Trade up and down the Malabar Coast, we met with no Loss whatever at Sea, except of a small Pilot Sloop, which was surprized by Two Gallivats, under the Colours of the Suddee of Ragapore, our Friend and Ally, not knowing at that Time of our being at Hostilities with the Marattas.

As your Honours, &c. had desired particular Information regarding the several Places ceded to us, I will conclude with it, the Account of our Situation at this Period.

Ceded for ever by the Treaty with the Paishwa,		
Salsette, with Caranjee, Elephanta, Hog Island, and Canary — —	3,50,000	
Basiien with its Dependencies —	4,00,000	
Orpad — —	3,50,000	
Jambuseer — —	4,00,000	
Baroach the Guicawars Shaw	3,50,000	
To be paid annually from Occlaseer	75,000	
		19,25,000
Presented to the Company since by Ragonaut Raw and Futty Sing, on the Conclusion of the Treaty between them; viz.		
Corial near Baroach —	50,000	
Chickley near Surat —	1,00,000	
Verion near Surat —	28,000	
Ahmood adjoining to Baroach	1,50,000	
		3,28,000
Ceded to the Company for ever — Rupees		22,53,000

Made over by the Paishwa for the Payment of the Subsidy, viz.		
Ahmood, since entirely given up, and therefore the others remain as a Pledge for the Payment of the Subsidy — —	1,50,000	
Occlaseer, the Remainder of its Revenues	1,00,000	
Hansoot — —	1,27,000	
Versal — —	1,00,000	
		4,87,000

From the Southernmost Part of Bassien to the Point of Chaul, the Land forms a deep Bay, in which are situated the Islands of Salsette, Bombay, Caranja, Hog Island, Elephanta, and Canary; Bombay being situated about Eight Miles from the Continent, forms the Harbour to which it gives its Name.

Salsette lays North of Bombay, from which it is divided only by a narrow Channel of about Half a Mile in Breadth; it is about Twenty Miles long, and the same Breadth on a Medium. Its chief Produce is Rice; it is capable of much Improvement, not being above Two-thirds cultivated, and great Part of it also breached by the Sea. The Fort of Tannah commands a fordable Channel, dividing Salsette from the Main, and is about the Middle of the Eastern Side of the Island.

Caranja is a small Island on the East of Bombay, forming Part of the East Side of the Harbour; its chief Produce is also Rice; it is at present worth about 60,000 Rupees per Annum, and is capable of Improvement.

Elephanta is a small Island, valued at about 800 Rupees.

Hog Island and Canary are little more than barren Rocks; the latter is in the Mouth of the Harbour. Of all these, except Canary, which is not worth the Trouble of reducing, we have Possession of the regular Sunnuds for them on the Paishwa.

Bassien is a Peninsula formed by a large River on the North, by the Sea on the West, and a River which divides it from Salsette, and to which it gives its Name, on the South; a Rivulet which fills makes it an Island in the Time of the Rains. It produces Rice, many Fruits, and particularly fine Sugar Canes: The Soil is exceedingly fine. An extensive Fort on the South commands the River. The District of Bassien extends to Baldapalby Northward, within Eight Coss of Damaun, including Dannoo, Terrapore, Mahim, Kelme, Almole, and some other Towns situated on Rivers flowing from the Gauts. We have the Sunnuds for Bassien and its Districts; but as we had not sufficient Force to reduce them after the Departure of our Army to the Northward, and as the conducting the Paishwa to Poona was the great Object which would insure to us the peaceable Attainment of these Places, it was not thought prudent to delay that, or diminish our Force by the previous Reduction of them; they are not therefore in our Possession as you imagined, but still in the Hands of the Ministerial Party.

These are all our Acquisitions to the Southward of Surat, forming a continued Chain with Bombay, of about Eighty-six Miles from North to South. Two additional Battalions of Sepoys, I imagine, will be sufficient for the necessary Posts, which being called in on any Apprehension from the French, will be a considerable Reinforcement to the standing Garrison of Bombay.

From Bassien, Donnoo, and the Rivers between, comes great Part of the Timber indispensably necessary for the Construction of the Ships. Salsette, &c. with Bassien and its Districts, are only estimated at 7 ½ Lacks, but under our Government they will, I doubt not, in a few Years produce at least Ten.

For all the Cessions to the North stipulated by the Treaty with the Paishwa, we have not only the Sunnuds, but absolute Possession; the Sunnuds for Corial, Chickley, and Variow, were just received by the very last Accounts, and no Doubt we had Possession soon after we were in Possession of Ahmood, and all the Places assigned for Payments of the Subsidy.

Orpad, Variow, and Chickley, laying contiguous to Surat, I see no Increase of Expence that will be requisite on their Account, except the necessary one for Collection.

The Cession of the Guicawar's Share of the Baroach Revenue, is only what is Choutiah, collected from the same Towns we did, so that this is all clear Profit. Jamboseer is a large commercial Town, situated on a small River to which it gives its Name. Its Territory adjoining to that of Baroach, very few Changes will be requisite, as the same Garrison which defends the Territory of the one, will serve for the other. Ahmood is a large Town; its Districts, and that of Corial, are all contiguous to that of Baroach from Occlaseer, where the Subsidy is paid; we have only to send a Man to collect annually 75,000 Rupees.

Occlaseer, the First of the Purgunnahs from which we are to reimburse ourselves for the stipulated Subsidy, lies between Surat and Baroach: Hansoot adjoins to our Purgunnah of Orpad: Versaul is about 40 Miles to the Southward of Surat, situated on a River, from which a great Quantity of Timber is exported. As it is from the Nett Produce of these Assignments that the Company are to be paid, the necessary Charges of Collection will be on Account of the Paishwa.

Although these Cessions are not literally the Maratta Share of the Surat Revenues, by which it is to be understood those collected by the Paishwa; yet, as they generally answer the

the Views of the Company, it was preferred accepting them for many Reasons. Different Persons collect in many of the other Districts, which might have involved us in Disputes; Baroach being reduced since the Date of their Orders, they could have no Views or Interest then in the District ceded adjoining to it; but another still more forcible Reason is, that in order to have completed the Sum we had in View, the Paishwa must have taken from the Guicawar Dominions; and at that Period it was very material to conciliate the Affections of that Family, who may be made useful Allies to the Company, should you deem this a fit Juncture to form a System for counteracting any future Design of the Poonah Durbar.

At the Conclusion of the Treaty with Futty Sing, the general Aspect of Affairs was very flattering to the Hopes of Ragoba; he had already experienced, that with the greatest Force they could ever hope to collect, the Confederates had never dared to make a bold and determined Stand against our Army as it then was, although for Want of Pay his own Troops had never been brought to act with any Degree of Efficacy. This Army would have been increased after the Rains by Captain Kelly's Battalion of Sepoys from Madras, which, from the Experience given of the Activity and Conduct of its Commander, the Attention of his Officers, and the excellent State of Discipline the Men were in, was judged by the Military Gentlemen to be little, if any Thing, inferior in the Field to Europeans; add to this, the Junction of Futty Sing's Troops, and the effectual Service that might be expected from those of the Paishwa, when they found him enabled to satisfy their Arrears; it was natural to imagine the Confederate Army would not dare to face us; the Guicawar Country extending far on the Road to Poona, secured our Rear and Provisions to the Army. With this Force alone, it might not be very rash to pronounce that we should have reached our Destination during the Course of the ensuing Campaign, had we received the requested Reinforcement from Madras; it seems to me there could not have been the least Doubt of it.

To increase his Hopes by the latest Accounts, Moodajee, who by the Death of his Brother Shabajee now enjoyed undisturbed Possession of the Bonsalo Dominions, was advancing with a very respectable Force to his Assistance, as was also Ishmael Cawn, at the Head of 4,000 good Horse; Appajee Gunnis, then in Charge of Ahmadabad, was in Treaty for the Surrender of it to the Paishwa, Part of whose Troops were gone to take Possession of it, which when effected, would leave him free from any Enemy to the Northward of the Nerbedah.

But above all, the Conduct of the Nizam at this Juncture most fortunately co-operated with other Events, to give us a most perfect Assurance, of conducting our Engagements with the Paishwa to a happy Issue; it was perfectly of a Piece with that Policy which had attentively watched every Turn in the Maratta Affairs, to retrieve what their Government had usurped from him in its Prosperity. On the Defeat of their Army, and the bad Aspect of their Affairs, when the Paishwa repassed the Nerbeda, the Confederates, who would advance nothing of their own, thought to bribe the Nizam to Action, by the Cession of the strong and important Fortress of Dowletabad, with Buranpore Assiry, and some Districts formerly conquered by the Marattas: He accordingly entered into a solemn Engagement with them; they had actually evacuated Dowletabad, and were withdrawing their Troops from the other Cessions. In Point of Territory, it seems he had now got all he wanted; but judging, that if the English entered generally and heartily into the Re-establishment of Ragoba, his retaining it might be very doubtful, in order to secure himself more thoroughly, he applied to the Nabob of Surat, to sound whether he could not compass his Admission into the Party of Ragoba: His Terms were, the Confirmation of all that the Ministers had ceded to him, for which the English were to become Guarantees; for this he offered to act against the Ministers with all his Force, consisting of 50,000 Horse, 15,000 Sepoys, and a Train of Artillery, which were to be further joined by 8,000 good Horse of Moodajee Bonsalo, should the Terms be accepted. Should the Nizam be once determined to act against them, the Confederates must lose all Hopes; and there seems no Reason to doubt that he would, with the Guarantee of the English to secure him in the stipulated Cession, as without it he could have little Hopes of peaceably retaining them any longer than just during the Continuance of the present Divisions.

Exclusive of this Application to the English, the Nizam also sent Vackeels to Ragoba, with Proposals for a general Accommodation between all Parties, on the following Plan: That Ragoba was to enjoy all the Honours, and sufficient Revenue to support the Dignity of the Paishwa, but the Government to be carried on in the Name of his Son Imcut Raw, and the Administration of Affairs to be with Moraba Tournese; as Duan, all

 Places

Places stipulated to be ceded by the Ministerial Party, to be confirmed to him by Ragoba and the Confederates fully pardoned and secured in Possession of their Fortunes and Effects.—Exclusive of the Policy of it, which alone suffices to account for the Conduct of Nizam, it is imagined the Death of his Neeziee Ruckna ul Dowla, who was said to be deeply bribed by the Ministers, was partly the Occasion of these Overtures.

Far different from this flattering Situation was the State of the Confederacy; they had been deserted by Mhadojee Sindia and Tocajee Holkar, on whom rested their chief Dependence; Naroo Uppah, the Governor of Poona, a Man well respected, was dead; Morava Tournise, a Minister of the first Consideration, with several others, could not be brought to join the Confederacy, and his Influence was so high, that they dared not molest him even in Poona: Already, some in their Party, by no Means inconsiderable, had quitted it; such were Appajee, Gumies, the Governor of Chmadabad, and Futty Sing Guicawar, to whose Knowledge and Influence in the Guzerat Country, they were solely indebted for the Success they met with, previous to our Junction with Ragoba: Shabajee Bensalo, who had been formerly of great Service to them, was dead: Always doubtful of the Nizam, the Death of Ruckna ul Dowla now defeated all their Hopes in that Quarter; they knew the utter Impossibility of resisting the united Efforts of the English; add to this, the Jealousy entertained of the Views and Ambitions of the leading Members of the Confederacy, made several dread their Success, almost as much as that of Ragoba. Such was the State of Politics at Poona.

Their Reliance on their Army was nothing better: The Maratta Chiefs who had been brought to engage in the Confederacy, were given to hope for Supplies of Cash from the Ministers; but here again the Brahmin Avarice combated the general Interest; for though they have large Sums of their own, yet no one being perfectly assured that any particular Benefit would accrue to him by parting with it, constantly refused every Application, and referred to the Treasurers of the Circar, which being only the temporary Collections, were soon exhausted in Subsidies to the Nizam. Hurry Punt Furkia foreseeing the Confusion this Want of Money would create, absolutely made pacific Overtures to the Paishwa, at the Head of his Army, when it was in its most flourishing Condition. However fit the Maratta Troops may be for predatory Incursions, strong Reasons may be assigned why they will never willingly be brought to act against an Army with a well-served Artillery; for these Reasons, and from the little Prospect they had of plundering, the Army of Hurry Punt Furkia very soon shewed strong Disinclinations to serve; and having lost Numbers of Horses in the different Attacks we had made on them, their Men now became clamorous on their Leaders for Arrears of Pay, who again importuned Hurry Punt Furkia: By the Account of Persons sent for Intelligence, and to watch his Motions, the Ministers had sent Bills for 15 Lacks of Rupees, but the Shroffs had refused to answer them, from whence may be justly inferred, they had not even in this Situation advanced the Amount. Hurry Punt Furkia had designed to winter to the Northward, in order to be at Hand to watch our Motions on the Opening of the Campaign, but his Troops had absolutely refused. By the last Accounts, he was at Indoor, in full March towards Poona, with between 20 and 30,000 Men, Horse and Foot. In his Way through Tookajee Holcar's Country they had violent Disputes regarding some Money which Furkia demanded, but Holkar could not be induced to furnish; and under Pretence that the Death of Siga ul Dowla, and his Third Son being in Arms, might render his Presence absolutely necessary in his own Jaghier, he drew off his Troops from the Confederacy.

Saccaram Bapoo, and Nanna Furneze, had sent Two Vackeels to treat of an Accommodation; but from the Indisposition of one of them, and afterwards of the President, they had not mentioned their Offers; and though it was rather wished to secure to the Company the late Cessions by the Ways of Peace than of War, yet the Precipitancy of dispensing with the President's Negociations, was thought might have bespoke too great an Eagerness on our Part, and an impolitic Doubt of Success in the Undertaking we were then engaged in.

Such, Gentlemen, was the Situation of the Paishwa on the Receipt of your Letter of 31 May last; I leave you to judge how different from that desperate, friendless, and forlorn State you seemed to apprehend him in. Had you been pleased to signify to the Government of Bombay alone your pacific Determination, there is no Doubt but a general Accommodation might soon have been effected with Honour and Credit to the Company, and all the Cessions and Advantages secured to them, which was stipulated for in the Treaty with the Paishwa. As the Terms of that Treaty were never understood by either

Party

Party to extend further than our Assistance to defeat the Ministerial Confederacy, and by conducting him to Poona, to reinstate him in the Paishwaship, whether this was effected by Force or Negociation, the Company were equally entitled to the several Benefits which induced them to form these Engagements.

But much do I fear, that whatever your future Resolves may be in Consequence of these my Representations, the Letter from the Honourable the Governor General to Saccaram Bapoo, and your positive Orders to withdraw our Troops from the Paishwaship, will utterly destroy all the fair Hopes of Success which from Circumstances we had a Right to conceive. Nothing can give a stronger Idea of the unfavourable Consequences which may probably ensue, than the triumphant Insolence of the Confederates, as expressed in their Offers subsequent to the Receipt of Governor Hastings's Letter. Instead of permitting us to retain Salsette and Bassien (the last of which I observe is not in our Possession) they demand Ragoba to be delivered up to them, Salsette and our other Acquisitions to be restored; for which they will deign to reimburse our Charges. But a few Days before, I may venture safely to assert they would have been glad to have compounded for the Guarantee of the English to the Safety of their Persons and Property. It is not in their Nature to conceive, that a Spirit of Justice dictated this apparent Concession; they attribute it to Fear, or a conscious Inability of performing our Engagements.

As the Ministers will make every Advantage of this Circumstance, and no Doubt highly exaggerated, I must confess myself at a Loss to judge with Precision what Consequences may ensue.

The First that strikes me is, that Futty Sing will fly off from all his Engagements, retain such Part of his 26 Lacks as are not paid, and refuse the Company quiet Possession of the several Districts he had ceded to them. By this Means the Paishwa will lose all the Dependence he had in Guzerat; for, having been obliged in some Measure to disappoint Govind Row in his Expectation on that Province, in order more effectually to secure so important an Object as having the whole Guicawar Family at his Devotion, it is not to be doubted but that Govind Row, when he finds the Paishwa incapable of performing his late Promise, will accommodate Matters with his Brother Futty Sing, and both decline any further Interference.

By our Desertion, that of the Guicawars, and probably most of his Troops for Want of Money, the Paishwa will really find himself for a Time that forlorn and abandoned Man which you, Gentlemen, imagined him to be. Whatever Part he may take, must be detrimental to the Interest of the Honourable Company in the West of India, and perhaps dangerous to their Possessions in the East.

If he embraces the Offer of the Nizam, and is reinstated by his Means, the Company must not only forego all Hopes and Title to further Possessions, but relinquish Salsette, or encounter all the Difficulties and Inconveniencies of a Maratta War, which are by no Means counterbalanced by the Revenues of that Island. Exclusive of this, we shall lose about 12 Lacks, which will become due for Arrears of Subsidy; and as we shall have every Thing to expect from the just Resentment of Ragoba, the Commerce of the Honourable Company, and the English in general, will be impeded, if not totally interrupted, by Discouragement it will be in his Power to give without coming to an open Rupture.

The same Consequence will ensue should he throw himself on the Protection of Hyder, with the additional Disadvantage of encreasing the Power of a Man whose mortal and declared Aversion to the Company and their Ally, and his open Partiality to and Encouragement of declared Rivals, render every Accession of Country or Connection the just Objects of our Jealousy. Hyder has already assisted him of late with Money, and it is thought would willingly undertake his Cause for much smaller Concessions than have been made to us, with 30,000 excellent Horse, and a Body of well-disciplined Infantry, a good Artillery, served with about 600 Europeans, and those he lately is said to have agreed for with the Dutch. This Force joined to the Allies of Ragoba, would be irresistible by the Confederates; and then it rests with you, Gentlemen, to determine with the combined Armies of Hyder and the Paishwa, in what Safety would be our Possessions in the Carnatic.

His other Resources are in his ancient Ally, Mondajee Bonsalo, in Holkar and Sindia, always inclined to his Party, and now utterly discontented with the Confederates; in Morabah Fourneze and his Party, and even in Hurry Punt Furkia, whose Treatment by the Poona Junto, has led them to make frequent Overtures to Ragoba, and lately in an Application

tion to the Portuguese; all which equally deprive us of the Advantages of the stipulated Cessions, and are pregnant with Dangers to the Honourable Company's Settlements.

But there is another Object, Gentlemen, on which I would wish to fix your serious Attention; it is the sacred Honour of the English Nation and the Company, and that firm Reliance which this hitherto unviolated Faith has given all the Powers around, on our Word and Engagements; it is well known among the Princes of Hindostan; the Violation of the most solemn Compacts enters into the common Course of Business, and therefore they are lightly formed, and little relied on: Far different with the English, they have beheld them backward to engage, making no Treaties but with the most deliberate Consideration; but then they have ever found them stedfast to their Word, and of Faith inviolable.

The Marattas have beheld us in the very Zenith of their formidable Power, with not Half our present Force, bid Defiance to all their Threats, and boldly oppose ourselves in Aid of an inconsiderable Ally: After a Two Years Siege, we hoisted our Colours on Gingerah, which they were on the Point of reducing; they admired our good Faith, and respected our Resolution, by withdrawing their Troops, though not without Murmur and strong Discontent.

In what Light will they then regard our Desertion of Ragoba, after the solemn Treaty so publicly entered into with him? For, whatever Errors there may be in the Conduct of the Government of Bombay, the Application of the Nizam of the Guicawar, and the Behaviour of all the neighbouring Powers, strongly bespeak their Idea of the Force and Solemnity of the Engagements of the English; they can hardly be brought to comprehend the Nature of the limited and discretional Power, the exact Explanation of which can alone clear the President and Council of Bombay in their Minds, of an unworthy and intended Fraud, in forming Engagements they must know were invalid. By this and by the public Manner in which you have proclaimed their Dependence, I am afraid that the Respect and Opinion of their Authority, which are necessary in the common Conduct of their Affairs, will be totally destroyed; and should they lose their Opportunity of accomplishing the View of the Company in the West of India, we may for ever bid adieu to all Hopes of it, how much soever the Directors may recommend a Continuance of our Attention to them; for it is only by availing ourselves of such Circumstances as must be embraced the Moment they present themselves, that I foresee any Probability of bringing Matters into the happy Train they were, previous to the Receipt of your Orders of the 31st May. The Intention of the Legislature in the Clause of Exception before quoted, will, I apprehend, be utterly frustrated. Who again will ever apply to us? They must be sensible the whole Face of Things may be changed before your Consent can be obtained.

Exclusive of our Breach of Faith with the Paishwa, which would be rendered doubly glaring by espousing a Man who was the notorious Contriver and Conductor of the Plot against Naron Row, with which the Confederates now affect to stigmatize the Character of Ragoba; exclusive of this, there appear to me many strong Objections against acknowledging the Administration of Sacram Bapoo and the Poona Junto: Sacram has always shewn himself the determined Enemy of the Company. Besides that Dread and Jealousy of their Advancement in the West of India, common to every Maratta who has a just Sense of the Interest of their Government, another good Reason may be assigned for it; whether it was from the Poverty of his Parents, or the Duties of the menial Employ he was brought up in prevented him from giving the necessary Application, but unfortunately he does not possess the requisite Advantages of Education, scarce being able to read or write. This necessarily, when he came to the Charge of great Affairs, compelled him to repose a Confidence in some Person who could: His Confidant is one Veilagee Punt Saler, a Bramin, who having long been Supreme Governor of the Concan, in which are Salsette, Bassien, and its Districts; this Man knowing the Views of the Company, has ever opposed with all his Influence the least favourable Inclination in the Durbar at Poona to comply with them, and has ever fomented Disturbances and Jealousies between us: Being a Man of Intrigue and Ability, he is said to have great Sway with Sacram; and as he is from Interest deeply concerned in preventing our Acquisition of these Places, I imagine, that should we utterly abandon Ragoba, and the Confederates perceive his other Resources likely to fail him, whatever they may promise us at first, should they at length have no Fears from him, they will never acquiesce in any of the Cessions made by the Paishwa; indeed their Offers before-mentioned sufficiently bespeak their Intentions. I leave you, Gentlemen, to judge, what will be the Sentiments of our honourable Employers on this Occasion, after such a Sacrifice of Men, Money,

Honour,

Honour, and national Faith, to become the Contempt and Ridicule of all the Powers in the West of India.

Bad and disgraceful as this may be, it appears to me yet trifling to the serious Consequences that may ensue to their Territories in the East, on the undisturbed Possession of which the very Existence of the Company depend. I hold it as a political Maxim, that all the Powers in India are interested in the Continuance of the Bramin Government. The Jealousy which, from various Causes, ever subsists between the Maratta Chiefs and the Bramins, will prevent that Union of the whole Empire which must be most formidable and dangerous to the rest of India. The surprizing Rapidity with which they overrun almost the whole Dominions of the Mogul, the numerous Armies they send forth to all Quarters, and the Bravery of the Rajepouts under their own Raja, and led forth by Chiefs of their own Cast, are sufficient Circumstances to make us deprecate their Reunion. Should the Administration continue in the Hands of the confederated Bramins, what with their own Disunion, and other Circumstances, it seems to me very probable that some of the Maratta Chiefs will expel them from the Government, and either re-establish the Raja, or reign themselves. Moudajee Bonsalo, whose Bravery, Policy, and daring Character are well known and dreaded, was suspected of this Design: Disincumbered from his Brother Shabajee, he may perhaps turn his Thoughts to effecting it. Should such an Event take Place, and the whole Power of the Maratta Empire be collected in one Hand, what Prospect of a lasting Tranquillity can there be to the other States of India? The Government of a Paishwa, under proper Checks and Limitations of Powers, seems to me the only certain Way to avert this Evil; and should this Object be deemed worthy your Attention, I apprehend the present Crisis to be the fittest that may ever again offer for effecting it.

I have thus, Gentlemen, as fully and clearly as is in my Power, explained to you the Rise, Progress, and present State of our Undertaking with the Paishwa Ragonaut Row. On one Hand, you will perceive the Interest of the Company and the Honour of the English Nation deeply concerned in fulfilling our Engagements; on the other Hand you may judge of the Detriment, Danger, and Dishonour, attending the utter abandoning of them. I am happy to perceive, that the general Manner in which the Letter from the Honourable the Governor General to Sacaram Bapoo is worded, by implying you unacquainted with the Nature of our previous Acknowledgment of Ragoba as Paishwa, on which is founded the Equity of our late Treaty, reserves as yet inviolate the Honour and good Faith of the Company, and leaves you free in the Choice of Measures. I do therefore most solemnly intreat you, in the Name of the Government of Bombay, to warrant and assist them to fulfil their Engagements with the Paishwa; as in their Opinion, and in mine, on the most mature Consideration, this appears to be the only safe and honourable Expedient at this Juncture, and is perhaps the only Opportunity that may ever offer again of accomplishing the several important Objects before explained to you, and establishing the Affairs of our honourable Employers on that System in the West of India, which they have so frequently and strenuously recommended.

But whatever may be your Intention, I must earnestly recommend to you, Gentlemen, instantly to revoke your Orders for withdrawing our Army from Ragoba. This may prevent the Effects to which they are immediately liable, by keeping all Parties in Suspence till your final Determination is known; and whether you may be led to terminate this Affair by Arms or Negociation, it is equally important to your Success, and pardon me if I add, to our National Reputation, not utterly to abandon him; the Desertion of all his Allies would be the infallible Consequence of ours, and his Death most probably of both; which the World, judging only by Appearances, would lay to our Charge.

In a Word, Gentlemen, whatever Judgment you may entertain of the original Measure, this seems to me to be no longer the proper Object of your Consideration. If we have unnecessarily engaged in a War to which we had no just Provocation, yet its Continuance is now become necessary to our Safety; for the Recall of the Army will not only throw us at the Mercy of a perfidious Enemy, who will not fail to take the basest Advantage of our Weakness, but it will cut off all our Hopes of future Resources by so dreadful an Example held out to those, whose Alliances we may hereafter find it necessary to solicit. If you suppose that we have violated former Engagements, and any Neutrality which the Company may have recommended to be maintained with the Maratta State, by the Treaty lately formed with Ragoba, permit me to say, that we have the Plea of these very Engagements to justify us in the Part we have taken with the only legal

legal or known Representative of the Maratta Nation, and that having executed a new Treaty with him, in all its Forms, we have pledged the National Faith and Honour for the Performance of it. The Government of Bombay is alone responsible, and willingly takes upon itself the Responsibility for the past; and for the future, it is our Duty to set before you the Alternative which we know depends on your Resolutions. On the one Hand, we are convinced that Conquest and Honour, the Acquisition of Revenues, and an Influence in the first State of India, will be the Issue of the Enterprize, which we have happily prosecuted to this Time, if we are allowed to carry it to a Conclusion: On the other Hand, Weakness, Disgrace, and Ruin, will inevitably follow the Retreat of our Forces, unless an Accommodation shall have first taken Place, by which the Interests of each Party shall have been secured, and their Safety effectually guarded against all future Claims and Hostilities.

I have the Honour to be, with the greatest Respect,

Calcutta, (Signed) William Tayler.
9th October, 1775.

The Governor General begs Leave to put the following Questions to Mr. Tayler:

Q. Is it known whether Sacaram Bappoo and his Party concerted the Plan of the late Revolution, and the Assassination of Narron Row with Ragoba, or was it brought about without his Knowledge or Intervention?

Mr. Tayler—It is not known whether it was or not; but by the best Accounts we have, it appeared that Ragoba was very desirous of saving the Life of his Nephew.

Q. Who had the Charge of Ragoba's Person when he was in Confinement?

A. He was confined in the Palace at Poona; but I don't know the Name of the Officer who had Charge of his Person.

Q. In whose Service were Mahomed Esaph and Summer Sing, the Murderers of Narron Row?

A. In the immediate Service of Narron Row himself, and belonged to some of his Troops called Guardees.

Q. To what Family did the Slave belong, whose Resentment is said to be the Cause of Narron Row's Death?

A. He had belonged to Madhoorow, and on his Death he became the Property of Narron Row.

Q. Is it certain that Sacaram Bappoo directed the Assassination of Narron Row, or is this a Point of common Belief?

A. It was universally believed to have been brought about by his Means; and Mr. Mostyn, who was Resident there at the Time, is as certain of it as a Person can be without having seen the Fact.

Q. On what Authority do you learn that Orders were given to the Maratta General to seize Madajee Sindia?

A. It was wrote to the Governor at Bombay by the Chief of Surat, and other Persons that he employed to gain Country Intelligence; and the Intelligence was confirmed by his immediately quitting the Army of the Ministerial Pay.

Q. What Symptoms has Tuckoojee Holcar given of a Defection?

A. He has all along shewn himself wavering; and it appears from Mr. Mostyn's Letters, that he did so at the Beginning: And a few Days before I left Bombay, a Letter was received from the Chief of Surat, dated the 27th of July, with this Paragraph:

Extract of a Letter from Mr. Robert Gambier to the President, &c. Members of the Select Committee at Bombay; dated Surat the 27th of July 1775.

The People I sent to enquire after Fenkia are just returned from Hindoor, where they left him making the best of his Way towards Poona, with, in all, about Twenty to Thirty thousand Men, Horse and Foot. His Troops are very mutinous for their Pay, and highly discontented, and in his Way through Holcar's Country he had some violent Disputes with him about some Money he demanded, and which Holcar could by no Means be induced to furnish.

A true Extract from the Copy of a Letter delivered to the Governor General and Council by Mr. Tayler.

Wm. Bruere,
Assistant Secretary.

And

And this Advice is confirmed by repeated Letters from Colonel Keating.

Q. On what Authority do you learn that Nizam Ally Cawn had made Overtures to the Nabob of Surat, for an Accommodation with Ragoba?

A. By a Letter from the Nizam to the Nabob of Surat, forwarded by him to the Governor of Bombay, of which I now present you a Persian Copy. Also by the following Letter from the Chief of Surat to the Select Committee at Bombay.

The following is the Translation.

Extract of a Letter from the Nabob Zabit Jung, commonly called Dhosa, written by Order of the Nabob Nizam Ally Cawn Bahadre, to his Excellency; received some Days ago.

After the Expulsion of Ragonaut Row, and his crossing the Nirbuddah and returning to Burrhanpore, the Nabob Nizam Ally entered into a Treaty with the Ministers of Madha Row and Narrain Row, to join their Party and canton at Kojistah Bunyead, on Condition of their giving up to him the Fort of Doulutabad and other Mahals; and he went into Cantonments there accordingly. Ragonaut Row, at the End of the rainy Season, being in the Country of Kandace, sent a Message to the Nabob, that if he would join him, he would resign to him the Fort of Doultabad, Asur, &c. together with Burhanpore and other Mahals in his Rear, which he had conquered by an Engagement, in which the Nabob Shokut Jung lost his Life; and that if he assented to his Proposals, to march to Alorah, and immediately conclude the Treaty: But of regard to his Engagements with the Ministers of Narrain Row and Madha Row, and to the bad Character as well as bad Faith of Ragonaut Row, the Nabob would pay no Attention to his Proposals; but since the English have sided with Ragonaut Row, although the Nabob has an Army of 50,000 Cavalry and 15,000 Infantry, and a Train of Artillery consisting of 100 Pieces of Cannon, with all Kinds of Ammunition and Necessaries of War, and is besides attended by Madajee Bonsalo at the Head of 8,000 Horse, whose Son he has adopted; and though the Ministers of Narrain Row and Madaha Row have evacuated the Fort of Doulutabad, and are ready to resign Aseer, Burumpore, &c. to him; yet as there is a Treaty subsisting between his Excellency and the English, that they shall not employ their respective Forces against each other, and he is desirous that they should daily encrease; and although Ragonaut Row is the Son of Mazee Row, and his Excellency was much his Enemy, on account of the Instability of his Disposition, yet if through your Means the Governor of Surat, or the General of Bombay, will cause Ragonaut Row to engage to give up to his Excellency the Fort and Places aforementioned, and will become Guarantee for the Performance thereof, his Excellency will be enabled to depend thereon, and will undoubtedly attach himself to the Party of Ragonaut Row, and procure for him the Accomplishment of his Views; for the Enemy's Forces are so numerous that they will surround the European Army, and prevent any Provisions being conveyed to them, in which case it will be difficult for them to preserve Guzzerat, much more to reduce Poona: Without the Aid of the Nabob's Army, Ragonaut Row can never obtain Possession of the Country; it is necessary therefore that you should make this Proposal privately to the English: I will likewise give every Aid in my Power. I conjure you by your Grandfather, that you will not communicate this Secret to any Person whatever. Let me have your immediate Answer to this.

Copy of a Letter from the Nabob Meer Hafiz ul Dein, Ahmud Cawn Bahader, Nabob of Surat; dated 22d of Jummadee ul Awul (or July).

It is a long Time since I have had the Pleasure to receive any Account of your Welfare: May this have proceeded from no disagreeable Cause. I have written concerning several Affairs of Consequence to the trusty Govind Ram, my Muttesedy, who will represent them to you. I am hopeful that having paid Attention thereto, you will favour me with an immediate Answer, and with any Commissions or Business you may have in this Part; in the Execution of which I shall receive great Pleasure. As at this Season of the Year there is no Passage for Boats, and the Difficulty of Land Carriage is well known, it was necessary to send this Letter with the greatest Care and Secrecy; I have therefore not inclosed it in a Rimcab Rarctah, according to Custom, which I hope you will be so kind as to excuse. May your Prosperity and Happiness daily increase.

APPENDIX, Nº 83.

Extract of a Letter from the Chief of Surat to the Select Committee.

Honourable Sir, and Sirs,

My last Address, of which a Duplicate accompanies this, was under Date the 15th Instant, since when I have received none of your Commands.

This I dispatch to give Cover to a small Packet in Cypher, received the Day before Yesterday, via Benares, to your Honours, &c. Address from the Governor General, &c. Council at Bengal, which, agreeable to your Orders, I have had opened, and fair transcribed.

The 25th I received a Letter from Colonel Keating, dated at Balampore Calicut, near Brodeara, the 13th Instant; in which he writes, That the Treaty with Futty Sing was the preceding Night signed and sealed; and that Futty Sing had further given the Company the Cusbah of Beriow, with all its Districts and Revenues; and that he hopes to send me a Sunnud for it in a few Days. He further writes, that Futty Sing had received Advices of Hurry Punt, with the Remains of his Forces, being about 105 Coss off, some on the Northern and some on the Southern Banks of the Nerbedah: That he had received Bills from Poona for 15 Lacks of Rupees, with which he had proposed to remain where he was till the rainy Season was over; but his Army, one and all, refused; and that the Shroffs, on whom his Bills was drawn, had refused to accept or pay them, which had caused a great Deal of Distress and Confusion amongst his People.—This is all the Colonel writes. But I hear from them Quarters, that Ragoba had detached a strong Party of his own Forces to Ahmudabad; for the Surrender of which Place the present Governor, Apajee Gunnes, was in Treaty with him; and this once effected, the Country to the Northward of the Nerbedah will be entirely reduced to Obedience to Ragoba.

The Nizam's Vackeels have been with Ragoba, and are, I understand, returned to their Master for further Orders. If your Honour, &c. approve it, I believe it would be no difficult Matter to negociate through the Nizam a general Accommodation between all Parties. I am informed, that a Proposal of this Nature has been made by the Nizam Ragoba on the following Plan: That Ragoba himself is to enjoy all the Honours, &c. sufficient Revenues for the Support of his Dignity of the Paishwaship; but the Government is to be carried on in the Name of his Son Amret Row, and the Administration of Affairs put into the Hands of Moraboy as Duan; and all Places stipulated to be ceded by the ministerial Party to the Nizam, are to be confirmed to him by Ragoba, &c. all the ministerial Confederacy to be fully pardoned, and left in Possession of their Fortunes and Estates. I do not suppose that Ragoba would easily consent to giving up the actual Government, though I believe he would sacrifice a great deal to secure the peaceable Possession of it to his Son. And I understand that Morabah, the proposed Duan, is in great Esteem with Ragoba; and though strongly solicited by the ministerial Party, has always refused to join against him. On the Whole, I am fully of Opinion, that a general Accommodation might be brought about, and more speedily and effectually through the Mediation of Nizam Ally, than by any other Means. And I therefore much wish to receive your Honour, &c. Orders, in respect to the proposed Treaty with him, and whether you would chuse that general Pacification should be made Part of it.

I much fear these Pattamas will find great Difficulty in getting to you, as a Gentleman lately come from Dauraun tells me, that all Communication between Bombay and that Place, has been stopped for some Time past; for which Reason I would transmit it by a Boat, but the Weather will not allow.

Surat, 27 July 1775.

I am, &c.
(Signed) Robert Gambier.

Q. Do you know, on any good Authority, what Terms the Vackeels of Saccaram and Nanah Funoze were directed to propose to the Government of Bombay?

A. We do not know the direct Terms they meant to propose; but from a Variety of Conversations it was imagined, that they would have agreed to let Ragoba conduct the Affairs of the Government, provided he agreed to let the Sicca be in the Name of the Infant, whose Party the Ministers espoused, and would engage for the Security of their Persons and Fortunes.

Q. In

Q. In what Instance has Saccaram ever shewn an Enmity to the Company?

A. I have the Minutes of some Conversations held by Mr. Mostyn at the Poona Durbar, wherein some are particularly related; and he has been remarkable in appointing all Negociations which we have had Occasion to make with the Paishwa; and after having obtained Sunnuds, his Intrigues have operated to prevent their ever being of any Use.

Q. What Resources have the Ministers for carrying on the War?

A. I have mentioned in my Letter, that they have hitherto relied on the Revenues of the Sircar, and would not employ their own Money; besides which, I believe their principal Reliance to have been on Nizam Ally, Tokajee Holcar, and Madajee Sindia.

General Clavering begs Leave to ask, If Mr. Tayler has got the Court of Directors Letter? 6th April 1772, appointing Mr. Mostyn to Poona?

A. I have the Paragraphs of it that relate to Mr. Mostyn's Appointment.

Read Extracts from the following Letters:

18th March, 1768.
31st Ditto, 1769.
1st April, 1772.

Governor General—I observe by these Paragraphs, the Company declare that they limit their Views on that Side of India to the Possession of Salsette, Bassein, and certain Islands and Districts round Surat; What was the Inducement of your Presidency for the Enterprize against Broach?

A. The Nabob having voluntarily broke through a Treaty which he made with the Governor and Council on his coming to Bombay for that Purpose.

Question by General Clavering—What Reason had you to conclude, that Salsette was ceded by the Crown of Portugal, by the Marriage Contract with Charles the Second, to the Crown of England?

A. From the Names of several Places mentioned in the Marriage Contract, which are in Salsette, and not in the Island of Bombay.

Q. Did Ragoba immediately after Execution of the Treaty, put the Presidency into Possession of the Lands which he agreed to cede to the Company?

A. He gave us the Sunnuds immediately, and we took Possession of them accordingly, except Bassein.

Q. Do you know how much has already been received from those Lands?

A. I do not, as the Accounts had not been transmitted from Surat and Broach.

Q. Have you Reason to believe that the Company was in immediate Receipt of the Revenues of those Places?

A. I most firmly believe it; and have a private Letter from Captain Abington to Mr. Draper, mentioning, that a Part of the Revenue for Orpad had been received, even in the Month of May last.

"I am very uneasy lest I should be blamed in not having been more expeditious in collecting the Grain; but I flatter myself both the Board of Surat as well as Bombay, will make great Allowances, when they consider the State of this Purgunnah. When I arrived, Overtures by the Marattas, the Inhabitants fled, and the Grain all buried. Things now bear quite a different Aspect, though I have often been interrupted by the Detachment of Maratta Horse. However, I have collected from the Villages situated near this Town, about 150 Candys of Wheat, have sent about 30 Carts to Randeer, and about One hundred more ready at different Villages."

Q. Has the Subsidy been regularly paid agreeable to the Treaty?

A. No, it has not; but I conclude we must be entering upon the Receipt of it, as we are in Possession of the Places.

Q. Have you the Instructions that were given to Colonel Keating, when he took the Command of the Army?

A. I have them not.

Q. Was Brigadier General Gordon consulted concerning the Operations of the Campaign?

A. I have Copies of the Minutes that passed on the Occasion, which I think imply his having been consulted.

Read, the Proceedings of the Select Committee, 11th February 1775, as follow:

 Extract

APPENDIX, N° 83.

Extract Proceedings of the Select Committee, dated 11th February 1775.

The Brigadier General and Mr. Halsey are now made acquainted of the Negociation depending with Ragoba; the Letters and Papers relative thereto, with our several Resolutions, and the proposed Treaty, being read to them, and particularly the Select Committee's Letter to the Governor General and Council of Fort William, of the 31st December last; they are also made acquainted of every other Particular in our Power to inform them of on this Subject, as well as of our Application to the Presidency of Madras, for a Reinforcement of Troops, and of our Request to Commodore Hughes, to come armed with his Squadron to this Court.

After mature Deliberation, the Brigadier General declares, that the Object to be gained for his Employers, by the Measures now pursuing, as far as he is acquainted with it, appears to him so considerable, and so much to the Advantage and Interest of the Honourable Company, that he joins with the Board, in thinking that it ought to be pursued, and brought to the speediest Conclusion; and in this Opinion Mr. Halsey also concurs.

The Resolution of our Yesterday's Consultation, of accepting Jewels to the Amount of Six Lacks of Rupees, in lieu of the Deposit of that Sum in Money, as Money cannot be procured, it is again unanimously accorded to, and confirmed for the Reasons then given; and the Treaty must be drawn up here as soon as possible, for being sent to Surat.

The Board then take under Consideration, the Force now to be sent to Ragoba's Assistance; and it is unanimously agreed, that it shall consist of the following;

Artillery	80
European Infantry	350
Sepoys	800
Lascars	160

Which, with their proper Officers, Non-commissioned Officers, &c. will compleat the Number to full 1,500 Men, being the Force that it is resolved at present to send; and as the Whole cannot be spared from hence, it must be compleated by Detachments from the Garrisons on Salsette, at Surat, and Broach; and it is agreed, that we leave it to the President with the Brigadier-General to determine as to the Number to be detached from the several Places; but that Part which goes from hence and from Salsette, must absolutely set out some Time before the next Spring.

The Brigadier-General now offers his Service to command this Detachment of our Forces, provided the Business could be accomplished within the Time he proposes staying in India. But the Board, as well as the Brigadier General, concluding that it will take up much longer Time than he proposes for his Stay, it is therefore considered who is the most proper Officer for this Command; and the President nominates Lieutenant Colonel Keating for it; which is agreed to by the Board, Brigadier General Gordon only excepted: For it is observed, that Colonel Egerton, ever since his Arrival in India, has been very unfit for any such Command, owing to his ill Health: Twice only indeed has he ever been ordered on any Service since he has been in the Company's Pay, now upwards of Six Years; the first of which was no more than to take the Command of the Garrison of Broach on the coming away of Lieutenant Colonel Brewer, which he at first declined, under the Pretence of its not being a Command equal to his Rank, though the General was of a contrary Opinion; and afterwards, on the Order being repeated to him, he then urged ill Health for his Excuse: The second was on the Expedition to Tannah, from whence he returned sick in Seven or Eight Days after he set out: For these Reasons, we deem Colonel Egerton a very unfit Officer for the Command; and Lieutenant Colonel Keating, from the Commission he has brought out from the Company, is next in Rank on the Establishment to Colonel Egerton, until Lieutenant Colonel Brewer may arrive from England.

Lieutenant Colonel Keating is therefore appointed Commandant of the Forces to be detached to the Assistance of Ragoba.

Brigadier General Gordon begs Leave to assign the following Reasons for his Dissent to this Appointment:

That it is not common in the Course of Service, that the commanding Officer of Artillery, or Chief Engineer, as Lieutenant Colonel Keating is, should command a Body of Infantry in Line:

That

That the Offer of this Command should, in his Opinion, be made to Colonel Egerton; when, if he says that his Health will not admit of his going, that it then by Rotation falls to Lieutenant Colonel Cay, and after him to Lieutenant Colonel Cockburn, who are the senior Officers in the Infantry.

The Board therefore observes, that there have been many Instances in India of Officers in the Artillery commanding Troops in Line, amongst which are the following, and no such Objections were then raised as the Board know of: Major Maitland, of the King's Artillery, commanded the Expedition to Surat in the Year 1759; Major Mare of the Artillery, and Chief Engineer, came to be Commanding Officer of the Forces of this Presidency on Sir James Fowlis's going to Europe; and Captain Pemble, who was Commandant of the Artillery, commanded the Forces detached to Bengal in the Year 1763. And besides, as we are satisfied with his, Lieutenant Colonel Keating's Conduct in the Reduction of Versarva and Carnejah, we think he merits such a Mark of our Favour as we confer on him in this Appointment.

A true Copy,

W. G. Farmer.

Q. It does not appear from those Consultations, that he was consulted upon the Operations; it appears only that he was consulted upon the Treaty, and the Number of Troops that should be sent there. I beg Leave to ask of Mr. Tayler, if he was afterwards consulted upon the Operations of the Army at any Time?

A. No, I believe not after that Day. On the 14th there was another Consultation, to read a Letter from Brigadier General Gordon, an Extract of which Consultation I beg Leave to read.

Extract Proceedings of the Select Committee, with Brigadier General Gordon's Letter, dated the 14th February 1775.

Resolved, by the Majority, after due Deliberation, That the Appointment of Lieutenant Colonel Keating to the Command of the Forces proceeding to the Assistance of Ragoba, be adhered to. We have however a just Sense of the Offer the Brigadier General has now made, and shall mention the same in our next general Address to our Honourable Employers.

Messrs. Halsey, Garden, and Fletcher, are of Opinion, as Brigadier General Gordon has now made a Tender of his Services, and to bring the War to a Conclusion, that the same should be accepted, and that he ought in consequence to be appointed to the Command of the Force going into the Field.

The Appointment of Lieutenant Colonel Keating being thus adhered to, the Brigadier General then immediately produced a Paper, containing a Dissent thereto, and his Reason for concurring on Saturday last in the Measure now pursuing: Ordered, as the General desires it, That the same be entered after this Consultation, for the Notice of our Honourable Masters; though we must just remark, that the Reasons for his acquiescing in the Plan we are pursuing, appear now very different from what they were on Saturday last. The general Motives for this Difference may be very obvious to all who may peruse this Day's Resolution.

As the Brigadier declares in the Dissent that he has now delivered, that Lieutenant Colonel Keating is so very unfit for the Command to which we have appointed him, it is remarked to the General, that it is very extraordinary that he did not make this Objection before our Appointment took place; and he is now desired to declare his Reasons for his Opinion. To this he replies, that the boasted Success at Verseva was really destitute of every military Merit but Resolution; for that had the Enemy done their Duty with any Spirit or Fidelity, the whole Party under Colonel Keating's Command, instead of coming off with Success must have absolutely been all cut to Pieces, while they were in Confusion and Noise under the Walls, when in attempting to erect Ladders which they could not effect, as he has been assured by Officers who were on that Service. But the General adds, that as he never was on Service wherein Lieutenant Colonel Keating was employed, he knows nothing further of his military Capacity.

The

The General being asked, whether he had any Objection to Colonel Keating's Conduct at Caranjah? he replies, He has not; that he confines his Remarks to his Proceedings at Versava.

The necessary Orders for the Embarkation of the Forces and Stores proceeding to Surat under Lieutenant Colonel Keating, are this Day given us, will appear on our public Diary, and the whole will be ready in about Three Days.

Honourable Sir, and Sirs,

As you have been pleased to resolve, that a large Part of the Troops shall take the Field immediately, I beg Leave to offer my Services to command them: This I hope you will think from my Rank here I have a Right to.

It is true that I have desired Leave to resign, when Opportunity which is agreeable to me offers for my proceeding to Europe by the way of China; but that Zeal which I have for the Service, added to the Respect which I owe to those Friends who so warmly supported my Appointment in the General Court of Proprietors, makes me wish most earnestly to render some further Service to the Company; I am therefore to request, that your Honour, &c. will be pleased to permit me to take upon me the Command of the Forces, which are immediately to be employed.

I am, &c.

Bombay, 12th February, 1773. (Signed) Robert Gordon, Brigadier General.

Brigadier General Gordon declares, that nothing would have induced him to give his Consent to the Troops taking the Field, or to enter into either Treaties or Wars, without the Orders of the Supreme Council, except this Consideration, namely, That as by the Attack of Salsette (on the Expediency of which Measure he never was consulted) Hostilities were actually commenced against the Marattas, after which it became necessary to make the most of Affairs. On this Principle he consented to entering into the Treaty which was laid before the Board last Council Day, and recommended as the most advantageous that could then be made for the Company's Interests. He therefore claimed the Command of the Troops which are to take the Field, as his undoubted Right; in the Execution of which, his best Endeavours shall be exerted to bring the Service to a speedy and honourable Issue.

The Appointment of Lieutenant Colonel Keating to command the Forces, is undoubtedly contrary to the Practice of the Army; either as Chief Engineer, or Commanding Officer of Artillery, he is entirely out of the general Line of Command. Brigadier General Gordon therefore dissents and protests against the Appointment, and hereby declares he thinks Lieutenant Colonel Keating so unfit for it, that if it is given to him, the General will in no respect whatever deem himself responsible for any Part of the Measure, either as to entering into the Treaty, the Troops taking the Field, or of the Consequences which may arise therefrom.

Bombay, 14th February 1773. (Signed) Robert Gordon, Brigadier General.

Question. When did the Government of Bombay receive public Advice of the late Act of Parliament for regulating the Affairs of India?

Answer. In the Month of August 1774.

Question. When did the Government of Bombay receive the Letter of the Governor General and Council of Bengal, of the 25th October 1774?

Answer. I cannot pretend to charge my Memory with the Date.

Question. Do you remember when you received Mr. Henshaw's Letter, advising you of the hostile Designs of the Portugueze on the Island of Salsette?

Answer. I believe about the latter End of November.

Question. Had you any other Information besides Mr. Henshaw's Letter, of the Designs of the Portugueze on Salsette?

Answer. We had many Reports, but no Advices so authentic as Mr. Henshaw's Letter; however, not only the Captain of the Fleet, but the Government at Goa, protested also against it; and there was a Letter from a Portugueze Priest intercepted afterwards, which proved their Intentions.

Question

Question by the Governor General. What was the Destination of the Portuguese Fleet?

Answer. They every Year send out a Convoy to Surat.

Question. How many Troops did you employ in the Reduction of Salsette?

Answer. I believe near Two thousand, but I am not certain.

Question. What Reason have you to suppose that the declared Son of Narron Row is a supposititious Child?

See Reference Page in printed Report, 27.

Answer. From the common Report of the Country, and Information given to me by Mr. Mostyn. Mr. Tayler then reads the Information as follows:

Soon after Narron Row was cut off, it was industriously reported that Gungaboy was near Two Months gone with Child; and she accordingly, at the End of her Seven Months, went through the accustomary Ceremony among the Gentoos; this was performed a very few Days before the Ministers carried her to Poona. I will not presume to say Gungaboy was not with Child, but her being accompanied with five Women, all big with Child, gave Rise to such a Conjecture; however, it might be only to secure a Boy, in case she should have a Girl. Be all this as it may; nay, even allowing Gunaboy to have brought forth a Boy, from the best Information I could get, and in which I placed much Confidence, as it came from the then Governor, Naroo Appair's House, that Boy certainly died, and Gungaboy adopted the Son of one Ramchunder, a Brachmin, that officiates at her Family Pagoda; and indeed it was much whispered about, and many concurring Circumstances persuaded me it was so; and I think there need be no better Proof of it, than the Nizam's Proposal to us, through the Nabob of Surat; that is, for the Maratta Government, in the Name of Amut Row, Ragoba's adopted Son.

General Clavering—I have put this Question to Mr. Tayler, because it appears by Mr. Mostyn's Letters of the 30th and 31st January 1774, entered in the Select Committee Proceedings of the 9th March 1774, that the Widow of Narron Row was Seven Months gone with Child; and by his Letter, dated in the Proceedings recorded of the Select Committee of the 8th September 1774, he says she was actually delivered of a Son.

The Board adjourn to proceed on this Business again in the Evening, and desire that Mr. Tayler will attend at Seven o'Clock.

Monday Evening. The Board being met according to Adjournment, now resume the Business of Mr. Tayler's Deputation.

Question by General Clavering,—Do you know what Inducement the Council at Bombay had to proceed in the Negociation with Ragoba, when it appears by the Letter that we received from that Council of the 31st December, that he was a Fugitive, abandoned by his Forces, and actually retreating towards Delhi?

Answer. He was not altogether abandoned at the Time we treated with him, although he had been defeated. Our Inducement was the Importance of the Object to the Company, and in Compliance with their repeated Injunctions.

Question. With how many Followers did he come to Surat?

Answer. I believe not more than 1000, but that his Army went with Gobindrow, and Conderow, and other Officers to a Place, called Copperwanjee.

Question. Had Mr. Gambier Instructions from the Council, to sign the Treaty with him?

Answer. The Treaty was sent up, signed by the Council, and interchanged by Mr. Gambier, afterwards with Ragonaut, he signed it officially as interchanged by him.

Question. I understand that after the Army landed in Cambay, a considerable Time was lost in treating with Futty Sing; had Colonel Keating Powers given him for that Purpose, or to treat with any of the Princes of the Country?

Answer. I don't know of any Time being lost in treating with Futty Sing; to the best of my Knowledge, nothing of that Kind appears in our Advices; but a Junction was made of our Forces with Ragoba's as soon as possible; the Instructions to Colonel Keating

Keating were, to do all he could for the Interest of Ragoba; but he had no express Powers to treat.

Question. Did the Council never express any Displeasure with Colonel Keating, for treating with Futty Sing?

Answer. They expressed their Displeasure at the Army's not moving faster to the Southward than it did; and Colonel Keating exculpated himself, by saying it was Ragoba's ardent Desire to take Ahmadabad. I don't recollect that the Council expressed any particular Instance of Displeasure at his treating with Futty Sing.

Question. Was it with an Intention of taking Ahmadabad, that the Army first moved to the Northward?

Answer. The first Motion to the Northward was to effect a Junction with Ragoba's Army; after the Junction that was the Reason assigned to us by him.

Question. Did they take the Place?

Answer. They did dot proceed again it.

Question. Are Colonel Keating's Reasons known for not proceeding further towards Ahmadabad?

Answer. The Governor and Council directed that he should not, if he could possibly avoid it.

Question. You have mentioned that the Territory which has been ceded to the Company is in Extant about 86 Miles, exclusive of the Lands lying contiguous to Broach and Surat, and that this Extension of Territory might be defended with Two Battalions; has this Information been given to the Council by any Military Men?

Answer. No, it has not; it was only my own Opinion which I presumed to offer; but I meant, that I imagined that Number sufficient to garrison the Forts, enforce the Collections, and protect the Country, supposing us to be in Peace with the Poona Government.

Question. Are you informed of the Loss the Company has sustained in Men during the last Campaign?

Answer. I do not know the exact Number; to the best of my Remembrance of the last Return that was received before I left Bombay, the Army exceeded 2,000 Men, but I cannot tell by what Number, as it came down in Cypher, and there was some Mistake in it, which prevented my paying more Attention than I otherwise should have done.

Question. Were the Sick included in that Return.

Answer. I believe they were.

General Clavering observing that his Reason for asking this Question is, that he heard the Men were very sickly; Mr. Tayler adds, That they have been sickly, but that they were on the Recovery, and some of them had joined the Army from the Hospital at Broach.

Mr. Barwell begs Leave to put the following Questions to Mr. Tayler:

Question. What is the Object of the War that has been entered into by the Government of Bombay; I mean so far as relates to the Service to be rendered to Ragoba, and when the Company will be entitled to the Benefit proposed to them by the Treaty?

Answer. The Benefit to be rendered to Ragoba was to fix him in the Government of the Maratta Empire at Poona; the Company were intitled to the Benefits from the Date of executing the Treaty, as appears by the 15th and 16th Articles.

Question. Was it meant, after fixing him in the Government at Poona, to accompany him any further with the English Troops?

Answer. No, it was not by any Means; if he had any further Occasion for our Services, he must have made fresh Overtures.

Question by General Clavering. Does it appear upon the Consultations, that the Question was ever agitated, whether or not you could enter into formal Engagements, and sign a Treaty with Ragoba, without the Consent of this Government?

Answer. The Subject was agitated, and we considered that we could, from the Reasons which have been already represented to this Board, which are the same as appear upon our Consultations.

Mr.

Mr. Francis begs Leave to ask Mr. Tayler the following Questions:

Question. Do you consider your conducting Ragoba to Poona, and putting him in Possession of that Town, as equivalent to fixing him in the Government of the Maratta Empire?

Answer. Yes.

Question. Would it have been inconsistent with your Engagements with Ragoba, to have withdrawn our Army after putting him in Possession of Poona?

Answer. No.

Question. You observe that the Acquisition of Salsette and Bassein was laid down to the Presidency of Bombay, by the Company, as the grand and sole Object of every military or political Engagement; that the Company declared these to be the utmost Limits of their Views on the West of India; and that they rather wished they could be obtained by Purchase than War—Have the Presidency of Bombay any Instructions, general or particular, to aim at Conquests or territorial Acquisitions on the Continent?

Answer. They have not other Instructions; the Company have said in their Letter, the 31st March 1769, that Salsette and Bassein, with their Dependencies, and the Maratta Proportion of the Surat Revenues, are all they seek for on the Western Side of India; and that these are the Objects we are to have in View in all our Treaties, Negociations, and military Operations, and what we must be ever watchful to obtain; always attentive to convince the Country Powers, these are, and ever will be, the utmost Limits of their Views on that Side of India.

Question by the Governor General. Are the Lands which have been ceded us by the Dependencies of Bassein, the ancient Territory of the Portugueze Government?

Answer. Yes, they were so understood.

Question by Mr. Francis. You observe that the Conveniency of the Harbour of Bombay has secured to the English almost the exclusive Trade in Indian Commodities, with the Country of the Marattas, as well as in the Cotton, with which Bengal and China are supplied; as we are already in exclusive Possession of the above Trade, in what Sense can the Commerce of the English, or of those who trade under their Protection, be improved or benefited by the territorial Acquisitions stipulated by the Treaty with Ragoba?

Answer. We before had the Trade, but we now have the Country, wherein the Articles of that Trade are produced.

Question. Have you formerly found any Difficulties in procuring Timber from Bassein, or Provisions from Salsette?

Answer. We have sometimes; but it always was in the Power of the Maratta Government to prevent our getting them.

Question. Have you lately received any Supplies of Timber from Bassein?

Answer. No, not since the Commencement of the War.

Question. On the 31st December last, the Presidency of Bombay were apprized of the Commencement of the present Government of Bengal; they had not then concluded any Treaty with Ragoba; on the contrary, they say in their Letter of the above Date, that they will accommodate Matters with the Government of Poona as soon as possible, and endeavour to reconcile them to our keeping Salsette—Was the Conclusion of the offensive Treaty with Ragoba a Case of such imminent Necessity as would have rendered it dangerous to postpone the Hostilities proposed by that Treaty, until the Orders from the Governor General and Council of Bengal might arrive? or had you any special Orders from the Company to engage in the above Treaty?

Answer. I am clearly of Opinion, that if it had been deferred till the Orders of the Governor General and Council had been received, that the Opportunity would have been lost; we conceived that the Orders of the Court of Directors were special on this Subject.

Question. Is it understood by the Presidency of Bombay, that the Exception made by the Legislature of a Case of imminent Necessity relates solely to the indispensable Defence of the Company's Possessions; or that it authorises them to commence Hostilities at their own Discretion, and without Provocation, against the neighbouring States?

Anſwer. The Preſidency of Bombay by no Means conſider that the Act authorizes them to commence Hoſtilities at their own Diſcretion, and without Provocation, againſt the Neighbouring States; but that having conceived it to be a Caſe of imminent Neceſſity, to poſſeſs themſelves of the Iſland of Salſette, to prevent it falling into the Hands of the Portugueze, they then thought it ſound Policy to enter into the Treaty they did with Ragoba, for ſecuring it, and obtaining the other Acquiſitions.

Queſtion. What Provocation had the Preſidency of Bombay received againſt the Government of Poona?

Anſwer. None.

Queſtion. Have any Part of the ceded Revenues been yet collected by us in ready Money, or is the Whole to be paid in Kind?

Anſwer. It is uſual there to receive the Rents Part in Money and Part in Kind. I ſuppoſe that the ſame Methods will be obſerved by our Agents as before; but the Seaſon having prevented any Advices being received from thoſe Parts before my Departure, I cannot be ſo preciſe as I could wiſh upon this Point.

Queſtion. Have any Part of Ragoba's Jewels been ſold towards defraying the Expences of the War?

Anſwer. Some Money had been raiſed upon ſome of them.

Queſtion. If Ragoba be the only legal and known Repreſentative of the Maratta Nation, why was Mr. Moſtyn continued as Reſident with the Government at Poona? and why do the Select Committee ſay in their Letter of the 31ſt December laſt, that they will accommodate Matters as ſoon as poſſible with that Government?

Anſwer. It did not appear to us to be at all neceſſary to recall Mr. Moſtyn, as the Miniſterial Party at Poona offered him no Moleſtation: What the Select Committee meant, by ſaying they would accommodate Matters with that Government, was, with whichever Party might prevail.

Queſtion. Whether the Governor and Council of Bombay, before they ſigned the Treaty with Ragoba, had ſeen the Inſtructions voted by the Court of Proprietors to this Council, in which we are particularly directed to fix our Attention to the Preſervation of Peace throughout India?

Anſwer. Yes, they had ſeen them.

Queſtion by the Governor General—Had any Overtures been made by the Miniſterial Party to the Preſidency of Bombay, before the Treaty was executed with Ragoba?

Anſwer. None.

Queſtion. Could an Alliance have been formed with the Miniſterial Party, conſiſtently with the Engagements actually exiſting between the Government of Bombay and the Maratta State?

Anſwer. In my Opinion it could not.

Queſtion. Did any Treaty of Friendſhip exiſt between the Preſidency of Bombay and Ragoba, before that concluded with him the 16th of March laſt?

Anſwer. Not with Ragoba particularly; there was a Treaty formed while he was Regent, during the Minority of Mahdoo Row.

Queſtion by Colonel Monſon—Did Ragoba make any Overtures to the Bombay Government, till after his Defeat by the Miniſterial Party?

Anſwer. Yes.

Queſtion. Of what Nature were they?

Anſwer. He then wanted us to aſſiſt him with a large Sum of Money, and did not make any Propoſals that we could liſten to of making Ceſſions to the Company.

Queſtion. Did he demand that Money as Chout, or as a Loan?

Anſwer. As a Loan.

Queſtion by the Governor General.—Were the Terms of the Treaty with Ragoba agreed upon before his Defeat, or after it?

Anſwer. Before the Defeat.

Mr. Tayler begs Leave to repreſent to the Board, that in Conſequence of their poſitive Orders to the Preſidency of Bombay, the Army will retreat from Ragoba the 15th of November, in their Way back to Broach and Surat, in order to proceed to Bombay, unleſs Orders are immediately ſent to prevent them; and that he conceives it to be neceſſary

necessary to keep them with Ragoba, whatever Determination the Board may come to.—Mr. Tayler withdraws.

The Question arising from the foregoing Minutes is, Whether the Orders sent to the Presidency of Bombay, to recall their Troops to their own Garrisons, shall be repeated, and their Recall for the present suspended?

Mr. Francis.—Every Part of the Information communicated to us by Mr. Tayler, confirms me in my former Opinion, that the Company's Troops should be withdrawn to their own Garrisons, without any Consideration whatsoever, but the Safety of their Retreat.

Mr. Barwell.—I think no Prejudice can arise to the Public Interests, by continuing the Troops in the present Situation; it may prove of great Utility to the Negociations Colonel Upton may enter upon. I am for sending immediate Orders, directing the Troops not to remain.

The Honourable George Monson.—From what has been submitted to the Consideration of the Board by the Presidency of Bombay, this, through Mr. Tayler, I find no Room to alter my former Sentiments on this Subject, that the Troops should be immediately ordered to withdraw to the Company's Garrisons, without any Consideration whatsoever but their immediate Safety. Their continuing longer in the Field will be a considerable Increase of Expence to the Company, without any Object of Advantage to them from it. The Ministerial Party by this Action will be sensible of our sincere Intentions to make Peace with them; and I have not the least Doubt but they will give due Attention to the Proposals made to them by Colonel Upton.

General Clavering.—There does not appear by any of the Answers which Mr. Tayler has made to the Questions which have been put to him, a single Reason to make me depart from the Opinion which I formerly gave, to direct the Presidency of Bombay to withdraw their Troops within their own Garrisons. He has indeed urged, that it would be a Breach of Faith on their Part with Ragoba; but he has not considered that the Breach of Faith would be much stronger on our Side, were we now to break off from the Overtures that we have made to the reigning Power at Poona, should we admit our Troops again to take the Field, and at the same Time should think proper to order Colonel Upton to proceed to Poona. One of the Two Cases must inevitably happen; either we should expose his Person to the Danger of being sacrificed, or our Negociations would be rendered fruitless, by the Suspicions that we should create in the Minds of the Ministers at Poona, that we were acting a perfidious Part by them. The Intention both of the Legislature and of the Court of Directors, is evidently that there should be an Union of as well as of Arms, between the Three Presidencies. If after the honourable Steps we have taken we should not succeed in our Negociation at Poona, it will be then Time enough to order the Troops of the Presidency of Bombay to act conjointly with the other Two Presidencies, to compel the Maratta State to submit to the Terms that we shall then think it adviseable to give them. At all Events, I never would advise that the Presidency of Bombay should hold Territories upon the Continent; unless it be some small Territory about Surat or Broach, merely to pay the Expences of those Garrisons; to hold more, would expose the Company to eternal Wars, in which nobody would profit but their Servants.

The Governor General.—I am confirmed in my Opinion, that our Army should keep the Field; that it should be strengthened with Supplies both of Men and Money, and that a Determination should be shewn by this Government, both to dictate and maintain the general Conditions of the Peace to which we should acquiesce; that a contrary Conduct would frustrate the Design of our Negociations, as is too apparent from the haughty Tone with which they dictated the Terms which were proposed by their Vackeels to the Government of Bombay, after having made Advances for Peace, while our Troops were in Opposition to them. I am convinced, that Fear only can operate upon the Minds of the Marattas; that if we miss the Advantage of which we are now in Possession, the Adherents of our Allies will abandon him; and that if our Negociation should afterwards fail, we shall have no Resource but in our own Strength for a future Defence.

Resolved, That the former Orders, transmitted to the Presidency of Bombay, shall remain in Force.

The Governor General.—As it appears from Mr. Tayler's Proposition, at his taking Leave of the Board, that the Presidency of Bombay have misunderstood the Order sent

sent them for withdrawing the Troops into their Garrisons, as meant to direct their Recall to Bombay, I submit to the Board the Propriety of explaining the Intentions of the Board in this Respect, which I suppose leave to the Presidency of Bombay the Option of such of the Company's Garrisons as they shall think most proper for the Reception of the Troops, whether Broach, Surat, Salsette, or Bombay, or to distribute them to each.

Agreed, That this be explained to Mr. Tayler, and mentioned to the Bombay Presidency.

The following Letters are accordingly written for this Purpose.

To William Tayler, Esq;

Sir,

After duly considering the Representation which you have been pleased to deliver to us, as well as the several Informations which you have communicated respecting the Nature, Motives, and Object of the Engagement of the Bombay Presidency with Ragonaut Row, and the present State of the Maratta Government at Poona; we have for the present to acquaint you, that we are confirmed in our Opinion of the Expediency of the Company's Troops being immediately recalled from the Service of Ragoba into their own Garrisons. Our Orders for this Purpose will therefore remain in Force.

But as you seem to understand, by the Proposition which you urged at taking Leave of the Board this Evening, that our Directions implied the Recall of the Troops to Bombay, we think it necessary to explain our Meaning to have been, that it should remain at the Option of the President and Council of Bombay to withdraw them to such of their Garrisons, and distribute them as they might see fit, for the Protection of the Company's Possessions, including Salsette.

Fort William, 9th October, 1775.

We are, &c.

P. S. We have ordered our Secretary to furnish you with a Copy of the Instructions which have been given to Lieutenant Colonel Upton, our Deputy to the Court of Poona; for your Information of the Conditions which we have prescribed for the proposed Treaty to be formed with that Government.

To the Honourable William Hornby, Esquire, President and Council.

Gentlemen,

We now acknowledge the Receipt of your Letter of the 23d August, delivered to us by Mr. Tayler.

It appearing by a Representation from Mr. Tayler, that he understood our Orders to you for withdrawing the Company's Troops from Ragoba, to imply the Recall of them to Bombay, we think it proper, lest you should put the same Construction upon them, to take this Opportunity of explaining our Intention to have been, that it should be left at your Option to withdraw the Forces to any of the Company's Garrisons which you might judge most proper for their Reception, or to distribute them to each; and to confine your Operations to the Protection of the Territories possessed by the Company previous to the Date of your Treaty with Ragoba, including Salsette.

Fort William, 9th October, 1775.

We are, &c.
Warren Hastings,
J. Clavering,
Geo. Monson,
Rich. Barwell.

APPEN-

APPENDIX, Nº 84.

Extract of Bengal Secret Consultations, the 18th October 1775.

PRESENT,

The Honourable Warren Hastings, Governor General, President,
Lieutenant General John Clavering,
The Honourable George Monson,
Richard Barwell, } Esquires.
Philip Francis, }

READ a Letter from Mr. Tayler, as follows:

Honourable Sir, and Gentlemen,

Agreeably to what you did me the Honour to notice to me in your Favour of the 9th, I have received a Copy of your Instructions to Lieutenant Colonel Upton. The Representations I had made to you, would, I flatter myself, have conveyed far different Ideas from those which dictated these Instructions; but it rests with you alone to determine on the Propriety of changing your Line of Politics; convinced as I am of the Detriment which must befal the present prosperous Situation of the Honourable Company's Affairs on the Western Side of India, If that Line which has been adopted, is continued to be pursued, I can only lament my ill Success: My Duty calls upon me to tell you, that the Moiety of the Revenues of the Town and Purgunnah of Broach, which has been ceded to us by Futty Sing, is in his Gift alone.

But as your Honour &c. have been pleased to appoint a Deputy from yourselves immediately to Saccaram Bapoo, and exclude the Government of Bombay from any Share in concluding the Peace, I am directed by the Honourable President and Council to represent to you that such a Measure will in their Opinion be a great Indignity to that Presidency, especially as the Honourable Company had themselves ordered a Member of their Board to reside there, and given repeated Approbations of his Conduct, as will appear more evidently from the accompanying Paragraphs of their Orders, and Copy of their Letter to Mahada Row.

Permit me therefore, in Justice to all the Gentlemen of the Board of Bombay, but particularly to those concerned in the Treaty concluded with the Peishwa, to remonstrate to you, that situated as they are in the Neighbourhood of the Marattas, having frequent Communication with them, and constant Opportunities of becoming acquainted with the Views, Connections, and Interests of the different Persons in the Poona Durbar, they certainly must be best qualified for negociating the several Matters intrusted to Colonel Upton, an entire Stranger to their whole System of Government; and I trust it will appear to your Honour, &c. that at the Time it pleased the Wisdom of Parliament to arm you with controlling Powers over the other Presidencies, it was by no Means their Intention that they should appear so much degraded and contemptible in the Eyes of the Country Government, as the Presidency of Bombay must do, unless you will commit the Treaty of Peace to their Management.

Our Honourable Employers, and the whole British Nation, may be naturally led to suppose, that in your Opinion the Members of that Government are devoid in every Degree of Integrity and Abilities; which would be the most cruel and unjust of all Imputations; for I can dare to affirm, not a Person who concluded that Treaty was actuated by any other Motive than their Obedience and Duty to their Employers, whose Interests appeared to them to be most materially benefited by their Engagements.

The Members who compose the Bombay Council have served the Honourable Company from 20 to 35 Years. The sole Dependance of some of them is still on the Service; and they have not yet been taxed with the Want of Abilities. Mr. Mostyn, who returned from England in the Year 1772, brought with him the Court of Directors Appointment as their Representative to the Poona Durbar.

For

For these several Reasons, Gentlemen, I earnestly conjure you to revoke your Orders to Colonel Upton, and by committing to the Management of the Government of Bombay whatever Negociation you may deem it necessary to enter into with either Party, support the necessary Respect to it, and not subject to so severe a Mortification, a Set of Gentlemen, against whom the only Faults that can be alledged are their having hastily carried into Execution their Zeal for the Interest of their Employers, and having been so unfortunate as to differ in Opinion from your Honour, &c. on the Necessity and Authority they had for it. I pledge myself to you for their implicit Obedience to whatever you may direct; and can only urge further in Behalf of this Measure, the very considerable Saving that will accrue by it to the Honourable Company, as it must be necessary to state to you the Difference between giving the Marattas a Peace, and becoming Suitors to them for one.

Calcutta, 12th October, 1775.

I am, &c.
(Signed) W. Tayler.

Copy of sundry Paragraphs of different Letters from the Honourable Court of Directors to the Presidency of Bombay.

Under the 18th March, 1768.

Par. 91. The Intimation you gave to our President and Council of Fort St. George, to use their Endeavours with the Marattas to obtain a Grant of Salsette and Bassein to us, we highly approve of; and we now recommend to you in the strongest Manner, to use your Endeavours, upon every Occasion that may offer, to obtain these Places, which we should esteem a valuable Acquisition; we cannot directly point out the Mode of doing of it, but rather wish they could be obtained by Purchase than War.

Under 31st March, 1769.

Par. 41. The opening a Negociation with the Marattas was a very proper Measure, and Mr. Mostyn acquitted himself therein highly to our Satisfaction.

42. The Demands made on them in Return for the Advantages they were to expect from our Successes against Hyder Ally, were also very proper. Salsette and Bassein, with their Dependencies, and the Maratta's Proportion of the Surat Revenues, were all that we seek for on that Side India.

43. These are the Objects you are to have in View in all your Treaties, Negociations, and Military Operations, and that you must be ever watchful to obtain; always attentive to convince the Country Powers, these are, and ever will be, the utmost Limits of our Views on the Western Side of India.

Under the 7th February, 1772.

Par. 16. Mr. Mostyn having represented to us, that his Health is so well established as to enable him to return to his Rank and Station in our Service, he now takes Passage for your Presidency in the Ship Duke of Cumberland.

17. We take this Occasion to apprize you, that it is our Intent Mr. Mostyn shall shortly proceed and reside at the Court of Mhada Row, not only to explain our Sentiments, but to endeavour to cultivate a good Understanding, and transmit such Business with him, as the Situation of Affairs may render necessary.

18. We are not at present prepared to transmit to you such Instructions for Mr. Mostyn as we may deem necessary, but shall not fail to do so by the latter Ships of the Season; mean while it is our Pleasure, and we direct, that on his Arrival at your Presidency, to be immediately appointed to such Post as he shall be intitled to by his Rank in your Council, which Post we also permit him to execute by a Deputy during his Residence at the Court of Mhada Row; and we further direct, that Mr. Mostyn be allowed the Sum of Rupees 5,000 per Annum, as Resident at Poona, to commence from the Time of his proceeding thither.

Resolved, That the following Letter be written to the President and Council at Bombay.

Gentlemen,

We think it proper to transmit you a Copy of the Instructions which we have given to Colonel Upton, that you may be acquainted with the Nature and Extent of the Powers and

and Commission entrusted to him, and the Terms which he is ordered to secure for the Company in his Negociations with the Maratta Government.

He has been directed to correspond with you; and as your local Knowledge and Experience may enable you to furnish him with useful Information, we request that you will communicate such to him whenever he may consult you.

The Guicawar Proportion of the Revenues of the Town and Purgunnah of Broach, and the Districts of Corial, Chickley, and Verio, having been made over to the Company by Futty Sing, who appears to be the Person possessed of the Right and Authority to make these Grants; and as we understand that they may be held without any material Increase of Expence, we desire you will retain Possession of them until a definitive Treaty of Peace shall have been concluded with the ruling Party at Poona.

Admitting the Possibility of Ragoba's being reduced by any unforeseen Misfortune to seek Refuge in some of your Garrisons, we would not have you understand from any Directions yet transmitted you, that we mean entirely to desert him; on the contrary, you will find, by a Paragraph of the enclosed Instructions to Colonel Upton, that our Intention is to obtain a suitable Provision for him; we therefore desire that you will afford him a Sanctuary for himself and his Domestics or Attendants, in Case he should ever be necessitated to apply for your Protection, in order to avoid any personal Danger.

We are, &c.

Resolved, That the Appointment of Lieutenant Colonel Upton cannot be repealed or changed consistently with the Orders of the Board already made public, and the Dignity of this Government.

Agreed, That these Resolutions be signified to Mr. Tayler as follows:

Sir,

We have received your Representation of the 9th Instant.

The Guicawar Portion of the Revenues of the Town and Purgunnah of Broach, and the Districts of Corial, Chickly, and Verio, having been made over to the Company by Futty Sing, who appeared to have possessed the Right and Authority to make this Cession, we have instructed the Presidency of Bombay to retain Possession of, until a definitive Treaty of Peace shall have been concluded with the ruling Party at Poona, as they may be held without Encrease of Expence to the Company.

With respect to the other Parts of your Letter, we are concerned to find you infer such Consequences to the President and Council of Bombay, as you seem to apprehend will result from the Appointment of Lieutenant Colonel Upton to Poona; we think it proper therefore to assure you, that it is our Wish to support the Reputation and Credit of their Government, as far as we can consistently with the due Execution of the Powers entrusted to us by the Legislature. It shall also be our Endeavour to secure the Presidency of Bombay from any Slight or Disrespect of their Authority. We are satisfied of the Knowledge and Experience of these Gentlemen in the political Views and Interests of the Maratta Government, nor do we question their Ability to conduct a Negociation for a Peace: Yet, however we may be influenced by these Motives, and by our Confidence in their Integrity and strict Desire to fulfil our Intentions, we do not think we can repeal or alter the Appointment of Colonel Upton consistently with the Orders and Resolutions which we have already made public, and signified to the Ministers at Poona, or with the Dignity of this Government, which he has been deputed to represent in his Character of public Minister at the Maratta Court.

As it is possible that Ragonaut Row may seek Refuge in some of the Company's Garrisons on the Malabar Coast, we have further directed the Presidency of Bombay to afford him an Asylum with his Attendants only, in Case he should find himself reduced to solicit this Mark of their Favour.

We are, &c.

APPENDIX, N° 85.

From the Nabob of Arcot; received the 14th October 1775.

AS soon as I learnt that you and the Gentlemen of Council were pacifically inclined towards the Ministers at Poona, and afterwards when I was informed that you had determined to send Col. Upton to conclude a Peace with them, I dispatched several Letters to you, under Dates the 16th of Jummadee ul Awal (or July) with a Duplicate of the 19th of the same Month; of the 13th of Jummadee Asianie (11th August) with a Duplicate thereof; of the 28th of the same Month, and of the 6th of Rujjub (2d of September); all of which have undoubtedly been perused by you and the Gentlemen of Council. I sent a Draft of Coulnâmâh, which in my Judgment should be obtained from the Marattas for the Tranquillity of the Carnatic, and for the Sircars, and other Possessions of the Company, to the Governor and Council of Madras, to be forwarded to you in a Letter from them; and for the greater Security, I now inclose you another Copy of it. By the Blessing of God I am an hereditary Prince, and a firm and steady Friend and Ally of the King of Great Britain, and am the most attached to the English Nation of all the Princes of India. My Friendship and sincere Regard to them has been frequently put to the Test, both in Times of Prosperity and Adversity, and through the strict Connection which subsists between me and the Company, our Concerns are the same, and my Country is independent of every Sirdar, however powerful, by Means of my Alliance with the King of Great Britain. By this the Country of Carnatic Paingaut, Tanjore, and all my other Dominions, are exempted from the Payment of Chout, either on Account of Time past or to come, as well as from all other Demands which would otherwise have been made on it. I therefore some Time ago requested you would send Instructions to Colonel Upton to consult with the Agent whom I should send there, and in Conjunction with him to exert his Endeavours for the Establishment of Peace with the Ministers at Poona. The Peace formerly concluded with the Nabob Nizam ul Dowlah, by General Calliaud and Mr. Stracey, was very soon broken; that concluded through me with the same Nabob, has not yet been shaken, though this is the ninth Year since it was first established; and, by the Blessing of God, were a Treaty concluded through my Mediation with the Ministers at Poona, there can be no Doubt but I should obtain great Advantages for the Company, because I am perfectly well acquainted with the Dispositions of the Powers of the Country, and in the Method of negociating and forming Treaties with them; and should, by the Blessing of God, exert myself to the utmost to establish it on the firmest Footing. The Advancement of the Prosperity and Interests of my Friends the English, in India, is the first Wish of my Heart; and this greatly depends on the present Treaty. The Poona Ministers some Time ago applied to me to take on myself the Part of a Mediator of Peace between them and the English. I am therefore desirous, for my own and the Company's Interests, and to remove all Doubts, to borrow Mr. Chambers (a good Man, and a Friend both to me and the Company) from the Governor and Council here, and to send him to Poona, accompanied by Shush Row, whose eldest Brother resides there on my Part. I request that you will be so kind as to send Orders without Delay to Colonel Upton to act in Conjunction with these Persons whom I shall send in the proposed Accommodation. I will transmit you a Copy of the Orders which I give to Mr. Chambers and Shush Row, as well as of the Transactions and Negociations of which I receive Intelligence from Poona. In the Treaty with the Marattas, it will not be proper to insert the Names of any other Countries, except those under the Dominion of the Company, myself, and the Successor of Sujah ul Dowlah; and it is for the Company's Interest that no other should be inserted; for the Nabob Nizam Ul Dowlah and Hyder Ally Khân, are very far from wishing the Increase of the Power and Authority of the English, to whom in their Hearts they are not Friends. And Hyder Ally Khân, in this Neighbourhood, incited thereto by the Consideration of the Greatness of his Forces, which he is daily augmenting, has gone beyond his Limits, of which you have been informed by my former Letters. He has lately formed a Resolution of marching from Serrungpatan,

and

and annexing the Countries of Kurpah, Kurnole, the Dominions of Morarow, and of the Zemindars dependent on Andoonie to his other Possessions. He is prevented carrying these Designs into immediate Execution, by the Necessity of repairing the Fort of Serrungpatan, Part of the Walls of which have been thrown down by an Inundation of the River Kâveerie; as soon as this Business is accomplished, he will certainly proceed to the Execution of the afore-mentioned Plan; and as the Chiefs of these Countries are not sufficiently powerful to make Head against him, there is no Doubt but he will quickly bring them under his Dominions. I enclose for your Information some Papers of Intelligence which I have lately received. At a particular Season of the Year, Horses and Cloaths were always brought into this Country to Tripotee, of which I used to make Purchases, and the People of the Country took off large Quantities; but for these last Two Years Hyder Ally Khân, in Consequence of his Intentions on Kurpah, has not permitted the Dealers in Cloth and Horses to come to Tripotee, but draws them into his own Country, and purchases their Merchandize himself. With the Approbation of the Governor and Council here, I raised several Troops of Cavalry, and by Reason of the Unhealthiness of this Climate to Horses, I have lost many in each Troop, which I cannot replace; and should Hyder Ally get Possession of Kurpah, &c. I shall not be able to procure a single Horse in Paingaut. This being the Case, it would be greatly for our mutual Interest that the Talook of Guntore, which is situated between my Possessions and the Sirkars, should be under the Company's Authority; and that Kurpah, which is from of old a Dependency of the Carnatic Paingaut (which is well known) should be put into my Hands. If by the Blessing of God this is carried into Execution, and the Fougedars of Kurnole, Morarow, and the Zemindars of that Quarter, who have altogether about 9 or 10,000 Horse, are under the Company's and my Protection, their Forces will be ready to join with us whenever we may have Occasion for them. I therefore think it would be proper that you should send a public Order to Hyder Ally Khân, to confine himself within his own Limits, and not to make any Attempt against the Dominions of others. You are apprehensive of the French: I am still more so from the Augmentation of Hyder Ally's Forces, who is their Supporter.

Enclosed in the above,

Draft of the Sunnud.

As the whole Country of the Carnatic Paingaut and Ballagaut, from the River Kishna to the Boundary of Muilewar, together with the Fort and Country of Tanjour, and all the Forts, Jaghierdars, Zemindars, Pykars, &c. are under the Government of the Nabob Wallah Jah, Ameer Ul Hind, Omdut Ul Mulk, Asoph Ul Dowlah, Anwar ul Dun Khân, Bahadre Zuffur Jung, Sepah Sallar, I, by the Order of Mahah Rajah, my Master, declare upon my Faith, and on the Oath by Bael Bhundhâr, that I renounce all Demands of Chout, Serdasemuckee, &c. on the Countries above specified; and that I have no Claim of Chout, &c. on Account of Times past or to come. It is hereby required of my Sons and Brothers who may succeed me, and of all the Officers of the Mahah Rajah's and my Government, and of all Ministers for Affairs, and Tassildars, that they strictly observe the Terms of this Sunnud, respecting the Renunciation of Chout, &c. from the Nabob Wallah Jah and his Posterity, and never on any Account, to the latest Generations, give them Trouble by a Demand of Chout, Serdasemuckee, Nalbundee, and other Taxes; but that they consider all the aforementioned Duties as absolutely renounced for ever. On this Occasion, knowing the most positive Injunctions, do not demand a fresh Sunnud every Year, and deviate not from the Orders contained herein.

Dated

APPENDIX, N° 85.

LIST of the Names of Maratta Chiefs, which it will be proper to insert as Guarantees for the Tranquillity of the Countries of the Carnatic, the Sirkars, and Bombay, and for the Observance of the Treaty of Peace to be concluded through your Means between Rajah Ram Raje Madho Row Sawae Pundit Purdhan, the Son of Narrain Row, and the King and Parliament of Great Britain, the Company, and English Nation, and the Nabob of Arcot.

Maodhajee Boosilah	Baboojee Naig
Futty Sing Guicawar	Taroo Sindkar
Govind Row Guicawar	Anund Row Rastah
Holdcar	Damun Row, Brother to Gopaul Hurry
Sindhia	Hurry
Siecaram Pundit	Nanna Purnaveesse
Morow Pundit Purnaveese	Hurry Pundit Purkeah.

Extract of Bengal Secret Consultations, the 9th November 1775.

PRESENT,

The Honourable Warren Hastings, Governor General, President,
Lieutenant General John Clavering,
The Honourable George Monson,
Richard Barwell, Philip Francis, } Esquires.

The Board, taking into Consideration the Nabob of Arcot's Application for Mr. Chambers to go to Poona, agreeable to his Letter received the 14th October, and entered in the Persian Correspondence;

Agreed, That Mr. Chambers be permitted to proceed to Poona, on the Part of the Nabob, to assist Colonel Upton in negociating any Points which the Nabob may think necessary to recommend to him to be made Conditions in the Treaty, but to transact his Business only through Colonel Upton.

Resolved, That the following Letter be written to Lieutenant Colonel Upton.

To Lieutenant Colonel Upton.

Sir,

The Nabob of the Carnatic has applied to us for Permission to depute Mr. William Chambers to Poona, to assist you in negociating any Matters on the Part of the Nabob, and to propose to you such Conditions as he may think necessary for the Interest of the Carnatic, to make Articles in the Treaty of Peace with the Maratta Government. We have allowed the Nabob to employ Mr. Chambers on this Service, in Case the President and Council of Fort St. George shall see no Objection to it; but we have thought it necessary to restrict him from transacting any Business, except through you: And we desire that you will conform to his Representations, as far as you may be authorized by the Tenor of our Instructions.

We understand that Colonel Keating has retired with the Troops under his Command to the South of Surat, and will there remain inactive; but that the Reasons alledged for this Movement are, to be in Readiness again to take the Field, or to embark for Bombay, as future Occasions may render necessary. If Colonel Keating should continue in this Situation until your Arrival at Poona, you will explain these Circumstances to the Ministry, and acquaint them that they may depend on our observing most rigidly the Pacification on our Part, and that we consequently require the same good Faith from them; but if they should order their Troops to be again put in Motion, with Intention to commence Hostilities afresh, we shall likewise be under the Necessity of breaking through

through the peaceful Measures which we meant to observe, and shall consider ourselves no longer bound to keep any Terms of Amity with them.

We are, &c.

Fort William, 9th November 1775. (Signed) Warren Hastings, &c. Council.

Extract of Bengal Select Consultations, 2d November 1775.

Extract of a Letter to Fort St. George.

The Nabob has applied to us for Permission to employ Mr. Chambers on a Deputation from him to meet Colonel Upton at Poona, and to assist him in negociating any Matters on the Part of the Nabob; also to propose such Articles as he may wish to have inserted as Conditions in the Treaty of Peace with the Maratta State. As we conceive this Attention due to the Nabob's Request, we have told him that we comply with it, if you should see no Objection; but that Mr. Chambers must transact his Business only through Colonel Upton, who has been ordered to attend to his different Representations, and to conform to them, as far as he may be authorized by the Tenor of our Instructions.

We are, &c.

Fort William, 9th November 1775. (Signed) Warren Hastings, &c. Council.

APPENDIX, N° 86.

Extract of Bengal Secret Consultations, the 29th November 1775.

PRESENT,

The Honourable Warren Hastings, Governor General, President,
Lieutenant General John Clavering,
The Honourable George Monson,
Richard Barwell, Philip Francis, Esquires.

THE following Letter from Lieutenant Colonel Upton was received since the last Meeting of Council, and immediately circulated.

Gentlemen,

I am honoured with your Letters of the 5th Instant; also the Letter from the Nizam.

In about Five Weeks from this Date, I expect to be at Poona; sooner if possible.

The Country about here is in the greatest Distress and Confusion. The Marattas have a small Army of about 3,000 Men, within 20 Coss of Calpee, their Free-Booters have plundered and laid Waste the Country all around within 5 Coss, and they daily expect the Town to share the same Fate. The Rajah of Calpee, Hamet Bahader the Gossain, (who, with his Brother Omro Gyr) has the entire Command and Direction of the Doaub, has lately marched with an Army of about 15,000 Men, to the Neighbourhood of Jansi, whether to secure a strong Pass there, or to besiege Jansi, is not known. The Marattas marched the 3,000 Men in Consequence of this Motion of Hamet Bahader's, and

and have got between him and Calpee. It is also said the Marattas have a large Force in Motion from Brampore, commanded by Hurry Pundit. In all Appearance, the Nabob Asoph ul Dowlah will soon have in his Country a considerable Maratta Army.

Calpee, 26th October 1775. I have, &c. (Signed) J. Upton.

APPENDIX, N° 87.

Bengal Secret Consultations, 29th November 1775.

THE following Letter from Mr. Tayler to the Board was received since last Council Day, and sent in Circulation.

Honourable Sir, and Gentlemen,

I have learnt that the Paishwa Ragonaut Row, has addressed you concerning his Pretensions from the late Treaty. Although the strict Adherence to that Treaty forms the chief Object of my Deputation; yet the Validity of it, and the National Obligation incurred by it, have already been so amply discussed, that I will only beg of you to bear in Mind, that however unauthorized and invalid the Engagements of the Government of Bombay may appear to you, a different Sentiment will prevail with the several Powers of Hindostan; for till the contrary was publicly announced, the ancient Constitution of the Company certainly existed with respect to them; and agreeably to that, Ragoba will in their Minds have a clear Right to every Advantage stipulated to him by the late Treaty. It must also be remembered, that the Ministerial Confederacy is by no Means a general Association of the most respectable Maratta Chiefs, to expel him from the Government for his Crimes or Incapacity, but a partial Combination of a few Individuals, brought into Office by his own Family, who, to gratify their own Ambition and Interest, first released him from Imprisonment, raised him to the Government of which he became the rightful Possessor; and then from the same Motives, entered into a rebellious Confederacy to expel him from that Government, in order to usurp it themselves.

Should these Considerations, and other Motives, induce you to make the Concerns of Ragoba a more leading Object in the intended Negociation at Poona, I think it incumbent on me to state you my Opinion, in what Manner this Point might be effected, most consistently with the Steps you have already taken, the good Faith of the Nation, the Interests of the Company, and how the present Differences might easily be terminated, so as to secure a permanent Settlement.

On no Footing whatever have the Ministers any Pretensions to the Government. If the Infant Mhadoo Row Narrain is really supposititious, the Title of Ragoba stands unquestioned; if he is the true Child of Narrow Row, surely the Guardianship of an Uncle is more natural and equitable, than that of Men who have been abetting to the Murder of his Father, and the Expulsion of that Uncle, merely to raise themselves on the Ruin of the Family, and must be deemed by all the Powers of India, a just Settlement.

To quiet all Parties, I would therefore advise, that the Acknowledgment of the Title of Mhadoo Row Narrain be the Basis of any future Treaty: That Ragoba possess the actual Government in Quality of Regent, in the same Manner as he did during the Minority of Mhadoo Row, and Narrow Row, the Uncle and Father of the Infant; and that in Case of the Death of the Infant and Ragoba, the Succession devolve on Imrut Row, Ragoba's adopted Son. To obviate any Objections that may arise to the Infant being put in the Power of Ragoba, a Battalion of Sepoys, or any certain Number of our Troops may be stationed there, for the Safeguard of his Person, under the Command of our Resident, the Expence of which must be paid by the Poona Government; or any other Plan may be pursued, which may be settled among themselves.

That

That the present Confederates be guaranteed by the Company, with Respect to their Lives, Fortunes and Offices; and even if required, an Asylum offered them in any of the Company's Territories, or as is usual among the Marattas, some Forts assigned them for the Security of their Persons and Property.

That the Cessions made by Ragoba to us be guaranteed by all Parties, as well as the Security of the Carnatic, and the Exemption of Mahomed Ally, from every Kind of Demands from the Marattas.

Whatever may be the Event of future Deliberation on this Point, I must again earnestly take the Liberty to recommend that our Army be permitted to remain with Ragoba till a final Pacification is effected. It will prevent him from Despair, and perhaps from throwing himself into other Connections; such a Shew of Determination will carry an Idea of Firmness and Confidence in this Government very necessary to give a Weight to Colonel Upton's Representations and Demands. The late Declaration of the Ministry indeed renders this but a Point of Prudence, in order to protect the Guzerat Country. Our Army might remain encamped with that of the Peishwa, under the Walls of Brodera. This would at once retain Futty Sing in our Party, defend the Guzerat Country, in Case of the Eruption of the Ministerial Army, and being at a proper Distance from them, prevent any Disturbance in collecting the Harvest and Revenues from our Pergunnahs. The Ministers might be acquainted with the Orders to do this, and that their Threats were the Occasion of it, as well as your Determination to continue the Army with the Peishwa till the final Pacification; since it appears so little Dependance is to be had on their Promises, and at the same Time they might be assured that was our sole Intention. As to the Expence, it could not be considerable, and we are besides in actual Collection of the Districts assigned for Payment of our Charges, which are rated at more than they amount to.

The Arrears from the 17th February last would also become secured.

Calcutta, 18th November 1775.

I have, &c.

(Signed) W. Tayler.

The Secretary also sent with the above, a Letter to him from the Governor-General, containing his Opinion upon Mr. Tayler's, and a Letter from Mr. Tayler to the Governor-General, as follows:

Sir,

Be pleased to send round the accompanying Letter from Mr. Tayler, with that in which he has lately addressed the Board, to the Gentlemen of Council, whose Opinions upon the Proposition contained in the Letter I wish to collect in this Way, unless they shall judge it necessary to discuss it in a formal Meeting.

My own Opinion upon it is clear. The Articles recommended for the Pacification appear reasonable, and likely to produce their Effect, because they accord with the Propositions which, as we understand from Mr. Tayler, were at one Time the Objects of the Ministers themselves, and it is not likely they will now refuse them, if a Determination is shewn on our Part to insist on them. By Colonel Upton's last Letter, we may expect him to have accomplished his Journey near a Month before our Orders on this Subject can reach him; if in that Space of Time he shall not have concluded a Treaty, it may be presumed that the Ministerial Party, seeing the Advantage in procrastinating the Issue of it, have purposely evaded it; and a Power thus granted to Colonel Upton to prescribe the ultimate Conditions, will bring his Negociation to a sure Crisis; and whether War or Peace be the Result, this Government will stand equally justified in their Endeavours to prevent the former, and to establish the latter.

I am, &c.

Belvidere, 22 November 1775.

(Signed) Wm. Hastings.

(Approved) R. B.

Honourable Sir,

As I have been given to understand that the Letter I did myself the Honour to address to yourself and the Council Yesterday, was deferred, on Account of your not being present at the Board; I hope you will excuse my taking the Liberty to urge to you the Importance of its being speedily decided on, especially if what I have proposed should meet with the Approbation of yourself and the Council, that immediate Orders may

be

be dispatched, so as to arrive in Time to prevent Ragoba from pursuing any other Measures.

I have, &c.

21st November 1775. (Signed) W. Tayler.

The following Desire having been returned by the other Gentlemen of Council, the Secretary begs Leave to bring on the above Business.

I desire the Consideration of Mr. Tayler's Letter may be postponed to the first Council, when I will give my Opinion upon it.

(Signed) J. H.
G. M.
P. F.

APPENDIX, N° 88.

Bengal Secret Consultations, 29th November 1775.

MR. Tayler now sends in a Letter as follows:

Honourable Sir, and Gentlemen,

Having Yesterday received a Letter from Lieutenant Colonel Keating, dated 29th Ultimo, containing Advices, which appear to me of the greatest Importance with respect to our present Situation with the Marattas, I herewith inclose for your Notice an Extract from it. I cannot here forbear remarking that this Event confirms the Advices and Conjectures of the Government of Bombay, regarding the State and Expectations of the Two Parties, which I had the Honour to communicate to you in my Address of the 9th Ultimo.

In the present critical Conjuncture of Affairs, it is much to be lamented that I was not so far successful as to induce the Revocation of your Orders for withdrawing our Army from Ragoba. This would have given him some Room to hope that you did not mean entirely to abandon his Concerns; and as I am convinced that he would at any Rate prefer a Restoration or Settlement under the Protection and Sanction of the Company to any other, I think, that notwithstanding the Offers of the Persons at Poona who have formed an Alliance to support his Cause, he would still have waited the Event of his late Address to you, before he withdrew himself from us to embrace their Protection.

But when I reflect on the Time at which Colonel Keating represents these Matters to be agitating, viz. the 29th Ultimo; and that about the 12th Instant, your final and absolute Determinations would arrive, which preclude him from all Hopes of Restoration through our Means, it seems to me that common Policy must plainly dictate his Reliance on the Junto formed by Moraba Furneese.

Should he adopt this Measure, there appears to me just Grounds of Apprehension, that what we have most of all to fear will happen; I mean the Re-settlement of the Maratta Empire, and the Restoration of Ragoba, without our Assistance, after the absolute abandoning of him, in direct Violation of the Treaty concluded with the Government of Bombay. In such Case, I think you must perceive, that Colonel Upton can form very little Hopes of Success in any one of the Points he is charged to negociate. I do not see on what Footing of Justice or Right he can pretend to any of the Cessions which form the principal Object of his Embassy, as they were the stipulated Price of Engagements we have found it convenient to recede from; and as to Stipulations regarding Mahomed Ally, I shall only remark, that the Carnatic has ever been too favourite an Object of Maratta Depredations to relinquish it but on Compulsion.

The

The only effectual Means I can devise in this Situation, is still to endeavour to become the Instruments of his Restoration, by acceding to the Treaty entered into with him by the Government of Bombay, leaving it to them to explain in the best Manner they may be able, the Cause of the Impediment on the Prosecution of our Engagements with him, the Mistrust that he has of all the Ministers, the Knowledge of their general Views, and of that Perfidy and Treachery; and which, from the leading Characteristics of his Nation and Cast, may perhaps yet induce him to wait the Event of his late Application to you, before he adopts that last and dangerous Measure of confiding his Life and Government with such doubtful Characters as these.

I have, &c.

Calcutta, 29th Nov. 1775. (Signed) W. Tayler.

Extract of a Letter from Lieutenant Colonel Keating, dated the 29th October 1775, and received the 28th November.

Though the Odds are greatly against this reaching you at Calcutta, yet at a Venture I shall communicate some little Matters which may be of Use.

Morabah Furneese has lately sent a Man to the Peishwa, with Assurance that he and the following are strongly attached to his Interest; Butchabhoy, Chintoo Wittol, Mallarjee Goparah, and Ramchunder Gunneis; all powerful Men. He adds, that the Situation of the Ministerial Party is nearly as bad as can be; that Hurry Punt Furkia, now at Aurungabad, has scarce five thousand Men under his Command, and, at the utmost, their whole Force doth not exceed 12,000, and those so dispirited and dispersed as not to be easily assembled. Saccaram Bappoo and Nanna Furneese are in Promder Fort, and afraid to trust themselves out of it: That he, Maroba, is collecting a Force which, by the Time we can ascend the Gotts, will amount to 10,000 of the best Horse lately in the Minister's Pay; with these he will join the Peishwa, and carry him to Poona without Bloodshed. These are the Accounts he daily receives from the Southward. Beesi Sing, the Raja of the Marwar Country, is now within 45 Coss of the City of Amedabad, on his Way to join the Peishwa; his Vackeel arrived here Yesterday, and says, his Master has with him Ten thousand of his Troops. We shall march To-morrow for our Pergunnah of Chickley, and leave the Peishwa's Army at Sangaaz. I hope in God you are by this Time successful. Nothing on Earth could please me so much as the Assurance of it.

A true Copy.

(Signed) W. Tayler.

The following Question is put, upon the First of the above Letters from Mr. Tayler:

Whether the Propositions contained in the said Letter, or any Part of them, shall be agreed to?

Mr. Francis—I think that the Resolution already taken by this Council, and on which our Instructions to Colonel Upton are founded, are not open to any Alteration, until we hear the Result of his first Negociation with the Ministry at Poona, or until he informs us in what Manner his Propositions are received by them, and whether the Negociation committed to him be likely to succeed or not.

Colonel Monson—The Situation of this Government with the Maratta State, and the Instructions under which Colonel Upton is sent to treat with the Ministerial Party at Poona, will not admit of any present Alteration. We should wait for the Result of his Negociations, before any such fresh Propositions of a different Nature from those which we have already made to the Ministerial Party are submitted to their Consideration. I therefore am of Opinion that the Propositions contained in Mr. Tayler's Letter cannot be admitted.

General Clavering—I cannot agree to the adopting at present the Plan proposed by Mr. Tayler in his Letter of the 18th Instant, because it would oblige us to vary the System of Pacification that we have proposed to the Ministers at Poona. It is necessary to wait for the first Advices from Colonel Upton before we alter the Measures we have already taken for his Negociation; should those fail, and Colonel Upton return, our Measures then must be adapted to the Circumstances; but at any Rate I think Mr. Tayler's Plan, of allowing our Army to remain with Ragoba, would defeat the present Negociation, and may eventually engage the Company in an endless War, in

order

order to establish Ragoba in his Peishwaship. What Reason Mr. Tayler may have for his Conjecture that Maderow Narrain is a supposititious Child, I cannot conceive. Mr. Mostyn, in his Letter of the 28th April 1774, recorded on the Select Committee Proceedings 15th June, speaks positively of his Birth; and again, in his Letter of the 20th May following, recorded on the Select Committee Proceedings of the 1st September 1774, confirms that Account, and the Effects that it had had upon Ragoba's Party, by his Forces having left him on that Account. This is the strongest Evidence that we can obtain of the Legitimacy of his Birth, both in the Mind of Mr. Mostyn at that Time, and in the Opinions that were entertained of it in that Country. As to Mr. Tayler's Scheme, of keeping a Battalion of the Company's Seypoys at Poona, it is too chimerical to require a serious Answer.

The Governor General—I still adhere to my Opinion delivered in my circular Minute of the 22d. The last Letter which we received from Colonel Upton, advised us that he was at Calpee on the 26th Ultimo, and expected to reach Poona in Five Weeks, which Period will have elapsed To-morrow. At all Events, any Letters which may be dispatched to him after this Day, will not be able to reach him until a long Time after his Arrival there, when every Negociation ought to be concluded, if he shall find in the Ministerial Party a sincere Disposition to Peace. These Propositions, accompanied with a peremptory Declaration that they are the ultimate Terms offered to them, I do not conceive would produce their Effect, and for that Reason I have recommended their being adopted. The Condition objected to by the General I should equally disapprove, but that I conclude the Alternative joined with it would preclude it from having a Moment's Consideration with either Party, and that they would both prefer an Accommodation of this Point between themselves, to any Interposition of our Force in an Occasion of so much Delicacy as the immediate Guard of the Person of their actual Sovereign.

Resolved, That the following Reply be sent to Mr. Tayler:

Sir,

We have received your Letters of the 18th Instant, and of Yesterday.

We are much obliged to you for communicating to us the Intelligence enclosed in the Letter from Colonel Keating. We hope that the Success of Colonel Upton's Negociation will obviate the Necessity of making any Alteration in the Instructions already given him; at any Rate, as he must be so near the End of his Journey, we think it absolutely necessary to wait for Advices of his First Interview and Negociations with the Ministry before we send him any new Instructions for his Conduct.

We are, &c.
Warren Hastings,
J. Clavering,
Geo. Monson,
Richard Barwell,
P. Francis.

APPENDIX, N° 89.

Copy of a Letter from William Tayler to the Honourable Court of Directors for Affairs of the United Company of Merchants of England trading to the East Indies.

Honourable Sirs,

BY the Advices from the Select Committee of Bombay, you will have been fully apprized of the Treaty entered into with Ragoonath Ballajee Row, the Paishwah of the Maratta Empire, for our Assistance with a Body of your Troops to act in Concert with his, in order to effect his Reinstatement in his Capital of Poona; which he had been obliged to abandon by the Violence of certain of his Subjects, who had entered into a rebellious Confederacy to expel him from his Government in order to usurp

it

it themselves. The Motives which guided the Conduct of your Servants at this critical Juncture, the Progress of their military Operations, and the general State of Affairs, have also, no doubt, been so fully stated to you by the Calcutta, that a Recital of them now would be an unnecessary Intrusion on your Time.

With the flattering Hopes they had then before them, of speedily accomplishing their Engagements with Ragoba, either by Arms or Negociation, and thereby effecting those Objects which had been so frequently and strenuously enjoined to them, as your ultimate Wishes in the West of India, it is not easy to conceive the Concern and Astonishment of your Servants on the Receipt of the following Letter from the Honourable the Governor General and Council, which arrived at Bombay on the 12th August last.

Copy of a Letter from William Tayler to the Honourable the Court of Directors.

From the very general Manner in which this Government had expressed themselves regarding the Measures pursued by your Servants at Bombay, it appeared to them impossible to judge with Precision of the Grounds of their Disapproval, which was indispensably necessary in order to remove their Objections to the Treaty with Ragoba; in the strict Adherence to which, the good Faith of the Nation and your particular Interests were deeply engaged. For the latter Purpose, as well as to give them every requisite Information regarding your Views and Interest at that Presidency, should they persist in their Determination to conclude a Peace with the Ministerialists, the Governor and Council of Bombay deemed it indispensably necessary to depute hither a Member of their Board; and, as I appeared to them duly qualified to answer their Intentions, they did me the Honour to select me. Pursuant to their Directions I therefore embarked on the Terrible Bomb Ketch, and arrived here the 1st Ultimo.

As the Ideas which appear to have guided the Resolutions of the Governor General and Council seemed to me to have arisen from Want of Knowledge, or Misconception of the Nature of the Maratta Government, the late Factions and Divisions in the Poona Durbar, the State of the different Parties, the Rank, Rights, and Connections of Ragoba, I thought it necessary to state these at large, together with your declared Views and Interests in the West of India, the Manner in which they would be accomplished by the Treaty with Ragoba, and also how far the Security and Welfare of your Territories in the East of Hindostan had been attended to in the Conclusion of that Treaty; I therefore addressed them the following Letter. *(See Appendix 83.)*

Copy of a Letter from William Tayler to the Honourable the Court of Directors.

Considering the Alteration of Circumstances, and the different Sentiments which the foregoing Address must doubtless have conveyed from those which seems to have dictated their Letter to the Government of Bombay of the 31st May last, I flattered myself that this Government would be induced to an Alteration of Measures: But it is with Regret I must acquaint you, that all I had urged was in vain; for under the 9th Ultimo they wrote me in Answer, that after duly considering the Representations which I had been pleased to deliver them, as well as the several Informations I had communicated respecting the Nature, Motives, and Objects of the Engagements with Ragoba, and the present State of the Maratta Government at Poona, they had, for the present, to acquaint me, that they were confirmed in their Opinion of the Expediency of the Company's Troops being immediately recalled from the Service of Ragoba into their own Garrisons. Their Orders for this Purpose would therefore remain.

The Reasons and Motives for the Conduct of this Government, are no doubt explained to you at large on their Records. For my Part, being totally ignorant of them, I can only here lament the ill Success of my Endeavours; being well convinced, that the Re-establishment of Ragoba, and the Completion of our Engagements with him, is the most effectual Means to insure the quiet and permanent Possession of the several Districts to be ceded to us.

Having expressed some Doubts regarding their Orders for the Recall of our Troops from Ragoba, they also acquainted me in their Letter of the 9th Ultimo, that, as I seemed to understand their Directions implied the Recall of the Troops to Bombay, they thought it necessary to explain their Meaning to have been, that it should remain at the

Option of the Government of Bombay to withdraw them into ſı and diſtribute them as they might ſee fit, for the Preſervation c cluding Salſette.

The Words " Company's Poſſeſſions" appearing to me inde willing to leave any Opening for the Government of Bombay tc tation of Diſobedience to the Orders of the Governor General a: it might be explained, whether they meant to include by the Diſtricts ceded to us by the Paiſhwa and Futty Sing Guicawar, a: or whether they meant to confine them only to Salſette, and Ter previous to our Engagements with the Paiſhwa: To which Anſwer, that their Meaning by the Company's Poſſeſſions, was, by the Company previous to the Date of the Treaty entered into they added including Salſette, becauſe the Government of Bomb of it before that Period. I have however the Pleaſure to inforı Deputation has not been in general ſucceſsful, yet, that I truſt it l effectual to the Advancement of your Intereſts; for on further R and explaining the Nature of the Tenure, and the particular Cor would be of to you, the Governor General and Council write Ultimo, that the Guicawar Proportion of the Revenues of the of Broach, and the Diſtricts of Corial, Chickley, and Veric over to you by Futty Sing, who appears to have the Right and Conceſſion, they had inſtructed the Preſidency of Bombay to re until a definitive Treaty of Peace ſhall have been concluded wi Poona; from which Circumſtance I hope they mean to retain venues of which are valued at ſo conſiderable a Sum as 5,28,000

I was regularly acquainted with the Deputation of Colonel Copy of his Inſtructions being ſent me. This Meaſure appear your Servants at Bombay in general, who, from their Proximit the daily Opportunities they have of becoming acquainted with actions, Intereſts, and Deſigns of the ſeveral Members of that ſuppoſed moſt fit for ſuch a Negociation; but particularly on M have done the Honour to appoint your Repreſentative there, have repeatedly approved. It alſo ſeemed to me highly derogato vernment there, and tending totally to ſubvert every Idea of Re thority in the different Powers around, which in its Conſequenc tended with Difficulties and Hindrances in the Conduct of your Expence of this Embaſſy, in Compariſon with the Trifle it woul gociation committed to the Management of your Servants at F pital Objection with me. For theſe ſeveral Reaſons I thought ſtrate againſt this Meaſure, to deſire the Recall of Colonel Up ſignify their Orders and Intentions, leaving the Execution of the of Bombay, for whoſe ready and implicit Obedience I confident ſorry I am to acquaint you, that my Repreſentations on this F for they acquaint me in Anſwer, that they are concerned to finc quences to the Preſident and Council at Bombay, as I ſeemed to from the Appointment of Colonel Upton to Poona; they thoug aſſure me, that it was their Wiſh to ſupport the Reputation and ment as far as they can, conſiſtently with the due Execution of them by the Legiſlature, that it ſhould alſo be their Endeavours of Bombay from any Slight or Diſreſpect of their Authority. ſelves ſatisfied of the Knowledge and Experience of your Se Views and Intereſts of the Maratta Government; nor did they to conduct a Negociation for a Peace; yet, however they may Motives, and by their Confidence in their Integrity and ſtrict tentions, they did not think they could repeal or alter the A Upton, conſiſtently with the Orders and Reſolutions which they lic, and ſignified to the Miniſters at Poona, or with the Digni which he had been deputed to repreſent in his Character of pul ratta Court. In Reply to this I can only remark, that if th Grounds on which I found my Objections, which the Governor not pretend to deny, the Reaſon they here aſſign for totally diſre me but unsatisfactory, as I do not conceive what Indignity can possibly ensue by their transferring the Management of this Negociation from Colonel Upton to a Deputation of your Servants at Bombay; their Supremacy in political Matters could have been as effectually explained. I can only further lament, that when the Mode and Terms of Accommodation were resolved on, they did not from the first signify their Intentions to the Government of Bombay, by which Means you might long ere now, I apprehend, have been at some Certainty with respect to your Affairs on that Side; whereas by the present Mode and Route, you are left in a very disagreeable Suspence, and likely to continue so for some Time; for though Colonel Upton, I understand, left this Place in July last, he was on the 27th Ultimo got no further on his Way to Poona than Calpee; and as it is probable the intermediate Country may be invested with Parties of Horse, and his Journey thereby delayed, it is impossible to say when he will arrive there.

With respect to the Matter and Objects of Colonel Upton's Instructions, I beg Leave to trouble you with the following Reflections:

If we may judge from the Tenor of Governor Hastings's Letter to Sackaram Bapoo, and from the Expressions he makes Use of, "My Employer the King of England," Colonel Upton will be esteemed at Poona the Representative of this sacred Character; I will therefore first proceed to examine how far his Actions will be consistent with the Dignity of it, and with those Ideas of Justice and Moderation, which no Doubt this Government will wish to convey of itself in this first Instance that is publicly brought forth to Action in the Face of all the Powers in India.

Every Circumstance, if well attended to, seems to confirm it beyond a Doubt, that consistent with Justice and Propriety, Ragoonath Row is the only Person whose Authority we can regularly acknowledge, with whom we can enter into any Treaty or Agreement relative to Maratta Affairs. On the Death of his Nephew Naron Row, being the only Male Survivor of the Family of Badjerow, he succeeded to the Paishwaship, and was regularly invested with the Office by every requisite Form, and acknowledged by the very Persons whose Interest and Ambition now lead them in Arms against him. This Acquiescence would by no Means be deemed a compulsive one; for at that Time it is well known he did not possess the Means of Compulsion: A Prisoner, without Money, and without an Army, he was solely indebted to them for his Release, and particularly to the Duan Sackaram. From the Justness of his hereditary Title, and this public Acknowledgment of the different Ministers and Maratta Chiefs, the Government of Bombay thought they might also with great Propriety recognize him. Accordingly the public Envoy of the Company at Poona, who then represented the English Nation, did, in the Name of that Nation, formally acknowledge him, and renewed with him the Treaties and Friendship entered into with his Ancestors. I conceive that this Act was as generally obligatory on the whole Nation, as any other Treaties of Peace and Alliance formed previous to the Existence of the Governor General and Council.

Exclusive of our public Acknowledgment of him as the ruling Power established at Poona by the Consent of all Parties, it must be observed, that we had in some Degree a previous Obligation to recognize him alone as rightful Heir of the Family of Badjerow. Our Agreement with the first Paishwah, Badjerow Ballajee, was rather, on his Part, a personal than a national one; nothing is mentioned in it of the Maratta Government; it was a Friendship between him and the Company, established by a Treaty signed in his Behalf by his Brother, Chimnajee Oppah, which Treaty is the Basis of all our Rights and Pretensions in the Dominions of the Paishwa. This personal Friendship is confirmed by a Minute on the Bombay Records, which declares all your Treaties null and invalid in the Extinction of the Paishwa Family. It was on this Footing that in the Year 1761 Ragoba, when Regent before, requested our Assistance against the Nizam in Behalf of the young Paishwa, Mhadoo Row. Nothing of the Maratta Government was mentioned; he pleaded, that in Virtue of our ancient Friendship with the Family, it was incumbent on us to assist him in that Time of Distress. Possessed with these Ideas, and deeming the reigning Divisions a fit Opportunity to compass the Views of the Company, the Government of Bombay early directed the Resident at Poona to sound whether Ragoba would want our Assistance; and at a Time when perhaps it might have been done to Advantage, they never once thought of treating with his rebellious Subjects, deeming it totally incompatible with our Engagements and Friendship with the Paishwa, and consequently a gross and open Violation of our Faith.

 On

On this Footing alone, the British Nation seems doubly bound to make the Restoration of Ragoba the primary Object of the intended Negociation. Though our solemn Acknowledgments of him, and the Renewal of Friendship pledged to his Ancestors, does not perhaps imply any actual Obligation to assist him; yet, in Honour and Justice we were certainly bound not to acknowledge any other Government at Poona till he had formally relinquished all Title to it; or till his utter Depression, by destroying all Hopes, had authorized our treating with the ruling Powers, in order to prevent a general Interruption to our Affairs. This virtual Obligation was confirmed by a solemn Treaty, whereby we not only renew our Acknowledgment of his Right, but engage to support him in it against the Usurpation of the Confederacy. Much has been already urged respecting the Validity of our Engagements to him by that late Treaty; and it yet remains to be ultimately decided how far that Treaty was legal and warrantable by the Act of the Legislature; but be that as it may, whatever may have been the Culpability of the Government of Bombay in concluding it, if any Regard is to be paid to national Faith, Ragoba has certainly a Right to every Advantage stipulated by it; for, till the contrary was publicly announced, the ancient Constitution of the Company certainly existed with respect to the Powers of India, and the Acts and Obligations of that Presidency became the Acts and Obligations of the Nation.

These Words of Colonel Upton's Instructions plainly acknowledge the Justness of Ragoba's Title, and clearly define the Nature of the Two Parties; Ragonath Row is the Peishwa, or Chief Ruler of the Maratta State, but he was obliged by the Ministerial Party to quit that Capital. It must be remembered that this Party was by no Means a general Association of the most respectable Maratta Chiefs to expel him from the Government for his Crimes or Incapacity, but a partial Combination of a few, who, to gratify their Ambition and Interest, first released him from Imprisonment, raised him to the Government of which he became the rightful Possessor, and then, from the same Motive, entered into a rebellious Confederacy to expel him from that Government, in order to usurp it themselves. To these worthy Characters is the Representative of the King of England to apologize for having assisted their lawful Prince, whose Right to Government his Nation had before in the most solemn Manner recognized, and renewed with him the Treaties and personal Engagements before entered into with his Ancestors. This sacred Character, against whom Rebellion is Death, consents to countenance and acknowledge their Usurpation in open Violation at a solemn Treaty previously entered into by his Nation, in which they engage to assist the rightful Prince in the Recovery of his Dominions from that very Usurpation.

Had the abandoning of Ragoba proceeded from a Detestation of his Crime, a pacific Disposition, or a Sentiment of the Justness of the Ministers to govern, the Equity of the Motives might have apologized for the Infidelity of the Act; but his Actions will effectually contradict every such Supposition, as the Price of our Neutrality is to insist on Part of the very Territories which was the stipulated Reward of our assisting Ragoba, and if this is refused, I am at a Loss to conceive what else he is to do, but contradict the pacific Declarations he set out with by a Denunciation of Hostilities; for surely he was not deputed in so exalted a Character, and with so much Parade and Expence, merely to apologize to the Ministers, and beg of them Salsette and Bassein.

But setting Honour and national Faith aside, I will proceed to the Consideration of the Purposes intended to be effected by Colonel Upton's Embassy.

The Words of his Instructions best define them, "to negociate and conclude a Treaty of Peace between the Maratta Government and the Presidency of Bombay," and "to obtain a Confirmation to the Presidency of the Islands of Salsette and Bassein." These Points he is to consider as indispensable. If I may venture to judge further of the Designs and Wishes of this Government, it is also no inconsiderable Object with them so to accommodate Matters, that after securing to the Company the Territories in Question, they may remain totally neutral and unconcerned in any further Parties or Resolutions which may arise in the Poona Durbar, and not be compelled to draw their Sword in future, but on the just Grounds of defending their own absolute and unquestioned Rights.

If by the Maratta Government, is meant the Ministerial Confederacy, there is no Doubt that Colonel Upton will succeed in being able to conclude a Treaty of Peace with them; Nine Men embarked in a rebellious Design to usurp a Government from its rightful Owner, will no Doubt, in the desperate Situation they were reduced to,

gladly

gladly embrace the proffered Friendship of the British Nation; but I cannot conceive how the usurped Power of these Nine Men, disavowed and abandoned by the most respectable Chiefs of the Maratta Empire, can well be deemed the Maratta Government, or a temporary Agreement with them a Treaty of Peace with it.

However pacifically inclined the Ministers may be for the present, I much doubt whether they will accede to the Conditions which are to be stipulated on the mere Footing of a Neutrality. Should any of the Maratta Chiefs have joined Ragoba, they certainly will insist on effectual Aid from us. Should he be deserted by all, and a Fugitive in one of our Garrisons, they will hardly consent to the Cessions to be insisted on by Colonel Upton; judging by themselves, they will give no Credit to his Menaces. The precipitate Manner in which the Apprehensions of this Government led them to direct the abandoning of Ragoba; the Excuses sent from hence; the Apologies to be made by our Ambassador; all bespeak us in their Opinion under the Influence of some secret Fear, or conscious Weakness. They know that with the Forces of Bombay alone, it is impossible to attack them with any Probability of Success. They are also sensible that unless we can retain the peaceable and undisturbed Possession of them, the Territories we demand will by no Means counterbalance the Losses we shall sustain by the Stoppage of Trade, the Ruin of our Merchants, and the Depredations it is in their Power to commit.

But whatever temporary Calm our present Accommodation may produce, many Circumstances concur to warrant the justest Apprehensions, that we must infallibly in the End either cede the Possessions we may now acquire, or have a much more difficult Task on our Hands, than the Re-establishment of Ragoba. I will suppose for a Moment every Thing adjusted with the Confederates, and Ragoba quietly acquiescing for the present in whatever we may choose to stipulate for him. To make this Tranquillity durable, we must be assured that his Resignation and Content will be lasting.—— The Character of Ragoba is rather propitious to such a Hope; he is something advanced in Years, and the various Turns of Fortune that he has experienced, has given his Mind so religious a Bent, that it would better suit his Disposition to be the ministring Brahmin of a Pagoda, than Conductor of the Maratta Empire.—It is not however in human Nature for him patiently and quietly to submit to the Usurpation of a Set of Men, whose only Views are to raise themselves on the Ruins of his Family: Were we free from Apprehensions on his Part, the Character of his Son Imrut Row, must preclude all Hopes of Tranquillity; he is a Youth of great natural Parts, and of an active, daring, and aspiring Genius: A firm Union of the Confederacy might perhaps enable them to withstand their Attempts, but it is composed of Men of such jarring Interests, that when they are not in Arms against Ragoba, they must naturally disunite. Their common Danger, when they had every Thing to fear from our Junction, could hardly contain their mutual Mistrusts and Jealousies of each other's Views, from dissolving their League. They consist of Rajahpute Chiefs and Brahmin Ministers; on a Settlement, the Rajahputes will be demanding Jaghiers; this the Ministers will be averse to, as such Grants diminish the Revenues, which is the principal Object of their Aims. Exclusive of this, it is well known that a rancorous and deadly Hatred has long subsisted between Sackaram Bapoo, and Nanah Furneeze, who are the Two leading Ministers in the Confederacy, and the latter is the Man of most Influence and Ability. Ragoba is generally esteemed by all Men for his charitable and unoppressive Character, and if he only quietly waits the Disunion of the Confederates, the Wishes of all Parties, aided by the Influence of those who have shewn themselves throughout particularly attached to him, must in the End I think infallibly restore him to the Government.—In such Case, it is easy to judge what Probability there is of our peaceably retaining the Cessions of the Ministers.

A Circumstance occurs to me, in considering the Plan of Colonel Upton's Negociation, which is not unworthy of Attention. It most unfortunately happens, that every one of the Districts which he is instructed to demand, are, from the Nature of their Tenure, either totally out of the Power of the Ministers to grant, or it would be totally inconsistent with common Justice for us to accept them at their Hands. The Nature of the Guicawar Tenure has been sufficiently explained, not to perceive at one Glance that the Poona Durbar cannot grant to us the Moiety of the Revenues of Broach, which is the sole Right and Property of the Guicawar. Salsette and Bassein are by no Means a Part of the Maratta Dominions; they are the Family Property of the Paishwa, granted by the Raja Shaa to his Predecessor Badjerow Ballajee; they

belong

belong as much to Ragoba in Quality of Heir, as the Districts of Calcutta do to the Company; from him alone can we with Justice and Propriety receive them: Or, from the indisputed Heir of the Paishwa Family, admitting for a Moment that the Infant Madoo Row Narrain could be clearly deemed so, can we with Justice accept his Patrimony from the Ministers, who have been accessary to the Murder of his Father; and expelled his Uncle from the Government, merely because they make his Name a Sanction to their Usurpations?

Such being the Reflections which occurred to me on the present Plan laid down to Colonel Upton, as the Object of his Negociation, I deemed it incumbent on me, as your Servant, and a Member of the British Commonwealth, ardently to embrace any Opportunity that might offer, to lead back this Government as far into what appeared to me the right Road of good Policy, as Circumstances would admit: And Ragoba having addressed them a Letter, regarding his Claim by the late Treaty concluded with him, I imagined they might again become the Subject of their Deliberations; I therefore under the 18th Instant proposed another Plan of Accommodation, which you will please to observe is a Medium between his conditional Re-establishment, and the Confirmation of the Authority of the Ministers.

Copy of a Letter from William Tayler to the Honourable the Court of Directors.

Though so many Days have elapsed since the Delivery of the above Plan, I have not yet been honoured with a Reply to it; and begin therefore to be apprehensive, should it even be approved, lest any Turn of Affairs may have produced an Accommodation, and Colonel Upton find Ragoba in the Government; how in such Case he could act with Propriety, and effect the Purposes enjoined him, I confess myself at a Loss to discover. The Arguments and Apologies stated in his Instructions can on no Account be enforced to Ragoba, who, on the Application for Salsette and Bassein, would naturally tell him, That he had been deceived by the Government of Bombay into a Treaty for their Assistance, and that depending on our good Faith, he had preferred our Nation to every other Resource; and that for the first Time it had been sported with, as the Government of Bombay must have well known their subordinate State: That therefore, he had only to express his Concern at the Delays having forced him into other Measures, and to form other Connections; and appealed to the Equity of our Nation, whether we ought not to restore Salsette, being his Family Inheritance, and all the Territories he had ceded to us, and aided us to get Possession of.

I have the Honour to be, with the greatest Respect,
Honourable Sirs,
Your most faithful and most
obedient humble Servant,
W. Tayler.

Calcutta,
26th November, 1775.

Copy of a Letter from William Tayler to the Honourable the Court of Directors for Affairs of the United Company of Merchants of England, trading to the East-Indies.

Honourable Sirs,

Since closing my Address to you of the 26th, I have received a Letter from Lieutenant Colonel Keating, dated the 29th Ultimo, containing some Advices, very important in the present Situation of your Affairs with the Marattas.

See Appendix 88.

As any Delay might render it uncertain whether this would reach the Salisbury, I take the Liberty to enclose you a Copy of my Address of this Date to the Governor General and Council on this Occasion, which will fully inform you of the Nature of these Advices, and of my Sentiments regarding them.

I cannot help here again lamenting the total Inefficacy of my late Representations to this Government with respect to our Engagements with Ragoba; for, in the delicate and critical Situation to which their Conduct has brought you, it seems to me very probable, that his Re-establishment without our Aid may ensue; in which Case we must

must probably for ever relinquish all Hopes of compassing your Views in the West of India.

I have the Honour to be, with the greatest Respect,
Honourable Sirs,
Your most faithful,
and most devoted Servant,
Wm. Tayler.

Calcutta,
29th November, 1775.

Copy of a Letter from William Tayler to the Honourable the Court of Directors for Affairs of the United Company of Merchants of England trading to the East Indies.

Honourable Sirs,

I have this Instant received the accompanying Letter from the Honourable the Governor General and Council, in Answer to mine of Yesterday; and as their Determination on this Point must be interesting to you, I send it by a Boat express, in Hopes it may yet overtake the Salisbury. Appendix 88.

The Remarks and Conjectures contained in my Letter to them of Yesterday, are sufficient Comments on their Resolutions not to alter their Conduct with the Alteration of Circumstances, as they point out all the evil Consequences that are likely to ensue.

I am, with the greatest Respect,
Honourable Sirs,
Your most faithful,
And most devoted Servant,
W. Tayler.

Calcutta,
30th November, 1775.

Copy of a Letter from William Tayler to the Honourable the Court of Directors for Affairs of the United Company of Merchants of England, trading to the East Indies.

Honourable Sirs,

By the Ship Hillsborough I now do myself the Honour to transmit you Duplicates of my several Addresses of the 26th, 29th, and 30th of November last.

I am sorry it is not in my Power to communicate any certain Accounts of the State of your Affairs in the West of India, for, notwithstanding that by their Letter to me of the 25th November, the Honourable the Governor General and Council deemed Colonel Upton to be near the End of his Journey, yet no Intelligence has been received of his Arrival at Poona. The Letter which has been lately sent from the Ministerial Party to this Government, has no doubt been duly forwarded in the public Advices by this Ship. I understand it contains a Menace to proceed to Hostilities, unless this Government comes to an immediate Accommodation of Matters, a preliminary Step to which, I learn, is to be the Restoration of Salsette, and the other Places ceded to us by the Paishwa, of which we have Possession. This I am inclined to think is rather a Bravado than their real Intentions; for, by Advice I received Yesterday from Gepal Row, the Brother-in-law of Ragoba, the Intelligence communicated to me by Colonel Keating, as mentioned in my Address to you of the 29th November last, is rather confirmed, with the additional Circumstance of the Paishwa's Army having given the Ministerialists a signal Defeat near the Pass of Soingur, which leads from Guzerat into the Districts of the Poona Durbar; but of this, though related on seeming Grounds of Authority, I am afraid to speak with Certainty, as I have not received Advices of this or any other Matter from the Government of Bombay; and it seems reasonable to expect, that had this Intelligence been well founded, they would doubtless have informed me of it.

Upon the Whole, I cannot help again lamenting that the Governor General and Council would neither permit the Government of Bombay to proceed in their Engagements with Ragoba, nor entrust to them the Accommodations they had determined on. In either Case I can confidently assert, that at this Hour you would have been in quiet Possession of an increased Revenue of 22 Lacks, with all the Advantages set forth in my First Address to this Government. Affairs would have been in Tranquillity in the West of India, and your commercial Concerns proceeding in their usual Channel; instead of which you may perceive the Uncertainty of your political Situation there, and the Probability there is of being either farther embroiled in military Operations,

Operations, or making Concessions equally inconsistent with your Interest and Honour. I learn by private Accounts, that the Vend of your Woollens and Staples is totally at a Stand, as (though contrary to their Agreement with the Government of Bombay) the Ministerialists do not suffer the Merchants to come down to trade: At any rate this Season bids fair to be a very unfortunate one for the private Merchants, from this Cause. And should the next produce another Scene of Hostilities, as this Effect would of course continue, I am afraid many new opulent Merchants of Bombay and Surat would be reduced to infinite Distress, besides a very considerable Loss that must ensue to you by the Failure of Customs.

I have the Honour to be, with the most profound Respect,
Honourable Sirs,
Your most faithful and
Most devoted Servant,
W. Tayler.

Calcutta,
20th January, 1776.

Extract of Bombay Secret Consultations, the 17th February, 1776.

PRESENT,

The Honourable William Hornby, Esquire, President and Governor,
The Honourable Dan. Draper, Esquire,
Thomas Mostyn,
Robt. Garden,
Andrew Ramsay,
Mr. Fletcher indisposed, Mr. Tayler at Bengal.

A Country Vessel being bound to Bushire, an Address was prepared to the Honourable Company, to be forwarded over Land as follows:

To the Honourable the Court of Directors for Affairs of the United Company of Merchants of England trading to the East Indies.

Honourable Gentlemen,

A Country Vessel proceeding to Bushire at a very short Notice, we can only advise your Honours of a few interesting Particulars. Colonel Upton arrived at Poona Dhur on the 30th December; and we wish we were able to give you a more satisfactory Account of his Proceedings; he is very reserved in his Advices to us, and has only acquainted us at Times with what Turn his Negociation was likely to take. In the Beginning of January he seemed to think that the Treaty would be concluded in a few Days; and on the 1st and 6th of this Month he advised us, that from Conversations he had held with the Ministers, it was very probable the Treaty would not take Place at all. Under the 10th he says, that Appearances are still against it, but proceeds to ask us, what Privileges we would wish to have stipulated in case Factories should be established at Bassein and Jamboofeer, supposing that the Cessions in the Guzerat Province should not be retained by the Company?

We know not what Circumstances may have occasioned these Resolutions in Colonel Upton's Negociations, but we begin to be apprehensive that he will conclude a Treaty upon Terms very injurious to the Company. We however immediately represented that your Interest required he should insist upon the Cessions made by the Treaty being confirmed: That he could not recede from his Demand for Bassein consistently with his Instructions; and that a Factory either at that Place or Jamboofeer would be attended with no Manner of Benefit to your Honours. If this Representation could have no Effect, we can only lament that the Time when the Existence of this Presidency is at Stake, we are not at Liberty to pursue our own Measures for its Welfare.

It has been our Study, ever since Colonel Upton's Arrival at Poona, to give him all the Information in our Power, so as to enable him to form the most competent Judgment of your political and commercial Interests at this Presidency; for, however inconsistent we may deem the Conduct of the Governor General and Council, in intrusting this Negociation to a Lieutenant Colonel entirely unacquainted with either, while a Member of our Board is expressly appointed by you Resident at the Maratta Durbar; yet it becomes our Duty to use every Precaution to prevent your Interest from suffering by this Conduct,

Conduct, which we are well satisfied it would do, were we, from a false Punctilio, to with-hold from Colonel Upton that useful and necessary Information which our Vicinity to Poona, our constant Intercourse and frequent Negociations with the Marattas, enable us to give him; and we cannot doubt, when your Honours are fully apprized of our Proceedings upon this Occasion, that you will not only do us the Justice to testify your Approbation thereof, but that you will likewise favour us with your Sentiments at large upon the Conduct of the Governor General and Council, in wresting out of our Hands the Management of a Treaty so immediately connected with this Presidency, and which must relate almost to its particular Interests.

Ragoba's Army and our Forces are now encamped near Surat. We thought it absolutely necessary to continue them with him until the Treaty is concluded, and Colonel Upton is convinced of the good Effects of this Measure. If, however, he suffers the Ministers to amuse him much longer, we are very apprehensive Ragoba's Distress for Money, which is become very great by this long Inaction, may cause his Friends to desert him, and his Army to disband for Want of Pay, which the Ministers would not fail to take Advantage of. We have particularly cautioned Colonel Upton on this Head, and strongly recommended to him to procure consistent and honourable Terms for Ragoba, without which we are assured the Peace cannot be permanent.

The Governor General and Council have authorized us to return the Cessions made by Futty Sing, being the Guicawar Share of the Broach Revenues of the District of Coral, Vercow, and Chickley, until a definitive Treaty may be concluded with the Ministers; but we have little Reason to hope they will depart from their original Plan for terminating our Differences with the Marattas.

Mr. Tayler having addressed your Honours very fully by the Salisbury, respecting the Negociations at Calcutta, it is not necessary for us to say any Thing further on the Subject.

We remain, with the utmost Respect,
Honourable Gentlemen,
Your most faithful and
Obedient Servants,
W. Hornby,
&c. Council.

Bombay Castle,
17th Feb. 1776.

APPENDIX, N° 90.

Extract of Secret Letter from Bengal, dated the 5th August 1775.

Par. 10. SOON after the Date of our last Dispatch, we received Information on private Authority, from various Channels, of a Treaty having been concluded between the Presidency of Bombay and Ragoba, the Competitor for the Peshwaship of the Maratta State at Poona; and that in Consequence their Troops had taken the Field to his Assistance. So extraordinary a Step on their Part, without any previous Communication with us, could not fail to alarm us; and we were preparing, on the Faith of that Intelligence, to write them, testifying our general Disapprobation of the Measures, when we received Advices from them, dated the 31st March, which fully confirmed the former Reports, and conveyed to us a Copy of the Treaty which they had actually concluded with Ragoba.

11. After maturely weighing these Advices, we were more confirmed in our former Opinion of the Danger and Impropriety of this Alliance. It appeared to us, that they had undertaken to conquer the whole Maratta Empire for a Man who is incapable of affording any effectual Assistance in it. The Plan which they had adopted for the Execution, seemed to aim at no decisive Conquest, but to portend an indefinite Scene of Troubles, without an adequate Force, without Money, or certain Resources for extricating them out of it; nor do we find they have any Plea of Injuries sustained from the Party which they have made their Enemy, or of their Obligation to defend him whose Cause they have espoused.

12. We therefore solemnly protested against the President and Council of Bombay, for all the Consequences of this Alliance, and peremptorily required them to withdraw the Company's Forces into their own Garrison, in whatsoever State their Affairs might be, unless the Safety of the Troops should be endangered by an instant Retreat. We also remarked to them the Indecency and Illegality of their Conduct in concluding an offensive Treaty, and engaging in actual War, without ever consulting our Opinion, or paying the smallest Regard to the Authority vested in us by a solemn Act of the Legislature, to superintend and controul the political Affairs of all India. We told them, that for the past we would content ourselves with leaving with them the Responsibility of their own Actions; but for the future, in Cases of the like Inattention, we would not fail to exercise the Power vested in us by the Act of Parliament for the Support of our Authority.

13. In order to render more effective our Resolutions on the Subject of these Measures, we agreed to depute a proper Person to Poona, to treat with the Rulers of that State for a lasting Peace between them and us; and that the Basis of this Treaty should be an instant Cessation of Arms, and a Confirmation to the Company of the Possession of the Islands of Salsette and Bassein. The Person we have chosen for this Commission is Lieutenant Colonel J. Upton, who is actually set out from hence on his Way thither, provided with proper Instructions and Credentials; he goes by the Way of Allahabad and Calpey, at which last Place he is ordered to wait for the necessary Passports from Sukeram Baboo, the ruling Minister at Poona, who has been written to for that Purpose, and previously acquainted with the Motives of his Journey. We have duly advised the Presidency of Bombay of this Appointment.

14. Since the Receipt of the first Advices of the Maratta War, we have had various Accounts of the different Operations in it: By the latest it would appear that Ragoba is in a prosperous Way, although he has met some Checks and Disappointments, particularly in an Engagement with the Enemy on the 18th of May last, in which a considerable Detachment of our Troops were surrounded and almost cut off; they suffered a Loss of no fewer than Six killed and Five wounded out of Fourteen European Officers who served in the Detachment. Seeing however a Possibility of Ragoba's being established at Poona before Colonel Upton's Arrival there, we thought it proper to add to his Instructions a Power of treating in that Case with that Chief, on the same Terms which we had prescribed for his Negociations with the opposite Party.

15. We have kept you regularly advised in the other Department, of the several Remittances we have made to the Presidency of Bombay. The Treasure we sent by the Seahorse arrived very opportunely for them; but as the new Troubles in which they have involved themselves encreased their Wants, they have made fresh Demands upon us; we have however refused to comply with them, till such Time as we have an Answer to our late Order, and a particular Account of their Operations in Consequence: We also informed them, we were greatly surprized at their Appointment of Mr. Mostyn, as a Deputy to attend Ragoba in the Field, without informing us of the Design and Object of his Commission; and we have directed them to transmit to us a Copy of his Instructions, and to order him to send to us by every Opportunity, successive Intelligence of the State of Ragoba's Affairs. We have further required of them Copies of their Correspondence with Colonel Keating, the Commanding Officer of the Troops in the Field.

Extract of Secret Letter from Bengal, dated 11th September 1775.

Par. 5. The President and Council at Bombay now finding that no Dependence can be placed on the Assistance of Ragoba's Forces, and that the whole Burthen of that extensive War is consequently fallen on the Company, have applied to us and to the Fort Saint George Presidency for a Reinforcement of Men, which they say Ragoba has earnestly solicited for, promising to make over additional Advantages to the Company for the Services of such extraordinary Assistance. They have also requested that we would furnish them with a liberal Supply of Money to carry on their Operations.

6. Having before ordered the Council at Bombay to withdraw their Army from the Service of Ragoba, in whatever Situation their Affairs might be, if it could retreat with Safety; and as Colonel Upton will in all Probability arrive at Poona, and enter upon his Negociations for a Peace with the Maratta State before any Force could be

brought

brought to join the Bombay Troops, even supposing them not to have been withdrawn; we directed the President and Council at Fort Saint George not to comply with the Request of the Bombay Presidency for a Reinforcement, and repeated our Orders to the latter to recal their Army immediately to their own Garrisons, and to confine their Views to the Protection of the Company's Possessions, including Salsette and that Moiety of the Revenues of Broach, lately held by the Guicawars, which Futty Sing, who by the latest Advices from Bombay appeared to have gone over to Ragoba from the Ministerial Party, had ceded to the Company. For a more particular Account of these Matters, we beg Leave to refer you to the Copy of our Consultation enclosed.

7. We have the greatest Reason to hope that Colonel Upton will find the Ministry at Poona inclined to listen to his Proposals for an Accommodation, and that he will be able to effect an honourable and advantageous Peace for the Company, as the Chief of the Maratta State at Poona has written to the Nabob of Arcot, to beg his Intercession with the English to desist from any further Hostilities, or continuing to afford any Succour to his Uncle Ragonaut Row.

8. You will see by our Proceedings, that the Governor General, who had hitherto concurred with the other Members of the Board in disapproving the Conduct of the Presidency of Bombay, and in ordering them to withdraw their Troops, as likewise in the Measure of the Negociation, which we are about to establish with the ruling Power at Poona, judged proper on this Occasion to depart from the System that he had before pursued, by giving it as his Opinion, that the Requisition of that Presidency for Troops and Money should be complied with. As his Reason for having adopted these Sentiments cannot well be abridged without altering the Force of them, we must beg Leave to refer you to the Consultations, not only for them, but the Opinions of the other Members of the Board in Reply to them.

9. We have agreed to extend our Supply of Money to the Bombay Presidency in the Course of this Year, commencing from the 1st May last, to 20 Lacks of Rupees, including a small Amount for which their Bills have been accepted since that Date, and we have authorized them to continue drawing on us for that Sum at the most reasonable Exchange in their Power.

Extract of Secret Letter from Bengal, dated 20th November, 1775.

Par. 21. The President and Council of Bombay on the Receipt of our Letter, which totally disapproved their Conduct in the Part which they had taken in Ragoba's Cause, deputed Mr. Tayler, One of their Members, to this Government, to represent in the fullest Manner their Motives for what they had done, and to exculpate their Actions in our Opinion; they advised us at the same Time, that Futty Sing, the Soubadhar of the Province of Guzerat, had come over to Ragoba's Party, and engaged to supply him with the seasonable Relief of 26 Lacks of Rupees, and that he had also made over in Perpetuity to the Company, the Guicawar Share in the Revenues of the Town and Purgunnah of Broach, besides the Districts of Coriaul, Chickley and Veriow.

22. Mr. Tayler on his Arrival was introduced to the Board, and delivered a long State of the Maratta Government and Connections, together with the Reasons of the President and Council of Bombay for having entered into an offensive Treaty with Ragoba, in the fullest Manner; we also put various Interrogatories to him respecting these Matters; all which will appear at full Length in our Proceedings, referred to in the Margin, and will throw a considerable Light upon the Subject.

23. We were by no Means induced to change the Sentiments we had formed of the Precipitancy and Impropriety in the Conduct of the President and Council of Bombay in the Measures they had adopted; we have therefore made no other Alterations in our former Orders to that Presidency for recalling their Troops within their own Garrisons, and confining their Operations to the Defence of the Company's Possessions, including the newly conquered Island of Salsette, than to extend that Line of Defence to the Countries lately ceded by Futty Sing to the Company.

24. Mr. Tayler conceiving that the President and Council of Bombay would suffer great Indignity by being wholly excluded from any Share in the Negociation with the Maratta Government, for a definitive Treaty of Peace; and as from their Vicinity and frequent Communication with that People, they had better Opportunities of becoming acquainted with the Views and Interests of the different Persons in Poona Durbar than

 Colonel

Colonel Upton, that they would therefore be the most proper Persons to conduct and execute the Business intrusted to him. We replied, with Assurances of our Wish to support the Reputation and Credit of their Government; and that, however we might be influenced by a Confidence in their Integrity, Abilities, and strict Desire to fulfil our Intentions, we could not, consistently with the Resolutions and Orders which we had published and signified to the Ministry at Poona, or with the Dignity of this Government, which must be affected by their Repeal, alter the Appointment of Colonel Upton, or recal him from the Duty on which he was engaged.

25. As there appeared to us a Possibility that Ragoba, after the English Forces were withdrawn from him, might, by unforeseen Accidents, be reduced again to apply for Protection to the President and Council of Bombay, we thought it right to provide for such an Event; and accordingly gave Directions that an Asylum might in such Case be granted to himself and Attendants.

26. We have heard from Colonel Upton, in a Letter dated the 26th October at Calpee; he then expected to reach Poona in Five Weeks. The Ministers at Poona are waiting with great Impatience for his Arrival, professing themselves as solicitous to forward the Peace on their Part as we can desire; at least it appears so from all the Letters and Declarations of Succaram Baboo and Bissarjee Pundit, the Ministers at Poona, to this Government. A total Cessation of Arms took Place immediately on the Knowledge of our Sentiments and Intentions. However, as Colonel Upton in his Letters to us mentioned a Report that a large Body of Marattas were in Motion from Brampee towards Calpee, we have directed him to acquaint Succaram Baboo, that the Pacification shall be rigidly observed on our Side, and that we expect the same good Faith from him; but that if he should put his Troops in Motion to commence Hostilities anew, we should consider ourselves no longer bound to keep upon any Terms with him.

27. The Nabob of the Carnatic hearing of our Intention to depute Colonel Upton on this Service, wrote to us through the Channel of Sir Edward Hughes, desiring, as the particular Friend and Ally of the English, to be included in any Treaty which might be formed with the Maratta Government. We accordingly directed Colonel Upton to insist on an Article in Favour of the Nabob, declaring, the long Duration of our Union with him; that it is supported by the strongest Ties of Friendship and Alliance; that the Company had ever considered his Enemies as their Enemies, and his Friends as their Friends: And we further directed him to require, that all the Maratta Chiefs should nominally and individually sign their Names to and execute the Treaty.

28. As the Nabob of the Carnatic also acquainted us, that he had many Articles to propose for the Treaty, wherein the Interests of his Government were deeply concerned, we requested that he would transmit them to us, and communicate them at the same Time to the President and Council at Fort Saint George, as the Company's Interest at that Place was so closely connected with his, that we might also have the Advantage of receiving the Sentiments of that Presidency upon them. We have since desired Permission to employ Mr. William Chambers, the Persian Interpreter at Fort Saint George, to proceed to Poona on his Part, and assist Colonel Upton in negociating such Articles as it might be necessary to propose for his Benefit. We have approved of his deputing Mr. Chambers, if the President and Council shall see no Objection to it; but we have positively forbid him from interfering in any Manner in the Negociations of Colonel Upton, or from proposing any Thing for the Treaty but through him. Colonel Upton has been ordered to attend to his Representations, as far as may be consistent with the Tenor of our Instructions to him.

APPEN-

APPENDIX, N° 91.

Extract of Bengal Secret Consultations, the 11th December 1775.

PRESENT,

The Honourable Warren Hastings, Governor General, President,
Lieutenant General John Clavering,
The Honourable George Monson,
Richard Barwell, } Esquires.
Philip Francis, }

RECIEVED the following Letters and Inclosures from Sir Edward Hughes:

Coventry, in Madras Road.

Sir, and Gentlemen,

I am honoured with yours of the 16th Day of August, acknowledging the Receipt of my Letters, dated the 5th, 13th, and 19th Days of July, and inclosing one from the Governor General, in Answer to the Nabob of the Carnatic, which at your Request I returned to his Highness; and I believe the inclosed from him, which I transmit at his particular Desire, is an Acknowledgment of the Receipt of that Answer, and of the perfect Satisfaction he found in the Perusal thereof.

On the 3d of this Instant His Majesty's Ship the Coventry joined me here from Europe, and on the 11th the Sea Horse arrived here again from the Coast of Malabar, where Captain Farmer (as well as Governor Hornby) informs me there was no Occasion for his Presence at the Time he left Bombay, the latter End of August. If there should be hereafter any Protection requisite for the Trade, as I mean to sail from hence on the 15th of the next Month for that Coast, with the Salisbury and the Two Ships abovementioned, where I am to be joined by the Dolphin and Swallow (the former in her Way to England) in order to refit at Bombay; whatever may then be in my Power, shall be done for the Service of the Company, and Safety of the Trade there; and I shall be particularly happy in receiving from you, Sir, and Gentlemen, any Commands you may wish to honour me with on those Heads, or relative to the Treaty now coming forward between your Board and the Ministerial Party of Poona.

I am, &c.
(Signed) Edward Hughes.

Madras, the 15th October 1775.

Sir, and Gentlemen,

I beg Leave to inclose you some Papers of Intelligence copied from what Captain Farmer delivered to me on his Return from Bombay, in his Majesty's Ship the Sea-Horse.

I have the Honour to be,
Sir, and Gentlemen,
Your most obedient humble Servant,
(Signed) Edward Hughes.

Warren Hastings, Esquire, Governor
General, &c. Council.

Sir,

Pursuant to the Orders I received from you, the following is what I have been able to learn concerning the East India Company's Affairs in the Gulph of Persia.

About Fourteen Years ago, Messrs. Shaw and Garden, the Company's Factors at Bussorah, sold a Quantity of Woollens on Trust to one Hodjee Esoof, a Turkish Merchant, who depending on his Influence with the Government, constantly evaded, and at last

last refused Payment for them: Whilst this Debt was depending, the Bashaw of Bagdad came down to Bussorah with an Army, in order to attack a certain Arab Shaik, called the Chaub, who with his Vessels and Forces threatened Bussorah. The Company's Chief there thinking this a good Opportunity, applied to the Bashaw for his Interference in procuring the Payment of Hodjee Esoof's Debt, which he promised, provided they would assist him with one of the Company's Cruisers to attack the Chaubs Vessels. The Company had till then appeared merely as Merchants at Bussorah, and the Attack of this Shaik was their first Deviation from that Character. The Chaub by their Assistance was driven away, and the Bashaw returned to Bagdad. The Chaub, watching his Opportunity in Revenge for acting against him, seized Two Merchant Vessels: This Hostility rendered the Trade to Bussorah unsafe, till he was reduced. Expensive Expeditions were fitted out for this Purpose, and after various Success on the Company's Side, the Chaub threw himself on the Protection of Kherim Khan, the present Regent of Persia, who is married to one of the Royal Family; and it is said keeps the right Heir to the Crown of Persia in Confinement.

Kherim Khan, after overcoming his Opponents, and quietly establishing himself at Sehyrash, it seems wished as much as was in his Power to restore the Trade of Persia; and accordingly, in the Year 1763 granted the English Permission to establish a Factory, with certain Privileges, at Bushire, a Place conveniently situated for the inland Trade with Persia. Here they resided without the least Molestation or Apprehension of it till the above Period, when an Envoy was sent to the Khan, to acquaint him that the Chaub was their Enemy, and that they rather hoped he would assist them than shew him any Countenance; but his Negociations being ineffectual, and from the Khan's Conduct the Safety of the Company's Property at Bushire seeming but doubtful, the Factory was withdrawn in 1769; and the Company, tired of the Charges attending on several Expeditions to the Gulf, directed that it should not be resettled, but that they should limit their Views and Settlements in Persia entirely to Bussorah. I could not find that the Company ever were at open Hostilities with the Khan. But the Object of Variance between them being long since removed by the Death of that Chaub, (although there is still a Chaub, who pirates as the former did, and has joined his Forces to Kherim Khan's against Bussorah) he has frequently pressed the Company to return to Bushire, offering every Advantage that they could ask; but the Company's Orders are positive against it. The Khan constantly resides at Sehyrash, which he has made the Capital of Persia; and from the Accounts I have been able to gather from the best informed Armenians, there is every Reason to suppose he would wish to be in Amity with the Company, as they all agree in allowing, that he seems by every Measure to wish the Re-establishment of Trade in his Dominions. He had however, and openly professed, a personal Enmity to Mr. Moore, the Agent at Bussorah, who was always against the Settlement, as it did not answer to the Company before, and whose Interest it certainly was not to effect a Reconciliation with the Khan, because, if the Factory at Bushire should be resettled, it might prevent Ships from going up to Bussorah, to dispose of the Cargoes; in every one of which he has a certain Profit, by one Means or another.

The Khan's Officers are in Possession of the Island of Carrack, and have a Fleet of Gallivats, which likewise pirate in the Gulf; but whether with or without the Khan's Consent is uncertain. It was Part of this Fleet that took one of the Company's Schooners, with Two Civil Servants on board, in 1773, when the Factors were obliged to fly from Bussorah, on Account of the Plague; they were not at Hostilities with the Khan, and he disavowed any Orders proceeding from him for this Action, but still retained the Two Gentlemen at Sehyrash, where he treated them very well. His Reason for detaining them was, that their Release might be a weighty Inducement for the Company to settle again at Bushire.

Mr. Garden was sent from Bombay, to endeavour to get these Gentlemen clear; upon his Application to the Khan, he released them, and promised to return the Schooner they were taken in; which however was not done at our Departure.

The Factory was in April last once more established at Bushire, and by what I could learn, it will never pay the Expence the Company must be at in keeping Servants there, as it appears to be a very poor Place, not being able to sell during our Stay there but very few of their Woollen Cloths; the rest came away under our Convoy, and which is the only Advantage the Company can expect from it: Whereas, from Bussorah they dispose of the chief of their Woollens to Merchants, that transported them to Bagdad, and all that Country which trade with the Bengal Piece-goods, and all the other Parts of India, will

will be entirely lost should Bussorah fall into the Hands of the Persians. The Agent of Bussorah is now upon an amicable Footing with Kherim Khan, but says, that he knows by long Experience that the Persians are a People not to be depended upon; for Instance, their taking one of the Company's Vessels, and detaining Two of their Servants at a Time of profound Peace; and that the Turks never deceived the English.

The Muskatters are the greatest Maritime Power in the Gulf; they have several square-rigged Vessels, besides one large Ship of 40 Guns, and a Number of Gallivats, with which they generally go to collect the Tribute due to the Prince of Muscat, who is called the Imaum, from certain Countries along the Coast to the Southward of Muscat. The Company has always been at Friendship with the Imaums of Muscat, who earnestly seek it for Two good Reasons; one, that they repair and build all their Vessels at Bombay, and the other, because they know the Company could at any Time, as they are bad Seamen (although the best in the Gulph) easily destroy their Vessels, without which they could not collect their Tribute to the Southward. They were fitting out with all the Expedition they could, and expected to sail in Five Days after our Departure, all their Fleet, which they said would consist of Twenty Sail of square-rigged Vessels, a Number of Gallivats and armed Frankies, amounting in the Whole to about One hundred Sail, with Twenty thousand Land Forces on board them, in order to relieve Bussorah, which in all Probability they will accomplish, if it is not taken before they arrive. They have detained one of Hyder Ally's Vessels that was going to assist the Persians against Bussorah; another of them was cast away on that Coast.

There is a Shaik at Ormus, who I understand has sent some Gallivats to assist Kherim Khan against Bussorah, although he looks upon himself as quite independent of him, as does many other petty Shaiks from thence up the Gulph, that have Gallivats and armed Boats who pirate and seize upon all Boats or Vessels whenever they can overpower them; those that I have mentioned are the chief of them.

I am, with all due Respect,
Sir,
Your most obedient
humble Servant,
(Signed) George Farmer.

Sea Horse, Bombay,
the 21st August 1775.

Sir Edward Hughes, Knt.
Commander in Chief of His Majesty's Ships in the East Indies.

Sir,

You mention in one of the Letters I am favoured with from you, that the President and Council of Bombay has wrote you relating the War, but very little or nothing concerning its Cause; give me Leave to inform you what I have been able to learn on that Subject.

The Marattas formerly inhabited the mountainous and interior Parts of India, and their Ministers, Men much famed for their Wisdom, were Bramins. It was contrary to their Cast ever to go to War; but whenever they had Occasion to send out an Army, the Operations were planned by them, and the Command given to Rajepouts or Princes among them of a different Cast. These Men, in Process of Time, feeling the Power they were invested with, one of them resumed the Regal Power from the Bramins, still keeping them as Counsellors of State, and the Head of them as a State Prisoner, who was treated with all the outward Shew of Royalty, and allowed a Revenue suitable to his Rank. He invested this Rajeput with the outward Appellation of the First Minister of State, when in Fact, by being at the Head of the Army, he had the whole Power in himself; however, to this Day this mock Shew subsists.

The Mogul Emperors were never able to conquer the Marattas; for when the Moguls worsted them in the Plains, they immediately retired to the Mountains where they could not follow them, and when recruited, poured down their Troops of Horse in Torrents. At this Time the Army was raised by the Prince, who always commanded them in Person; the Horses were all his own, of which consisted their Armies, and he never suffered any Fortification to be raised in his Dominions, for Fear an Enemy should get Possession of them, and by that Means maintain a Footing in their Country; whereas, if they entered it, as the whole Country was open to their Horse, which was their chief Strength, they would harrass the Enemy so much on every Side, that they were glad to get back

back as soon as they could. Upon the Downfall of the Mogul Empire rose the Maratta Empire. Upon their Divisions the Marattas poured down their vast Armies of Horse, by which Means they soon got Possession of all the open Country adjoining to them, with some few of the fortified Places, and penned those up so close that still adhered to the Moguls, that these Places were glad to pay them Tribute, otherwise they would destroy every Thing within the Reach of their Guns.

This great Extent of Dominion obliged them, like all other overgrown States, to send Governors to rule over the distant Provinces, which Governors by Degrees raised themselves to a Kind of Independence, as had happened to the Moguls before, and was the Ruin of that State. These Governors farmed the Revenues of the Province at a certain Price, and were likewise obliged to send to the Assistance of the Prince a stated Number of Horsemen fit for the Field; so that what he could squeeze out of the Ryots or Farmers over and above, was his own. Their continual Extortion upon these poor People soon depopulated the Country, and instead of their Horse, which formerly belonged to the Prince, they now contract with the chief Men of the Country for a certain Sum of Money, to bring such a Number of Horsemen fit for Action into the Field. These great Men agree with the common Men under them, they finding their own Horses, for as much less than what is allowed them as they can, so that the common Men's whole Fortunes consist in their Horses and Arms, as they are obliged to find another Horse if any Thing happens to the one they ride. I leave you to judge, Sir, thus circumstanced, whether it is not reasonable to think that they will avoid as much as possible coming to Action, especially against a regular Army, and a good Train of Artillery. Having given you the Outlines of what I have been able to get any Insight into concerning this People, I now come to inform you of what is said to be the Cause of the present War between the Company and them.

Ragoba's elder Brother governed those extensive Territories with great Prudence and Strictness, insomuch that I was well assured that you may leave all your Property in the Middle of the Highway, without any one's daring to meddle with it, let it lay there ever so long. To bring them to this, he was obliged to destroy whole Districts of Banditti, which struck such a Terror into others, that it stopped all pilfering of that Nature, although the great Men still kept grinding the Ryots as before.

At his Death he left Two Sons, the eldest of which reigned some Years after him with Reputation, and died about the Age of Twenty-five Years. Suspecting that his Uncle Ragoba was entering into some Cabals against him, he shut him up a close Prisoner, where he was at the Time of his Death. His Brother was then seated on the Throne, a young Man about Sixteen or Seventeen. At this Juncture Ragoba's Party, not thinking themselves or him well used, gathered to a Head, and attacked the Prince; he run for Protection to the Prison where his Uncle was confined, who took him in his Arms and promised his Protection: The Rebels followed, and threatened that they would kill them both if he did not immediately let him go, which he did, and they directly put him to Death. The Nephew left a Wife that proved to be with Child: Ragoba's Party placed him in the supreme Command; and the Ministers, who are chiefly Bramins, and ruled every Thing in the former Reign, fled, and raised what Troops they could. Ragoba soon found himself straitened for Want of Money, as the Treasury was quite empty; however he found Means to raise an Army, and marched after the Ministers. About this Time the Queen, who they had with them, was brought to Bed of a Son, that is now living, which, with the Odium he lay under as being thought accessary to his Nephew's Death, and the Want of Money to pay his Troops, occasioned the Desertion of them; so that without ever striking any effectual Stroke against the Ministers, after various Incidents which happened to him, he was obliged with only a few Followers to make the best of his Way to Surat, from whence he applied to the Government of Bombay to assist him in regaining the Possession of Poona, the Capital of the Maratta Dominions; which, as soon as he quitted, the Ministerial Army returned to and proclaimed the young Prince, whose Mother, an intriguing artful Woman, well supports the Pretensions of her Son.

Ragoba does not dispute his Right to reign, only alledges that he has the sole Right to be Regent during his Minority. What he would do had he him in his Power, is hard to say.

Just at this Time the Governor and Council of Bombay, sent some Forces, and took Sallette from the Marattas, under Pretence that the Portugueze, who had a large Armament at Goa, were going to attack it; and should they succeed, it was more than probable they should never have the same Opportunity of gaining it to Bombay, as undoubtedly

edly it is of the greatest Utility to it; but the Pretence for taking it cannot be justified according to our Notion of War and Peace. To support what they had done, considering the Divisions among the Marattas, they thought it right to join Ragoba, who promised them Chart Blank; and I was told, upon his depositing Twelve Lacks of Rupees, they promised to support him with 1,500 Sepoys and 700 European Troops, until they placed him in Possession of Poona; he paying to the Company a Lack and a Half of Rupees per Month, to defray the Expences of these Troops, and after the War was over, to give up as much Territory as would bring in to the Company a clear Revenue of Twenty Lacks of Rupees per Annum. Upon this Colonel Keating was sent with an Army a good deal short of the stipulated Number to Cambay: Ragoba went with him from Surat. After their Arrival at Cambay, and some Movements there, about Five thousand Horse, which was very far short of what Ragoba expected, joined Keating and him; with this Force they marched towards Brodera, where they made a Treaty with Futty Sing, by which Ragoba was to have received Twenty-six Lacks of Rupees from him for the Nabobship of Guzerat, and Leave to remain in Possession of Brodera (both which had been absolutely promised to Govindrow his elder Brother, who had ever been a faithful Friend of Ragoba's.) The Consequence of this Treaty was, that Govindrow has withdrawn his Forces from them, and refuses to give them any Assistance; on the contrary he does not scruple to say, that Keating and Shaw (Chief of Broach) are infamous Liars, and may meet with the just Reward of their Infidelity when they least expect it. On the other Hand, Futty Sing has passed the Day of Payment with a Tender of Three and a Half Lacks only, in Consequence of which, Keating has ordered out an Eighteen Pounder, a Six, and Two Howitzers, to attack him in Brodera the 11th August. This Advice arrived at Bombay the 23d, as the Proclamation for a Cessation of Arms between them and the Marattas was reading. The Orders for the Cessation came from Bengal, together with a very long Chawbuck or Letter.

Mr. Tayler, one of the Council, and a Member of the Secret Committee, was preparing to sail for that Place, in order to solicit Leave to proceed in the War, until all and every Part of the Treaty with Ragoba is fulfilled. This is no more than they owe to themselves, and indeed to the Interest of their Masters; for however rash and inconsiderate the Commencement of this War may have been, they are evidently gone too far to retreat without the greatest Danger of losing not only Salsette, but Bombay itself. Besides, their Arms on this Side India would ever after be held in Contempt. Only think of their expending so many Men, for they have lost a Number, without coming to any decisive Actions; such Sums of Money, and vast Quantities of Ammunition and Stores, at the Distance of 500 Miles from Bombay, whilst the avowed Object of the War is to be in Possession of Poona, and placing Ragoba on the Peshwash Mamud. Would a Stranger to the Geography of the Country believe then that Poona is only 70 Miles from Bombay, and only one Pass of any Difficulty between them, which is ill fortified and worse defended in Point of Troops? The real Case is, by all that I could any Way discover, that Half of Colonel Keating's Army could march from Bombay to Poona in Four Days, in Spite of all that they have in that Country to oppose him; so that nothing but the Expectation of a great Body of Horse joining Ragoba at Cambay, could induce him to take that round-about Way.

I am, &c.

Bombay, 24th August 1775. (Signed) George Farmer.

Sir Edward Hughes, Knight,
Commander in Chief of his Majesty's Ships in the East Indies.

Warren Hastings,
J. Clavering,
Geo. Monson,
Rich. Barwell,
P. Francis.

APPENDIX, N° 92.

From the Nabob of Arcot; received the 10th December.

I Some Time ago sent you Papers of Intelligence which I had received from the Army of the Nabob Nizam ul Dowlah, from Poona, &c. and I now enclose for your Perusal a News-paper from Poona, dated the 29th Shabaun (25th of October.)

Translation of a Letter from Kishen Row, dated the 29th of Shabaun (25th October) received the 22d of Ramzaun (16th November.)

Nannah Purnaveese is lately arrived at Poona, and having raised near Five Lacks of Rupees, will dispatch it to Hurry Pundit in a Day or Two; Hurry Pundit marched from Berhanpore, crossed the Teetie, and went to Turgaon. Having had an Interview with Sucaram Pundit, and consulted with him, he is on his Return to the Army.

A Detachment of 4 or 5000 Cavalry, which he sent into the Neighbourhood of Soonkur, have reduced Navabpore and all the other Garrisons of Gobind Row Kaunkwar to his Obedience; Amrut Row and Gobind Row, &c. having assembled 5 or 6000 Horse, are arrived in the Neighbourhood of Aklasore. This lays Hurry Pundit under the Necessity of supporting his Forces in that Part, and prevents his coming to the Presence.

During the Season of the Dussarah, several Persons undertook to satisfy the Forces here, and they will very shortly march from hence.

I formerly wrote you that the Nabob Nizam ul Dowlah was about to confer the Office of Dewan, on Sumsum ul Dowlah; the Particulars are as follows: The Nabob Nizam ul Dowlah at first sent a Message for that Purpose; the Negociators of this Business are, the Wife of the Nabob Shaheed, the Wife of Nizam ul Dowlah, Golum Sieed Khan, Nusseeb Yar Khan, Zabit Jung, &c. but the Mother of Sumsum ul Dowlah will not agree or even hear it mentioned.

Kishan Row Billal and Nannajee Pundit are arrived here. I hear that Kishen Row has concluded a Treaty on the following Terms, with the Nabob Nizam ul Dowlah, " Tha. the Remainder of the Jaghier, amounting to 65 Lacks of Rupees, which was " formerly stipulated, and of which 48 Lacks have been already given, shall now be com" pleted." A List of the Places to be given up in Consequence of this Agreement is preparing in the Dustar; they will probably be surrendered to the said Nabob. Should he come to the Aid of the Poona Ministers in Person, there is no Doubt of their resigning the said Places to him, but if he only sends an Army, I cannot say whether they will be given to him or not. As soon as I can gain any certain Intelligence on this Head, I will transmit it to you.

APPENDIX, N° 93.

Extract of Bengal Secret Consultations, the 8th of January 1776.

READ, the following Letter from Lieutenant Colonel Upton:

Gentlemen,

I was last Night favoured with your Letter of the 20th October. The Translation of the Letter which the Governor General was pleased to write to Succeram Baboo, in Consequence

sequence of my Application, was not inclosed (as you mentioned its being;) it is however of no great Consequence. I am greatly obliged by your having wrote to him.

I was prevented going the Jansi Road by the Gossaines having besieged that Place; and the Country between Jansi and Saugur (the intended Route) being all in Arms, the Raja and Jimmedars against each other, and the Whole of them trying to make themselves independent. I wrote to the Narwar Raja for Permission to travel through his Country, which he granted; but the Independent Rajas, &c. through whose Country I am to pass, made further Application necessary.

I had Permission from them to pass, but it retarded me much. From Narvah I travelled entirely through Ragoba's Country, obliged always to send forward for Permission to go on, the Country every where either in Arms, or ready to be so, or the People shut up in their Forts. I am now in the Country of a Patan, Nabob Fiaz Mahomed Cawn, who grants me a free Passage through his Country; but his People behave sturdily. I have not yet received a Line from Poona. The Sirdars of the different Districts have not been apprized of my travelling through their Country, or know any Thing of my Business. And I am now within 70 Coss of Berhanpore, the Head Quarters of their Army. On the Eugene Road, which you will observe in Jeffery's Map, and which is about Sixty Coss to the Westward of Bopall, they have an Army in Motion of about Fifteen thousand Men, I imagine marching to the Relief of Jansi. Twenty-five of the Nabob Asoph ul Dowlah's Horsemen have joined me; these I take on to Poona, and have wrote to countermand the rest of the Escort provided by the Nabob, which indeed I have repeatedly done since my having left Calpee. It might have appeared that I travelled slow, from not recollecting that at Benares I had to settle the Mode of being supplied with Money to fix my Route, and get proper People to attend me, expecting little or no Assistance from Poona. At Allahabad I was to receive the Nabob's Escort and Cattle to carry the Camp Equipage; from thence I was obliged to travel by Land (not being able to go up the Jumna) and laboured hard to get up the Tents, &c. from Calpee to Hemet Behaudre's Encampment, about 30 Coss; the Country quite laid waste, the People every where in Arms, and the Maratta Pendaries plundering on all Sides; we were obliged therefore to travel very circumspectly. I am now going on from 20 to 25 Miles a Day, over a Country very mountainous, and filled with Rocks and Jungles. I have wrote to Berhanpore, to ask the Sirdar to lay Bearers for me and Captain M'Pherson to Poona. If he complies with my Request I shall not be long getting there.

To the Second Paragraph of your Letter of the 20th October, I shall be very particularly attentive. Trivial Formalities or Punctilios shall never obstruct any Business I may have to transact.

Bopawl, I am, &c.
25th November 1775. (Signed) J. Upton.

Resolved, That the following Letter be written to Colonel Upton;

Sir,

We have received your Letter of the 25th November, dated at Bopawl.

We send you Copies of Letters which we have lately received from Madoo Row Narrain, and from Succeram Baboo, together with our Answer to the latter. We earnestly recommend to you the greatest Dispatch possible in bringing your Negociations to a Conclusion.

Fort William, We are, &c.
8th January 1776.

APPENDIX, N° 94.

From Madho Row; dated the 28th of Ramzaun (22d November); received the 1st January 1776.

ALTHOUGH I have repeatedly written to you, yet a long Space of Time is past without my having had the Pleasure of any Letter in Answer, for which I am very anxious. Several Letters addressed to my Ministers, Siccaram Pundit and Bellajee Pundit, on the Subject of increasing the Friendship between us, have been received, and Answers returned from this Quarter; since which, though a long Time is elapsed, nothing which I desired has been carried into Execution.

The aforementioned Ministers have the firmest Reliance on your Wisdom and Foresight, and have inspired me with the same Sentiments. Your Negligence in this Business is the Subject of the greatest Astonishment. It is the Desire of the said Ministers to establish the strictest Friendship and Connection between the Two States, which appears to them a Matter of mutual Advantage. You have been informed of all Particulars by the Letters already written you from this Quarter; in Consequence of which I have now to request, that you will not give Ear to the Representations of self-interested Persons, but will pursue such Measures as may conduce to the Advancement of our mutual Friendship, and to the settling of the Affairs now before us to our mutual Satisfaction. As I am the Cause of what has happened, I will exert my utmost Endeavours for the Establishment of Peace and Unanimity. Let me be speedily favoured with your Sentiments; for in Consequence of the Length of Time which has elapsed, the Ministers are filled with Uneasiness with regard to the Event of this Business, and are very anxious for an Answer. Any Delay will probably prove the Means of increasing the Troubles. For the rest, you are the Master to act as you think fit.

From Siccaram Pundit, of the same Date; received the 1st January 1776.

I have been favoured with your agreeable Letter, under Date the 28th of Rajub, or 23d of September; in which you inform me of the Departure of Colonel Upton, who being invested with full Power to negociate a Peace between the Two States, will proceed to Poona by the Route of Illahabad and Calpee; and you desire, that I will give Directions to the Foujidars, Gomastahs, &c. that no Objection be made to his Passage with such Things as he has with them, and that they will furnish him with every Kind of Necessary he may stand in Need of. This Letter reached me the 21st of Ramzaun (15th of November) and I perfectly understood the Contents. Agreeable to your Desire, the strictest Orders were dispatched to the Foujidars, Talookdars, &c.

Four Months, my Friend, are passed, since any News has been received of Colonel Upton, and though daily News-papers arrive from that Quarter, there is no Mention of him. This is Matter of great Surprize. In your first Letter you informed me, that you had written in express Terms to the Governors of Bombay and Surat, to recall their Forces from the Alliance of Ragonaut Row, and to cease Hostilities against the Armies of the Government, which they would doubtless comply with; and you desired, that I would forbid the Troops of this Government to commit any Act of Hostility against the English. Placing the utmost Confidence in what you wrote me, I gave Orders accordingly to the Commanders of the Forces for a Cessation of Arms, and informed the said Governors of the Subject of your Letter, to which they returned me an evasive Answer; of this I have already written you. They have not to this Time recalled their Forces from thence, but instead thereof have reduced several Towns in the Neighbourhood of Goujeraut, although the Roads to the several Ports are shut up, yet Ships are sent to collect Stores. This being the Case, the Vessels of this Government oppose and obstruct them in their Passage to and fro; this you may have heard from Report. The Sirdars of this Government have Lacks of Men under their Command, and are filled with Bravery: How long are they to remain idle Spectators of the greatest Losses? They will now set about recovering the Towns which have been taken from them. Did the said Governors pay any Attention to your Orders, they would without Hesitation give up all the conquered Towns. If they retain them, no Blame can be thrown on the Sirdars.

From the Fame of the good Faith of the English Nation, I made no Doubt that the said Governors would comply with your Directions; but the contrary appears, as they are every Minute committing Acts of Hostility. I had determined from what you wrote me, to set about accommodating the Disputes between the Maratta States and the English Nation, who in Violation of former Treaties have commenced Hostilities; but I am now of Opinion, that the said Governors are averse to an Accommodation, and have made interested and partial Representations to you, with a View to prevent its taking Place. The Delay in the Arrival of your Vackeel, and in putting a Stop to the Flames of War, are Reasons for my Belief; I therefore write, to request that you will weigh the Representations of self-interested People in the Balance of Wisdom, and will apply to the Accommodation of all Differences, which is the Part of true Wisdom. To sum up all in a few Words, the Governors do not recall their Forces from the Alliance of Ragonaut Row, or deliver up the conquered Towns; and although the Roads are shut up, Ships pass backwards and forwards, which Instances are not consistent with Peace and Friendship, but may be considered as the Foundation of a Quarrel; I therefore think it proper to give you Information of such Transactions.

From Ballagee Pundit; of the same Tenor and Date.

N. B. Duplicates of the Two last Letters of the same Date were received at the same Time with the Originals.

Extract of Bengal Secret Consultations, the 8th of January 1776.

The Honourable Warren Hastings, Governor General, President,
Lieutenant General John Clavering,
The Honourable George Monson,
Richard Barwell, } Esquires.
Philip Francis, }

Read, Two Letters from Mado Row Narrain, and Succeram Baboo, received the 1st Instant, and recorded in the Persian Correspondence.

Agreed, that the Governor General be requested to reply to these Letters in the following Terms.

I have received the Letter which you wrote to me the 22d November.

I have repeatedly written Answers to your several Letters, and dispatched them to you in Duplicate by different Roads, to ensure the Safety of their Conveyance. It is with Surprize I received the Information of your having given Orders for stopping the Ports, and for intercepting our Vessels on the Malabar Coast, as this Measure is so contrary to your Professions of Peace and Friendship. By a Letter received from Colonel Upton, written a few Days after the Date of yours, I learn that he had advanced as far as Bopaul, within Seventy Coss of Burhampore, but that his Journey had been very much retarded by the Obstacles which he had met with in the Way, for Want of the Passports which you had promised to supply him.

From a Principle of Justice, and from the Sentiments of Moderation which have been earnestly enjoined us by our Superiors, we have put a Stop to the Hostilities which had taken Place between the Government of Bombay and your Forces; we are in Hopes that you have imitated our Example, and that by a reciprocal Desire to promote an amicable Conclusion to these Troubles, all Differences between us may be happily settled, on the most equitable and permanent Footing: But if you shall resolve to adopt a different Conduct, and in Violation of your Promises renew the War against us, whilst our Forces remain in Peace and in Inaction, we shall then be remediless, and you must answer for the Consequences. We have given strict Orders to the Presidency of Bombay to abstain from all further Hostilities, and to withdraw their Forces to their own Possessions. We are informed that they have lately complied with these Orders, you can therefore have no Excuse if any Act of yours should be the Cause of reviving the War.

Agreed, that Copies of Mado Row Narrain's Letters, and of Succeram Baboo, together with the Board's Reply, be sent to Colonel Upton.

APPEN-

APPENDIX, N° 95.

Extract of Bengal Secret Consultations, 18th December 1775.

RECEIVED, the following Letter from Fort Saint George, together with a Letter from Bombay.

Honourable Sir, and Sirs,

We now enclose you a Duplicate of our last Letter, also a Packet, which we have received under your Address from the President and Council of Bombay.

Fort Saint George, 25th November 1775.

We have the Honour to be, &c.

Honourable Sir, and Gentlemen,

We had the Honour to address you the 4th Instant, and agreeable to what we then mentioned, we shall now proceed to reply more fully to your Letter, dated 18th July.

We are much concerned that you should still think you have Reason to complain of our not being sufficiently full and explicit in our Advices respecting our Proceedings in Consequence of the Treaty with Ragoba, which we cannot but in a great Measure attribute to your Honour, &c. as not having then received our Letter, dated the 30th April, of which you have not acknowledged the Receipt, and we flatter ourselves that all Cause of Complaint on this Head will be entirely removed by our succeeding Letters, and the Information Mr. Tayler will personally give you.

In Compliance with your Requisition, we now transmit a compleat Series of our Correspondence with Lieutenant Colonel Keating, beginning with the Instructions given him on his first Proceeding with our Troops to join Ragoba; and we shall not fail regularly to transmit Copies of all Letters that may in future pass between us. We also enclose a Copy of the Instructions we had prepared for Mr. Mostyn, by which your Honour, &c. will perceive that the Objects of his intended Mission were only to press Ragoba to march with all possible Expedition towards Poona, to hasten the Accomplishment of some Points of the Treaty, and to relieve the Commanding Officer from all Charge of Business with the Durbar, and Negociation with the Country Powers. The Treaty with Ragoba had been executed long before our Determination for sending Mr. Mostyn to the Army, and we did not conceive the Measures to be in the least repugnant to the Directions contained in your Letter of the 8th March, being solely intended to hasten the Conclusion of the War which had been already begun. Mr. Mostyn, however, was prevented from proceeding to join the Army by the unusual Severity of the Monsoon; and this Design was afterwards entirely dropt, upon the Receipt of your Letter dated the 31st May.

We most sincerely regret the Resolution your Honour, &c. have taken to send Lieutenant Colonel Upton to treat with Saccaram Bappoo at Poona, without waiting for further Advices from us. We did entertain Hopes we should have convinced your Honour, &c. of the Justice of Ragoba's Pretensions to the Peshwaship, and that we should have met with your Support and Assistance in the Prosecution of the War; when we did not doubt but in the Course of the next Campaign we should have conducted Ragoba to Poona, and fulfilled our Engagements with him. These Hopes we now fear are not only defeated by this Measure, but the Dignity and Consequence of this Presidency amongst the neighbouring Powers very sensibly injured. We cannot think we were unreasonable in our Expectations, that the Negociation in which the Interests of this Presidency were so materially concerned, should have been carried on in Concert with us, and which indeed we concluded to be your Intention from the Tenor of the Governor General's Letter to Saccaram Bappoo; but when we advert to the Extract you have favoured us with from Colonel Upton's Instructions, we find him vested with the most extensive Powers, and not the least Reference to be made to us for Advice or Information, the Want of which is avowed in these very Instructions, and which from the Vicinity of Bombay to Poona,

Poona, we could convey to him in Two Days. Notwithstanding this, we thought it our Duty to afford Colonel Upton every Information we could give to assist him in the Execution of his important Commission, being satisfied that he would only receive partial Accounts from Poona, both of Ragoba and Affairs in general; and we at first proposed to send a Gentleman fully instructed to meet him there, to confer with him respecting the Interests of this Presidency so far as you have committed them to his Charge; but not knowing whether this Step might be agreeable to your Honour, &c. we dispatched a Letter to him by different Routes, a Copy of which is enclosed, wherein we made him this Proposal; or if he preferred Information by Letter, we offered to give him the most full and satisfactory Advice on every Point he might wish to be informed of. We have not yet received an Answer to this Letter, or any Advices of the Colonel's Arrival at Poona, though we have heard so long ago as the 9th Ultimo, that he was arrived at Calpa, on the River Jumna.

The Letter from Colonel Keating, dated the 30th August, will shew you in what Manner Ragoba received the News of your Honours, &c. Determination to open a Negociation with the Ministry, and of your positive Orders for withdrawing our Forces from his Army, and a Cessation of Hostilities taking Place. This subsequent Letter, dated the 2d September, will apprize you of the Peshwa's Resolution to wait patiently the Result of the Negociation; but in the mean Time, he demands very pertinently from what Source he is to supply his Exigencies, until the Conclusion of this important Adjustment, which must necessarily take up some Months; and then makes the following Proposals, which we intend to communicate to Colonel Upton, when we hear of his Arrival at Poona; and we beg Leave strongly to recommend to your Honour, &c. to obtain them for him, as being in our Opinion extremely moderate, and strictly consistent with Justice.

Ragoba first proposes, that Half of the Country, the Produce of which is reserved for the Maintenance of the reigning Peshwa, should be put into his immediate Possession; or, lest this Proposal should take up too much Time in the Discussion, that a monthly Stipend be paid him from the Circar of Poona, for the Support of himself and his Adherents, until some Agreement may be concluded. This Stipend his Agent here proposed should be Lacks of Rupees per Month.

He next proposes, and entreats, that before you come to any Decision respecting his Pretensions to the Peshwaship, you will attend to every Evidence that can be produced by either Party; when, if it should be proved to your Satisfaction, that a Son of the late Narron Row does exist, let such Son be appointed Peshwa; but he then, as next of Blood, claims the Office of Dewan for himself, until the Minority of this supposed Son expires, at which Period he will rest satisfied with a Provision independent of any Employment; if on the contrary he should prove to your Honour, &c. that this Child, said to be the Son of Narron Row, is a supposititious one, and which he doubts not to make evident, he in such Case pleads, that as the Son of Bajerow, he is justly entitled to the Peshwaship of the Maratta Empire; with which if he is invested, he promises to fulfil the Whole of his Engagements with the Honourable Company.

We have sent Directions to Colonel Keating to retire with our Troops into our Purgunnahs contiguous to Surat or Broach, as soon as the Weather and Roads will permit; and as by the Agreement for the Cessation of Arms every Thing was to remain on the same State until a general Pacification might be concluded, we have ordered him to give effectual Protection to these Purgunnahs, and to repel any hostile Attempts that may be made on them. Mr. Tayler will have taken Possession of most of the Purgunnahs ceded to us so long ago as the Month of April last.

In the Course of Colonel Keating's Correspondence you will observe, that he has at different Times obtained Grants from Futty Sing and Ragoba, of some other small Districts contiguous to Surat and Broach. He lately obtained from the former a Grant of a Purgunnah called Siner, producing a Revenue of upwards of a Lack of Rupees a Year; but as it lay out of the Line of Territory we wished to possess, and your Honour, &c. had forbid us to aim at further Acquisitions, we immediately gave Directions for its being restored.

We beg Leave to observe, in Reply to a Remark in your Letter dated the 10th July, that we acquainted your Honour, &c. in our Letter, dated the 31st March, of Ragoba's having made a Deposit in Jewels, valued at Six Lacks of Rupees, as a Security for the Expences of the War; and by the Treaty it appears that several Districts were made over to the Company, the Revenues of which were to be particularly assigned for the Payment

Payment of the Monthly Stipend of Rupees 1,50,000. Ragoba has since paid a further Sum of about Two Lacks of Rupees, as mentioned in Colonel Keating's Letter, dated the 30th August, and we had every Reason to expect more considerable Sums would have been received from him, in Consequence of the Treaty with Futty Sing, who has already paid about Ten of the stipulated Twenty-six Lacks, and we are persuaded would have paid the Whole, and that Ragoba would have found no Difficulty in raising Money as he advanced, had we continued to support him.

Whatever may be your Determination with respect to the Matters at present in Agitation, we assure you we will most strictly conform to it; and we request in the most earnest Manner, that you will not continue to withhold the necessary Supply of Money for our Expences, from an Apprehension that we shall apply it to any Purposes inconsistent with your Directions; and likewise, that you will, if possible, assist us in paying off our Bond Debt, which, unless we are confirmed in Possession of the Places ceded to us by the Treaty, we see no Prospect of being able to effect ourselves.

We should have been more particular in explaining the Pretensions of Ragoba to the Peshwaship, had not Mr. Tayler been commissioned to give you full Information on that Head; he will also be able to acquaint you with many Particulars you may want to know respecting Futty Sing and Govind Row, the Sons of Dormajee, or, as they are commonly termed, the Guicawars, the Mention of whom so frequently occurs in the Letters from Lieutenant Colonel Keating. We shall only here observe, that this Family, till lately, collected a Share of Six Tenths of the Broach Revenues in Participation with us; and that it was their Share we wished to obtain, and not the Mogul's, as mentioned in your Instructions to Lieutenant Colonel Upton. The Mogul's Share devolved to us when we reduced the Town, and Futty Sing having lately given us a Phirmaun for the Guicawar Share, we are now entitled to the whole Revenue of that District.

We have the Honour to remain, &c.

Bombay Castle,
the 14th October 1775.

Ordered, That the foregoing Letter from the President and Council of Bombay lie for Consideration until the Arrival of the Original, the Letter now before the Board being a Duplicate, and no Inclosures having been sent with it.

APPENDIX, N° 96.

Extract of Secret Letter from Bengal; dated the 15th January 1776.

Par. 38. WE have received a Letter from Lieutenant Colonel Upton, dated 25th November, at Bepaul, about 70 Coss North of Berhanpore; in which he said, he had met with continual Obstacles in travelling through a Country where the People were all in Arms, and not having received any Passports from Poona, he had been much delayed.

39. Letters of the 22d November, very lately arrived from the Paishwa and Ministry at Poona, declare, that Orders to secure a free Passage to Colonel Upton had been issued to the Fousdars, &c. but that no Accounts of him had reached Poona. These Letters are so uncommon in their Nature, and the Style so different from any Thing we could have expected, that we take the Liberty to refer you to the Translations of them. They shew little pacific Inclinations at first professed by this Party; but seem to be written on the Grounds of false Information, as they accuse the Presidency of Bombay of Inattention to our Orders, in suffering the Army to act offensively after we had declared ourselves for Peace; though we are well assured, both by the Presidency and by Means of Colonel Keating, that all Operations were immediately suspended, and that the Army only waited for the fair Season to retire. The Ministry likewise think ill of our Ships sailing from Port to Port as in the Time of Peace; and tell us that they will be intercepted by the Maratta Vessels on the Coast, and the Ports shut against them: They further complain of the Suspence they are kept in; and threaten, unless the Places which

which we have taken be delivered back immediately, that they will set their Army in Motion for the Recovery of them.

40. We cannot reconcile these Declarations to the reduced State in which the Ministers appear, by Advices from Colonel Keating to Mr. Tayler, dated 29th October, which he communicated to us: The Contents of these are, that Moraba Furnesee, one one of the principal Persons in the Poona Durbar, had come over to Ragoba's Interest, with several other Men of Power; that the Ministerial Army was reduced to 12,000 Men at the utmost, and much dispirited; that the Ministers had retired to Poonder Fort, and were afraid to trust themselves out of it; and Ragoba's Party daily gained Ground. We believe both these Relations may be magnified by the sanguine Ideas of either Interest; but we hope that a general Equilibrium will be preserved until Colonel Upton's Arrival at Poona, to give Weight to his Negociations. In the mean Time, we have represented to the Ministers our Motives for putting a Stop to the late Hostilities on the Malabar Side of India, hoping they would entertain a reciprocal Desire to conclude Matters amicably; but if they resolve to pursue a different Conduct, and not to abide by the Promises they had made, we should be under the Necessity of opposing them, and leave them to answer for having drawn the Consequences upon themselves.

41. We have lately received a Letter from the President and Council at Bombay, containing an Account of Ragoba's Reception of the Intelligence of our having deputed a Person to Poona, and Proposals made by him in Consequence; the first of which is, that a District or monthly Stipend be immediately assigned him for the Support of himself and his Adherents until the Negociations are concluded: Secondly, That his Pretensions to the Paishwaship should be discussed; and in Case he proves that Mahda Row Narrain is only a suppostitious Child of the late Paishwa, his Title to it as next Heir should be acknowledged, otherwise, by the same Pretensions, he claims the Regency until the Son of the deceased Paishwa becomes of Age to act for himself, at which Time he will rest satisfied with a Pension. As the Letter which conveyed this Information to us is a Duplicate, and as none of the original Papers referred to in it were inclosed, we have suspended the Consideration of it until we receive the Original.

APPENDIX, N° 97.

Extract of Bengal Secret Consultations, dated the 5th February 1776.

PRESENT,

The Honourable Warren Hastings, Governor General, President,
The Honourable George Monson,
Richard Barwell, } Esquires.
Philip Francis, }

RECEIVED an Original Letter from the President and Council of Bombay, dated the 14th of October, Duplicate of which Letter is recorded in Consultation of the 18th December last; but as the Papers referred to in it did not arrive with the Duplicate,

Ordered, That they be entered after this Day's Consultation.

As the Correspondence with Colonel Keating is very voluminous, and as it must appear on the Proceedings of the Council of Bombay;

Ordered, That only Abstracts of it be entered on the Proceedings of this Board.

Ordered, That the Inclosures in the above Letter be entered after the Consultations.

APPENDIX, N° 97.

Abstract of Letters to and from Lieutenant Colonel Keating.

No. 1. His Instructions.

2. Letter from. Arrived with the Troops at Surat, 27th February; proposes marching to Cambay at the proper Season.

3. Letter from, to the President. State of the Engagement between Ragoba and the Ministerial Party; with its Consequences.

4. Letter to. To observe the Directions of the Chief and Council at Surat; and deliver them Copy of his Instructions.

5. Letter from, dated Surat 9th March. Proposed Attack on the Ministerial Forces in this Neighbourhood, deferred; is determined to proceed to Cambay the next Springs, and carries with him the 18 Pounders.

6. Letter from, dated off Sevally, 15th March. Is on his Way to Cambay; requests discretional Orders; his Reasons for it; delivers his Sentiments on the most eligible Means for affording Ragoba Assistance. Ragoba consents to pay the Expence of transmitting Stores and Provision. Has attacked the Marattas in the Neighbourhood of Surat, and put them to Flight.

7. Letter to, dated 23d March. Instructions for his Conduct when at Cambay. Disapprove of his having attacked the Marattas near Surat. Will send a Detachment of 150 Europeans to join him in Two Days.

8. Letter from, dated 21st March, near Cambay. Arrived and encamped at Narangzeer on the 20th. Ragoba received Advices from his Army, under Conderaw and Govindrow. The State thereof. A Party of Ragoba's dispersed Troops join him, and bring Account of more expected shortly. Has an Interview with the Nabob, who assures him of every Assistance in his Power. Relates Intelligence of the State of the Ministerial Party. Great Confusion in their Councils.

9. Letter to, dated 31st March. Send a Detachment of Sepoys. Require him to effect a Junction with Ragoba's Army, and proceed to Poona with all possible Dispatch.

10. Letter from, to the President, dated 30th March. Futty Sing desires Leave of the Nabob to send Two Men to Camp; on which Account he wrote him to join Forces. His Reason for it. Further Letters from Futty Sing. His first Letters intercepted by Henry Punt Fuckia. His Letters answered by Fuckia; their Contents. Expects Govindrow and Candarow will join him without Delay, the Enemy only 14 Coss distant. Receives hourly Intelligence of their Intention to attack him. Is well prepared to receive them. Requests more Subaltern Officers; Luxaman Gossaull appointed Vackeel to Dada Saib. Propose 5 Lacks to be sent Dada Saib, as the only Means of insuring Success. Means for Repayment, with the Advantages the Company are to reap from it.

11. Letter from, dated 31st March. Requests that the Time of the Springs may be fixed on for his Departure, should he not be able to effect a Junction with Ragoba's Army. Nothing but Money wanting to ensure Success to Ragoba's Affairs.

12. Letter to, dated 22d April. Complains of his Neglect in not advising them of the State, &c. of the Army. Are not able to supply Ragoba with Money.

13. Letter from, dated Gunnich 18th April. Is joined by a Party of Govindrow's Troops. Plan proposed for forming a compleat Junction. Futty Sing determined on entering into a Treaty. Madajee Scindia has offered his Assistance, and marches on the 27th to join the Army. Represents the Distress Ragoba is in for Want of Money, and the Terms he offers for obtaining it. Ragoba to defray the Expence of transporting Guns, &c.

14. Letter from, dated Darrah 19th April. Has joined the Whole of the Peishwa Army. Enforces the immediate Necessity of supplying Ragoba with Cash. Has resolved in assisting him out of the Military Chest; and writes to Surat for a Supply.

15. Letter from, dated 20th. Covering Triplicate of the above.

16. Letter from, dated 21st. Is joined by 10,000 of Govindrow's Troops; the Baggage, &c. left under Care of his Uncle Condaro, 60 Coss off.

17. Letter from, to the Governor, dated 23d. The Army 50,000 strong. The Treaty with Futty Sing under Signature.

18. Letter to, dated 3d May. Disapprove of his having supplied Ragoba with Money. Positively direct him not to advance any more. To transmit Copy of the Treaty with Ragoba, and a Cypher with which he is to correspond.

19. Letter from, dated near Hossam, the 28th April. His Reasons for not writing oftener. Comes to a Battle with the Confederate Army; Particulars thereof. Ragoba's Troops did not engage. Will send a more circumstantial Account of it in his next. Again urges the Necessity of supplying Ragoba with Money. The present Plan and Designs of Ragoba.

20. Letter from, dated Mawtrah, 3d May. Meets the Enemy on his March towards Kereah; engages them, and puts them to Flight, with the Loss of near 1,200 killed and wounded. Disadvantage of being incumbered with a large Bezar; on which Accouut, intends persuading the Paishwa to change his Route, and go towards Poona.

21. Letter from, dated Neriad, 10th May. Seanes Mantrah on the 5th, and encamped at Coomleah; which Place he leaves the next Morning; and after marching a few Miles, is interrupted by the Whole of the Ministerial Army. Comes to an Engagement; Particulars thereof. Left Hydrabad on the 7th, for Neriad; is suddenly attacked at Dabaun. Throws the Enemy into Disorder, and obliges them to retreat in the utmost Confusion; since which, they have not shewn themselves. Encamps at Neriad on the Eighth; Description of the Place. The Paishwa intends laying a Tax on it. Refers to Mr. Lovibond's Letter for the Particulars of the Treaty with Futty Sing. Wishes much to cross the Myhie before the Rains. Urges it to the Paishwa, who gives his Reasons against it. The Paishwa promises a Donation of 30 Lacks to the Army as soon as he is in Possession of Poona. Gives his Reasons for advancing the Paishwa Money. Has got a Deposit of Jewels to the Amount advanced.

22. Letter from Mr. Lovibond to Colonel Keating; relates the Treatment he met with while negociating the Treaty with Futty Sing.

23. Letter from, dated Betassee 19th May. Particular Account of their March from Neriad, with the shameful Retreat and Loss sustained in an Engagement near Nappier on the 18th; imputes the backward Behaviour of the Paishwa's Troops to their Want of Pay: Loss on the Enemy's Part very great.

24. Letter from, dated Suban the 26th May. His March from Battse to the above Place. Has not seen any Thing of the Enemy since the Engagement on the 18th; imagines the Loss they sustained that Day has totally dispersed them, if not entirely ruined their Cause. Is drawing near Broach; Supplies will be ready on his Arrival there. Is much solicited by Govindrow to form the Siege of Brodua; declines it. Expects to be on the Banks of Nubedah in Two Days. Has not been able to find out the Reason of the shameful Conduct of the 2d Company of Grenadiers. On the 18th a Party of the Enemy appear before the Camp, but on firing Two or Three Shot, they retired.

25. Letter from, dated Jarraseer 3d June. The Want of Money has caused almost a general Defection among Ragoba's Troops. Govindrow refuses to cross the Nubedah. The Arabs refuse to march without all that is due to them. The most eligible Step now to be pursued is, to oblige the Enemy to cross the Nubedar. Will be obliged to get a Reinforcement at Broach. Urges, in the most pressing Terms, that Ragoba may be supplied with Five Lacks.

26. Letter from. Has been confined by a severe Illness. On the 8th marched from Jerraseer, intending to cross the Nerbedah, but found it impossible. On the 9th reached Seruttah; there got Intelligence of the Enemy's being encamped close to the Pass of Bavapoor. On the 10th, discovered the Enemy, who on seeing them fled in Confusion. His Reasons for again attempting to march to the Southward. Ragoba determined on not crossing the Derbedah. Resolved on going to Duboy. On the 12th the Monsoon set in very violently, which prevented his reaching Duboy till the 19th. Govindrow desirous of reducing Brodera. Is in Hopes of obtaining Sunnuds for the Province of Ahmood. In Consideration of his acquiescing in Ragoba's Proposal at Bowa Peer, Futty Sing declares his Readiness to join him immediately; offers him a Pass for himself and Attendants. Is in Hopes of obtaining some valuable Acquisition for the Company, on whatever Terms Ragoba and the Guicawar Family may settle. Mr. Shaw joins him, and makes Ragoba a public Visit and Present. Ragoba encamped on the River Ore. The Ministerial Army gone to the Inalive Country, and are much disaffected. Report of many of them being drowned at the setting in of the Rains. State

 of

of his Army, &c. The Paishwa requests the Europeans may be compleated to the Terms of the Treaty, for which he will pay a further Sum.

27. Letter to, dated 13th July. Approve his Intention of crossing the Nerbedah and Tappy; concur in the Reduction of Brodera; the Conditions on which it is to be undertaken. Approve his having held a Court of Enquiry on the Second Company of Grenadiers, and request his Opinion on the Proceedings. Lament the Effects of the Irregularity of Ragoba's Troops. Do not think proper to alter their Resolution for not supplying Ragoba with Money. Disapprove of his having accepted a Phirmaund for a Donation to the Army.

28. Letter from, dated 8th July. Substance of the Treaty with Futty Sing.

29. Copy of the Treaty with Futty Sing.

30. Letter to, dated 6th August. Approve of the Treaty with Futty Sing. Desire him to be urgent for the Payment of the Arrears of the monthly Stipend, &c. On Ragoba's receiving the Sum stipulated in the Treaty.

From. July 22. Treaty between Ragoba and Futty Sing concluded the 18th Instant. All the Sunnuds, except for Verrow (which he hourly expects, are made over to the Company for ever. Request they will grant him a Reinforcement of Men and Stores.

From. The Paishwa's Family, and Essob Cawn, with 4000 Horse and Foot, are on their Way to join the Peishwa. Mhadajee and Mhadajee Bounsella, are ready to join, provided some Country is ceded to them. Appajee Gunness has sent Vackeels to treat. The Ministerial Party greatly distressed.

Letter to, 19th August. Have received Letters from the Governor General and Council, disapproving the Measures they were then pursuing; in Consequence, positively order him to desist from further Hostilities against the Ministerial Party, unless attacked by them, and to remain in his present Situation until further Orders. To assure Ragoba of their Protection and Support.

Letter from, 30th July. Futty Sing has paid near Two Lacks of the Sum stipulated, as mentioned in his Address of the 8th Instant. From the extraordinary Hardship of the Officers, hopes they may be allowed Double Batta. Has received the Sunnud for the Verrow Purgunnah.

Letter to, 5th September. Direct that he return, with Forces under his Command, into the Broach or Surat Purgunnah. To acquaint Ragoba, that it is their Advice that he continue with him till the Embarkation of the Troops.

Letter from, 6th August. The Ministerial Army is marched to Barrampoor.

——— From, 8th Ditto. Has had several Conferences with the Paishwa respecting Nizam Ally. The Paishwa is apprehensive of the Nizam's joining the Ministers. Is desirous of receiving Assistance from the English only, and granting Territory in Lieu. By a Compliance with his Terms he engages to increase the monthly Stipend. Has deputed Mr. James Forbes to proceed to Bombay, to settle this Business. The Paishwa requests that the Madras Presidency may be wrote to, to insist on Nizam Ally's remaining neuter, and that the Nizam may be wrote to, to the same Effect. Great Pains has been taken to prevent Futty Sing from paying the Sum of Money to the Paishwa, as per Agreement. Nothing shall divert his Attention from reaching Poona as soon as possible. His Opinion on the Behaviour of the 2d Grenadier Company on the 18th May.

Letter from, 9th August. Has had a particular Conversation with Govind Row, from which he is convinced of the deceitful Conduct of Futty Sing; has therefore resolved on making every Preparation for undertaking the Siege of Brodera. Is encamped with the Paishwa Army within Two Miles of Brodera, and is in Readiness to invest the Place.

Letter from, 21st Ditto. Captain Scott's and Captain Westphalls's Detachments are halted within 1000 Yards of Brodera; Futty Sing has proposed coming into their Camp, on Assurance of Safety; has prevailed on him with much Importunity to discharge his present Payment of Ten Lacks; desires such Villages as Govindrow has possessed himself of, may be restored to him, for the Possession of which, will pay Five Lacks more; to which the Peishwa has assented.

Letter from, 25th August. The Peishwa has received Intelligence of Saccaram Bapoo and Nana Farness having erected their Standard in the Field, with a Design of abolishing the Title of Peishwa; represents the Necessity of a Reinforcement to prevent the Consequences. The Peishwa appears averse to receiving Payment in Jewels, Elephants, and

and Piece Goods; is apprehensive of what may follow. The Peishwa has detached Ameen Cawn with 3000 Horse and 200 Foot towards Amadabad. Has defeated the Troops of Appajee Guinés.

Letter from, 27th August. The Peishwa appears desirous of going to Amadabad. Will not consent to it till he has granted a Sunnud for a Purgunnah equal to Ahmood. Has received Intelligence of Mamed Escobb's having defeated a Body of 7000 Horse, under the Command of Wornan Row, near the Banks of the Nerbedah.

——— From, 30th August. Has recommended a Residence at Bombay to the Peishwa, until the Event of the Treaty is known. Has received Futty Sing's Bond for Six Lacks, payable in Two Months. The fatal Consequences which may attend leaving the Country to the Mercy of the Peishwa's Army; how it may be obviated. Has ordered a Detachment to take Possession of Kurraul.

Letter from, 2d September. The Peishwa much distressed and perplexed to account for the sudden Reverse of Conduct towards him; his Advice to him on the Occasion. The Peishwa is determined to wait the Conclusion of the Treaty at the Head of his Army: His Propositions for supplying his Exigencies in the Interim: Wishes, prior to any Decision, that the Supreme Council would attend to every Evidence which he can produce respecting the lawful Son of the late Narrain Row: Conditions in Consequence. Futty Sing has declared his Readiness to afford Protection to the Country.

Letter to, 19th September. Express their Surprise at the Reason he assigns for not having retained a considerable Part of the Ten Lacks paid by Futty Sing to the Peishwa. Direct that the Forces may be withdrawn, which were sent to take Possession of Sinor, and that it be restored to the Person from whom he received it. To procure no further Grants for securing the Debt due from the Peishwa, and to enter into no further Negociations. Disapprove his Intentions with respect to Govindrow: Require his Reasons for this Part of his Conduct.

Letter from, 6th September. The Peishwa has infringed the Treaty with Futty Sing, not having delivered up to him the Whole of his Purgunnahs on the Payment of the Ten Lacks. The Peishwa still continues greatly depressed.

——— From, 10th September. The Partizans of Govindrow are anxious for an Accommodation between their Master and Futty Sing. Transmits a List of the killed, deceased, and deserted Sepoys.

——— From, 18th September. Futty Sing has agreed to give up to Govindrow, One Third of the Guicawar Possessions, on certain Conditions: Govindrow not satisfied, but insists on the Peishwa's ceding a considerable Part of his own Country; which he has refused. Futty Sing has ceded to the Company a Village called Der Battia. Ameen Cawn has resisted one Sally from the Besieged at Amadabad, who felt a material Loss. The Peishwa has desired Pattamars may be sent to Bengal, as he intends corresponding with the Supreme Council. Futty Sing has sent him the Sunnud for the Village of Dubattia.

Letter from, 27th September. Govindrow still refuses the Offers made him by Futty Sing and the Peishwa. The Peishwa has given up the Purgunnah of Harisoot in Lieu of one which had been promised to the Company. The Peishwa has discovered a Defection in Part of his Army; has applied to him for a Detachment, which he complied with. Govindrow has come down a little in his Demands.

Letter from, 1st October. Explains that Part of his Letter, dated 30th August, which regarded the Peishwa's Debt. His Reasons for a Change in his Sentiments with respect to Govindrow.

——— To, 8th November. Desire that he will use his Endeavours with Futty Sing to make over Batta to the Company instead of Duballio.

——— From, 30th October. The Peishwa has crossed the River with his Army, Has received further Assurances of Attachment of Moraba Dadda, also Offers of Service from Bejee Sing, Raja of the Marawar Country.

To Thomas Mostyn, Esquire,

Sir,

In order to attain the clearest Insight into Ragoba's Affairs, his Situation, Expectations, and Designs, as well as to give him such forcible and proper Advice as will induce him to proceed with all possible Expedition to Poona, his Capital, we have deemed

deemed highly necessary that a Gentleman of the Rank of Council should proceed to him; and having appointed you for these Purposes to proceed to and reside at Ragoba's Durbar, it is our Direction that you embark for Cambay as soon as possible, from whence you are to set out to join the Army with as much Expedition as the necessary Attention to your own Safety will admit. We make no Doubt when Ragoba is informed of your Arrival at Cambay (or at any other Port from whence it may be most convenient to join his Army) that he will readily concert proper Measures with Lieutenant Colonel Keating, for sending an Escort to conduct you with Safety to the Camp; or you are otherwise to take such proper Measures as will insure your Arrival there in Safety.

From the Knowledge you have acquired of the Country People, it is almost unnecessary for us to remind you that the Influence we hope you will acquire over Ragoba, and those who are most in his Esteem and Confidence, will much depend on your endeavouring to conciliate his good Opinion, which we accordingly expect you to do.

Sensible as we are that the War can only be terminated by Ragoba's moving speedily towards Poona, you are therefore strenuously to urge him to do so, by setting forth in proper Colours the great Disadvantage to his Affairs, by his continuing so long so very far distant from his Capital, thereby putting it entirely out of his Power, either to procure Money for his own Occasions, and what ought to be as material to him, it also puts it out of his Power to provide for the Payment of the Stipend monthly due by Treaty to our Honourable Employers, for the Expences of their Forces which are now assisting him.

A Copy of the Treaty we enclose, that you may act conformable to it; but there are a few Points, to the Accomplishment of which we expect your particular Attention.

1st. That you endeavour as soon as possible to procure the Payment of the Arrears of the monthly Stipend of One and a Half Lack of Rupees, and that the same be punctually made good to you in Time to come.

2dly. That you procure from the Peishwa a sufficient Body of Horse to be sent to the Chiefs of Surat and Broach, for putting the Company in effectual Possession of the Territories by Treaty ceded to them.

3dly. That you procure from the Peishwa the Sunnud, that he has bound himself to obtain from the Guicawars, for their Share of the Revenues of the Town, and in the Purgunnahs of Broach.

These Points once accomplished will be of very material Advantage to our Employers, and they are no more than he has bound himself to perform. On our Part, every Thing we engaged for has been fulfilled, and even more; notwithstanding which, Ragoba by Letter has pressed us for a Loan of Money, and this Request has been most urgently and frequently repeated by Lieutenant Colonel Keating, the Commanding Officer of our Forces now with Ragoba. What makes this Matter more extraordinary is, that after we had acquainted Colonel Keating of our Inability to furnish this Loan, and that we also deemed it inconsistent with the Interest of the Company to do so, he has again urged us on this Head, and adds, that he is afraid to acquaint Ragoba of our Refusal.

As we shall not supply Ragoba with Money for the Reasons given above, you are to advise him accordingly in a proper Manner, leaving him no Hopes however of any pecuniary Assistance on the Part of the Company. If you find that he has received any Assurances of our assisting him with Money, acquaint us of it, and let Ragoba know that they have been given without our Knowledge and Permission. Urge him to march towards Poona without any further Delay, and in doing so, he will doubtless shortly be able to supply himself with Money for his own Occasions, as well as to enable him to fulfil his pecuniary Engagements to the Honourable Company.

You are well acquainted how much we have disapproved of Lieutenant Colonel Keating's Conduct, by intending to march to Amadabad, which is the opposite Route to Poona. Notwithstanding we explained our Sentiments hereon in our Letter of the 23d of March, yet, by his last Advices, it appears that he persists in that Opinion, and actually intends to proceed thither; you are to make due Enquiry of the Paishwah, and of Lieutenant Colonel Keating, as to their Motives for this Proceeding, of which you are to advise us.

Although Lieutenant Colonel Keating was in nowise authorised by us to enter into any Treaty or Negociation of any Kind with any Powers or Persons whatever; yet from his Advices it appears that he has done so, and particularly with Futty Sing; indeed, he acquaints us that he has been under the Necessity of making the Company a Party in a Treaty between Ragoba and Futty Sing. How or in what Manner the Company were to be Parties, he has not yet advised; and as he was quite silent on the Subject in the Letters he has wrote us, we do not know whether the Treaty has taken Place or not; we therefore deem it necessary that you should require the Colonel to acquaint you of every Step he took regarding this Treaty, and to lay before you in Writing his Proceedings with Ragoba, and his Correspondence with all or any of the Country Powers that he may have corresponded with, in order that we may receive the same through you, with your Sentiments at large thereon. Should any Proposals or Applications in future be made to any of the Country Powers, they must all be made to you, and not to the Commander of our Forces; and whenever the Company's Interest may be concerned, they are to be transmitted to us with your Sentiments. In these Matters the Military Commanding Officer must not interfere; but we shall rely on you to take Care to support his Consequence in every consistent Manner, sensible as you must be that much will depend on his Conduct.

As we direct that you only in future shall have Intercourse with Ragoba, or that all Intercourse shall be through you, so it will be necessary that the Military Commanding Officer shall be under your Controul, except in the Execution of every Military Operation; and we accordingly lay down the following Rule for your Conduct in respect to the Military Commanding Officer, to whom Instructions are accordingly given.

Whenever it may be resolved and agreed between Ragoba and yourself to march, to encamp, or to make any other Movement with the Army, you are to signify the same to the Commanding Officer of our Forces in Writing, and he is ordered to obey; but in respect to the Mode of the March, of the Encampment, or the Method of carrying any Military Measure into Execution, the Military Officer is of course the more proper Judge how it should be effected, and therein you are not to interfere, nor in the Detail of the Duty of the Army.

As the Expences of our Forces must amount to a very considerable Sum monthly, we esteem it very necessary that you should superintend and controul the Accounts of the Commissary and Paymaster, which we accordingly direct you to do; and those Officers, through Colonel Keating, are now ordered to lay their Accounts before you monthly, or oftener if you call for them, and never to make any Payments out of the ordinary Course of the Service which you shall disapprove of.

Inclosed is a Copy of our Instructions to Lieutenant Colonel Keating of the 17th February last, and of this Day, by which you will observe that he is directed to render to you an Account of his Proceedings in general, and to produce to you the Copies of his Letters hither, and our Replies.

We rely upon you constantly and frequently to advise us of every Particular within your Knowledge, as well respecting Ragoba, his Motions, Forces, and our general Prospects of Success by this Expedition; in short, from you we now expect every requisite Information, as it is unnecessary, after you arrive at Ragoba's Durbar, that the Commanding Officer should correspond with us.

Lieutenant Colonel Keating, on your demanding it, will appoint such a Guard to attend you, as you shall think necessary.

Returns of the Forces are regularly to be delivered to you, and through you transmitted to us.

Mr. Charles Brome, Senior Merchant, and Mr. Francis William Pemberton, Writer, are appointed to your Assistance; and we direct, that you keep an exact and regular Diary of all your Proceedings, wherein all Letters, whether from the Country Powers or others, are to be inserted, and the Motives of the Advices noticed in it; Two Copies of this Diary are to be delivered to us on your Return.

Lieutenant Colonel Keating is ordered to deliver up to you the Seal of the Company, the Cypher, and the Letter of Instructions to the Cypher; and as the Communication by Sea will shortly be shut, your Correspondence with us must be carried on by trusty and careful Pattamars.

The Allowance you enjoyed at Poona will be continued to you as long as you are engaged on this Service, and your Expences will be defrayed by the Company; but we rely on you to observe every necessary Frugality; you are also to take Care, that no unnecessary Expence be incurred in the Department of Commissary and Paymaster to our Forces.

The

The Sum of Rupees 5,000, has been advanced you here, on Account of your Expences, for which you are to give due Credit in your Accounts; and until you receive Money from Ragoba, as we hope you shortly will, in Consequence of what is mentioned in the former Part of these Instructions, you may draw for such further Sums as you shall require, on this Place, or on Surat Factory, or the Paymaster or the Commissary to the Army.

Bombay Castle, May 1775.

We are, &c.

To Colonel Upton.

Sir,

In a Letter from the Governor General and Council of Bengal, dated the 10th July, they acquainted us of their having appointed you to proceed to Poona, and of the Object of your Mission; at the same Time, they transmitted an Extract of such Part of their Instructions to you, as they said was necessary for our Information.

The Governor General and Council, in their Letter to us, mention that they are much uninformed as to the then Situation of Affairs; and it appears by their Instructions, that in most Points they have been able to give you discretional Orders only; in this Case we think it becomes a Duty we owe to our Honourable Employers, to offer you every Information that you possibly want, for enabling you to discharge the high Commission with which you are entrusted; and as we learn by some of the Ministerial Agents now here, of your Arrival at Calpay, on the River Jamma, from whence they shortly expect you at Poona; and as we are fully satisfied that you will receive very partial Accounts from the Ministerial Confederacy, of the real State and present Situation of the Affairs of Ragonath Row, and of the Company, so far as they are connected, we will therefore most readily give you, on your signifying your Desire for it, every Information that you can wish for relative to both, either by a Letter, or by deputing a Gentleman to you, from hence to Poona, properly instructed and fully acquainted with the Whole. Should you prefer the latter, we request that you will procure the necessary Passports for him, and on your sending them hither, he shall proceed immediately; at any Rate, we wish you would take no material Step in the Business entrusted to you, relative to this Presidency, till after we may receive your Reply to this Letter.

In Case you should prefer our only writing to you on the Subject abovementioned, it will be then necessary that you should acquaint us, whether you are in Possession of the Company's large Cypher for your Correspondence.

We transmit this Letter in Quadruplicates, by different Routes, in Hopes that it may safely reach you.

Bombay Castle, 11th September 1775.

We are, &c.
(Signed) President and Council.

A true Copy.
(Signed) Edward Ravenscroft, Sec.

Continuation of the Correspondence between Lieutenant Colonel Keating and the Bombay Presidency, abstracted, inclosed in the Letter from Bombay of the 17th November 1775.

Letter to Lieutenant Colonel Keating, 8th November, acknowledging the Receipt of his Letters of the 4th, 8th, and 16th October, desiring him to use his Endeavours to procure a Grant of Batta, instead of Duballia, taken Possession of by Mistake.

Letter from, 30th October. He has prevailed on the Paishwa to cross the River, and will endeavour to induce him to proceed without Delay to the Surat Purgunnahs. The Peishwa has received further Assurances of Morabah Dadda, and of Bejee Sing's Attachment; the latter has made Offers of Services, and is encamped within 45 Coss of Amadabad, with 10,000 Men, and wishes to join the Paishwa. The Ministerial Confederates have violated the Cessation of Hostilities; Instances given.

Honourable

Honourable Sir, and Sirs,

I have been honoured with your Commands of the 15th Instant, and in Reply thereto, beg Leave to acquaint you, that the Place I mentioned to the Colonel, as a proper Possession for the Honourable Company, if any further Cessions of Territory were obtained from the Guicawars, was a Village called Batta, and not Duballia, which he through Mistake applied and obtained Futty Sing's Sunnud for; Batta is a large Village, or rather Town, with a considerable District belonging to it, which affords an annual Revenue of about 20,000 Rupees, situated near the Banks of the River, on the opposite Side, a little below the Honourable Company's Garden House; it formerly I am told belonged to the Orpad Purgunnah, on which it borders; and as that Purgunnah borders on Hensote, Batta is the only District which prevents the Honourable Company from enjoying without Interruption the whole Territory, for a considerable Breadth, between the River of Surat and Broach; and on this Account I mentioned it to Colonel Keating, when I found he was negociating with the Guicawars for Territories to be ceded to the Honourable Company, as a Place which it would be both convenient and advantageous to be annexed to our other Possessions. Most unluckily, he somehow mistook the Name, and accepted Sunnuds for a Village called Duballia, which is a very trifling Farm, situated on the Banks of our River, on the Surat Side, a little below a well known Place called Veriew, now belonging to the Honourable Company, as ceded to them by Futty Sing. Not imagining that such a Mistake could arise as to the Name, immediately as I received Advice from the Colonel, that he had procured the Sunnuds, I concluded they were for Batta, and sent to take Possession of that Place; and not till some Time afterwards, when I got the Sunnuds translated, did I find out the Mistake, which I then noticed to the Colonel, and begged him to rectify it; and as I imagined that to effect this could be no difficult Matter, I determined still to keep Possession of Batta; but as he has lately wrote me, that on Account of your Orders, not to apply for any further Grants of Territory, and moreover, his being at present deeply engaged in negociating an Accommodation between Futty and Govindrow, he cannot do it, I shall be under the Necessity of withdrawing our People from Batta, if the Guicawars Agent insist on it; and as to Duballia, for which I have still the Sunnuds, I have yet done nothing, as I concluded, that when the Mistake was rectified, and the Sunnuds obtained for Batta, of course Duballia would be restored, and therefore I now request your Orders what I am to do with them. The annual Revenues of this Village amount to about 4,000 Rupees. For the Reasons I have assigned, I imagine your Honour, &c. will agree with me, that the Possession of Batta would be I can convenient and advantageous.

We have begun to collect the Revenues of Chicoly and Versaul, which Purgunnahs produce Batty and early Grain, and have already recovered from these two Places about 35,000 Rupees, and more is daily coming in from Orpad; we shall begin to collect in about a Month more, as soon as the Grain it produces is fit to cut. The Purgunnah of Chicoly contains 72 Villages, and is situated to the Eastward of Gundaire and Versaul, on which Purgunnahs it borders. Its annual Revenues amount, from the best Information get, to about a Lack of Rupees.

It is very necessary that all the Lands of the ceded Purgunnahs should be surveyed and measured, before any proper and particular Account can be taken of their Produce and Value; and I therefore beg you will be pleased to send a proper Person with the necessary Instruments for this Service, when I will endeavour to procure, as soon as possible, an exact State of all your Possessions under the Management of Surat.

Surat, 30th October 1775.

I have, &c.
(Signed) Robert Gambier.

A true Copy.
Edward Ravenscroft,
Secy.

Warren Hastings,
Geo. Monson,
P. Francis.

APPENDIX, N° 98.

Extract of Bengal Secret Consultations, the 12th February, 1776.

RECEIVED the following Letter from Lieutenant Colonel John Upton:

Gentlemen,

I have delayed writing a few Days, as I was desirous of doing myself the Honour of addressing you, to say somewhat more than barely that I was arrived at Poona. The Journey was considerably longer than we before imagined; Mr. Smith makes it 948 Miles from Kalpee, and we were never able to procure a Relief of either Beans, Colies, or Cattle for our Camp Equipage, and very little assisted in any Way. The Miscarriage of Orders from our Ministers here, and the disturbed State of the Country, was the Occasion of this.

I was met about Eight Coss from Poona by a Vacquil (a Man of Rank) from Sicca Ram Baboo and Bellajee Pundit. He told me the Peshwa and Ministers were at Poona Dhur, a Fort about Ten Coss from Poona; that it was their Request I would stay a Day or Two to refresh my People, and travel by small Stages, so that I might pass about Four or Five Days before I reached Poona Dhur, as they were waiting a lucky Day for the Meeting; which happened the 30th December, the Day after my Arrival, when I was conducted to the Peshwa's Durbah. On the Way I was met by Sicca Ram Baboo and Bellajee Pundit. On this Occasion a full Durbar was assembled. The Professions of Friendship from the Governor General and Council were made on the Part of the Company, and returned by Sicca Ram Baboo and Bellajee Pundit on the Part of the Maratta State.

The next Day was appointed for reading the Credentials, when all the Chiefs that could be collected were to be assembled in Durbar. This was accordingly done.

In debating with the Ministers preliminary to the Treaty being entered upon, which must necessarily be delayed some Days, as will appear in the Sequel, they urge strongly Reasons against the Signature of their Chiefs individually to the Treaty. The Conversations and the Reasons they give I inclose; also the Rise and Progress of the present Dissensions and Disturbances in this Country, as related by themselves.

In my Instructions I am directed to insist on the Signature of their Chiefs nominally and individually, which I imagine will be attended with many Difficulties, or perhaps not attainable; you will be pleased therefore to give me further Directions respecting this Article: I am myself of Opinion it might be dispensed with. In concluding the Treaty I shall endeavour, and I hope with Success, to keep open some separate Articles, in Case any Thing further should occur to you, or for your future Approbation of what may to me.

The Ministerials have in their Hands almost all the Collections of the Country; consequently the Interest of a great Majority of their Chiefs: Indeed I hear of very few that are connected with Ragonath Row, and these of the Guzerat Country only; so that a Peace in the Country will soon be established, upon the English withdrawing their Protection from Ragonath Row.

At the Request of the Ministers I have wrote to the Presidency of Bombay, to know if their Force is entirely withdrawn from Ragonath Row, as they have Intelligence here that yet some Troops remain with or near him, which enables him to commit Hostilities; and they declare on their Part, they have not moved a single Horseman from their Army since the Receipt of the Governor General's first Letter, now near Six Months ago.

Enclosed is a Letter I received from the Governor and Council of Bombay. My Reply requested every Information they could possibly give me, and which I expect in Four or Five Days. I have also the Honour to enclose the Copy of a Letter I received from

from the Nabob of the Carnatic, by which you will perceive he is sending an Ambassador to negociate at this Court. I shall be particularly attentive to the Instructions I have received respecting the Nabob. I was much disappointed in not meeting a Vackeel of his at Poona, as the Ministry here are very desirous to conclude the Treaty as expeditiously as possible, and which my Instructions in every Part direct me to do.

The last Letter I received from the Board, is dated 20th October 1775. If any Orders has been sent to Bombay, or Minutes have passed in Council respecting the Business of my Deputation, since that Date, I have not been informed of them.

I hope in a few Days to acquaint you with the Sense of these People regarding the Treaty; at present I cannot see a single Person that is not entirely devoted to them.

Much Uneasiness has been expressed at my not having brought some Present on the Part of the Company. They say it is not only the Custom of this Country, but they conceive of ours, and all the World, on such Occasions; and that it leaves too much Room for their People to form mistaken Notions. This was intimated to me by one of their Chiefs appointed to reside with me, and who is present at all our Debates at the Peshwa's Durbar: He observed, that they were afraid their Nation was not considered so honourably, or of the Consequence they could wish it to be. I told him it had not escaped the Gentlemen at Calcutta, and requested he would satisfy Sicca Ram Baboo and Ballajee Pundit of this, but that the Business was too urgent to admit the Delay of a Fortnight or Three Weeks to make such Preparation; that I had been hurried, as they well knew, with a very long Journey before me; that I had been desired to assign these Reasons for what they might think a Neglect, and that I had received Directions to send to Bombay, and provide this customary Compliment. I have accordingly given Orders for different Articles, to the Amount of about Fifteen thousand Rupees. I wish you may think this right.

I have the Honour to enclose the Form in which I mean to draw up the Treaty. You will please to return it me with your Remarks and Alterations, should you think any necessary.

Poona Dhur,
5th January 1776.

I have, &c.
(Signed) J. Upton.

P. S. It is with extreme Grief I advise of the Death of poor Dr. Banks. He had been in a declining Way these Two Months past, and expired this Morning early.

Conclusion of a Debate respecting the Maratta Chiefs individually signing the Treaty, 3d January 1776.

The Colonel asked, If they had considered his Proposal of calling their Chiefs together to sign the Treaty? They replied, They had; but looked upon it as a Request which could not be complied with, without Danger to the Tranquillity of the State. That they have now in their Possession Treaties between their Peshwa and the Kings of Delhi, as far back as the Reign of Aurungzebe, as well as Treaties with all the other Powers of Indostan, which they were ready to produce; that the Colonel might see the Seals which have been affixed on all such Occasions, and that the same will now be used; and that they also bind themselves by a most solemn Oath, which they take at the Time of putting their Seals or Names to the Treaty, to abide faithfully by every Article therein contained;—I hope the Colonel in his Letter to Calcutta will acquaint the Gentlemen with these Circumstances.—They declared these were the invariable Rules observed in all Treaties that had ever taken Place between their State and any other Power; that were they now to deviate from them, the Consequences might be fatal, as it would induce the Chiefs, who are now entirely dependent on the Peshwa, and liable to be deprived of their Dignity and Country at his Pleasure, to think themselves of Consequence enough to demand a Share in the Government, instead of obeying the Orders of their Masters, and cause Dissensions rather than unite them.

That there were Three or Four Chiefs whom they could not call to the Peshwa's Durbar, though they acknowledged in most respects his Superiority, and were obliged to to join him with their Forces whenever he made War upon any Power adjoining to or near their respective Countries. Their Names and Countries as follows:

Madajee Bhonsalo,	— Durbarow Cattach.
Guccawar Govendram, and Futty Sing	Half Guzerat,
Mirarow, —	Part of the Carnatic.

They further declared, That they wished nothing so much as a lasting Peace with the English, and that the Colonel might depend upon their taking every Measure in their Power consistent with the Honour and Safety of their Country to establish such a Peace.

The Colonel observed to them, that the Presence of the Chiefs was a Circumstance which the Honourable the Governor-General and Council considered as indispensable; that if the Arguments he had made Use of heretofore were not of Force sufficient to bring them to his Opinion, he would, as he had already mentioned, write to the Governor-General and Council, and receive their further Instructions on this Article, which he hoped would be more favourable to their Wishes; in the mean Time the Treaty may be carried on, so as to enable them to withdraw their Army, and reduce the heavy Expence they at present complain of.

J. Upton.

His Highness the Nabob Wallajaw Ummur ul Hind, Candath ul Mulk, Bahader ul Dowlah, Anweer ul Deen Cawn, Bahadre Zuffer Jung, Sepah Salaur Subahdar of the Carnatic, to Colonel John Upton, Embassador at Poona, from the Governor-General and Supreme Council at Bengal.

Upon hearing of your Appointment as Embassador, to negociate a Peace with the People at Poona, I wrote to the Governor-General, desiring a Letter from him to you, to keep the Tranquillity of the Carnatic in View; the Governor-General, in Friendship to me, has sent me an English Letter, directed to you, and has informed me, that he has sent you a Duplicate thereof, which I hope you have received. I send you inclosed, Translation of his Letter to me; that to you I will send by trusty Persons, who are soon to set out. My Friendship and Regard have been for a long Time established with the King, the Company, and the English Nation, as have been their Favour and Regard to me. They consider me as themselves, and in their Kindness to me included me in the 11th Article of the Treaty made at Paris, with the other Kings; I am therefore convinced that I am the first Friend to the English Nation; and as there is no Prince in India so firmly attached to them as myself, and as the Governor-General has wrote to you to negociate jointly with my Embassadors, I request that you will wait a little for their Arrival, as they will soon set out, and by them I will write particularly, after which you will include the Peace and Tranquillity of the Carnatic in the Treaty between the Company, the English Nation, and the People of Poona, or Ragonaut Row, agreeable to a Draft I shall send you; and you'll oblige the Chiefs of the Marattas, not to demand any Chout, Surrdare, Mokee, &c. either for the past or the future. I never will forget your Friendship in this Affair, and I will be much obliged to you. What can I say more?

Given at Chepaute,
8th November 1775.

TREATY between the Honourable the English East-India Company, and the Maratta State.

Poona, January 1776.

Whereas Differences have arisen amongst the Chiefs of the Maratta State, and the Presidency of Bombay having taken a Part therein, by sending Forces into the Maratta Dominions, which the Honourable the Governor-General and Council of Fort William disapprove, we are desirous of conciliating the Differences, and have determined accordingly to enter such Measures as may most effectually contribute to so desirable an End.

The

The Governor-General and Council of Fort William, for this Purpose therefore have authorized, deputed, and given full Powers unto Lieutenant Colonel John Upton, in the Service of the Honourable English East-India Company, to conclude a Peace between the Presidency of Bombay and the Maratta State; and the following are the Articles of Convention between the said Lieutenant-Colonel John Upton, on the Part of the Honourable the English East-India Company, and the Ministers and the Chiefs respectively of the Maratta State, whose Names are hereunto subscribed, on the Part of the Maratta State. Done at Poona, this . . . . Day of 1776.

L. S. The Seal of the Peshwa.
L. S. A. B.
L. S. C. D. (Signed) J. U.
L. S. E. F.

Present, when the above was signed,
A. M. Persian Interpreter.
J. P. Secretary.

Article the 1st.
It is agreed, That
Article the 2d.
That
Article 3d.
That, &c. &c.
Signed as before.
Present when signed, as before.

Separate Articles.
No. 1.
2.
3.
&c. &c.

Signed as before.
Present when signed, as before.

N. B. In the Preamble to the Articles I have said " to settle a Peace between the Presidency of Bombay and the Maratta State, agreeable to the Tenor of my Instructions;" you will please to signify if you approve this Method, or would prefer its being drawn up only, " a Peace with the Honourable English East-India Company," as the Maratta Ministers seem very desirous of settling a full and lasting Peace with the English Nation; and there may be some Articles in which the Bombay Presidency may not be considered more particularly than either of the other Settlements.

Resolved, That the following Form of a Preamble to the Treaty with the Marattas, be sent to Colonel Upton.

ARTICLES of a Treaty of perpetual Peace and Friendship between the Maratta State and the English East-India Company, signed, sealed, and ratified by Rajah Ramraujee, Mahederow Seway, Pundit Purdham, the Son of Narrain Row, Peshwa, and Succaram Pundit, Maraba Pundit Turnavess, &c. &c. &c. (Babooje Naick Naroo, Sucker Amundrow Rasta, Darunnun Row, and Nanâ Turnavess) for themselves, and on Behalf of the other Chiefs and People of the Maratta State, on the one Part, and by Lieutenant Colonel John Upton, who is invested with full Powers by the Governor-General and Council of Bengal, on Behalf of the English East-India Company, on the other Part.

Whereas Differences have arisen between the Chiefs of the Maratta State, and the Governor and Council of Bombay have taken a Part therein by sending Forces into the Maratta Dominions; the Governor-General and Council of Bengal, from an earnest Desire to conciliate the said Differences, and to restore a firm and lasting Peace between the Chiefs of the said State and all the Governments of the English Company committed especially to their Charge, have deputed Lieutenant Colonel John Upton, and invested

invested him with full Powers from them, and on the Behalf of the English I Company, to conclude a Treaty of perpetual Peace and Friendship with th and other Rulers of the Maratta State; and the following are the Conditions by both Parties respectively; viz.

I.

II. &c.

N. B. The Treaty, when executed agreeable to the foregoing Form, shou livered to the Paishwa of the Maratta Government. In the Duplicate signe Governor-General and Council, the Precedency in Rank should be give Company.

The Names of the Maratta Ministers and Chiefs mentioned in this Pre only for the Sake of Form. Those should be inserted by whom the Treat ratified.

APPENDIX, N° 99

RESOLVED, That the following Reply be written to Colonel Upton:

Sir,

We have received your Letter of the 5th January from Poona.

Our Reasons for insisting on the Signature of all the Maratta Chiefs to th were founded on the undivided State of that Government, and the Infan Peishwa, who is supported by the Regency at Poona. We still think that t currence is equally desirable; but we would not let this Point be made any O to the Conclusion of the Treaty, and the Distance is too great for you to refer t Difficulty which may occur to you in the Course of your Negociations, and tc our Orders. On all such Occasions, you will conform as nearly to the genera our Orders as Circumstances will admit.

On the present Subject we authorize you to accept of the Ratification of the the Peishwa, his Ministers, and the Persons whose Signatures are usually fi Treaties of that State; and we wish also to obtain those of all the other C are present, and are possessed of sufficient Power to oppose the Execution o would still have you require, that the others should be Parties, and that th may be signified by Writings, or by Persons properly authorized on their Be as we are sensible that this may be impracticable with respect to all the Chi cially those who espouse the Interest of the opposite Party, we only express that the Whole may be included, and leave it to your Discretion to recede Requisition such Degree as you shall find it unattainable.

We enclose a proper Form of a Preamble to the Treaty which you may con the Peishwa.

We are, &c.

General Clavering.—When Colonel Upton's Instructions were drawn u directed to use his Endeavours to obtain the Cession of Bassein, on the Suppo the Government of Bombay was actually in Possession of it. From later A have been informed, that although the Cession of the Island of Bassein was Article of the Treaty between Ragoba and the Government of Bombay, the of it had never been yielded to the Company.

We have been informed by Mr. Tayler, that of all the Possessions of the Empire, the Ministers are more tenacious of preserving the Islands of Salsette a than of any other of their Territories; because the Conquest of those Isla made by the Peishwa's Ancestors from the Portugueze, they considered the of them as an Honour which it would be a Disgrace for them to relinqui am apprehensive that if the Terms in Colonel Upton's Instructions relativ Island of Bassein remain unrepealed, and that he be not instructed to relinqui mand of Bassein in Case the Ministers should absolutely object to cede it to the Company, the Treaty must be broken off, and consequently the desirable Object which we have in View, of obtaining Peace for the Government of Bombay, be postponed for a considerable Time; I beg Leave to propose, that discretional Orders be now given to him, not to insist on the Island of Bassein being granted to the Company in the future Treaty of Peace; unless the Ministers have already consented to acquiesce to the Demand that he has made for it, or that he perceives a Disposition in them to yield the Possession of it to the Company.

Mr. Francis.—I understood that the Object of Colonel Upton's Appointment was to settle and conclude a definitive Treaty of Peace with the Maratta State, on Terms equitable to them, and also in some Degree honourable and advantageous to the Company. We undoubtedly meant to relinquish many of the Advantages stipulated by the Presidency of Bombay with Ragoba; but we also meant to obtain some other beneficial Articles in Return for those Concessions, otherwise I see no Subject for a Negociation. A Peace, by which one of the contracting Parties yields every Thing, might have been obtained without a formal Embassy, or even without a Treaty. The Acquisition of Salsette and Bassein must have appeared to us to be an equitable Condition, since, in our Instructions to Colonel Upton, we have declared, that "we were determined on no Account" to relinquish the Possession of those Islands, and that he would "at no Rate" agree to restore them. It does not appear to me, that the Circumstance of Bassein's not being actually in our Possession makes any Difference with respect to the Propriety of our adhering to our first Plan. Our Right to demand the Cession of that Island, would not have been improved by our previously taking Possession of it. We are forming a Treaty of perpetual Peace, in which each of the contracting Parties must be expected to yield something reciprocally for the Public Good.

I think that the Cession of Salsette and Bassein should be insisted on; and as Col. Upton has not suggested to us that he expects to meet with any Difficulties on either of those Points, I hope they will both be obtained.

Col. Monson.—When I gave my Consent to the First Draft of Instructions to Col. Upton, I understood, from the Representations of the Presidency of Bombay, that they were in Possession, in Consequence of the Treaty with Ragoba, of Bassein and its Dependencies. I have since learned, that although that Cession was one of the Conditions of the Treaty, that Ragoba had no Power to put the Presidency of Bombay in Possession of that Place; and that if they obtained it, it must be by Force of Arms. My Object in the Mission of Col. Upton to Poona, was to restore Peace on the Western Side of India, which I think should be obtained on any Terms, as a War carried on there can only be expensive to the Company, and prejudicial to the general Trade of Hindostan. I therefore am of Opinion, that Col. Upton should have Instructions to obtain Bassein and its Dependencies, if he can, from the Ministerial Party; but not to make it an Article on which to break off the Treaty he is now instructed to conclude.

Governor General.—The Company have invariably joined Bassein and Salsette in all their Instructions to the Presidency of Bombay, to obtain Possession of the latter. Of its Importance in a commercial Light, we have been informed by Mr. Tayler, in his Letter to this Board, recorded in Consultation 9th October. It appears to be of still greater Consequence as a political Acquisition, from its Connection with the Continent, and its Contiguity to the Passes which lead directly to Poona. We have repeatedly declared to Col. Upton, that we would not depart from our Claim to Bassein; nothing has since occurred to induce the Board to change a Declaration so peremptorily made, nor do I conceive that Colonel Upton will find any Difficulty to carry it into Execution. The Ministers have no personal Interest to serve, nor Family Pride to gratify, in the Detention either of Salsette or Bassein.

They were conquered by the Ancestors of Ragoba, who has already consented to relinquish them. The Infant Peishwa, who might be swayed by the same Considerations, is incapable of forming any Opinion upon them; and every Argument which can justify our retaining the Possession of Salsette, combats equally in Favour of our Right to Bassein, and of the Propriety of asserting it. I am therefore of Opinion, that no Alteration should be made in our original Instructions upon this Subject.

I am against the Question.

Resolved, That no Alteration be made in the Instructions already given to Lieutenant Colonel Upton, for requiring the Cession of the Island of Bassein, as a Condition of the Treaty of Peace.

General Clavering. — I must protest against this Resolution of the Board, a the fatal Consequences that I am afraid will ensue from it. By one Act of In we have taken the Island of Salsette from the Marattas, and by another we ref make Peace with them, without they relinquish the Possession of an Island whi have no Right to claim from them, by any Equivalent that we can cede to th return.

General Clavering requiring to refer to the Letter from the Court of Directors Presidency of Bombay, which arrived this Day in the Grenville Packet, to enabl to finish his Protest; the Secretary informs him, that with the Approbation c Board he has just sent it to Mr. Tayler for his Perusal. The General therefore compleating his Minute until he can obtain a Reference to it.

Ordered, That the Secretary wait on Mr. Barwell with the above Debate, a quest his Opinion upon the Question proposed by the General.

The Secretary having waited on Mr. Barwell with the Whole of this Consult agreeably to the Orders of the Board, he declared that he acquiesced in the Senti expressed by the Governor General and Mr. Francis.

Warren Hastir
J. Clavering,
Geo. Monson,
P. Francis.

APPENDIX, N° 100.

Extract of Bengal Secret Consultations, the 14th February, 1776.

PRESENT,

The Honourable Warren Hastings, Governor General, President,
Lieutenant General John Clavering,
The Honourable George Monson,
Richard Barwell, } Esquires.
Philip Francis, }

GENERAL CLAVERING having referred to the Letter of the Co Directors of Bombay, dated 12th April, now delivers in a Continuation Minute of the 12th Instant, as follows:

The Letter from the Court of Directors to the Council at Bombay of the April, which we have just been reading, contains their positive Commands not t Possession of the Island of Salsette without their Permission, but by Negociatio the Island of Bassein can be obtained by the same Means, I shall be glad; but I t neither consistent with the Orders of the Court of Directors, given so particul this Letter to the Council of Bombay, or to us, in their Instructions to preser Peace of India, to continue a War merely to acquire Territory. On the same ciples, the Propriety of restoring of Salsette, it may be said, might be inferred; that, one Injustice will not authorize our committing another. I confess I wis ardently that the Board would even obviate the Objection I feel to our insisting on ing Salsette, without giving some Equivalent for it either in Money or in Territo believe Fort Victoria was once proposed by the Company themselves as an Equ for it; but whatever the Board may think proper to do in this Matter, there tainly a very great Difference between relinquishing a Place of which we are in Posi and our insisting on obtaining another Island of much more Value and Strength, t might perhaps have much Difficulty to acquire by Force. The Board must ref the Consequence of the Ministers at Poona refusing to comply with our Demand the War must be continued, the Effects of which are already so severely felt

Presidency of Bombay, in its Trade in all its Branches. Are we resolved in what Manner the War shall be conducted, to compel the Maratta State to submit to our Terms? Are we determined to send Twenty Lacks annually to Bombay till Peace is concluded? For these, and many other urgent Reasons, I think the Board's Resolution to insist on the Surrender of Bassein of so much Importance, that it deserves to be reconsidered. I therefore move, that the Orders to Colonel Upton, to insist on the Surrender of Bassein, may be discretional, in Case it can be obtained by Negociation, but not otherwise.

Mr. Francis—The System on which I have invariably acted, has been hitherto honoured with the Concurrence and Approbation of General Clavering and Colonel Monson. The former Protest now made by General Clavering against a Resolution of the Board, in which I concurred, cannot therefore fail to bring the Consistency of my Conduct into Question both here and at Home. I do not think that I have departed from any one of the Principles which I have avowed and set my Name to. I think that in adhering to the Instructions originally given to Colonel Upton, I did no more than support the same Plan, which was approved and confirmed by every Member of the Board. I must, however, beg the Indulgence of the Board to take a little Time to consider and draw up a Defence of my Conduct, as I know no Period of my future Life in which the Transaction that appears on the Records of Monday last may not affect my Character. I have the greatest Reason to expect this Indulgence, as General Clavering himself has taken Two Days to consider and introduce some new Arguments in his present Motion, which were not before the Board on Monday. Late in the Afternoon of that Day I did earnestly and repeatedly request of the Board to delay the Debate and Decision of the whole Question till the next Morning: That Proposal was not agreed to. I did also urge, that Mr. Barwell's accidental Absence might not prevent the Questions being determined by a full Board; but that his Opinion might be taken into the Determination of the Board, as has been practised upon some other Occasion. This Conduct shews how unwilling I was to hurry the Decision of a Question in which I had the Misfortune not to agree with General Clavering and Colonel Monson—No Time was allowed me. After a more careful Review of the whole Subject, I must declare, that I do not even now see any Reasons for adopting General Clavering's first Motion, which ought not to have weighed with him and with the Board at the Time when he signed the following Instruction to Colonel Upton:

" We are determined on no Account to relinquish the Possession of Salsette and
" Bassein; therefore should the Peishwa hold out against yielding them to the Com-
" pany, you are at no Rate to agree to restore them."

A Circumstance is now mentioned, which alone is supposed to justify a Departure from the Spirit of this Instruction; viz. that when it was given, the Board conceived that Bassein was actually in our Possession. I myself do not think the Difference material. But those Members of the Board who think it material, should, as I humbly apprehend, have moved for an Alteration of the Instructions as soon as they discovered their Mistake. I believe it was discovered so long ago as the 9th October, when Mr. Tayler was before the Board. From that Time to the present, no Step has been taken to obviate the fatal Consequences which are now foretold to our adhering to the Demand of Bassein. No other new Matter of any Kind respecting this Question has yet come before us. Colonel Upton does not suggest to us the Apprehension of any Difficulty whatsoever on this Point. I cannot therefore, without departing from that Consistency of Conduct which I have hitherto endeavoured to maintain, consent to any Alteration in Colonel Upton's original Instructions; let me add, that I cannot do it without opposing my own Opinion to the unanimous Sense of the Board, deliberately, not hastily taken, as I find it expressed in our Letters to Colonel Upton of the 21st June and 17th July. At the same Time, however, I am far from opposing the present Motion for bringing the Question again under Consideration. I am at all Times ready to give every Member of this Board an Opportunity of reconsidering his Opinion on any important Question; we owe such Compliance mutually to each other; we owe it also to the public Service. Neither am I myself so obstinately fixed in my own Opinion, as not to be open to hear and yield to Argument.

Mr. Barwell—I do not understand General Clavering's Motion to be a Reconsideration of the Resolution to insist on the Surrender of Bassein, but a Proposition to alter the original Instructions given to Colonel Upton. I am against the Motion.

Colonel Monson—Mr. Francis, in his Minute, accuses the Board of having hurried him into a hasty Opinion, without being allowed sufficient Time to digest his Thoughts upon the Question then under Deliberation. I was present at the Board on Monday last during the whole Time of the Board's sitting, and do not recollect any Proposition being made for an Adjournment. I believe it will not appear from the Proceedings of that Day, that such a Proposition was made. Mr. Francis, in order to prove a Consistency in his own Conduct, charges me with a Neglect of mine. It is true I was acquainted by Mr. Tayler so early as the 9th of October, that we were not in Possession of Bassein and its Dependencies. It would certainly then have been proper to have sent Colonel Upton Instructions not to have insisted upon the Cession of that Place to the Company, as the ultimate Terms of the Treaty. I do not think I can be accused of deviating from that System of Consistency which I have laid down. I declared on Monday last, that my Object in the Mission of Colonel Upton to Poona, was to restore Peace. My Intention in giving a discretionary Power to Colonel Upton, is consistent with that Declaration. I think that Colonel Upton should endeavour to procure Bassein, but not to make it the final Condition of his Treaty. If he should perceive a Disposition in the Ministry at Poona to relinquish Bassein for an Equivalent, or what may be thought so, I would recommend even that Broach and its Dependencies should be ceded for Bassein and its Dependencies. Upon the Whole, I think it so much for the Interest of the Company, and so consonant to their Instructions to acquire Peace throughout India, that I would even consent, should it be insisted on, to restore the Island of Salsette. I should be sorry to preclude any Gentleman from delivering his Sentiments upon a Question which I think, considering the critical Situation of Affairs in Europe and this Country, of the utmost Consequence to the Company. I therefore am for the Motion; not that I have any new Matter to offer to the Consideration of the Board, but shall be ready to yield to any Arguments which may be used in Support of a contrary Opinion to that which I have given.

Mr. Francis—I beg Leave to assure Colonel Monson, that I never had a Thought of bringing a Charge of any Kind against the Board, or against himself. No Man is more ready than I am to acknowledge and bear Testimony to the Integrity and Consistency of his Conduct. I have often availed myself of his superior Judgment: I hope still to be guided by it. With respect to the Question before the Board, my Object is simply the Acquisition of Bassein with Salsette; I have expressed no Opinion, I have proposed no Limitation to the Concessions which it may be proper to make to the Marattas in Return for this Acquisition. I think the Situation of these Places makes the Acquisition of them so essential to the Security and beneficial Possession of Bombay, that I am willing to purchase it upon the Terms proposed by Colonel Monson, and so far forth I yield to his Opinion.

With respect to what I have said, of my Request that the Debate of Monday last might be postponed till the next Morning; it is very true, that no formal Motion appears on the Proceedings to that Effect. That I did make such a Request, is a mere Matter of Fact, for which I can only appeal to the Recollection of the other Members of the Board. But I beg it may stop here.

General Clavering—In deciding on the important Question now before us, it seems very immaterial, whether the Protest I have entered this Day on the Consultations was finished on Monday or not; the Reason of my deferring it to this Day, was to obtain the precise Words contained in the Letter from the Court of Directors to the Government of Bombay, prohibiting them to take Salsette by Force if they could not obtain it by Negociation. I have introduced no new Matter into it which would not have appeared at that Time, had I recollected the Terms in which the Court of Directors Commands were expressed. I wished only to be accurate, and not to take up the Time of the Board a Second Day on a Business which I could not have wished might have been concluded immediately. In regard to the Desire which Mr. Francis expresses he had to postpone the Decision of my Question on Monday, till there was a full Board; it certainly only depended on himself and the Governor General to have done it, if they had pleased, as they then formed a Majority. I mentioned in my Minute on Monday, that the Orders for insisting on keeping Bassein as well as Salsette, were given in Consequence of the full Persuasion that we were in, that the Island of Bassein had been ceded and relinquished to the Company along with the other Possessions which Ragoba had actually surrendered to the Government of Bombay. It is true that the Mistake was discovered so early as in October, but neither at that Time nor since did it ever occur to me, that

wo

we had given Orders so peremptory to Colonel Upton, not to relinquish the Possession of Bassein. The Word not to "restore," plainly implies our Conception of our being in Possession of it. The first Duty that we owe both to those who employ us and ourselves, is to correct a Mistake as soon as we discover it; it was only on Monday last that I observed, on reading over the Instructions to Colonel Upton, the Error that we had committed; I no sooner observed it, than I made a Proposition to the Board to have it rectified, hoping that it would have met with no Difficulty from any of the Members, and particularly from one with whom I had hitherto concurred in every Sentiment since my Arrival at Bengal, in the strict Observance of the Company's Orders, and in the Principles of Public Justice. I still hope that both he and the other Members of the Board, on a Review of the Consequences (which I cannot help thinking will be very fatal) of the Orders given to Colonel Upton, unless they be rescinded, will still permit that they be made discretional.

The Governor General—I certainly remember that Mr. Francis more than once expressed a Reluctance to decide on the Propositions contained in Colonel Upton's Letter at the last Meeting of the Board in this Department, and he will do me the Justice to acknowledge that I declared myself equally desirous of postponing it; and had a Motion been made to that Effect, I should certainly have voted for it, for the Purpose of affording sufficient Leisure for every Member of the Board to weigh and deliberate maturely on a Point of so much Importance as that contained in the General's Question; but no such Motion was made, and for my own Part I had no Motive to make it, because I was already clearly determined in my own Opinion. I have already assigned the Reasons which induced me to oppose the General's Question. I could add many others of equal Strength, and could place those which I have already urged in a much stronger Point of View; but I conclude that the Judgment of the Court of Directors will, ere this, have been made known to the Presidency of Bombay, concerning the Propriety of the Design formed by that Presidency for possessing themselves both of Salsette and Bassein. I shall be therefore very brief in what I have further to add on this Subject.

I have always understood it to have been an invariable Injunction of the Court of Directors to the Presidency of Bombay, to seize every favourable Occasion for acquiring Possession of Salsette and Bassein, either by Treaty or Arms, and conceive the Acquisition of Bassein to be of equal, if not of greater Consequence, than that of Salsette. In the Instructions therefore which were given to Colonel Upton, I assented to the Declaration, that the Possession of Salsette and Bassein should on no Account be relinquished, regarding the Possession of both as an inseparable Object both of the Company's Intentions and Wishes; nor do I recollect whether I understood Bassein to have been still in the Possession of the Marattas at the Time when these Instructions were drawn, or in ours; it yet does not appear from the Bombay Letters which were received to that Date; nor would it have made any Change in my Opinion of the Propriety of insisting on the Cession both of Salsette and Bassein; yet I should with less Reluctance have yielded, at that Time, to any Proposition that had been made for the Surrender of the latter, as the Wish of the Majority of the Board was to remove every Obstacle to the Restoration of Peace, and the Concession might have been then made on our Part, without any Circumstances of Humiliation; but having declared our Resolution in such peremptory and decided Terms, having repeated it in Two separate Paragraphs in the First Instructions, and again in the Second which were delivered to Colonel Upton on the 17th July, I have no Doubt that Colonel Upton will have made the Demand both for Salsette and Bassein in Terms equally peremptory. I dread therefore the Consequences of relinquishing a Point on which we have already made the future Event of Peace or War to turn. The Marattas will be obviously led to conclude, with such a Promptness to change a Resolution of such Consequence, that we shall be equally disposed to yield to any Demands which they may make, rather than hazard the Renewal of the War. From what has passed, I feel myself as solicitous as the other Gentlemen of the Board may be, to bring Colonel Upton's Negociation to a speedy and peaceable Conclusion; and from the Character of the People with whom we are in Treaty, I believe that we shall be more likely to attain that End by an undeviating Adherence to the Requisitions and Declarations which we have already made, than by Concessions of any Kind, but more especially by such as are

 spontaneously

spontaneously made, through the Apprehension only that they may be in the future Course of the Negociations exacted from us.

Mr. Francis moves, That this Debate be adjourned till to-morrow.

Agreed to.

Warren Hastings,
J. Clavering,
Geo. Monson,
P. Francis.

Extract of Bengal Secret Consultations, the 15th February 1776.

PRESENT,

The Honourable Warren Hastings, Governor General, President;
Lieutenant General John Clavering,
The Honourable George Monson,
Richard Barwell, } Esquires.
Philip Francis, }

Resumed the Debate of Yesterday.

Mr. Francis—I have already expressed my Willingness to make a Compensation to the Marattas for the Cession of Bassein, if the Possession of that Place cannot be obtained on any other Terms. Colonel Monson has expressed an Opinion to the same Effect. I would therefore propose, that Colonel Upton, in Case he should find insurmountable Difficulties in obtaining Bassein without a Compensation, may be authorized to propose certain Concessions to the Poona Government in Return for their Compliance with his first Demand. I think that a Surrender of our Right and Interest in Broach might be made the Condition of that Compliance; but he should at the same Time be particularly instructed to reserve this Concession until he shall find it absolutely impossible to succeed without it. In the mean Time he may propose other Compensations, if any should be demanded, and not come to this but in the last Extremity.

Mr. Barwell—I adhere to the Opinion that I have already given; I cannot conceive that we have it in our Power to offer the Marattas any Thing beyond the Company's Alliance for the Cessions demanded from them. The Ministers of the Maratta State must be fully sensible of the Interests we sacrifice in quitting the Party of Ragoba, and withdrawing our Forces from his Cause; any Thing beyond this, I apprehend, will speak rather a Weakness in the English Government; and I shall not be surprized if, presuming on such a Principle, they should demand to be paid even for the Expences of the War. The most favourable Occasion that could have offered for promoting the Interests of the Company on the Western Side of India, we propose to forego for the Sake of Peace, and only insist on such a Condition from the Maratta State, as is absolutely necessary to the very Being of Bombay. I am against the Motion.

Colonel Monson—When Proposals of Peace are made to a Nation, to which they have it not in their Power to accede, it is the same Thing as a Declaration of War, or a Continuation of Hostilities. This I conceive to be the Nature of the Proposal which is to be the final Condition on which Colonel Upton is to make his Treaty with the Marratta State: The Fort of Bassein I understand to be of very considerable Strength, and in the Possession of a Person who neither acknowledges the Ministerial Party or that of Ragoba; it is certain, from our not having been put in Possession of it, that he pays no Regard to the Treaty the Presidency of Bombay have made with Ragoba, or we should have been in Possession of that Place many Months. My Wish in giving a certain Latitude to Colonel Upton's Instructions, is to attain an honourable and lasting Peace; therefore, I could wish that the positive Orders under which he is now to act might be extended; but at the same Time, that he should be instructed to obtain the desirable Object of Bassein and its Dependencies, without giving any Equivalent for them; but if he finds that is not to be done, then to enter into a Negociation for an Exchange of Broach and its Dependencies for Bassein and its Dependencies, but not to cede the former until the Company are put in Possession of the latter, without

without any Expence or Assistance afforded by the Company; that is, not to receive the Right only without the Possession.

If Peace is not to be obtained from the Marattas but by the Cession of Broach for Bassein, I think it should be accepted on those Conditions. I am therefore for the Motion.

Mr. Francis—I beg Leave to observe, that there is no Fact or Instance before the Board, on which I could ground a Supposition that the Commandant of Bassein would not think himself bound to comply with the Orders of the Poona Government: His not having acquiesced in the Treaty made between the Presidency of Bombay and Ragoba, proves only that he is not a Dependant of that Prince, which I never understood he was; but it does not follow, that he will not obey the Orders of the Paishwa and his Ministers, whom, as I have always understood, he acknowledges for his Superiors. I undoubtedly meant that the Cession of Broach, or any other Place now held by the Company, should not be made until the Company were put in Possession of Bassein.

Colonel Monson—I have no Right to say that the Person who commands in the Fort of Bassein, will not obey the Orders of the Ministerial Party, for by doing that, I should declare him a Rebel; but it is my Opinion that he will not, as I believe there are few Instances in this Country where Persons who are in Possession of strong Forts, do give them up by the Orders of any Person, without having first made Terms for themselves. I make no Doubt, but if the Ministerial Party would make over their Right to the East India Company, of Bassein and its Dependencies, and that the Company's Army was to appear before the Place, that the Commandant would deliver it up to the Army, on certain Advantages for himself; but then the Company must be at the Expence of the Conquest; and in this Manner, they might take Possession of any Place in this Country.

General Clavering—The Proposal made by Mr. Francis to exchange Broach for Bassein, is perfectly agreeable to the Object I had in View, in acquiring the latter by Negociation; but I must observe, that Mr. Francis has not explained himself, whether he would still persevere instructing Colonel Upton to break off the Treaty with the Ministers, in Case they should refuse to cede that Island to us upon these Terms.

Mr. Francis—I have always considered the Acquisition of Salsette and Bassein as the fundamental Article of our Negociations with the Marattas; considering all Circumstances, I do not foresee a Probability of their being refused; if, however, Colonel Upton should find the Maratta Government inflexibly determined not to yield Bassein, he may in that Case suspend his Negociations, and wait for further Orders from this Board, but there will be no Necessity for his entirely breaking them off, or quitting Poonah.

Governor General—I object to the Question, because Broach is already the Company's Property, purchased at great Expence, and with the Loss of the Lives of an Officer of distinguished Merit and many British Subjects; because I have Doubts whether there be a Power in this Board to give up the Possession of Broach, the Acquisition of which has been confirmed by the Court of Directors; because I believe that in the Comparison, the Possession of Broach will be found to be yet more advantageous than even that of Bassein; at least, we know it to be a rich and fruitful Country, abounding in many valuable Productions and Manufactures, especially in the Article of Cotton, with which it supplies the greatest Part of the Country in that Article from the Malabar Coast; because it is a much frequented Port of Trade, and the Key to the Provinces of Adjemore, Jessemore, and the Western Districts of Hindostan, which it supplies with Broad Cloth, bought at the Company's Sales; because our present Possession of it is known and visible to the whole World, and the Surrender of it will be an implied Imputation of a Want of Power in the Company to retain it; and lastly, because I am clearly of Opinion that the Treaty may be obtained without it, and that even if it could not, we should be justified, after the many Concessions which have been made to the Ministers, were we to be reduced to the Necessity of renewing the War, there being every Reason to believe that the Contest would be of very short Duration.

Resolved, That Lieutenant Colonel Upton, in Case he should find insurmountable Difficulties in obtaining Bassein without a Compensation, be authorised to propose certain Concessions to the Poona Government, and that in Return for a Compliance with his first Demand, a Surrender of our Right and Interest in Broach be the Condition of that

Compliance;

Compliance; but that he be particularly instructed to reserve this Concession until he shall find it absolutely impossible to succeed without it.

Ordered, That Instructions agreeable to the above Resolution be sent to Colonel Upton.

Mr. Francis—I request the Sense of the Board, whether it should make a Part of the Instructions to Colonel Upton, that in Case he should find the Maratta Government inflexibly determined not to yield Bassein at any Rate, he should suspend his Negociations, and wait for further Orders from the Board, or whether he should intirely break off the Treaty, and quit Poona? I agree that he should suspend his Negociations, and wait for Orders.

Mr. Barwell gone Home.

Colonel Monson thinks he should wait for further Orders.

General Clavering—I agree to it with Reluctance, because I think it will tend to protract the Conclusion of the proposed Treaty.

Governor-General—I do not object, although I think that a more firm and decided Conduct is more likely to accomplish the Ends which we have all in View.

Agreed in the Affirmative, to this additional Proposal of Mr. Francis.

Resolved that the following Letter be written to Lieutenant Colonel Upton.

Sir,

In Addition to our Letter of the 14th, which accompanies this, we think it necessary to give you farther Instructions, to obviate if possible the Occasion of any farther Reference.

If you should find the Ministers totally averse to make the Surrender of Bassein a Condition of the Treaty, after using every other Means in your Power to engage them to it, we authorize you to offer some Concessions to them in return, which you will endeavour to make as moderate as possible; and ultimately we empower you to cede the Fortress and Dependencies of Broach in return for the actual Cession of the Island of Bassein and its Dependencies, if you shall find it unattainable on inferior Terms; but you are not to propose this final Concession until it appears absolutely impossible to succeed without it. If this should also be rejected, we desire you will give us immediate Information, and not leave Poona, if you can continue there with Safety, until you receive our farther Orders.

We are, &c. &c.

Warren Hastings,
J. Clavering,
G. Monson,
P. Francis.

APPENDIX, N° 101.

Extract of Bengal Secret Consultations, the 26th February, 1776.

PRESENT,

The Honourable Warren Hastings, Governor General, President,
Lieutenant General John Clavering,
The Honourable George Monson,
Richard Barwell, } Esquires.
Philip Francis, }

RECEIVED the following Letter from Bombay:

Honourable Sir, and Gentlemen,

We addressed you in Duplicate by the Ships St. Helena and Union, under the 17th Ultimo, and have since been honoured with your Commands, dated the 25th May, 17th July

July, and 9th October, all of which arrived on the 28th Ultimo, and on the 6th Instant we received your Letter, dated the 7th September, addressed to the Select Committee.

The Irregularity and Delay with which both your and our Advices have been mutually received, have been very perplexing to us; and as the Two first-mentioned Letters are of so very old a Date, and your Honour will have since received such full Information from our late Letters, and from Mr. Tayler, it is only necessary to observe in Reply to that Date, the 25th May, that we certainly should have addressed you by the same Vessel which conveyed the Return of our Forces to General Clavering, had we not understood she was to make a trading Voyage, and would probably have a long Passage to Bengal, and we then shortly intended to dispatch the Company's Vessel the Tannah Schooner, directly to your Presidency, which however was unavoidably detained longer than we expected.

Before we received the Explanation of your Orders for recalling the Company's Troops to our own Garrisons, we did not understand they absolutely implied their Return to Bombay, and therefore proposed letting them remain in the Surat or Broach Purgunnahs until we were favoured with your final Answer to the Representations Mr. Tayler was commissioned to make you. Our late Letters and Correspondence with Lieutenant Colonel Keating, transmitted by the Royal Charlotte, will likewise have apprized you of the Advice we gave to Ragoba, to accompany our Troops with such Part of his Army as he might be able to maintain, being sensible that the Separation of our Forces from his at that Time, would have exposed him to immediate Destruction, entirely defeated the Purpose for which you had deputed Colonel Upton to Poona, and rendered ineffectual the Representations we intended making to your Honour, &c. in his Favour.

By our last Advices the Two Armies were arrived at Corode, a Place only 15 Coss from Surat, belonging to the Nabob. And when our Commanding Officer was preparing to march to the Quarters assigned for them in Chicoley, one of the Purgunnahs ceded to us by Futty Sing, the Peishwa acquainted him, that he could not quarter in that Purgunnah without certain Ruin to his Cause, and insisted on remaining in their present Situation, until he could explain his Reasons to us, and receive our Determination.

We beg Leave to enclose a Copy of the Letter Ragoba addressed our President on the Subject, and the Continuation of our Correspondence with Lieutenant Colonel Keating, which will inform your Honour, &c. of his Motives for refusing to quit the Encampment at Corode; and having considered with the most deliberate Attention what Conduct we should observe on the Occasion, the following most forcible Reasons occurred to us, to induce us to permit our Troops remaining for the present in the Encampment they now occupy:

That we hourly expected to receive full and precise Orders from your Honour, &c. in Answer to the Representations made you by Mr. Tayler, and we could foresee no bad Consequences from our Troops remaining in their present Situation until that Time, whereas many might be apprehended from their precipitately quitting Ragoba:

That the most probable Consequence of their taking this Step appears to be, that his Adherents, discouraged by your deserting him, would likewise instantly forsake him, and the several Officers who before were inclined to embrace his Cause, would give up all Thoughts of supporting him, which would not only make his Situation desperate and irretrievable, but also have a very bad Effect on Colonel Upton's Negociation, by encouraging the Poona Government to demand Terms very different from those we are clearly of Opinion they may now be induced to agree to, as they will certainly either raise or lower their Demands according to Ragoba's Situation, and this your Honour, &c. seem to be aware of, by your Instructions to Colonel Upton:

That on the other Hand, should Ragoba, notwithstanding the Separation of our Forces, be still able to keep his Army together, and his Friends remain firm to his Interest, the Honourable Company would lose all their Influence with him, and the Maratta Armies, no longer awed by the Presence of British Troops, would very probably again commence Hostilities, whereby your Honour's, &c. Hopes of effecting a general Pacification, would be entirely defeated:

That Corode, though not actually the Company's Purgunnah, belonged to our Ally the Nabob of Surat, and our Troops would be there equally ready to embark for the Presidency, or disposed of as might be necessary in Consequence of your Orders, as if they had been at Chicoly; and being situated on the Banks of the River Tappey, the Army

Army having the Country open to them, would be plentifully supp and Provisions, and the Company's Territories be preserved from the ways committed by Maratta Armies.

For the above Reasons we conceived the Good of the Service absolu permitting the Company's Troops to remain with Ragoba in their prese until we received the expected Letters from your Honour, &c.; and we you will approve our Determination.

Ragoba also warmly solicited us to permit our Forces to accompan the Candeish Country, to levy Contributions; but though we are sen much in Want of Money, no Provision having been yet made for hi the Adjustment of the Treaty, we did not think ourselves authorized Step, and acquainted him, it was totally out of our Power to comp quest.

From the best Intelligence we can procure of the Situation of the M we learn, that on the 14th Instant Hurry Punt Furkia, with 13 or 1 Foot, Five Cannon, and Three Swivels, mounted on Hackeries, wit were encamped near the Village Conquella, on the Banks of the Ri Coss from the Pass of Candibana. Annant Row Rasta, and his Brot with about 5,000 Horse and Three Pieces of Cannon, were encampe Coss from the said Pass; and Derhajee Nonibalhar, with about 12 or Two Elephants, were at Boundigom, one Coss from the Pass: That th little Signs of Spirits, and kept exceeding watchful Guards, so that finite Difficulty the Halcarrahs could enter the different Camps, even of Grass-cutters; and Col. Keating's Letters mentioned, that they ployed in sinking Shafts in the Pass, to prevent the Passage of Stores c

The Ministerial Party have not made any Overtures to us for an since those mentioned in our Letter dated the 23d August; nor had w expect they would, as your Honour, &c. have signified to them your Inte Col. Upton to treat with them at Poona; and the several Acts of Hostili their Troops, as mentioned in Col. Keating's Letters, give us great R the Sincerity of their Intentions.

The many Overtures and Offers of Assistance made to Ragoba by and other most considerable Men of the Confederacy, and the Diffe between the Chiefs of that Party, have caused so great an Alteration Affairs in Favour of Ragoba, that we beg Leave to submit it to you, Opinion, that a Treaty with him would be more advantageous to the mises more Stability and Permanency, and is more likely to ensure th of India, than one with the Ministers. The Reasons on which we g nion, are fully stated in a Letter we have dispatched to Col. Upton, necessary he should be apprized of the true Situation of Ragoba's A commenced his Negociation: And in this Letter, a Copy of which have freely offered our Sentiments to the Colonel; but as he may no himself at Liberty to adopt them, we request, if your Honour, &c. in Opinion, you will send him Directions accordingly. We have not him, but within these few Days have received certain Intelligence Brampore, on the Road to Poona.

The Cessions of Territory made by Ragoba appear to us Objects of to the Company, that we are greatly alarmed at your Intentions them. The Company's Right to them is indisputable, as being de Grants made by the lawful Sovereign of the ceded Countries; and that if Colonel Upton shews a Determination not to part with then Obstacle to the Conclusion of a general Peace, which ever Party he The compact and convenient Situation of the several Purgunnahs, wit Settlements of Surat and Broach, will enable us to collect the Rev Expence; and a very small Addition to the Garrisons at those Plac sufficient for their Defence. The Revenues will defray the Expences, Investments of this Presidency; the Company will possess many valu Commerce with their own Territories, and be able greatly to ext Woollens and other Staples of Great Britain. We have been some Ti Possession of all the ceded Territories (except Bassein); the Revenue without any Difficulty, and the Marattas already consider them as di their Empire. Your Honour, &c. must before this Time be so well informed on the Subject, that it is unnecessary for us to add more; but we hope soon to be able to send you an accurate Account of their Revenues, and a correct Chart. Colonel Keating has succeeded in obtaining a Grant from Futty Sing of Batta, the Village mentioned in our Address dated the 17th Ultimo; and there being Four Villages called the Autgoms, situated in the very Center of the Broach Purgunnah, which formerly composed a Part of it, until they were wrested from the Moguls by the Guicawars, about Forty Years ago, we conceived that our Sunnud for the Town and Purgunnah, entitled us likewise to these Villages, or at any Rate that it was improper they should be possessed by any other Power, as they might prove a constant Source of Disputes. We therefore instructed Colonel Keating to state our Pretensions to them to Futty Sing, and to obtain a Sunnud for them, and likewise if possible for the remaining Eight Autgoms (there being Twelve in all) which border close upon the Purgunnah, and would be a very convenient Addition to the Company's Territory. We do not know the Amount of the Revenues produced by the Autgoms, but we believe it is not very considerable.

Colonel Keating's Letters contain all the Information we possess respecting Govind Row and Futty Sing; and we have the Pleasure to observe, that the Dispute between them is nearly compromised, which will be a Circumstance very favourable to Ragoba.

We have the Honour, &c.

Bombay Castle,
29th December 1775.

(Signed) William Hornby, D. Draper, J. Mostyn, B. Fletcher, Robert Gardin, W. Ashburner. Andrew Ramsay.

Translation of a Letter from Ragonath Row, Bajee Row, Pundit Pradan, to the Honourable William Hornby, Esquire, President and Governor of Bombay; dated the 28th November, and received 4th December 1775.

After Compliments:

Your Honour having sent Mr. Tayler to Calcutta this long While ago, I thought that an Answer would soon be received from him: I marched further to receive his Answer on the Way. With this Intention I marched from Nurmada, and encamped at Codadah upon the Jappee; but your Order is not come as yet. Colonel Keating desired me much, on my Arrival here, to march and to go to Chickly; but our marching thither will tend to my Disadvantage, as all the Officers and Ministers who have sent their Proposals to me (by your Honour's Help) promising to come and join me, will become hopeless; and my Army will, on my going to Chickly, starve there; the Country will be ruined, and I shall be distressed for Money for my Expences. I did, for these Reasons, very much desire Colonel Keating to remain at this Place; but he refuses to do so without your Honour's Order. There is no Danger in complying with my Proposal, which will not infringe the Cessation; and I can get Money by levying Contributions; and it will be much to my Advantage to remain near the Pass of the Gaut, as far as Bhondgam, because several Officers intend coming to me there from the Gaut; but Colonel Keating will not do this without your Order. I have therefore wrote your Honour this Letter, hoping you will send him an Order to do any Business (agreeable to my Desire) that may be for my Advantage, and such as can be done without fighting; as also to go near the Gaut to prevent the Army (which intend coming to join me on my reaching there) from despairing. Your Honour will please to send this Order directly; and as you have taken my Business upon you, you should consider, that if I return back, what the People will say; whether the Officers who have promised to come and join me will or not be hopeless; and whether it will or not be difficult to persuade them to join me again? My Enemies are, by your Help, entirely broke. On our going as far as Bhondgam, the Business will be done without fighting. As you have taken all the Burthen of my Business upon you, you ought to act for its Advantage. Your Honour will give general Orders to your Commanding Officer here, to continue doing such Business as can be done through threatening; as also to go to Caundas, and as far as Bhondgam, near the Country of of Guzerat, where the Pass of the Gaut is called Barey. Should my Army as well as yours be ready there, the Revolters will come hopeless, not join together, and submit to me; but if we shall remain into our Mahall of Chickly, they will think that a Dispute has arose between our Friendship, by which they will be animated to join together; our marching further is therefore very convenient; the Business is for the most Part done. If the English Army will march with my Forces to the Gaut, even without fighting, the Revolters will be separated through Fear, and never be able to stand to fight. What I thought I have mentioned to your Honour, and I will act agreeable to your Sentiments. As our going to Chickly will hurt our Purpose, I have therefore taken the Liberty to write you all the Particulars. Please to send me an Answer, as also one to Colonel Keating.

A true Copy,
(Signed) Edward Ravenscroft,
Secretary.

To Colonel Upton.

Sir,

On the 11th September last, being informed by the Ministerial Agents at this Place that you were shortly expected to arrive at Poona, we dispatched Letters to you by Four different Routes, one of which at least we suppose must have reached you; and having lately received certain Intelligence of your being advanced as far as Brampore, we wait with the utmost Impatience to receive your Answer to that Letter, as we much wish to communicate many Matters of great Importance to this Presidency, before you bring your Negociation to any Conclusion; and for that Purpose are ready, as we therein acquainted you, either to depute a Gentleman fully instructed to confer with you at Poona, or to convey our Information by Letter, whenever you signified to us which Method you prefer.

But as your being apprized of the true Situation of Ragoba's Affairs before you commence your Negociations, may be of the utmost Importance, we dispatch this express, to convey to you the most authentic Intelligence we possess respecting him; and, in order to give you the more perfect Idea of his Situation, shall begin our Detail from the Time we received the Governor General and Council's Prohibition for carrying on the War, and Advice of their having deputed you to treat with the Ministers for a general Pacification.

Ragoba's Army and our Troops were then cantoned during the rainy Season at Duboy; a Place about Twenty Coss from Brodera, after having carried on a very successful Campain against the Ministerial Army, whose Forces were so broken and dispirited by repeated Defeats, that we are persuaded their Chiefs would have found the utmost Difficulty in bringing them again to act against us. Ragoba likewise had lately detached Futty Sing from the Ministerial Party, and concluded a Treaty with him, by which he not only gained a powerful Ally, but stipulated for a Subsidy of Twenty Lacks of Rupees; a considerable Part of which was paid before the Receipt of the above-mentioned Letter from the Governor General and Council; and by this reasonable Recruit to his Finances, he would have been enabled to have taken the Field the ensuing Campaign with great Advantage.

Upon Receipt of the Governor General and Council's Orders for recalling the Company's Troops into our own Garrisons, we gave the necessary Directions for their marching from Duboy, into the Purgunnahs adjacent to Surat or Broach, whenever the Season would permit; and at the same Time advised Ragoba to accompany and remain with them, with such Part of his Forces as he could maintain, until we received an Answer from the Governor General and Council, to the Representations we had deputed Mr. Tayler, a Member of our Board, to make to them; for we were sensible, had we abruptly withdrawn our Forces from him, his Adherents, alarmed and discouraged by our Desertion, would have instantly forsaken him, and his Destruction become immediate and inevitable, which would have greatly embarrassed you in your Negociation, as the Ministers, relieved from all Apprehensions of Ragoba, would have demanded Conditions very different from what we are clearly of Opinion they may now be easily brought to, should you think it expedient to treat with them.

The Event has justified our Conjectures of the good Effects that would attend the Appearance only of our Forces continuing in Concert with Ragoba; during the March from

from Duboy towards Surat, he received repeated Overtures from many of the Ministerial Chiefs, who were ready to return to their Allegiance to him. Under the 16th October, Colonel Keating, the Commander of our Forces with Ragoba, write us that Moriba Dada Badjaba, Chinto Vittul, Ramchundra Gunnis, and Mallarjee Gorparah, all principal Men and Officers in the Confederacy, and then in the Neighbourhood of Poona, had entered into an Association to support Ragoba's Cause, which they had signified to him, with strong Assurances of joining him with 25,000 good Horse. Beejee Sing, Rajah of the Marwand Country, likewise sent a Vackeel to the Peshwa on the 28th October, with the warmest Assurances of Friendship, and Offers of immediately joining him with 10,000 Men, then encamped within Forty-five Coss from Ahmedavad.

Every Day almost brings favourable Accounts to Ragoba; Differences are continually arising amongst the Chiefs of the Ministerial Party, and most of the principal Men in the Maratta Empire, are ready to acknowledge him as Peshwa; Madajee Sindea has sent to inform him, that if the English continue with him, he will immediately join him with a large Body of Forces; and if they should abandon him, he then requested the Peshwa would retire with his Army to Ugeen, where they would concert the necessary Measures for the Good of his Cause: Appajee Madeu, one of Ragoba's Adherents, who had been at Ugeen, to negociate with Mhadjee Scindy, returned to Camp about Ten Days ago, with a Body of Two thousand Horse. The Beginning of this Month, Two Vackeels arrived with Ragoba, from Marabah Furnees, Butcheba Proonder, Shajee Bonsto, Darah Scinta, Apparaw Pattanher, Mallarjee Gosparah, Vessejee Punt Benewallah, Chintoo Vittule, Wittol Sewdew, and Ragopunt Row, Men who formerly were attached to the Ministerial Interest, and who had empowered these Vackeels to assure Ragoba of their Determinations to join him with 15,000 good Troops, provided the English supported him.

The English and Peshwa Armies are now encamped at Carode, on the Southern Banks of the River Tappey, about Fifteen Coss from Surat, where we propose they shall remain, until we receive final Orders from the Governor General and Council, or your Negotiation is brought to some Conclusion, for which we have stated our Reasons very fully to them.

We think it necessary to mention to you, that notwithstanding the Agreement for the Cessation of Arms, which has been religiously observed both on our Part and Ragoba's, the Ministerialists have violated it in several Instances; Vessels with English Passes and Colours are daily insulted by their Gallivats, who have even taken Three or Four of our Merchant Vessels, and they make no Scruple of firing from their Batteries at Bassein on our Boats in Salsette River. They take every Method in their Power of distressing this Settlement, by prohibiting all Supplies of Grain, Timber, and Provisions; and Ragobah has lately complained of their having actually committed Hostilities against Two of his Partizans, Mahomed Esoof and Chimman Row: The First they attacked in the Malway Country, totally dispersed the Forces he commanded, and have since cut him off; and Chimman Row has given the following Account to Colonel Keating of the Attack made upon him: "That he was attacked with about 15,000 Men, near the "Pass of Candabarow, and knowing of the Cessation, he was not apprehensive of any "Danger; but contrary to every Expectation, he was attacked in the Night of the "20th October, by about 2,500 Men, commanded by Anant Row Rasta, who had "forced a March of 25 Coss for that Purpose, and in this Action he had near 500 "Men killed and wounded, many taken Prisoners, and lost all his Baggage." On the 15th Instant a Body of about 800 Horse, detached by Hurry Punt Furkia, again attempted to surprize Chimman Row, but being timely apprized of their Intentions, he retreated to Sungur, with very little Loss. Colonel Keating likewise advises, that the Billdars belonging to the Ministerial Army are employed in sinking Shafts in different Parts of the Candibarra Pass, to prevent Cannon, Carts, &c. from passing.

In these critical Circumstances, your Arrival at Poona, being so long protracted, keeps us in a State of the most anxious and disagreeable Suspence, and gives the Ministerial Party every Advantage they could wish for, collecting and recruiting their dispersed and broken Army, and shaking the Resolution of those who are inclined to embrace Ragoba's Cause. We have ventured to defer separating our Forces from Ragoba before your Negociation was set on Foot, being convinced that Step would have given such a Turn to Affairs, as to render all your Efforts ineffectual to bring the Ministers to any reasonable Terms of Accommodation; but we now flatter ourselves, that from the

 present

present favourable Situation of Affairs, you will find no Difficulty in securing for the Honourable Company, all the Advantages stipulated for them in our Treaty with Ragoba, and such Conditions for him as may be perfectly satisfactory, should you not think it more eligible to treat with him, instead of the Ministerial Party; for we do not hesitate in giving our Opinion, that a Treaty with him would in every Respect be most advantageous for the Company, not only as it promises more Stability and Permanency, and would more effectually secure the general Tranquillity of India; but even supposing the Infant the Ministers have set up, to be really the Son of Narron Row, which we can by no Means allow; yet Ragoba is in that Case entitled to the Office of Duan, or Regent, during the Minority, and therefore the proper Person to treat with; and there is little Room to doubt but the Ministers would acquiesce, when they found that you supported him; whereas, should Ragoba not be satisfied with the Stipulations you may make for him, there is every Reason to apprehend, that from his numerous Adherents, and former Consequence in the Maratta State, he will be constantly raising Disturbances, and forming Intrigues with every Power from whom he can expect any Support, which in their Consequences may materially affect the Company's Possessions.

During this long Cessation of Hostilities, Ragoba has found the utmost Difficulty in raising Money to supply the Exigencies of his Army, no Provision whatever having been made for his Support, during the Discussion of the Treaty; and his Enemies being in Possession of Poona, and the Kircar Treasures, deprives him of all Resources: We therefore earnestly recommend to you, to insist upon it as a preliminary Point, that the Ministers immediately assign him a suitable Revenue, which we think at least should be Seven or Eight Lacks of Rupees per Month.

When we receive your Answer to our Letter, dated the 11th September, we shall immediately take the necessary Measures for informing you of what we have to offer, regarding the Interests of this Presidency; and the Advices we have received from Bengal, since your Appointment.

Bombay Castle,
29th December 1775.

We are, &c.

A true Copy.
(Signed) Edward Ravenscroft,
Secretary.

To the Honourable the President, &c. Council of Bombay.

Gentlemen,

I take the immediate Opportunity of my Arrival at this Place, of acknowledging the Receipt of your Letter of the 11th September, which came safe to Hand Yesterday. I also forwarded a Letter which I brought with me from the Governor General and Council of Fort William.

As you request, you may depend upon my not taking any material Step in the Business on which I am deputed relative to the Presidency of Bombay, till I am honoured with another Letter from your Board, which I am convinced will give me every Information I can desire. Should it hereafter appear necessary, I shall gladly embrace your kind Offer, of a Gentleman's being deputed to Poona; but I should rather wish this Business should be done by Letter.

As you mention being already informed of the Particulars in my Instructions that relate to your Presidency, the repeating them now will be quite unnecessary.

I have in my Possession the Company's small Cypher, but there is not the least Reason to fear an Interruption of any of our Letters, as the People here are fully satisfied of the Necessity of my corresponding with your Presidency, and have given the most positive Orders that our Caussits may pass every where uninterrupted. The Subject of the Letters will, however, determine the Manner in which you may chuse to write.

Poona Dhur,
30 December 1775.

I have the Honour, &c.
(Signed) J. Upton.

A true Copy,
(Signed) Edward Ravenscroft,
Secretary.

APPEN-

APPENDIX, N° 102.

Extract of Bengal Secret Consultations, the 6th March 1776.

PRESENT,

The Honourable Warren Hastings, Governor General, President,
Lieutenant General John Clavering,
The Honourable George Monson,
Richard Barwell, } Esquires.
Philip Francis, }

RECEIVED the following Letter from Colonel Upton:

Gentlemen,

I take the earliest Opportunity of acquainting you of what I conceive is the Disposition of these People regarding the Terms of Accommodation. The Letters they received from Calcutta before my Arrival, had persuaded them fully, that I was deputed to treat with them on equal Terms, without making any Demands whatever; however, at a few Meetings I made them sensible that they had understood these Letters too literally.

A Delay to our Business of some Days was occasioned by a Death in the Family of Sicca Ram Baboo, and a Marriage in Ballajee Pundit's. The necessary Information from Bombay (to which Correspondence they readily assented) occasioned a further Delay. We were yet somewhat getting on with the Business preliminary to the grand Articles of the Treaty, and I had every Reason to expect that a Peace, both honourable and advantageous for the Company, would take Place; but I am now fully convinced they will never agree to our keeping Salsette, or to surrender Bassein. On these Islands, they say, they have expended many Crore of Rupees, particularly on Bassein, which they appear determined at all Events to keep, and indeed they declare against parting with Salsette, and the four small Islands in the Bay, and that they will never grant the Sunnuds for such of them as we have already so unfairly taken from them, and will render Salsette in a great Measure useless to us, by prohibiting all Connection with it from the Continent. These have been their Resolutions at our Two or Three last Meetings, and I conceived it owing to their imagining that I must treat with them at any Rate, and that I had vastly exceeded my Instructions, by asking a Surrender of these Islands. They ask me a Thousand Times, why we make such Professions of Honour? how disapprove the War entered into by the Bombay Government, when we are so desirous of availing ourselves of the Advantages of it?

They say the Governor General and Council of Calcutta have deputed me to negociate with them on Terms honourable to both Nations; yet all Advantage and Honour is confined to ourselves.

In short, I find Salsette and Bassein are the only Impediments to a Treaty's taking Place that might otherwise be very advantageous; for I am fully convinced that they would readily cede to us some Country in the Neighbourhood of Broach or Surat in Lieu of them; also cede to us their Share of Collections in the Broach Purgunnah, defray the Expences of the War, and give up all Demands on the Chout in every Part of the Company's Possessions, and all future Right and Title to such Claim.

When my Instructions were made out, it was thought we had got Bassein, and I was therein ordered on no Account to give it up. But as the Company are not in Possession of this Island, the Stipulations regarding it must take a different Turn. I think if they allow the Company to settle and maintain a Factory, with certain Privileges in Trade, on Bassein, and totally exclude all Foreigners, and give some Country near our Settlements of Broach or Surat in Lieu of it, it would be quite as advantageous, and possibly may be effected; and to this Purpose all my Endeavours will be used.

I shall insist on the Company's keeping Possession of Salsette, agreeable to the Orders in my Instructions, and of their giving up the Four small Islands mentioned therein, situated in in the Bay of Bombay. If these Terms are refused, the Treaty must of Course be broke off for the present, or perhaps altogether, for they intimate they will wait no further References to Calcutta, but again commence Hostilities within a few Days, as the Letters they have already received from thence have so much misled them.

I see in the Bombay Correspondence an Order for that Government to keep Possession of the Cessions made in the Guzerat Country. I have had repeated Conversations on that Subject with the Ministers, who declare that no one in the Country can have any Right to give Grants of any Part thereof; that Futty Sing is not the Proprietor of the Country, but was appointed the Sirdar of it on Terms similar to all other Sirdarries. They must say that most of the Concessions have been made since the Cessation of Arms has taken Place; that Futty Sing advised them repeatedly that he should be obliged to comply with the Demands of the English, and Ragonaut Row, if he was not assisted with more Troops. This they would not comply with, as they had determined strictly to adhere to their Obligation of preventing all Hostilities, and were assured that any Places taken or ceded during the Cessation of Arms, would be restored.

We therefore have agreed to leave the Guzerat Country quite undetermined on, till your further Pleasure shall be known. I shall take the first Opportunity of forwarding to you the Names of the Places ceded in that Country, by whom, and at what Time. The Ministry are satisfied, that if they prove what they assert respecting it, you will make no Demands therein further than what they themselves may grant in the Treaty.

Should the Treaty be now concluded, a separate Article must be kept open for this Business.

I had the Honour to write to you, Gentlemen, on the 5th of last Month; I hope my Letter has been received. I send this by Way of Masulipatam, in Expectation of its getting sooner to Calcutta than by the other Route. In a Day or Two, as soon as I am further informed of the Intention of these People, I shall write again by Way of Benares, and send a Duplicate of my Letter of the 5th Ultimo.

These People, I imagine, are by no Means in the deplorable Situation that had been thought; they have a very numerous Army, and no Want of Money; they have engaged in an Alliance with the Nizam, who has lately marched a Body of Twenty-four thousand Troops, and Thirty-five Guns, to join Hurry Punt Tuckia; by this Time the Junction must be effected, though I imagine the Nizam's Troops will not be easily brought into Action. The Commandant of these Troops, Nabob Fazil Beg Cawn Dhowsa, sent to me to know if our Treaty was likely to take Place with the Ministers, and many Questions, all of which tended to guide their Actions; so that they might save Appearances, yet not be led into the Field against the English. I may mistake in my Conjecture, but I have every Reason to suppose not.

If we cannot agree upon Terms of Accommodation, and Hostilities again commence, I shall go to Bombay, and wait your Orders either to return immediately to Bengal, or execute what further Instructions you may have to give.

Phoona Dhur,
2d February 1776.

I have, &c.
(Signed) J. Upton.

P. S. They will agree to allow to Ragonaut Row a Houshold, consisting of One thousand Horse, to be under his Direction, and obey all his legal Orders, Two hundred Domestics to be named by himself, and Twenty-five thousand Rupees a Month. He is to live at his former Residence on the Ganga, or name where he rather chuses to reside.

I enclose an Account given by the Ministry of the Succession of the Guicawar Family to the Command in Guzerat.

Establishment, &c. of the Guicawars, in the Command, &c. of the Guzerat Country.

Fermuck Row Dobarry, being a Chief of high Rank, under the Sahou Raja, he bestowed on him the Guzerat Country; but some Commotions arising between him and Bajerow the Paishwa, a Battle ensued, in which Fermuck Row was killed, and his Army dispersed; he had a Son or Two, who made their Escape, and took Refuge with the Moguls.

Damajee

Damajee Guicawar, who was the principal Chief under Fermuck Row, and managed the Guzerat Country in his Life-time, promised a proper Submission to the Paishwa immediately after his Master's Death, which was accepted of, but commenced a Rebellion soon after against Tara Boi, Mother to the Ram Raja. The Paishwa marched against him with an Army, and gained a complete Victory, and made Damajee himself Prisoner. He had been but a few Days in Confinement, when he found Means to sooth the Peshwa, and prevail upon him to accept of his Services, producing a proper Security for his future good Behaviour, and paying down Fifteen Lacks of Rupees. The Peshwa gave him a Grant of Half Guzerat, on a Promise of being his Vassal, paying Six Lacks of Rupees a Year, and having Ten thousand Horse always ready for his Service. Damajee died some Years after. He left Three Sons he had by Two Wives. Govinrow was the Son of the First Wife, but younger by some Years than Syajee and Futty Sing, who were the Sons of the Second Wife. They began to dispute who should succeed the Father in the Chiefship, and not being able to settle amongst themselves, they repaired to Poona, and laid their Claims before Madarow, then Paishwa. He ordered their Law Books to be examined; by which it appeared that the First-born (whether of the First or Second Wife) was to succeed to the Father's Rank and Fortune. Syajee was the Eldest Brother, but being blind, the Sunnuds for Half Guzerat were given to Futty Sing, the next Heir, for which he paid Seventy Lacks immediately, and promised Obedience to the Peshwa.

Govinrow, who had been in Expectation of obtaining these Sunnuds, remained at Poona, and refused a Jaghier of Six Lacks a Year offered him by Madarow.

After the Death of Narrain Row, Govinrow applied to Ragoba, for the Chiefship of Guzerat, which he gave him on receiving Twenty-two Lacks of Rupees.

Govinrow immediately commenced a War against his Brother.

After Ragonaut Row was supported by the English, he marched towards Guzerat, where he was joined by Govinrow, and Futty Sing with his Forces joined the Ministerial Army, and continued with them, till in Consequence of the Calcutta Letters a Cessation of Arms took Place, Futty Sing returned to his own Country. Ragoba and the English attacked Futty Sing. He immediately wrote to Poona for Assistance, but the Ministers having stopped all Acts of Hostilities in Obedience to the Calcutta Letters, refused to send any Reinforcement to Futty Sing; who being unable to repel the Force of his Enemies, found himself under the disagreeable Necessity of coming to such Terms as they thought proper to demand, particularly with the English, who engaged to prevent his Country being disturbed either by Govinrow or Ragoba.

Govinrow seeing this Treaty settled with his Brother, had no further Hopes, therefore quitted Ragoba, and marched across the River Mahie, where he established his own Authority, and on this Side of the Mahie Futty Sing's Country is still disturbed by Ragonaut Row.

N. B. The Guicawars were Servants of Dobarry; Dobarry a Servant to the Raja; and all the Chiefs under the Rajaship have for a long Period been subordinate to the Peshwa, and renewable by his Sunnuds. Eswant Row, the Son of Dobarry, died amongst the Moguls, and left behind him one Son, who arrived at Poona Three Years ago, and applied to the Peshwa for his Country, and we are now about giving him Part of it.

APPENDIX, N° 103.

Extract of Bengal Secret Consultations, 6th March 1776.

READ a Letter from Mr. Tayler, as follows:

Honourable Sir, and Sirs,

In a Dispatch from the Honourable the President and Council of Bombay, there are forwarded to me Copies of their several Addresses to you of the 4th, 14th, and 31st October,

October, 17th November, and 29th December, and one to Colonel Upton, dated the 29th December, which I believe has likewise been enclosed in a Packet to you.

I beg Leave to remark to you, Gentlemen, that these Advices confirm the Truth of the Intelligence I had the Honour to communicate to you in my Address of the 29th November last, with the additional Circumstance of the Overtures of Mhadajee Scindea, and of Brahmin Ministers, and Rajapute Chiefs. On a Settlement being made, it seems probable that the latter will be demanding either large Sums or a Grant of Territory in Reward for their Services; both of which the Ministers will be equally averse to grant. It is well known, these have already been so backward in the Performance of their Engagements to the Army, that at the Time they were in Arms against the Peshwa, great Dissensions prevailed among them. Their Leader, Sacram Bapoo, whose Influence and Abilities render him the great Support of their Cause, is already advanced in Years, and very infirm, and his Death it is thought would dissolve the Confederacy. In either of the above Causes operating, I can foresee no other Consequences but the Restoration of Ragoba.

Should you utterly abandon his Interests, there seems to me a great Probability of this Event taking Place, in despite of the Efforts of the Ministerialists. One great Reason why he prefers a Restoration by Means of the Company is, because it will be effected by a much smaller Sacrifice of his Influence and Dominions. He well knows that the Demands of those who offer their Aid would be very exorbitant; but abandoned by you, he will have no other Resource than to submit to these Demands. You have already been apprized of those who are now in his Party; and I am informed that Holkar has offered his Assistance on certain Conditions. I leave you to judge, Gentlemen, whether it is probable that the Ministers will be able to cope with the united Force of those he will then have in his Party.

Should he effect his Restoration, I must again repeat, that there seems little Probability of the Company's quietly retaining the Cessions of the Ministers; at any Rate, his Efforts will occasion a Scene of Confusion in the Maratta Dominions, very destructive to the Commerce of the Company, and of this Country, which have already suffered very considerably by it.

Such is the Light in which I view the present State of Affairs, and future Prospects; considering therefore the Obligations of the English Nation to him by Treaty, the Fairness of his Conduct hitherto, the Justice of his Proposals to us, and the general Face of Things as they appear by the Advices from Bombay, together with the Idea that must be entertained by all the Country Powers of the Breach of our Engagements with Ragoba, I trust you will deem it equally consistent with Equity and sound Policy, at least to adopt some Plan of Accommodation satisfactory to him, and immediately instruct Colonel Upton accordingly, as it may not yet be too late for Advices to him to prove effectual.

But whatever may be your Determination on this Point, I doubt not, Gentlemen, you will agree with me in my Opinion, that in the present State of Affairs it seems hardly probable the Confederates will hesitate complying with all the Conditions stipulated for in the Treaty with Ragoba, if Circumstances are well availed of. I have already been too explicit on the Utility of the several Cessions to the Honourable Company for you not to perceive the Importance of them; and I therefore earnestly conjure you to insist also on whomsoever you may treat with confirming and guaranteeing all the Cessions made with Ragoba and the Guicawars.

Should your Informations, by the Advices of Colonel Upton, differ from those transmitted by the Government of Bombay, I beg Leave to observe, that he dates from the Fort of Pronder, where he is surrounded by the Ministers and their Creatures, whose Interest it is to misinform him with respect to their own Strength and Importance, and to secrete from him every Circumstance favourable to Ragoba and his Partizans. Their Patience, Skill, and Dissimulation, in conducting political Negociations, are very well known in India. It is almost useless to insist on the different Credibility that is due to Informations collected under those Disadvantages, and those communicated by Gentlemen, in whose Honour you have a Security from intentional Deceit, and whose Caution is warranted by the Dangers they incur, should their ill-grounded Intelligence mislead you into Measures that might not otherwise be deemed expedient.

I have, &c.

5th March 1776. (Signed) W. Taylor.

APPENDIX, N° 104.

Extract of Bengal Secret Consultations, 6th March 1776.

GOVERNOR General—I have waited to hear whether any Proposal upon the Subject of the Letters now before the Board, should be made by any of the Members who have hitherto had the chief Guidance in the Measures which have been adopted respecting the Transactions of the Government of Bombay with the Marattas, for the Purpose of preserving a Consistency in the Resolutions of the Board. I have thought it my Duty rather to follow than take the Lead in this Business in which I may be obviously led to follow my original Ideas, as every other Member will be as obviously Inclined to such Measures as shall be consonant to those to which they have already given their Assent. But as no Proposition has been yet made by any other Gentleman, and as the Letter from Colonel Upton requires a speedy and decisive Answer, I shall offer my Sentiments upon it, leaving it to the Board to adopt them, if they shall find them to correspond with their own, as much Time has already been consumed in Colonel Upton's Negociation; and we cannot, were we inclined to it, expect that we shall be able to protract the Conclusion of it so long as to admit repeated References from him to this Board, and repeated Instructions in return. I am of Opinion that whatever Orders are now sent to him in Reply to his Letter before us, they should be peremptory and conclusive; that he should be directed to bring the Business of his Negociation to an Issue, either by an immediate Conclusion of the Treaty, or by demanding his Dismission, and retiring to Bombay: There he may still remain and wait the Orders of the Board for his future Proceeding; but as such an Event must be certainly followed by the Renewal of Hostilities with that Party of the Maratta State with which we are now in Treaty, it will next remain to be considered, what Provision shall be made for such an Event. I see no Alternative but to withdraw wholly from the War, or renew the former Treaty with Ragoba; the latter appears to me unavoidable in the Case which I have supposed. In the mean Time I would recommend, that Colonel Upton be referred to the Instructions which he has already received, and directed to conform literally to them. In proposing this, I own I feel a Repugnance to the last Order which was sent to him respecting the Exchange of Broach for Bassein; but as this is a Measure already resolved on, I shall make no new Objection to it; but I think it nevertheless my Duty to state one Objection, which I have already intimated, from Recollection only, on Grounds which have since occurred to me of greater Certainty, in the Consultation 15th February. I expressed a Doubt whether there was a Power in this Board to give up the Possession of Broach, the Acquisition of which had been confirmed by the Court of Directors. Of this I have no longer any Doubt, as I think the following Clause in the Act of Parliament clearly limits the controlling Powers of this Government over the other Presidencies, to the commencing of Hostilities, the declaring of War, the negociating or concluding of Treaties of Peace; but does not authorize this Government to order the Surrender or Exchange of any of the Company's Possessions dependent on the other Presidencies, to obey such Orders. I beg Leave to subjoin the Words of the Act of Parliament, leaving it to the Board to draw such Conclusions from them as they may think necessary and applicable to the Case in Question. "And be it further "Enacted by the Authority aforesaid, That the said Governor General and Council, or "the major Part of them, shall have, and they are hereby authorized to have Power "of superintending and controlling the Government and Management of the Presidencies of Madras, Bombay, and Bencoolen respectively, so far and in so much as "that it shall not be lawful for any President and Council of Madras, Bombay, or "Bencoolen, for the Time being, to make any Orders for commencing Hostilities, or "declaring or making War against any Indian Princes or Powers, or for negociating or "concluding any Treaty of Peace or other Treaties, with any such Indian Princes or "Powers, without the Consent and Approbation of the said Governor General and "Council first had and obtained; except in such Cases of imminent Necessity as would "render it dangerous to postpone such Hostilities or Treaties until the Orders from the "Governor General and Council might arrive, and except in such Cases where the "said Presidents and Councils respectively shall have received special Orders from the "said United Company: And any President and Council of Madras, Bombay, or "Bencoolen, who shall offend in any of the Cases aforesaid, shall be liable to be suspended from his or their Office, by the Order of the said Governor General and "Council; and every President and Council of Madras, Bombay, and Bencoolen, for "the Time being, shall, and they are hereby respectively directed and required to pay "due Obedience to such Orders as they shall receive touching the Premises, from the "said Governor General and Council for the Time being; and constantly and diligently to transmit to the said Governor General and Council, Advice and Intelligence "of all Transactions and Matters whatsoever that shall come to their Knowledge relating to the Government, Revenues, or Interest, of the said United Company."

Mr. Francis—I cannot admit the Governor General's Construction of that Clause of the Act of Parliament which he has quoted. A Power to make Peace, must in its Nature include a Power to agree to the only Terms on which in some Cases Peace can be obtained. This, or any other State, may be reduced to Extremities, in which it may have no Alternative but relinquishing a Part of its Possessions or hazarding the Whole. With respect to the Business before the Board, I observe, that Colonel Upton informs us in his Letter of the 2d February, that the Ministry have intimated to him, that they will wait no further References to Calcutta, but again commence Hostilities within a few Days. From this Passage, and from the general Tenor of his Letter, I conclude that one of the two Events must have already taken Place, either he has concluded a Treaty of Peace, relinquishing our first Claim to Bassein, but obtaining the other principal Objects of his Instructions, or he must have withdrawn to Bombay; in either Case, a Question between Peace on any Terms, and the Continuance of Hostilities, is not entirely open to the present Decision of this Board; if it were, (or in order not to differ with any Member of the Board who may still think it is, supposing the Question entire before us) I should think that, whether to obtain an honourable Peace, or to conduct a War with Advantage if that should be unavoidable, it is indispensably necessary that we should order Colonel Upton to withdraw to Bombay. I mean always on the Presumption that the Ministry have given a peremptory Denial to our keeping Salsette, or accepting of the Exchange proposed to them by our last Letter; it seems to me, from the Intelligence now before us, that we treat with great Disadvantage, while Colonel Upton is at Poona; and I say this from a Suspicion that they avail themselves of the Circumstance of having him and his Party in their Power; otherwise it is inconceivable to me, that when we offer to relinquish the greatest Part of the Advantages stipulated with a Prince whose Title to the Peshwaship, or at least to the actual Government during the Minority of Mhada Row Narrain, is in Competition with theirs, they should absolutely refuse to make us any Compensation for so great a Sacrifice to them; at least it is such, whatever we may deem it. This is my general Opinion of the Line which this Board ought to pursue, but as I have not yet heard the Sentiments of the other Members of the Board, and as so great a Question as Peace or War is under the Deliberation of the Board, I shall reserve my final Vote upon this Question until I have the Advantage of hearing the Sentiments of the other Gentlemen.

Mr. Barwell—Though there is not regularly any Question before this Board, as Mr. Francis has thought it necessary to comment so largely on the Sentiments expressed by the Governor General, it may be expected that I should give my Ideas upon the Measures this Government ought to pursue on the present State of the Company's Affairs in the Western Side of India. This Council has been very moderate in the Proposals made to the Ministerial Party at Poona, for withdrawing their Forces from the Field, and relinquishing the Advantages which, under the Sanction of a solemn Treaty, the Company are entitled to reap. From the Letters we have received from Colonel Upton, it seems not to be left to our Option to effect a Pacification, on any other Terms than by submitting to such as may be dictated by the Poona Durbar. I confess I should be concerned to see the Company involved in an expensive War, but when I consider the Dishonour that must arise to the English Arms, by appearing to yield that through Fear which we have it in our Power to over-rule, we sacrifice both the Interests of the Company, and our Military Reputation, by such Tameness. We offer to yield to the Maratta Government certain Benefits to be derived to us by a certain Mode of Conduct, and consequently have a Right to expect that some small Equivalent, however inadequate it may be to our Concessions, should be made to us, for deviating from that Conduct. I will not enter into the Principles that first led the Bombay Government to

adopt

adopt the Cause of Ragoba, but being engaged, I judge we have a Right to take Advantage of the present State of the Maratta Government, to the Advantage of the Company. I do not think any Part of Broach should be yielded up in Exchange for Bassein, admitting that the Power was unquestionably in this Board to cede or transfer the actual Possessions of the Company. In the present State of Colonel Upton's Negociations, I do not see any Steps that this Government can take in it, further than to authorize the Government of Bombay, provided his Negociation does not prove successful, to pursue such Measures for their own Defence, and the Support of this Ally, as they may judge prudent and consistent with the general Interests of their Settlement.

Colonel Monson—The Governor General, by the Act to which he alludes, admits a a Power in this Government to make Peace. The Means of doing it must therefore be inherent in it, and if it can only be effected by making Cessions of any of our present Possessions, undoubtedly we have a Right to yield them up. Colonel Upton's Letters leave no Option in this Board in what Manner they may continue their future Negociations; he acquaints us, that he shall stipulate certain Terms for the Company on the Island of Bassein, to the Exclusion of other European Nations, but that he apprehends the Poona Durbar will not be prevailed upon to allow of the Cession of Bassein and Salsette, in which Case he purposes to retire to Bombay. This Event must have taken Place before he can receive any further Instructions from us. If his Negociation should not have taken Place, on the Terms mentioned in his Letter, it will then be for the Board to consider, whether they will continue the War in Conjunction with Ragoba, or act upon the defensive. When that becomes a Question, I shall be ready to give my Sentiments upon it.

General Clavering—On the Decision of the Question, whether the Orders which have been already given to Colonel Upton shall be confirmed or modified? depends the final Events of Peace or War with the Maratta State. Our first Instructions to him were conveyed in Terms which breathed a different Spirit from those which have lately animated this Board. We directed Colonel Upton to assure the Ministry of Poona, of the Regret that we felt at the Commencement of Hostilities on the Part of the Government of Bombay; that we disavowed its Negociations with Ragoba; and that we wished for nothing more than to unite with them in Friendship. On the 7th September we began to change our Language, and since that Time, and since Mr. Tayler's Arrival, some Gentlemen have suggested, that the Honour of the English Name was more concerned in procuring and maintaining Conquests, than in either paying a Regard to the Instructions of the Court of Directors to preserve the Peace in India, or to set an Example of Justice and Moderation, by relinquishing Possessions that had been obtained by the Infraction of a Treaty of Peace. Those who now persevere in those Measures, must be responsible for the Consequences of them, and ought, when they send their final Orders to Colonel Upton, to consider on the Means for carrying on the War, and instructing the Bombay Council accordingly.

Governor General—I meant not my Minute as a formal Question for the Determination of the Board; but as the Sense of the individual Members of the Board seem to have been delivered in the several Minutes which have followed mine, and as it is necessary that some Answer should be given to Colonel Upton, I beg Leave to propose the following Question for the Determination of the Board: Whether Colonel Upton shall be ordered to conclude a Treaty of Peace with the Maratta Administration at Poona, under the Instructions which have been already transmitted to him, or, in Case of their Refusal to accede to the Treaty, to require his Dismission, and retire to Bombay?

Mr. Francis—I have already given my Opinion on that Point.

Mr. Barwell—I think Colonel Upton should be instructed conformably to the Question.

Colonel Monson—I think he should, unless he has concluded a Treaty before he receives our last Instructions; in which Case, if the Conditions of it are not conformable to his last Instructions, it should not be cancelled; he should make a peremptory Demand conformably to his last Instructions; and if the Poona Durbar will not give him a categorical Answer, he should demand his Dismission, and retire to Bombay in Six Days after the Receipt of the Letter now proposed to be wrote to him.

General Clavering—I agree with Colonel Monson, that whatever Conditions we may have agreed upon, they should not be cancelled by the subsequent Orders that Colonel Upton has received from us; but if he has not been able to obtain the Island of Bassein unconditionally,

unconditionally, or in Exchange for the Town and Territory of Broach, I am of Opinion that he should not insist upon it. With regard to the other Part of his Instructions, I think he ought not to insist absolutely on any Thing more than the Island of Salsette, and the other Islands in the Bay; however, to obtain such other Advantages in the Neighbourhood of Surat or Broach as he may find they will readily yield. His Retirement to Bombay must follow of Course, if the Conditions I have proposed are not complied with.

Governor General—I agree to the Question, and to the Qualification proposed by Colonel Monson; namely, that if Colonel Upton shall have concluded a Treaty in the Manner which he has advised us in his last Letter he intended, before the Receipt of our Letter of the 15th February, that Treaty should be confirmed. I likewise approve of the Limit of Time proposed for his Departure.

Mr. Francis—This Government will undoubtedly be bound by any Treaty which Colonel Upton may conclude; of Course I presume it can never be proposed to cancel or alter it. I think, however, that supposing it concluded before the Receipt of our last Instructions, and that he shall have relinquished the Demand of Bassein, he might still be instructed to propose the Exchange of Broach for that Island, if he should find the Ministry disposed to comply with such a Proposal.

Agreed, That in Case Colonel Upton shall not have already concluded a Treaty, he be ordered to conform to his former Instructions; and if the Ministry at Poona should not accede to those Conditions, that he require his Dismission, and retire to Bombay within Six Days from the Receipt of these Orders: But if a Treaty shall have been concluded before the Arrival of the last Instructions, without obtaining a Cession of Bassein to the Company, he be ordered to offer them the Terms of Exchange therein mentioned.

APPENDIX, N° 105.

Extract of Bengal Secret Consultations, the 7th March, 1776.

PRESENT,

The Honourable Warren Hastings, Governor General, President,
Lieutenant General John Clavering,
The Honourable George Monson,
Richard Barwell, } Esquires.
Philip Francis, }

READ, and approved, the Consultation of Yesterday:

Received the following Letters from Lieutenant Colonel Upton:

Gentlemen,

I had the Honour to write you on the 2d Instant, and herewith forward a Duplicate of that Letter.

By the Conversation that passed last Night at the Durbar, which accompanies this, you will perceive that the Negociation is entirely at an End. The Ministers are determined never to grant the Sunnuds for the Company's keeping Salsette, or for their possessing the Four small adjacent Islands. They offered in Exchange for Salsette, a Country of Three Lacks of Rupees in the Neighbourhood of Broach, but would not wait my referring this Business to the Board, as I requested; though they were told, and understood, that by laying a Dauk to Benares they might get a Reply as soon as the Answer to our former Reference (under Date 5th January) could arrive. They could not wait for that either; they said they had already expended immense Sums, and had been deceived by the Letters from Calcutta; that full Powers were vested in me, me, and from me they expected an Anſwer. I obſerved to them, that full Powers, It was true, were veſted in me, provided I did not deviate from the Inſtructions that were given me, and I had all along told them, that Salſette could not be given up, and that they might be aſſured I ſhould never abuſe the Powers they conceived me poſſeſſed of. That they had yet an Opportunity left of aſking this Exchange; they replied no, poſitively.

In Five or Six Days more I am to leave Poona Dhur, and they will then fix the Time for the Expiration of the Ceſſation of Arms. I told them I expected a ſufficient Time to adviſe all our Settlements before the Renewal of the War; however, I ſuſpect them of taking every Advantage.

I wrote the laſt Week to the Governor and Council of Bombay, to prepare them for this Event; alſo to Colonel Keating, that he might guard againſt any Surprize. His Majeſty's Squadron being here at this Time is a fortunate Event; and I think, if the War is to be proſecuted, if Three or Four Companies of Europeans, a ſmall Detachment from the Corps of Artillery, and Two or Three Battalions of Sepoys were embarked from Bengal to join the Army from Bombay, we might ſoon command Peace on our own Terms; for the Chiefs of this Country are quite at a Loſs which Side to take, and are waiting to ſee what the Engliſh do.

I incloſe a Letter I received Two Days ago from the Governor and Council of Bombay, with an Extract of a Letter they had received from Colonel Keating, and further Offers made by Ragonaut Row. In Three or Four Days I ſhall write again by Way of Benares.

Poona Dhur, 7th February 1776.

I have the Honour to be, &c.

(Signed) J. Upton.

P. S. I ſhall write to the Governor and Council of Fort St. George and the Nabob of Arcot, to inform them of the Treaty's being broke off with the Miniſterial Party.

Debate at the Peiſhwa's Durbar, February 6th, 1776.

Colonel Upton went to the Durbar this Evening at Half paſt Six o'Clock. After the uſual complimentary Queſtions, the Converſation turned on the Time and Delay it would occaſion ſending Letters to Calcutta, and receiving Anſwers, before the Treaty could be concluded; that they had already expended Crores of Rupees for theſe Seven Months paſt, waiting the Colonel's Arrival; and continuing that Expence to receive further Accounts from Bengal, would condemn them in the Eyes of the whole World: That the Colonel came to treat with them with full Powers, why therefore refer to others?

The Colonel obſerved to them, that by the Plan he propoſed of laying a Dauk from this to Benares immediately, Anſwers would arrive as quick, if not quicker, than the Replies to the Letters ſent ſoon after his Arrival. Regarding their Objections to aſſembling the principal Chiefs to ſign the Treaty, that although he was of Opinion the Supreme Council would, after reading his Repreſentation, be ſatisfied with the uſual Signatures as mentioned by the Gentlemen here, yet it was neceſſary for him to receive their Letter to that Purpoſe, before he would deviate from that Article of his Inſtructions; and that being the Caſe, there could be no Time loſt in continuing the Ceſſation of Arms for another Month, particularly as they might, if they pleaſed, withdraw what Part of the Army they thought proper to reduce their Expence, and that the Colonel would be anſwerable that the Engliſh Army would ſtrictly attend to the Terms of the Ceſſation; and further, that he propoſes this Meaſure of referring to the Supreme Council, becauſe they (the Miniſters) did not ſeem to credit that his Demands were in Conſequence of his Inſtructions: That he himſelf could not deviate from theſe Inſtructions, but it was very probable the Gentlemen of Calcutta would, by their own Repreſentations and his, be diſpoſed to comply with their Propoſals, or refer them to England if they thought neceſſary, by which Means the Miniſters would be ſenſible, that he acted with ſtrict Honour from the Beginning: That he alſo would engage for the Continuance of the Ceſſation of Arms for a Month

or

or more after the Replies arrived from Calcutta; if the Alternative was to renew the War, to give them full Time to assemble their Troops.

They declared they had been already so much disappointed by the Letters from Calcutta, and drawn into such very heavy Expence, from a Certainty that no Claims whatever should be made upon their Country; and that Salsette, which had been so unjustly taken from them, would be again restored; that they had no Idea or Intention of suffering the like Inconvenience any more. That as the Colonel had come so great a Distance to settle a Peace with them, they wished to shew a Disposition to do every Thing in their Power to conclude a Peace: That from these Considerations they would give up the Country mentioned Yesterday in Lieu of Salsette; but could not make Peace upon any other Terms: That it rested with the Colonel to agree or not as he pleased, as he was come with full Powers to treat with them.

The Colonel assured them, that though he had full Powers, he was determined not to abuse them, and that he was not authorized to give up Salsette; that he must again observe to them, the Supreme Council might, and it was probable they would, agree to their Offer; but it was not in his Power to part with Salsette.

They replied very shortly, God will determine as he thinks best.

The Colonel asked their absolute Determination. They declared, they knew of none but War.

The Colonel said, He was very sorry he could not act more to their Satisfaction, for it would give him great Pleasure if he could.

It was then agreed that the Colonel was to stay Five or Six Days near Poona Dhur, by which Time they would assemble a Durbar for him to take his Leave.

The Colonel observed, that from the Day he took his Leave, it would be necessary to fix a certain Day, not nearer than a Month or Twenty Days, to give a reasonable Time for all Parties being properly informed with the Renewal of the War.

They said, when the Colonel came to take his Leave, they would fix a Day for the Commencement of Hostilities.

N. B. It was remarked in this Evening's Conversation, that finding the Colonel could not (or would not, as they termed it) restore Salsette, they never opened their Lips about any Thing else.

(Signed) J. Upton.

A true Interpretation.
Ar. Macpherson, Persian Interpreter.

From the above Advices, which supersede the Orders of Yesterday, it appears most probable, that the Treaty with the Ministerial Party of the Maratta State has been broke off, and Hostilites renewed; it is also probable that these sudden and abrupt Declarations of the Ministers, may have been a Feint, for the Purpose of trying what Impression it might make on the Mind of Colonel Upton, and that finding him determined, they may ultimately consent to an Accommodation, upon the Terms which he has proposed to them; but this the Board can state only as a possible Event, and it now becomes necessary to suppose the War renewed, and to provide the Means of conducting it with the greatest Probability of Success. From the Returns now laid before the Board by the Commander in Chief, it appears, that the whole Military Force at the Presidency of Bombay, exclusive of the remote Factories, is as follows, including Officers:

	Artillery.	Infantry.	Sepoys.
At Bombay — —	112	450	1776
Madras Detachment at ditto —	—	—	893
In the Field — — —	114	378	1454
Madras Detachment ditto —	—	106	—
At Salsette — —	75	193	955
At Caranja — —	1	29	240
	302	1156	5318

The Presence of His Majesty's Squadron appears a Circumstance most favourable to the Design of reinforcing the Detachment in the Field, as the Garrison at Bombay will require but very few Men to defend it, and the rest (the Board think) may be conveniently and safely spared to be sent into the Field.

APPEN-

APPENDIX, Nº 106.

To Colonel Upton.

Sir,

WE have received your Letter, dated the 24th Ultimo.

Immediately on the Cessation being proclaimed, we gave Instructions to the Commanders of all the Company's Vessels not to molest any Boats or Vessels belonging to the Marattas; and as no Act of Hostility has been committed on our Side, there is not any Occasion for repeating these Orders.

We are much pleased to find you are convinced of the Propriety of the Company's Troops not being entirely withdrawn from Ragonath Row's, before the Conclusion of the Treaty, and we are sensible you will experience the good Effects of this Measure in your Negociation.

The several Cessions from Futty Sing (except Batta) were made long before the Receipt of the Governor General and Council's Orders for discontinuing the War.

The Treaty between him and Ragoba was executed on the 18th of July last, near Brodera, whereas those Orders did not reach Bombay until the 12th of August; and it was stipulated in that Treaty, that the Guicawar Share of the Broach Revenues, and the Villages of Cordi, Chickley, and Periow, should be ceded to the Honourable Company. Futty Sing, before this, was openly connected with the Ministerial Party; but when he found Ragoba supported by the English, he was glad to make his Peace with him, and return to his Allegiance; and these Cessions were made to the Honourable Company, for the Services rendered him in accommodating Matters between him and the Peshwa. He has lately made many Professions of his Attachment to the Company; and in a Letter to our President at the Time, expressed his Satisfaction at the Accommodation effected by Colonel Keating. The only Cession obtained since the Cessation, was the Village of Batta, which is so connected with our other Possessions, that a Grant of it was requested from Futty Sing in the Room of Sinore, a Place producing a much more considerable Revenue, which we voluntarily relinquished because it was not so conveniently situated. We have also lately requested him to give up his Pretensions to the Autgoms, some Villages situated in the very Center of the Broach Purgunnah, which he does not seem to consider as included in his Grant of that District, but we are not yet apprized of the Success of this Application. We never authorized, nor do we believe any Compulsion was ever used to obtain these Grants from Futty Sing.

We must again strongly urge to you the Propriety of your insisting upon the Ministers settling an Establishment for Ragoba immediately, for we may venture to foretel, that if you recede from this Point, they will protract and retard the Negociation by every Artifice in their Power, in the Hopes of Ragoba's Army disbanding for Want of Pay, which would intirely frustrate the good Effect we with so much Reason expected from our late Measures, and we are also apprehensive it will be a difficult Matter to prevent an Army without Pay, in a plentiful Country, from committing some Irregularities, which the Ministers will be very ready to term an Infringement of the Cessation.

We have lately received a Letter from Colonel Keating, containing some Proposals made by Ragoba, of which we think it proper to transmit a Copy for your Notice, and likewise an Extract from another Letter alluded to therein; but the Orders from the Governor General and Council arriving about that Time, Mr. Forbes did not deliver Ragoba's Proposals. You have never acknowledged the Receipt of our Letter, dated the 29th Ultimo.

We hope you will prevail with the Ministers to give immediate Orders for opening the Communication; and remain,

Sir, &c.

Bombay Castle,
1st February 1776.

(Signed) Wm Hornby,
Dl Draper,
Robt Gordon, &c.
Council.

A true Copy.

Extract of a Letter from Lieutenant Colonel Keating to the Select Committee of Bombay dated the 5th September 1775, from Muckerpore Camp, Three Miles from Brodera.

I Had the Honour of addressing you last the 6th Instant; since when, I had severa long Conferences with the Peshwa, respecting Nizam Ally, who is in Treaty wit both him and the Ministers. The Peshwa says, that without Nizam Ally joins the Mi nisters, they cannot again make any formidable Head against him, so that him only is h apprehensive of, being possessed of a great Number of Cannon, and a large Body of goo Country Infantry.

The Nizam would most willingly join the Peshwa, provided he agrees to his Terms, bu the latter says he wishes for no other Friends than the English alone, who have don every Thing for him, therefore is desirous of receiving Assistance from them only, an grant Territory in Lieu thereof. Our last Conversation on this Subject was on the 6th Instant; he then requested me to appoint a proper Person to proceed to Bombay imme diately, accompanied by a Man of his own to settle this Business. His Wish is to hav an Augmentation to the Number of Forces already stipulated for, of at least Two hun dred Europeans and One thousand Sepoys, besides their Officers, also Four Field Pieces Two Royal Howitzers, and Ammunition in Proportion. Upon your granting him thi Supply, he is ready to engage to increase the monthly Stipend, also to grant and mak over to the Company for ever, such Country as you shall esteem most proper, having an exact Affinity to the Number of Troops, &c. formerly agreed for, and now required.

In Compliance with the Peshwa's Request, and judging it proper so to do, I have ap pointed Mr. James Forbes to proceed to Bombay on this Business. He is the Bearer o this Letter, and having acted as my Secretary since Mr. Holmes went to Bombay, he i able to give your Honour, &c. every Kind of Information you may require; and I re quest he may return to the Army, when this Affair is concluded on.

The Peshwa desires me to request, that you will be pleased to write to the Governo and Council of Madras to insist on Nizam Ally remaining neutral in the Dispute between him and the rebellious Ministers: Also, that the Governor of Bombay will write to the Nizam to the same Purpose, and if necessary, send a Gentleman to him; but adds, that should the Nizam, in Defiance of such Remonstrance, persist in taking an active Part against him, he doubts not, with the Blessing of God, and the Reinforcement above-mentioned, to be able, in the Course of the ensuing Campaign, to reduce the Ministerial and the Nizam's joint Force, and compel him to make ample Restitution; in which Case, he assures me the Company may depend upon reaping considerable Advantages.

A true Extract,

(Signed) Edward Ravenscroft, Secretary.

Honourable Sir, and Gentlemen,

I had the Honour to address you last the 18th Instant.

Since the Dispatch of the 5th Instant, by which your Honour, &c. received full Powers to treat with the Supreme Council of Calcutta, in the Person of Lieutenant Colonel Upton, the Peshwa has been considering with great Attention on the best Grounds for establishing a Treaty with that Council. He frequently mentioned the Subject to me, signifying his Intention of extending his Designs with the Assistance of the English; and this he declared, not from Views entirely confined to himself, but also with those of enlarging considerably the Interests and Advantages of the Honourable Company, to whom he acknowledges himself highly indebted. In Consequence of these Considerations, he Yesterday made known to me the grand Outlines for the Basis of this new Treaty, desiring at the same Time that I would explain the Whole to your Honour, &c. since he intended the same to answer to you, as Guides in the Management of the Treaty. He concluded

concluded with observing, that he had designed and proposed something similar to the present Propositions the Beginning of August last, and which I communicated in Part under the 8th of that Month, by Mr. James Forbes, who was further instructed on that Occasion.

The following are the Articles as explained by the Peshwa.

1. That he the Peshwa doth confirm and guarantee to the Honourable Company, the Treaty of Surat, in the most full and ample Manner.

2. That he Ragonath Badjirow shall grant, cede, and for ever make over unto the Honourable Company, all that Part of the Cocanny Country immediately appertaining to the Poona Government, except the Port of Ghiriah, and a Territory thereunto annexed, sufficient for the Uses of the Port.

3. That the said Ragonath Badjirow Peshwa shall, as soon as possible, put the Honourable Company's Troops in full and ample Possession of any one of the Gauts or Passes that lead from the Cocanny into the high Part of the Maratta Dominions; and which Gaut or Pass shall be determined on by the Honourable Company, and ever after considered as belonging to the East India Company.

4. That the said Ragonath Badjirow Peshwa doth agree, that the Honourable Company shall receive the Sum of 10 per Cent. per Annum, out of, and from the gross Produce of every Jaghire that has been, or may hereafter be granted to any Person whatever, who is or may hereafter be dependent on the Maratta Government; and the said Sum of 10 per Cent. per Annum shall be paid in Cash, without any Deductions whatever, to such Person or Persons as the Honourable Company, or their proper Agents, shall appoint; or such Lands and Territories as the said Company may esteem most convenient to be made over to them, within the Course of One Year from the signing of the Treaty, in the most full and ample Manner, by the said Ragonath Badjirow, or his Heirs.

5. That the said Ragonath Badjirow Peshwa doth engage, for himself and his Heirs, to take from the Honourable Company to the Amount of Ten Lacks in Woollens annually, paying for the same an Advance of Fifteen per Cent. upon the Prime Cost.

6. That in Consideration of the above Cessions, Grants, and Advantages to the Honourable Company, they on their Part shall engage to add to the Army now in the Peshwa Service, such a sufficient Force, as may be able, with God's Blessing, to place him in Possession of the Seat of his Father, the Government of the Maratta Dominions.

7. And that the said East India Company do agree to advance him, Ragonath Badjirow Peshwa, the Sum of Ten Lacks of Rupees, the better to enable him to prosecute and fulfil these Engagements; and which Ten Lacks are to be repaid within One Year after his resuming Charge of the Government.

8. And that as it is well known the Family of Nizam Alli Cawn are Encroachers and Usurpers of the natural Rights of the Hindoos, as also declared Friends to the French Nation, the Power of the said Nizam Alli Cawn shall be curtailed, as the contracting Powers may judge proper, for the Ease and Safety of the Common Cause; and further, that whatever Country it may be necessary to dispossess him of, One-fourth Part of its gross Annual Revenues shall be paid nett to the Honourable Company, in the Manner laid down with respect to the 10 per Cent. from the Jaghiers, or Lands and Territories granted in Lieu thereof: Also is provided,

9. That all Troops provided by the Honourable Company for the Assistance of Ragonath Badjirow, or his Heirs, for the Purpose above-mentioned, or any other that may hereafter be necessary, shall be paid and allowed for in the same Proportion as is provided for by the Treaty of Surat, except the Expence of carrying Ordnance Stores and Provisions, which are ever to be esteemed distinct, and allowed as a separate Charge.

10. That from the Day of signing the Treaty upon which these Articles depend, the contracting Parties shall esteem themselves as mutually bound to assist and support each other in their just Rights and full Possessions, to the End of Time; and the said Ragonath Badjirow Peshwa doth, of his own free Will and Accord, further agree, for himself and his Heirs for ever, That in Case the English Nation were at any Time attacked either by a foreign or Indian Power, in any Part of their Settlements or Possessions in India, that he or his Heirs will and shall assist them with Six thousand Horse, free of all Expence whatever, and with the Whole of his Fleet, that may belong to the Port of Ghiriah.

The Peshwa desired me to observe to your Honour, &c. that the gross Amount of the Jaghire proceeding from the Maratta's Government, amount at present to about Two Crore of Rupees per Annum.

From the certain Advantages that will arise to the Honourable Company by this proposed Treaty, the Peshwa doubts not but the same will be readily agreed to; and as a principal Part of it was framed so long ago as the Beginning of last August, and at that Time mentioned to your Honour, &c. it cannot be regarded as extraordinary that it is now renewed.

I am, &c.

Camp near Maudave,
24 Jan. 1776.

Thomas Keating,
Lieut. Col.

APPENDIX, N° 108.

RESOLVED, That the following Letter be written to Mr. Bristow:

To Mr. Bristow.

Sir,

By a Letter received from Colonel Upton, under Date the 7th of February, we are informed, that the Ministers at the Poona Durbar have peremptorily refused to accede to the Terms of Accommodation, which he was instructed to propose to them. That they positively insisted on the Restitution of Salsette, and a Renunciation of the Four small Islands adjacent to it; and would not agree to wait the Result of a Reference of this Point to us; in short, that they were determined to hear of Peace on no Conditions, that should not be exclusively honourable, and advantageous to themselves; Colonel Upton's Negociation is therefore entirely broken off; he was to receive his Dismission, and retire to Bombay within Six Days from the Date of his Letter; but the further Interval to be allowed before the Renewal of Hostilities was not then determined. The Ministers having resolved to send their Army again into the Field, we have no Alternative left, but a vigorous Prosecution of the War against them, in Conjunction with Ragonaut Row, on the Presumption that the Resolution of the Ministerial Party is final. We have agreed to support the Pretensions of that Prince, and have taken every preparatory Step that has occured to us, for providing Means to carry on the War with Vigour and Success.

The immediate March of the Brigade from Owde to the Frontier of the Province of Corah, nearest to Calpee, appearing to us a Measure likely to be attended with good Effects, not only from the Appearance of Resolution which it will convey to the neighbouring Powers, but also for the Conveniency of detaching the Party hereafter-mentioned, if the Situation of Affairs should absolutely require it, we desire you will represent to the Nabob the State of our Transactions with the Marattas, and that we judge it necessary, for the Security of his Dominions, to remove the Brigade from its present Cantonments to Corah. In this Station they will be ready to oppose any Attempts which Radajee Sindia, or any other Maratta Chief, might be encouraged, by the present Disposition of the Company's Forces, or by other Circumstances, to make against his Possessions; and in this Light we desire you will represent this proposed Movement of the Brigade to the Nabob, as a Measure calculated for his Security, rather than for any direct Purpose of our own.

As soon as you have obtained his Consent to the Motion of the Brigade, you will advise Colonel Stibbert, who is ordered to hold himself in Readiness, to march.

We have written to all the neighbouring States to engage their Assistance against the Ministers at Poona, or at least to secure their Neutrality.

Madajee Sindea, and Touckoojee Holcar, have been referred to you for Particulars. If they have Vackeels at the Nabob's Court, you will sound them with respect to their Master's Attachment to Ragoba's Interest, and endeavour to discover their real Intentions, whether they mean to take any, and what Part in the War. You will also open a direct

direct Correspondence with their Chiefs; the Object of which must be to explain to them our late Transactions with the Ministry at Poona. That not having approved of the Proceedings of Bombay in their Declaration of War against the Ministerial Party, we had endeavoured, from Motives of Moderation, and of general Amity to the Maratta States, to restore Peace in that Part of India. That for this Purpose we had deputed Lieutenant Colonel Upton to Poona, with ample Powers to conclude a Treaty with the Ministers there, and offering to relinquish many important Advantages stipulated by the Presidency of Bombay in their Treaty with Ragonaut Row; but that the Ministers, notwithstanding the Success of our Arms in the last Campaign, have peremptorily refused to listen to any Terms of Accommodation, but such as left us without any Advantage of any Kind, and which we could not accept without dishonouring ourselves in the Eyes of all Indostan: That the pacific Measures we had hitherto pursued had produced no Effect, but to demonstrate to all Indostan the Moderation and Justice of the Principles on which we act. That we are now compelled, by the determined Obstinacy of the Ministers, to renew the War: That being reduced to this Necessity, we have resolved to support the Cause of Ragoba with the utmost Vigour, and with a general Exertion of the whole Power of the English Arms in India: That our grand Object still is Peace; and that we are determined to act in all Quarters at once; and by the Decision and Rapidity of our Proceedings, bring the War, if possible, to a speedy Conclusion: That as we are well assured of the Fidelity and Attachment of Madjia Sindia, and Tuckooje Holcar to the Cause of Rogoba, we have thought it adviseable to give them the earliest Knowledge of the actual State of Affairs, and of our future Intentions; and that we hope and expect they will not fail to make an immediate and public Declaration in Ragoba's Favour. That to encourage them to take this Step, we have ordered the Brigade in Owde to march towards the Frontiers of their Country, where it will be ready to give them effectual Support, if the Events of the War should make it necessary; and that you are instructed to receive and transmit to us any Proposals which they may think fit to offer for the Advantage of the Common Cause. Your Correspondence with the Maratta Chiefs will be formed out of these Materials. That you may not, however, be unprovided with specific Instructions to guide you in your Negociations with them, we authorize you to acquiesce in any Requisition made directly by them for the Assistance of our Forces to the Extent of Three Battalions of Sepoys, to join and co-operate with them in such Military Operations as they may recommend, and be disposed to engage in for the Interest of Ragoba. At the same Time we in Confidence acquaint you, that this is a Measure which nothing but the apparent Necessity of Affairs could induce us to adopt. You will therefore take Care not to make any Proposals of this Kind yourself, but merely yield your Consent to it on their Solicitation. In that Case you will give immediate Notice to Colonel Stibbert, who is furnished with Directions to act in Conformity to the Advices he may receive from you.

We are, &c.

Fort William, (Signed) Warren Hastings,
7th March 1776. &c. Council.

Mr. Francis—I yield my Assent to the latter Part of the proposed Letter to Mr. Bristow, in which he is impowered to bind us to a Measure which may engage the Company's Arms beyond the Line of the Guarantee of the Nabob of Owde's Dominions, solely upon the Ground of Necessity.

Colonel Monson—I agree to all the Measures proposed by the Governor General, as thinking the War now unavoidable, but most seriously lament the Situation in which this Country is thrown by the precipitate and ill-advised Measures of the Presidency of Bombay. I can now devise no Means by which we can extricate ourselves out of this War, but by a vigorous Exertion of all the Company's Force.

General Clavering—Since the Commencement of Hostilities between the Government of Bombay and the Maratta State, my utmost Endeavours have been employed to put an End to them by a Peace. But as the Negociation is now broken off with the Maratta State, I think it an indispensable Duty in me to give my Concurrence to Measures which seem best calculated to extricate the Government of Bombay out of the Difficulties in which they have engaged their own Government, as well as the other Presidencies. I think it necessary to enter this Declaration to obviate any Objection that may be made to me against my consenting to carry the Company's Arms beyond the Line of Defence prescribed by them. Nothing but the Necessity of the Case should have obliged me to it; and

and to prevent our being dazzled by the Lucres which Ragoba has thrown out to the Government of Bombay, of various Cessions which he will make to the Company as soon as he is in complete Possession of the Maratta Government, I think that the Government of Bombay should be instructed to make a Renunciation of every Cession that he has made, excepting the Islands of Salsette and Bassein, and their Dependencies, together with so much Territory in the Neighbourhood of Surat and Broach, as will be just sufficient to pay the Expences of those two Establishments.

The Governor General—The particular Appellation which Colonel Monson has made of my Name, in the Assent which he has expressed to the preceding Resolutions, makes it necessary for me to disclaim any separate Concern in them from the other Members of the Board. I consider myself only as the Instrument of the Board in collecting and dictating their concurrent Sentiments. I think it necessary to say thus much, not only as I look upon the Measures now proposed to be adopted, as the joint Composition of the Board, but as I wish most heartily that in all Cases which may arise, that have a Relation to the Object now before us, we may always proceed with the same Unanimity; however different our Sentiments have been on the past Measures, Chance or Causes independent of this Board, have at length concentred both our Opinions, Views, and Wishes in the same Point; and I declare, that as in the late Debates I laid it down as a Rule to follow rather than take the Lead, in the Support of Measures which did not originate from myself, or with my Participation, in like Manner it is my Intention to yield up my own Opinion, and to join most heartily with the rest of the Board in the future Conduct of the War, excepting in such Points only as shall very materially affect the Interests of the Company, or the Safety of their Possessions. I think it necessary to remark upon Mr. Francis's Minute, that I should give with equal Reluctance my Assent to the discretional Order proposed to be sent to Colonel Stibbert and Mr. Bristow, for the March of a Party of our Forces beyond the Defensive Line of the Dominions of the Nabob of Owde, were not the present a Case which requires the most vigorous Exertion of every Power of this Government, for extricating the Company from the Troubles in which they are involved, or were the Measures which has been proposed applicable in my Sense of it, either to the Letter, or the evident Spirit of the Company's Orders, which have invariably forbidden remote Expeditions, on the express Consideration of the Danger to which their own Possessions were exposed by the Absence of the Forces necessary for their Defence. I think it not likely that the Maratta Chiefs will require the Aid of our Forces; but we have no other Condition of our Alliance which we can either offer or assent to. Should they make the Requisition, the Refusal would impress them with Doubts of our Sincerity; our Acquiescence would rivet them to the Cause, and the Report of such a Junction, and of the British Forces arming in all Quarters of Indostan and Decan, would give Credit to the Party which we have espoused, and influence the other Powers of Indostan, who are now hesitating to which Side they shall adhere, to unite with us in Confidence of our Power, and the Probability of our future Success. Such a Detachment cannot properly be called a Diminution of our Military Strength, since it consists only of the native Troops, whose Places will be immediately supplied with others. I shall only add, that every other Proposition resolved on in this Day's Consultation, has my entire and hearty Concurrence.

Agreed, That Colonel Stibbert be advised of the Orders sent to Mr. Bristow, as follows;

To Colonel Stibbert, or Officer commanding the Army in the Field.

Sir,

The Ministers at Poona having refused to listen to the Terms of Accommodation proposed to them by us, and having endeavoured to impose Conditions on this Government exclusively honourable and advantageous to themselves, we take it for granted that Colonel Upton has, in Consequence of his Refusal to comply with such Conditions, received his Dismission from their Court, and that Hostilities are actually renewed; on this Presumption, we have ordered Mr. Bristow to obtain the Nabob's Consent, and to give immediate Information of it to you, that you may march with the Brigade under your Command to the Frontier of the Province of Korah, nearest to the Pass at Calpee; you will therefore hold yourself in Readiness for this Purpose.

Mr. Bristow has been further ordered to open a Correspondence with Madajee Sindia and Tuccojee Holkar, with a View to engage them to espouse the Interest of Ragoba; and

and in Case of their Solicitation for the Assistance of a Part of our Military Force, we have authorised Mr. Bristow to yield to such Requisition, and to give immediate Notice of it to you; upon the Receipt of which, we desire that you will detach from the Brigade under your Command a Force not exceeding Three Battalions of Sepoys, to join and cooperate with Madajee Sindia and Tuccajee Holkar, or either of them, as may be agreed on against the Ministerial Party; and you will supply the Place of such Force, by raising an equal Number of fresh Battalions, to keep entire the Strength of the Brigade.

We are, &c.

Fort William, 7th March 1776. (Signed) Warren Hastings, &c. Council.

Resolved, That the following Letter be written to Fort Saint George:

Gentlemen,

By a Letter received from Colonel Upton, under Date the 7th February, we are informed, that the Ministers of the Poona Durbar have peremptorily refused to accede to the Terms of Accommodation which he was instructed to propose to them; that they positively insisted on the Restitution of Salsette, and a Renunciation of the Four small Islands adjacent to it; and would not agree to wait the Result of a Reference of this Point to us; in short, that they were determined to hear of Peace on no Conditions that should not be exclusively honourable and advantageous to themselves. Colonel Upton's Negociation is therefore entirely broken off; he was to receive his Dismission, and retire to Bombay within Six Days from the Date of his Letter, but the further Interval to be allowed before the Renewal of Hostilities was not then determined. The Ministers having resolved to send their Army again into the Field, we have no Alternative left but a vigorous Prosecution of the War against them, in Conjunction with Ragonaut Row, on the Presumption that the Resolution of the Ministerial Party was final: We have agreed to support the Pretensions of that Chief, and have taken every preparatory Step that has occurred to us for providing Means to carry on the War with Vigour and Success.

We recommend it to you to succour them immediately with a Reinforcement of Two Battalions of Sepoys, or more if you can spare them, either by the Way of Anjengo, if the Season be not too far advanced, or by what other Route you may think more eligible; and to alleviate any Danger which you might apprehend from being deprived of so large a Body of your Military Force, you will, if you deem it adviseable, raise new Corps to supply the Place of such as you may send on this Service, during their Absence; and we are willing to defray any extraordinary Charge that you may incur on this Account.

We have written to Nizam Ally Cawn, Hyder Ally, Morary Row, Moodajee Booncla, Suckajee Holcar, and Madajee Sinda, with a View of engaging their Assistance in favour of Ragoba; or at least to secure their Neutrality. We request that you will open a Correspondence with the Three first, and concur in using your joint Efforts with us to induce them to second our Views for the Re-establishment of Ragoba in the Government of Poona.

Our Resident at Oude has been ordered to open a like Correspondence with Madajee Scinda and Suckajee Holcar; and in order to keep them firm to our Party, we have removed the Brigade from Oude to the Frontier of Corah nearest Calpee, under the Pretence of affording them any Assistance that the Exigency of the Case may require.

While we lament the Necessity which has compelled us to undertake this War, and which has frustrated our Endeavours to maintain a general Peace in India, so strenuously recommended by the Company, we rely on your Efforts to co-operate heartily and effectually with u in bringing it to a speedy Conclusion.

We are, &c.

Fort William, 7th March 1776. (Signed) Warren Hastings, &c. Council.

Resolved also, That Sir Edward Hughes be addressed as follows:

To Sir Edward Hughes, Knight, Commander of His Majesty's Squadron in India.

Sir,

We formerly had the Honour to acquaint you of the Principles in which the President and Council of Bombay entered into an Allianca with Ragonaut Row, to assist him with the

the Company's Troops in Support of his Pretenſions to the Paiſhwaſhip of the Maratta Government at Poona, that not having approved the Proceedings of that Preſidency in engaging the Company's Arms in Hoſtilities againſt the Miniſterial Party.

We had deputed Colonel Upton to Poona, with full Inſtructions and Powers to conclude a Treaty of Peace with that Party, on Terms reciprocally honourable and advantageous; but by a Letter juſt received from Colonel Upton of the 7th February, we are informed that the Miniſters would liſten to no Conditions but ſuch as they might think fit to impoſe for their own Honour and Benefit excluſively, and to leave us no Alternative but to acquieſce in them with Diſhonour to ourſelves, or to renew the War. Colonel Upton was to receive his Diſmiſſion, and retire from the Poona Durbar, in 5 or 6 Days after the Date of his Letter; but no Period had then been fixed for the Renewal of Hoſtilities.

On the Preſumption that the declared Reſolution of the Miniſterial Party to proſecute the War was final, and that Colonel Upton has actually broke his Negociations, and retired to Bombay, we take the earlieſt Opportunity of adviſing you that we have releaſed the Preſident and Council of Bombay from the Reſtrictions which we had laid upon the Operations of their Army, and have authorized them to continue the War in Conjunction with Ragoba againſt the Miniſters.

As this is a Meaſure to which we are unavoidably reduced, after having ſought by every honourable Means to prevent it, we are determined, by a vigorous Exertion of our Powers, to bring the War to as ſpeedy a Concluſion as poſſible. We have therefore taken every preparatory Step that has occurred to us for carrying it on with Succeſs, by providing Supplies of Men and Money, to be immediately ſent to Bombay; and by writing to all the Country Powers, to engage their Aſſiſtance in the Cauſe of Ragoba, or at leaſt to ſecure their Neutrality. We entertain great Hopes that they will not oppoſe him, as we underſtand, from repeated Informations, that moſt of the Chiefs of the Maratta State were wavering in their Determination which Side they ſhould eſpouſe.

We have only to requeſt the Favour of you to continue with His Majeſty's Squadron under your Command on that Coaſt during the Continuance of theſe Troubles, and to grant all the Aſſiſtance in your Power to the Operations of the Preſident and Council at Bombay.

Fort William,
7th March 1776.

We are, &c.
(Signed) W. Haſtings, &c. Council.

Agreed, That the Governor General be requeſted to write to Nizam Ally Cawn, Hyder Ally Cawn, Moodajee Booſila, Moodajee Sindia, Succojee Holkar, and Morrary Row, to engage their Aſſiſtance in the Cauſe of Ragoba, or to induce them to remain neuter.

Agreed alſo, That Succajee Holka and Moodajee Booſila, be referred to Mr. Briſtow for Particulars.

And agreed, That a Letter be written to Ragoba, and forwarded to Surat, as follows:

Gentlemen,

To Surat. If Colonel Upton ſhould have been obliged to break off his Negociations with the Miniſters at Poona, and a Continuation of the War ſhould in conſequence have been reſolved on, we deſire you will immediately forward the incloſed Letter by a ſafe Conveyance to Ragonaut Row; but if on the contrary a Treaty of Peace ſhould have been concluded, you will deſtroy it.

Fort William,
7th March 1776.

We are, &c.
(Signed) Warren Haſtings, &c. Council.

To Ragonaut Row.

The peremptory and repeated Injunctions which this Government has received from the Company, to maintain the Peace of all their Poſſeſſions in India, and eſpecially to avoid every Occaſion of Difference with the Maratta Nation, compelled myſelf and the Council, on the firſt Advices of the Engagements which the Governor and Council of Bombay had entered into with you, without our Knowledge or Participation, and of the War which was the Conſequence of thoſe Engagements, to ſuſpend the Continuance of it until we should have used our Endeavours, by every fair and honourable Means, to obtain a peaceable Accommodation of all Differences; and for this Purpose Colonel Upton was deputed on the Part of this Government with full Powers to negociate and conclude a Treaty of Peace with the Ministers at Poona. It was with much Reluctance that I found myself under the Necessity of appearing to counteract your Views, while the Negociation continued; but I had not been inattentive to your Interests in the Instructions which I gave to Colonel Upton, who had express Directions to stipulate such Conditions as you should approve, and as might insure your future Safety and Welfare. By Letters lately received from the Gentleman, I am informed by the Ministers at Poona, either presuming on our Moderation, or relying with as much Confidence on their own Strength, have rejected his Offers of Peace, and declared their Intentions of renewing the War. How much soever I have sought to avoid this Brunt, while the Orders of my Superiors impelled me to it; yet, as my Endeavours have proved unsuccessful, and as I now deem myself freed from all former Restraints, I feel the highest Satisfaction In offering you, in the Name of this Government, the perpetual Friendship and Alliance of the Company, and the Assistance of their Arms in all Parts of India, to replace you with full Authority in the Seat of your Government at Poona; and for that Purpose Letters have been written to the Presidency of Bombay, authorizing them to renew their Negociations with you for a Treaty of Alliance, the Ratification of which is to be referred to myself and the Council appointed for the Superintendance of the Company's Affairs in India, that the Conditions of it may be equally binding on all their Governments and Dependencies; and Orders have been given both to that Presidency, to the Presidency of Madras, and to the Commander of our Forces in the Provinces of Oude, to co-operate in the Execution of your Designs, and particularly to form Connection with Nizam Ally Cawn, Hyder Ally, Morrary Row, Moodajee Boosila, Succajee Holcar, and Madajee Sindia. I have also sent Supplies, both of Men and Money, to Bombay, and have neglected no Means to insure you the completest Success; for the next I refer you to the Governor of Bombay, of whose Zeal and Attachment you have already received the strongest Assurance and Conviction.

We are, &c.

Agreed, That the following Letters be written to Bombay and to Colonel Upton:

Gentlemen,

By a Letter received from Colonel Upton, under Date the 7th February, we are informed that the Ministers at the Poona Durbar have absolutely and peremptorily refused to accede to any Terms of Accommodation, but such as should be exclusively honourable and advantageous to themselves; being therefore left without any Alternative, he was to receive his Dismission from their Court in Five or Six Days, when a further Interval would be fixed for the Renewal of Hostilities.

On the Presumption that Colonel Upton's Negociations are entirely broken off, that he has retired to Bombay, and that Hostilities are in Consequence renewed, we think it necessary to take the earliest Opportunity to release you from the Restrictions which we formerly laid on your Operations, and to provide every Means in our Power for carrying on the War in Conjunction with Ragoba with Vigour. We therefore authorize you to treat with him, and to give him the strongest Assurances of our full Assistance and Support; which he has also been given to expect in a Letter from this Government, whereof we transmit you a Copy enclosed.

One of the most important Services you can render to the Company, is to obtain the immediate Possession of Bassein, provided it can be done by Negociation with the Killadar, and by offering him advantageous Terms for himself; but we do not mean to make this the present Object of your Military Operations, which should be directed to one Point only, the Restoration of Ragoba; nor would we have your Attention drawn off to any other till that shall be accomplished.

We recommend it to you to send into the Field all the Force you can possibly spare (and if you deem it necessary) to bring a Body of fresh Sepoys for the Duty and Defence of your own Garrisons. Although we shall leave the Detail and immediate Conduct of the War entirely to your Direction, while the Scene of its Operations lies in your Neighbourhood; yet, as we are entrusted with the general Controul and ultimate Charge of it, as it is likely from the Nature of it to involve the Company's Possessions in every Part of India,

India, and the Means of conducting it must principally rest on the Resources of this Government, we think it incumbent upon us to require and insist that you assign the Command of the Army to General Gordon, whom alone we deem fit to be intrusted with a Charge of such Consequence to the Interest, Honour, and Safety of the Company, by whose express Choice and Nomination he was appointed to it; and we also recommend that you give him immediate Orders to join the Troops with Ragoba, and march the combined Forces with all possible Expedition to Poona, suffering no Object to divert his Attention from this main Point, which we hope will put a Conclusion to the War. The Occasion is too critical and important to suffer us to stand on personal Respects. We hereby declare that we shall consider you answerable to the Company for the Consequences, if our present Recommendation of General Gordon should not be complied with.

We have written to Sir Edward Hughes, to request that he will remain with his Squadron on your Coast, and afford you all the Assistance in his Power; to this Request, you will of Course add your own Solicitation to him, and we have no Doubt of his Compliance; we have also desired the Presidency of Fort Saint George, to send you as large a Reinforcement of Troops as they may be able to spare, and if the Season will permit, to dispatch them either by the Way of Anjengo, or by other Roads which they may prefer; you are as well able to judge as we are, how far it may be prudent to depend on receiving this Reinforcement in Time.

We have further written Letters to Nizam Ally Cawn, Hyder Ally, Moodajee Boosila, Moodajee Scindia, and Succoojee Holkar, to engage their Assistance, or at least their Neutrality in the present War. The Two First of these Chiefs will receive Applications to the same Effect from Fort Saint George; and we have ordered our Resident at the Court of Oude, to open a Negociation with the Two last, and if they should concur heartily with us, he is authorized, on their Solicitation for Assistance from us, to grant them the Aid of Three Battalions of Sepoys, to co-operate in any Military Operations which they may recommend, and be disposed to engage in for the Service of Ragoba. In the mean Time, we have ordered the Brigade in Oude, to march to the Frontiers of the Province of Corah, nearest to the Calpee Pass, professedly to be in Readiness for this Service, if the Situation of Affairs should absolutely require it also, but with a View to keep them in Awe if they should be inclined to counteract our Measures.

To supply you with Funds for carrying on the War, we propose to remit to you immediately, either in Specie or Bills, Five Lacks of Rupees, and One to authorize you to draw on us to the Amount of Five Lacks more, the Whole to be solely appropriated to the Operations of the War. And that we may be satisfied that these great Supplies are not only expended with Oeconomy, but strictly appropriated to the Service for which they are given, we expect that you will keep a separate Account of the Disposition thereof, and of all other Sums which you may hereafter receive from us on this Account, and that you do transmit the same to us; for the rest we leave it to you, to form new Connections, and to induce the several Chiefs of the Maratta Empire to espouse the Cause in which we are now unavoidably embarked.

The Succession of Events which have involved the Company in this Quarrel, has sprung from Measures in which we had no Concern, and for which we are not answerable; but while we lament the Necessity to which this Government is reduced, of engaging in War, we are equally sensible of the Expediency of pushing it with Vigour, and to this Object you may be assured our utmost Efforts shall be directed.

We are, &c.

Fort William, 7th March 1776.

(Signed) Warren Hastings, and Council.

To Lieutenant Colonel Upton.

Sir,

We have received your Letters of the 2d and 7th February. From the Contents of the latter, we conclude that your Negociation has been entirely broken off with the Ministers; that you are returned to Bombay, and that Hostilities have in Consequence unavoidably taken Place; we have therefore, on this Presumption, released the President and Council at Bombay from their former Restraint, authorized them to renew the Treaty of Alliance with Ragoba, and to support his Pretensions to the Paishwaship with all the Force they can send to his Assistance; we have also desired the Governor and Council

Council at Fort Saint George, to grant them a Reinforcement of Men, and have taken ſuch Meaſures on our own Part, as we thought neceſſary to give Life and Vigour to his Cauſe, by writing to the ſeveral Country Powers, and removing the Brigade from its Station in Oude, to the Frontier of Corah neareſt Calpee.

We wait with Impatience the Arrival of the further Advices which you promiſed to ſend us; and ſuppoſe they will contain News, either of your having quitted Poona, or that the Miniſters have yielded to your Propoſals, and a Treaty has been concluded with them. On the Receipt of this Letter, we ſhall write further to you; in the mean Time, we ſhall only add, that if this ſhould find you ſtill at Poona, and that no Treaty has yet been finally concluded, you will conform to the Inſtructions which you have already received.

Fort William, 7th March 1776. (Signed) W. Haſtings, &c. Council.

Mr. Francis—I would beg Leave to recommend it to the Board, that in authorizing the Preſidency of Bombay to treat again with Ragoba, they may be confined to the agreeing upon preliminary Articles of a Treaty, which Articles they may execute with him; but that the definitive Treaty may be reſerved to be ſettled and executed with Ragoba by this Government, as it is probable that the Views of this Council, particularly with regard to Territorial Acquiſitions, may not be ſo extenſive as we have Reaſon to think may be propoſed by the Bombay Preſidency.

Agreed, That the above Propoſal lie for Conſideration till next Council Day.

Warren Haſtings,
J. Clavering,
Geo. Monſon,
P. Francis.

APPENDIX, N° 109.

Extract of Bengal Secret Conſultations, the 11th March 1776.

PRESENT,

The Honourable Warren Haſtings, Governor General, Preſident,
Lieutenant General John Clavering,
The Honourable George Monſon,
Richard Barwell, Philip Francis, } Eſquires.

READ, and approved, the Conſultation of the 7th Inſtant.

The Secretary having received the following Papers and Note from General Clavering on Saturday, ſent it, agreeably to his Requeſt, in Circulation to the other Members of the Board.

General Clavering deſires Mr. Auriol to circulate to the Governor General, and the other Members of the Council, the incloſed Paper, in order that they may form their Opinion on the propoſed Meaſure of ſending 30 of the Artillery Corps, and 50 of the firſt Regiment, to Bombay; the Expence, the Length of the Voyage, and the late Seaſon at which they can arrive at Surat, being taken into Conſideration.

He will be able to inform the Board To-morrow, of the Quantity of Field Pieces and Howitzers which are in Store. By the Return of the Field Bombay Train it appears, that there are

lb. 12	lb. 6	lb. 3		lb. 12		lb. 6		lb. 3
[illegible]	[illegible]	[illegible] 4;	of which ſerviceable,	3;	in the Field,	4	and	4.

It is necessary to consider the Pay and Batta of the Troops during this Voyage, and their Establishment afterwards. The General recommends to the Governor General and the Members of the Board, to determine what Batta should be given to the private Men and what to the Officers during the Voyage, and after they join the Bombay Army, to prevent every Occasion of Animosity on Account of the Difference in the Batta received by their Officers and ours.

The Question that arises is, Whether, first, any Stoppages should be made from the Private, for the Provisions furnished to them on Board?

2d. Whether any, and what, Advance of Batta should be made to them to enable them to purchase Necessaries for the Voyage?

To enable the Board to decide on the Two Questions, he has procured the best Information (not having any Precedent before him) of what appears to be proper.

That on the Supposition of a Voyage of Three Months, One Month's full Batta should be paid to the Men in Advance, and One Month after their Arrival at Bombay, and the Third Month appropriated towards the Payment of their Provisions; afterwards, to conform to the Allowances in the Bombay Service, which he understands is the same as ours.

With regard to the Officers who will be entitled to the full Double Batta as soon as they go on Board, it is proposed that they should have Three Months paid in Advance; and after their Arrival at Bombay, to be paid only the Batta of the Officers on that Establishment, but to have the Assurance of Government that they will be entitled, at their Return, to the same Allowances as were given to the Detachment which went to the Decan in the Year 1768.

To whom are the Officers to apply for Orders when they arrive at Bombay? The President and Council, General Gordon, or Lieutenant Colonel Upton?

The Board will be pleased to decide immediately on these Points, as the necessary Orders must be given.

I approve intirely of the above Proposals. I think the Officers and Men of the Detachment ought to be put under the immediate Orders of General Gordon as soon as they join the Army.

(Signed) Warren Hastings,
Philip Francis,
Richard Barwell.

There are many Instances of Troops belonging to One Presidency serving at another: Whatever has been the Custom should be followed as a Precedent. The General Orders to the Troops while at Bombay, must, as I conceive, be given by the Governor and Council, and communicated to them by the usual Channel of the Fort Major. The private Orders will be given by the Senior Officer of the Corps.

(Signed) Geo. Monson.

I approve of the Proposals of sending a small Detachment to Bombay, but refer it to the Consideration of the Board, whether it would be more proper to make the whole Detachment consist of Infantry, as there appears, from the Return, to be already a Number of Artillery Men at Bombay, sufficient for the Service. If the Vessel proposed to carry the Detachment should touch at Madras, she will be infallibly detained in her Voyage, and obliged to go to the Southern Passage, which will prevent her arriving in Time to be of real Service. The Indian Queen being in Readiness to depart immediately, appears the fittest Vessel for the Purpose.

(Signed) Warren Hastings,
Richard Barwell.

I agree to the Proposal made by the Commander in Chief, if on farther Consideration he should think the Number of Artillery Men now at Bombay insufficient.

(Signed) Philip Francis,
Geo. Monson.

Agreed, That Two Brass Twelve Pounders, Two Brass Six Pounders, with Carriages, Limbers, Tumbrils, and a spare elevating Screw for each Gun, be equally divided on the Ships Indian Queen and Saint Helena.

Resolved, That a Lieutenant, and a Lieutenant Fireworker, with Thirty Artillery Men, a Lieutenant and an Ensign, with Fifty European Infantry, be also sent with the Guns on the Ships above-mentioned; Half the Number on each Ship.

Resolved also, That on the Arrival of the Troops at Bombay, the Infantry be put under the Command of Captain Allan M'Pherson, who is now with Lieutenant Colonel Upton. And

Agreed, That a complete Camp Equipage be sent with them.

Agreed also, That the Quantity of Provisions specified in the above Paper, with every Thing necessary for the Voyage, be furnished from the respective Offices, under the direct Orders of the Comptroller.

Resolved, That Three Months Pay and Double Batta be paid in Advance to the Officers, from the Date of their embarking. That on their Arrival at Bombay, they shall receive the same Batta as the Officers on that Establishment: And Resolved, That they be assured that on their Return they will be intitled to the same Allowance of Batta as was made to the Detachment which went to the Decan in 1767.

Agreed, That the Officers on their Arrival at Bombay shall receive their Orders from the President and Council, but when in the Field, from the Commander in Chief, if he be present, or from the Officer commanding on the Spot.

Agreed, That Two Months Pay and Double Batta be issued to the Non-commissioned and Private of the Detachment, One Half to be paid to them, the other to remain in the Hands of the Officer commanding each Corps, and to be issued on their Arrival at Bombay; they are afterwards to conform to the Allowances in the Bombay Service.

Mr. Francis's Proposition in last Consultation, relative to the Limitation of the Power to be delegated to the President and Council at Bombay, for negociating a Treaty with Ragoba, being now taken into Consideration, is unanimously agreed to.

The Board proceed to consider the Articles proposed by Ragoba in the Letter recorded in the last Consultation from Colonel Keating to the Presidency of Bombay, and transmitted to this Board by Colonel Upton;

Agreed to the First Article.

General Clavering—I think the Treaty of Surat should be confirmed as far as it relates to Salsette and Bassein, and the Islands; but I am of Opinion that no more Territory should be obtained in the Neighbourhood of Broach or Surat, than what will be sufficient to pay the Charges of those Two Establishments. The Country of Guzzerut, in which I understand is centred a great Part of those Cessions that have been yielded to the Company by Futty Sing, is open, and will always require a considerable Body of Troops to defend it. An Establishment of Troops adequate to the Protection of so large a District, always exposed to the Incursions of Cavalry, would absorb the Amount of the Revenues that may arise from them. This Opinion, I confess, is not consonant to the Company's Orders, which limited their Views on the Western Side of India to the Maratta Proportion of the Surat Revenues, but at that Time Broach had not been taken; and the same Reasons which in the Year 1769 influenced the Court of Directors to obtain the Maratta Proportion of Surat, I cannot doubt would now prevail with them to acquire a sufficient Territory to support the Expence of Broach, had a Treaty with the Maratta State come under their Consideration since that Time.

Governor General—I think it will be proper to confirm the Treaty as it stands. The Countries yielded by the Territory in the Neighbourhood of Broach and Surat, appear to me of too little Importance either to be insisted on or relinquished, unless the Possession of them should be an Impediment to the new Treaty.

Mr. Francis—As I unite the Idea of Security to that of Acquisition, it has been my invariable Opinion, which I believe conforms to the declared Policy of the Company, that the Territorial Possessions on the Western Side of India should be confined to Salsette and Bassein, and the other small Islands near Bombay, the entire Revenue of Broach, and a Territory round Broach and Surat sufficient to support the Expence of the Company's Establishment in those Places. If however it should be the Opinion of the Majority of the Board to accept for the present, (and in order to support the immediate Expences of the War) of the additional Concessions proposed by Ragoba, I shall not

 oppose

oppose it, as it will depend upon this Government, or the Company, to relinquish them hereafter.

Mr. Barwell agrees to accept this Article.

Colonel Monson—The peremptory and hasty Refusal of the Poona Durbar to the Proposals of this Government for Peace, leaves us no Alternative: I therefore am of Opinion, that all Advantages tendered to the Company for their Assistance in this War should be accepted. I should act on different Principles, had we had Option as to what Conduct we might pursue. There can be no Harm in accepting any Cessation, as the Company may at any Time, if they think them improper, relinquish them. I agree to accept this Article of the Treaty.

General Clavering—I cannot agree to accept of more Territory till the Court of Directors Pleasure be known upon it. At the same Time I admit, that the Acquisition of the Concany Country would be very convenient, both for the Support of Bombay in Time of War, for the Supply of Provisions, and likewise a great Protection to Salsette, in order that it may become an useful Conquest to the Company; but I think myself bound, by the peremptory Orders of the Company with regard to the Acquisition of Territorial Possessions, not to yield my Consent to it.

Governor General—I disapprove of accepting this Cession, as it will extend our Possessions to a Distance unwarranted by the general Spirit of the Company's Orders, and disproportional to our Means of Defence.

Agreed, That the Second Article be not accepted, as it would extend our Possessions to a Distance not warranted by the Spirit of the Company's Orders.

To the Third Article.

The Board having resolved not to accept the Country, the Gaut is unnecessary.

To the 4th Article.

The Governor General observes, that this should be totally disapproved, as it can by no Means be enforced, but such as would render the Company obnoxious to every Person of Consequence in the Maratta State, whose Confidence and Attachment it is our Interest to conciliate, not to alienate them from us by an Opposition of Interests, and an Encroachment on their Rights.

Mr. Francis objects to it for the same Reason.

Mr. Barwell—I would accept of it.

Colonel Monson rejects it, because he thinks it would involve the Company in a constant Scene of War with the Maratta Jaghiredars.

General Clavering objects to it.

Agreed, That it be rejected, as it could be enforced by no Means but such as would render the Company obnoxious to every Jaghiredar in the Maratta State, whose Confidence and Attachment it is the Company's Interest to conciliate, not alienate by an Opposition of Interest, and by Encroachments on their Rights.

To the 5th Article.

Mr. Francis—I suppose that Prime Cost includes all Expences to the Landing of the Cloth in India, and I agree to it.

Mr. Barwell agrees to it.

Colonel Monson—In Consequence of our relinquishing the advantageous Offers made in the former Articles, I think the Quantity should be encreased to 15 Lacks.

Mr. Barwell acquiesces in Colonel Monson's Proposition.

General Clavering—I consider Ragoba's Situation to have been so desperate when he made these Propositions, that I am afraid little Dependence can be placed on the Performance of them. When he is reinstated, I cannot object to Offers which are so evidently advantageous both to the Company and to Great Britain.

Governor General approves of this, if it can be obtained with the free and unconditional Assent of Ragoba.

Agreed to.

To the 6th Article.

Agreed to, understanding the putting Ragonaut Row in Possession of Poona to be the ultimate Object of the Treaty, and of all the Operations entered into with him.

To

To the 7th Article.

Rejected. The Supply of Ten Lacks of Rupees, which the Board have already resolved to send to the Presidency at Bombay, being all they have in their Power to spare, they expect that it be solely appropriated to the Military Operations of that Presidency.

Article the 8th not agreed to.

To the 9th Article.

Agreed, That the Monthly Subsidy to be paid for the Troops furnished by the Company, be fixed at Two Lacks per Month, without Reference to the Number in the Field; but in Consideration of this, we will assist him with our Forces in all Parts of Hindostan and the Decan, which will produce a much greater Expence to the Company.

To the 10th Article.

The Board cannot agree to bind the Company to such extensive Engagements as those specified in this Article; but as the Whole is now going Home to the Court of Directors, their Orders shall be requested upon this Article.

Agreed, That another Letter be written to the President and Council at Bombay, enclosing a Copy of the above Articles, with the Resolutions of the Board upon them, and directing them to conclude a preliminary Treaty with Ragoba agreeable thereto.

The Letter to Bombay having been drawn up by the Secretary, he sent it in Circulation for the Approbation of the Board, as follows:

To the Honourable William Hornby, Esquire, President, &c. Council, at Bombay.

Gentlemen,

Understanding from the Returns of your Ordnance, which have been laid before us by the Commander in Chief, that you will have Occasion for Field Pieces to prosecute the War, we have sent, by the Indian Queen and Saint Helena, Two Brass Twelve Pounders and Two Brass Six Pounders, with an equal Number of Carriages, Limbers, and Tumbrils, also a spare elevating Screw to each Gun; we have also embarked a Lieutenant and a Lieutenant Fireworker of Artillery, with Thirty Artillery Men, a Lieutenant and Ensign, with Fifty European Infantry, and a complete Set of Camp Equipage. This Force is equally divided on each Vessel; and we have appointed Captain Allan M'Pherson to the Command of the Infantry on their Arrival at Bombay. We have agreed for their Passage at 2½ Rupees per Man per Day, and have furnished them with Provisions and other Necessaries for the Voyage, agreeable to the enclosed Account; if any Overplus should remain, you will receive it from the Commanders.

We have received from Colonel Upton, and read with Attention, the Letter which Colonel Keating addressed you, under Date 24th January, containing Proposals from Ragoba for a new Treaty; but considering the Circumstances under which they were drawn up, we wish in general to decline accepting them. Our Sentiments are expressed upon each separate Article, and we transmit a Copy of them for your Information. We authorize you to conclude a preliminary Treaty with Ragoba, conformably to the Conditions now agreed to, and those contained in the Treaty of Surat, and desire that you will transmit the new Treaty so concluded to us, as we mean to make it the Basis of a definitive one, which we propose to execute with him ourselves. You will assure Ragoba at the same Time, that we do not mean by this Mode to exact further Concessions from him, or to enlarge the Conditions; of this our Intention he may be convinced, if he considers how ready we have been to relinquish spontaneously most of the advantageous Offers which he made through Colonel Keating, but we do it with a View of rendering the Engagements more solemn, obligatory, and lasting.

We presume you understand of course, that the Part we take in the present War, and the Assistance we mean to afford to Ragoba, are founded on the Supposition, that he does not depart from such of the Conditions proposed by himself as we have assented to.

Fort William, 11th March 1776.

We are, &c.

(Signed)

APPEN-

APPENDIX, N° 110.

Extract of Bengal Secret Consultations, the 11th March 1776.

ORDERED, That the List of Stores be entered after the Consultation.

General Clavering having proposed the following additional Paragraph to the above Letter, the Secretary forwarded the same to the Governor General, and the other Members of the Board, and received back their separate Opinions, as follow the Paragraph.

Additional Paragraph proposed by General Clavering to the Letter to Bombay.

" We shall direct Lieutenant Colonel Upton to send the Two Companies of Sepoys, " under the Command of Captain Wroe, which he took with him as his Escort, to " strengthen your Army, and to command the Troops from this Presidency; and re- " commend it to you that he may be appointed Second in Command in your Army; his " Military Talents may be exerted usefully in that Station, under Brigadier General " Gordon; perhaps he may be able to augment the Two Companies at Surat to a com- " pleat Battalion. In that Case we doubt not but you will afford him all the Assistance " in your Power with the Chief at that Place."

If this Paragraph be approved of, and the Measure included in the Letter to Bombay, Colonel Upton ought to be made acquainted with the Military Arrangements that have taken Place, and are proposed from this Presidency with respect to the Third Battalion to be detached from the Brigade in the Province of Owde, to join Madajee Holcar, &c. and to acquaint him, that we shall direct the Officer who may be appointed to command these Three Battalions, to join the Bombay Army on the first favourable Occasion; under which Circumstances the Command of those Battalions will of course devolve upon Colonel Upton, as belonging to the Troops from this Presidency.

J. Clavering.

Agreed to. (Signed) Geo. Monson.
P. Francis.

I object. (Signed) Rich. Barwell.

I entirely disapprove of the Proposition; and that I may not detain the Letter to Bombay, I shall deliver my Objections in a separate Minute, with such other Observations as I shall judge it necessary to make on the present Draft of the Letter to Bombay.

(Signed) Warren Hastings.

The above Paragraph having been approved by a Majority of the Board, it was accordingly inserted in the Letter to Bombay, and the following Letter was in Consequence thereof written to Lieutenant Colonel Upton.

To Lieutenant Colonel Upton.

Sir,

We desire that you will send the Two Companies of Sepoys, which you took as an Escort from hence into the Field, under the Command of Captain Wroe, to strengthen the Army with Ragoba. We have embarked Fifty Artillery Men and Fifty European Infantry from the Presidency for Bombay, and have appointed Captain M'Pherson to command the latter, on their Arrival. The chief Command of all the Troops which we may furnish, will of course belong to you; and we have recommended it to the Presidene and Council at Bombay, to appoint you Second in Command of the Army with Ragoba, under General Gordon.

In case you should have it in your Power, by recruiting new Sepoys, to augment your Two Companies to a complete Battalion, we think this Measure adviseable. We have removed the Brigade in Owde to the Frontier in the Province of Corah, nearest Calpee,

and

and authorized the Commanding Officer to detach a Force, not exceeding Three Battalions of Sepoys, to the Assistance of Madajee Scindia, or Tuckoojee Holcar, if they should make a Requisition for them in Support of the Cause of Ragoba. In case of such a Detachment being sent, we shall order the Commanding Officer to take the first favourable Opportunity of joining the Bombay Army, when the Command of them also will of course devolve no you.

We are, &c.

Fort William,
11th March 1766.

(Signed)

The Governor General having sent the following Note to the Secretary, with his Dissent to the above Appointment, it was circulated, and returned, with the Opinions of the different Members as follow the Dissent.

To T. P. Auriol, Esquire.

Sir,

I send you inclosed my Dissent from the Paragraph in the Letter to Bombay, regarding Colonel Upton, which I desire may be sent round, and entered on the Consultations to go Home by this Dispatch.

I am,
Sir,
Your most obedient Servant,
(Signed) Warren Hastings.

14th March,
1776.

I am sorry that so early an Occasion should have presented itself, to compel me to object to any Measure proposed by the Majority of the Board, for the Conduct of so important a Service, as that in which we are now likely to be engaged; but how studiously soever I may endeavour to avoid an Appearance of Disagreement in ordinary Cases, the present is of a Nature and Tendency which will not admit of such an Acquiescence, without a Sacrifice of my Duty. I therefore declare my Dissent from the Resolution of the Board, as it is expressed in the Letter to the President and Council of Bombay, of the 11th Instant, in Recommendation of Lieutenant Colonel Upton, for the eventual Command of the Army employed by that Presidency, against the Marattas; for the following Reasons:

1st. Because a Recommendation from this Government to that of Bombay, under the present Circumstances of their Affairs, and the Consequences, both public and personal, which they will have Cause to apprehend from a Refusal to comply with it, has all the Effect of an Order.

2dly. Because this Government has no Right to order or to prescribe to that of Bombay, the Appointment to Commands on their own Service, nor any other Measure of Detail.

3dly. Because they cannot comply with such an Order, without a Deviation from the Practice of the Military Service; and a Breach of the Company's Orders, which ought not especially to receive Encouragement from the controlling Government.

4thly. Because Lieutenant Colonel Upton is Junior in Rank to Three Officers on that Establishment, namely, Colonel Egerton, Lieutenant Colonel Cockburn, and Lieutenant Colonel Kay, of whose Abilities this Board have had no Experience, and cannot therefore be the Judges.

5thly. Because this Board have had no Experience, and cannot be the Judges of the comparative Merits and Abilities of Lieutenant Colonel Upton, which ought to have been established by unquestionable Proofs, to entitle him to so extraordinary and invidious a Preference.

6thly. Because it is contrary to the very Principle on which the Board have already censured the President and Council of Bombay, for their partial Appointment of Lieutenant Colonel Keating to the Command, in Prejudice to the Rights of General Gordon, and contrary to that declared to them on this Occasion, in the following Words, "The "Occasion is too critical and important to suffer us to stand on personal Respects," unless it can be clearly demonstrated that personal Respects were not the Inducement for the Recommendation of Lieutenant Colonel Upton.

7thly.

7thly. Becauſe it cannot fail to give high Diſguſt not only to thoſe Officers who are immediately ſuperſeded by Colonel Upton, but to every other Officer on the Eſtabliſhment, who will naturally look upon it as a Precedent which may operate hereafter to the general Prejudice of the Service, excluſively of the Concern which every Military Man of Spirit muſt feel for the Honour of the Corps of which he is a Member; and ſurely this is not a Time to give Offence to thoſe on whoſe Zeal and Attachment to the Service, the Safety of the Company's Intereſts ſo eſſentially depends.

8thly. Becauſe the immediate Conduct and Reſponſibility of the War depend wholly on the Preſidency of Bombay, and the latter more eſpecially, ſince the ſolemn Proteſt and Declaration ſignified to them in the Letter from this Government, of the and 6th Inſtant; but to dictate to them the irregular Choice of an Officer for the Command of their Army, is to preclude them from the Means, and diſcharge them from the Reſponſibility, ſince he will conſider himſelf, and be conſide ed by them, as ſupported by an Authority ſuperior to that under which he immediately acts, and therefore leſs accountable to them for his Conduct, than one of their own Nomination.

Laſtly. Becauſe the Service on which Colonel Upton was originally employed, muſt obviouſly impreſs Ragoba with Prejudices againſt him, and with Suſpicions of his Attachment; and univerſal Experience has ſhewn, that nothing has a more fatal Tendency to defeat the Succeſs of great public Meaſures, than a Miſunderſtanding between thoſe who are immediately charged with their Execution. I think it but a Juſtice due to Colonel Upton, and to myſelf, to declare, that though I have ſtrongly objected to the Indulgence, which it has propoſed to ſhew him, I have no perſonal Diſlike to him. On the contrary, I hold him in great Eſteem, becauſe I know him to be poſſeſſed of the general Eſteem of his Brother Officers, which is the beſt Teſt in Default of Experience, of an Officer's real Merits.

(Signed) Warren Haſtings.

The Proteſt entered by the Governor General, to the Letter written to the Government of Bombay, recommending Lieutenant Colonel Upton to be appointed Second in Command in their Army, is grounded on a Fact ſo very erroneous, that one cannot help ſuppoſing that in the Hurry of his Buſineſs, he has not given it an attentive Peruſal.

He is pleaſed to ſay, that Lieutenant Colonel Upton is recommended to the eventual Command; whereas the Words are, that he is recommended to be Second in Command, that the Chief Command is of courſe to devolve to him. Any one of the Officers whom Mr. Haſtings has mentioned, may be ordered, on the Death or Removal of the Chief, to take the Command, without deviating from the expreſs Senſe of the Recommendation contained in our Letter. As this Government is now ſending Troops to join the Bombay Army, it is proper that an Officer of Rank ſhould command them. The Two Companies, when augmented to a Battalion, as the ſame Letter imports, will, together with the Europeans detached from this Preſidency, form a Body equal to a Third of the Forces in the Field; and will be more than equal to them, if the Three Battalions which it is propoſed ſhould act with Madgee Sindia and Tocojee Holcar, ſhould ever join them.

But Mr. Haſtings now urges that this Government has no Right to order or to preſcribe to that of Bombay the Appointment to command in their own Service, or any other Meaſures of Detail. That this was not Mr. Haſtings's Sentiments on the 7th Inſtant, the Conſultations will bear Witneſs. He dictated the Intentions of the Board to remove Colonel Keating, and to appoint Brigadier Gordon, in Terms ſo harſh, that one of the Members objected to them; and on that Account they were ſoftened.

Mr. Haſtings may plead on this Occaſion, as he has done on others, when he has altered his Opinion, that he endeavours to adopt the Senſe of the Board when it is not totally repugnant to his own. This Plan of Conduct is evidently a ſafe one, becauſe it may accommodate itſelf to every future Contingency. A few Months hence he may diſapprove the Meaſures that we are now taking to ſupport Ragoba, as he did thoſe which the Board unanimouſly adopted at firſt to oppoſe him.

Mr. Haſtings declares, that he has no perſonal Diſlike to Colonel Upton; but on the contrary, that he eſteems him. The Diſlike and Eſteem which is here denied and affirmed, may be weighed againſt each other by the Words of the Context, and Credit given to that which ſhall preponderate. In one Scale may be placed the Allegation of Inexperience, which to an Officer is highly detrimental to his Credit; and in the other, Mr. Haſtings's Profeſſion of Eſteem, becauſe he ſays he is poſſeſſed of the general Eſteem of his Brother Officers; whether Mr. Haſtings's Profeſſion of Eſteem thus eſtabliſhed,

can

can compensate the Attempt to hurt an Officer's Reputation, must be left to Colonel Upton himself to determine; he knows his Services, and how unjustly they are depreciated. To efface, however, any Impression which may be made to Colonel Upton's Disadvantage during his Absence, by Mr. Hastings's Suggestion, it is sufficient only to mention, that he was bred up in the King's Army; and on his Arrival in India was immediately employed on the Expedition to the Decan, under the Command of Colonel Peach.

(Signed) J. Clavering.

The Governor General, in his Dissent to the Letter to the Presidency of Bombay, appears to me to have intirely misunderstood the Recommendation of Lieutenant Colonel Upton's Services to them. The Words of the Letter are, "We recommend it to you that he (Colonel Upton) may be appointed Second in Command in your Army; his Military Talents may be exerted usefully in that Station, under Brigadier Genertl Gordon." This Expression by no Means gives the eventual Command of the Army to Lieutenant Colonel Upton: In combined Armies the Ranks of Officers are according to the Dates of their Commission. I consider the Forces of the different Presidencies, when united, to form an Army of that Nature. I therefore think Lieutenant Colonel Upton has a Right to the Rank derived from the Date of his Commission at this Presidency, when he shall be serving in any Army where a Part of the Troops of this Presidency are employed.

If Lieutenant Colonel Upton were to be ordered away, and the Troops of this Presidency continued on the Bombay Service, it would be an implied Censure on him in this Presidency. The Governor, in his Fourth Objection, has mis-stated a Fact; for Lieutenant Colonel Upton is Senior in Rank to Two out of the Three Officers which he has mentioned. Lieutenant Colonel Upton has served many Years with an unimpeached Reputation; and Candour obliges me to think him, and I ever shall (until his public Conduct may give just Reason to alter my Opinion) an Officer to be trusted with the Conduct of any Command that his Rank may intitle him to.

(Signed) George Monson.

I again object to the additional Paragraph proposed by General Clavering; and I think the Governor General perfectly right in the Objections he makes to the Recommendation of Colonel Upton.

(Signed) R. Barwell.

In Military Appointments, the Recommendation of the Commander in Chief will always have considerable Weight with me, as I think it ought to have with the Board. I have no Knowledge, nor do I pretend to be a Judge of Colonel Upton's Merits as an Officer; I therefore yield implicitly to the present Opinion of General Clavering, who is the proper official Judge of the necessary Qualifications for a Military Command, since I have no personal Knowledge of my own to oppose to it. A great Part of the Governor's Objections to Colonel Upton, seems to be founded on a Mistake of Terms and Facts. It is not expressed or meant that Colonel Upton should command in chief in case of the Removal of General Gordon; and I take it for granted that Colonel Monson is not mistaken when he asserts, that he is Senior in Rank to Two of the Three Officers mentioned by the Governor, neither is our Recommendation of Colonel Upton, in my Opinion, equivalent to an absolute Order. At the same Time I expect it will be complied with, since, independent of the superior Authority vested in this Council, it would be highly unreasonable that, even on the Footing of a combined Army, the Party from which the chief Support of the common Cause is expected, should have no Officer in that Army on whom they can directly depend. There is no Ground for supposing that Colonel Upton will oppose or counteract that Authority under which he is immediately placed, much less that the Service on which he was originally employed must impress Ragoba with Prejudices against him, and with Suspicions of his Attachment. After failing in a Negociation for Peace, which he undoubtedly had at Heart, it seems probable that the Obstinacy of the Ministers, to which he will attribute his Want of Success, will have filled his Mind with Disgust and Resentment. I have a Right to oppose one Supposition to another, and on this Ground conclude that Colonel Upton will be cordially received by Ragoba, as a Man slighted and disappointed by the other Party.

(Signed) P. Francis.

The Governor General's Dissent having been returned to him agreeable to his Desire, with the several Observations of the different Members for his Information, he sent them back, with the following Note to the Secretary.

I desire the Secretary to send round my Reply to the Minutes concerning the Recommendation of Colonel Upton, that it may be recorded with them in this Place.

(Signed) Warren Hastings.

If I have misunderstood the Intention of the Board in their Recommendation of Lieutenant Colonel Upton, the Explanations which have been furnished me of it have not enabled me to discover my Mistake, since I still conceive an Appointment of Second in Command to be the same in Effect as an Appointment to the eventual Command.

I readily acknowledge the Error which has been pointed out to me by Colonel Monson, with respect to the Ranks of Lieutenant Colonels Cockburn and Hay. I had been informed, that the Dates of those Gentlemen's Commissions were prior to Lieutenant Colonel Upton's; but I since understand the contrary from the same Authority, on which I can safely rely. This removes a Part, yet but a small Part of my Objections. It was for the Purpose of amending this Part of my Minute that I wrote to the Secretary to return it; but I did not receive it back until the other Members had written their Replies to it.

I should be sorry to waste my own Time, or to lay Claim to that of the Court of Directors, by a minute Refutation of the General's Arguments; but I am compelled, in my own Justification, to reply to a Fact asserted by him, which is directly contrary to my Resolution of it. He says, that I "dictated the Intentions of the Board to remove Colonel Keating, and to appoint Brigadier General Gordon, in Terms so harsh that one of the Members objected to them, and on that Account they were softened."

As I remember this Subject, and I think I can venture to trust to my Remembrance of it, the Proposal of recommending the Removal of Lieutenant Colonel Keating, and the Appointment of General Gordon to the Command, originated with one of the other Members of the Board. I myself objected to the Terms in which it was proposed, as pronouncing a severe Censure on Lieutenant Colonel Keating, in which we were not warranted by any Proofs before us.

The first Draft of the Letter to Bombay was not written or dictated by me. In that the Passage relative to the present Subject stood thus:

"As the general Conduct of this War, and Provision of Resources for carrying it on, now remain with us, and the Honour and Interest of the Company are so deeply concerned in the Operations of the Army, we think it proper to inform you, that we cannot place so much Confidence in the Knowledge and Skill of Lieutenant Colonel Keating, as to trust the future Operations of the War to his Charge: We therefore expect, and insist upon it, that you assign the Command of the Army to General Gordon, and direct him immediately to join the Troops with Ragoba," &c.—This Passage I erased entirely when the Secretary brought the Draft to me for Correction, and substituted the following in its Stead: "Although we shall leave the Detail and immediate Conduct of the War entirely to your Direction, while the Scene of its Operations lies in your Neighbourhood, yet, as we are intrusted with the general Controul, and ultimate Charge of it, as it is likely from the Nature of it, to involve the Company's Possessions in every Part of India, and the Means of conducting it must principally rest in the Resources of this Government, we think it incumbent upon us, to require and insist that you assign the Command of the Army to General Gordon, whom alone we deem fit to be intrusted with a Charge of such Consequence to the Interest, Honour and Safety of the Company, by whose express Choice, and Nomination, he was appointed to it. We also recommend, that you give him immediate Orders to join the Troops with Ragoba," &c.

This Extract is sufficient to shew the Principle on which I joined in the Recommendation of General Gordon, for the Command of the Bombay Forces, and to prove that my Opinions have been consistent.

(Signed) Warren Hastings.

APPEN-

APPENDIX, N° III.

Extract of Bengal Secret Consultations, the 11th March 1776.

MR. Tayler sends in the following Letter:

To the Honourable Warren Hastings, Esquire, Governor General, &c. Members of the Council at Calcutta.

Honourable Sir, and Gentlemen,

As the Refusal of the Ministers, to treat on satisfactory Terms, has determined you to embrace the Cause of Ragoba, and to commit the intire Management of all future Transactions with him to the Government of Bombay, I beg Leave to represent to you, that before they are entirely terminated, many Points of Discussion may arise with different Persons, which will require much local Knowledge of Affairs in the West of India: As from my long Residence, and the Share I have for some Years past had in the Administration of Bombay, I may make bold to say, that I possess this requisite Knowledge, you have done me the Honour to make me fully acquainted with your Views and Sentiments, and I have also been publicly deputed from the Government of Bombay to represent the Company's particular Views and Interests at that Presidency; should you, from these different Circumstances, deem me fit for the important Charge of conducting future Negociations, I beg Leave to tender my Services on this Occasion, not doubting, from the Confidence shewn in the particular Selection of me, and the Approbation they have testified of my Proceedings, the Governor of Bombay will readily concur in Opinion with you, regarding the Propriety of it.

I beg Leave to observe, that as the future Conduct of Affairs is to be entrusted with the Governor of Bombay, they alone will become responsible for Events; it seems but reasonable therefore, that they should have Persons on whom they can absolutely depend, and in some Shape command, employed under them; by your Appointment of me, they will be perfectly satisfied in this Point; and I beg Leave further to remark, that as it may seem now material to impress the Paishwa with a Confidence in us, my Return to him, after having been especially deputed to promote his Pretensions, will go far to effect this End.

Should you think fit, Gentlemen, to accept this Offer of my Services, besides the Credit I should hope to obtain by it with my honourable Employers, the Honour you do me in reposing this Confidence, will be a strong additional Incitement to exert all the Ability and Activity I may be possessed of, to settle Matters in the West of India on the most permanent Footing; and so much convinced as I am of your Desire to bring them to a speedy Conclusion, I beg Leave to assure you, that this shall be a particular Object of my Attention, for which Purpose I will proceed by the most expeditious Route to join the Paishwa.

As by the present Appearance of Things I do not now see the Necessity of my further Stay here, I purpose, if it is agreeable to you, at any Rate returning to Bombay; and take this Opportunity to assure you, that I entertain the most grateful Sense of the many Marks of Respect and Civility with which you have publicly and individually honoured and obliged me, during my Residence here; I return you my Thanks for them, and with the sincerest Wishes that Success may attend all your Undertakings,

I remain, very respectfully,
Honourable Sir, and Gentlemen,
Your most obedient humble Servant,
W. T.

Calcutta,
11th March 1776.

Agreed,

Agreed, That the following Reply be written to Mr. Tayler.

To William Tayler, Esquire.

Sir,

We have received the Letter which you this Day wrote to us.

Having already advised the President and Council at Bombay very fully of our Sentiments in respect to the future Treaty to be entered into with Ragonaut Row, we think that it would be improper to charge you with any separate Commission from this Government to negociate with him; but we leave it to you to return to Bombay in whatever Manner you may judge most expedient, and to act according to the Orders which you may receive from that Presidency. We wish you a safe and pleasant Journey, and remain,

Sir,

Fort William, the 11th March 1776.

Your most obedient Servants,
Gov. Gen. & Council.

APPENDIX, N° 112.

Extract of Bengal Secret Consultations, 1st April 1776.

GENERAL CLAVERING having proposed the Two following Paragraphs to be added to the General Letter to be dispatched by the Talbot, they were circulated, and returned to the Secretary, with the Minutes which follow them, and inserted in the Letter.

" As it does not seem clear to us, that either by the Act of Parliament, or by the Charter, a Power is given to the Judges to issue a Writ of Habeas Corpus, we submit it to your Opinion to take the Sentiments of your Standing Council on this Point.

" Some Part of the Conduct of the President and Council of Bombay seems not to be free from Objection. Whilst they were under the Injunctions of our Orders, to observe the Suspension of Arms, and to withdraw their Army into their own Garrisons, or at least into the Purgunnahs belonging to them, Colonel Keating had furnished Two Eighteen Pounders for the Siege of Amadabad, and the Company's Troops remained the whole Time encamped with those of Ragoba."

I declare, that for my own Part, I have no Doubt of the Powers inherent in the Supreme Court to issue Writs of Habeas, but I cannot object to the Reference proposed to be made upon this Point to the Court of Directors, if any other Member of the Board think that the Court are not possessed of such a Power.

I believe it will appear, that the Siege of Amadabad was begun, and the Two Pieces of battering Cannon lent for the Service, before the Order arrived with Colonel Keating for the Cessation of Arms; that on the Receipt of that Order, Ragoba, at the Instance of Colonel Keating, sent Orders to discontinue the Siege. How those Orders were obeyed does not appear.

It is past a Doubt that our Forces did remain with Ragoba, because he could not accompany them, nor be secure against Hostilities if he had remained behind, and they had quitted him. If this Paragraph is agreed to, I desire that a Copy of the Letter from the President and Council of Bombay, dated the 29th December 1775, which contains their Reasons for this Measure, may be sent a Number in the Packet, for the fuller Information of the Court of Directors.

(Signed) W. H.
R. B.

I have no Objection to the Question mentioned in the First of the Two Paragraphs proposed by General Clavering, being stated as Matter of Doubt to the Court of Directors,

rectors, if any Member of the Board has a Doubt on the Subject. For my own Part, I cannot suppose that a Court, vested with such extraordinary Powers as those of the Supreme Court of Judicature, should want one so material to the Liberty of the Subject, and which, in England, is trusted to every Judge of the King's Bench and Common Pleas; I mean always when the Person in whose Favour the Writ of Habeas Corbus is granted is legally an Object of the Jurisdiction of the Court.

I agree to the Second Paragraph, and to the Governor General's Motion thereupon.

(Signed) P. F.

If there be any Doubts in the Mind of any of the Members of the Board, with regard to the Right of the Power of the Supreme Court, to issue Writs of Habeas Corpus, the Reference may be made as stated by the General.

I think the Second Paragraph should be inserted in the General Letter, and I agree to the Governor General's Motion.

(Signed) G. Monson.

The following Letter from Bombay, with its Inclosures, was received since last Council, and circulated with a Proposal from General Clavering, that a Letter should be written to Bombay.

Honourable Sir, and Gentlemen,

On the 21st Instant we were favoured with your Letter, dated the 20th October.

Colonel Upton has not yet imparted to us any Intelligence of the Progress or State of his Negociation, but we have given him every Information that we think can prove of Service to him in bringing it to a happy Conclusion.

We have very strongly urged to the Colonel, the Propriety of insisting upon the Ministers confirming our Treaty with Ragoba in every Article, and settling honourable and satisfactory Terms for him. We cannot more fully explain our Reasoning and Sentiments on this Subject, than we have in the inclosed Copy of our Letter to him, to which we therefore beg Leave to refer you.

A Continuation of our Correspondence with Colonel Keating since the 29th Ultimo, is now enclosed with Duplicates of the Papers transmitted with our Address of that Date.

Bombay Castle,
20th January 1776.

We are, &c.
(Signed) Wm. Hornby,
President, &c. Council.

Ordered, That the Inclosures be abstracted, and entered after the Consultation.

The foregoing Letter having been returned from Circulation to the Secretary, he prepared the Draft of a Letter to Bombay, which he circulated for the Approbation of the Board, and received back the Minutes which follow it.

Gentlemen,

Since closing our Letter to you of Yesterday, we have received yours of the 28th January.

From your Correspondence with Lieutenant Colonel Keating, which was inclosed in it, we are concerned to observe, that the Ministers at Poona did not complain without Reason of Hostilities on the Part of Ragoba, after the Cessation of Arms had been proclaimed. His persisting with any Appearance of our Concurrence after that Period in the Siege of Amadabad, is a Circumstance so inconsistent with the general Assurances which have been repeatedly given by us, that we cannot avoid taking Notice of it. It further appears by Colonel Keating's Letter of the 4th November, that Two of the Company's Field Cannon of 18 Pounders, had been employed against that Fort, which is an additional Matter of Surprize and Concern to us, as it must at least convey the Idea, that the Siege was carried on with your Aid and Participation, and that we connived at it. We think, for your Honour and ours, that this Matter should be cleared up, and that if Lieutenant Colonel Keating acted therein without your Sanction, he should be made accountable

accountable for his Deviation from the Orders which you had given him to forbear all Hostilities.

We are sorry likewise to remark, that our Injunctions were not better observed for withdrawing our Troops within your own Districts. It is needless to urge to you the Necessity of a Compliance at all Times with the general Orders that we send to you, as without it the comptrolling Authority vested in us would become absolutely nugatory, and rather tend to embarrass the Company's Affairs than promote them.

We are, &c.

I object to the Letter proposed to be written to Bombay, because I am of Opinion that the Correspondence between the President and Council of Bombay, and Lieutenant Colonel Keating, does not afford Grounds for charging either Ragoba or Colonel Keating, with having committed Hostilities after the Cessation of Arms had been proclaimed, but it is very evident that the Ministerial Forces did commit Hostilities in more than One Instance.

I cannot subscribe to the Censure past upon the Presidency of Bombay, for suffering their Army to remain with Ragoba after the Orders received from this Board, because I I think they would have been highly culpable had they abandoned him.

(Signed) W. H.
R. B.

I approve the Letter to Bombay, as Colonel Keating's Correspondence furnish the Declarations which are made in it.

(Signed) G. M.

Extract of the Continuation of the Correspondence with Colonel Keating, from the 4th November, 1775, to 25th January, 1776.

Letter from, dated Kisnapoor, 4th November, 1775.	The Paishwa satisfied with the Terms of the Governor General and Council. The Attack of Amedabad begun previous to the Agreement for a Cessation of Hostilities. Difference between Futty Sing and Govind Row adjusted.
Letter from, dated Bowoon, 13th November.	Futty Sing has consented to give Pitlad to Govind Row.
Letter from, dated Wrgachaw, 20th November.	Thinks encamping at Candeish will be preferable to the Chicoly Purgunnah.
Letter to, dated 2d December.	To obtain from Futty Sing the Four Aistgooms in the Heart of the Purgunnah of Broach; also to prevail on him to make a Cession of the remaining Eight in the Room of Sinor.
Letter from, dated Corrode, 26th November.	The Paishwa refuses marching his Army into Chicoly Purgunnah.
Letter from, dated 29th November.	Buckebah will join the Paishwa with Five thousand good Troops on his Arrival in the Candeish Country.
Letter from the Paishwa to Col. Keating, 25th November.	His Reason for not marching the Troops into the Chicoly Purgunnah.
Letter from Col. Keating to the Paishwa, 26th Nov.	Strenuously recommending him to proceed to Chickley.
Letter from the Paishwa to Colonel Keating.	Is determined not to march to Chickley.
Letter to, dated 6th December.	Consents to the Troops remaining at Corrode, but cannot comply with Ragoba's Proposal for marching them into the Candeish Country.
Letter from, dated Corrode, 8th December.	The Paishwa much dejected.
Letter from, dated 22d December.	Has obtained a Sunnud from Futty Sing for the Purgunnah of Batta; has great Hopes of obtaining the Four Villages of the Autgom. The Ministerialists have violated the Cessation of Arms.

Letter

Letter from, dated Corrode, 24th December.	A Party of the Ministerial Forces has advanced within Five Coss of their Camps, and attacked Monackjee Sindia, when hunting.
Letter from, dated Corrode, 28th December.	Monackjee Sindia has made his Escape from the Ministerial Party—The Nizam wavering in his Conduct.
Letter to, dated 8th January 1776.	Positively forbid committing any Acts of Hostility. Require full Information relative to the Complaint made by the Ministers, of small Parties being detached for plundering the Villages.
Letter from, dated Corrode, 5th January.	The Paishwa delegates his Authority to the Governor and Council of Bombay, to treat with Colonel Upton.
Letter from, dated near Mandavia, 13th January.	Had forwarded the Sunnud obtained from Futty Sing for Batta to Surat.
Ditto, Ditto, Ditto, 18th January.	Information relative to the Complaint mentioned in the Letter to him of the 8th Instant.

To the Honourable William Hornby, Esquire, &c. Council, Bombay.

Honourable Sir, and Gentlemen,

Agreeable to your Orders, communicated to me by your Secretary, I now proceed to inform your Honour, &c. how the Honourable Company's Two Iron Eighteen Pounder Cannon came to be employed in the Siege of Ahmadabad, and why the Siege was continued after the Cessation of Arms took Place.

Early in the Month of July, 1775, and long ere the Cessation of Arms was thought of by me, Ragonaut Bajerow acquainted me, "That he had determined on the Reduction of Bowesett, a Fort then in the Possession of the Ministerial Party, about "Twelve Coss from Cambay; that he had appointed Ameen Khân, a Partizan of Note, "to command this Service, and desired I would furnish him with the Two Eighteen "Pounder Iron Cannon then at Cambay; as I knew that Bowesett might be easily reduced, also that it was of great Consequence to Ragonaut Bajerow to have Possession thereof, I readily agreed to his Request, the more so, being sensible that the Wish of your Honour, &c. was to support him to the utmost. Ameen Khân received the Cannon, Three hundred Shot, and Twenty Barrels of Powder, by my Desire, from Mr. Malet, and proceeded to Manadabhad; there he was successful, as I had the Honour to acquaint you under 25th August. Flushed with this Success, instead of pursuing his first Design, Ameen Khân marched against, and formed the Siege of Ahmedabhad.

As soon as the Cessation of Arms was known to me, I requested of Ragonaut Bajerow to give Orders to cease Hostilities against Ahmedahabad, and send the Two Eighteen Pounder Guns to Cambay. This he assured me should be done; and I can venture to say he kept his Word, so far as issuing his positive Orders; but it was his Misfortune, as it ever happens to unfortunate Asiatic Princes, to have his Mandate little attended to when in Distress, especially by those who were at any Distance. Ameen Khân, soon sensible of Ragonaut Bajerow's true Situation, no longer expecting his Favours, or dreading his Power, set up a Kind of Independence, and, by various Excuses, put off the Return of the Cannon, or raising the Siege.

On the 25th October I received a Letter from the Honourable the President, wherein he mentioned the Two Eighteen Pounders, and desired me, by every Means, to get them returned to Cambay, that no Time should be lost; I immediately wrote the inclosed Note, marked No 1, to my Interpreter, then at the Durbar, and the same Evening enforced the Contents to Ragonaut Bajerow in Person; and I can positively assure the Honourable Board, that no Endeavours on my Part have been wanting in order to recover the Two Cannon.

No. 2 is Ragonaut Bajerow's Application to me for the Loan of the Cannon, &c. and Number 3 is his Obligation to be responsible to your Honour, &c. for them. These Precautions, I flatter myself, will convince your Honour, &c. that I proceeded regularly regarding this Business, and was actuated only by proper Motives for the Welfare of the Cause I had the Honour to be employed in.

I have the Honour to remain, with all possible Respect,
Honourable Sir, and Gentlemen, &c.

Bombay,
21st June, 1776.

Thomas Keating,
Lieut. Colonel.

Note,

APPENDIX, N° 112.

Note, marked No. 1, being a Message from Lieutenant Colonel Keating to the Peshwa, through his Interpreter at the Durbar.

Wiswanath,

Present best Respects to the Peshwa, and tell him, that I have just received Letters from Bombay and Broach; the first give an Account that Hurria Punt Furkia has marched from Brampore, and is coming to the Northward; in the same Letter the Governor orders me to bring our Two Eighteen Pounders from Ameen Cawn to Cambay, and send them from thence to Surat, to be in Readiness in case we want them with this Army. I therefore desire you will give my Compliments to the Peshwa, and request he will give immediate Orders for the Two Guns to be sent directly to Cambay, otherwise the Governor will be very much displeased. The Broach Letter is from the Chief, who says, that Part of the Peshwa's People are plundering in the Occlaseer Purgunnah, therefore I request that he will give strong Orders that none of his Troops do go near any Country in our Possession, and order those at or near Occlaseer to return to the Army, and assure him that I cannot accompany him in any March that leads us towards any of the Purgunnahs in our Possession; and that, as soon as any of his Troops begin to plunder them, I must withdraw our Troops from his to give Protection. As soon as you have done, come to me, as I want you on particular Business.

Yours, &c.

25th October, 1775. Thomas Keating.

No. 2 and 3 were the original Letters, with the Peshwa's Seal affixed.

True Copies.
(Signed) Edward Ravenscroft,
Secretary.

Warren Hastings,
J. Clavering,
Rd Barwell,
P. Francis.

Extract of Bombay Secret Consultations, the 8th January 1776.

PRESENT,

The Honourable William Hornby, Esquire, President and Governor,
The Worshipful Daniel Draper, Robert Gordon,
——— Brice Fletcher,
——— Robert Garden,
William Ashburner, Andrew Ramsey.

N. B. Mr. Mostyn indisposed, Mr. Tayler at Bengal.

Keating, Lieut. Colonel Thomas, Letter to.

To Lieutenant Colonel Keating.

Sir,

We have duly received your Letters dated the 22d, 24th, and 28th Ultimo.

We have now received Advice from Colonel Upton, of his Arrival at Poona Dhur, and of his having commenced his Negociation; and therefore think it necessary positively to direct, that you do not on any Account commit any Act of Hostility against the Ministerial Forces, unless the Company's Troops are actually attacked by them, which we are willing to believe will not be the Case.

Colonel Upton has represented to us, that the Ministers have complained to him of Ragoba's having detached a Part of his Army to besiege Ahmedavad, and that small Parties of his Forces are plundering and laying Waste some Villages belonging to the Circar; and though we cannot but think the Ministers have misinformed him, especially regarding the Attack of Ahmedavad, which you acquaint us in your Letter, dated the 4th November,

November, the Peshwah had upon our Remonstrance promised to discontinue; we must nevertheless direct, that you give us, without Loss of Time, full and explicit Information on these Points; for the Ministers declare, that on their Part they have not detached a single Horseman from the Army that opposed the English, and Ragoba, since the Receipt of the Governor General's first Letter, now near Six Months ago, nor committed any Acts of Hostility against Ragoba.

We are
Your loving Friends,
William Hornby,
&c. Council.

Bombay Castle,
8th January 1776.

Extract of Bombay Secret Consultations, the 22d January 1776.

PRESENT,

The Honourable William Hornby, Esquire, President and Governor,
The Worshipful Daniel Draper, Esquire, Robt. Gordon,
Tho. Mostyn, Brice Fletcher,
Robert Garden,
William Ashburner, Andrew Ramsay,
Mr. Tayler at Bengal.

Keating, Lieut. Colonel Thomas, Letter from.

Honourable Sir, and Gentlemen,

Yesterday, I had the Honour to receive your Commands of the 8th Instant, and agreeable thereto, now transmit the Information you require.

This Afternoon I had a Conference with the Peshwa, respecting Amadavad, &c. He assured me, That agreeable to what I wrote your Honour, &c. under the 4th November last, he had sent repeated Orders to Ameen Cawn, to desist from further Acts of Hostility; that for a long Time past, little or no Molestation had been given to that Place; that it is true the Army still continues close to it, proceeding from the Insufficiency of Authority to recall them, since he is not able to discharge any Part of the large Debt due to that Army. He at last observed, That by the Cessation of Arms, his Power is dwindled nearly to nothing.

As to giving Trouble to the Villages under the Sircar, he said, That he supposed the Ministers allude to his collecting Money, &c. for the Maintenance of his Army, if so, they are right; but observes, that all he is able to raise, falls infinitely short of a mere Support, and from Purgunnahs in his Possession, previous to the Cessation of Hostilities. He added, that he could not but observe, that the Ministers holding such Language, is highly improper on every Account, and particularly with respect to himself extremely insolent, knowing him, as they do, to have a lawful Right to act so, and themselves absolutely his Servants, usurping a Power they have not the smallest just Claim to; and he desired me to request that your Honour, &c. will be pleased to write to Lieutenant Colonel Upton, not to countenance them in such Acts of Haughtiness, otherwise they will never be reduced to a proper Standard of Behaviour, which must be very detrimental to the Interest of the Honourable Company, as well as to him.

The Peshwa remarked, that the Minister's Assertion, of never having detached any Force against his since the Period alluded to, is uniform with their whole Conduct, glaringly erroneous; it being notorious, that Two Bodies of his Troops have been destroyed by those of the Confederates, one under Mahomet Esoff in the Malwa Country, the other commanded by Chimman Row, on this Side the Candibarra Gaut, as advised your Honour, &c. in my former Addresses.

The Peshwa requests, that your Honour, &c. will be pleased to let him know, from Time to Time, the Progress of the Negociation, and how it is likely to terminate.

I am, with the greatest Respect,
Honourable Sir, and Gentlemen,
Your highly obliged, and
most devoted Servant,
Thomas Keating,
Lieut. Colonel.

Camp, near Mandavie,
18th January 1776.

APPENDIX, N° 113.

Extract of Bengal Secret Consultations, 1st April 1776.

THE Secretary begs Leave to record in this Place the following Letter, received from Lieutenant Colonel Upton since last Council.

Gentlemen,

I had the Honour to write to you on the 7th Instant, and now take the First Moment to remove the disagreeable Impressions that Letter must have made. The Ministry have at length agreed to the Conditions mentioned in my Letter of the 2d Instant, but they intend writing to you, Gentlemen, to ask an Exchange for Salsette, and the small Islands in the Bay, for which they mean to offer Three Lacks of Country near to Broach or Surat; perhaps they mean also to make some further References, for they think all the Demands made are of my own Accord, as they are persuaded you meant to ask no Country or Concessions of any Kind whatever from them.

I shall take Care, however, that the Articles of the Treaty be clear, and not admit of Equivocation, and this they readily agree to; they say, if they are insisted on, it must be so.

As Peace must be firmly and fully established, there is no waiting any Reference: As mentioned in my Letter of the 2d Instant, respecting the Guzerat Province, I shall examine all the Sunnuds minutely, and take Copies of such as are necessary, by which that Country was made over to this Government, and also those that have been since granted to the different Sirdars. When I am fully satisfied that Futty Sing had no Right to make over Grants of any Parts of that Country, I shall agree to the restoring of all made by him and Ragonaut Row, except what is now stipulated for, viz. the entire Purgunnah of Broach, and a Country of the annual Amount of Three Lacks of Rupees, near or adjoining to Broach.

I am so desirous of sending this off, that I shall at present say no more, intending to write again in Three or Four Days, by which Time I hope to have the Articles ready.

Poona Dhur, I have, &c.
24th February, 1776. (Signed) J. Upton.

P. S. The Governor and Council of Bombay advising that a Factory in Bassein would be of no Use to the Company, I have dropped that Demand, but all Foreigners are to be for ever excluded a Residence thereon.

General Clavering having directed the Secretary to circulate his Opinion, that a Letter should be immediately written to Colonel Upton, approving the Terms of the Treaty which he proposes to conclude with the Ministers, and to request that the Members of the Board will give their Opinions upon this Proposal; it was accordingly circulated, and the Opinions of the Board returned as follows:

The Approbation of this Board is not necessary to the Confirmation of any Treaty, which may be concluded by Colonel Upton; neither would it be proper or consistent to express an Approbation of it, before the Terms of it were known, Colonel Upton having too imperfectly notified his Intentions in this Respect.

(Signed) W. H.

The Terms of the Treaty which Colonel Upton proposes to conclude with the Ministers, are, as I understand, that the Cession of Salsette and the Islands in the Bay, and the entire Purgunnah of Broach, and a Country to the Amount of Three Lacks of Rupees adjoining to Broach, be made to the Company. It is necessary that we signify to him our Satisfaction of those Terms; otherwise if he should receive our Letter, which ordered him to continue to insist on the Island of Bassein, or at least in Exchange of Broach for it, he might be prevented concluding the Treaty on the Terms which he has adjusted with the Ministers.

(Signed) J. C.

I shall

I shall undoubtedly think this Government bound to ratify any Treaty that shall be concluded by Colonel Upton, by which Salsette shall be secured to the Company. But I apprehend that as the Treaty is not before us, we cannot now safely or regularly give any Opinion upon it, and as it was to have been signed within Three or Four Days after the 24th of February, the Conclusion of it cannot be effected by any Instructions sent at this Time.

(Signed) P. Francis.

I agree with the General's Proposition, because I find that our Letter of the 15th Ultimo, did not notify to Colonel Upton the Resolution of the Board, to insist on the Cession of Bassein, but proposed the Exchange of it for Broach.

There is little Probability that the Negociation shall have been protracted, at the Time in which this Letter may reach Colonel Upton; but in Consideration of the bare Possibility of its arriving in Time to prevent the Loss of Broach, I wish to empower him to accept the Conditions mentioned in his Two last Letters, and to conclude the Treaty upon them; these Conditions I gather from his Letters as follows:

The absolute Surrender of the Island of Salsette, &c. to the Company, with the Cession of that Portion formerly enjoyed by the Marattas of the Revenue of Broach, the entire Purgunnah of Broach, additional Lands adjoining to it yielding a Revenue of Three Lacks of Rupees; to indemnify the Company for the Expences of the War; to stipulate the Exclusion of all European Foreigners from Bassein; and to obtain a Province for Ragoba, not less than that specified in Colonel Upton's Letter of the 2d of February; to this should be added a solemn Assurance of Safety to Ragoba. An Exemption from the Chout is not a proper Object for this Government to require, because it implies a Right which has never been allowed to the Marattas.

Lest I should have mistaken the Terms of the General's Question, I think it necessary to explain my Sense of it; viz. that Colonel Upton be authorized, in case he shall not have concluded the Treaty with the Ministers at Poona, to conclude it on the Terms which we understand to have owed their Assent, by his Letter now before us, and to pay no Regard to our Letter of the 15th Ult. To this Proposition I agree.

(Signed) W. Hastings,
R. Barwell.

Colonel Monson—I shall think myself bound by any Treaty which Colonel Upton may conclude with the Ministers; and I shall approve of any Treaty that he may make agreeable to the first Orders which he received. Our subsequent Orders to him have been to relinquish Bassein and its Dependencies, for Broach and its Dependencies. If he should have concluded a Treaty before the Receipt of our last Letter, it will be agreeable to the Orders he received from the Board, excepting the single Instance of his insisting upon Bassein; for which, in his Letter 2d February, he proposes to have an Equivalent.

In Consequence of the above Minutes, the following Letter was dispatched to Lieutenant Colonel Upton:

Sir,

We have received your Letter of the 24th of February, which has relieved us from the Suspence in which we had been left by your former Advices of the 7th; and we have in Consequence given Orders for disembarking the Troops whom we had directed to proceed to Bombay.

If your Negociations should still remain open when this Letter reaches you, we authorize you to conclude the Treaty on the Terms which, by your Letter now arrived, and that of the 2d of February to which it refers, we understand to have received the Assent of the Ministers, and to pay no Attention to our Instructions of the 15th Ultimo.

25th March. We are, &c.

In Consequence of the Treaty of Peace having been concluded, General Clavering directed the Secretary to send round the following Paper to the Members of the Board:

In Circulation.

That no Time may be lost in re-landing the Troops who had been embarked for Bombay, particularly from the Indian Queen, which Ship had gone down the River, General Clavering sent an Order early this Morning to the Master Attendant for that Purpose, as well as to return the Salt Provisions which had been borrowed of Captain Snow. He hopes that these Orders will meet the Approbation of the Board.

I also request the Opinion of the Board, whether the Treasure should be brought back from the Ships, or suffered to proceed to Bombay. That Presidency has been supplied this Season with 27 Lacks, instead of the Twenty which were promised. The next Season will not commence till the 1st of May.

(Signed) J. P. Auriol,
Secretary.

I refer to my Minute sent in Circulation.

(Signed) W. Hastings.

I think the Treasure should be landed.

(Signed) J. Clavering.

I think the Treasure should be landed. I have not seen the Governor's Minute.

Half past 5 o'Clock. (Signed) G. Monson.

I have seen and approved the Governor General's Proposals.

(Signed) R. Barwell.

I think the Treasure should be landed.

(Signed) P. Francis.

Soon after the above was sent in Circulation, the Secretary received the following Proposal from the Governor General; which he also circulated, and received back the Opinions as entered after it.

The Governor General submits it to the Consideration of the Board, whether it may not be expedient to disembark the Detachments now on Board the Neptune and Indian Queen, and remand them to the Garrison, as the Object of their original Destination no longer exists.

At the same Time he wishes the Board to consider, whether it may be so proper to repeal the Destination of the Treasure and Stores. In any probable Situation of Affairs, the former may be of considerable Service. If there is a Peace, it may be directed from the Supplies of next Year; if War, such a Supply will be immediately and indispensably necessary. From the latter Consideration, he inclines to the Opinion, that it would be proper to let the Guns and Stores also proceed. From the Duplicity of Conduct which we have already experienced in the Ministers of Poona, Prudence requires that we should guard against another Reverse, and still afford such Aids to the Presidency of Bombay, as may prove of essential Use to them in the Case of a Second Rupture with the Poona Government, and at the same Time avoid the Appearance either of Suspicion or Deception on our Side, which might be the Consequence of our sending the Detachments, if the Ministers should prove firm to their Engagements.

(Signed) Warren Hastings.

I approve R. Barwell.

I think

I think that the Treasure and Guns should be landed, and Orders sent to Bombay to withdraw their Troops into their Garrisons; and this Order should be insisted on.

(Signed) J. Clavering.

The Guns, Detachments, and Treasure, should be landed. If Letters are now written to Bombay, they should contain Orders to that Presidency to adhere strictly to the Terms of the Treaty, supposing it actually signed. It is my Opinion, and, if necessary, I desire it may be circulated as a Motion from me, that the Two Ships should be detained until we receive the Letters by which Colonel Upton promises to send an Account of the Conclusion of the Treaty in Three or Four Days.

(Signed) P. Francis.

I agree with Mr. Francis, that the Detachment, the Guns, their Carriages, the Tumbrils, Limbrils, and Stores, with the Treasure, should be re-landed; and that if Letters be now wrote to Bombay, that Orders should be given to that Presidency to adhere strictly to the Treaty concluded by Lieutenant Colonel Upton.

I agree also to his Motion, provided the Owners of the Ships can be prevailed on to detain them until we shall hear again from Colonel Upton; but not to lay an Embargo on them.

(Signed) G. Monson.

I cannot agree to Mr. Francis's Motion. The Expence will be great and useless. If the Presidency of Bombay have not already received Orders to conform to any Treaty concluded by Colonel Upton, I have no Objection to such an Order to be now written; although the Obligation will not be strengthened by it, since they are constitutionally bound to observe the Terms of every Treaty made by the Superior Government, and will be criminal if they infringe it.

(Signed) W. Hastings.

Orders having been issued to the Master Attendant, to disembark the Troops from the Indian Queen and Saint Helena, the following Letter was received from him:

To J. P. Auriol, Esquire.

Sir,

The Indian Queen, Captain Boyle, having sailed before the Orders for disembarking the Troops, and for taking out the Treasure, could reach her, I transmit you enclosed the Bill of Lading for the Treasure, signed by Captain Boyle, who kept One Bill, saying that it was necessary to do so, as he had not received any Orders either for taking the Troops on Board, or for receiving the Treasure.

The other Bill of Lading was enclosed in the Governor General and Council's Letter to the President and Council of Bombay, received under a flying Seal for that Purpose; which Letter, when closed, was delivered to Captain Boyle by Mr. Wallis, a Master in the Pilot's Service, sent by me on that Service. The Troops on board the Saint Helena were disembarked as soon as the Orders of the Board were received.

I am, &c.

Calcutta, H. Wedderburn,
27th March, 1776. Master Attendant.

APPEN-

APPENDIX, N° 114.

ANOTHER Letter from Lieutenant Colonel Upton having been received since last Council, it was circulated, and is now recorded as follows:

Gentlemen,

I am made very happy by sending the Copy of the Treaty concluded with the Ministers.

We waited some Days for a lucky Hour to sign the Articles, and during that Period I had every Reason to believe they wanted to recede from their Agreements; they wished and urged, by every little Means they could devise, to make me refuse the Terms, which however I was not in the least disposed to do, and took Care they should not, though they insisted on crouding the Articles with Abundance of Repetitions and Suspicions. I was attentive to their not being very glaring or too trifling, and then was obliged to admit them. I had drawn out the Articles in English, but here we had many Difficulties to surmount; they so perplexed me with Doubts and Alterations, that I was forced to give it up. They were made out out in Persian, a Language understood, they said, by all. The English is therefore a Translation from the Persian; I could have wished the reverse.

The small Island, Canary, I understand is not now in our Possession; in that Case we do not get it; I find it is of no Value. The Ministers not knowing the English Names of the small Islands in the Bay of Bombay, and my being unacquainted with the Maratta Names, prevented our inserting them nominally in the Treaty. I have wrote to Bombay to get the English and Maratta Names, and it is then agreed to insert them: This is absolutely necessary, to prevent any Misunderstanding hereafter; as soon I have got this Information, I will forward the Names to the Board.

The Ministers write to you, Gentlemen, to offer a Country of Three Lacks per Annum in Exchange for Salsette, and the small Islands in the Bay. I told them of the Impropriety of proposing a Country of much less Value than the Islands; they replied, they trusted entirely to the Honour of the Gentlemen of Calcutta, who must be conscious of their having no Right to these Islands, and would therefore restore them; however they have thought fit to send a Vackeel, who I suppose is authorised to make other Proposals; they have had little Reason from me to hope Success in this Negociation. They made me promise to write; and as we act, they say, from Principles of Honour and Justice, enforce the Arguments they have to urge for their being restored. I think they will of themselves let none escape them, if I may conclude from what I have experienced of them.

I before wrote the Impossibility of waiting a Reply to my Letter of the 5th January. The Ministers have promised to write to procure Letters from their principal Surdars, signifying their having received the Treaty, and promising Obedience to the Articles of it. They say this was never done before, or Treaties ever signed in any other Manner than the present, and it will hurt them very much with the Peshwa's Subjects.

Bassein not being, as you imagined, possessed by us, has made you long since, I hope, give up all Thoughts of our obtaining it; they say we cannot have the smallest Claim to it, and that nothing but Force shall ever get it from them. It will be impossible by any other Means ever to obtain it. I understand it is not an Island, as all along supposed, but a very considerable District, reaching from Salsette almost to Surat; a Nullah at the back Part of it, which fills in the Rains, has given Rise to its being thought an Island. The Fort is very large, and stands on an Isthmus, divided from Salsette by a River, the Breadth of which secures Salsette from ever being incommoded by this Fort.

I observe this, as much Pains has been taken to persuade to the contrary, and the Necessity of our having Bassein for the Security of Salsette.

The Stipulations for Ragonaut Row amount to about Ten Lacks per Annum; but they insist on paying his Houshold Troops, &c. as he might otherwise collect in a short Time Money sufficient to engage them in fresh Troubles.

The

The Ministers request you will be pleased to appoint a Gentleman to reside at Poona, to adjust all Ragonaut Row's Business with them, as well as any public Business they may have to transact with the Presidency of Bombay, &c.

I inclose a Copy of one of the Sunnuds granted by Futty Sing, also the Treaty concluded by him with Ragonaut Row; these I received from the Governor and Council of Bombay.

I have wrote to Futty Sing, to send me the Copy of a Sunnud, for any District granted by him in the Guzerat Province to the English, also the Copies of the Sunnuds by which he holds Half of the Guzerat Country, that I may compare them with those in the Peshwa's Office. I have requested of him also to let me know how far he considered himself as Proprietor of any Part of that Country; and if he ever thought himself authorized to alienate from the Maratta Government, any Purgunnah of Guzerat. Should this Right be vested in him, he will be careful how he denies it, as it may endanger to him the Loss of his Country altogether. I have desired that these Papers may be attested by the Casi.

I have forwarded to the Governor and Council of Bombay, Extracts from the Treaty of such Articles as concern that Presidency, and request that they would depute Two Gentlemen, to fix with the Two Persons sent from this Government, the Boundaries of the Country ceded near or adjoining to Broach. The Marattas agree to our taking this District where we like, so that we do not pitch upon Jaghire Land: I have also transmitted to the Presidency of Fort Saint George, such Articles of the Treaty as concern that Presidency.

I was much concerned at not being able to insert the Articles you proposed for the Nabob of Arcot. The Ministers are afraid it might engage them in some Dispute with the English, and they positively refused admitting it: They will be careful, however, in their Conduct towards him. I inclose the Reasons they gave at our last Conversation on this Subject. They say they are ready to treat with the Nabob, and if he will restore Tanjore, &c. through their Mediation, which it seems they have proposed to the Rajah, (a Relation of the Ram Rajah's) they will then resign Part of the Chout, &c. I forward also another Article the Nabob of Arcot desired me to obtain for him.

As the Articles of the Treaty will be made out at Calcutta, to be signed by the Board, permit me, Gentlemen, to observe, that Ram Rajah's and Peshwa's Seal (in One) is always at the Top of all Treaties; I mention this, that the Company's Seal may not by any Accident be otherwise fixed. The Ministers or Servants to this Government we never suffered to sign or seal on the same Side of the Paper with the Peshwa. Except the Exchange for Salsette should take Place, may I request you will not alter the Words of any of the Articles; there are many that want it; but it is inconceivable what Jealousies and Suspicions these People harbour.

I am honoured with your Letter of the 8th January, with the Translations of the Letter from Sacaram Baboo, and Baliajee Pundit, and the Reply, &c. and the Copy of the Letter from Soy Madee Row; also the Packet for the Peshwa, which was forwarded to him. This is the only Letter I have received from the Board since the one dated 9th of November, 1775, advising that Mr. Chambers had Permission to come to Poona, on the Part of the Nabob of Arcot. That Gentleman was not deputed: The Nabob's Business was transacted through his Vackeel here.

This Packet goes away by Way of Masulipatam; I dispatched a Letter by the same Route on the 24th Ultimo, and herewith send a Duplicate of it.

In Two or Three Days the Ministers will forward some Dispatches on our Camels, by Way of Benares, when I shall have the Honour to write again, and send Duplicates of all Letters, &c.

Poona Dhur,
3d March 1776.

I am
(Signed) J. Upton.

APPENDIX, N° 115.

From Siccaram Pundit: Received the 1st April 1776.

THE All-wise Creator and Protector of the Universe formed Man superior to all other of his Creatures, and endowing him with Reason, made him Lord over all, and by the Gift of Speech, adorned by the Gem of Veracity, put into his Hands the Authority over the whole Terrestrial World; it is consequently the Duty of all Magistrates, and those invested with Authority, to provide for, and protect the People of God intrusted to their Charge. As this is not to be effected without making Use of the apparent Means, wise Men established the Mode of corresponding with each other by Letters and Messengers. It was therefore my earnest Desire to lay the Foundation of such a Correspondence with you; and although certain weak and little Minds considered this Design as the Effect of Timorousness and Want of Spirit, yet in the Sight of Wisdom, it will be regarded as a Proof of a great Soul; and as it is incumbent on the first Projector of any Plan to carry it into Practice, I was debating with myself on the Means of effecting it, when your agreeable Letter arrived, informing me that the King of England had given Orders to all his Servants in this Part of the World, not to engage in Hostilities, or form Treaties, without the Approbation of the Governor General of Bengal, and to take no Step which might be the Cause of Disputes with any Chief of the Maratta Nation; that you had sent Orders to put a Stop to the Proceedings of the Bombay People, and to recall their Troops from the Field of Battle; that you proposed to depute some one to adjust all former Causes of Dispute, and to negociate a strict Friendship in future, as soon as you learnt if it would be agreeable to me; and that I, on my Part, should give Directions to the Forces of this Government, to refrain from all Acts of Hostility. The Receipt of this Letter, in an auspicious Hour, inspired me with the greatest Joy.

I had afterwards the Pleasure of repeated Letters from you, on the Subject of the Establishment of a firm and lasting Friendship, and the Conciliation of the Disputes which subsisted between the Two States.

Induced thereto by Friendship, I recalled my Generals into the Neighbourhood of Cundase, and waited Seven Months in Expectation of your Deputy's, (viz. Colonel Upton's) Arrival. During this Interval, the English from Bombay and Ragonaut Row, attacked Setajee Hankwar, a Chief in my Trust, and obliged him, being unable to oppose them, to enter into written Engagements for the Delivery of a Sum of Money, and a certain Territory. They moreover ravaged the whole Country of Goojeraut, and arbitrarily levied large Contributions. My Generals were desirous of preventing this, but preferring your Satisfaction to all other Considerations, and relying on your Promises, I positively forbad any Act of Hostility, and patiently bore the Expences of Crores of Rupees to which the Support of the Army amounted. It causes me the greatest Surprize, that the English at Bombay, notwithstanding your Orders to them, continued in Alliance with Ragonaut Row, and even increased their Ravages. After the Colonel's Arrival, they plundered Nowapoorah. This bad Faith and Disobedience of Orders, so contrary to the Character I had heard of the English, at first greatly surprized me; but I have now learnt that this is nothing more than a Report, which amuses the Vulgar; and that they don't act up to this Character. Let what is past be forgotten.

On the 4th of Zekaida, (28th of December) Colonel John Upton arrived in the Neighbourhood of Poorunder: Some Days were past in Expectation of an Answer from the Governor of Bombay; as soon as it was received, the Negociation was commenced. In respect to Ragonaut Row, the Colonel said, that Satisfaction must be given to him. Reflecting on the Vicissitudes of Fortune, and the Uncertainty of all human Affairs, this Request of the Colonel's was agreed to. I enclose you a Copy of the Memorandum relative to this Affair, by which you will be fully informed of the Subject. If this is complied with, it's well: But should Ragonaut Row refuse his Assent, let strict Orders be given to all the English to afford him no Manner of Assistance, nor to protect him. Enclosed is the original Memorandum of Propositions made by the Colonel. He has made a Request of the Island of Salsette. The Circumstances are these: In the first Place, the said

said Island is the Inheritance of Seremunt Sahib, and was recovered with infinite Trouble out of the Hands of the Portuguese. Although the Governors of Bombay entered into a Treaty, in Consequence of which the Trade of all other Europeans was prohibited, and for the Space of 100 Years their Trade has flourished there more than ever, by the Encouragement of this Government, and though between the Government and former Chiefs, Three several Treaties have been contracted, and the sincerest and steadiest Friendship been ever shewed to their Settlement; yet, losing Sight of all this, and observing a Breach in this Government, and the Chiefs at the Head of their Armies engaged in Contentions, they took the Opportunity to seize perfidiously on Salsette. It is likewise stipulated in their Treaties, that if any Subject of this Government shall fly to them for Protection, though it may be ever so necessary to afford it him, they shall nevertheless deliver him to the Officers of Government. Disregarding this, notwithstanding they had been Witnesses of the Conduct of Ragonaut Row (Thomas Mostyn was present, and an Eye Witness of every Transaction) and Letters had been written from the Presence to the Governor of Bombay, on the Accession of Seremunt Row Pundit Purdhan to the Musnud, to which a Letter of Congratulation on this Event was received in Answer; I say, disregarding every Consideration of good Faith or Friendship, they assisted Ragonaut Row; they considered the Possession of Salsette as superior to every Consideration. This Event caused me the utmost Astonishment. I am convinced that you will not insist on this improper Request. By the Instigation of the Bombay Gentlemen, the Colonel is very earnest on this Point. I considered the Engagements of the English as inviolable; it was the Duty of Friendship to have made the Bombay People suffer for their ill Conduct, and to have obliged them to restore the Government Possessions, that so others might have been deterred in future from Breach of Faith, and the Integrity and Justice of the English Faith have been deeply implanted in the Minds of their Friends. This Method of Conciliation has been set aside. You have moreover expressed in your Letter of Credence, a Desire that the Honour and Satisfaction of both Parties should be equally attended to; but losing Sight of this also, you have introduced the above Demand. Notwithstanding the Suspension of Hostilities whilst the Affair of Salsette remains unsettled is highly impolitic; yet, as the protracting of the Disputes till an Answer could be received from you, who are at such a great Distance, would be very prejudicial to both Parties; and as I place entire Confidence in you, that you will undoubtedly give Orders to the Government of Bombay to restore the Place with all its Wealth, thinking it adviseable, and importuned thereto by the Colonel, I have agreed to an Expedient, and have referred the Affair to your Justice. The Delivery of Salsette into the Hands of the Government will be the Means of a perfect Conciliation. The Perusal of the Second Article gave me infinite Surprize; I was astonished at this new Pretension, which favours neither of Friendship nor good Faith. After long Arguments and Negociations on this Subject, an Expedient was found, and I at last was obliged, in Consideration of your Friendship and Justice, to agree to this also. It is accordingly inserted in the List. Notwithstanding Satajge Raukwar was invested with no Authority for that Purpose, he was compelled to execute a written Engagement for the Cession of the Country under him; and the Division of Broach in that Country, which is the Property of the Government, is now demanded, and by another Artifice this has been confirmed. I am astonished that the Colonel should propose such heavy Conditions of Friendship.

He demands to be reimbursed the Charges of the Army. Justice points out that the Person who violates his Engagements, should be responsible for the Expences incurred on both Sides. In Opposition to this Rule, to demand it from us, is a new Pretension introduced from Europe. The Answer given concerning the defraying the Expences of my Army was, that such Demand was inconsistent with Justice and Generosity, and that the Ryots of the Country would compensate to the Government the Charges which it had been put to. Were I to give such an Answer, it would be just; but, prompted by Sentiments of Generosity, and out of Regard to you, I have agreed to its being inserted in the Treaty. You will act herein as the Duties of Friendship dictate to you.

He has addressed me on the Subject of the Nabob Mahomed Ally Khan. Between us and the said Nabob a strict Friendship had long subsisted, and in the War with the French we afforded him every necessary Assistance of Forces and Firmauns from his Majesty; notwithstanding which Services, the Chout, Serdasmukky, &c. which he was from of old liable to, are many Years in Arrears. Moreover he has seized on the Country of Tanjore, Arnie, &c. the Raja of Bhosilah, as well as on Ramnautpory, our Place of Worship, Acts highly inconsistent with Friendship. I am hopeful that you will write to him in effectual Forms, to deliver Tanjore and the other Places, with their Rajahs, into the

the Hands of Officers of this Government, and to adjust the Affair of Chout and Serdasemukky at Poona. Where is the Necessity of sending the Troops of this Government to that Quarter? For these many Years I have preserved my Friendship for him inviolable; but it is not enough that this should be kept on one Side only. If he will make Payment of what is justly due from him, no unfriendly Measures will be pursued by this Government. Be yourself the Judge of the Proposal relative to Bengal, and observe that Bhoosilah is a Chief over 25,000 Cavalry, and the Support of our Power, and that induced thereto by Friendship for him, we have given up to him the Bengal Tribute. It is incumbent on you not to be wanting in Friendship to Bhoosilah.

To sum up all in a few Words; notwithstanding the Reasonableness of our Claims, and the Justice of our Cause, merely with a View of putting your Professions to the Proof, the Army was recalled from the Field. We have long had an Intercourse of Friendship with the English Chiefs, and at last, instead of receiving Advantage therefrom, are Losers by it. This has made me wish to transmit all these Particulars, with Copies of the Treaties entered into by the Bombay People, together with your Letter and Colonel Upton's Propositions to the King of England and his Council, and to form such an Engagement with them, that no such Instances of Breach of Faith may occur in future. As you are invested with the Authority of your Sovereign, and are desirous of my Friendship, I have first written to you.

In former Times the Emperor Aurungzebe, and other inland Powers, joined by the Portuguese, and other Maritime Powers, conceiving evil Designs against this Government, were defeated, and met with the just Reward of their Actions. Their Breach of Friendship was the Cause of their so shortly losing all their Conquests. The Bombay People seeing the Weakness of Ragonaut Row, and the Minority of Seremunt Row Pundit Purdhan, took this Opportunity of effecting their Purpose. I have referred the Remedy to your Justice. Act in such a Manner that Friendship may take firm Root between us. If you suffer the Affair of Salsette to remain unsettled, it will be prejudicial to the Establishment of Friendship, and the Cause of continual Quarrels with the Descendants of the present Chief. From the sincere Regard which I bear you, and with the greatest Integrity, I have fully explained my friendly Sentiments to you. I flatter myself, that on the Perusal of this Letter you will write to the Governor of Bombay to restore the Island of Salsette. Should you have any Doubt of what I have written, my Vackeel will soon arrive at Calcutta, and will explain every Particular to you.

You may depend on this, that it is my earnest Desire to obtain the English Friendship.

N. B. In the above was enclosed Copy of a Letter from the Governor of Bombay to Madho Row Pundit Purdhan, acknowledging the Receipt of his Letter, and congratulating him in the usual Terms on his Accession to the Peishwaship.

Memorandum of Eight Propositions made by Colonel John Upton.

1st, Salsette and the Four small Islands shall be ceded by Treaty to the English. After which Siccaram and Balajee Pundit, and the Bombay Gentlemen, shall write a full State of the Affair of Salsette and the Four Islands, to the Governor General and Council of Bengal. I will also write to support your Letter. If the Gentlemen of Calcutta will give up the Island of Salsette, and the Four small Islands in Exchange for some other Country, it it well, otherwise they shall remain in the Possession of the English. If the Gentlemen of Calcutta do not restore Salsette, &c. the Maratta Sirdars shall have no Claim on the English, and shall not engage in Quarrels with them. Salsette, with the other Islands, shall remain in the Hands of the English.

Names of the Islands.

Caranja,	Kennery,
Elephanta,	Hog Island.

2d, The Gentlemen of Calcutta having heard that the Port of Lissey was fallen into the Hands of the English, directed me, in Consequence, on no Account to give it up. This Account has proved to be a Mistake, and Lissey is in the Possession of the Maratta Chiefs. I am therefore desirous that an English Factory for the carrying on of Trade, be established at Lissey; and a Part of that Country, yielding a Revenue of Three Lacks of Rupees, be given to us. The Factory shall not be included in this, but shall be be agreed to separately. No other European Nation shall be allowed to have a Factory at Lissey.

3d, The Expences of the English Army, from the Day of its joining Ragonaut Row, shall be paid me agreeable to a separate Account under the Signature of the Paymasters and Officers of the Army, and the whole Council of Bombay.

4th, The Marattas shall never claim Chout of any of the Countries under the Company's immediate Authority.

5th, The Affair of Ragonaut Row shall be settled in the Manner on which we formerly discoursed.

6th, The English conquered Broach from the Mogul, that Part of the Country belonging to the Marattas, and the Purgunnahs subordinate to Broach, shall be unconditionally ceded to the English.

7th, With respect to the Nabob Wallah Jaw, Sirdar of the Carnatic: As he has long been the Ally of the English Company in every Change of their Fortune, it is necessary that the Marattas also consider him in the same Light as he is considered by the English.

8th, No Claim of Chout or other Tax shall be made by the Marattas on any other Country which they shall cede to the Company.

From Ballajee Pundit; of the same Tenor and Date.

From Siccaram Pundit; Received 4th July 1776.

Since Colonel Upton's Arrival, I have addressed to you Four Letters, which contain a full Relation of all Particulars; but I am surprized that I have not received an Answer to either. Let there be no Delay in your Correspondence.

Being very anxious for the Restoration of Salsette and the small Islands, from the Possession of the English, I was desirous of sending a Vackeel to Calcutta. In the mean Time, a Copy of the Treaty which had been drawn out and transmitted to you by Colonel Upton, arrived under your Seal. The last Article, which has been written differently from our Wish, I have perused. However, as the Introduction of Scruples, and a Refusal to exchange Copies of the Treaty, might possibly be a Vexation to you, and create Suspicions of a Difference, I have, with a View to the Establishment of Friendship, avoided the Utterance, and even the Admission of a Doubt into my Breast; and accordingly, on the 3d of Rubby-ul-sani, 1190 Hegira, I delivered one Instrument of the Treaty, on the Part of the Government, to Colonel Upton, and accepted for the Government the Instrument which was sent from Calcutta. If an Article of the Treaty should have been written in different Terms, it is no Matter; however, I am assured, when I reflect upon the Sincerity of your Friendship, that I shall obtain Salsette and the small Islands, and that you will, from your Favour, deliver them up. The Settlement which has been made between Seremunt Row and the English, has founded a firm Friendship, and will tend to the best Effects. But I am very much surprized at Two Circumstances, which I will now describe. My Friend, the Governor of Bombay, effaced all Treaties from his Memory; and in a Time of Peace, when I had no Suspicion of his Design, availed himself of the Advantage which our Family Disputes afforded, as well as of the Infancy of Seremunt Row; and before the present War, seized Salsette by Artifice. He felt no Compunction at the Disgrace which such a Measure must unavoidably reflect upon the good Faith of the English. Besides which, he connected himself with Ragonaut Row, and the English took the Field. When the War raged between us, and the Flames of Contention ascended, you wrote to me, with a View of putting an End to it; and repeatedly to the Gentlemen of Bombay, directing them to withdraw their Army from Ragonaut Row. But there was nothing but Evasion on their Part, till at length Colonel Upton arrived, and became sensible of the Artifice and Deceit of the Governor of Bombay. However, instead of correcting him, he demanded Salsette, the Country of Seremunt, since the Negociation proceeded from you; and Colonel Upton insisted upon it, an Article was inserted in the Treaty, respecting Salsette; for I thought that you would have shewn a Resentment at the Infraction of Treaties by the English at Bombay, and ordered the Restoration of Salsette. But this has not happened; and you have written a last Article in the Treaty, that the English shall possess Salsette, and the Islands for ever.

 Another

Another Circumstance is this, I have heard that the Chief of Surat now entertains Seremunt Ragonaut Row, and Two hundred Dependents in Surat. This has the Appearance of a great Deviation; for it has been stipulated in former Treaties, and you may have known it, that if any Native Refugee from the Maratta Government shall seek an Asylum with the English, he shall not be permitted to stay, but be delivered up to the Government's Men; and an Article in the late Treaty expresses, that the former Treaties which may not have been annulled or varied by the present, shall be held in full Force. What the Colonel writes is not attended to, and disregarded. It is their Purpose to detain Ragonaut Row. How then is the good Faith of the English preserved? The Trade in this Country was formerly in the Hands of the Dutch East India Company; but the Government relying upon the good Faith of the English, stopped their commercial Dealings with the Dutch, and established the Trade of the English; and the Government has behaved always so as to merit their Friendship. I was assured, that if any other European Nation should attempt to seize Places belonging to the Government, the English would afford it their Assistance. But it appears that I was mistaken, for the English at Bombay have themselves seized Places belonging to the Government, forgetful of their former and late Engagements, and persisting in a Resolution not to restore them. Being sure of Unanimity amongst themselves, they are encouraged to raise Disturbances. You are wise, and prudent, and desirous of my Friendship; weigh well these Circumstances, and bring the Governor of Bombay to Reason.

One of the good Qualities for which the English are celebrated, is that of rigid Adherence to what is right. For in the Instance where Mahomed Ally Khân unjustly possessed himself of the Country of Tanjour, and also where the English took the Rohilla Country, in both Instances when the News reached the Company, they immediately restored those Countries. I therefore request, that upon understanding fully all Circumstances with respect to Salsette, which is Seremunt's Country, you will deliver it up entire, together with the Islands, to Seremunt the Peishwa. A Country shall be granted in Lieu of them in the Vicinity of Broach, out of which the Revenues are received without Difficulty, and which will not require an Expence of Sebundy, or Establishment of Servants. I request that you will positively forbid the Governor of Bombay to permit Seremunt Ragonaut Row to remain at Surat. A Compliance with these Two Requests will confer a Pleasure, attended with the best of Consequences to our Friendship, and encrease it by additional Sincerity and Strength.

I feel with Pleasure a Regard for the English, which gains upon me by daily Augmentation. What other Person shall dare to breathe a different Sentiment? But you will learn all Particulars from my Vackeel, who will arrive within a small Period. I request that you will render me happy by frequent Letters.

From Bollajee Jenardun; a Letter of the same Tenor and Date.

APPENDIX, N° 116.

THE following Letter from Lieutenant Colonel Upton, which arrived on the 23d of last Month, with the Treaty enclosed, was immediately circulated.

Gentlemen,

I have the Honour to forward a Copy of the Treaty of Peace concluded this Day with the Marattas.

The Conditions of it meeting with your Approbation, will make me exceedingly happy.

Poona Dhur,
1st March 1776.

I have, &c.
J. Upton.

Treaty

APPENDIX, Nº 116.

Treaty between the Honourable the English East India Company, and the Maratta State.

Poorunder, 1st Day of March, 1776.

Whereas Differences have arisen amongst the Chiefs of the Maratta State, and the Government of Bombay having taken a Part therein, by sending Forces into the Maratta Dominions, which the Honourable the Governor General and Council of Fort William disapprove; and being desirous of conciliating these Differences, have determined accordingly to enter into such Measures as may most effectually contribute to so desirable an End: They have for this Purpose therefore authorized, deputed, and given full Powers unto Lieutenant Colonel John Upton, in the Service of the Honourable the English East India Company, to conclude a Peace between the Government of Bombay and the Maratta State. And Colonel Upton having accordingly arrived at Poorunder, has concluded a solid and firm Peace, on the Part of the English Company, with the Ministers Siccaram Pundit and Ballajee Pundit, on the Part of the Peshwa Row Pundit Purdhaun, and all the Maratta Chiefs; and the following are the Articles of Convention which they have engaged into.

Article 1st.

Peace shall be established and take Place from this Day, between the Honourable the English East India Company in general, and the Government of Bombay in particular, and Row Pundit Purdhaun, and his Ministers Siccaram Pundit and Ballajee Pundit, on the Part of all the Marattas; and the following Articles are to be observed inviolably by both Parties.

Article 2d.

The Peace is to be forthwith proclaimed between the Honourable Company and the Maratta State, at the Presidency of Bombay, and at all its Dependencies, at the Head of the English Troops encamped at Mandavie, and in every Part of the Guzerat Province where there are British Subjects. The Maratta Government will also order Proclamations to be made throughout all their Dominions.

Article 3d.

The Peshwa Row Pundit Purdhaun, and his Ministers, being desirous of having Salsette, and the small Islands, subdued by the English in this War, restored to them, do offer to give in Exchange, a Country of Three Lacks of Rupees, with its Chout, &c. in the Neighbourhood of Broach. Colonel Upton having declared, that he could not restore the said Islands, it is therefore agreed, that they shall remain as they now are; and that they shall write to the Honourable the Supreme Council of Fort William, and both Parties engage to abide by their Determination.—If the Governor General and Council of Fort William do not restore them, they shall continue in the Possession of the English, and the Marattas will then give up all Right and Title to the said Islands; should the Governor General and Council of Calcutta restore Salsette, with the said Islands, the English will accordingly deliver them over to the Paishwa.

Article 4th.

The Marattas do agree to give to the English Company for ever, all Right and Title to their entire Share of the City and Purgunnah of Broach, as full and complete as ever they collected from the Moguls or otherwise, without retaining Claim of Chout, or any other Demand whatever; so that the English Company shall possess it without Participation, or Claim of any Kind.

Article 5th.

The Marattas do agree (by Way of Friendship) to give for ever to the English Company, a Country of Three complete Lacks of Rupees, near or adjoining to Broach, on which there is to be no Claim of Chout, or any other Demand whatsoever; Two Persons on the Part of the Company, and Two Persons on the Part of Row Pundit Purdhaun, to proceed and determine the Place and Boundaries, when the Peshwa will give the Sunnuds.

Article

Article 6th.

The Paishwa and Ministers agree to pay to the Company Twelve Lacks of Rupees, in Part of the Expences of the English Army, in Two Payments, viz. Six Lacks within Six Months of the Date of this Treaty, and the other Six Lacks within Two Years of the same Date.

Article 7th.

The English do agree, that every Part of the Guzerat Country, ceded to the Company by Ragonaut Row, or taken Possession of by them, shall be forthwith restored, with all the Forts and Towns thereunto belonging, except what is settled by this Treaty; the Country ceded to the English by Seaguor, or Futty Sing Guicawar, shall also be restored, when it is proved by their Letters and Copies of the Sunnuds granted by the former Paishwa's, now in their (the Guicawar's) Hands, that they do not possess Power or Authority to make such Cessions. The Purgunnahs of Chickley and Coral, with the Town of Veriow, Three Villages of the Purgunnah of Churrassey, and the Village of Batta Gang, are to continue as Pledges in the Possession of the English, till the Sunnuds for the Country of Three Lacks are made over. All Treaties and Agreements subsisting between the English and Ragonaut Row, are hereby annulled, and those of Seajee and Futty Sing Guicawars are to be also annulled, when the above-mentioned Proofs are produced. And these Treaties are to be destroyed in the Presence of the Peshwa's Ministers when they come to Hand.

Article 8th.

The English do agree, the Troops from the Presidency of Bombay are to be marched immediately into their own Garrisons and Districts.

Article 9th.

It is agreed that Ragonaut Row is to disband his Army within One Month of this Date; his Followers and Adherents, except the Servants about his Person, are to separate within the same Time; and Proclamation is to be made by the Maratta Government, granting a full Pardon to all the Adherents and Followers, and all such as have been in Arms with Ragonaut Row, the Four following excepted, viz. Abajee Mahadu, Nair Cawn Gardie, Toola Khedmutgar, and Kurrig Sing Chokydar, who for Crimes and Misdemeanors committed against the State, are for ever banished the Maratta Dominions.

Article 10th.

If Ragonaut Row refuses to disband his Army, the English are to withdraw their Forces, and are not to assist him.

Article 11th.

The Conditions of the Ninth Article being complied with, the Peshwa and Ministers then consent to establish a Houshold for Ragonaut Row, consisting of One Thousand Horse and some Foot, who are to be paid and relieved at the Pleasure of Government, but to obey all legal Orders given them by Ragonaut Row; also Two Hundred Domestics, to be chosen by Ragonaut Row, and paid by Government. They will also cause to be paid to Ragonaut Row, to defray his other Expences, Three Lacks of Rupees, per Annum, by Monthly Payments, at the Rate of Twenty-five Thousand Rupees per Month; conditionally, that he resides at Cooper Gang, on the Banks of the Gungha Gudomy. If at any Time he may want to change his Place of Residence, Application is to be made to the Paishwa, without whose Permission such a Change is not to take Place; and he is not to cause any Disturbance, or carry on improper Correspondence with any Person.

Article 12th.

It is agreed that no Assistance is to be given by the English to Ragonaut Row, or to any Subject or Servant of the Paishwa's, that shall cause Disturbances or Rebellion in the Maratta Dominions.

Article

Article 13th.

The Peshwa Row Pundit Purdhaun, and his Ministers, do declare, that the Chout of Bengal and its Dependencies has, for Time out of Mind, been Part of the Jaghire of the Bounsello, they therefore cannot withdraw it; but if the said Bounsello, or any of his Descendants or Successors, or any other Person, cause Disturbances, by claiming or demanding the Chout on Bengal or its Dependencies, they do engage never to assist them themselves, or permit any Maratta Chief, dependant on them or the Rajahship, to give them any Assistance.

Article 14th.

It is agreed, That in case of Shipwreck of any English Ships or Vessels, or Ships or Vessels trading under their Protection, on any Part of the Maratta Coast, every Assistance shall be given by that Government, and the Inhabitants, to save as much as possible; and the Whole that may be saved shall be returned, all reasonable Charges being defrayed by the Owners. In like Manner the English Company engage their Assistance, should any Maratta Ships or Vessels be shipwrecked on any of their Coasts.

Article 15th.

The Treaties between the Government of Bombay and the Marattas, dated July 1739, and 12th October 1756, are to be held and continued in as full Force as when they were first entered into, unless any Article or Articles of either of them should, in other Manner, be provided for by this Treaty; in such Case, such Article or Articles are to be rejected, and those of this Treaty abided by.

Article 16th.

All other Treaties or Agreements, subsisting between the Government of Bombay and the Maratta Government, not having undergone Alteration, or otherwise provided for by this Treaty, are to be held and continue in as full Force as when they were first entered upon.

Article 17th.

It is agreed, That if Ragonaut Row has lodged any Jewels belonging to the Peshwa Row Pundit Purdhaun in the Hands of the English, they are to be restored, on the Obligation being complied with for which they were lodged.

Article 18th.

The Honourable the English Company shall be considered as the sole Lords and Proprietors of all the Places ceded by this Treaty, from the Dates of the respective Sunnuds or Grants, and are therein accordingly to exercise their own Laws and Authorities. And the Marattas are not to cause any Disturbance in any of the ceded Countries, nor shall the English occasion any Disturbance in the Maratta Dominions.

Article 19th.

In the Places hereby ceded to the Honourable Company, and in all the Places restored to the Maratta Government by the English, it is agreed that both Parties shall commence to collect the Revenues thereof from the Day in which they are delivered, and no Demand of Collection for any past Time shall be made.

Article 20th.

A Copy of this Treaty, under the Seal of Colonel Upton, shall remain with the Minister of the Maratta Government; and a Copy shall be sent to Calcutta, to be signed and sealed by the Honourable the Governor General and Members of the Supreme Council of Fort William, and afterwards given to the Peshwa.

A Translation. (Signed) J. Upton,

(Signed) A. M'Pherson,
Persian Interpreter.

The Signature of Saccaram Pundit. The Signature of Ballajee Pundit.

Here it is dated.

Th:

APPENDIX, N° 116.

The Board now proceeds to consider the Treaty concluded by Colonel Upton, and recorded above.

To the 3d Article,

Resolved not to relinquish Salsette, and the other conquered Lands.

Agreed, That this be added as a Clause at the End of the Treaty.

Whereas it is declared by the 3d Article of the foregoing Treaty, that "the Peshwa "Row Pundit Purdhaun, and his Ministers, being desirous of having Salsette and the "small Islands subdued by the English in the late War restored to them, do offer to "give in Exchange a Country of Three Lacks of Rupees, with its Chout, &c. in the "Neighbourhood of Broach." And further, that "if the Governor General and "Council of Fort William do not restore them, they should continue in the Possession "of the English; and the said Peshwa Row Pundit Purdhaun, and his Ministers, will "then give up all Right and Title to the said Islands:" The said Governor General and Council hereby declare their Resolution not to relinquish the said Islands of Salsette, Caranja, Elephanta, and Hog; or to accept the Territory offered in Exchange for those Islands. And the said Islands are accordingly to remain for ever in the Possession of the English, by Virtue of the present Treaty.

Signed { W. H.
H. G. M.
P. F. R. B.

5th Article agreed to; understanding they are to put the Company in quiet Possession of this Territory.

7th Article. The first Condition approved of, with the following Reservations: That our withdrawing our Troops and Officers from the Countries ceded by Ragoba or Futty Sing, shall be deemed as a Performance of the Treaty regarding these Cessions: With regard to the last Condition of this Article; viz. And these Treaties are to be destroyed "in the Presence of the Peshwa's Ministers when they come to Hand."

Mr. Francis proposes that Colonel Upton be instructed to represent to the Ministers, that as we have declared the former Treaty concluded by the Presidency of Bombay with Ragoba void, and as it is in Fact annulled by the present Treaty, we deem it highly offensive to us, and totally useless to them, that we should be required to destroy it in their Presence. That as Ragoba is in Possession of a Duplicate of his Treaty, our destroying one Copy of it can answer no End whatsoever, and may be liable to an Interpretation derogatory to the Dignity of this Government; that he should therefore exert his utmost Efforts to have the Words above-mentioned omitted; but that if ultimately he should fail of Success, we have left a Blank sufficient to insert them: That in this Case, and supposing the Ministers to adhere inflexibly to the Omission of the Words in Question, he is to declare to them, that we shall comply with the Article as it stands, when all the other Terms of the Treaty are completely executed on their Part.

Mr. Barwell—From what I have seen of the Treaty in general from what Colonel Upton mentions in his Letter, I conceive there is no Option in this Government to make any Alteration in the Terms of the Treaty: In this Idea I shall subscribe to it. At the same Time I would recommend from the Opinion I entertain, that the Maratta Government, if sincerely disposed to a Pacification, will gladly admit the principal Points that it is expected the English shall bind themselves to. I disapprove entirely of all the Matter introduced of a foreign Nature; and think it should be specified, that the English Government is to reap such specific Advantages, upon Condition that they withdraw their Forces from the Aid of Ragoba; that Articles of a Treaty upon this simple Principle should be drawn out, such as this Board can approve, and transmitted to Colonel Upton; leaving to him to judge the Necessity of delivering that which he has sent for our Ratification, or withholding it entirely, and insisting on their receiving of the One framed by this Government.

Colonel Monson—I approve that the Proposition made by Mr. Francis should stand as an Instruction to Colonel Upton.

General Clavering—I agree to the Proposition made by Mr. Francis. I could have wished the exceptionable Words had been omitted in the 7th Article of this Treaty. If the Ministers will agree to the Omission of these Words, or to the substituting simply, That we annul Treaties made by the Presidency of Bombay with Ragoba and Futty Sing, my my Objections to it will be entirely removed; but at all Events I had rather agree to the Article as it stands, than engage in a War, if that is to be the Alternative of our accepting or refusing it.

Governor General—I do not agree to the Clause in the 7th Article, by which it is stipulated that the Treaties with Ragoba and the Guicawars, shall be torn in the Presence of the Peshwa's Ministers; nor do I agree to the Proposition now made, to leave it at the Option of Colonel Upton, to insert the Clause in the Treaty to be executed and sent from this Government. The Ministers can gain no real Advantage from such a Concession; but it would prove a real Loss to this Government, in the indelible Disgrace that it would stamp on them, for having consented to such an Indignity. I am therefore of Opinion, that the Treaty should be executed without that Clause; and that Colonel Upton should declare to them, in the most peremptory Terms, that we will not submit to it. If they will go to War for such a Trifle, a Trifle to them, but of very great Consequence to us, they will go to War with us even in Spite of the Treaty, which has left many Pretences for it.

Agreed, That Colonel Upton be written to, agreeable to Mr. Francis's Proposition.

General Clavering—I cannot agree with the Governor General in Opinion, that should the Ministers refuse to comply with the Omission of the Word "Consent," or to substitute the other Words I proposed, that an indelible Disgrace will be stamped on us for having consented to such an Indignity. The Treaty in Question was made by the Government, and was of no Effect, unless it has been confirmed by us. When every other Means had failed of engaging the Company in a War with the Maratta State, it was no impolitic Step to embarrass the Negociation with as many Difficulties as could be created. It is proper the Court of Directors should know, that the Intrigues of the Presidency of Bombay have been employed at this Place, from the Outset of the Negociation to this Time, sometimes by displaying in the most lively Colours the Force of Ragoba, and that of his powerful Dependants; and lastly, by positive Assertions, that whatever Demands we made of the Ministers, they certainly would be complied with. The Preparations that we were making only a few Days ago, to enter upon this War, together with the great Extent of the Operations proposed, will prove to the Company how nearly these Intrigues were succeeding, and the immense Difficulties and Expence that we should have been engaged in, if they had had their Effect.

Governor General—All that the General has said is so totally foreign from the Question before us, that I am at Loss to reply to it; but as it immediately follows my Minute, and begins with expressing a Disagreement from the Sentiments which I have expressed in mine, I cannot understand it, but as applying throughout to myself. If the General means to charge me with endavouring to embarrass the Negociation, it is a Charge which he cannot know to be true, and which, from the Testimony of my own Conscience, I declare to be without Foundation. I could bring Proofs of this even from the Articles of the Treaty which have been read; there are many Passages in it which I disapprove, and many Expressions which I think highly injurious to us; yet having given full Power to Colonel Upton to conclude a Treaty, and being almost as anxious at this Time perhaps as the General can be, that the Treaty should be concluded, I pass them over without Observation. I disapprove of the Clause which immediately precedes that to which I now except, because it is a wanton and unnecessary Triumph on the Part of the Marattas, and ought not to have been assented to by Colonel Upton; at least the Reason should have been assigned, instead of the simple Expression of the Annihilation of an old Treaty being made the Condition of a new; but as it expresses no more in Effect, than we have already declared in our Letters to the Poona Ministry, I have consented that it should stand. But the Clause in Question appears to me to be fraught both with the most disgraceful and dangerous Consequences: I have hitherto only objected to the Indignity of allowing a Treaty, solemnly executed by a Part of the British Government, to be torn in the Face of a public Durbar; but the Consequences appear to me to extend much farther; it appears evidently to be the Design of the Ministers to discourage and intimidate, by every Artifice, all those who may be hereafter inclined to form Engagements with the English; for this Purpose they have insisted on a Declaration to be entered in the Treaty now executed with them, that the former Treaty with Ragoba, the Incompetency

tency of which he could not know, is annulled, and to be publicly torn: The Exception of Four Persons from the Pardon granted to Ragoba's Adherents in the 9th Article; the fallacious Concessions of the 11th, by which Ragoba is to become a Prisoner at their Mercy; and the 17th, by which we are made to give up to his Enemies the Jewels pledged by him under the Faith of Government; are all Proofs of the same dangerous Policy in the Maratta Ministers. I shall make no further Reflections in this Place on the Treaty, as it now stands submitted to us; I will agree to confirm it, so far as it respects Concessions, which we can in Honour grant, or which we have a Right to yield. These I do not conceive to be included in the Obligation of the full Powers granted to Colonel Upton. It will rest with Ragoba to be a Party, if he chuses, in the Treaty; I shall therefore think myself obliged to confirm that Part of the Treaty which respects him, but will not agree to the 17th Article, because the Pledge is not ours to give; yet as it is made an Article in the Treaty, and the Refusal to comply with it may be quoted as a Pretence for breaking off the Whole, I do propose that an Equivalent in Money, on a fair Appraisement, be given to the Ministers in Lieu of the Jewels deposited by Ragoba, but that they remain his Property, to be disposed of according to the original Conditions on which they were trusted to our Charge. The rest of the Treaty I am content to leave as it stands.

General Clavering—The Governor General has been pleased to apply the Words I made Use of in my last Minutes to himself. I will not contradict him, but shall appeal to those very Consultations to which he has referred, for the full Vindication of what I have asserted. I will not take up the Time of the Board in refuting several Circumstances that appear in the Governor General's Minute, but shall content myself with remarking, that it appears to me, that he has totally mistaken the Meaning of the 17th Article, which only expresses that the Jewels pledged by Ragoba are to be restored on the Obligation being complied with. By the Word "restore," it evidently can mean to Nobody but Ragoba himself, at least, that is the Sense in which I understand it. It matters not to whom the Jewels belong; the fulfilling the Engagement on our Part can only be performed with the Person with whom the Engagements was made. It was Ragoba who lodged the Jewels with the Government, and it is to him that they are to be restored, on his paying the Money for which they were pledged.

Governor General—I have not misunderstood the Meaning of the 17th Article; I have compared the Persian Original with the Translation, and I find both suppose a Right in the Paishwa to the Property of the Jewels, which the Treaty says we are to restore. The Context sufficiently shews that the Property shall be restored to the Proprietor of it. If in the opposite Sense, the Article would have run thus, "It is agreed that the Jewels which were lodged by Ragonaut Row in the Hands of the English, are to be restored on the Obligation being complied with for which they were lodged."

Mr. Barwell—To prevent any Interruption in the Discussion of the different Articles of the Treaty, I concur with the Governor General in the Objections he makes to the 17th Article; the rest of the Treaty I shall make no Objections to.

13th Article.

The Board do not think it adviseable to accept the Concessions made by this Article, and agree therefore that it be left out in the Treaty: And

Agreed, That Lieutenant Colonel Upton be directed to decline any Explanation upon it; but if that cannot be avoided, to inform the Minister, our Reasons for omitting it are, that we apprehend it may be understood to contain an Acknowledgment of a Right which does not exist, and which they themselves, we conclude, by proposing the Article, have no Thoughts of insisting on.

17th Article,

Mr. Francis—With respect to this Article, I think that Colonel Upton should be directed to inform the Ministers, that these Jewels were deposited with the Governor and Council of Bombay by Ragoba, and that we considered them as his private Property; that we cannot therefore, in Justice or Honour, return them to any Body but him; that we consider it as not an Object of Importance in any other Sense: And if he finds that the Ministry insists upon it, that he shall give them proper Assurances, that upon a further Reference to us, it shall be accommodated to their Satisfaction.

Agreed

Agreed to this Proposition, and that the 17th Article be left out in the Treaty.

Ordered, That a Treaty be drawn out in Conformity to that now received from Colonel Upton, with Alterations made by the above Resolutions; and that a Letter be accordingly written to Colonel Upton, as follows:

Sir,

We have received your Letters of the 1st and 3d March, with a Copy of the Treaty which you have concluded with the Peshwa.

As you inform us that the Articles of this Treaty are to be made out here, and signed by us, we have accordingly drawn them up in the Form of a Treaty which we had executed, omitting however the concluding Words of the 7th Article, and the 13th and 17th Articles entirely.

With respect to the first Omission, we desire that you will represent to the Ministers, that as we have declared the former Treaty entered into by the Presidency of Bombay with Ragoba, void; and as it is in Fact annulled by the present Treaty, we deem it highly offensive to us, and totally useless to them, that we should be required to destroy it in their Presence; besides, as Ragoba is in Possession of a Duplicate of this Treaty, our destroying one Copy of it can answer no End whatsoever, and may be liable to Interpretations derogatory to the Dignity of this Government.

We think this a Point of so much Consequence to us, that we direct you to exert your utmost Efforts to have these Words totally omitted, as they are in the enclosed Treaty, but if you should ultimately fail of Success, we have left a Blank sufficient for Insertion of the Words in Question. You will declare to them, that we shall comply with the other Terms of the Treaty when they are compleatly executed on their Part.

As we do not think it adviseable to accept the Concession which is proposed to be made to the Company by the 13th Article, we have caused it to be left out of the enclosed Treaty, to which we apprehend the Ministers can have no Objection. We wish you to decline entering into any Explanation with the Ministers on the Reasons of this Omission; but if you cannot avoid it, you may acquaint them, that our Motives for it is the Apprehension that it might be understood to convey the Acknowledgment of a Right which does not exist, and which they themselves, by proposing or admitting the Article, we conclude have no Thoughts of ever insisting on.

The Cause of our not having assented to the 17th Article is, that the Jewels in Question having been deposited by Ragoba with the Governor and Council of Bombay, we consider them as his private Property, which we are bound to return to him; we cannot therefore, in Justice or Honour, part with them to any body else. We look upon this as an Object of no Importance in any other Sense, and desire you will urge our Reasons to the Ministers, and endeavour to induce them to acquiesce in them; but if you find that they still insist on this Article, you will give them proper Assurances in our Name, that upon a further Reference to us it shall be accommodated to their Satisfaction; and immediately advise us.

We have added a Declaration at the End of the Treaty, importing that we are resolved not to relinquish Salsette and the conquered Islands, in Exchange for the Territory offered to us in Lieu of them near Broach. This Clause will clear up and fix the Point left undecided in the 3d Article.

All the rest is exactly conformable to the Draft which you have sent us; but we think it necessary to observe, that we understand by the 5th Article, the Ministers are to put the Company in quiet Possession of Territory therein ceded; and by the First Condition in the 7th Article, that our evacuating and quitting Possession of the Countries thereby stipulated to be given up, by withdrawing our Troops and Officers of all Denominations from them, is all that is required on our Part for the Performance of it.

Colonel Monson having sent a Minute to the Secretary Two Days after the above Letter to Colonel Upton was written, he desired that it might be entered immediately after the Letter, and is as follows:

I sign this Letter with a Declaration, that I do, with as much Reluctance as the Governor General, give my Consent to an Act that would fix indelible Disgrace on this Government.

The latter Part of the 17th Article is in my Opinion of no Manner of Consequence, unless we make it so by our Animadversions.

The Papers in Question I disavow as Treaties; they are Stipulations entered into by Persons not vested with an Authority to make solemn Engagements. If abrogating an unlicensed Act be considered as disgraceful and dishonourable to the British Nation, I am at a Loss to form a Judgment of what may be deemed honourable for it.

The destroying of these Papers in public will be so far from being a Disgrace to this Government, that it will be an honourable Declaration to the Potentates of the East, that it is determined not to sanctify any Act done but by proper Authority.

A Doctrine established on the Principles laid down by the Governor General, would be annulling the Power of this Government, and subverting the Intention of the Act of Parliament. I should have said this on Monday, but was unwilling to take up the Time of the Board in Discourse on Points in which I cannot agree with him.

I must beg Leave to observe, that not many Days since, he was as ready to yield up the Honour of this Government to the Commandant of Chandernagore, as he seems in the present Case desirous to assert it.

(Signed) G. M.

Resolved in the mean Time, That a Copy of the Treaty received from Colonel Upton be sent to the Secretary of the Court of Directors, in a short Letter from the Secretary, which he accordingly wrote as follows, and dispatched by the Talbot.

Sir,

By the Commands of the Honourable the Governor General and Council, I have the Honour to enclose a Copy of the Treaty concluded by Lieutenant Colonel Upton with the Peishwa and Ministers of the Maratta State at Poona; it arrived late last Night, and was read this Morning in Council. As a Counterpart is to be made out here, executed by this Government, and transmitted to Poona for the Peishwa, the Board have agreed to omit the concluding Words of the 7th Article, together with the Whole of the 13th and 17th Articles, for obvious Reasons, which they have directed Lieutenant Colonel Upton to explain to the Satisfaction of the Ministers; and have further resolved to add a Clause to the Treaty, importing that they decline to accept the Exchange of Territory offered in Lieu of Salsette and the small Islands adjacent to it.

I have, &c.

Fort William, the 1st April, 1776.

(Signed) P. Auriol, Secretary.

APPENDIX, N° 117.

RECEIVED the following Letter from Bombay:

Honourable Sir, and Gentlemen,

Enclosed is a Duplicate of the Letter we had the Honour to address you on the 28th Ultimo.

We also transmit in a Series, Copies of the Letters that have passed between us and Colonel Upton since that Date; and it gave us much Satisfaction to observe by his Letter, dated the 24th Ultimo, that the Ministers were reconciled to our Forces continuing with Ragoba in their present Situation, and perfectly satisfied that the Terms of the Governor General's Letter to Sacram Baboo had been fully complied with. The Colonel observes, that was our Army to be withdrawn entirely from Ragoba, the Ministers would not fail to take Advantage of it, and that they would, in such Case, have little Occasion to enter into any Treaty.

From what Information the Council has given us, it seems rather dubious whether any Treaty will take Place with the Ministers. In the Beginning of January he seemed to think the Treaty would be concluded in a few Days, but in his subsequent Letters, dated the 1st and 6th Instant, he gave us to understand it was very probable it would not

take

take Place at all. In his last Letter, dated the 10th Instant, he says Appearances are still against it; though whatever Circumstances may have occasioned the Obstacle to the Conclusion of the Treaty, we begin to be alarmed, lest it should be surmounted by Concessions very injurious to the Company. The Questions he has put to us respecting Bassein, and the Cessions in the Guzerat Country, and the Privileges necessary to be stipulated in case of Factories being established at that Place and Jambooseer, give us Reason to imagine that he entertains Thoughts of relinquishing those Cessions; and we therefore esteemed it our Duty to represent to him, that the Interest of the Company required he should insist on the Cessions made by the Treaty being confirmed; that he could not recede from his Demand of Bassein consistently with your Instructions, and that Factories either at that Place or Jamboosеer, would be attended with no Manner of Advantage to the Company. No Investments can be provided there for Europe; and from the Vicinity of the former to Bombay, and of the latter to our Settlements of Surat and Broach, no Increase of the Vend for Europe Commodities can be expected. We have sufficiently set forth to him the Importance of the Cessions made by the Treaty, fully explained the political and commercial Interests of this Presidency, and given him likewise an ample Account of the present Situation of Affairs; and we cannot depart from our Opinion, that by a resolute and steady Conduct the Ministers might be brought to confirm these Cessions, and to reimburse us the Expence of the War, rather than break off the Negociation, unless he suffers them to amuse him, and gain Time until Ragoba's Army disbands for Want of Pay, but as he recedes they will advance.

Every Argument that can be advanced to shew the Necessity of a Revenue being acquired for this Presidency adequate to its Expence, and have effectually this great End, might have been answered by our Treaty with Ragoba, has been already fully stated to your Honour, &c. both by us and Mr. Tayler; and it has also been fully represented to you how much the Consequence and Dignity of this Presidency will suffer by your entrusting the Management of this Negociation to Colonel Upton, when a Member of our Board is expressly appointed by the Company Resident at the Maratta Court, and repeated in their late Commands by the Gatton. We can only lament that these Representations have not been attended with better Success; but we have this pleasing Reflection, that we have discharged our Duty to the Company as far as we could, by giving Colonel Upton every Information that our Experience and Knowledge of their Interests at this Presidency could dictate, to assist him in the Execution of his important Commission.

During this long Interval of Inaction, our Presidency has laboured under every Disadvantage that could have attended a State of actual War with the Marattas. All Intercourse of Trade and Correspondence with their Dominions is more rigorously prohibited than during the Continuance of the War, to the great Detriment of the Company's and private Trade, though we have represented to Colonel Upton the Propriety of insisting upon the Communication being opened. But the Inconveniences to Ragoba have been still greater: His Enemies being in Possession of Poona, and the Circar Treasuries, deprive him of all Resources for the Maintenance of his Army, and his Distress for Money has lately arose to so alarming a Height, as described in Colonel Keating's Letter, dated the 6th Instant, inserted in the Correspondence now forwarded, that to prevent the Purpose being entirely defeated, for which we had so long continued our Troops with him, we deemed it absolutely necessary to advance him the Sum of Eighty thousand Rupees, with which we hope he will be able to appease the Clamours of his Army, at least for a few Days. This Sum we advanced upon the Security of a Supply of about 24,000 Pagodas furnished him by the Nabob Hyder Ally, and which is since arrived upon one of the Company's Cruizers.

It appears to us to be evidently the Intention of the Ministers to protract the Negociation as long as they possibly can, in Hopes of Ragoba's Friends deserting him, and his Army disbanding for Want of Pay, by which all their Apprehensions of his Reinstatement will be removed. We have more than once apprized Colonel Upton of this Circumstance, and inforced to him the Necessity of making it a preliminary Point with them, immediately to assign an adequate Revenue for his Support during the Negociation, which we cannot think is an unreasonable Demand, as we presume no Treaty will be concluded, without stipulating proper Terms for him; and it is but equitable that a Portion of the Revenues should in the mean Time be made over to him. The Colonel seems rather doubtful of Success in this Point; and if at last he should be unable to bring the Ministers to proper Terms, and be reduced to quit Poona, we shall

very

very much regret your not having complied with our Request for a Reinforcement, which we think could not have failed giving a favourable Turn to the Negociation, or at any Rate would have been in Readiness to prosecute the War without losing a whole Season.

We transmitted to Colonel Upton, for his Notice, a Copy of Colonel Keating's Letter, dated the 24th, containing some Proposals made by Ragoba. What Colonel Keating calls full Powers from Ragoba, to treat with your Honour, &c. in the Person of Colonel Upton, is no more than a Letter from him to our President, requesting we will exert our Influence to obtain consistent Terms for him; for we should not think ourselves at Liberty to accept any such Powers from him.

We still continue to receive Complaints from our Army, of the Acts of Hostility committed by the Ministerial Forces, as you will find particularly mentioned in Colonel Keating's Correspondence.

The Revenues are coming in very fast from the ceded Purgunnahs, and we expect to receive, in the Course of this Month, 2,86,000 Rupees, from one Assessment made on the Districts of Hansood, Occlaseer, and Jamboseer, dependent on Broach; and by the End of next Month we hope to be at a Certainty how much the Whole will produce this Season, which we will not fail to advise you of.

We have Advices from Bushier, dated the 28th December, when Matters at Bassora were still in a very uncertain Situation. The Turks were very obstinate in their Defence of the Town, expecting Relief from Bagdat; and Career Cawn seemed as determined to reduce it, declaring his Intention of marching against it in Person, rather than raise the Siege.

We have, &c.
(Signed) William Hornby,
&c. Council.

Bombay Castle,
18th February, 1776.

Ordered, That the Correspondence with Lieutenant Colonel Keating be abstracted, and that it be entered after this Consultation, together with the Correspondence with Lieutenant Colonel Upton.

APPENDIX, N° 118.

Abstract of the Continuation of Colonel Keating's Correspondence, from the 24th January to 14th February 1776.

LETTER from, dated near Mandavie, 24th January. Transmits an Explanation of the Articles of a new Treaty proposed by Ragoba.

Letter to, dated 31st January. Futty Sing has kept up a constant Correspondence with the Ministers; desire he will keep a watchful Eye over his Conduct.

Letter from, dated Mandavie, 6th February. The Paishwa's Distresses increase daily. The Ministerialists still continue to commit Ravages.

Letter to, dated 14th February. Determine to advance Ragoba 80,000 Rupees.

Continuation of the Correspondence between the Select Committee of Bombay and Colonel Upton, from the 28th January.

To the Honourable the President and Members of the Select Commitee, Bombay.

Gentlemen,

I have received your Letter of the 18th Instant, with the Copy of the Memorial, &c. delivered to the Governor General and Council of Fort William. I am much obliged by the very full Information you have been pleased to give me, and shall endeavour to make every Use of it, to the Honour and Advantage of our Honourable Employers.

From

From a Death in Siccaram Baboo's Family, and a Marriage in Ballajee Pundit's, the Durbar has not been assembled for some Days past. I sent to desire they would immediately issue an Order to the Officers of their Grabs and Gallivats, not to molest any Vessels or Boats with English Passes or Colours. The Order was to be sent off last Night; they request in Return, that their Vessels, &c. may pass unmolested.

I have perfectly satisfied these People of the Propriety of our Troops remaining where they are, and that the Terms of the Governor General's Letter have been fully complied with, by withdrawing our Troops from Ragonaut Row's, and by your having publickly proclaimed the Cessation of Hostilities. Till the Terms of the Treaty about to take Place were made known, I observed to them, were we to withdraw our Forces entirely, they would have little Occasion to enter into any Treaty. They were, as I have already said, quite satisfied that our Troops should remain, observing strictly that no Hostilities were committed; was the Army to be withdrawn intirely, they would immediately take the Advantage of it. At first, they asked this of me, till they were convinced of the Impossibility of its being complied with.

I shall be much obliged to you, Gentlemen, to inform me, if the Cessions made by Futty Sing were antecedent to your Receipt of the Governor General's Letter, ordering the Troops to discontinue Hostilities. Futty Sing has all along, according to the Account of the Ministry, and they offered to produce his Letters, corresponded with them; and advised, that unless more Troops could be sent to him, he must give up such Places as were demanded: They say he was compelled to this, after the Cessation of Arms had taken Place.

By my Instructions you will observe, that the Power of treating with either Party is not vested in me (except conditionally). I observe this, as you mention, "if I still "prefer treating with the Ministers at Poona," &c.

I am afraid I shall not be able to get any Establishment for Ragonaut Row, previous to the Treaty's being settled; they will have much to urge against it.

Poona Dhur, I have, &c. &c.
24th January, 1776. (Signed) J. Upton.

To Colonel Upton.

Sir,

We have received your Letter, dated the 24th Ultimo.

Immediately on the Cessation being proclaimed, we gave Instructions to the Commanders of all the Company's Vessels, not to molest any Boats or Vessels belonging to the Marattas; and as no Act of Hostility has been committed on our Side, there is not any Occasion to repeat these Orders.

We are much pleased to find you are convinced of the Propriety of the Company's Troops not being entirely withdrawn from Ragonaut Row's before the Conclusion of the Treaty; and we are sensible you will experience the good Effects of this Measure in your Negociation.

The several Cessions from Futty Sing, (except Batta) were made long before the Receipt of the Governor General and Council's Orders for discontinuing the War. The Treaty between him and Ragoba was executed on the 18th of July last, near Brodera; whereas these Orders did not reach Bombay until the 12th of August; and it was stipulated in that Treaty, that the Guicawar Share of the Broach Revenues, and the Villages of Corat, Chickley, and Veriow, should be ceded to the Honourable Company. Futty Sing was before this openly connected with the Ministerial Party; but when he found Ragoba supported by the English, he was glad to make his Peace with him, and return to his Allegiance. And these Cessions were made to the Honourable Company for the Services rendered him, in accommodating Matters between him and the Peshwa. He has lately made many Professions of his Attachment to the Honourable Company; and in a Letter to our President at the Time, expressed his Satisfaction at the Accommodation effected by Colonel Keating. The only Cession obtained since the Cessation, was the Village of Batta, which is so connected with our other Possessions, that a Grant of it was requested from Futty Sing in the Room of Sinore, a Place producing a much more considerable Revenue, which he voluntarily relinquished, because it was not so conveniently situated. We have also lately requested him to give up his Pretensions to the Autgoms, some Villages situated in the very Center of the Broach Purgunnah, which he does not seem to consider as included in his Grant of that District; but we are not yet apprized of the Success of this Application. We

never

never authorized, nor do we believe any Compulsion was ever used to obtain these Grants from Futty Sing.

We must again strongly urge to you, the Propriety of your insisting upon the Ministers settling an Establishment for Ragoba immediately; for we may venture to foretell, that if you recede from this Point, they will protract and retard the Negociation by every Artifice in their Power, in the Hopes of Ragoba's Army disbanding for Want of Pay, which would entirely frustrate the good Effects we, with so much Reason, expected from our late Measures; and we are also apprehensive it will be a difficult Matter to prevent an Army without Pay, in a plentiful Country, from committing some Irregularities, which the Ministers will be very ready to term an Infringement of the Cessation.

We have lately received a Letter from Colonel Keating, containing some Proposals made by Ragoba, of which we think it proper to transmit a Copy for your Notice, and likewise an Extract from another Letter alluded to therein; but the Orders from the Governor General and Council arriving about the Time, Mr. Forbes did not deliver Ragoba's Proposals.

You have never acknowledged the Receipt of our Letter, dated the 29th Ultimo.

We hope you will prevail with the Ministers, to give immediate Orders for opening the Communication.

I remain, &c. &c.

Bombay Castle, (Signed) W. Hornby,
1st February, 1776. &c. Council.

To Colonel Upton.

Sir,

We shall now reply to your Letter received last Night.

We were struck with the utmost Surprize by the Questions you put to us respecting Bassein. We never imagined that you could entertain an Idea of stipulating for our having a Factory only at that Place, when your Instructions are so peremptory for your insisting upon the absolute Cession of It to the Company. A Factory there would not be attended with the least Benefit or Advantage to them; and it is our Opinion that the Interest of the Company requires you should insist upon this Cession, and that you cannot, consistently with your Instructions, act otherwise. The Papers you have been already furnished with, will shew you the Importance of Bassein, and the Desire the Company have for so many Years expressed to obtain it. Salsette will never prove of much Advantage, and the Inhabitants will never think themselves in a State of Security, unless we get Possession of Bassein, and its Dependencies, as described in Mr. Tayler's Memorial, and we think that Circumstance only can effectually exclude other Europeans, from either forming a Settlement there, or making themselves Masters of the Place. In the Treaty concluded with the Maratta State, in October 1756, of which we observe you have got a Copy, it was expressly stipulated in the First Article, that the Dutch, who was the only European Power we were then apprehensive of, should not form any Settlement in their Dominions; and we do not think that any Treaty that can be formed with the Ministers, will afford us better Security against such an Event.

We were equally alarmed and concerned at the Supposition you have made, that the Cessions in the Guzerat Country should not be retained by the Company. We have sufficiently explained the Importance of these Acquisitions in our Letter dated the 18th Ultimo; and in that Letter, and the one dated the first Instant, we particularly mentioned the Names of the ceded Places, and plainly distinguished by whom, and when, ceded. For your full Satisfaction, we will repeat these Particulars; premising, that what is termed the Guzerat Province, commences from the River Tappy, or Surat River, extending from thence to the Northward, and that consequently some of the Northern Cessions are not, strictly speaking, situated in that Province.

APPENDIX, N° 118.

Cessions in the Guzerat Province by the Treaty with Ragoba, executed in March 1775.

Orpad.
Jamboosеer.
The Guicawar Share of the Broach Revenues, and since confirmed by Futty Sing.
An annual Collection from Occlaseer of Rs. 75,000, presented by Ragoba since the Conclusion of the Treaty.
Ashmood, presented in the Month of June last.
Hansood, granted in the Month of July, with the Proviso that the Company's Right should not commence until the 6th October, it having been farmed out until that Time.

These Two Places, with Versault, and the Remainder of the Occlasee Revenues, were taken Possession of in the Month of April, being mortgaged by the Treaty, for Security of the Monthly Stipend.

Versault is situated to the Southward of Surat, and therefore is not in the Guzerat Province.

Cessions made by Futty Sing, agreeable to the Stipulation in his Treaty with the Paishwa; executed the 18th July.

Ragoba's Grant of the Guicawar Share of the Broach Revenues, confirmed as abovementioned.
Coral, near Broach.
Chickley and Veriow. } To the Southward of Surat River.

Ceded by Futty Sing in November.

Batta, situated between the Purgunnahs of Orpad and Hansood, which it connects, and for that Reason a Grant of it was requested from Futty Sing.

We likewise, to prevent Disputes hereafter, solicited the Grant of some Villages called the Autgoms, situated in the Center of the Broach Purgunnah, as Futty Sing did not seem to consider them as included in the former Sunnud. We are not yet apprized of the Success of this Application, though we think the Company's Right to them indisputable, as they formerly belonged to that Province in the Time of the Moguls. We before observed, that we did not imagine the Cessions made by Futty Sing could be effected by your Negociations, and we have forwarded to you a Copy of the Governor General and Council's Letter to us on that Subject.

We cannot see any possible Advantage that will arise to the Company, from having a Factory at Jamboosеer, and therefore wish not for any Privileges there, upon that Footing; we might have formed a Settlement there many Years ago, had we thought it eligible.

The Revenues of the Northern Purgunnahs have been collected by and for the Use of the Company, ever since the Month of April last, and very considerable Sums have lately been received.

We have thus given you very explicit Information on our Parts; and are, &c. &c.

Bombay Castle, 15th February, 1776. (Signed) Wm. Hornby, &c. Council.

True Copies.
(Signed) Edw. Ravenscroft, Sec.

APPENDIX, N° 119.

Extract of Bombay Secret Consultations, the 11th March, 1776.

PRESENT,

The Honourable William Hornby, Esquire, President and Governor,
The Honourable Daniel Draper, Esquire, Robert Gordon,
Thomas Moystyn, ———
——— Robert Garden,
Andrew Ramsay.
N. B. Mr. Fletcher indisposed, and Mr. Tayler at Bengal.

MET to read the Letter received last Night from Colonel Upton, advising his having concluded a Treaty of Peace with the Ministers, and enclosing an Extract of such Parts of which, as he says, relate to this Presidency.

The Extract of the Treaty was then read, and considered with the utmost Attention.

It is remarked, as extraordinary, that although the Treaty is dated the 1st Instant, it was not received here until the 10th in the Evening, and Ragoba has only a Month allowed him to disband his Army.

The Opinion expressed in our Letters of the 15th and 26th Ultimo, respecting the Extent of Colonel Upton's Power with regard to the Cession of Bassein, was founded upon his written Instructions transmitted to us by the Governor General and Council, and not upon any private or verbal Instructions he might have received at Calcutta, for we never imagined he had any Instructions whatever respecting this Presidency, which had not been communicated to us. If the Governor General and Council have wrote to him since Mr. Tayler's Arrival in Bengal, we hope he would have had Cause to have deviated from such verbal Instructions.

We cannot think that an Escort of One hundred of the Company's Troops, or the Residence of an English Gentleman at Poona, will prove any Security for the Safety of Ragoba's Person at Cooper Gung, if he should venture to trust himself in the Power of the Ministers; and their Motives for the Request, concerning the Advice to be given by Colonel Keating, Hurry Punt Furkia, appear very obvious.

As to the Ministers sending a Vackeel thither upon the Plea assigned by Colonel Upton, it appears very extraordinary, as we think the Treaty should not be explained by a Marratta Vackeel.

We think the Ministers might have placed so much Confidence in us, as to have ordered the Communication to be opened without waiting for Advice of our Troops having returned into Garrison.

Two Gentlemen will soon be appointed for the Purpose mentioned in Colonel Upton's Letter, but we apprehend the Condition, that the District to be ceded is not to be Jaghire Land, will be a great Obstacle to our getting such as may be most convenient and advantageous.

Colonel Upton must be acquainted with the English and Maratta Names of the Islands in our Possession.

It is then considered what Orders are immediately necessary to be given in Consequence of the Treaty; when the following occurs to us:

The Peace must be proclaimed To-morrow Morning at the Head of this Garrison, and Orders immediately sent to the Army and Subordinates for the same Purpose.

Orders must likewise be immediately sent to Colonel Keating to march our Troops into the Company's Districts dependant on Surat, and to give Advice thereof to Hurry Punt, and whether Ragoba accepts the Terms stipulated for him.

Ragoba

Ragoba must be apprized of these Circumstances and Conditions, and acquainted that it is not in our Power to continue our Forces with him any longer: He must also be desired to let us know his Resolutions and future Intentions.

The further Discussion and Considerations of the Treaty is deferred till our next Meeting, when it will be entered, with our Sentiments at large upon each Article.

As it yet remains a Doubt whether Salsette will be retained by the Company, no more Money must be expended on Works or Buildings of any Kind upon that Island.

Extract of Bombay Secret Consultations, the 12th March 1776.

The Peace was this Day proclaimed at the Head of the Garrison.

Extract of Bombay Secret Consultations, the 15th March 1776.

PRESENT,

The Honourable William Hornby, Esquire, President and Governor,
The Honourable Daniel Draper, Esquire; Robert Gordon,
Thomas Mostyn, ———————
Robert Garden, Andrew Ramsay.
Mr. Tayler at Bengal, and Mr. Fletcher deceased.

Re-perused the Articles of the Treaty concluded by Colonel Upton with the Ministers at Poona, when the Brigadier General lays before us some Remarks and Observations thereon; which are likewise read, and at his Request ordered to be entered after this Consultation.

The Board then proceed to make their Remarks upon the Treaty, which are ordered to be inserted in this Place, in Columns opposite to each other.

Extracts from the Treaty concluded between the Honourable Company and Maratta State at Poorundur, the 1st Day of March 1776.

Article 1st.

Peace shall be established and take Place from this Day, between the Honourable the East India Company in general, and the Government of Bombay in particular; and Row Pundit Purdhan, and his Ministers, Siccaram Pundit and Ballagee Pundit, on the Part of all the Marattas; and the following Articles are to be observed inviolably by both Parties.

Bombay Castle, the 15th March 1776.

Remarks made by the Honourable the President and Council of Bombay on the Extracts of the Treaty concluded by Colonel Upton.

Remarks on the 1st Article.

The Name of the Peshwah with whom the Treaty is concluded, is not mentioned in this Article; the Term Row Pundit Purdhan being only Titles annexed to that Office, and applicable to every Peshwah. This appears to us a most material Omission; and though we suppose the Infant, said to be the Son of Narron Row, is the Person meant, we think if Colonel Upton has received satisfactory Evidence of his Legitimacy, there should have been an express Article in the Treaty acknowledging him Peshwah. Colonel Upton has been totally silent on this Part in his Correspondence with us; he also seems to have departed entirely from the Clause in his Instructions, dated the 16th of August, which directs as an indispensable Point, that whatever Treaty he may enter into with the Maratta State, shall be signed nominally and individually by all the Chiefs; and we must conclude the Treaty is only signed by the Two Persons mentioned in this

this Article: And this Precaution was the more necessary in the present Case, as the supposed Peshwah is an Infant of Two Years of Age.

Article 2d.

The Peace is to be forthwith proclaimed between the Honourable Company and the Marratta State at the Presidency of Bombay, and all its Dependencies, at the Head of the English Troops encamped at Mandavie, and in every Part of the Guzerat Province where there are British Subjects. The Maratta Government will also order Proclamations to be made throughout all their Dominions.

Remark on the 2d Article.

This Article has already been complied with on our Part.

Article 3d.

The Peshwah Row Pundit Purdhan, and his Ministers, being desirous of having Salsette and the small Islands subdued by the English in this War, restored to them, do offer to give in Exchange a Country of Three Lacks of Rupees, with its Chout, &c. in the Neighbourhood of Broach. Colonel Upton having declared that he could not restore the said Islands, it is therefore agreed that they shall remain as they now are, and that they shall write to the Honourable the Supreme Council of Calcutta, and both Parties engage to abide by their Determination. If the Governor General and Council of Fort William do not restore them, they shall continue in the Possession of the English, and the Marattas will then give up all Right and Title to the said Islands. Should the Governor General and Council of Calcutta restore Salsette, with the said Islands, the English will accordingly deliver them over to the Peshwah.

Remarks on the 3d Article.

Colonel Upton in this Article has again acted in direct Breach of his Instructions, dated the 21st June and 17th July, which enjoin him in the most positive Terms to insist upon the Cession of Salsette and Bassein. Indeed the Reference at all upon this Point, should not in our Opinion have been admitted upon any Consideration, though we flatter ourselves, as the Company have so repeatedly recommended to us to obtain Possession of Salsette and the adjacent Islands, the Governor General and Council will on no Account agree to restore them. As for Bassein, we must now give up all Hopes of obtaining this favourite and desirable Object. Unless some Advantages, unknown to us, are obtained for the other Presidencies, we cannot think this Reference will be agreeable to the Governor General and Council; and the Inconveniences and Loss to the Company at this Presidency, from the Delay occasioned thereby, will be very great. Whilst our retaining these Possessions remains in Doubt, no further Steps can be taken for their Improvement either in Cultivation, Population, or in stocking them with Cattle, &c. which they stand much in Need of; and the Time now approaches for leasing out the Farms again, which we cannot expect can be done on any tolerable Terms in this State of Uncertainty, so that at any Rate the Company will lose great Part of the Revenues for this Season. The Compensation offered for Salsette, &c. is also in every Respect inadequate, as Three Times the proposed Exchange in the Neighbourhood of Broach, or any where else, would be no Equivalent for these Islands, whose Situation gives them Advantages we could not meet with in any other Territory. In case of Differences with the Marattas, or a War with France, they will, in the former Case, form an excellent and secure Barrier to preserve this Island from all Insults, and supply us with a large Quantity of Grain; and in the latter, we shall have the Advantage of keeping our Military Force more compact, and be able to withdraw a considerable Number to reinforce this Garrison, which could not be done from a more distant Possession. The Improvements made to the Fortifications at Tannah, by forming a Glacis and Esplanade, would also prove a powerful Argument for not putting this Place again into the Hands of the Marattas. We must further remark, that in case we do not retain Salsette, and the other Islands, it will be absolutely necessary to ascertain the Royalty of the River between the former and Bassein, otherwise there will be a continual Subject for Altercation and Dispute; and, on the other Hand, should we relinquish this Island by Orders from the Governor General and Council, there seems to be a great Defect in this Article, in not recapitulating, in the latter Part, that the Marattas shall at the same Time give us the proposed Territory in Exchange.

Article 4th.

The Marattas do agree to give to the English Company for ever, all Right and Title to their Share of the City and Purgunnah of Broach, as full and complete as ever they collected from the Moguls, or otherwise, without retaining Claim of Chout, or any other Demand whatever; so that the English Company will possess it without Participation or Claim of any Kind.

Remarks on the 4th Article.

This Article appears specious at first Sight; but when it is considered that the Poona Government have no Right or Title whatever to any Share in the Town or Purgunnah of Broach, the Value of this Cession is entirely destroyed. In the Partition of the Guzerat Country, made in the Year 1759, between the Poona Government and Damajee, the Father of Futty Sing, and Govin Row, the Town and Purgunnah of Broach were included in the Share allotted to Damajee, with whom and his Successors therefore, the Sovereignty and the Power of ceding them only rested; which was plainly acknowledged by Ragoba in the Treaty of Surat, as he therein only engaged to procure this Cession from the Guicawars for us; and by Virtue of their Sunnuds alone, we have for some Time enjoyed full Possession thereof. We cannot discover in the Treaty of Broderah, the smallest Trace of the Acknowledgment mentioned by General Gordon in his Remarks upon this Article. The Company do not therefore derive any great Benefit from this Article, further than a Security against any Demands the Ministers might hereafter have made on this Territory. If upon Examination of the Sunnuds, as mentioned in the 7th Article, it should appear the Guicawars have a Right to make

make Cessions, this Gift of the Ministers will be of no less Consequence; and in this Case, we hope Colonel Upton will insist upon a proportionable Territory being assigned in Exchange, and the nearer to Surat the better.

Article 5th.

The Marattas do agree (by Way of Friendship) to give for ever to the English Company, a Country of Three complete Lacks of Rupees, near or adjoining to Broach, on which there is to be no Claim of Chout, or any other Demand whatever. Two Persons on the Part of the Company, and two Persons on the Part of Row Pundit Purdhan, to proceed and determine the Place and Boundaries when the Peshwah will give the Sunnuds.

Remarks on the 5th Article.

We apprehend much Difficulty and Trouble in carrying this Article into Execution; and we think either the Places to be ceded, or the Method in which the Revenue of Three Lacks is to be ascertained, ought to have been settled. The further Clause mentioned in Colonel Upton's Letter, that the Country of Three Lacks ceded by this Article, is not to be Jaghire Land, will prove another very great Obstacle to any Adjustment, or to our getting such a District as may be most convenient and advantageous; the best Lands adjoining to Broach being all Jaghire, and mostly to Saccaram Bappoo Pundit, which accounts for this Exception.

Article 6th.

The Peshwah and Ministers agree to pay to the Company Twelve Lacks of Rupees, in Part of the Expences of the English Army, in Two Payments, viz. Six Lacks within * Months of the Date of this Treaty, and the other Six Lacks within Two Years of the same Date.

Remarks on the 6th Article.

The Sum of Twelve Lacks is very inadequate to the Expences of the War, and the distant Periods fixed for the Payment very exceptionable, and even disgraceful, as the Ministers proposing such Terms must have proceeded from an Opinion that Col. Upton would agree to any Thing rather than continue the War. So many Events may happen before the End of Two Years, that our Hopes of receiving the Second Payment are not very sanguine; and if the Ministers were not able to pay so small a Sum in a much shorter Time, their Power cannot be very formidable. This Article is also very defective in not stipulating where or to whom the Money is to be paid.

Article 7th.

The English do agree that every Part of the Guzerat Country ceded to the Company by Ragonath Row, or taken Possession of by them, shall be forthwith restored, with all the Forts and Towns thereunto belonging, except what is settled by this Treaty; the Country ceded to the English by Seajee, or Futty Sing Guicawar, shall also be restored when it is proved by their Letters and Copies of the Sunnuds, granted by the former Peshwahs (and now in their Guicawar's Hands) that they do not possess Power or Authority to make such Cessions. The Purgunnahs of Chickly and Coral, with

Remarks on the 7th Article.

By this Article the Company are at once deprived of Jambooseer, Hansood, Ahmood, Occlaseer, Orpad, and Versaul, now in our quiet Possession, and producing a Revenue of at least Fifteen Lacks of Rupees a Year. We are to remain in uncertain Possession of Coral, Veriow, Chickly, and Batta, ceded by Seajee and Futty Sing, and to wait the Discussion of a tedious Adjustment before we receive the Country of Three Lacks, made over to the Company by the 5th Article. But the most striking Inconsistency is, that the Pledges assigned by the Ministers to remain in our Hands for this said

* The Number of Months for the Payment of the first 6 Lacks of Rupees, is omitted.

with the Town of Veriow, Three Villages of the Purgunnahs of Chureassy, and the Village of Batta Gang, are to continue as Pledges in Possession of the English till the Sunnuds for the Country of Three Lacks are made over. All Treaties and Agreements subsisting between the English and Ragonath Row are hereby annulled, and those of Seajee and Futty Sing Guicawars are to be also annulled, when the abovementioned Proofs are produced, and these Treaties are to be destroyed, in the Presence of the Peshwa Ministers, when they come to Hand.

said Country, are (except the Three Villages of Chureassy) the very Places just before stipulated not to be restored but in case of a certain Contingency, and are alone in the Gift of Guicawars, by Virtue of whose Sunnuds they already belong to the Company, which Colonel Upton was not ignorant of. This very Article shews it was a Doubt with him, whether the Guicawars had or had not a Right to make Cessions; therefore he should not have accepted such doubtful Security. Besides, even if it should be proved that the Guicawars have not a Right to make Cessions in the Guzerat Country, it does not follow that the Ministers have, though they will probably derive sufficient Influence from this very Treaty to make the Guicawars disavow their own Acts, and produce any Proof or Voucher they may require, especially as their own Interest is so much concerned. We also apprehend it will be found very difficult to judge of the Authenticity of Letters and Sunnuds, in case of any Collusion between them and the Ministers. Exclusive of the Instance quoted in our Remarks upon the 5th Article, we have other undeniable Proofs that the Guicawars possess an unquestioned Right to make Cessions, as we have now in our Hands Four Sunnuds from Damajee Guicawar, by which we have collected Revenues from so many Districts adjoining to Surat, ever since October 1759, one of which is Veriow; and another Proof is the Conduct of the Durbar at Poona at the Time we first became possessed of Broach, and concluded a Treaty with Futty Sing in February 1773; for although Mr. Mostyn was then actually at Poona in Quality of Resident for the Company, that Government did never, as that Gentleman assures us, make any Objections to our Treaty with Futty Sing, or call in Question his Power of making any Engagements he thought proper.

The Stipulations in the latter Part of this Article, that Treaties made by the Presidency shall be destroyed in Presence of the Peshwah's Minister, we consider it as highly injurious to the Honour of the Nation and the Company; and we cannot but reflect, with Astonishment, that Colonel Upton should ever listen, and much less agree, to so disgraceful a Concession. The evil Tendency of this unnecessary, impolitic, humiliating, and dishonourable Condescension, is too obvious to need any further Comment. However, the Execution of it seems to rest with Colonel Upton; for we cannot conceive that he will demand

Article 8th.

The English do agree, that the Troops now in the Field, from the Presidency of Bombay, are to be marched into their own Garrisons and Districts.

Article 9th.

It is agreed, that Ragonath Row is to disband his Army within One Month after this Date. His Followers and Adherents (except the Servants about his Person) are to separate also within the same Time; and Proclamation is to be made by the Maratta Government, granting a full Pardon to all the Adherents and Followers, and all such as have been in Arms with Ragonath Row; the Four following excepted, viz. Abagee Mahadu, Noor Cawn Gardie, Toola Hudmutgar, and Hurrig Sing Chokydar; who, for Crimes and Misdemeanors committed against the State, are for ever banished the Maratta Dominions.

Article 10th.

If Ragonath Row refuses to disband his Army, the English are to withdraw their Forces, and not to assist him.

Article 11th.

The Conditions of the 9th Article being complied with, the Peshwa and Ministers then consent to establish an Houshold for Ragonath Row, consisting of 1,000 Horse, and some Foot, who are to be paid and relieved at the Pleasure of the Government; but to obey all legal Orders given them by Ragonath Row. Also Two hundred Domestics, to be chosen by Ragonath Row, and paid by Government. They will also cause to be paid to Ragonath Row, to defray his other Expences, Three Lacks of Rupees per Annum, by Monthly Payments, at the Rate of Twenty-five thousand Rupees per Month; conditionally, that he resides at Cooper Gang, on the Banks of the Gungha Gudowry. If at any Time he may want to change his Place of Residence, Application is to be made to the Peshwah, without whose Permission such a Change is not to take Place; and he is not to cause any Disturbance, or carry on improper Correspondence with any Person.

demand the Original from us, to be applied to such a Purpose.

Remark on the 8th Article.

Orders have already been issued to carry this Article into Execution; but we think the Communication should have been opened immediately.

Remarks on the 9th, 10th, and 11th Articles.

Colonel Upton, in the first of these Articles, has stipulated for what is out of his or our Power to perform; for the disbanding Ragoba's Army must in a great Measure depend upon himself, notwithstanding any Advice we might give him for that Purpose; and Ten Days of the limited Month were expired before we received the Treaty. The Tenth Article is comprehended in the 8th, and must be complied with.

The Provision made for him in the Seventh is in every Respect so inadequate to his Rank and Station, and so very inconsistent with what he had a Right to expect, that we think he will never accept of it. If he does, he never can consider himself but as a State Prisoner; and there is every Reason to believe his Life would not be of long Duration, considering that his Houshold is to judge of the Legality of his Orders, and to be appointed, paid, and changed, at the Pleasure of the very Men who rebelled against him, and who must therefore dread the very Idea of his ever regaining his former Power. Many good Consequences would have ensued, and the Permanency of the Peace have been rendered much more secure, had the Colonel stipulated that Ragoba should have had the Option of residing at Bombay, which the Ministers could not have objected to, had their Intentions been good; and he would have proved a most useful Instrument in our Hands, to have alarmed their Fears, and the best Security for their observing the Peace.

However, as it seems very probable Ragoba will apply to us for Protection, and the Governor General and Council, in their Letter of the 20th October, have given us Permission to afford him Sanctuary, in case he should ever be necessitated to demand it, and as we think it would reflect the highest Disgrace upon the Company, to expose him to the Mercy of his Enemies, we shall receive him, upon his requesting it, with his Family and Domestics only; and it must be strongly recommended to Colonel Upton, in that Case,

Case, to get his Establishment continued to him here, that the Company may not be at the Expence of supporting him. The Four Persons mentioned in the 9th Article must not be received. We think the Whole of the Stipulations respecting Ragoba particularly inglorious; and that the Breach of Faith to him will fix the most indelible Stain on the Honour of the British Nation through Indostan.

Article 12th.

It is agreed, That no Assistance is to be given by the English to Ragonath Row, or to any Subject or Servant of the Peshwah's, that shall cause Disturbance or Rebellion in the Maratta Dominions.

Remark on the 12th Article.

Must of course be complied with.

Article 14th.

It is agreed, That in case of any Shipwreck of English Ships or Vessels, or Ships or Vessels trading under their Protection on any Part of the Maratta Coast, every Assistance shall be given by that Government, and the Inhabitants to save as much as possible; and the Whole that may be saved shall be returned, all reasonable Charges being defrayed by the Owners. In like Manner, the English Company engage their Assistance, should any Maratta Ships or Vessels be wrecked on any of their Coasts.

Remark on the 14th Article.

This Article is more advantageous for the Company than the Stipulations made in former Treaties on this Head, as before all Wrecks were shared equally between the Marattas and us; and we therefore hope it will be faithfully complied with.

Article 15th.

All Treaties between the Government of Bombay and the Marattas, dated July 1739, and the 12th October 1756, are to be held and continued in as full Force as when they were first entered into, unless any Article or Articles of either of them should in other Manner be provided for by This Treaty; in such Case, such Article or Articles are to be rejected, and those of this Treaty abided by.

Remarks on the 15th Article.

If there had been any Articles in the Treaties herein mentioned, which interfered or clashed with the present Treaty, it certainly would have been better to have pointed them out, than leave them to the Construction of the contracting Parties; though however, it does not appear, that the Treaties mentioned in this Article do clash with the Articles transmitted to us by Colonel Upton.

Article 16th.

All other Treaties or Agreements subsisting between the Government of Bombay and the Maratta Government not having undergone Alteration, or otherwise provided for by this Treaty, are to be held and continued in as full Force as when they were first entered upon.

Article 17th.

It is agreed, that if Ragonath Row has lodged his Jewels belonging to the Peshwah Row Pundit Purdhan in the Hands of the English, they are to be restored on the Obligation being complied with for which they were lodged.

Remarks on the 17th Article.

This leaves open a Door for much Altercation and endless Cavil; for, should any of the Jewels deposited be claimed by the Government, and Ragoba should insist they are his personal Property, Who is to determine this Matter?

Article 18th.

The Honourable East India Company shall be considered as the sole Lords and Proprietors of all the Places ceded by this Treaty, from the Dates of the respective Sunnuds of Grants, and are therein accordingly to exercise their own Laws and Authorities. And the Marattas are not to cause any Disturbances in any of the ceded Purgunnahs; nor shall the English occasion any Disturbance in the Maratta Dominions.

Article 19th.

In the Places ceded to the Honourable Company, and in all the Places restored to the Maratta Government by the English, it is agreed, That both Parties shall commence to collect the Revenues thereof, from the Day on which they were delivered; and no Demand of Collections for any past Time shall be made.

John Upton.

Alex. Macpherson,
Persian Interpreter.

Remark on the 18th and 19th Articles.

These Articles seem to have secured, upon good Terms, the Stipulations therein made; and we can only express our Hopes there will be no Delay in giving the Sunnuds.

As the Extracts of the Treaty sent us by Colonel Upton are only signed by him and his Persian Interpreter, he must be desired to send us an authentic Copy under the Peshwah's Seal, as we may some Time find it necessary to produce this Treaty.

After the most serious Consideration of all Circumstances, we are entirely of Opinion that the Treaty is inadequate, and highly injurious to the Reputation, Honour, and Interest of the Company, particularly in the Stipulations respecting Ragoba; and we are afraid that Peace is very far from being secured on a permanent Footing, even after such mortifying Concessions. We are satisfied the Ministers, before they heard from Bengal, would have given a Crore of Rupees to have obtained such Terms; and even now, had Colonel Upton alarmed their Fears by threatening to treat with Ragoba instead of them, we have not a Doubt but much more adequate Terms might have been obtained, and Ragoba admitted to some Share in the Government, according to his Right; however, as the Treaty is concluded, and Colonel Upton has sent us an Extract of such Articles as he says concern the Presidency of Bombay, it becomes our Duty to carry them into Execution, as far as may depend upon us; and the necessary Orders were therefore immediately given for withdrawing our Forces from Ragoba, and proclaiming the Peace at this Place, and the subordinate Settlements.

Mr. Garden acquiesces in the Propriety of affording an Asylum to Ragoba, on his requesting it; but as he wishes the Governor and Council should avoid engaging themselves further than they can perform, he thinks they should not commit themselves in this Instance, before they have communicated their Intentions to Colonel Upton; as he fears the Ministers may term this Step an Infringement of the 12th Article of the Treaty.

The Board remark upon this, that the Exigence of the Case will not admit of their waiting for an Answer from Colonel Upton, as the Orders for withdrawing the Army cannot be delayed, and the Permission for affording Ragoba an Asylum must accompany these Orders, or it may arrive too late to be of any Service.

Adjourned.

Edward Ravenscroft,
Secretary.

William Hornby,
D. Draper,

Andrew Ramsay,

APPENDIX, Nº 119.

Brigadier General Gordon's Remarks and Observations on the Treaty concluded by Colonel Upton.

Brigadier General Gordon having carefully perused the Treaty concluded between the Honourable Company and the Maratta Empire, begs Leave to make the following Remarks thereon:

That the 1st Article, immediately by restoring Peace, is perfectly consistent with the Spirit and Tenor of Colonel Upton's Instructions, and the Object of his Embassy; as Is the 2d Article, directing the General Proclamation thereof.

By the 3d Article, Salsette, and all the other Islands which were conquered during the War, are reserved for the Company till the Pleasure of the Supreme Council is known. As it is to be supposed that they are well informed of the Company's Sentiments respecting Salsette, the Possession of it, which has been so long earnestly wished, is virtually secured by this Article.

The 4th Article cedes to the Company the Maratta Share of the Broach Revenues in the amplest Manner. A considerable Addition of annual Income is thereby secured to the Company; all Subject of Contention from Interference in Collection is removed; and as by the 7th Article, the Peshwah and his Ministers engage to prove, that the Guicawar's Family have no Right to make Cessions, that Power must be vested in the Maratta Government established at Poona, which indeed seems to be acknowledged in plain Terms by Futty Sing, in the Treaty which he concluded with Ragonath Row on the 18th July 1775.

In the 5th Article, it is very honourable and advantageous, as the Company thereby gain perpetual Possession of a Tract of Country producing Three Lacks of Rupees per Annum, with Power to chuse the Districts most convenient and advantageously situated for them in the Neighbourhood of Broach.

By the 6th Article, the Company are to receive from the Peshwah Twelve Lacks of Rupees to defray in Part the Expences of the War. Two Years seem rather a distant Period for the Payment of the Second Moiety; but it ought to be attended to, that this War was carried on against the Peshwah and his Ministers.

By the 7th Article, the Company agree to restore all the Cessions made to them in the Guzerat Country by Ragonath Row and Futty Sing, on its being proved that they had no Right to make such Cessions. If such Proofs are exhibited, Justice directs that a Restitution should be made.

The Company are however in the mean Time to retain Possession, particularly of certain Villages and Purgunnahs, as Pledges, till the Sunnuds for the Country, agreed by the 5th Article to be ceded to them for ever, are made over. If it is proved, that Ragonath Row and Futty Sing had no Right to make the Treaties which they have done, it is reasonable that they shall be declared null and void.

The 8th Article directs the drawing the English Troops into Garrison. As a Peace is concluded, that is certainly proper.

By the 9th Article, Ragonath Row is required to disband his Army, within a Month from the Date of the Treaty. This Measure seems necessary to ensure Peace; and it is believed the desperate State of his Finances would render it difficult for him to keep them together.

By the 10th Article, the Company engage, that if Ragoba should refuse to disband his Army, they will withdraw their Troops, and not assist him. The Expediency and Necessity of this Article are evident; without it no Peace could take Place.

The 11th Article provides an Establishment for Ragonath Row, on his complying with the Terms of the 9th Article. On this it is to be remarked, that his Guards, being paid and appointed by the Peshwah, and his Ministers, must be totally dependent on them. Incensed as they and he are against each other by repeated mutual Injuries, he will have much Danger to apprehend from being so entirely in their Power. If therefore his annual Allowance, which Colonel Upton states to amount to Ten Lacks, was to be paid to himself, with Permission either to retire to the Place of Abode fixed upon for him by the Treaty, or to any English Settlement, it would tend to ensure the Safety of his Person; and should he take the latter of these Steps, the Company could always guard against his Infringement of the Treaty.

 The

The Company engage by the 12th Article, not to assist Ragonath Row, or any Person in Rebellion against the Maratta Dominions. This is certainly just, proper, and consistent, as long as they adhere to the Treaty; as are also the Stipulations contained in the 14th Article, respecting Ships wrecked on the English or Maratta Coasts.

The 15th and 16th Articles contain Confirmations of former Treaties, except in such Parts as they are altered by the present one; as this is always usual on such Occasions, no Remarks occur upon it.

In the 17th Article it is stipulated, that the Peshwa shall have any Jewels belonging to him which have been deposited as Pledges by Ragonath Row, on fulfilling the Conditions whereon they were lodged. This seems reasonable and just, as perhaps they are a Part of the Regalia.

The 18th Article declares the English sole Lords and Proprietors of the Territory ceded to them, and this in the most express Terms.

The 19th ascertains the Time when each Party is to begin to collect the Revenues, which is done in the clearest Manner.

Having thus gone through the Treaty, Article by Article, it remains to be considered, whether more advantageous Terms ought reasonably to be expected, when every Circumstance relative to the Rise, Progress, and Management of the War, the Resources for carrying it on, the present State of the contending Parties, Colonel Upton's Instructions, and the Sentiments of the Company, are attended to.

'As to the First of these; the Brigadier General apprehends, that it will be difficult to defend the Attack made on Salsette, by which the War was begun, on Principles of good Faith and Justice. That on the 16th March, 1775, previous to which Brigadier General Gordon had entered a Dissent, disclaiming all Share of Responsibility for the Measures pursued when the Treaty was concluded and signed with Ragonath Row, he was by no Means in a Condition to fulfil his Part thereof.

That the Views and Intentions of the Honourable the President and Council, which it is to be presumed had only for their Object the Advantage and Interest of their Employers, were by no Means seconded by the Officer intrusted with the Command of the Troops employed in Support of Ragonath Row; on the contrary, that Officer, Lieutenant Colonel Keating, did, by repeated Acts of Violence and Misconduct, waste much Time and Ammunition in wandering, without any Object of Importance to the Service in View, through the Guzerat Province, instead of marching towards Poona, to which alone his Operations should have been directed; during which the Lives of many gallant Officers and Men were lost, large Sums of Money squandered away, and all this without obtaining one permanent or essential Advantage. If a Judgment therefore may be formed of what would have been done in a succeeding Campaign by Lieutenant Colonel Keating, from what happened in his last, no great deal ought to be expected.

That the Resources of Men and Money whereof this Presidency were possessed, seem not sufficient for so vast an Undertaking, paying due Attention at the same Time to the Safety of their different Settlements. The Truth of this Remark is plainly evinced by the repeated Demands which the Board have been unanimous in making for large Supplies from the other Presidencies, to enable them to carry on the War.

That Ragonath Row, weakened by the Defection of his Friends, Govind Row, who was disgusted by the Treaty of Broderah, in the utmost Distress for Money, and without a Prospect of Relief in this absolutely necessary Article, is ill able to contend with his rich and powerful Opponents, whose Cause it is believed the Nizam is ready to espouse with a large Army.

The Instructions given by the Governor General and Council to Colonel Upton, mark throughout their Intentions immediately to establish a Peace; indeed it seems to be the grand Object of his Mission. That they had been led into a Belief that Bassein is actually in Possession of this Presidency, is evident from the express Words of their Instructions. This however being a Mistake, Colonel Upton is certainly at Liberty to exercise the discretional Power given to him respecting that Place, which never was in the Hands of the Company, and consequently it cannot be restored, nor Possession of it relinquished, by them.

The only Restriction that Colonel Upton seems under about a Provision for Ragonath Row and the Broach Districts, is, that he is not to prolong the Negociations for a Day, for any Conditions, except those which are expresly mentioned. The only Conditions expresly mentioned are, the keeping Possession of the conquered Countries, and this is done by the 3d Article of the Treaty.

The

The pacific Intentions of the Court of Directors, are sufficiently evident from their Decisions respecting the Rohilla and Tanjore Wars, and if possible, still more so from their express Commands, received by the Ship Gatton, relative to Salsette, and to the very War wherein this Presidency has just now been involved.

Brigadier General Gordon, from a Review of all these Circumstances, begs Leave to offer it as his Opinion, that the Peace concluded by Colonel Upton is, in whatever relates to the Company's Interests, honourable, advantageous, and expedient. That the Alteration which he has proposed in these Articles, which relate to an Establishment for Ragounath Row, should be recommended to Colonel Upton's particular Attention, who is however sufficiently and entirely justified by the Letter of his Instructions, for the Steps which he has taken. And Brigadier General Gordon desires to conclude his Opinion on the Whole of this Business, by reminding the Board, that the Governor General and Council, charged as they are with the general Care, Management, and Direction of whatever appertains to the Honour and Interests of the British Nation throughout Indostan, may have Views for the Good of the Whole, whereof a Part cannot be competent Judges.

Robert Gordon.

Bombay,
15th March, 1776.

APPENDIX, N° 120.

To the Honourable the President and Members of the Select Committee, Bombay.

Gentlemen,

I HAVE received your Letter of the 14th Instant, and the Copy of Colonel Keating's Letter to you, dated the 6th Instant.

Very repeatedly I have desired of the Ministers a Supply of Money for the Use of Ragoba during the Cessation of Arms, but have never been able to procure a Rupee. To me the Request appeared unnatural. I had no Argument to enforce what I asked. What have we to urge when desiring our Enemies to supply us with the Means of carrying on a War against themselves? It is true, Gentlemen, you have said that it is but reasonable that a Portion of the Revenues, so unjustly withheld from Ragoba, should be made over to the Maintenance of him and his Adherents.

The Merits of this Argument I shall not enter into; however good they appear at Bombay, I am afraid the Force of them would be lost at Poona. The dispersing of Ragoba's Army must be shortly expected: This evinces the Necessity of concluding the Peace with all possible Expedition; in Two or Three Days it will either be established or entirely broke off.

With your Letter of the 15th Instant I am also favoured. Permit me, Gentlemen, to refer you in Turn to my Instructions. You will perceive I am directed to act as appears to me best (particularly regarding this very Island of Bassein) for the Honour and Benefit of the Company; and this I am determined to do. We have little just Claim to any Thing. If the Peace should take Place it will be both honourable and beneficial. You know as well as myself the Sense of the Governor General and Council regarding this War; you will therefore, Gentlemen, easily conclude what it must be respecting the Treaty they wish to have concluded with the Marattas: They are ever mindful of the Honour as well as Advantage of the Company.

I have the Honour to be, &c.

Poonah Dhur, (Signed) J. Upton.
20th February, 1776.
Received the 23d following.

P. S. I have to request the Favour of your forwarding to me a Copy of one of the Grants or Sunnuds by which Futty Sing made over to the Company any Part of the Guzerat Country, as the Ministry maintain no such Powers were ever vested in him, and therefore that such Sunnuds are of no Force or Value.

To Colonel Upton.

Sir,

WE have received your Letter dated the 20th Instant.

As you therein acquaint us that the Treaty will either be established or entirely broke off in Two or Three Days, we should wave entering further into the Discussion of the Question, Whether you have or have not, according to your Instructions, a discretional Power to recede from the Demand for Bassein? did we not differ so widely in the Construction of your Powers on this Head, that we deem it necessary, in Support of our Opinion so decisively given, and to remove all Imputation of Omission from us hereafter in this important Point, to shew you upon what Grounds it was formed.

According to the Copy we possess of your Instructions, dated the 21st June, the Third Paragraph, to which we suppose you mean to refer us, runs as follows: "If there is "any Foundation for the Intelligence which we have lately received, and which we "believe to be authentic, of some signal Advantages which have been gained by Ragonaut Row over the Ministerial Army, we apprehend you may be able to obtain the "Cession of Salsette and Bassein, with the other conquered Islands, without much "Difficulty; and in this Case, you may also have it in your Power probably to gain "more substantial Advantages to be yielded to the Company. Your next Object, "therefore, must be to obtain a formal Surrender of the Moiety held by the Marattas "of the Revenues of the Town and Purgunnah of Broach; but we must leave *these*, or "any other Points, which you may be able to secure for the Interest and Advantage of "the Company, to your Discretion," &c. &c. This is the only Passage we can discover in your Instructions, in any Shape tending to give you this discretional Power with respect to Bassein; though in our Opinion the Word *these* evidently relates to the other Advantages to be secured in Addition to Salsette and Bassein, and does not include these Places, the Cession of which, in the preceding Article, is made a principal Object of your Deputation: But whatever Construction may be put upon that Expression, the Intention of the Governor General and Council is clearly explained in the very next Paragraph, in which your Power of relinquishing these Cessions is particularly excepted against in the following very explicit Terms; viz.

"Though we do not mean absolutely to insist upon all these Concessions, if manifest "Advantages should have been gained against the Company's Arms, yet we are determined *on no Account* to relinquish the Possession of Salsette and Bassein; therefore, "should the Paishwa hold out against yielding them, you are at no Rate to agree to "restore them, declaring to them, if necessary, that the Matter having been referred "to the Honourable Court of Directors, *it is impossible to relinquish these Places* without "their express Permission."

But in the Second Sett of your Instructions, of a much later Date, this Matter is, if possible, placed in a still clearer Light, and every Possibility of a Doubt of the Governor General and Council's Intentions on this Head removed. The Copy transmitted us by them is dated the 17th July, and the Paragraph we mean to allude to runs as follows:

First, "The direct Purposes of your Appointment are to negociate a Treaty of Peace "between the Maratta Government and the Presidency of Bombay, and to obtain "a Confirmation to that Presidency of the Islands of Salsette and Bassein to the Company. *These Points you are to consider as indispensable.*" We do not think that the Company's Right to Bassein, or the Force of your Instructions respecting it, are in the least impaired by the Circumstance of our not having Possession, though the Difficulty of prevailing with the Ministers to consent to this Cession may be increased; and we have already apprized you how very anxious the Company are to obtain this Acquisition, without which, their Views upon this Coast will remain unaccomplished: Therefore, upon the most thorough Conviction, we persevere in the Opinion we before expressed, that you cannot agree to any Treaty wherein this Cession is not included,

without

without acting inconsistently with, and we will now add, in direct Breach of, your Instruction.

We readily allow, that if a Treaty is to take Place with the Ministers, it had better be concluded before Ragoba's Army disperses; but we do not mean by this Acknowledgment, that it is necessary a Treaty should be concluded at all Events; we are far from considering Ragoba's Cause as irretrievable, if the Treaty with the Ministers was off, and the Company to continue to support him.

We will not say any Thing on the Company's Right to the Cessions made by the Treaty, and that Question cannot be decided either by us or you.

We entertain the highest Opinion of the Governor General and Council's Regard for the Honour and Advantage of the Company; and we flatter ourselves we possess the same, and are competent Judges of both at this Presidency.

We enclose a Copy of the Treaty concluded with Futty Sing and Secajee Row Shumsheer Bahader, by which the Guicawar Share of Broach, and the Districts of Corah, Veriore, and Chickley, were ceded to the Company; and also a Copy of one of the Sunnuds executed by the latter in Consequence of the Treaty.

Sir Edward Hughes has acquainted us that His Majesty's Ship Dolphin will sail for England about the 15th of next Month.

We are, &c.

Bombay Castle, (Signed) William Hornby,
25th February, 1776. &c. Council.

To the Honourable the President and Members of the Select Committee, Bombay.

Gentlemen,

I am honoured with your Letter of the 25th February, and with the Copy of the Treaty concluded by Ragoba with Futty Sing, and Seagee Row Shumshaw; also the Copy of one of the Sunnuds executed by Seagee Row.

I am sorry we differ so widely regarding the Sense of my Instructions; you will permit me to observe, that the Words "relinquish, restore, and confirm," imply having Possession, which never was the Case; and I am quite clear also, that I have acted very consistently with the (private verbal) Instructions I received before I left Calcutta, and I never had or seen Cause to deviate from them.

The Treaty of Peace between the Honourable Company and the Maratta Government was signed Yesterday Afternoon; such Articles of Convention as concern the Presidency of Bombay I have the Honour to forward.

Your Influence with Ragoba, that he may quietly acquiesce in the Conditions stipulated for him, will, I am convinced, not be wanting. If he expresses any Fear or Uneasiness at going to the Residence appointed for his Reception, with the Maratta Sirdars sent to escort him, they consent to his being accompanied by an English Gentleman, with an Escort of One hundred of our Troops.

The Establishment made for Ragonaut Row amounts to about Ten Lacks of Rupees per Annum. It was impossible to procure for him any Part in the Government of this Country. The Ministers have most solemnly promised to live ever on friendly Terms with him, unless he should occasion Disturbances in the Country. An English Gentleman being here, will be the Security for their good Behaviour towards him. The Ministers request, when the English Army march into their own Garrisons, &c. Colonel Keating will advise Hurry Pundit Furkia of it, and at the same Time inform him if the Conditions obtained for Ragonaut Row are accepted of by him, and if he is putting the Part depending on himself in Execution.

A Vackeel will be sent in a Day or two from this Government to Bombay, to explain any Thing that may not be fully comprehended.

Broach is the Place appointed for the Two English Gentlemen and the Two Marattas to meet at, to fix the Boundaries of the ceded Country, amounting to Three Lacks per Annum. The Persons sent by this Government will be furnished with a Letter from me, signifying their being the People appointed by them to assist in carrying the Agreement into Execution.

As soon as Advice is arrived at Poona, of the English Army having marched into their own Garrisons, they will order the Communication to be opened.

I shall

I shall be much obliged to you, Gentlemen, to favour me with the English and Maratta Names of the small Islands in or near the Bay of Bombay, now in our Possession. Not knowing them by each other's Names prevents their nominally being inserted in the Treaty. We are to keep only such as we now possess.

I have the Honour to be, &c.

Poona Dhur, (Signed) J. Upton.
2d March 1776.

Received 10 following, at Night.

P. S. You will be pleased to appoint Two Gentlemen to proceed to fix the Boundaries of the Purgunnah to be ceded near or adjoining to Broach. The Ministers agree to our taking any District that is not Jaghire Lands.

J. Upton.

APPENDIX, N° 122.

SIGNED the following Letters to Lieutenant Colonels Keating and Upton.

To Lieutenant Colonel Keating.

Sir,

We are now to acquaint you, that we received Advice from Colonel Upton late in the Evening of the 10th Instant, that he had concluded a Treaty of Peace between the Honourable Company and the Ministers at Poona, on the 1st.

Enclosed is a Copy of an Extract from the Treaty, as transmitted to us by Colonel Upton; and it is necessary for us to give you the following Orders in Consequence.

The Peace must be proclaimed at the Head of all the Company's Forces under your Command, agreeable to the 2d Article.

You are immediately to march our Troops into such Quarters as will be assigned them by the Chief and Council at Surat within the Company's Districts. The Detachments from Broach and Surat are to return to those Garrisons, and the Remainder is to be held in Readiness to embark for the Presidency, as Opportunities offer.

The Stipulations respecting Ragoba must be communicated to him in a proper Manner; and the absolute Necessity of our separating the Company's Forces from his, explained to him. The Honourable the President has wrote to him upon this Occasion; and if he expresses any Fear or Uneasiness at going to the Place appointed for his Reception with the Maratta Sirdars sent to escort him, the Ministers consent to his being accompanied by an English Gentleman, with an Escort of One hundred of our Troops. Colonel Upton tells us, the Ministers have most solemnly promised to live ever on friendly Terms with him, unless he should occasion Disturbances in the Country. You will lose no Time in acquainting us with what Resolution Ragoba may now take, and with his future Intentions.

If Ragoba refuseth to accept the Conditions stipulated for him, in Apprehension of Danger to his Person, and in Consequence thereof applies to you to be received into any of the Company's Garrisons, you may receive him with his Family, and a suitable Number of Domestics only; but the Four Persons mentioned in the 9th Article must on no Account be protected.

When our Troops march into Garrison, you will advise Hurry Punt Furkia thereof; and at the same Time inform him, if Ragoba accepts of the Conditions stipulated for him, and if he is putting into Execution the Part of defending himself.

The 13th Article is omitted in the Extract sent us by Colonel Upton.

You will acquaint us what Part of the stipulated Twenty-six Lacks have been paid to Ragoba, by Futty Sing, and how you have disposed of the Goods and Jewels you mentioned in your Letter, dated the 30th August, to have retained in your Hands on Account

Account of Ragoba's Debt to the Company. We have received your Letters, dated the 31st, 16th, and 25th Ultimo.

We are your loving Friends,

Bombay Castle, 15th March 1776.

William Hornby, &c. Council.

P. S. We have just received your Letter of the 11th Instant, to which the above will serve as a Reply.

To Colonel Upton.

Sir,

Late in the Evening of the 10th Instant, we received your Letter of the 2d, with the enclosed Extract of the Treaty you have concluded between the Honourable Company and the Ministers at Poona.

The 13th Article is omitted in the Extract you sent us; and as all the other Articles follow each other in a regular Series, we wish to know if this Omission is accidental.

The Peace was publickly proclaimed here on the 12th Instant.

The Intention of this Letter is principally to enclose a Copy of a Letter just received from Colonel Keating, which justified our Apprehensions that Ragoba would not accept the Terms stipulated for him, as he is of Opinion his Person will be endangered by putting himself so much in the Power of his Enemies. We shall therefore afford him an Asylum, with his Family and Domestics, in one of the Company's Settlements, agreeable to his Request, and the Latitude given us by the Governor General and Council, in their Letter dated the 20th October, of which you have a Copy; for we think ourselves bound, by every Tie of Honour and Humanity, not to deny him the Protection he has demanded; but we have given Orders that the Four Persons mentioned in the 9th Article must on no Account be received.

We recommend it to you to endeavour to stipulate with the Ministers, that Ragoba may have an Establishment continued to him, to the Amount mentioned in your Letter, viz. Ten Lacks of Rupees per Annum; and you must be sensible of the Advantages that will result to the Company from his Residence with us, as so long as he is in our Hands the Ministers will be very cautious in their Conduct, though at the same Time we shall not countenance him in fomenting any Disturbances against the Maratta State.

The English and Maratta Names of the small Islands in the Harbour of Bombay, now in our Possession, are enclosed.

We are,
Sir,
Your most obedient Servants,

Bombay Castle, 15th March, 1776.

William Hornby, &c. Council.

Received the following Letter from Lieutenant Colonel Keating:

Honourable Sir, and Gentlemen,

The 9th Instant at Night I received a Letter from Lieutenant Colonel Upton, a Copy of which is enclosed.

Yesterday I had a long Conference with the Peshwah, who positively declares he will never accede to the Terms stipulated for him by Lieutenant Colonel Upton. He writes to your Honour, &c. by this Conveyance, and desires me to represent to you as follows:

That on the known and long experienced good Faith of the English Nation, he had entered into a solemn Treaty and Covenant with the Honourable Company, whereby they are bound to punish his rebellious Subjects, and to restore to him his just and lawful Right, the Government of the Maratta Empire.

In respect to himself, he has agreed to grant certain Advantages to the Honourable Company, the Particulars of which are too well known to your Honour, &c. to need recapitulating, that nothing on his Part has been wanting, or ever will.

By Lieutenant Colonel Upton's Letter to him, he finds the Stipulation alluded to is neither more or less than his receiving from his rebellious Ministers the paltry Sum of Three Lacks per Annum, in Consideration of his remaining their discretional Prisoner for the rest of his Life, which he has every Reason to suppose would in such Case be of short Duration.

He has a firm Reliance on the good Faith of the English Nation, and relies on their fulfilling Engagements made in the Face of Heaven; but should he, by untoward Fate, be for a Time disappointed by Means not in his Power to account for, he is still resolved to reject every other Proposal, and appeal for Justice to England; in the mean Time throws himself on the Protection of the British Nation, in full Confidence of receiving proper Support and Maintenance at Broach, Surat, or Bombay, until the Determination from England can be obtained.

Lieutenant Colonel Upton having mentioned to the Peshwah that the Circar of Poona will be at the annual Expence of Ten Lacks of Rupees by his whole Establishment, he wishes the Company to receive it towards defraying the Expence they may be put to on his Account, until a final Determination takes Place.

He observed, as his firm Opinion, that the Terms agreed to by Lieutenant Colonel Upton were not voluntary, but compulsively obtained by the Ministers, in Consequence of having him entirely in their Power.

I have received a Letter from Hurry Punt Furkia, informing me, that in Consequence of Lieutenant Colonel Upton having agreed to surrender to the Maratta Circar all the Purgunnah granted by Ragonath Row Peshwah to the Honourable Company, he is preparing to come as far as Sungar, to receive them from me. I replied, that I shall always act in strict Conformity to your Honour, &c, Orders; and that as yet you have not instructed me relating to his Expectations.

I am, with the greatest Respect,
Honourable Sir, and Gentlemen,
Your greatly obliged, and most devoted Servant,

Mandavie Camp, the 11th March 1776.

Thomas Keating, Lieut. Colonel.

To the Honourable the President and Members of the Select Committee, Bombay.

Gentlemen,

I am honoured with your Letter of the 15th Instant, together with the Paper containing the English and Maratta Names of the small Islands in the Bay of Bombay, in our Possession; also Lieutenant Colonel Keating's Letter to you, dated the 10th Instant.

I forwarded Extracts only of such Articles as concerned your Presidency. The entire Treaty I take for granted will be sent you by the Governor General and Council.

I am much concerned to hear Ragoba will not accept the Terms stipulated. It was long before I could get the Ministers to grant these; and I have endeavoured all in my Power since to procure for him a Change of Abode. It was not likely they would agree to his residing in any of our Settlements, after what had passed; nor could it be expected that they would encrease the Stipend. They must always fear his stirring up fresh Commotions; and they certainly would not themselves furnish him with the Means. How would he have been provided for, had the Army been withdrawn conformably to the original Order?

The Conditions of the Peace, stipulating with the Ministerial Party, are "for our Neutrality," what was agreed upon for it; Ragonaut Row, "if it made One Article in the Treaty, would of course be guaranteed by the Company; such Terms were to be obtained for him as it might appear to me reasonable to expect, and which might not frustrate the immediate Objects to my Negociations."

You will excuse, Gentlemen, my making these Observations: I could not get other or better Conditions for Ragonaut Row; and it was with the utmost Difficulty I effected the Business on which I was deputed.

You will of course, Gentlemen, use every Argument to persuade Ragonaut Row to accept the Terms stipulated for him. The Ministers make the most solemn Protestations, that his Person shall be safe, and that he shall receive every Indulgence he can

expect.

expect. They say Ragonaut Row and the World must be convinced, that they would not break a Treaty so solemnly entered into with Gentlemen possessed of such Power, Rank, and Honour, as the Members of the Supreme Council are; and that they asked to have a Resident, chiefly to see their Obligations towards him (Ragoba) performed.

I am almost convinced the Governor General and Council will not consent to his residing in any of our Settlements; and am much afraid the Ministers will withhold his Stipend, unless he agrees to the Conditions provided for him by the Treaty. I shall continue to exert myself in endeavouring to procure Terms more agreeable to Ragoba, but with little Hopes of Success.

I have the Honour to be, &c.

Poonah Dhur, (Signed) J. Upton.
19th March 1776.
Received the 22d following.

To the Honourable the President and Members of the Select Committee, Bombay.

Gentlemen,

I am honoured with your Letter of the 17th Instant, together with a Copy of Lieutenant Colonel Keating's Letter of the 12th Instant. I shall take the earliest Opportunity of acquainting the Ministers with Ragoba's Determination.

I am writing to the Governor General and Council, and shall enclose your Letters for their Information respecting Ragoba.

I have the Honour to be, &c.

Poona Dhur, (Signed) J. Upton.
March 21st, 1776.
Received the 26th following.

APPENDIX, N° 123.

Extract of Bengal Secret Consultations, the 6th May 1776.

PRESENT,

The Honourable Warren Hastings, Governor General, President,
Lieutenant General John Clavering,
The Honourable George Monson,
Richard Barwell, } Esquires.
Philip Francis, }

READ, and approved, the Proceedings of the 2d Instant.

Received the following Letter from Lieutenant Colonel Upton:

Gentlemen,

I have the Honour to forward a Duplicate of the Treaty, also Duplicates of my Letters, &c. of the 3d Instant.

I received a Letter Yesterday from the Governor and Council of Bombay, also a Letter from Lieutenant Colonel Keating to the Select Committee, Bombay, dated the 11th Instant: These I forward for your Perusal.

It should seem by these Letters, that great Terms were expected to be gained for Ragonaut Row, rather than that Peace was to be concluded between the Presidency of Bombay and the Maratta State for our Neutrality.

I was long in getting the Conditions now stipulated for Ragonaut Row; and this will not be Matter of Surprize, when we consider how often he has been in Arms against the State, even so long ago as in the Peshwaship of Madu Row, Uncle to the present Peshwa: He

He was then defeated, taken Prisoner, and pardoned; he has repeatedly offended and been pardoned; and why it should be supposed now, when he is secured by so solemn a Treaty, that his Person should be in such Danger, I cannot conceive. After what has passed they certainly would not let him reside in any of the Company's Settlements, nor would they furnish him with the Means of occasioning fresh Troubles to the State.

I enclose my Reply to the Select Committee of Bombay; I hope they will try every Means to reconcile Ragonaut Row to accept the Conditions stipulated for him.

I have not seen the Ministers since the Receipt of this Letter. Ragonaut Row's residing in any of our Settlements, I am sure will give great Umbrage.

I send this Packet by Way of Masulipatam. The Ministers will dispatch Letters by Way of Benares in a few Days: I shall then advise how they receive the Report of Ragonaut Row's refusing the Terms stipulated. Perhaps they may make some favourable Alterations in them; but I think they will not. As I have repeatedly and very lately asked this, they always replied they thought the Conditions very proper. His future good Behaviour, and nothing else, would ever get him any other.

I have the Honour to be, &c.

Poonah Dhur,
30th March 1776.

(Signed) J. Upton.

The English and Maratta Names of the small Islands in the Bay of Bombay, ceded by the Treaty with Ragoba, and now in our Possession.

English Names.	Maratta Names.
Caranja,	Oran and Seva,
Elephanta,	Gance Porne,
Hog Island.	Nauva.

(Signed) Edward Ravenscroft,
Secretary.

Read, the following Letter from Bombay.

Secret Department.

Honourable Sir, and Gentlemen,

We had the Honour to address you on the 18th Ultimo, and have since forwarded a Duplicate of our Letter under that Date.

A Continuation of our Correspondence with Colonel Upton since that Time, is now enclosed, and though we imagine the Advice from that Gentleman of the Conclusion of the Treaty, will have reached you before this Letter, we enclose a Copy of the Extract he transmitted to us, which we did not receive till the 10th Instant.

Colonel Upton has differed very much in Opinion with us in his Interpretation of your Instructions respecting Bassein, from the Tenor of which we ever considered that the Cession of that Place was to be an indispensable Point in any Treaty he might conclude with the Ministers. Your Directions on this Head appear to us very clear and express, but Colonel Upton argues that they were founded on the Supposition of our being in actual Possession, which never was our Case, and from whence we conclude he infers their Force is destroyed. He added further, that he was quite clear he had acted very consistently with the (private verbal) Instructions he received, before he left Calcutta.

We have carefully examined our Advices to your honourable Board, and are at a Loss to conceive upon what Foundation you entertained the Idea of our being in Possession of Bassein; but though you do seem to have misconceived this Point, we were of Opinion, that had the Force of your Orders to Colonel Upton, for insisting upon this Circumstance of our being in Possession, you had sufficient Time after the Arrival of Mr. Tayler to have explained or altered his Instructions; we rather thought the Peremptoriness of your Orders proceeded from your Attention to the Honourable Company's Commands to this Presidency, dated the 31st March 1769, and 1st April 1772, respecting their Views on this Side of India, which will remain unaccomplished, until we are confirmed in the Possession both of Salsette and Bassein.

Immediately upon Receipt of the Extract of the Treaty, we ordered the Peace to be proclaimed at all the Company's Settlements under this Presidency, and at the English Camp; and at the same Time, gave Directions for our Troops being marched into Garrison, agreeable to the 8th Article.

The Maratta Vackeel mentioned in Colonel Upton's Letter of the 2d Instant, is not yet arrived.

The

APPENDIX, N° 123.

The Stipulations made for Ragoba were in every Respect so inadequate to his Rank and Station, and so very inconsistent with what he had a Right to expect, that we never supposed he would accept of them, and consent to put his Life and Liberty entirely in the Power of his Enemies, who must dread the Idea of his ever regaining his former Power. Many good Consequences would have ensued, and the Permanency of the Peace been rendered much more secure, had the Colonel stipulated that Ragoba should have had the Option of residing at one of the Company's Settlements, with a suitable Appointment. This the Ministers could not have objected to, had their Intentions been good, and he would have proved a most useful Instrument in our Hands for alarming their Fears, and the best Security for their observing the Peace; however, we thought ourselves bound by every Tie of Honour and Humanity, and authorized by your Letter of the 20th October, to afford him Protection in case he should apprehend his Life in Danger, and request it, and in that Case we should have received him and his Family; but though on the first Intelligence of the Conditions stipulated for him, he determined to throw himself upon our Protection, as mentioned in Colonel Keating's Letter, dated the 11th Instant, yet on further Consideration, and after consulting with his principal Ministers and Officers, he signified the following Sentiments and Resolutions to our Commanding Officer, which he declared to be final:

That he had the most ample Dependance upon us for the Performance of the Treaty of Surat; the more so, as we must be perfectly convinced that he has punctually fulfilled every Part of his Promise, so far as had hitherto depended upon him:

That he is fully determined never to accept of any Compromise, much less so inglorious a one as that mentioned to him by Colonel Upton:

That should we refuse to fulfil the Treaty of Surat, he then appealed to the Honourable Company for Justice; and in the mean Time was resolved, as far as possible, and with God's Assistance, to defend his just Rights against the evil Designs of his rebellious Servants; and waved that Part of his former Resolutions of placing himself under our Protection, until the Company's Determination could be obtained.—

Thus are our Apprehensions, that the Peace would not be of a long Duration, already in some Measure confirmed, and a Prospect of a destructive War commencing on the very Verge of the Company's Possessions, which it cannot fail materially to affect. We have not yet heard of any Steps taken by either Party in Consequence of Ragoba's Determination; but we understand it was founded upon his Dependence of Assistance from the Nizam and Hyder Ally, and the Defection of one of the principal Ministerial Officers, who has promised to join him with a large Body of Horse. We leave to your Honour, &c. to judge, what must be the Situation of this Presidency, should Ragoba prove successful by the Assistance of these Powers, incensed as he must be against the English for their Breach of Faith with him.

The Company by this Treaty will be deprived of Jamboseer, Ahmood, Hansood, Occlaseer, Orpad, and Versaul, producing a Revenue, which could be collected with very little Difficulty and Expence, of at least Fifteen Lacks of Rupees a Year. The Cessions made by the Guicawars are also to be restored, when it is proved they had no Right to make such Cessions (which we suppose they will readily allow, when it is so much for their Interest, though we never before heard their Right called in Question, and have held Lands under their Sunnuds since the Year 1759); these are Chickly, Coral, Veriow, and Batta, producing a Revenue of about 1,98,000 Rupees a Year; but it is very remarkable, that although the Guicawar Cessions are not to be restored but in Case of the above Contingency, and would of course remain in our Hands until the Doubt of Futty Sing's Power was cleared up; yet are there Four Places with Three Villages in the Purgunnah of Churcasy, belonging likewise we believe to Futty Sing, accepted as Security for the Performance of Engagements entered into by the Ministers at Poona, and we are immediately to make Restitution of the Territories ceded by Ragoba, retaining only in our Hands the above doubtful Security for the Performance of their Part of the Treaty.

After the positive Manner in which you were pleased to enjoin Colonel Upton to insist upon the Cession of Salsette and Bassein, we were struck with the utmost Surprize, when we perceived that our retaining Possession of the first, and Caranja, Elephanta, and Hog Island, remains a Matter of Doubt. Our Duty to the Company leads us to express our Hopes, in the most earnest Manner, that you will on no Account agree to restore these Places. The Compensation offered for them is in every Respect inadequate; and Three Times the Value of the proposed Exchange in the Neighbourhood

of

of Broach, or indeed elsewhere, would be no Equivalent for these Islands, whose Situation gives them Advantages we could not meet with in any other Territory. Salsette is only divided from Bombay by a River, not above One hundred Yards wide, and Caranja lays in our Harbour directly opposite the Castle; and in case of future Differences with the Marattas, they will not only form an excellent and secure Barrier to preserve this Island from all Insults, but we shall also have Resources of Grain and Provisions within our own Power; and in case of a War with France, or any other European Power, we shall have the grand Advantage of keeping our Military Force more compact, and shall be able, at the shortest Notice, to withdraw a considerable Number to reinforce this Garrison, which could not be done from a more distant Possession. We have likewise made very considerable Improvements to the Fortifications at Tannah, by forming a Glacis and Esplanade, which should be a most powerful Reason for not putting this Place again in the Hands of the Marattas; and we can with great Safety assure your Honour, &c. that these Islands will, in a very short Time, produce an infinitely more considerable Revenue, than the Territory proposed to be given in Exchange; for all which Reasons, and the great Desire the Company have expressed to obtain these Islands, we repeat our Wishes, that you will not on no Account agree to restore them.

The present Inconveniency and Loss to the Company occasioned by this Reference will be very great. No further Steps can yet be taken for the Improvement of these Islands, either in Cultivation, Population, or in stocking them with Cattle, &c. which they stand much in Need of; and the Time is now approaching for leasing out the Lands again, which we cannot expect will be done on any tolerable Terms, in this State of Uncertainty; so that at any Rate, the Company will lose great Part of the Revenues for this Season.

Since writing thus far, we have received another Letter from Lieutenant Colonel Keating, which is added to his Correspondence now forwarded; wherein he acquaints us of his having communicated to Ragoba the full Contents of the Treaty; and that when he was made sensible of his real Situation, he declared, that from a Confidence in the well-known good Faith of the English Nation, he had repeatedly rejected Offers of Assistance from Nizam Ally, and other powerful Men, who were capable of restoring him to his Right; and that he had nothing now left, but a Reliance on the Justice of the Nation at large, to whom he should carry his solemn Appeal; and therefore claimed our Protection and Support, until their Determination was known. He is to proceed to this Place as soon as proper Opportunity offers.

Colonel Upton seems to think, that your Honour, &c. will not consent to Ragoba's residing in any of the Company's Settlements; but we beg Leave to submit to your most serious Consideration, the everlasting Shame and Disgrace which will be entailed on the Nation, if we were to surrender him up into the Hands of his Enemies, after having given him Protection, and any Accident was to happen to him in Consequence. We cannot consider the Protestations of the Ministers as a proper Security for the Safety of his Person, if he was to put himself absolutely in their Power, as settled by the Treaty.

Our Troops were to march into Garrison on the 26th of this Month; but the Communication with the Maratta Dominions still remains shut.

We are, &c.

Bombay Castle, (Signed) William Hornby,
30th March, 1776. &c. Council.

APPENDIX, N° 124.

GOVERNOR General—I cannot help noticing the extraordinary Allusion made by Colonel Upton to the private verbal Instructions which he says he received before he left Calcutta, which I remark in this Place, for the Purpose of declaring, that he received no private verbal Instructions from me; and I move, that Colonel Up-

ton

ton be asked to what Instructions he alludes by this Expression, and from whom he received them?

Mr. Francis—It appears to me, that Colonel Upton does not appeal to any private verbal Instructions, supposed to have been received by him, as if they were contradictory to, or inconsistent with the public Orders of the Board; he could not but know that such Instructions were of no Force, and he could not plead them as Authority to act against his formal Orders. As I understand it, he mentions them merely as a Confirmation in his Mind of the same, and Construction which he himself affixes to his Orders. I do not believe that any Member of this Board would have taken upon himself to have exceeded these Limits; and I think the Enquiry useless.

Mr. Barwell—As Objections have been started to the Motion, and the Information can be of no public Utility, any private Sentiments that may have been expressed on the Tenor of the Board's Instructions to Colonel Upton, are no more than the Sense of an Individual of the Government which gave those Instructions: For my Part, I have never presumed to interpret the Orders of this Government, nor to discuss with Colonel Upton the particular Part he should act in carrying them into Execution. Indeed I do not recollect I ever held any Discourse with the Colonel upon the Subject of his Instructions; but, as I have said before, that as Objections have been started to the Motion, I am of Opinion it should be waved. The Enquiry can answer no Purpose.

Colonel Monson—The Question proposed to be put to Colonel Upton, can be of no public Utility, and is in itself of no Consequence, any more than gratifying private Curiosity; as the Governor General wishes to be informed to what Colonel Upton alludes, I have no Objection to the Question being put to him.

General Clavering—The private Instructions alluded to, refer to the Board's Orders to retain Possession of Basicin. When Colonel Upton left this Place, it was believed by every Member of the Board, that we were then in Possession of that Place; and there was then no Difference in Opinion amongst any of the Members on the Propriety of the Orders for establishing a Right to a Place, of which we thought we were in Possession. From this Circumstance, I am convinced that Colonel Upton cannot mean that he had private Orders from any individual Member of the Board, to relinquish a Place which, by his Orders, he was instructed to retain; he can only allude to those general Words contained in his Instructions, that we left these or any other Points which he might be able to secure for the Interest and Advantage of the Company, to his Discretion. The Latitude given to him by those Words, may probably have been repeated to him by every Member of the Board, in Answer to certain Doubts which he submitted to the Board for Explanation. If it could answer any Purpose whatever, I would readily assent to the Proposition; but as I think it cannot, I agree with Mr. Barwell and Mr. Francis, that the Enquiry would be useless.

The Governor General—I desire to recall my Motion; it was not from my own Inclination that I made it.

General Clavering—As the President and Council of Bombay acquaint us that they have offered Ragoba an Asylum in one of the Company's Factories, being authorized so to do by our Letter to them of the 18th of October, and as his Residence there may have Consequences either to disturb the Friendship lately established between the Poona Government and the Company, or at least that it may occasion a certain Expence to the Government of Bombay for his Maintenance, seeing that by the 11th Article of the Treaty lately concluded with the Poona Government, he will not be entitled to receive any Part of the Sums therein stipulated for him, unless he shall reside at Coopergong, on the Banks of the Gungha Gudowry, I could wish the Board would be pleased to consider what Instructions it will be necessary to give the President and Council of Bombay, with regard to the Two Subjects above-mentioned.

The Governor General—I beg Leave to state the Propositions included in the General's Minute, in distinct and formal Questions; and beg the Favour of the General to correct me if I err in my Construction of them, my Meaning being to draw the Subject into precise Points, to fix the Resolutions of the Board upon them.

Question 1st. Whether, by the following Paragraph of our Letter, of the 18th October, viz. "Admitting the Possibility of Ragoba's being reduced, by any unforeseen Misfortune, to seek Refuge in some of your Garrisons, we would not have you "understand, from any Directions yet transmitted you, that we mean entirely to desert "him; on the contrary, you will find, by a Paragraph of the enclosed Instructions to "Colonel

" Colonel Upton, that our Intention is to obtain a suitable Pro
" therefore desire that you will afford him a Sanctuary for himsel
" or Attendants, in case he should ever be necessitated to apply t
" tection, in order to avoid any personal Danger;" the President a
bay were authorized to grant the Protection of their Governmen
the Situation of Affairs at the Time in which his Application was m
Protection?

2d. Whether the Board shall approve of the Protection grante
President and Council of Bombay, or whether they shall be direc
from him?

General Clavering—I beg Leave to add a Third Question, whic
be suffered to remain at Bombay, whether the Council at Bombay
to grant him a Pension for his Maintenance at the Company's Exp

Mr. Francis—I think that the Presidency of Bombay were u
rized to give Ragoba a Retreat within the Company's Territorie
nothing in the late Treaty, which precludes us from granting hi
sent; at the same Time, several Considerations induce me to wish,
have been avoided: The first and principal one is, that, as long a
our immediate Protection, and particularly at Bombay, the Recor
and the Maratta State will probably be open to Jealousies and Susp
which at present may prevent a cordial Union between us, and ev
casion of a Rupture. If, however, Ragoba be at present at Bom
that we are either obliged by Treaty, or that it would be consiste
to dismiss him from thence; but as the utmost we are then bound t
Retreat, it should not be accompanied with any Conditions burth
pany, or which may induce him to continue there. This contain
First and Second Questions, and to the Third I answer, No.

Mr. Barwell—To the First Question I answer, that I think
Bombay was authorized.

To the Second, I am of Opinion that this Government oug
the Protection offered to Ragoba.

To the Third, that he should not be allowed any Pension by the

Colonel Monson—To the First Question, the President and Cou
authorized to give Protection to Ragoba, under certain Limitatio
pressed in our Letter of the 18th October; I think Ragoba was n
stances, for he rejected the Terms stipulated for him by Colonel
solved, " as far as possible, with God's Assistance, to defend his j
" evil Designs of his rebellious Subjects," and waved that Part
lutions of placing himself under the Protection of the Gentlemen

To the Second Question, I disapprove of the Protection given
Bombay, as I think it impolitic, and a Measure by which they
lish Company in Disputes and Differences with the Maratta State
given to a considerable Person at this Presidency, drew on them th
Country Government, and annihilated the Company's Establishm
The Gentlemen at Bombay, with such a Precedent before the
with more Caution. I think them very censurable for the Prote
Ragoba, as they might very well have avoided it, it having been
him. As I suppose that Ragoba is already at Bombay, I would a
tlemen of that Presidency should recommend to him to withdraw
the Protection of their Flag, and on no Account grant him any
his Subsistence.

General Clavering—The President and Council of Bombay were
by the Letter of the 18th of October, to afford Protection to Rag
or the Suspension of Arms, or until a Treaty could be concluded
of Poona. The Conditions contained in our Letter were not to
of an unforeseen Misfortune happening to him, and they were
Assurance that we did not mean to desert him, but on the contrar
was to obtain a suitable Provision for him. This Intention has
Stipulation contained in the 11th Article; I conclude therefore,
of Bombay was not authorized, after the Treaty took Place, to

Ragoba; and I think they should be told, that we do not approve of their altering the Stipulation which has been made in his Favour in the 11th Article.

The Second Question is answered in the above; and further, they should be acquainted that we do not understand how Ragoba can be made a most useful Instrument, as they declare in their Letter of the 30th of March last, in their Hands, if they do not mean to employ him to carry on Intrigues against the Maratta State, and thereby endanger the Continuance of the Peace, which we have just established.

To the Third Question, I am clearly of Opinion, that the Court of Directors will not approve of any Pension being granted him from the Company's Treasury.

Governor General—To the First Question, I reply, that the President and Council of Bombay were generally authorized, by our Letter of the 18th October, to grant their Protection to Ragoba.

To the Second Question, That though I regret the Necessity which impelled the President and Council of Bombay to grant their Protection to Ragoba, I still approve of it, and think this Board ought to approve of it.

The Third Question does not fall within my Construction of the controlling Powers vested in this Government over the other Presidencies, who require not our Authority for the Disposal of the Company's Treasure entrusted to their Charge.

Extract of Bengal Secret Consultations, the 9th May 1776.

PRESENT,

The Honourable Warren Hastings, Governor General, President,
Lieutenant General John Clavering,
The Honourable George Monson,
Richard Barwell, and Philip Francis, Esquires.

Read, and approved the Proceedings of the 6th Instant.

The Secretary having prepared the Draft of a Letter to Bombay, in Consequence of the Minutes of last Council, which was circulated and corrected by the Members of the Board, he now lays it before them for their Determination.

To the Honourable William Hornby, Esquire, President, &c. Council at Bombay.

Gentlemen,

We have received the Letters which you addressed to us under Dates the 18th February and 30th March.

We observe with Concern that Ragoba had resolved to put himself under the Protection of your Government, and to retire to Bombay. You alledge that you were authorized, by our Letter of the 20th October last, to grant him an Asylum. We admit the Fact, but we cannot allow that this Authority could be interpreted to extend beyond the Time of the Cessation of Arms, whilst the Negociation was carrying on. The Terms of our Letter were "admitting the Possibility of Ragoba's being reduced by any "unforeseen Misfortune to seek Refuge in some of your Garrisons;" in that Case "we desire you would afford him a Sanctuary for himself, and his Domestics or Attend-"ants, if he should ever be necessitated to apply for your Protection, in order to avoid "any personal Danger." The Sense of these Expressions is fully explained by the intermediate Words, "that our Intention was to obtain a suitable Provision for him." This Provision has been secured by the 11th Article of the Treaty now concluded, and we think that the particular Stipulation therein made in his Favour cannot be construed, but by a Perversion of our Meaning, to understand an urgent Necessity, on which Exigency alone our Authority for his going to Bombay can be established. If the Use you mean to make of him be as you say, to render him an useful Instrument in your Hands for alarming the Fears of the Ministers, we are apprehensive that such an Effect being produced in them, must of course expose the Possessions of the Company to the Danger of being involved in a new War. Can it be supposed that whilst you are harbouring

bouring a Person so obnoxious to the Ministers, that they will receive a Minister on your Part, or send one of theirs to your Presidency?

We hope that these Arguments will have their Weight with you, but at all Events we shall deem you answerable to the Court of Directors and the British Nation, if the Ministers should, upon hearing of your Intention, refuse to ratify the Treaty, and renew the War in Consequence of it.

In your Letter now before us, you maintain the independent Right of the Guicawar to make the Cessions which they had yielded by their Treaty with you to the Company; and you say, that you never before heard this Right called in Question; yet in the original Plan of your Treaty with Ragoba, as set forth in your Letter to us of the 31st December 1774, the Share collected by the Guicawars from the Territories of Broach is demanded *of Ragoba* as one of the Conditions on which he was to receive the Company's Assistance: And it further appears, by the 5th Article of the Treaty with Ragoba and Futty Sing, to which Colonel Keating made himself a Party in Behalf of the Company, that the Government and Revenues of the Purgunnah of Broach were ceded to the Company by the former; which Cession Futty Sing is expressly directed not to dispute.

If Ragoba, whom you then considered as Peshwa, had Authority to make this Cession, it follows that Futty Sing is a Dependent of the Maratta State, and that he can have no Power to alienate any Part of the Territory under his immediate Government, without the Authority of the reigning Peshwa.

With respect to our Mistake, in supposing that you were in Possession of Bassein when we drew up the Instructions given to Colonel Upton, as you say that " you are at " a Loss to conceive upon what Foundation we entertained that Idea," we must acquaint you that it took its Rise from the Terms of your Letters of 31st December 1774, and 31st March 1775. In the former you said that " you had insisted on the Com- " pany's being put in Possession of the Places to be ceded by Ragoba as soon as the " Treaty should be executed;" and in the latter, that " the Treaty with Ragoba had " been made out in the Terms you proposed, and executed, and that the necessary " Sunnuds were delivered for the several Districts and Territories the Company were en- " titled to in Virtue of it." And the Information was further confirmed to us by our Advices from Fort Saint George.

In Reply to the Reference made to us by the Ministers in the 3d Article of the Treaty of Poona, we have already directed Colonel Upton to signify to them, that we cannot assent to the Exchange of Territory therein proposed, to be ceded in Lieu of Salsette, and the small Islands in the Bay, and we have inserted an explanatory Clause to this Effect, at the End of the Treaty which Colonel Upton transmitted to us for Signature.

As we did not approve of some other Parts of the Treaty, we have struck them out, and enjoined Colonel Upton to state our Reasons for so doing to the Ministers, and to use his Endeavours to obtain their Consent also to the Omission of them. The Parts to which we refer are the concluding Words of the 17th Clause, and the 13th and 17th Clauses entirely. When the Treaty shall be executed with these Alterations, Colonel Upton will furnish you with a regular Copy of it.

We are, &c.

Fort William, 6th May 1776.

General Clavering—A Doubt having arisen in the Minds of some of the Members of the Board on the Result of the Governor General's First Question, entered on the Consultation of the 6th Instant, viz.

Whether by the following Paragraph of our Letter of the 18th October, viz. " Ad- " mitting the Possibility of Ragoba's being reduced, by any unforeseen Misfortune, to " seek Refuge in some of our Garrisons, we would not have you understand, from any " Directions yet transmitted you, that we entirely mean to desert him; on the contrary, " you will find, by a Paragraph of the enclosed Instructions to Colonel Upton, that our " Intention is to obtain a suitable Provision for him; we therefore desire that you will " afford him a Sanctuary for himself and his Domestics or Attendants, in case he " should ever be necessitated to apply for your Protection, in order to avoid any perso- " nal Danger."—The President and Council of Bombay were authorized to grant the Protection

Protection of their Government to Ragoba, under the Situation of Affairs at the Time in which his Application was made to them for their Protection.

And as it is necessary that the Letter to be written to the Government of Bombay should be formed on the Resolution which a Majority of the Board may take on that Question; I must beg it may be re-considered, and a clear and precise Opinion given upon it.

Mr. Francis—The Question does not state what Application, nor when, because there were different Applications made by Ragoba when the Terms of the proposed Treaty were first communicated to him; and before it was concluded he declared his Resolution of retiring into the Company's Territories; which Resolution he afterwards waved. The intended Draft of the Letter to Bombay admits that they were authorized to receive him under the Circumstances mentioned in ours of the 18th October. I meant to condemn, in the strongest Terms, their receiving him at all since the Conclusion of the Treaty, and I assign my Reasons for it: If he be at Bombay I do not think he can be forced from thence; but I think that we ought to enjoin that Presidency, in the strongest Terms, not to give him any Encouragement to stay there.

Mr. Barwell—I have no other Opinion to deliver upon a Re-consideration of this Subject, than that which I have already recorded.

Colonel Monson—I adhere to the Opinion I gave to this Question at the former Debate, which I think was clear and precise.

General Clavering—The Permission given in our Letter of the 18th October, was restricted to the Cessation of Arms only; I am clearly of Opinion that the President and Council of Bombay are not authorized by that Letter to receive Ragoba, after the Conclusion of the Treaty with the Maratta Government; their Intention in harbouring him there is obvious. If the Ministers refuse to ratify the Treaty on that Account, the President and Council of Bombay, who have given their Sanction to his Reception there, contrary to the Spirit and Letter of our Orders, must answer for the Consequences. An Opinion given by any Member of this Board, will not justify them to the Public.

The Governor General—I adhere to my Opinion already given; still I object to the Letter, because it is not drawn up conformable to the Resolutions of the Board; but, to avoid a long Debate upon this Subject, I desire that the general Sense of the Board may be taken, Whether the Draft shall pass as it now stands or not?

Mr. Francis—As the Doubt concerning the Sense of the Board, expressed in their Resolutions of the 6th, still continues, I was going, in order to obviate all Differences in Point of Form, to propose that those Resolutions should be annulled, and that the Question should be taken up afresh; but the Governor's Motion seems to me to answer the same Purpose; I agree that the Letter shall stand.

Mr. Barwell—I cannot agree to a Draft of any Letter that does not conform to a Vote of the Majority of this Board. The present Draft is not founded upon the Resolutions of the 6th; and till the Resolutions of the Majority is fully and explicitly rescinded, I shall be very cautious how I put my Name to any Letter that may in any Respect counteract such Resolutions of the Majority.

Colonel Monson—The first Measure of the Board is to revise the Proceedings of the preceding Day, and every Member I conceive to have a Right to correct, revise, or alter his Opinion. The Letter as it now stands, is consistent with a Resolution of the Majority; I therefore approve of it.

General Clavering—I approve of the Draft of the Letter.

Governor General—I object to it in Point of Form; the Resolutions of last Council should be rescinded, and the Opinions contained in the Draft of the Letter now in Question taken as Answers to the Questions upon which those Resolutions were formed; but as it is the Substance and not the Form to which I object, and as the Second Resolution, though not formally, is subsequently repealed by the concluding Part of the Minute delivered this Day by Mr. Francis upon the First Question, I understand the whole Resolutions of the last Day to be virtually repealed, and shall wave any further Objections to it in this Place.

Ordered, That the Draft of the Letter to Bombay, recorded in the former Part of this Consultation, be written fair, and dispatched.

APPENDIX, N° 125.

RECEIVED a Letter from Colonel Upton, as follows:

Gentlemen,

I am honoured with your Letter of the 12th February, and its Continuation in Cypher, dated the 15th February; also the Preamble to the Treaty.

I am greatly concerned I was not before informed to how great a Degree you was desirous of possessing Bassein; I perceive now you wish to have it almost at any honourable Rate, though this Knowledge would have perplexed me exceedingly.

No Concession on the Part of the Company could have got us Bassein; and Eight-and-forty Hours only were left to determine, whether we chose to renew the War, or make Peace, on the Conditions I wrote on the 2d February last, which I with the greatest Difficulty had obtained, and thought very honourable and advantageous.

I conceived I fully understood the Sense you entertained of this War, and your absolute Determination to prevent the Company's being engaged in a general one with the Marattas, by putting an End to it. I thought, and still hope, I understood my Instructions thoroughly. Salsette and Bassein were not to be restored. Our never possessing Bassein, put it out of my Power to restore it; and the Ministers would not consent on any Terms to surrender it. If this was insisted on, Hostilities were immediately to have been commenced; and the Ministers swore, in the most solemn Manner, that they would carry Fire and Sword through Bengal, though the Loss of their own Country should be the certain Consequence; and that they would grant a Residence to the French, even in Poona itself. This might be the Effect of Passion only; but they seemed to have been making Preparations for the carrying Part of this Threat into Execution.

There was no Time for a Reference; Peace must take Place, and that without Delay; besides, I thought the Conditions, as I have already observed, very honourable and advantageous.

Had the Letters of the 15th February arrived soon enough for me to have proposed the Exchange for Bassein, we should have offered for it more than Twice the Value.

Broach, with the Maratta Collections granted to us, and a Country of Three Lacks per Annum ceded (in Fact in Lieu of Bassein) amount to about Nine Lacks and an Half of Rupees, besides the Twelve Lacks granted towards defraying the Expence of the War, which never would have been given whilst we were making such Offers for Bassein. Salsette we possessed, they could not get it from us: This was not the Case with Bassein.

Salsette and Bassein are the Property of the Paishwa by Inheritance, independant of the Ram Rajah. This must have been a great Bar to our ever obtaining them by Treaty, while the Brahmins are in Possession of the Peshwaship; and was now a principal Reason for their not suffering any Proposals to be made about Bassein.

I yet lament, Gentlemen, not having been better acquainted with your Sentiments before the Peace was concluded; though I hope, and am persuaded, you will approve the Measures I have taken.

I had the Honour to write you on the 21st March, advising of the final Determination of Ragonaut Row. Three Days ago I received the accompanying Letter from the Select Committee of Bombay. You will perceive, Gentlemen, Ragonaut Row has again claimed the Protection of the English. I have enclosed my Answer to the Select Committee, also a Letter from the Peshwa to me on this Subject, and Extracts the Ministers have sent me of former Treaties.

Your full Directions to the Presidency of Bombay are necessary, otherwise I fear the Articles of the Peace will with great Difficulty be carried into Execution.

The Ministers say they cannot withdraw the Army; that subsisting this Army (including the Nizam's Forces) amounts to Thirty Lacks of Rupees per Month; that we

occasion

occasion this heavy Expence to them by protecting or rather taking Part in the Disputes between them and Ragonaut Row. They declared long ago, and desired I might inform you, that should it be the Fate of Ragonaut Row to be taken by them in Battle, his Person should ever be safe.

The Sunnuds and Letters from Futty Sing are not yet arrived, the Ministers expect them daily.

The Ministers, Gentlemen, have been for some Time past expressing their great Desire to write to His Majesty; I conceive to prefer a Complaint against the Presidency of Bombay, for their unjust Attack on Salsette, &c. (though they declare not.) They hear the Nabob of Arcot has made a firm Friendship by this Means, and they wish to do so also. I have satisfied them that full Powers on the Part of the King, as well as the Company, were vested in the Supreme Council; they acknowledge this; but the Paishwa wishes to pay his Respects to the Throne. They either have or will write to request your Permission and Assistance to their putting this Wish in Execution.

Commodore Sir Edward Hughes sails with the Squadron on the 15th Instant for Madras.

I have the Honour to be, &c.

(Signed) J. Upton.

Poorunder,
10th April 1776.

P. S. At the Request of the Ministers who were desirous of writing to the Honourable the Governor General, I have delayed till this Day sending off my Packet.

I forward the Copy of another Letter from the Peshwa, on the Subject of Ragonaut Row's residing at any of the Company's Settlements.

(Signed) J. Upton,
13th April.

Copy of a Letter, bearing the Seal of Mahdoo Row Peshwa. Received by Colonel Upton on the 17th Suffer 1190 Hegira.

I have been informed by Captain Macpherson, that the Governor and Council of Bombay have brought Ragonaut Row to that Port, where they have Intentions of detaining him; since by an express Article of the Treaty he is excluded from the Protection of the English, unless he lives in Coppercanoon, and it is stipulated, that not one of the English shall afford him Assistance, notwithstanding what has been written from Calcutta, and the Powers with which you were invested, and the Character of the English for good Faith. Such a Manner of regarding Friendship and Peace was never before heard of. You are prudent, and invested with Powers from Calcutta, and will therefore attend to the Terms of the Treaty agreed to by yourself, and not afford Ragonaut Row a Place amongst the English.

Copy of a Letter, bearing the Seal of Madhoo Row, the Peshwa. Received by Colonel Upton on the 23d Suffer 1190 Hegira.

I understand that Ragonaut Row is accompanying the English Army to Bombay, where he will be permitted to live by the Governor and Council. A Peace was concluded with the English for this Reason, that Ragonaut Row might live entirely out of the Way of Family Disputes, and by no Means make himself a Party therein. What is become of the Peace now, if the Governor and Council of Bombay, who formerly assisted Ragonaut Row, now carry him to Bombay? In what Manner are the Disputes of our Family settled, while the Cause of those Disputes remains with the English? Since the Governor General and Council have deputed you to this Place, invested with full Powers, the Crime of Intrigues, of which Ragonaut had been guilty, was at your Desire forgiven, and a suitable Allowance settled for him. While he remains quiet, and fixed in the Place assigned him, the Terms of the Treaty shall not be infringed by me. He complains that his Life is in Danger. When Engagements are entered into by Men of Character, shall they not be observed? Should he fall into my Hands in the Field of Battle, his Life shall be secure.

In a Treaty which was concluded between this Government and the English of Bombay, the English engage not to protect, or in anywise assist Refugees from us, and we engage

gage to do the same; and the last Treaty, in its 15th and 16th Articles, conforms to all Sunnuds and Treaties which are not annulled or varied thereby, the same Degree or Validity as on the Day when they were executed; and the Spirit of the whole Treaty lately concluded is, that the English shall not support the Cause of Ragonaut Row; that they shall be entirely disunited from him; that they shall not afford him a Place in any of their Ports; and that the Family Dispute shall be left to me. I will write these Particulars to the Governor General and Council of Calcutta, who have concluded Peace with me. Should the Governor and Council of Bombay refuse at your Requisition to separate Ragonaut Row from them, give it under your Hands, that they do not regard your Words; and the Governor General and Council at Calcutta, will not assist the English at Bombay. What shall I write more? I before represented to you these Circumstances summarily, and have now represented them fully.

First Treaty concluded in the Time of Serrimunt Pundit, and in the Government of Mr. Stephens, by Capt. Hecherbar, at Bassein, in the Year 1140, Bachupoory.

Article the 7th. The English shall not in any Shape assist the Enemies of the Sircar (Maratta Government) not even if they should be their own Friends. In the same Manner, the Enemies of the English shall not be assisted by the Sircar.

Second Treaty concluded at Poona on the Part of the English, by John Spencer and Thomas Byefield, Esquires, in the Year 1157, at Beechipory.

Article the 18th. The Engagements which subsisted in former Years between the Sircar and the English, shall now be in Force between the Parties.

Third Treaty between the Sircar Row Pundit Purdhan, and Charles Crommelin, Esquire, President and Governor General of Bombay, concluded in the Year 1162.

Article the 3d. The Dependants of the Circar have been strictly ordered, in case any of the Servants of the English, whether principal Servants or inferior, shall desert from the English and come to them, to confine them, give Notice to the General, and deliver them over to the Company's Men. In the same Manner, if any of the Servants of the Circar, principal or inferior, except Europeans, shall seek the Protection of the English at Bombay, the English shall also deliver them over to me. This is agreed between the Parties. The English shall give their Word to their Servants, and carry them away.

A True Translation.
(Signed) Henry Vansittart,
Act. Pe. & Translator.

From Balajee Jandarun. Received 17th May 1776.

I hope that by the Arrival of my former Letter you have been informed of all Particulars.

It is stipulated in the Treaty, that the Governor and Council of Bombay shall remove their Army from an Alliance with Serumunt Ragonaut Row, immediately upon the Establishment of the Peace; but more than a Month has elapsed, and the Troops have not yet withdrawn from his Assistance. Serrenaut is on his Way to that Quarter, and the English are united with him. What Colonel Upton has written for the Removal of the Army, has had no Effect. Hurry Pundit sent a Letter, with a View of adding Strength to the Peace; to which he received an Answer from Colonel Keating, the Commanding Officer of the Troops, by Lait Loll.

Being guided by Wisdom and Judgment, you have written various Letters for the Establishment of a Peace, and the Settlement of Differences, and probably some to the Governor and Council of Bombay; this is therefore surprizing. I desire that you will write in such Terms to the Governor and Council of Bombay, as may constrain them to desist from every Act which may be inconsistent with the Friendship between us; and direct them to make it their Study to strengthen the Union.

Inclosed is Colonel Keating's Letter; written on a separate Paper.

My Friend, Hurry Pundit, is obliged to retain a War Establishment, which is an Expence to the Government of 30 Lacks of Rupees per Annum: By whom shall we be indemnified for this enormous Sum?—The English have not yet desisted from Hostilities, and collect by Severities in the several Districts of Guzerat. Should Hurry Pundit

establish

establish the Authority of the Maratta Aumils, it will be said that he is causing Variances. We have been treated in this Manner before our very Eyes. You will weigh these Circumstances in the Balance of Wisdom, and write to the English at Bombay, ordering them to forbear Hostilities.

Copy of a Letter from Colonel Keating to Hurry Pandit. Received the 2 Suffer 1190 Higera.

I received your Letter of the 22d and 24th Mohurram, on the 27th and 28th of the same Month. Since the Receipt of the first Letter, which you wrote me on the Occasion of the late Transactions, I have written to you these Letters, which I hope have arrived safe.

I have there mentioned what was within the Compass of my Knowledge; but I have not to this Time received my Orders from Bombay, respecting the Peace; but I very well know that the Peace will not be approved by Serrimunt Pundit Purdhan Paishwa. He performs what it is incumbent on him to do; but what cannot be seasonably done will be seen. You write, "Let the Palm Plantation of Friendship and Union flourish:" When the Seed has not been sown, how can we reap Fruit? It is my Wish that Peace may be established in the Zellæ, in a Manner which may be be right and proper.

Copy of a Letter from Colonel Keating, in Answer to Hurry Pundit, dated the 3d Suffer, 1190 Higera; and received the 6th of the same Month.

I have this Day received Orders from the Governor and Council of Bombay, together with the Treaty; the Contents of which shall be explained to Serrimunt Paishwa. You will not march from the Place where you now are, until you hear from me, nor cross the Cuttil.

Since, agreeable to the Treaty, no Part of the Army is to molest any Part of the other, you will give Orders to all your Army not to molest any of the Servants who may pass or repass of Serremunt Paishwa. Should they meet with any Molestation, it will be known that you have not acted according to the Treaty.

Written on a separate Paper.

Since the Close of my Letter, Hurry Pundit has received a Letter from Colonel Keating, the Contents of which are so inconsistent with the Treaty that I cannot comprehend them. I am surprized, when your Superiors have invested you with the supreme Authority over the different Posts, and you have delegated that Authority in this Instance to Colonel John Upton, by whose Negociations a Treaty has been concluded, that the Governor and Council of Bombay should disregard it, and behave in Contradiction to the Rule of Obedience. I therefore conceive it to be evident, that neither Orders from Calcutta, nor even Orders from the King of England, would affect them; for Colonel Keating, a Commanding Officer amongst Men subject to your Orders, notwithstanding your repeated Letters and those of Colonel Upton, persists in a Disposition of Enmity, and would not recede from his Purposes. I refrained from Hostilities Eight Months, Five of which have passed in Negociation, Three in concerting Peace, and more than a Month has elapsed since the Conclusion of Peace. I have submitted to a very heavy Expence of my Army from a Desire of Friendship, but am under Apprehensions, if the Governor and Council of Bombay will not desist from their Measures at a Time when Colonel Upton is here, how will they behave when he leaves me? I request you will order them to observe the Conditions of the Treaty.

Copy of a Letter from Colonel Keating to Hurry Pundit, dated 8 Suffer 1190 Higera, and received the 10th.

Agreeable to the Orders I have received from Bombay I am now to advise you, that Serrimunt Ragonaut Baje Row Paishwa, in no Respect approves the Treaty which has been concluded between him, and Colonel Upton, and the Mutseddies are by no Means satisfied with it. By Article 9th he is to disband his Army within a Month. The Treaty did not arrive till Twenty-four Days after its Date, and Ragonaut was not before this Time informed of it; so that the Period remaining for the Performance of this Condition is very

very short. He is now dismissing his Officers and using Expedition, but he must exceed the Time limited by Two or Three Days, more or less; I therefore request that you will not press him to an inconvenient Haste, nor come over from the other Side of the Cuttil, but remain in your present Situation until you hear from me. In the 9th Article it is written, that after Serrimunt Ragonaut Row shall have disbanded his Army, he shall, without meeting with any Molestation, travel where he pleases, and that no one shall disturb him: I therefore enjoin you to a strict Observance of this Condition, that there may not be the least Deviation from it; should there be any, it will be an Infringement of the Treaty between you and the English.

From Saccaram Pundit. Received the 20th May, 1776.

I have addressed to you various Letters, the Contents of which you must have fully understood.

Although the Behaviour of the Bombay Gentlemen did not merit the Re-establishment of Friendship, yet your Letters, the Embassy of Colonel Upton, the Assurances which he made of your Friendship, and the Consideration of your Dignity and Superiority over the other Settlements, induced me to assent to some of Colonel Upton's Proposals, and refer others to your Justice, as I have particularly informed you in the Letter which I have before written on this Subject. Colonel Upton wrote in the customary Manner to the Gentlemen of Bombay.

The Letters received from Colonel Keating by Hurry Pundit, of which I had before transmitted you Copies, contain Subjects of Dispute, and the Gentlemen of Bombay continue to support Surrimunt Ragonaut Row, and are desirous of carrying him to Bombay. This very much surprizes me, for it is not the Nature of the English to be disobedient to Orders. However, they pay no Regard either to your Orders or Colonel Upton's Letters, and persist in their former unfriendly Disposition. If we are to judge by their Behaviour, what Opinion can be entertained of your Orders? The Rules which used to direct the English no longer exist. Consider those Orders. It is neither acting up to the Character of great Men, nor to the Principles of Sirdars; nor is it a Custom in Europe, that writing should be one Thing, and speaking another, concluding a Treaty another, and performing the Conditions of that Treaty different from all. Under these Circumstances Peace is impossible. My Army has been without Employment, and occasioned a Loss to me of Three Crores of Rupees, all which has happened in Consequence of your writing; besides which the Country of Guzerat has sustained much Damage, and the Bombay Gentlemen have, in Violation of other Treaties, been exciting Troubles. It very much surprizes me that at a Time when your Letters have been received, and Colonel Upton has written pressingly on the Subject of ceasing to support Sirrimunt Ragonaut Row, still that this should not have effected the least Change in their Behaviour, except indeed by promoting stronger Inclination to Disorders. What I have written may be the Dictates of Resentment, but Colonel Upton, who has been Witness to all Transactions, will write to you. I hope, however, for the Prevention of such Behaviour, that some effectual Measures will be adopted in Europe, and by you, that it may never be experienced in future; and that you will positively forbid every Englishman to support Serrimunt, or to have any Connections with him, or to interfere in the Affairs of our Family, or obstruct the Collections of the Chout, which is the Right of our Government; that you will order Saslty to be delivered up, and write a favourable Answer to the other Particulars contained in my former Letter, and which were referred to your Justice, and that you will take such Measures for the Establishment of the Affairs in this Quarter as may found a lasting Friendship and Confidence between us.

APPENDIX, N° 126.

To the Honourable the President, &c. Members of the Select Committee, Bombay.

Gentlemen,

I HAVE the Honour to enclose the Copy of a Letter from the Peshwa, written to me in Consequence of my having made the Ministers acquainted with the Paragraph in your Letter of the 31st of last Month, respecting Ragonaut Row's having claimed your Protection, and that he intended proceeding to Bombay. The Ministers have also sent Extracts of former Treaties, which I forward for your Perusal.

You will be pleased to observe, I had before informed the Ministers with Ragonaut Row's final Determination, of which you advise me in your Letter of the 17th Ult. This, therefore, in a great Measure becomes a fresh Engagement with Ragonaut Row, and I cannot help thinking, as I mentioned in my last, as an Infringement of the Treaty—"We are not to take any Part in the Maratta Disputes"—as few Obstructions as possible should be put in the Way to prevent carrying into Execution the Articles of the Treaty.

In the Extract you have been pleased to forward me of Lieutenant Colonel Keating's Letter, dated 25th March, 1776, I cannot help noticing the Two following:

Paragraph 1st. "This Morning, agreeable to your Orders, Peace between the Honourable Company and the Poona Ministers was proclaimed at the Head of the Honourable Company's Forces now under my Command."

Is it possible Colonel Keating could have proclaimed the Peace in the Manner related by this Paragraph? The First Article of the Treaty informs, when the Peace had taken Place, and the Names of the Ministers who acted on the Part of the Maratta State. The Second Article directs, that Peace shall be forthwith proclaimed between the Honourable Company and the Maratta State, &c. &c.

If Colonel Keating has proclaimed the Peace in the Manner he writes (between the Honourable Company and the Poona Ministers) it may be productive of Doubts and many Inconveniences; what these may be, will occur to you, Gentlemen, without my further remarking.

Paragraph 5th. "In Consequence of the Claim of Ragonaut Row, I made him acquainted that I had received your Honour, &c. Orders to afford him Protection; he will proceed to Bombay as soon as proper Opportunity offers. His own Elephants, Horses, &c. he means to send into the Neighbourhood of Broach, under Escort of the Detachment belonging to that Garrison."

All I shall observe on this Paragraph is, that it will be a fortunate Circumstance if the Detachment escorting Ragoba's Elephants, Horses, &c. is not attacked by Hurry Punt Furkia, or some detached Part of his Army; as (if Ragonaut Row did not accept the Compromise) he had Orders to be very attentive to his Motions. I have not mentioned the latter Part of this Paragraph to the Ministers, and wish it may have passed unnoticed.

I cannot close this Letter without observing, that I wrote on the First of last Month to Ragonaut Row, informing him that Peace was that Day concluded with the Ministerial Party, and acquainted him with the Terms stipulated for him. To this Letter I received his Answer. Colonel Keating wrote to you, Gentlemen, on the 11th and 12th March, advising of Ragonaut Row's Determination in Consequence of what was agreed upon for him; yet I perceive by the 4th Paragraph of the Extract of Lieutenant Colonel Keating's Letter, that Ragonaut Row had supposed he was to have been supported by the English so late as till the 24th March. To what End could Colonel Keating's prior Conversations on the Subject of the Peace and Stipulation have tended?

I understand the Ministers have not sent a Vackeel to Bombay as they promised, to have explained any Difficulties that might have arisen, and they now refuse to send one.

I have the Honour to be, &c.

(Signed) J. Upton.

Poorunder,
8th April 1776.

APPENDIX, N°. 127.

Extract of Bengal Secret Consultations, dated the 16th May 1776.

PRESENT,

The Honourable Warren Hastings, Governor General, President,
Lieutenant General John Clavering,
The Honourable George Monson,
Richard Barwell, and Philip Francis, } Esquires.

THE Proceedings of the 15th Instant read, and approved.

Resumed the Consideration of the Letter from Colonel Upton, received and recorded Yesterday.

General Clavering—In the Letter that was read Yesterday from Lieutenant Colonel Upton of the 10th April, he acquaints us, that our full Instructions are necessary to the Presidency of Bombay to prevent their receiving Ragoba, otherwise he fears that the Articles of the Peace will with great Difficulty be carried into Execution. It is true the Board have already expressed their Sentiments on this Subject in very strong Terms to the Gentlemen of Bombay; they have set before them the Consequences which they apprehend will ensue from their receiving Ragoba, and have left it with them to answer for the Event. Such an Admonition would probably suffice to enforce a Compliance with our Directions from the other Presidencies; but the President and Council of Bombay, who have presumed to violate a solemn Peace in Opposition to the known Intentions of the Court of Directors; who in the Face of an Act of Parliament gave Orders to commence Hostilities, who signed the Treaty of Surat, and gave their Sanction to that of Brodea, concluded and guaranteed by Colonel Keating; who evaded our Orders to withdraw their Troops into their Garrisons when Colonel Upton was deputed to Poona, and still more, who furnished their Cannon to carry on the Siege of Amadahad during the Suspension of Hostilities; I repeat, that after such Proof of Contempt of all Authority, I think it is not merely sufficient to caution them; we should add our positive Orders that they should send away Ragoba from the Company's Settlements. If it should be objected, that those who have on so many Occasions been disobedient before, will not scruple to be so again, under Pretence of their Faith being pledged to Ragoba, together with the Danger which they affect to entertain for his Person, it may be answered, that we have it particularly in Charge to preserve the Peace of India, and that we cannot suffer the Danger of exposing the Company's Possessions to the uncertain Event of a War, to stand in Competition with their Scruples, if they were even well founded.

They ought to know, that a great Nation is as jealous of its Honour as it is of its Rights; that receiving the Pretender by any Potentate in Europe was deemed in England to be equivalent to a Declaration of War; and that if it were permitted to the dependent Parts of any State not to acknowledge the Conditions of a Treaty, or not to carry them into Execution, a Peace could never be established or maintained between one Nation and another.

I submit these Considerations to the Wisdom of the Board, and whether it be not expedient to prohibit expressly the Presidency of Bombay, to receive Ragoba in any of the Company's Possessions, and in case he should be there before this Letter reaches them, that they be commanded to send him away.

Notwithstanding Colonel Upton has already remarked, in his Letter to the Presidency of Bombay of the 8th April, the Impropriety of Colonel Keating's Publication of the Peace, which he ought to have proclaimed by virtue of the Second Article in the Name of the Honourable the East India Company and the Maratta State, instead of that of the Poona Ministers; yet, lest the Presidency of Bombay should not have altered the Terms of the Proclamation in their Orders to their several Subordinates, I beg Leave to offer it as my Opinion, that it would be adviseable, in order to obviate all Doubts and Uncertain-

 ties

ther concerning the Authenticity of the Treaty, that they should be directed to proclaim it expresly in the Manner of the Maratta State.

I further submit it to the Consideration of the Board, whether it would be likewise adviseable to inform the Ministers at Poona, through Colonel Upton, with the Orders we have given to the Presidency of Bombay.

The Question contained in the General's Minute being put, the Members of the Board deliver their Opinion as follows:

Mr. Francis—I have already delivered my Opinion of the Conduct of the Presidency of Bombay, in offering a Retreat to Ragoba, and of the Consequences which that Measure may produce. If he be not actually at Bombay, I agree that we should give them positive Injunctions not to receive him; not that I think the Terms of the Treaty expresly preclude us from suffering him to reside within the Company's Territories, but because I deem it impolitic and hazardous. If he be now at Bombay, I would not order him to be removed by Force; but I would insist upon their not affording him the least Support, Countenance, or Encouragement to remain; and I would declare them answerable for all the Consequences of their retarding the Ratification of the Treaty. In that Case I believe there is no Likelihood of his remaining long in so disgraceful a Situation, or that the Presidency of Bombay will venture to keep him: Our Intention in this Respect, and our Resolution never to afford Ragoba the least Assistance against the Maratta Government, may be fully explained to them by Colonel Upton.

I think, if Colonel Keating has proclaimed the Peace in the Terms mentioned by Colonel Upton, he is highly blameable; and that Proclamation should be again made in the Manner proposed by General Clavering.

Mr. Barwell—I think it is immaterial, whether Ragonaut Row be at this Instant at Bombay or in the English Camp. He has already put himself under the Protection of the English Government, and I think that Protection should be continued to him while he chuses to remain under it. The Circumstances of Ragonaut Row, under which he chuses to decline accepting the Establishment proposed for him by the Poona Ministers, plainly indicate that his Acquiescence is denied simply under the Apprehensions he entertains of the Acts of his Enemies. The Choice that is left to him is to submit himself a State Prisoner to the People, whom he stiles himself his Subjects, to put his Life to the Risk, by unreservedly placing himself in their Hands; or to demand an Asylum with those who were lately bound, under a solemn Engagement, to place him at the Head of the Maratta State. He has chosen the latter; and I think it will neither be consistent with the Honour or Justice of this Government, to become either the Instrument of his Imprisonment or his Death. If such Sacrifices are expected from the English Nation, to purchase a Peace from the ruling Faction of the Maratta State, I disclaim and protest against them; and I conceive the Demand now made for the delivering up Ragonaut Row, as well as the continuing the Maratta Army in the Field, as obvious Marks of the Spirit of Enmity and Resentment that I expect will break out as soon as the Maratta Government is so established as to allow the present ruling Faction to pursue Measures against the English, with the least Probability of Success. The Letters from Ballajee Pundit and Siccaram Baboo, on the Treaty executed by them, I cannot view in any other Light than as a strong Protest against the Treaty itself, and a plain, open, and avowed Declaration, that they will esteem the State authorized to proceed to Hostilities, as soon as its political Interests may admit of such a Measure. I am against the general Proposition for dismissing Ragonaut Row from Bombay, should he be there, or for directing that Presidency to refuse to receive him, should he seek an Asylum in their Settlement: At the same Time I would give the strongest Assurances to the Poona Government, that no Assistance of any Kind shall be afforded to Ragoba, or any Pretensions he may advance abetted by the English Government; but that they are determined, to the utmost of their Power, to give such Security as they may be enabled to the Person of Ragoba; and that they cannot, in Justice or Honour, refuse him a Residence in Bombay, or at any of the other Presidencies.

I think such a Proclamation of the Treaty of Peace, as is recommended by the General, should be directed.

Colonel Monson—I agree to the First and Second Propositions made by the General they being in a great Measure consistent with an Opinion I gave some few Days since;

 they

they are the best Proofs that can be given to the Maratta State, of the Intentions of this Government to preserve inviolate the late Treaty concluded with them. While Ragonau remains at Bombay, they will have sufficient Cause to mistrust our Intentions. He must have been received there with a View to encourage Intrigue, and occasion Jealousies and Suspicions between the Maratta State and the English Government. I approve of the Two last Propositions mentioned by the General.

Governor General—I object to all the Terms of the General's Proposition; to the Two First, namely, to refuse to Ragoba Protection if he should require it, and if granted already, to withdraw it from him, because it is contrary to good Policy, and not required by the Terms of the Treaty. I object generally to all, because, from the very extraordinary Declaration made by Siccaram Baboo, in his Letter received the 1st April, read in Consultation the 17th, and recorded in the Persian Correspondence, No. 6, I doubt the Validity of the Treaty on the Part of the Maratta State, and shall never think it binding on the Company while a Latitude is avowedly claimed by the opposite Party to declare it null, whenever the Caprice or Interest of the Rulers shall excite them to break it.

General Clavering—Although the Terms of the 10th Article in the Treaty concluded by Colonel Upton, express no more than that we shall not assist Ragoba, yet I agree with the Poona Ministers, in the Letter from the Paishwa, in thinking that the Spirit of the Treaty implies, that he should not be received by us. This Treaty, which confirms those between the Government of Bombay and the Marattas, dated in July 1739 and 12th October 1756, which are probably referred to in those Articles which they have sent to us; the First concluded with Mr. Stevens; the Second with Messrs. Spencer and Byfield; the Third, which they have likewise referred to us, and which appears to be the same that is entered in the Book of Treaties, No. 12, expresly declares in the Third Article, "that whatever People, Europeans of all Nations excepted, who are in the Service of Maddoo Row, shall be delivered up on the same Terms and Conditions." If therefore the Gentlemen of Bombay thought themselves bound by the Conditions of former Treaties, they certainly should not have received him, unless they meant to give him up. I should be sorry to see the Conditions of these Treaties enforced so far, although I cannot feel that Respect for a Man who has been represented to the Court of Directors, by the late President and Council, as the Murderer of his Nephew. Mr. Barwell has said, that he "conceives the Demand now made for the delivering up Ragoba, "as well as the continuing the Maratta Army in the Field, as obvious Marks of the "Spirit of Enmity and Resentment that he expects will break out as soon as the Maratta Government is so established as to allow the present ruling Faction to pursue "Measures against the English with the least Probability of Success." If that should be the State of the Case, though I cannot admit any Design of delivering up Ragoba, he must allow that the Government of Bombay has reduced the Company into that disagreeable Dilemma of either not making Peace with the Ministers, or the supporting the Claim of a Man whom the late Administration have declared, in their Letter to the Court of Directors, dated 17th January 1774, Par. 6, was "the Murderer of his Nephew;" and in another from the Select Committee, dated 17th March 1774, Par. 6, that "he had obtained the Command by exceptionable Means." I leave the Argument there, contenting myself with having used my utmost Endeavours to establish a firm Peace with the Maratta State, in Opposition to the various Means that have been employed both at Bombay and at this Place, to prevent its taking Effect.

Governor General—I shall never acknowledge any implied Terms by Deductions from former Treaties, in a Treaty expresly concluded between the present Rulers of the Maratta State and this Government, as applicable to the Person of Ragoba, who was the principal Object of it; neither do I allow the Construction put on the 3d Article of the Treaty of 14 September 1761, which stipulates, "that the Servants of Maddoo Row, "who desert to the English, shall be delivered up to him." Ragoba, the Competitor of the Peshwa, can by no Construction be said to be his Servant. Much Stress has been laid upon an Expression in one of the General Letters of the late President and Council, in which Ragoba is stiled the Murderer of his Nephew; as if it made it criminal in this Government to hold any Connection with him: The Words alluded to are as follows: "By these Advices we learn, that there prevails great Distractions among the Maratta "Powers; that Ragoba, the Murderer of his Nephew, has marched with an Army of "60,000 Men to attack Nizam Ally." These Words, which have no immediate Relation to their Context, were certainly neither meant to convey a formal Charge against Ragoba,

Ragoba, nor an Acquittal of his Accomplices.—The Fact, as I have always understood it, and as it is generally admitted, is, that Ragoba obtained the Peshwaship by the Murder of his Nephew, perpetrated by the immediate Authority of Siccaram Bappoo and his Partisans; that these, who were at that Time in the Possession of the Offices which they have ever since held, were the principal Authors; and Ragoba, who at that Time was a Prisoner, was their Accomplice; there is therefore at least as strong an Objection to any Kind of Connection to the Party of the Ministers as with that of Ragoba; but in Truth, I hold the Objection to have no great Weight on either Side. The Company would have much to answer for indeed, were it necessary to adopt all the Vices and Crimes of those with whom they have at any Time been engaged by any political Tie or Connection; for the rest, I declare that I do most firmly and sincerely wish for a sure and lasting Peace with the Marattas; but I differ from the General, and other Members of this Board, in my Opinion of the Means by which it is to be effected; believing in my Heart, that every Concession beyond the strict Letter of Right, will eventually prove an Acceleration of the Breach which it is intended to prevent.

General Clavering.—I have carefully examined all the Records in this Council, to ascertain the Fact of the Murder of Narrain Row. Mr. Mostyn, in his Letter, 31 August 1773, to the Select Committee at Bombay, says, "That Ragoba was upon the Stairs "when his Nephew ran into his Arms, and begged of him to save his Life, and take "the Government." And in his Letter, 9th September 1773, to this Government, he declares, "That Two Soubahdars, Mahomed Esoof and Summer Sing, had been "brought over to Ragoba's Interest, who had been closely confined for some Time past "by his Nephew, fled to the Palace with about 500 Men, on Pretence of being mustered; and after having cut off the Guards at the Gates, rushed in and killed Narrain Row: About an Hour after, Ragoba was proclaimed in the Town without Bloodshed." He however adds, "That from what he can learn, most of the Ministers "were concerned in this Affair." I perceive likewise in a Letter from the late Vizier, entered in Consultation 26 November 1773, that speaking of this Murder, he says, "That "the Peshwa was assassinated by Order of Ragonaut Row." I do not suppose that the late President and Council meant to convey any Charge against Ragoba when they spoke of this Fact to the Court of Directors on Two separate Occasions; they intended probably to inform the Court of Directors of the Facts, as they understood them at that Time.

Whether the Governor General has formed a different Opinion of this Business, I cannot conjecture; he probably can refer to the original Correspondence, which gave him the Information.

Governor General—I should be sorry to lose more of my own Time, or to swell the public Records with the Discussion of so unimportant an Argument; I shall therefore conclude my Part of it by remarking, that I could produce from the Persian Correspondence, Evidence as good as that of the late Vizier, against Siccaram Bappoo and his Associates; and by declaring, that my Opinion of the Concern which Ragoba had in the Assassination of his Nephew, was precisely the same when I first heard of that Event as now, as it will evidently appear, even in those Minutes in which it is disputed.

Resolved, That the following Letters be written to Bombay, and to Lieutenant Colonel Upton.

To the Honourable Wm. Hornby, Esquire, President, &c. Council, Bombay.

Gentlemen,

By the Letter which we wrote you on the 9th Instant, you have been fully apprized of the Sentiments we entertain of the Protection afforded by your Presidency to Ragoba, and of the Consequences likely to result from it.

We have been advised by Colonel Upton, since the Date of that Letter, of the Disgust which the News of this Measure had given to the Ministers. In the Letters to him upon that Occasion, written under the Seal of the Paishwa, they have exclaimed loudly against it, as being repugnant to our Professions of Amity, and contrary to the obvious Spirit of the Treaty. The Distrust and Jealousy which you have raised in their Minds, cannot fail to work upon them, and to prevent any cordial Union between us, and probably to produce more fatal Consequences if the Cause of them be not removed; we therefore direct, that if this Letter should reach you before Ragoba has taken Refuge in Bombay,

or

or any of your subordinate Settlements, that you on no Account receive him; and in case he should be actually at Bombay, or elsewhere within the Limits of the Company's Territories, when you receive this Letter, we insist that you do not afford him the least Support, Countenance, or Encouragement, to continue there; and we must at the same Time repeat, that we shall hold you answerable for all the Consequences of this imprudent Step, should it prove the Cause of retarding the Ratification of the Treaty, or be the Occasion of a Renewal of the War.

We observe a Paragraph in Colonel Upton's Letter to you of the 8th April, expressing his Suprize that Colonel Keating should have proclaimed the Peace as having been established between the East India Company and the Poona Ministers, instead of the Maratta State. The Impropriety of using these Terms on our Part, is so obvious, that we can scarcely credit Colonel Keating's having made Use of them; but if he did, we direct that a Proclamation of Peace be made, if not already done, in all the Company Possessions under your Controul, expresly in the Name of the Maratta State.

We request that you will cause Copies to be made of all the Treaties which are now in Force between your Presidency and any of the Country Powers, or which may at any Time have been guaranteed by you, and take the first Opportunity to transmit them to us.

We are, &c.

Fort William,
16th May 1776.

To Colonel Upton.

Sir,

We have received your Letters of 20th and 21st March, and 10th April, with a Postscript of the 13th.

We enclose Copies of Two Letters which we have written to the President and Council of Bombay, and refer you to them for our Sentiments and Directions, respecting the Protection which they have tendered to Ragoba.

We desire you will inform the Ministers, that we have given peremptory Directions to the President and Council of Bombay, not to receive Ragoba under the Company's Protection; and in case he should be actually at Bombay, or at any of their subordinate Settlements, when they receive our Letter, we have ordered them not to give him the least Support, Countenance, or Encouragement, to remain there. You will accompany this Communication with the most solemn Assurances in our Name, that we are determined never to give him the least Assistance against the Maratta Government.

We are, &c.
Warren Hastings,
J. Clavering,
Rich. Barwell,
P. Francis.

Fort William,
16th May 1766.

APPEN-

APPENDIX, N° 128.

Extract of Bengal Secret Consultations, the 2d May, 1776.

PRESENT,

The Honourable Warren Hastings, Governor General, President,
Lieutenant General John Clavering,
The Honourable George Monson,
Richard Barwell, } Esquires.
Philip Francis, }

READ, and approved the Consultation of the 29th Ultimo.
Received the following Letter from Fort Saint George.

Honourable Sir, and Sirs,

By the Swallow Sloop of War that arrived here Yesterday, we received a Letter from the Governor and Council of Bombay, together with an Extract of the Treaty concluded by Colonel Upton with the Maratta Ministry at Poona, Copies whereof come enclosed.

As this Event renders it unnecessary for us to reinforce that Presidency as we intended, with Two Battalions of Sepoys, we shall countermand the Orders we had given those Troops, to hold themselves in Readiness to march to Anjengo.

We have the Honour to be, &c. &c.

Fort Saint George, (Signed) George Stratton,
15th April 1776. &c. Council.

My Lord and Gentlemen,

The last Letter we received from your Presidency was dated the 13th of December, and we have not yet heard of the Grenville's Arrival upon the Malabar Coast.

On the 1st Instant Colonel Upton concluded a Treaty of Peace between the Honourable Company and the Ministers at Poona; and for the Information of your Lordship and Council, we enclose a Copy of the Extract transmitted to us by him.

We have given Orders for our Troops returning into Garrison, and as Opportunities offer we shall send round the Detachment of Europeans, and Captain Kelly's Battalion of Sepoys belonging to your Presidency.

His Majesty's Ship Dolphin, Captain Pigot, failed for England the 22d of this Month.

We are with Esteem, &c.

Bombay Castle, (Signed) William Hornby,
24th March 1776. &c. Council.

Extract of Bengal Secret Consultations, 20th May, 1776.

PRESENT,

The Honourable Warren Hastings, Governor General, President,
Lieutenant General John Clavering,
The Honourable George Monson,
Richard Barwell, } Esquires.
Philip Francis, }

Read, and approved, the Proceedings of the 16th Instant.
Received the following Letter and Enclosure from Fort Saint George.

Honourable Sir, and Sirs,

We have this Day received a Letter from the President and Council of Bombay; Copy thereof we have the Honour to enclose for your Information

We are, &c.

Fort Saint George, (Signed) Geo. Stratton, &c.
2d May 1776. Council.

To

To the Right Honourable George Lord Pigot, President and Governor, &c. Council at Fort Saint George.

My Lord, and Gentlemen,

We have lately received a Letter from the Governor General and Council, wrote upon a Supposition that Colonel Upton's Negociation was broke off, and that Hostilities were renewed between us, and the Ministerial Party: In this Case they have taken off the Restraint they formerly laid us under, and seemed determined to prosecute the War with the utmost Vigour. It appears they have signified their Intentions upon this Head to your Lordship and Council; and they have also declared to Ragoba, in the most express Manner, their Resolution to support his Cause.

Though by the Treaty concluded by Colonel Upton, so contrary to their Expectations, the State of Affairs is become very different from what it was imagined by the Governor General and Council at the Date of these Letters, we think our Situation is still rather precarious. Their Declarations to Ragoba being very unreserved, lead us to expect Applications from him, which we shall be embarrassed how to answer; and the Overtures they have ordered to be made to Hyder Ally, Nizam Ally, Moodajee Bouncello, Mahadajee Scindea, and Tookajee Holkar, will naturally alarm the Ministerial Party, and give them Cause to doubt our Sincerity. We do not think the Ministers shew much Inclination to perform their Part of the late Treaty; and indeed we doubt their Ability in some Points. Their Grabs have very lately made Prize of some Merchant Boats from under Convoy of a Company's Cruizer, and all Intercourse of Trade or Correspondence with their Dominions is still prohibited. Ragoba is so largely in Arrears to his Army, that he will find the utmost Difficulty in disbanding them; and he has refused to accept the Terms stipulated for him by Colonel Upton. Thinking his Life would be endangered by putting himself so entirely in the Power of his Enemies, he has claimed our Protection, which we esteemed ourselves bound, by every Tie of Honour and Humanity, to grant him; and this the Ministers pretend to term an Infringement of the Treaty.

There is also every Appearance of further considerable Commotions in the Maratta State, owing to a Party being formed in Favour of Subida, a Descendant of the Paishwa Family, and next in Succession to Ragoba; with whom, it is said, he means to associate, in Opposition to the Ministers.

While Affairs are in this uncertain Situation, we think it highly expedient to maintain a respectable Force, and to be provided against all Events; we have therefore determined to defer returning the Madras Detachment, as we at first intended, until we can judge how far this Presidency is likely to be affected by any of the above Circumstances.

We remain with Esteem, &c.

Bombay Castle,
15th April 1776.

(Signed) William Hornby, &c.
Council.

A true Copy.
(Signed) D. Baine, Dy. My. Sy.

APPENDIX, N° 129.

Honourable Sir, and Gentlemen,

WE had the Honour to address you on the 30th Ultimo, by His Majesty's Ship Sea-Horse, and have since received your Letter, dated the 29th January.

We have lately received repeated Accounts that Sudaba, who has been kept in Confinement for many Years by the Poona Government, has effected his Escape from Rhotna Gheriah, and is already joined by several Maratta Chiefs, and a considerable Body of Forces. It is said, that he claims the Office of Regent of the Maratta State, either for himself singly, or jointly with Ragoba, during the Minority of the young Paishwa, in Opposition to the Pretensions of the Ministers; but we have yet no further Particulars of of his Proceedings, than what are contained in the enclosed Copies of Two Letters from the Resident at Fort Victoria. Sudaba is the Son of Chimmajee Oppah, the Brother of Bajerow, who was Ragoba's Father, and consequently, next to Ragoba, is entitled either to the Peshwaship or Regency of the Maratta Empire. At the famous Battle of Paniput, in the Year 1761, Sudaba was supposed to be killed; but some Time afterwards a Person made his Appearance at Poona, greatly disfigured with Wounds, who asserted that he was Sudaba, and of which, it is said, he gave most convincing Proofs; but the Government did not think proper to acknowledge him, and have kept him in Confinement ever since. This is the Person who is started up in Opposition to the Ministers, and we apprehend will occasion much Commotion in the Maratta State.

We have the Honour to be, &c.

Bombay Castle, (Signed) Wm. Hornby, &c. Council.
10th April 1776.

Honourable Sir, and Gentlemen,

Enclosed are Duplicates of our Letters, dated the 30th Ultimo, and 10th Instant.

We have since had the Honour to receive your Letter, dated the 7th of March, with the enclosed Copy of that to Ragoba, and we must confess we greatly regret, that Affairs are not in the Situation you imagined, because the Treaty concluded by Colonel Upton so contrary to your Expectations, appears to us inglorious, and dishonourable to the Company, and the Terms thereof entirely inconsistent with your Instructions to him.

We conceive our Duty to the Company now calls upon us to give you our Opinion of this Treaty, and it is grounded upon the Articles respecting Ragoba, the Stipulation for our Treaties being destroyed in Presence of the Maratta Ministers, the valuable Restitution to be made, all the Conditions on our Part to be immediately performed, the distant Periods assigned for the Ministers Performance of their Part, the general Superiority given them throughout, the entire Omission of Bassein, and the Reference respecting Saisette.

The Treaty also appears to us to be defective in other essential Points, which we think may affect its Validity; the Name of the Paishwa is not inserted in the Extract transmitted to us, the Terms Row Pundit Purdhan being only Titles annexed to that Office, and applicable to every Paishwa; neither does it seem to us that the Treaty has been signed nominally and individually by the Maratta Chiefs, agreeable to your Instructions, which was particularly necessary in the present Case.

We observed to Colonel Upton in the Course of our Correspondence, that it was by no Means necessary a Treaty should be concluded at all Events, as we were far from considering Ragoba's Cause as irretrievable if the Negociation with the Ministers was to break off; and we have not a Doubt, if the War had been prosecuted upon the vigorous Plan you had adopted, it would soon have been brought to an honourable Conclusion, the Company have secured great and solid Advantages, and a general Peace have been established upon an equitable and permanent Footing; which, we are sorry to say, seems far from being the Case at present.

We have not yet experienced any good Effects from this Treaty. The Ministers do not permit of any Communication or Intercourse with the Maratta Dominions, to the great Detriment of the Company's, and private Trade, and we hear lately, that no Persons dare apply for Permission to come to Bombay from the neighbouring Parts, even with the trifling Articles of Vegetables and Fruit. Within these few Days, they refused Permission for Major Wear, of your Establishment, going to the Hot Wells for his Health, which has ever hitherto been freely allowed of. This Conduct does not shew much Disposition in the Ministers to be upon Terms of Friendship with us, and is, we think, very injurious to the Credit and Reputation of the Company, after the Peace has been so long concluded; but the Proceedings of the Maratta Fleet afford still less Demonstration of their pacific Intentions.

They very lately took Six Merchant Botellas, with English Passes and Colours, in their Passage from Goa to Bombay, and carried them into Gheriah. These Vessels had been under Convoy of the Company's Ship Gatton, which arrived here from the Coast the 7th Instant, but had separated from her by some Accident.

On the 4th Instant the Terrible, in her Passage from Bengal, fell in with their Fleet off Gheriah. Their Ships immediately run up on each Quarter and under the Stern of the

the Terrible, while their smaller Vessels carried off two Merchant Boats with English Colour, notwithstanding the Commander acquainted the Maratta Commodore they were under his Protection. The Maratta Commodore also demanded that the Commander, or one of the Officers of the Terrible, should come on board his Ship; which being refused, he made an Effort to take two other Vessels which were under her Convoy. But for your more full Information of the whole Transaction, we beg Leave to refer you to the enclosed Copy of the Report delivered to us by the Commander of the Terrible.

We have represented to Lieutenant Colonel Upton these Infringements of the Treaty, and recommended to him to insist upon the immediate Restitution of the Eight Vessels, and full Satisfaction for the Insult offered to a Company's Cruiser; but we do not yet know what Answer the Ministers have returned.

Colonel Upton has acquainted us, in his Letter dated the 8th Instant, that the Ministers absolutely refuse to send a Vackeel to Bombay, which he before advised us, in his Letter dated the 2d Ultimo, they intended doing, "to explain any Thing that might not "be fully comprehended."

Their Reason for this Refusal proceeds from our having afforded the Company's Protection to Ragoba, which they term an Infringement of the Treaty; and Colonel Upton has likewise embraced that Opinion, and taxed us with forming a new Engagement with Ragoba, and with interfering in the Maratta Disputes. We flatter ourselves your Honour, &c. will not view our Conduct in this Light, and that you will do us the Justice to acquit us of these Imputations; for, after the most attentive Consideration, we cannot discover that we have acted in the least repugnant to any Part either of this or former Treaties, and we could not have denied Ragoba a Sanctuary, with any Regard to the Honour of the Nation, or the Principles of Justice and Humanity. We also conceived, that your Orders of the 18th October were alone a sufficient Warrant to us, and these Orders we long ago communicated to Colonel Upton, which makes us surprized at his supporting the Ministers in such a Demand; instead of which we think they should have suggested to him the Propriety of stipulating in the Treaty, that Ragoba's Place of Residence should be left at his own Option. Ragoba is certainly under no Obligation to abide by Terms so full of Danger to his Person, settled for him without his Authority or Consent; and the Solicitude of the Ministers to get him into their Possession evinces the Justice of his Apprehensions: They refuse giving him a single Rupee, unless he will accept the Terms, and reside at the Place allotted for him. The Language they make Use of in their Representation to Colonel Upton on the Subject, is very extraordinary; they desire a Certificate from him of our Refusal to give up Ragoba upon his Application, and then that your Honour, &c. shall not assist us. This Representation is termed a Letter from the young Paishwa; and if the Ministers should break with us in Consequence of our protecting Ragoba, as this Menace seems to imply, we hope we shall be fully justified by your Honour, &c. in resisting them.

Exclusive of the other Defects in the Treaty before-mentioned, we have further to observe, that the Ministers have engaged for more than they have Ability or Right to perform. We mean, by stipulating to give up the Maratta Share of the Broach Revenues, which is in the Gift of the Guicawars alone, and thus swelling the Treaty with an imaginary Advantage. In the Division of the Guzurat Province, made in the Year 1759 between the Poona Government and the Guicawar Family, the District of Broach was assigned to the latter, and we have held several small Places ever since by Virtue of their Sunnuds, a Copy or Two of which we enclose. After the Reduction of Broach, we concluded a Treaty with Futty Sing in February 1773, wherein the Proportion of Revenues to be collected by each, was settled without any Reference to the Poona Government; and though Mr. Mostyn was then at that Durbar in Quality of Resident for the Company, no Objections were started against the Right of the Guicawars to form any Engagements they might think proper. Ragoba, in his Treaty with us, would only engage to obtain from the Guicawars a Grant of their Share, and a Vacqueel is lately arrived here from Futty Sing, to demand Restitution of the Cessions made to the Company by his Treaty with Ragoba, as the Conditions thereof are not fulfilled, and this Man positively denies all Right of the Poona Government to alienate the Guicawar Territories.

Ragoba is now in Surat, and so greatly in Arrears to his Troops that he is not able to disband them; and they are now in the Neighbourhood of that City: It is not improbable but the Ministerial Army may attack them. And to secure the Company's

Settlements

Settlements from Danger and Molestation in the Troubles likely to ensue, we have resolved to quarter our Troops in the Garrisons of Surat and Broach, during the approaching Monsoon, instead of bringing them to Bombay as we at first intended. This has obliged us to detain the Madras Detachment.

We have not any further Accounts of the Proceedings at Sudaba since our last of the 20th Instant. The Party formed in his Favour seems to be very considerable, and if this is the real Sudaba, which we have great Reason to believe, he will prove a very dangerous Adversary to the Ministers in Conjunction with Ragoba; he was always esteemed a Person of uncommon Capacity and Abilities, and formerly conducted the Administration of the Maratta Government with great Reputation. The enclosed Letter from the Resident at Fort Victoria contains an Account of his Escape from the Battle of Paniput, and of the Circumstances that happened to him afterwards, and affords some other Proofs of his being the real Sudaba.

Your Offers to Ragoba of the Company's Alliance and Support being very unreserved, lead us to expect Applications from him, which we shall be embarrassed how to answer; and the Overtures made to Hyder Ally, Nizam Ally, Moodagee Bouncello, Madajee Scindia, and Tookajee Holcar, will naturally alarm the Ministerial Party, and make them doubtful of our Sincerity. When your Intention of supporting Ragoba is published, it will doubtless add great Weight to his Cause, and weaken the Influence of the Ministers, by detaching many Chiefs who were before wavering.

From the above Representation we flatter ourselves it will appear to you, that the present Treaty is dishonourable and insecure; that it is concluded on Terms which your Substitute was not authorized to agree to; that the Ministers have not Inclination or Ability to perform their Part; that they have even actually infringed it by taking our Vessels; that they themselves, by taxing us with infringing it, and by their Menaces, deem it void; that their Government is far from being universally acknowledged by the Marattas, and does not promise much Stability; that there is every Appearance of further considerable Commotions in the Maratta Empire, by which the Company's Interest must suffer; and that there is no other Method of effecting a general Peace but by their Interference; we therefore request you will take these Circumstances, and our present precarious and disreputable Situation, into your most serious Consideration, submitting to you, whether it will not be more eligible, and more consistent with the Honour and Advantage of the Company, not to ratify the Treaty formed by Colonel Upton, but to permit us to enter into Engagements with Ragoba upon the Plan laid down in your Letter of the 7th Ultimo?

We request you will favour us with your immediate and express Directions for our Conduct; and that these Advices may be conveyed to you with all possible Expedition, we dispatch the Drake Snow with them, and also to afford Mr. Tayler an Opportunity of returning to his Station, under whose Orders we have therefore placed the Commander; but should Mr. Tayler have left Calcutta, we request your Honour, &c. will return the Vessel to us.

A Continuation of our Correspondence with Colonel Upton is enclosed; and our Troops, being now in the Surat Districts, we have received no further Letters from Lieutenant Colonel Keating.

We have the Honour to remain, &c.

Bombay Castle, (Signed) Wm. Hornby, &c.
22d April, 1776. Council.

Honourable Sir, and Sirs,

Since closing our Address of the 22d Instant, Futty Sing's Vacqueel therein mentioned, has delivered us a List of the Demands he was instructed to make by his Master; to which we shall return for Answer, that we have referred the Matter to you, and shall wait your Determination. We therefore enclose a Copy of this Paper, and request to be favoured with your Directions upon the Subject.

Ragoba has also acquainted us, that he has received Promises of Assistance from Nizam Ally Khan, upon Condition that we will engage not to assist the Ministerial Party, and therefore requested we would give him an Assurance to that Effect. A Copy of this Letter is enclosed; and likewise of another received from Ragoba, requesting that the Jewels deposited by him may be restored; but we shall wait your Honour, &c. Directions on the Subject of both these Letters.

 The

The great Loss that arises to the Company on the Remittances made from your Presidency in Specie, when reduced into Bombay Currency, occasioned by the high Batta charged on Sicca Rupees, and the Expence of Freight, induces us to request, that in your future Consignments you will send us the Patna Sonat Rupees, which for the above Reason turns out a better Remittance; and to relieve the Company from the Expence of Freight, we shall, in the Month of August next, send round one of our Cruizers to receive what Treasure you may have to send us on Account of next Year's Supply; and in the mean Time the Drake, as we before mentioned, will serve for that Purpose.

We have just received your Letter of the 11th Ultimo, and beg Leave to observe to you, that we disavowed, in the most express Manner, Ragoba's Attack on Ahmadavad, and insisted upon our Two Eighteen Pounders being returned, which had been lent him by Colonel Keating long before the Cessation of Arms had taken Place; this will be evinced by our Letter to Colonel Keating, dated the 20th October, transmitted to you by the Talbot: And Ragoba, upon our Remonstrances, acquainted us, that he had sent repeated Orders to Ameen Khan, his Officer before Ahmadavad, to discontinue the Siege, and restore the Guns; but that such Orders had not been obeyed, and that he had lost all Authority over that Army, owing to their being so largely in Arrears. We can assure you that we have avoided, with the utmost Caution, giving the least Cause for Complaint to the Ministers on our Part, and that we shall ever pay the utmost Attention to your Orders. The Reasons assigned for the Deviation in the Instance mentioned by you, will, we hope, prove satisfactory, the Necessity being so obvious, and the good Effects thereof acknowledged by Colonel Upton.

We have the Honour to remain, &c.

Bombay Castle, (Signed) Wm. Hornby, &c.
24th April, 1776. Council.

Demands made by Sadeshew Punt, Vackeel of Futty Sing Guicawar. Delivered in the 2d of April, 1776.

First. I beg that your Honour will favour me with your Letters to the Nabob of Surat; and Mr. Gambier to deliver the Office of Choutea, relating to Secajee Row, Guicawar Shumshier Bahadur, and Futty Sing Row Guicawar, to the People who they may send to take Charge of the same on the Receipt of your Letters, and that they may not be molested therein.

Secondly. My Master has granted you Sunnuds for the Purgunnahs of Chickly, Veriow, Batta, and Three Villages in the Purgunnah of Chureasy; but as nothing has been settled, I desire you will order them to be returned, and favour me with your written Orders to the Persons in whose Charge the above Purgunnahs are, to return them to the said Secajee Row, and Futty Sing Guicawar.

Thirdly. The Amount paid by Means of Colonel Keating, was in Goods, Gold, Gold Rupees, Piece Goods, Cash, Jewels, &c. conditionally, that Ragoba should get all my Master's Tannahs Property settled; which was not done; my Master's Business is unfinished, and the Money lost: I therefore request that you will either order the aforesaid Money to be returned, or get Ragoba Dadee to refund what he has received; you being a Mediator, will I hope see this done.

Fourthly. Nicorah Tupah has always been separated, and never under Broach; notwithstanding which, your Gentlemen at that Place hinder my Master's People there. Your Honour will therefore send an Order to them for to continue it to the Guicawar in the same Manner as before.

Fifthly. The Customs of Kem Cuttodrah, on the other Side of the Tappee, belongs to my Master; whereas now, the Gentlemen of Surat and Broach have turned out our Chokydeers, and have placed their own there. Your Honour will therefore order them not to hinder our Chokydeers, and to take away theirs.

Sixthly. Rodrajee Dessoy, of Chureasy, has several Accounts to settle with my Master: He owes a Balance, and we want also to receive of him such Revenues as he has recovered; but he has taken your Protection, and become an Aumildar of Chickly. This is not right; because my Master's Credit will not be preserved: Your Honour will therefore write to Mr. Gambier, not to employ him in your Business; he is a Zemindar, and must go to the Guicawar to settle with him.

Further

Further Demands made by Sadesbew Punt, on Account of his Master Futty Sing Guicawar. Delivered in on the 18th April, 1776.

First. The Guicawar's Share of the Purgunnah of Broach for the last Year, remains in the Hands of the English, which I beg may be paid to my Master, Futty Sing.

Secondly. The Merchants of Surat pay Customs in the Phorza of that Place, in which my Master has a Share; some of them, under your Protection, clear their Goods without paying what is due to my Master. Your Honour will therefore, I hope, settle this Business.

True Copies of the Translates.
(Signed) Edw. Ravenscroft, Secretary.

Translation of a Letter from Ragonath Row, Bajerow Pundit Pradhum, to the President; dated from Surat the 7th April, 1776, and received the 22d following.

After Compliments:

I am arrived at Surat, and am so much distressed for Money to pay my People, &c. that I cannot express it to you. I deposited in the Hands of Mr. Gambier, when at this Place before, my Jewels to the Amount of Six Lacks and a Half of Rupees, which I beg you will order to be returned to me, and I will then pawn them to carry on my Expences for a few Days. As these my said Jewels were deposited in trusty Hands, I hope that no Dispute will be made about returning them to me. Luxaman Appajee will give your Honour every Information about them.

Translation of another Letter from Ragonath Row, Bajerow Pundit Pradhum, to the Honourable the President; dated from Surat the 9th April, 1776, and received the same Day as the above.

After Compliments:

Jaffarood Dowleet Bahadre, an Officer belonging to Nizam Ally Khan, corresponds with me; and now informs me, that the said Nabob is willing to come and assist me; but is afraid that you will take the Part of the Ministers at Pronder: If this is done, the Business cannot go on properly; he therefore requests you will give him your Assurance, not to assist them on any Account, and then my Business will be done according to my Wishes. I have acquainted him, that I shall request you to give me this Assurance; and I have wrote Luxanam Appajee, in what Manner he is satisfied, which he will tell your Honour. I therefore beg of you to write to the said Officer, to Mr. Gambier, and to me, upon this Business, agreeable to what I have mentioned above; then will my Business be done; I shall look upon you as having effected it; and by it your Name will be exalted. I hope the above-mentioned Letters will come soon, and you may depend upon my keeping them a profound Secret; which I have no Doubt will also be done on your Part. I have sent to Luxanam Appajee a Copy of my Letter to Jaffarood Dowleet Bahadre, that he may shew it to your Honour. The Nabob of this Place refuses to pay the Amount of the Chout due to me; he wants a general Release from my Camawisdar of my Chout in full, and then he will pay him a Fourth Part thereof. Although I am in the greatest Want of Money, I cannot get my just Demands paid me; and Mr. Gambier does not interfere therein. The Nabob being under your Protection, I cannot force him; therefore, request you will write to Mr. Gambier and the Nabob about this Business.

True Copies of the Translates.
(Signed) Edward Ravenscroft, Secretary.

APPENDIX, N° 130.

GOVERNOR General—As it appears to me inconsistent with the Character of the Supreme Government, 1st. To continue a Series of verbal Disputations, much more to descend to its own Justification with its Inferiors, I submit it to the Consideration of the Board, whether it would not be most becoming, as well as regular, to decline a Reply to the Strictures upon the Treaty which are contained in the Letter from the President and Council of Bombay, dated 22d April, and merely to inform them, that we shall transmit them, with such Remarks as we shall judge necessary, to the Court of Directors. As in many Points my Opinion agrees with that of the President and Council of Bombay upon this Subject, I conceive myself not competent to answer their Arguments, but shall leave it to such of the Members of the Board as may conceive themselves more immediately affected by the Objections urged against the Treaty.

2d. I offer it as my further Opinion, that a Peace and Treaty having been concluded with the Maratta State, the President and Council of Bombay should be informed, that we are determined to abide by the former, and the Conditions of the latter, and that they should be peremptorily enjoined to abstain from every Act that may be construed an Act of Hostility against the Marattas, and that upon these Grounds we forbid their giving any Protection to Ragoba's Army, or to any Part of it, or to allow it to encamp within any Part of the Company's Territories, as this could not fail to be imputed to them as a Breach of the 12th Article of the Treaty.

3d. I offer it as my further Opinion, that the Assurance of our Neutrality required by Ragoba, in the Case of his accepting the Offers of Assistance made him by Nizam Ally Cawn, should be given to him, as it may prove the most likely Means of inducing him to relinquish the Protection of the British Flag; and further, because I see no great Cause of Apprehension from his Alliance with Nizam Ally, but the contrary; since it might eventually prove an Impediment to his contracting the like Engagements with Hyder Ally, who appears to have been even to the last the warmest Friend of his Party.

4th. I offer it as my further Opinion, that the President and Council of Bombay should be authorized to restore to Ragoba the Jewels deposited by him as a Pledge in the Hands of the Chief of Surat, as the Engagement for which they were pledged has been set aside, and the Charges of the War have in Effect been transferred, by the 6th Article of the Treaty, from Ragoba to the acknowledged Paishwa.

5th. I offer it further as my Opinion, that as this Government supposes the supreme Authority of the Maratta State to be united in and represented by the Peshwa, and the Possessions reclaimed by Futty Sing are all stipulated either to be restored to the Maratta State, or to be ceded to the Company, the President and Council of Bombay should be directed to reject the Pretensions of Futty Sing, to the Restoration of the Guicawar Moiety of the Town and Purgunnah of Broach, and for the Purgunnah of Chickley, Veriou, Batta, and the Three Villages in the Purgunnah of Chuneasy, as inadmissible; the rest of his Demands respecting Matters independant of the Treaty, and depending on Circumstances, of which we are furnished with no Materials to form any Judgment, no Instructions are required from us upon these Points, the President and Council of Bombay will of course settle them in the most equitable Manner; these being all Points of a political Nature, contained in the Letters from the President and Council of Bombay, I beg Leave to state them as distinct Propositions for the Substance of the Letter to be written in Reply to them.

Fort William, 20th May 1776.

Mr. Francis—The Preservation of Peace in India has at all Times been inculcated by the Company's Instructions to their Servants, and ought to be the constant Object of the Policy of this Government; to which a controlling Power over the political Measures of the other Presidencies was given, as I conceive, for this express Purpose. A steady Adherence to the pacific System we have hitherto pursued, seems particularly incumbent on us at the present Season, when our Advices from Europe give us too much Reason to presume,

presume, that the Nation is already in a State of Anxiety and Alarm, in which every Man, who has a just Sense of Duty to his King and Country, must take Part.

I should depart as widely from the Dictates of this general Duty, as from the real and immediate Interests of the Company, if I consented to any Measures, which, by hazarding the Security of the British Empire in India, might increase those Difficulties which now surround the Councils of the Nation. If the Peace with the Maratta State had been less advantageous than it is, I think that every Consideration of Justice, Policy, and Expediency, obliges us to carry it strictly into Execution. The Presidency of Bombay have thought fit to call it *inglorious and dishonourable*. The whole State of Facts, from the taking of Salsette to this Time, will enable the Court of Directors to determine, whether this peremptory Declaration is founded on solid Reasons, or on a Partiality to former Engagements, and an Inclination to continue the War, at all Events, in Support of Ragoba. We are not bound to justify our Conduct to them; and on this Point I agree with the Governor General, that it would ill become the Dignity of this Government to descend to an Altercation with them. But I think they should be told, that, as we are resolved to adhere strictly to the Terms of the Peace, and as *we* alone are responsible for the Consequences of that Resolution, they on the other Hand are answerable for nothing but their Obedience, which we expect shall be instant and implicit; and that we are determined not to suffer the Decision of Peace or War in India to depend on any Authority but that to which it is committed by the Legislature.

The preceding Opinion agrees with that of the Governor General, stated in the Second Proposition, so far as it goes; but I am further of Opinion, that as Ragoba has not disbanded his Army, (which until the Receipt of the present Letter I took for granted) we are expresly precluded, by the 10th Article of the Treaty, from giving him any Assistance; and that therefore he should be peremptorily required to quit Surat, and the Company's Territories.

I certainly would not take a voluntary Part in any Quarrel between Nizam Ally and the Maratta State; but I think that our giving the proposed Assurances to Ragoba might be liable to Inconveniencies. Since we are determined to detach ourselves from all Connection with him, I would not take any Step that might furnish the Maratta Government with the least Colour for suspecting our good Faith.

I think it would be beneath the Dignity of this Government to retain Ragoba's Jewels on Account of the Expences of the War; but if any Sums of Money have been advanced to him personally, those Jewels, or a sufficient Portion of them, should be answerable for the Debt.

I see no Objection to the Remainder of the Governor General's Proposition.

(Signed) P. Francis.

Mr. Barwell—I adopt entirely the Propositions submitted by the Governor General to the Approbation of the Board; they appear to me to have no other Object than giving Security to the Company, and ensuring a good Understanding between the Maratta State and the English Government. I think the Article that proposes the Restoration of the Jewels lodged by Ragoba, should be qualified; for in case the Company have any Demands upon Ragoba for Money advanced him, the Jewels are the only Security they hold for the Payment of such Loans.

Colonel Monson—I agree with the Governor General in his Proposition, that it would be inconsistent with the Dignity of this Board, to enter into Altercation with the Presidency of Bombay, upon Matters which depend entirely upon the Authority of this Board; but I am for acquainting them that our Sentiments of the Peace will not be altered by their Interpretation of the Treaty; that we shall state our Opinion of it to the Court of Directors, with our Reasons for the Propriety and Necessity of making it; that we acquire Obedience from them in all Matters; and that we shall deem them responsible to their Employers, for an Infringement of the late Treaty; and if they should be guilty of a Violation of it, that we shall be under the Necessity of exerting the Authority vested in us; that we clearly perceive they are bent on War at all Events, and will give a justifiable Cause for the Re-commencement of Hostilities, by giving Protection to Ragoba, when at the same Time that they received him, he kept his Army embodied within a few Miles of Surat, on the frivolous Pretence that they would not disband for Want of Pay; the first Instance I have ever heard given as a Reason for an Army remaining together; the Want of it is commonly the Cause of their disbanding. Such Excuses will undoubtedly

undoubtedly be regarded by the Ministers as a Violation of the Treaty, and they will in Consequence renew Hostilities, in which Measure they will be justified by the Treaty.

The Second Proposition is already answered in the foregoing.

To the Third Proposition: The Situation of Ragoba does not entitle him to make any such Requisition of us. I think it would be impolitic to make a Declaration on this Subject, as I think it might be considered as an Interference in his Favour, which would be contrary to Treaty.

To the Fourth: The Jewels should be restored to Ragoba, on his repaying the Money which has been advanced to him on their Security.

I agree to the Fifth Proposition.

General Clavering—In Answer to the Representation made to us by the President and Council of Bombay, that the Treaty lately concluded by Colonel Upton is dishonourable and Insecure; and in Answer to the Opinion, which they have offered to us, that there is no Way of securing a Peace that shall be at the same Time honourable and permanent, but by the Company interfering, and suffering their Presidency to contract new Engagements with Ragoba, I think we should confine our Answer to the following Points:

That we will not enter into a Contest with them, whether the Terms of the Treaty be honourable or not; that we are answerable to the Court of Directors for the Rectitude and Expediency of our Measures, and only require of them a strict Compliance with our Orders; and further, that we should observe to them that it would be impossible for this Government ever to establish a Peace that can be permanent, if the different Presidencies, under the Controul of this Government, shall think themselves at Liberty to cavil on the Propriety of our Measures, and refuse directly or indirectly to execute our Commands: That the Peace with the Maratta Empire, which they violated by the taking of Salsette, and their subsequent Engagements with Ragoba, was as permanent as any that we could possibly make, were even their Wishes to be accomplished of establishing Ragoba in the Peshwaship, without which they seem to think that no Peace can be permanent; but that on this Occasion we will not hesitate to declare to them, that the peremptory Orders that we now give them, to avoid every Thing which may impede the Conclusion of the Peace with the Maratta State, proceed as much from our Adherence to the positive Injunctions of the Court of Directors, as to the Consideration of the Embarrassments in which the Crown of Great Britain is now involved, which renders the Peace of India more expedient than ever: That it appears to us that the Refuge which they have afforded Ragoba and his Army at Surat, will, from their own Account, be attended with the most dangerous Consequences, since they think it not improbable that the Ministerial Army may attack that of Ragoba: That we hope that the Regard to good Faith, which the Ministers have shewn during the Suspension of Arms, will still continue, notwithstanding the Provocation they have received; but that we cannot possibly answer that they will persevere to maintain that Reserve, when they perceive that the Presidency of Bombay do not intend to perform the Conditions of the Treaty on its Part.

The Second Proposition is answered above.

The Third: I cannot agree to this Proposition, because we are engaged by Treaty not to interfere in the Disputes of the Maratta Government.

To the Fourth: That the Jewels should be restored to Ragoba, upon his paying the Money for which they were pledged.

To the Fifth: The Treaty concluded at Poona has directed what shall be restored and what retained; the Government of Bombay itself has acknowledged the Powers of the Peshwa over the Countries possessed by the Guicawars, and as I acknowledge no other Peshwa than him who is in Possession of the Government of the Maratta State, my Opinion is, that the Government of Bombay should literally comply with the Terms of the Treaty.

Agreed, That the Resolutions of the Board be collected from the foregoing Opinions, in the following Letter to Bombay:

To the Honourable William Hornby, Esquire, President, &c. Council at Bombay.

Gentlemen,

We have received your Letters of the 10th, 22d, and 24th Ultimo, by the Drake.

We think it unnecessary to enter into any Discussion with you on the Terms of the Peace lately concluded with the Maratta State; had they been less advantageous than we

are

are assured they will appear to the Company, we deem ourselves bound, by every Consideration of Prudence, Policy, and Justice, to adhere strictly to them. The Preservation of Peace in India has been at all Times the Object of the Company's Policy, and is particularly inculcated in their Instructions to us. The Difficulties with which, as you cannot but know, the Councils of the Nation are now surrounded, make it indispensably our Duty not to encrease them at so alarming a Crisis, by engaging in Measures which may affect the Tranquillity of the Company's Possessions in this Part of the World. We alone are answerable to the Company for the Consequences of the pacific System which we are determined to pursue; you, on the other Hand, are answerable for nothing but your Compliance with our Injunctions, which we expect shall be instant and implicit.

We do therefore hereby expresly direct, that you conform strictly to the Terms of the Treaty, as far as depends on your Presidency, and that you carefully avoid any Step whatsoever which may give Occasion of Distrust or Jealousy to the Maratta Government.

We had no Doubt that Ragoba would have disbanded his Army before he received Protection in Surat, until the Arrival of your Letter of 22d April. The Reasons assigned for his not doing it, seem to us very unlikely to produce the Effect you attribute to them. We have heard of Indian Armies disbanding for Want of their Pay, but never that an Army unpaid had long kept together. At all Events, your granting Ragoba the Company's Protection under such Circumstances, and suffering his Army to remain encamped within the Company's Territories, is directly contrary to the 10th Article of the Treaty, and has but too evident a Tendency to disturb the Union which has been formed with the Marrattas. Your own Words are sufficient to confirm us in this Opinion. You say, that "it is not improbable that the Ministerial Army may attack them, (Ragoba's "Army) and that Dangers and Molestations are likely to ensue to the Company's Settle- "ments." To prevent Consequences so hazardous to the Interests of the Company, we direct that you peremptorily do require him forthwith to quit Surat, and to retire out of the Company's Possessions.

Although it is by no Means our Intention to take any Part in the Quarrels between the Peshwa and Ragoba, yet we deem it impolitic and unnecessary to give Ragoba the Assurances which he has demanded from the Satisfaction of Nizam Ally. Such a Declaration would be productive of no good Consequence to us, but might raise Suspicions in the Maratta Government of our good Faith towards them.

With respect to the Jewels pledged by Ragoba, which he has now applied for, we desire, that after liquidating out of them any Advances that may have been made to him from the Company's Treasury, you will order the Residue to be returned to him.

As we suppose and admit by the Treaty, that the supreme Authority of the Maratta State is united in and represented by the Paishwa, and as the Possessions claimed by Futty Sing are all stipulated either to be restored to the Maratta State or ceded to the Company, we desire you will reject the Pretensions of Futty Sing to the Restoration of a Moiety in the Revenues of the Town and Purgunnah of Broach, and his Demand for the Purgunnahs of Chickly, Veriow, Batta, and the Three Villages in Chuneasy, as inadmissible. The Rest of his Demands respect Matters independant of the Treaty, and rest on Circumstances of which we are not furnished with any Materials to form a Judgment of; we must therefore leave it to you to settle them in the most equitable Manner.

We have taken Care to prevent the Consequences which you apprehend will result from the Measures we had adopted when we wrote to you on the 7th March, by desiring the Chief and Council of Surat to destroy the Letter written to Ragoba in case a Treaty should have been concluded, and by suspending the Dispatch of the Letters we intended to write to the other Chiefs until we found it unnecessary to dispatch them.

We are, &c.
Warren Hastings,
J. Clavering,
Richard Barwell,
Philip Francis.

Fort William,
20th May 1776.

APPENDIX, N° 131.

Extract of Bengal Secret Consultations, the 6th June 1776.

PRESENT,

The Honourable Warren Hastings, Governor General, President,
Lieutenant General John Clavering,
The Honourable George Monson,
Richard Barwell, } Esquires.
Philip Francis, }

RECEIVED the following Letter from Lieutenant Colonel Upton:

Gentlemen,

' The Peshwa has not yet been put in Possession of any of the Purgunnahs restored by the Treaty. It was necessary, it seems, that our Troops should remain in Guzerat, for the Security of the Company's Possessions in that Province; they are disposed of in Surat and Broach; the Commanding Officer at Surat, and Ragonaut Row with him there, and his Troops are encamped all around it.

' The Ministers could not conceive that this was separating from Ragonaut Row, or not taking Part in the Maratta Disputes; they had authorized Hurria Pundit (their Commandant) to receive the Purgunnahs that were to be made over. He wrote almost daily to Colonel Keating, to know when he might advance to take Possession of these Districts; and was as constantly answered, that he must remain where he was, and on no Account advance; if he did, it would be a Breach of Treaty, and he must answer the Consequences; or Answer to some such Purpose.

' Thus foiled, the Ministers complained heavily; they insisted on my writing to the Presidency of Bombay, that they might know, at a Certainty, if the Articles of the Treaty were to be permitted to be carried directly into Execution. The Answers of that Board was to determine the Part the Ministers meant to take, as well as my longer Stay at Poona.

' The Ministers had certainly very just Cause of Uneasiness; they lost their Collections in general, they were obliged to keep up their Army, they lost great Part of their Collections throughout their whole Country, and their Influence was every where visibly on the Decline; they began to suspect that we had brought them into this Lull, to take the Advantage of it. It is very certain the Sirdars in general said the Peace was not a firm one, and that the Ministers had been imposed upon.

' Their being put in Possession of their Purgunnahs, which I hope will immediately take Place, will restore that Confidence and Security they have for some Time past been deprived of.

' The accompanying Letters and Papers will inform you, Gentlemen, fully and progressively, how the Delays have been occasioned: To these permit me to refer you.

' I enclose the Substance of a Message in Confidence, to be made known to the Supreme Council only. It is a most vague, scandalous Scheme, and even their Sincerity in it greatly to be doubted. The Vackeel insisted on its being forwarded to the Board. May I request you will please, Gentlemen, to give me a few Lines in Answer for the Nabob? The Knowledge of this intended Enterprize may be of material Consequence.

I am collecting and comparing Futty Sing's Sunnuds, &c. and the Letters from the different Sirdars, acknowledging their having received, and their Obedience to, the Treaty. These I shall have ready to send off with the Treaty, which I propose doing by Lieutenant Paterson, as it will not be safe trusting them to Hircarrahs in the rainy Season, and as Lieutenant Paterson's Services will be very little wanted at that Time here.

Since

Since writing the above, I have received the Treaty executed by you, Gentlemen, with a Letter, dated 1st April. I have no Doubt but I shall be able to get the Ministers to assent to the Alteration you require. A Duplicate of this Letter of 1st April being also sent, makes me conclude some other Letter was intended, and this Duplicate by Mistake put up instead of it. I shall this Day forward the Packet for the Governor and Council of Bombay.

I am, &c.

Poorundur, (Signed) J. Upton.
6th May 1776.

Mirza Jan and Mahomed Afzil Khan delivered the following Message from the Nabob Fazil Beg Khaun Daissa, on the Part of the Nizam.

29th April 1776.

If the English are desirous of placing Ragoba in Poona in the Course of the Rains, I will join him with the Nizam's Troops. In the mean Time Ragoba, with the English Army, should proceed to Bombay, which is only about 40 Coss from Poona, and prepare their Stores, &c. On their informing me that they are ready, I will join them with all Expedition, and when he is placed in Poona, the English will have what they desire, viz. Salsette, Bassein, a Country of Twelve Lacks, the Maratta Share of Broach and its Purgunnah, with a Country of Six Lacks in the Neighbourhood of it, and keeping Possession of the Country granted by Futty Sing; also be paid a Lack of Rupees a Month for the Army, during the Time it may be with Ragonaut Row, with the Payment of the Twelve Lacks agreed to by Sacaram Bapoo. Ragonaut Row agrees to grant to the Nizam a Country of Thirty Lacks, the Fort of Asseer, the City of Burhampore, and the Forts of Shoulapore and Mulhere. The Particulars of these Places are known to Kain ud Dowlah Bahadar, Soubadar of Surat.

If the Colonel agrees to these Terms, he will, under Pretence of going to see the present Treaty carried into Execution, leave Poona, and proceed to Ragoba at Surat, where every Thing will be settled through Kain ud Dowla. The Colonel is to keep up the Appearance of Friendship with Sacaram Bapoo till the Rains come on. Moribba Pumavier is joined in the Scheme of fixing Ragoba in Poona; no Doubt he has before mentioned these Matters.

The English must protect Ragonaut Row till all these Circustances are ripe for Execution.

The Nabob has Twelve thousand Horse and Twelve thousand Infantry, with Thirty Guns, ready to join the English and Ragoba when required, after which Hurry Pundit and Saccaram Bapoo, &c. will not be able to face us; and, with the Blessing of God, we will fix Ragonaut Row in Poona without Bloodshed.

After Ragoba is settled in Poona, the Nabob does promise to make him grant to the English Company Sunnuds for the Cattack Country, and relinquish all Claim of the Chout.

The Nabob has Possession of the Fort of Aumeer, about 20 Coss from Naugpore; and if the Bhonsula should make any Opposition, he engages to subdue him, with very little Trouble to the English, if they will assist him with the following Troops; viz. Three hundred Europeans, Two thousand Sepoys, and Six Guns from Masulipatam. He will pay these Troops for the First Year 30,000 Rupees per Month; for the Second Year, Rupees 40,000 per Month; for the Third Year 50,000, and for the Sixth Year 60,000 Rupees per Month, until the Cattack Country is in Subjection.

As a Security to the Company for the due Performance of all these Conditions, the Nabob Dhaussa will give his Son as a Hostage to be in the Hands of the English, lodged in the House of Haussin Ally at Masulipatam, till the Whole is fulfilled; and the Company to be Security that Ragoba will perform his Engagements with the Nizam.

But on the other Hand, if the English are determined to keep firm to the present Treaty, and decline joining Ragonaut Row, the following Conditions are proposed:

That for these Two Months, till the Rains are fairly set in, the Time is to be taken up in settling about Ragonaut Row with the Saccaram Bapoo, &c.; he (Ragoba) is to continue in Surat till Govinrow (who is also well-affected to his Cause) comes near that Place, when the English are to remove him from themselves, and he will immediately

 cross

crofs the Tapty and Nurbudda with Govinrow. Hurry Pundit will not be able to purfue him acrofs thefe Rivers till the Rains are over.

After the Rains are fet in, the Englifh fhould difcharge Two Battalions of Sepoys, which will be entertained by Ragoba.

Hulkar and Sindea are fincerely difaffected to Siccaram Bapoo and Ballajee Pundit, and have propofed to canton near Auringabad during the Rains, and that if I would join Ragoba they would.

It is required, that as foon as the Nizam my Mafter takes Ragoba by the Hand, the Englifh will not, in any Degree whatever, affift Siccaram Bapoo or Ballajee Pundit, or afford them Protection, even were they to offer them Fifty Lacks in Money, and a Country of Fifty Lacks of Rupees more.

This to be given under the Signatures and Seals of the Councils of Bengal, Madras, and Bombay. When this Treaty is clofed, I will in the End of the Rains join Ragoba with the Nizam's Army, and with the Bleffing of God fix him in Poona.

But if the Colonel fhould not agree to fpin out the Time as above, till the Rains fet in, or to Ragonaut Row's remaining in Surat until he could join Govinrow, or to difcharging the Two Battalions of Sepoys, Ragonaut Row fhould be embarked in a Ship, and fent to Mafulipatam, there to remain until I fend for him; which I will do as foon as the above Treaty, figned by the Surat Councils, arrives to my Satisfaction, and place him in Poona by the Affiftance of the Nizam's Army.

If Saccaram Pundit and Ballajee Pundit fhould fay to the Colonel, It is agreed upon between you and us, that if Ragoba will not difband his Army, and refide on the Banks of the Gunga, the Englifh are to feparate from him, Why don't you act accordingly? The Colonel muft reply, That Ragonaut Row came under our Protection, which we cannot refufe him; but if he raifes any Commotions, you muft chaftize him. The Englifh will not affift him.

I fhould now be able to place Ragonaut Row in Poona, and the Minifters could not prevent it; but the Intention is, to fecure the Engagements of the Englifh againft affifting or protecting them, as no other Power will venture to do either.

After Ragonaut Row is fettled in Poona, I will be anfwerable for his duly fulfilling all the Articles of the Treaty entered into by Siccaram Bapoo and Ballajee Pundit, alfo granting Sunnuds for the Cattack Country, and relinquifhing the Chout.

The Cattack Country will be put in Poffeffion of the Company, on their fending Troops, &c. as already mentioned. My Son will be given as a Hoftage for the due Performance of the Conditions of the Second Propofal.

In a former Treaty, it is agreed between the Englifh and the Nizam, that the Friends and Enemies of one fhall be the fame to the other. It is requefted, that the Englifh will be attentive to their former Engagements, and now confirm them, and not join or affift any Power on which he makes War.

If the Nizam fhould carry Ragoba to Poona, the Englifh Company are not to give any Affiftance to Siccaram Pundit and Ballajee, or any of Row Pundit Pardhan's Officers, nor take any Part in the War; were they to offer them Fifty Lacks of Rupees, and a Country of Fifty Lacks of Rupees more, no Affiftance or Protection muft be given them.

It is requefted Colonel Upton will write to the Supreme Council of Calcutta, and get a Treaty under their Signatures and Seals to that Purpofe.

(Signed) An. Macpherfon,
Perfian Interpreter.

The Subftance of Colonel Upton's Reply to the Meffage fent by the Nabob Fazil Beg Cawn Dhauffa; 29th April 1776.

If the Nabob had not joined the Minifterial Army, and had fent a Vackeel to him on his Arrival at Burhampore, or immediately after his Arrival at Porunder, it might have been productive of much better Terms for the Company from the Minifters, and the Nizam's Treaty with them might have been fecured to him; but the Nabob having joined Hurry Pundit with 24,000 Men and 30 Guns, after his Arrival, made the Minifters talk high and indifferent to Peace or War; confequently, the Colonel found much Difficulty in fettling a Peace with them. Their coming now, after the Peace is eftablifhed with the Minifters, to propofe an Alliance fuch as is now offered, is fo

difhonourable

dishonourable to the English, that he must decline agreeing with them in any one Part of the Terms they propose: That he would, agreeable to the Nabob's Desire, keep it a Secret, and write to the Supreme Council; but he would not have the Nabob flatter himself with their doing any one Thing to the Prejudice of the Treaty they had lately entered into; and that he could assure him, they would not commit any Action that would reflect Dishonour on themselves or their Country.

(Signed) An. Macpherson,
Persian Interpreter.

APPENDIX, N° 132.

Extract of Bengal Secret Consultations, the 20th June 1776.

PRESENT,

The Honourable Warren Hastings, Governor General, President,
Lieutenant General John Clavering,
The Honourable George Monson,
Richard Barwell, }
Philip Francis, } Esquires.

READ again, the Letter and Enclosures from Lieutenant Colonel Upton, recorded in Consultation the 6th Instant.

Resolved, That the following Letter be written to Lieutenant Colonel Upton:

Sir,

We have received your Letter of the 6th Ultimo.

Although we approve of the Answer which you gave to the Proposal delivered to you on the Part of Fazel Beg Cawn, yet we wish that you had avoided giving so much Countenance to it as you did, in promising to transmit it to us; you would have done well if you had peremptorily rejected it. For the future we direct that you hold no Kind of Communication or Correspondence either with Nizam Ally Cawn, or any Agent in his Behalf, or indeed with any other foreign Prince or Power, during your Continuance at Poona; as such, an Intercourse would not fail to excite the Jealousy of the Maratta Government. The President and Council at Bombay, in a Letter dated 24th April, advised us of a Requisition made to them by Ragoba, which appears to have an intimate Relation with the Proposals delivered to you by the Emissaries of Fazel Beg, and was probably an Effect of the same concealed Plan. The Words of their Letter are: "Ragoba has also acquainted us, that he has received Promises of Assistance from Nizam "Ally Cawn, upon Condition that we will engage not to assist the Ministerial Party, "and therefore requested we would give him an Assurance to that Effect." In Reply to this Paragraph we told them, that "although it was by no Means our Intention "to take any Part in the Quarrel between the Paishwa and Ragoba, yet we deemed "it impolitic and unnecessary to give Ragoba the Assurances which he had demanded "for the Satisfaction of Nizam Ally; such a Declaration would be productive of no "good Consequence to us, but might raise Suspicions in the Maratta Government of "our good Faith towards them."

We have given you the above Extract from our Letter to the President and Council at Bombay in this Place, as it may serve you for a general Rule, to be applied to every similar Case that may occur during the Time of your Negociations. You will receive with this a Copy of our Letter 20th May, wherein this Subject is contained.

As Ragoba refused to be a Party in the Treaty, and has declined to accept the Conditions stipulated for him in it, we have no Right to complain of the Design declared by the Ministers to disperse his Army; we hope, however, that the President and Council of Bombay will have taken Precautions to obviate an Event so discreditable to their

their Government as the Execution of this Measure whilst Ragoba's Troops remain within the Company's Possessions, by formally requiring their Removal from thence before any Hostilities had taken Place between the contending Parties.

You do not inform us whether the Letter you received from Lieutenant Colonel Keating, of which you complained to the Government of Bombay, had been written in Reply to one from you, or what was the Cause of it; we should be glad to be informed of this Circumstance.

We are pleased to observe in your Letter to Bombay, dated the 4th May, that you had obtained an Order for the Restitution of the Vessels which had been taken upon the Maratta Coast, and that the Ministers disavowed having given any Directions which could have authorized the Seizure of them.

We are, &c.

APPENDIX, N° 133.

Extract of Bengal Secret Consultations, the 6th June 1776.

Extract of a Letter from the Honourable the President, &c. Members Select Committee at Bombay, to Colonel Upton; dated 16th April 1776.

WE acted agreeable to the Dictates of Honour and Humanity in affording the Company's Protection to Ragoba, when he solicited it, and apprehended the Safety of his Person would be endangered by accepting Terms stipulated for him without his Authority or Consent; and we think the Solicitude of the Ministers to get him into their Power evince the Justice of his Apprehensions. His residing in one of the Company's Settlements will be a much better Security against his forming Intrigues to the Prejudice of the Ministers, than we conceive their Protestations would prove for the Safety of his Person, was he to put himself in their Hands. The Letter from the Governor General and Council, dated the 20th October, is a sufficient Warrant, and we cannot allow that our merely giving him a Sanctuary is either an Infringement of the Treaty, a new Engagement with Ragoba, or taking any Part in the Maratta Disputes.

Ragoba is so largely in Arrears to his Army, that he will find the utmost Difficulty in prevailing upon them to disband. By our last Advices the Company's Forces were arrived at Domus, near Surat Bar, for the Purpose of embarking for the Presidency, but on Account of the numerous Bodies of Forces in the Neighbourhood of Surat and Broach, we have since thought it expedient to give Orders for quartering them in those Garrisons during the approaching Monsoons, to preserve the Company's Territories from Molestations.

The Communication with the Maratta Dominions is still kept shut, and all Intercourse rigorously prohibited, though the Company's Forces have been some Time within their own Districts. We do not think this shews any Disposition in the Ministers to be upon Terms of Friendship with us, &c.

We have within these few Days received a Letter from the Governor General and Council, wrote upon a Supposition that your Negociation had been broken off, and Hostilities renewed. We at the same Time received Copy of a Letter they had addressed to Ragoba, offering the Alliance of the Company, and the Assistance of their Arms to fix him in the Seat of his Government at Poona. Transcripts of both which we think it necessary to enclose for your Information.

By these Letters, the Governor General and Council shewed the strongest Determination to prosecute the War with the utmost Vigour, in Conjunction with Ragoba, rather than make a Peace upon Terms not honourable and advantageous; and it appears to be evidently their Intention that the Conditions for Ragoba should have been such as he would himself approve, and which would have insured his future Safety and Welfare. We shall expect Applications from Ragoba in Consequence of this Letter.

A true Extract.

(Signed) A. M'Pherson.

Extract

APPENDIX, N° 133.

Extract of a Letter from Lieutenant Colonel Upton to the Honourable the President, &c. Members of the Select Committee of Bombay; dated 22d April 1776.

The Ministers absolutely refuse opening the Communication into their Country, till the Army of Ragonaut Row shall be disbanded or separated entirely from the English.

The Letter you have received from the Governor General and Council was in Consequence of my Letter to them on the 7th of February. I had previously advised of the Terms I should insist on stipulating for the Company. If the Ministers refused these, the Negociation was entirely to have been broken off. In Consequence of this Refusal the Letter of the 7th of February was written, with my fullest Remarks. I had no Doubts if the Peace had not taken Place, that the most vigorous Measures would have been pursued to have secured an honourable Peace; there appeared no Alternative, it must have been made Sword in Hand.

You are already acquainted, Gentlemen, with my Sentiments regarding Ragoba's residing in any of our Settlements. The Ministers now inform me, that his Army is in the Neighbourhood of Surat. If this is true, it stands thus: Our Army is in the Guzerat Province (to this separately there can be no Objection;) the Commanding Officer, (and I presume the greatest Part of his Army) is in Surat; Ragonaut Row also with him there, and his Army under Cover of this Garrison.

I hope, and am almost persuaded, there can be no Truth in this Information. It is expressly contrary to the true Meaning of the 8th and 10th Articles of the Treaty. As I have repeatedly given my Opinion on this Subject, I shall not in future presume again to oppose it to your's; but you will please to observe, that I must bear no Part of the Blame, should this Mode of carrying these Two Articles of the Treaty into Execution be attended with any destructive Consequences.

The accompanying Paper, containing a Conversation that passed last Night with a Person deputed by the Ministers, will acquaint you better than I can otherwise do, with the Sense they entertain regarding the carrying into Execution the Articles of the Treaty.

A true Extract,

(Signed)

A. M'Pherson.

Copy of a Letter from Lieutenant Colonel Upton to the Honourable the President, &c. Members of the Select Committee of Bombay, dated the 26th April, 1776.

The Ministers have requested of me to forward to you the Copies of two Letters received by Hurria Pundit from Col. Keating.

The Ministers have now got beyond complaining; they threaten; and I conclude will not wait many Days longer inactive, if the Articles of the Peace are not permitted to be carried into Execution. They are not only losing their Collections in the Guzerat Province, but their Influence throughout their whole Country. Were they to attempt taking Possession of the restored Purgunnahs, they suppose it would occasion some Disturbances between their Troops and Ragonaut Row's, who are in the very Neighbourhood of these Purgunnahs. This they say would be of little Consequence; but as the English Troops are also near, and Ragonaut Row with them, of more fatal Consequences. They wait your Reply to my Letter of the 22d, and will then come to some Determination.

The following is an Extract of a Letter I received Yesterday from Lieutenant Colonel Keating:

" It ever affords me the utmost Satisfaction to engage in any Business that redounds to my Country's Honour, and the Interest of my Honourable Employers; but for Reasons that must be obvious to you, I must decline advising Ragonaut Bajerow to accede to the Terms stipulated for him.

" Prior to our taking any Part in the Maratta Disputes, Ragonaut Bajerow ofttimes rejected Terms preferable to those the Ministers now offer him. Before we gained any Advantage over the Confederate Army, one of the Agents made a Proposal for his being Regent, provided the English would guarantee their Employments and Property. This too he positively refused.

" During

" During the Life of Madow Row Peshwa, Ragonaut Bajerow declined a Settlement of Sixteen Lacks of Rupees per Annum, besides the Possession of Thirty-two Forts, because there was tacked to it a Clause similar to that of residing on the Banks of the Gunga, which he esteems as nothing less than a Prisoner at the Devotion of his Enemies.

" It is at Ragonaut Bajerow's Request I now write you; and which I the more readily do, since Huria Punt Furkea, in one of his late Letters to me, wishes to be informed which Part of the Treaty Ragonaut Bajerow objects to, and what he wants. He objects to every Part and Point of the Treaty, and has appealed to the Supreme Council of Calcutta, the Honourable Company, and to his Majesty, for Redress; but as a long Time must consequently elapse before a Decision can be known, during which a Provision for his Maintenance is necessary, and being desirous of preserving the Friendship of the English Nation, and avoiding a War so destructive to the Maratta Empire, and to Commerce in all its Branches, he is therefore come to this final Resolution, To accept either of the Two following Conditions, until an ultimate Settlement takes Place: The Establishment offered him by Mhadow Row Peshwa, with the Difference of residing under the English Protection; or The Poona Shaw of the Guzerat Province in its ruined State.

" If these Conditions are agreed to, Ragonaut Bajero is determined to remain in perfect Tranquillity, until all Matters are regularly settled; but if they are refused, to support his just Rights in the best Manner he is able."

The Army being withdrawn, I did not conceive Col. Keating had any further Part to take in the Business of my Deputation, as I never was informed by you, Gentlemen, that he was appointed to assist in carrying any Part of the Treaty into Execution. As this, however unknown to me, must have been the Case, I am greatly surprized to find the executing or declining what you may have directed, has been so optional to the Colonel, as the First Paragraph of the Extract plainly shews, the Whole of which I cannot well comprehend.

The Whole of this Extract requires your Consideration, as an immediate War between the contending Maratta Parties seems inevitable, without the speedy Exertions of your Presidency. I am suspected by the Ministers of being privy to the Designs of Ragonaut Row; nay, they now suspect the Supreme Council must have had Views further than to treat with them by this Delay, &c. and they have not the least Doubt of Ragonaut Row's receiving from Bombay every Assistance.

My Arguments, my Assertions to the contrary, have lost all their Force: The constant Answer is, Why the Delay in carrying the Articles into Execution? Why do our Troops all remain in Guzerat, Ragonaut Row received into Surat, and his Troops encamped around it?

As I think myself no longer safe at Poona, I have to request the Favour of your calling a Board, and coming to some immediate Determination respecting the making over the Country, restored by the Treaty to the Peshwa in the Guzerat Province. I shall impatiently wait the Resolutions of your Meeting, which will determine my longer Continuance or immediate Departure from the Place.

I have, &c.

Poorunder, (Signed) J. Upton.
26th April, 1776.

Extract of a Letter from the Honourable the President, &c. Members of the Select Committee, Bombay, to Lieutenant Colonel Upton, dated 27th April, 1776.

Our Troops have been long ago separated from Ragoba's Army, and have no Connection with it; therefore, according to the Promise of the Ministers, we have a Right to expect the Communication being immediately opened.

We assure you, that it is entirely contrary to our Inclination or Desire, that Ragoba's Army continues so near to Surat; and we are very anxious to remove them, if we knew how to effect it. Directions will be sent to the Chief and Council at Surat, to represent to him, in the strongest Manner, the Impropriety of his Troops remaining in their present Situation, and to insist upon their being removed to a proper Distance; but from his present Circumstances we are apprehensive little Regard will be paid to his Orders.

We

We remain in our Opinion, that our giving Ragoba and his Domestics an Asylum, is not contrary to any Article of the Treaty: His Army continuing so near one of our Settlements is, as we before said, entirely against our Inclination, and we will do all in our Power to remove them. Any Conferences he may have with Col. Keating, can be of no Consequence, as the latter is entirely under the Orders of the Chief and Council at Surat, and is now shortly expected at Bombay.

We hope you will not give the smallest Degree of Credit to the Information of the Ministers, that Ragoba has been supplied with Guns and Military Stores; as we never gave the least Authority to Colonel Keating, or any other Person, for that Purpose.

They complain, without Reason, of the Purgunnahs not being restored according to the Treaty; it is entirely their own Fault that they have not received them long ago, as we sent Orders on the 16th of last Month, to the Councils at Surat and Broach, to evacuate them whenever Persons properly authorized on the Part of the Ministers came to receive them. For your Satisfaction we enclose Copies of these Orders, which we know have been received at both Settlements; and by the best Advices, dated the 11th Instant, from Broach, and the 20th from Surat, no Agents had then arrived from the Ministers for that Purpose. Colonel Keating had nothing to do with the Purgunnahs.

A true Copy.

(Signed) An. Macpherson.

Copy of a Letter from Lieutenant Colonel Upton to the Honourable the President, &c. Members of the Select Committee at Bombay, dated 4th May, 1776.

Gentlemen,

I received your Letter of the 27th Ultimo, Two Days ago, and acquainted the Ministers with such Parts of it as concerned them; viz. that their not having Possession of the Purgunnahs restored by the Treaty, was owing to their Agents, who had not presented themselves to receive them: That Orders had long since been sent to the Chiefs of Surat and Broach to give these Purgunnahs up, whenever they were demanded by Persons properly authorized by the Ministers to receive them: That it was entirely contrary to your Inclination, and without your Concurrence, that Ragoba's Army continued so near to Surat.

The enclosed Copy of a Letter from the Peshwa will inform you with their Determination respecting Ragonaut Row's Troops, which is to wait Fourteen Days, and then order Hurria Pundit Furkia to disperse them. They wait Fourteen Days, that yet sufficiently longer Time may be had to disband them, and that they may avoid incurring the Punishment they will be liable to, if found in Arms after that Date.

I have, &c.

(Signed) J. Upton.

Extract of a Letter from the Honourable the President, &c. Members of the Select Committee, Bombay, to Lieutenant Colonel Upton, dated 1st May, 1776.

However, to leave the Ministers without the Shadow of a Plea for Complaint, we now enclose fresh Orders for the Restitution of the Purgunnahs in Guzerat, which you will please to deliver to them; and we have sent Directions to the Chief of Surat, to make the strongest Remonstrances to Ragoba, on the Impropriety of his Troops remaining in their present Situation, and to insist upon their being removed.

The Extract you have inserted from Colonel Keating's Letter appears to be an Answer from one to you, which we have never seen. He never had any Instructions from us to authorize him to write to you in the Manner he has done, or to take any Part in the Business of your Deputation, as you seem to take for granted.

It appears by the inclosed Extract of a Letter from Ragoba, that he has got some Intimation of the late Intentions of the Governor General and Council in his Favour, and we conclude the Ministers must have received the same Intelligence; which, with the Motives assigned in our last Letter, will easily account for their late Conduct.

A true Extract.

(Signed) An. Macpherson.

Extract of a Letter from Ragonaut Row Badjerow Pundit Pradhan, to the Honourable the President; dated 23d April, and received the 29th following.

It is reported, that you have undertaken my Business again: I therefore think that the Rebels will make an Attempt to fall upon me; all which you will take into your Consideration, and do what you think proper.

My Vackeel at Calcutta has forwarded express from thence a Packet directed to you, which he informs me is about my Business. I now send the same to you, and upon Receipt you will know the Contents. My chief Dependance is on you.

A true Extract.

(Signed) Edward Ravenscroft,
Secretary.

*Part of a Conversation that passed last Night between Colonel Upton and * Mhaderow Sadashew (on the Part of the Ministers) 22d April 1776.*

Mhaderow complained heavily, that the Articles of the Treaty were not carried into Execution on the Part of the English; on the contrary, that Ragonaut Row was in Surat, and his Army round the Walls; that Colonel Keating was daily in Conference with Ragoba, who was furnished with Powder and all other Military Stores, even Guns; that the English had not restored the Purgunnahs, &c. ceded by Ragoba, agreeable to the Treaty; and that all the Guzerat Country was destroying and burning: That the Ministers were desirous of knowing what the Colonel said to all these Circumstances, and what was to be done.

The Colonel replied, Some of these were Circumstances he was perfectly acquainted with, and that he was very much concerned to see them; but what they mentioned relative to Military Stores, &c. must be impossible: that he had done every Thing which depended upon himself, viz. concluding a Treaty of Peace with the Marattas on the Part of the English, and making the Representations of the Ministers as well as his own, of the full Sense and Meaning of that Treaty, to the Governor and Council of Bombay; but that it was the Business of the Two Governments to carry the Articles into Execution, which he made no Doubt would be the Case on the Part of the English if they would have Patience; and that he could assure them the Peace was very firmly established; but that he could not be answerable for the Conduct of other People, which the Ministers seemed to think, and had blamed him accordingly.—— Yesterday he (Colonel Upton) sent to inform them that the Governor and Council of Bombay had advised him, that they had given Ragonaut Row Protection in Surat; at the same Time they wrote to him to assure the Ministers that he could not cause any Commotions in the Maratta State whilst he remained under the Company's Protection, and that they would only admit his Family and Domestics; that his Army being round Surat was by no Means by Choice, but they were so much in Arrears they would not disband; further, that the Governor and Council of Bombay assured him that they would carry the Articles of the Treaty into Execution without Delay. If the Ministers were not satisfied with this, they should write the Colonel a Letter that such and such Articles of the Treaty were not carried into Execution, and what they meant to do.

Mhaderow declared they would write no more Letters on the Subject, for they found no Advantage from those they had wrote; but that the Ministers were desirous of knowing what the English were determined to do, for their Army had been idle at a Lack of Rupees a Day for these Ten Months past, owing to the Letters from Calcutta and the Colonel's Arrival; and that now there was a heavy Loss to Government in the Revenues of Guzerat not being collected; and that the English must not be surprized if they made the Twelve Lacks pay for Part.

* On the first Arrival of Colonel Upton at Poorunder, Maderow Sedashaw was appointed by the Ministers to reside near him, and to transact any Business between the Ministers and the Colonel; and that whatever he said or did was to be looked upon as said or done by the Ministers, in the fullest Sense.

The

The Colonel said, He could not help observing the Ministers themselves were in a great Measure instrumental in many of the Delays they urged against the English, by being constantly in the Fort on the Hill; I never giving him an Opportunity of consulting with them on any Business. That it was now about a Month since he had seen either of them, whereas it was his Opinion they should see one another very frequently till the Business was over, even once a Day if it appeared at all necessary; and that he would, according to their Representations, write to Bombay as often as Three Times a Day if required.

Maderow said that they were nowise dependant on the English; that he did not see the Necessity of their meeting so often, as they neither expected or asked any Thing from them but to fulfil their Engagements; that they were ill-treated by the English, for the Council of Bombay appeared to be preparing to do every Thing in their Power to take an Opportunity of seizing upon more of the Maratta Dominions: Whether the Governor General and Council and the Colonel were concerned, they could not pretend to say; but if the Supreme Council had not sufficient Authority over the Governor and Council of Bombay, so as to have their Orders through the Colonel obeyed, they should not have interfered, but have left them and the Government of Bombay to settle their own Differences; but on the other Hand, if the Colonel had Power vested in him, he should either go to Bombay, or depute a proper Person to know the Occasion of Delay to carrying the Articles into Execution, and afterwards proceed to Surat, &c. to see them carried into Execution; without which he was sure nothing could be done; for Hurry Punt Furkia had wrote Twenty Letters to Colonel Keating about separating from Ragoba with the English Army, and to beg to be informed when he marched, that People might be sent to take Possession of the Country to be restored, and that he might be left to settle with Ragoba if he did not retire to Cooper Gang as agreed upon. That the only Answers he could get to his Letters were, desiring him to continue with his Army where he then was; that Ragoba was discharging his Troops, and if he (Hurry Punt) marched with his Army to disturb them, it would be breaking the Peace with the English. That these were such evasive Answers as shewed little Disposition to amicable Terms.

The Colonel declared to him that he acted all along upon the strictest Honour with them in every Respect, and that he again assured him that the Peace was firmly established on the Part of the English, which they would find if they would wait a little, the Articles being carried into Execution; that however they might suppose themselves ill-treated, he thought it nevertheless their Business, as well as that of the English, to do every Thing in their Power to establish the Peace, and in the mean Time to forget as much as they could their Grievances.

The Colonel asked, When they had received a Letter from Hurry Pundit? and begged to see the last. Maderow replied, They received them daily, and would send one of the last; but no good Effects were expected from Letters; they were afraid they would at last be reduced to the Necessity of following the Example of Hyder Ally, who secured his Peace with the English in a very honourable Manner to himself.

The Colonel observed to him, that such Conversation was rather improper. He replied, It might be so; but he must observe to him, that it was the Intention of the Ministers, should the War again take Place, to carry Fire and Sword throughout the Whole of the Country possessed by the Company in India, and entirely lay it Waste, be the Consequence ever so fatal to themselves.

(Signed) An. Macpherson,
Persian Interpreter.

APPENDIX, N° 134.

Extract of Bengal Secret Consultations, the 3d July 1776.

PRESENT,

The Honourable Warren Hastings, Governor General, President,
Lieutenant General John Clavering,
The Honourable George Monson,
Philip Francis, Esquire.
Mr. Barwell indisposed.

RECEIVED the following Letter from Colonel Upton:

To the Honourable the Governor General and Council, Fort William.

Gentlemen,

I did myself the Honour to write to you last on the 6th Instant.

The Ministers have consented to omit the 13th and 17th Articles, and the concluding Words of the 7th Article, and have signed the Treaty, which will be sent in a few Days by Lieutenant Paterson, as I advised in my Letter of the 6th.

They requested on their Part that a few Alterations might be made. I informed them, that the Treaty being executed by the Supreme Council, it was impossible for me to make or admit of any Alterations. They therefore write to you, Gentlemen, requesting this; but their principal Motive is, to continue the Correspondence about negociating for an Exchange for Salsette: This they have much at Heart, and I am persuaded will offer largely to effect. They mean to send a Vackeel to Calcutta, a Man of more than usual Consequence, with full Power respecting this Exchange; they intend he shall reside always at Calcutta, as they express a very great Desire of having a firm and lasting Friendship with the English. May I be permitted to express my Wish, that in Reply to their Letter you will acquaint them their Vackeel shall be received, and his Proposals heard; for though an Exchange should not take Place, yet it will have the good Effect of knowing how far it might answer to the Company, and will keep the Door open for further Conferences if necessary; it will also soften a Number of rather disagreeable Circumstances that have happened, and restore a Confidence with Bombay, which is much required. I have to beg, Gentlemen, you will excuse my having on this Occasion expressed my Wishes; they are submitted altogether from observing the Necessity of Harmony being restored between the Presidency of Bombay and the Marattas.

The Alterations the Ministers wanted should took Place in the Treaty (which as I could not comply with, they insisted I should write to ask might be granted) were in the Third Article, the Words "subdued by the English in this War," as they declare they were not at War with the English when these Islands were taken. They want any other Words rather than "taken in War," or "in this War." This had been discussed a Hundred Times before, and I had convinced them, that expressing it in other Terms could not be admitted, more particularly as we did not know the Marratta Names of the small Islands in our Possession in the Bay of Bombay, nor did they know nor would consent to our inserting the English Names; that these Islands had certainly been taken in War, and in this War, for there was no separating or making Two Wars of it; and further, to what Purpose to them could tend the Alteration, as they were now, as much as they then could be, at Liberty to treat about these Islands.

In the Sixth Article they say, the Words "in Part of the Expences of the English Army" imply, that some further Sum on that Account remains due; this had also before been repeatedly Matter of Debate. I have quite satisfied them by signing a Paper, that the true Meaning of the Sixth Article is, that the Peishwa will have complied with his Obligation respecting it when the 12 Lacks are paid: In this Article therefore,

fore, now, no Alteration is required; though a Reply to their Request respecting the Third Article may be necessary.

The Ministers are advised by Hurry Pundit, that the greatest Part of Ragonath Row's Troops have joined him: This has made them very happy, as they now expect soon to see an End to their Disturbances; for they conclude Orders will soon arrive to forbid Ragonath Row's residing at any of the English Settlements.

I enclose Extracts of Letters from Hurry Pundit to the Paishwa, received about Six Days ago, by which you will perceive they had then much Cause of Uneasiness.

The Ministers required in no other Manner to be put in Possession of the Purgunnahs to be restored to them than by our evacuating them, but they were not able securely to take Possession whilst our Army was in the Field, and Ragonath Row's not disbanded, and remaining with or near the English Troops.

You will please, Gentlemen, to direct where or to whom the 12 Lacks of Rupees, towards defraying the Expence of the War, are to be paid. It was agreed to receive this Money in Putachaule Rupees, the current Rupee of this Country, which is in general here somewhat better than the Arcot Rupee.

Some further Papers are expected from Futty Sing; as soon as these arrive, Lieutenant Paterson will receive his Dispatches. I hope to have the Pleasure to acquaint you by him, that the Articles of the Peace have been all (except that of the 12 Lacks) carried into Execution.

I have just received the enclosed Note; it is the first Intimation I have had of Succaram Baboo's Intention of retiring: I imagine (as he is old and infirm) he takes this Method of letting Morobah Furnice succeed to his Appointments, who has all along declined taking any Share in the Business of Government with Succaram Pundit. It is evident, therefore, they look on their Disturbances as nearly at an End.—Permit me to request you will forward these Passports and Letters as soon as convenient; I should suppose they would not set out on their Journey till the Beginning of November. The Name of the late Peshwa Madowrow's Mother is Goupkaboy, and should be inserted in her Pass.

I have the Honour to be, &c.

Poorunder, 27th May 1776. (Signed) J. Upton.

Resolved, that the Board cannot consent to any Alterations at this Time in the Treaty, which are in themselves of no Consequence, and which could not be made without cancelling the Treaty already ratified on both Sides.

Resolved, that the following Letters be written to Colonel Upton, and to Bombay.

To the Honourable William Hornby, Esquire, President, &c. Council, at Bombay.

Gentlemen,

Since our Letter to you of the 1st Instant, we have received Advices from Lieutenant Colonel Upton, dated 27th May; and in Consequence of his Desire, that we would determine the Mode and Place of Payment of the 12 Lacks of Rupees, stipulated for the Expences of the War, we have directed him, before he quits Poona, to settle for the Payment of it at your Presidency, at the Periods when it shall become due; and to prevent any Disputes respecting the Value of the Coins, we think it necessary to desire that you will take whatever Money shall be offered you on this Account, giving a Receipt for the same in the Specie in which it may be paid; and if you shall think that there is any Deficiency in the Amount, you will be pleased to report the same to us.

Fort William, the 3d July 1776. We are, &c.

To Lieutenant Colonel Upton.

Sir,

We had written to you on the First Instant; but before the Dispatch of our Letter, we received your's of the 27th May.

We cannot now give our Consent to the Alterations in the Treaty which the Ministers have desired; they are in themselves of no Consequence, and if agreed to, must cancel the Treaty which has been already ratified on both Sides.

As

As we have already desired you to inform the Ministers, that we had resolved not to accept their Proposition for an Exchange of Territory, in Lieu of Salsette, Caranga, Hog, and Elephanta, and a Declaration to that Effect was added at the Foot of the Treaty, we cannot enter into any further Negociation with them on that Subject; but as all our Proceedings must be referred to the ultimate Decision of the Honourable Company, they will signify their Directions in Consequence. However, we should deem ourselves wanting in Candour, to suggest to the Maratta Government Expectations which we do not believe will be realized; we therefore desire you will intimate to them our Opinion, that the Company will never consent to relinquish these Islands.

We are much pleased with the Intention of the Ministers to send a confidential Vackeel to reside in Calcutta, and desire you to encourage this Intention, by the strongest Assurances of our Wish to maintain the Peace established between us, to cultivate their Friendship, and to remove every Subject of Doubt or Distrust that may arise on either Part; and we think nothing more likely to contribute to this End, than establishing a direct Communication between us in the Manner which they have proposed.

Before you leave Poona, we direct that you settle the Payment of the 12 Lacks of Rupees to be made at the Presidency of Bombay, as it becomes due.

We have applied to the Nabob Vizier, and to Rajah Cheyt Sing, for the Passports desired by Succaram Pundit for himself, and Goupkaboy the Mother of the late Peshwa, which will be forwarded to you by Mr. Bristow and Mr. Fowke. We desire that when you deliver them, you will assure both these People of our Protection, and every Mark of Attention and Respect in our Power, if they shall chuse to reside either in the Dominions of our Ally the Vizier, or in the Territories dependant on this Government.

This Resolution of Succaram Pundit, to proceed to Benares, and to leave the chief Direction of the Maratta Government in the Hands of Moraba Furness, a Person who is generally supposed to be in the Interest of Ragoba, appears to us so strange, that we cannot acount for it. We desire that you will furnish us with your Opinion of this Measure, of Succaram's Motives for it, and of the Effects which are likely to be produced by such an Event.

We are, &c.
Warren Hastings,
R. Barwell,
P. Francis.

Fort William,
the 3d July 1776.

APPENDIX, N° 135.

Extract of Bengal Secret Consultations, the 24th July, 1776.

RECEIVED the following Letter from Lieutenant Colonel Upton:

To the Honourable the Governor General and Council, Fort William.

Gentlemen,

Lieutenant Paterson will have the Honour to deliver the Treaty executed by the Ministers.

The Name of the Peishwa having been but once mentioned in the Treaty (in the Preamble) and that not appearing in the English Translation, the Words "Maratta "State" having been substituted, I thought it necessary to insert it a Second Time; and, with the Consent of the Ministers, have accordingly again inserted it (where he is mentioned) in the last Line but one of the Preamble.

The Season is too far advanced to delay Lieutenant Paterson's Departure any longer, as intended, in Expectation of receiving shortly more Attests from Futty Sing, who is ordered to come without Delay to Poona, and is to bring with him all the Papers that have any Relation to the Business yet unsettled in the Gozerat Country.

I herewith forward Articles of Obligation between the Peishwa and Guicawar Family; also a Letter, &c. from Futty Sing; and Letters from Syndia, and Tucogee Hulker, in Reply to the circular Letter sent by the Peshwa, on concluding the Peace.

The Peshwa is in Possession of all the Purgunnahs ceded by Ragonaut Row, that were to be restored by the Treaty, except Jamboofeer, which we are to remain possessed of, until the Country of Three Lacks is made over.

My last Letter to the Board was dated 27th May, but not dispatched until the 1st Instant, owing to the Peishwa's delaying the Caussfeds.

I have the Honour to be, &c.

Poorunder, (Signed) John Upton.
June 3d, 1776.

Ordered, That the Treaty be deposited among the Records in the Secretary's Office; and that the other Persian Papers be sent to be translated: And,

Agreed, that the following Reply be sent to Colonel Upton.

To Lieutenant Colonel Upton.

Sir,

We have received your Letter of the 3d Ultimo, by Lieutenant Paterson, with the Treaty, and the other Papers which accompanied it.

In our Letter of 1st July, we directed you to proceed to Bombay, and on your Arrival there to use your Endeavours to compleat what should remain to be executed of the Treaty; this done, we see no Cause for your continuing longer at that Place, but desire that you return to this Presidency by whatever Route, whether by Land or by Water, you may prefer. If you should chuse to return through Poona, you will not fail to repeat to the Peishwa and his Ministers, in our Name, the strongest Assurances of our Resolution to maintain the Peace concluded with them, and to preserve every Condition on our Part inviolate.

It did not occur to us, that, according to the universal Practice of the East, a Return of Presents would have been tendered to you by the Court of Poona, on your Departure from it; nevertheless, it may not be yet too late, to inform you of the Conduct which we wish you to observe on such an Occasion. Although you are precluded by the Law from accepting of Presents for your own Use, yet as Presents have been made on the Part of the Company, we shall approve of your accepting, in like Manner, of any which shall be made to you from the Ministry at Poona, in the Name and on Behalf of the Company.

We desire you will make the like Assurances of Friendship on our Part, to any Chiefs of the Maratta State whose Dominions you may pass through, in case you should resolve to return by Land.

Fort William, We are, &c.
24th July, 1776.

APPENDIX, N° 136.

Extract of Bengal Secret Consultations, the 22d July 1776.

RECEIVED the following Letter from Bombay:

To the Honourable Warren Hastings, Esquire, Governor General, &c. Council at Fort William.

Honourable Sir, and Gentlemen,

Since our last of the 10th Ultimo, we have received your several Letters, dated the 12th and 26th February, 11th and 16th March, and 16th April, with the Consignment of Treasure by the Indian Queen, and the Bill inclosed in the last-mentioned Letter.

This

This is chiefly to acquaint you, that on the Ship Hodges we now return the Detachment of Europeans under the Command of Lieutenant Taylor, having shipped on Board Forty Days Provisions for their Use, as per inclosed Account. We request your Honour, &c. will settle with the Commander for the Passage of this Detachment.

Ragoba's Army is entirely disbanded, and he is now in Surat, with Two hundred only of his Domestics and Servants. We have strongly urged to Colonel Upton to use his Endeavours to induce the Ministers to assign him a suitable Establishment to relieve the Company from the heavy Expence they will otherwise incur by his Maintenance.

The Communication with the Maratta Dominions still remains shut, notwithstanding the Promise of the Ministers that it should be opened as soon as the Company's Forces had retired into their own Districts.

By our Advices from Surat and Broach, we conclude that the Restitutions stipulated by the Treaty are by this Time made.

We are, &c.

Bombay Castle, 10th June, 1776.

(Signed) William Hornby, &c. Council.

Warren Hastings,
J. Clavering,
R. Barwell,
P. Francis.

Extract of Bengal Secret Consultations, dated the 5th August 1776.

Received the following Letter from Bombay.

Honourable Sir, and Gentlemen,

We enclose a Duplicate of our last Letter, dated 10th Instant, and have since had the Honour to receive your Letter, dated the 21st March, enclosing an Extract from your Minutes of Council respecting the Allowances to be made to the Bengal Detachment.

This Detachment we returned by the Hodges, as before advised, and we found the Expence of the Madras Battalion so great a Drain upon our Treasury, and having no Certainty of speedy Assistance from your Honour, &c. since you have been pleased so peremptorily to forbid our drawing upon you, that to prevent the Inconvenience to which we might otherwise be exposed, we determined to send back this Battalion likewise, and a considerable Part thereof has been already embarked, and the Remainder will very shortly proceed.

We enclose Copy of a Letter from Colonel Upton, received since our last, and of our Reply, and we doubt not your Honour, &c. will concur with us in Opinion, that there appears in the Whole of this Gentleman's Correspondence, a too great Readiness to listen to the trifling Complaints of the Ministers, and a Want of Confidence in our Representations.

Sudaba still continues to the Southward, being prevented from advancing by the Monsoon; he has lately sent Two Vackeels here to request the Company will assist him with a Battalion or two of Sepoys, and a Supply of small Arms. He says Ragoba's Cause and his are the same, and that his Object is to deprive the Ministers of the Power they have so unjustly usurped, and to restore the Family of Badjerow to their just Rights. Sudaba is now in Possession of great Part of the Conkan Country, and his Army is said to consist of about 18,000 Men. We shall shortly write your Honour, &c. more fully on this Subject.

Shortly after the Return of Colonel Keating, we thought it incumbent upon us, in Consequence of your Letter of the 11th March, to call upon him to explain the Attack of Ahmedavad, and the Circumstance of Two of the Company's Cannon being employed upon that Siege after the Cessation of Arms had taken Place. Enclosed is a Copy of his Reply, which with our Letter to him, dated 20th October, formerly transmitted, we hope will clear up this Affair to your Satisfaction.

Colonel Upton's Letter will inform you, that the Ministers have at last given Orders for Communication being opened between the Company's Settlements and the Maratta Dominions,

Dominions, but they have so long deferred it, that it will be of little Advantage to our Commerce till the Opening of the Season.

We have the Honour to be, &c.

Bombay Castle, (Signed) Wm. Hornby,
30th June 1776. &c. Council.

Ordered, That the Enclosures be entered after the Consultations.

Continuation of the Correspondence with Colonel Upton, from the 10th June.

To the Honourable the President, &c. Members of the Select Committee, Bombay.

Gentlemen,

I am honoured with your Letter of the 2d Instant.

The Ministers have repeatedly declared, that they will strictly observe the Obligation they have engaged in respecting Ragonaut Row, but they will not make or admit of any Alteration therein. I am afraid I have not sufficient Influence here to get his stipulated Allowance, or any Part of it paid, unless he complies with the Conditions on which it was granted; I shall, however, try all in my Power to effect this. The Ministers have consented, and given Orders accordingly, to open the Communication on the 18th Instant, observing the same Customs and Duties as heretofore.

I have this Instant received a Letter from the Ministers, acquainting me, that they are informed by Hurria Pundit that a Thousand Cavalry, a Thousand other People, with Artillery, Elephants, Camels, Horses, &c. have been received into Surat with Ragonaut Row. I hope this is no more than Report; and have to request, Gentlemen, you will write me, that I may satisfy the Ministers accordingly.

They advise me also, that a Man, who calls himself Sadashaw Row, is raising Disturbances in the Cokun Country. I acquaint you with this to prevent the Inconveniences that might otherwise happen on the first Opening of the Communication.

The Ministers further inform me, that Hurria Pundit had a Vackeel at Surat, who has been ordered to retire. They wished and hoped that the Establishment of the Peace would have been succeeded by a full Confidence and Friendship.

I have the Honour, &c.

Poona, (Signed) John Upton.
June 1776.

To Colonel Upton.

Sir,

We have received your Letter dated the 13th Instant.

We still hope you will meet with Success in your Endeavours to obtain the stipulated Allowance for Ragoba.

The Ministers have so long deferred opening the Communication, that the Company will not derive any commercial Advantages from it this Season.

The Fears of the Ministers make them very ready to adopt Suspicions of our Conduct upon every Occasion, and we could wish you would not shew so much Attention to their frivolous Complaints that respect us. We enclose an Extract of a Letter from the Chief of Surat, which will remove all Doubts respecting the Number of People received into Surat with Ragonaut Row, but we know nothing of Hurria Pundit's Vackeel being ordered to retire from thence. We are sensible the Ministers entertain a Belief that the Company approve of our supporting Ragoba, and that we shall renew the War in his Favour after the Rains; and through this Medium do they view all our Actions.

Two Vackeels arrived here on the 17th Instant from Sadashew Row; and we apprize you of this Circumstance, as we suppose the Ministers Fears will instantly be alarmed; but you may assure them, that we shall not pursue any Measures in Consequence that may be repugnant to the late Treaty, and which indeed is the proper Answer to return to all their Complaints.

We are, &c.
Wm. Hornby, &c. Council.

Bombay Castle,
20th June 1776.

APPENDIX, N° 137.

Copy of the 48th Paragraph of the Separate Letter to Bengal, dated 15th December 1775.

BY this Conveyance we transmit you Copy of Advices received from our Servants at Bombay, relative to the Capture of Salsette and Caringa, and to the subsequent Cession of those Places to the Company by Ragoba the Maratta Chief; and although the Materials before us do not enable us to give you particular Instructions on every Point relative to those important Events, we however approve, under every Circumstance, of the keeping of all the Territories and Possessions ceded to the Company by the Treaty concluded with Ragoba; and direct that you forthwith adopt such Measures as may be necessary for their Preservation and Defence.

Extract Bengal Secret Consultations, 3 July 1776.

Read again, the 48th and 49th Paragraphs of the Company's General Letter in the Secret Department; dated 15th December 1775.

The Board having, so long ago as the 31st May 1775, unanimously declared their Opinion, That the Treaty formed by the Presidency of Bombay was invalid; and having in Consequence of that Resolution concluded and ratified a Treaty in the Name of the Company with the Ministers of the Maratta State, are no longer at Liberty to carry into Execution the Intentions of the Court of Directors, expressed in the 48th Paragraph of their Letter, by keeping all Territories and Possessions ceded to the Company by the Treaty concluded with Ragoba, since many of those Territories have been ceded to the Maratta Government by the above Treaty with them, and cannot either be retained or resumed consistently with the public Faith of this Government, except in the Case of a direct Violation of the Treaty on the Part of the Marattas.

The Board are further of Opinion, That the Presence of Colonel Upton at Poona is no longer necessary; and that his Services may be more effectually employed at Bombay, for the Accomplishment of what yet remains to be carried into Execution of the Treaty on both Sides, than by a longer Residence at Poona.

It is therefore resolved, That the following Letter be written to Colonel Upton.

To Lieutenant Colonel Upton.

Sir,

We are of Opinion, that your Residence at Proonder is no longer necessary; but that your Service may be more useful at Bombay, in promoting the Accomplishment of such Articles of the Treaty as remain still to be carried into Execution; we therefore direct, that you demand your immediate Dismission from the Peshwa's Court, and proceed to Bombay as soon as you can with Convenience, after the Receipt of these our Orders. You will inform the Ministers, that we have judged your Presence to be no longer necessary at Proonder, as your Interposition may be more effectually employed with the President and Council at Bombay, in urging them to a speedy Compliance with the Conditions of the Treaty, which remains to be accomplished on their Part, and which we are sorry to see have been so long delayed. You will also formally require of the Ministers, to put the Government of Bombay in Possession of the Territories, which are stipulated by the Treaty to be ceded to the Company, and to settle a Provision for the Payment of Six Lacks of Rupees, which, by the 6th Article of the Treaty, will become due on the 1st September next; but you must not express or shew any Distrust of their Intentions, nor suffer any Thing which they may say to you in Reply to your Requisitions, to induce you to defer your Departure from Proonder. On your Arrival at Bombay, you will exert your Endeavours to effect the Conclusion of the

the different Articles required by the Treaty, and remain there till further Orders, to carry on any Negociations which may be necessary with the Ministers.

We are, &c.

Fort William,
1st July, 1776.

Resolved, That a Copy of the 48th Paragraph of the General Letter, and of the above Resolution, be transmitted to the President and Council of Bombay, with the following Letter:

To the Honourable William Hornby, Esquire, President, &c. Council at Bombay.

Gentlemen,

We have received your Letter of the 18th May. The Honourable the Court of Directors having signified to us by the Greenwich their Orders, in Consequence of the Capture of Salsette, and of the Treaty which at the Date of your Advices to them you were negociating with Ragoba, we think it proper to enclose a Copy of these Orders for your Information, and of the Resolutions which we have come to on reading them.

As the Treaty of Poona has not left us at Liberty to follow the apparent Intentions of the Court of Directors on this Occasion, we leave you to act agreeable to our Resolutions, which will point out the Plan we have judged it necessary to adopt in Consequence of their Directions; to which we must add, that if you shall not have put the Officers of the Paishwa in Possession of the Districts ceded to the Maratta State by the 7th Article of the Treaty, before the Receipt of this Letter, we peremptorily repeat our Injunctions, that you cause these Districts to be delivered up immediately, and that you admit of no further Delay in this Point, or in executing any Article that remains unaccomplished on your Part, but observe with the most scrupulous Fidelity every Condition required of you by the Treaty.

Colonel Upton, whom we have recalled from Poona, has been ordered before his Departure, to require of the Ministers the punctual Execution of the Stipulations on their Part; but if they should evade complying with his Demand, or be guilty of any Acts of Hostility, we direct that you take no Steps of your own Authority to retaliate the Injuries or Affronts which may be received from them or their Dependents, except you shall be compelled to it in your own immediate Defence, but that you give us the earliest Information, and wait for our Instructions; contenting yourselves in the mean Time by amicable Remonstrances to the Ministers, to endeavour to obtain a suitable Redress.

We have directed Colonel Upton to proceed to and continue at Bombay till further Orders, that he may finish any Negociations with the Ministers which remain unsettled at the Time of his Departure. We recommend him to your Attention; and as we have not communicated to him the Orders of the Company, and the Measures we mean to pursue, we request that you will impart them to him on his Arrival at your Presidency.

We are, &c.

Fort William, 1st July 1776.

Mr. Barwell—I have no particular Objection to the Resolution of the Board, as far as it binds this Government to pacific Measures: Policy in the present Situation of the Company's Affairs requires it, and I think our utmost Endeavours should be used to secure the Advantages expected to result from the Treaty concluded with the Poona Ministers; but I mean not, by subscribing to this Resolution of the Board, to allow that this Government is not at Liberty to adopt hostile Resolutions, and to seize the first Opportunity that offers to execute the Company's Intentions.

Warren Hastings,
Jno. Clavering,
Rd. Barwell,
P. Francis.

APPENDIX, N° 138.

Extract of Bengal Secret Consultations, the 8th July 1776.

READ a Letter from Mr. Tayler, as follows:

To the Honourable Warren Hastings, Esquire, Governor General, &c. Council at Fort William.

Honourable Sir, and Sirs,

I have received from your Secretary a Copy of the 48th Paragraph of the Honourable Company's Commands of the 15th December last, and of your Resolutions in Consequence of them.

With respect to the first, I can only say, that, in my Conception, nothing can more forcibly express their Ideas of the Situation in which they wished to see their Affairs in the West of India; and it is therefore with infinite Concern I lament, that the Treaty concluded by Lieutenant Colonel Upton with the Ministerial Confederacy, leaves them so widely distant from that Situation. With the former Orders of the Company before them, and this strong Confirmation of their Sentiments, I doubt not but the Government of Bombay would wish to bring them as near to it as such Part of the Territories ceded by Ragoba, that remain in their Possession, will admit; and if they are deterred from so doing, by your declining that Assistance enjoined by the Orders of the Company, it is you alone who must be answerable for the Consequences.

In my own Justification, I think myself bound, in Behalf of the Honourable the Court of Directors, and the Bombay Presidency, to remonstrate and protest against your Non-compliance; especially as the Conduct of the Ministers, since the signing and concluding of the Treaty on the 1st March, by having in the Month of April taken several Vessels with our Passes and Colours (and some of them from under the Convoy of the Terrible Bomb Ketch, whose Captain is now here in Command of the Drake) by their not having permitted any Intercourse or Communication with Bombay till the 19th of May, the Date of my last Advices, nor having till that Time sent any Persons to deliver the Lands to be given in Exchange for those ceded to us by Ragoba, gives you as fair an Opportunity as can be desired, of placing Matters on the respectable Footing so much wished for by our Honourable Masters, instead of the very contrary one they are placed in by the Treaty negociated by Lieutenant Colonel Upton.

I must here beg Leave to recall to your Recollection the Treaty concluded by the Government of Bombay with Ragoba, and approved by you and their Superiors, the Honourable the Court of Directors; and contrast it in a few Instances with that negociated by Lieutenant Colonel Upton. By the Bombay Treaty, Ragoba, the rightful Paishwah, makes over to the Company for ever certain appointed Districts, the Revenues of which amount to Rupees 19,25,000, and with the Villages of Corial, Chickly, Veriow, and Arnood, and the Chout of Surat, since obtained from him and Futty Sing, to about Rupees 23,00,000 per Annum; all which they were in Possession of, except Bassein, estimated at 4 Lacks: Lieutenant Colonel Upton obtains from Rebels, who you are pleased to term the Poona Government, Cessions, some of them very vague, to the Amount of Rupees 9,50,000. The Bombay Treaty secures a lasting Peace to the Carnatic and these Provinces; Lieutenant Colonel Upton leaves them to be plundered and laid Waste, as soon as the Rebels may find it convenient. The Bombay Treaty provides for and secures, by actual Possession of Lands assigned for the Purpose, the entire Expence of the War in favour of the lawful Prince: Lieutenant Colonel Upton is content with a Promise of 12 Lacks, which will be about Half the Amount, and no Security at all; and to conclude the History of Lieutenant Colonel Upton's Treaty, it is made with a Man, (Saccaram Bappoo) who is immediately about to resign his Share in the Administration to Morabah Furneese, a declared Partizan of Ragoba's, and retire to Benares, to pass the Remainder of his Days under your Protection.

I have

I have only further, Gentlemen, to urge you to re-consider the gross Indignity you are offering to the Presidency of Bombay, by directing that Lieutenant Colonel Upton shall reside there, for the Purpose of concluding whatever may remain unfinished of the Treaty; and I beg you to recollect, that the Company have appointed a Select Committee there, expressly for conducting all political Measures; and that by their having excluded you, since the Act of Parliament took Place, from having any Interference in restoring the King of Tanjore to his Dominions, it is evidently their Intention that you should not interfere in the Manner you think yourselves entitled to do, in the Affairs of the other Presidencies; and from the very great Difference in the Sentiments of the Court of Directors and yours, on the Treaty with Ragoba, it is also evident the Bombay Council have acted conformably to their repeated Instructions and Wishes, and ought not, if in Compliment only to the Court of Directors, to be subjected to the Disgrace you are about to attempt to inflict on them.

I have the Honour to be, &c.

Calcutta, the 5th July 1776. (Signed) W. Tayler.

The above Letter having been sent in Circulation immediately after its Receipt, the following Opinions were returned upon it.

In Answer to Mr. Tayler's Letter, wherein he says he thinks himself bound in Behalf of the Honourable Court of Directors, and the Bombay Presidency, to remonstrate and protest against our Non-compliance with the Orders of the Company, my Opinion is, That we ought to desire him to produce the Powers with which he is vested on the Part of the Honourable East India Company, to authorize him to protest against the Acts of this Government.

(Signed) J. Clavering.

Agreed. (Signed) P. Francis.

Mr. Tayler should be required to produce the Powers and Authority to the Board, which entitle him to remonstrate and protest, on Behalf of the Honourable the Court of Directors, and the Bombay Presidency, against the Acts of this Government.

(Signed) Geo. Monson.

Mr. Tayler has certainly exceeded the Authority delegated to him by the President and Council of Bombay, and indeed any which they could give; but I think it not unnecessary to propose the Question to him which is the Substance of the above Minutes, as the Board well know, that he has not the Powers alluded to in them; and in my Opinion, the Dignity of Government would be best maintained by a direct Censure, than by the Implication of it.

(Signed) Warren Hastings.

Mr. Barwell—The President and Council of Bombay expressly deputed Mr. Tayler, a Member of their Board and of their Select Committee, to this Government, for the sole Purpose of engaging its Concurrence to the political Measures which were adopted at that Presidency, to secure the Prosperity and future Welfare of the Company's Settlements on the West Side of India. Mr. Tayler has been received as the public Deputy of that Government, in Behalf of which he now acts, and in Support of a Policy, that a Majority of this Board totally condemn: How far Mr. Tayler may be blameable in his Representations, I for my Part will not pretend to decide; but leave to the Company to determine on the Propriety of this Address now under Consideration, and whether it is consonant to their Views. I apprehend the passing a Censure on Mr. Tayler by this Government is unwarrantable, and I judge unbecoming in the present Instance; because in so doing we vindicate Opinions contradicting the Sense of the Company, who have approved of the Marratta War, a War that under any other Circumstances than the present, we must have countenanced and prosecuted; and which I fear will be revived by the Marrattas at a Period when we shall be deprived of that Faction in their State, which now favours the Prince with whom we were lately in Alliance.

I reluctantly add a short Observation on the preceding Minute, solely for the Purpose of obviating any Misconception of the Opinion given in mine. The Censure which I thought

thought the Board might with Propriety pass on Mr. Tayler, was not for any Sentiments expressed by him, concerning the late Treaty, or the last Orders of this Board, but for the Tone of Authority which he has assumed in his Address to the Board; in this he is surely wrong. Upon the former, I did not mean to offer an Opinion.

(Signed) Warren Hastings.

Agreed, That the following Letter be written to Mr. Tayler:

To Mr. Tayler.

Sir,

We have received your Letter of the 5th Instant. You inform us, that "in your own Justification you think yourself bound in Behalf of the Honourable Court of Directors, and the Bombay Presidency, to remonstrate and protest against our Non-compliance with the Orders of the Company."

We desire you will be pleased to inform us, by what Power or Authority you deem yourself entitled to protest in Behalf of the Court of Directors and the Presidency of Bombay, against any Act of this Government; and that, if you are possessed of such Power and Authority, you will communicate to us the Instruments or Instructions which vest you therewith.

As soon as we receive your Answer to this Enquiry, we shall consider what Reply it may be proper for us to make to the Remainder of your Letter.

We are, &c.

Fort William,
the 8th July 1776.

Extract of Bengal Secret Consultations, the 10th July 1776.

PRESENT,

The Honourable Warren Hastings, Governor General, President,
Lieutenant General John Clavering,
The Honourable George Monson,
Philip Francis, Esquire,
Mr. Barwell indisposed.

Read the following Letter from Mr. Tayler:

To the Honourable Warren Hastings, Esquire, Governor General, &c. Council at Calcutta.

Honourable Sir, and Sirs,

Yesterday Evening I received your Letter of the 8th; and in Reply do myself the Honour to acquaint you, that I have been deputed to this Place by the Honourable the Governor and Council of Bombay, who are the Representatives of the Company on that Side of India; being appointed a Government on their Behalf to conduct their Affairs there, they cannot be superseded without altering the Form of Government established by the Company. I conceived the Appointment of Lieutenant Colonel Upton to reside at Bombay and to treat publicly, independent of them, to be a direct Supercession of that Government: In their Letter of the 22d August they acquaint you of their having appointed me to represent to you at large the particular Interests of that Presidency, and as their Deputy, and as a Member of that Government, I could not but be sensibly affected at such a Measure, and thought it my Duty to remonstrate.

As the Orders of the Honourable the Court of Directors for maintaining the Cessions made by Ragoba have not probably reached Bombay by this Time, either by the Way of Aleppo or Madras, and the Governor and Council, who will conceive themselves fully authorized, will think it their Duty to act immediately in Obedience to those Orders, and must have taken Measures accordingly before the Receipt of your late Directions for a contrary Mode of Conduct; I considered the Embarrassment they may suffer under such Circumstances, and I thought it incumbent on me to urge you in the strongest

ſtrongeſt Manner to alter your Reſolutions; and I can with the greateſt Truth aſſure you, that I am actuated by no other Motives than the Zeal I entertain for the Honour and Intereſt of our Employers, and the Reputation of that Government of which I have the Honour to be a Member; had I neglected to act as I have done, I ſhould have expected their ſevereſt Cenſure.

I muſt beg Leave to add, that I am convinced, from the Actions and Declarations of Succaram Baboo, &c. ſince the Treaty, that it is not their Intention to obſerve it longer than may ſuit their own Convenience; and that if a proper Truſt was repoſed in the Governor of Bombay, the Company's Views on that Side might ſtill be obtained with great Facility; under the preſent Circumſtances they will be obliged to ſubmit to every Inſult, except an open Attack, in any of the Settlements for the Space of Three Months, which will be required to receive your Determination.

It may be alledged, in Favour of continuing the Powers veſted in Lieutenant Colonel Upton, that the Miniſters will be averſe to negociate amicably with the Governor of Bombay, but as a Treaty is now concluded with them, I cannot deſire a ſtronger Proof of their unfriendly Diſpoſition.

have the Honour to be, &c.
(Signed) William Tayler.

Calcutta,
10th July 1776.

Read again, the Letter from Mr. Tayler recorded in the laſt Conſultation.

Agreed, That the following Reply be written to Mr. Tayler:

To Mr. Tayler.

Sir,

We have received your Letter of this Day.

In your Addreſs of the 5th Inſtant, you declared yourſelf bound to proteſt and remonſtrate in Behalf of the Court of Directors, againſt our Non-compliance with their Orders. In your preſent Letter, you have not only dropped the Word *proteſt*, but even ſhifted the Object of your Remonſtrance. Colonel Upton's Continuance in a public Character at Bombay, has no Relation to the Point on which your Proteſt was founded; neither have you produced any Powers from the Company for making that or any other Declaration in their Behalf, againſt an Act of this Government. We conclude, that ſuch Powers have not been delegated to you, and that in aſſuming them, you have acted without Authority.

We ſhall avoid entering into an Argument with you upon the general Subject of your Proteſt. We cannot, however, paſs unnoticed the Appellation of *Rebels*, by which, in your Letter of the 5th Inſtant, you repeatedly deſcribe the Government of Poona. The Members of which that Government is compoſed, are the ſame Perſons with whom the Preſidency of Bombay entertained a Reſident, and whom they acknowledged, even after the Recall of Mr. Moſtyn, as they informed us in their Letter of 31ſt December 1774, that "the Preſident, agreeable to their Reſolution, would explain "to the Miniſterial Party at Poona the real Motives for their Proceedings, and that "they ſhould be aſſured, in Caſe they gain the Advantage in the preſent Conteſt, by "the Overthrow of Ragoba, that the Preſidency of Bombay would reſign the Iſlands "to them;" and finally, it is with theſe Perſons that this Government hath negociated, concluded, and ratified a Treaty, by which the Preſidency of Bombay is bound, and for which we ſhall be anſwerable to the Court of Directors.

We do not underſtand to what Order you allude, when you ſay that "ſince the Act of Parliament took Place, the Court of Directors have excluded this Government from any Interference in reſtoring the King of Tanjore to his Dominions," nor conſequently can we admit the Inference you draw from that Order, "that it muſt be their Intention we ſhould not interfere in the Manner we think ourſelves entitled to do in the Affairs of the other Preſidencies." Your Deciſion on the Company's Intentions with reſpect to the Diſpoſition of Tanjore, ſeems to us not leſs arbitrary and unauthorized, than your proteſting without Powers, in Behalf of the Court of Directors, againſt the Acts of this Government. We alſo are of Opinion, that you have equally miſtaken the Inſtructions and Wiſhes of the Court of Directors, previous to their Directions of the 15th December laſt; and in Support of our Opinion, we refer you to their Letter

of

of the 12th April 1775, to the Bombay Presidency, in which you will find the following Paragraphs:

Par. 43. "There is no Part of your Conduct more reprehensible than that of engaging, without absolute Necessity, in Military Expeditions; the large Sums which "have been expended at Broach, and on the Coolies, are an immediate Inconvenience "to the Company, and the Consequences of your Proceedings embarrassing in the "highest Degree; and after succeeding against the Place, it is mortifying to observe "that our Affairs are in a much worse Situation than they were before those Expe- "ditions were undertaken, as we do not find that the Charges incurred in conquering "the Country, and the Expences of keeping the Conquest, are likely to be defrayed "from its Resources in a reasonable Time, without oppressing the Inhabitants."

Par. 53. "It is with much Concern we learn from your Records, that we are not "likely to obtain Salsette from the Marattas by Negociation. We however disapprove "your Resolution to take Possession of that Island by Force, in Case of the Death "or Deposition of Ragoba, and hereby positively prohibit you from attempting that "Measure under any Circumstances whatever, without our Permission first obtained for "that Purpose."

Prior to the Receipt of a Copy of this Letter from the Court of Directors, we acted in Obedience to their General Instructions for the Preservation of the Peace of India; but since that Period, these Orders have been the more immediate Guide of our Conduct with respect to the Object in Question.

With regard to the Orders transmitted to Colonel Upton, our declared Intention was, that he should remain at Bombay to compleat any Articles of his Negociation with the Government of Poona, which he might leave unsettled at the Time of his Departure; he is the immediate Agent of this Government, and was deputed expresly on that Service; our employing him to conclude it at Bombay, could not be meant, nor ought to be deemed a Supercession of that Government; and if you consider the Offence which the State of Poona hath justly taken at their receiving Ragoba with his Army within the Boundaries of Surat, after the Conclusion of the Treaty, and the Impossibility, from this Circumstance, of their deputing any Person to Bombay, to carry into Execution the Articles of the Treaty which were to be performed on their Part, you cannot but seriously approve of a Measure which places a Minister from this Government between your Presidency and them, to effectuate those Ends which probably could not be attained by that Presidency alone, without such an Interposition.

Fort William, 10th July 1776. We are, &c.

Extract of Bengal Secret Consultations, the 15th July, 1776.

PRESENT,

The Honourable Warren Hastings, Governor General, President,
Lieutenant General John Clavering,
The Honourable George Monson,
Richard Barwell, } Esquires.
Philip Francis, }

Read, and approved, the Proceedings of the 10th Instant.
Mr. Tayler sends in the following Letter:

To the Honourable Warren Hastings, Esquire, Governor General, &c. Council at Fort William.

Honourable Sir, and Gentlemen,

The 13th Instant, in the Evening, I received your Letter of the 10th.

From a due Deference to your Opinion, it gives me much Concern that you should conclude I have acted without Authority, in protesting against your not complying with the Orders of the Honourable the Court of Directors, dated 15th December 1775, for keeping,

keeping, under every Circumstance, all Territories and Possessions ceded to the Company by the Treaty concluded with Ragoba, and adopting all such Measures as might be necessary for their Preservation and Defence; but as a Question, I presume it still remains to be decided, with respect to the Propriety of it on my Part, by that Government under whose Authority I immediately act, and ultimately by the Honourable the Court of Directors.

In Vindication of my Description of the present Government at Poona, by the Appellation of *Rebels*, permit me to refer you to the 4th Article of your Instructions to Lieutenant Colonel Upton, dated 17th July 1775, which begins with this Passage: "Ragonath Row is the Paishwa or Chief Ruler of the Maratta State, but was obliged, "by the Ministerial Party at Poona, to quit that Capital; and they have since proclaimed in his Stead the Son of Narrain Row, the late Paishwah, who is still an "Infant." Allowing this Infant to be the Son of Narrain Row, which, when I had the Honour of attending you in Council, I acquainted you Mr. Mostyn was assured he is not, Ragonath Row, during the Minority of his Uncle, Mhadow Row, and Father, Narrain Row, was Regent of the Maratta Empire. At his Accession to the Paishwaship, on the Death of Narrain Row, it rested with him to continue or remove Saccaram Bappoo and Ballajee Pundit from their Offices: He continued them, and they acted as his Ministers for several Months, and now withhold the Government from him. Under the Sanction of these Circumstances it is that I venture to describe them by the Appellation of *Rebels*.

The Honourable the Governor and Council of Bombay, of themselves, and through me, have repeatedly assured you, that you might depend on their shewing the strictest Observance to any Directions you should be pleased to send them, relative to the Treaty which Lieutenant Colonel Upton has been employed to negociate. As the Representatives of the Company on that Side of India, I must still think that Confidence ought to have been placed in them, and am sure they are on every Account entitled to it; and from the Ministerial Party having sued to them for Peace, I am fully persuaded, that had you been pleased to repose the necessary Trust in them, it could have been long since settled on more respectable, advantageous, and permanent Terms than it now is.

I have the Honour to be, &c.

Calcutta, (Signed) W. Tayler.
15th July 1776.

APPENDIX, N° 139.

From Ragonaut Row; Received 14th November 1776.

I HAVE dispatched to you Seven or Eight successive Letters, but have not to this Time been favoured with an Answer to either, which surprizes me; indeed, from remaining in Expectation of an Answer, I have incurred a very considerable Loss; and being remedilefs I left Surat, and am arrived at the Fortress of Dummen. I have received repeated Letters from the Sirdars of Poona, but being unwilling to consent to any of the Propositions without Advice, I have returned no Answer. I have been informed by my Vackeel at Bombay, that the Gentlemen of the Council at Bombay and at Calcutta, have been directed by the Company in Europe to support me, agreeably to the former Engagement; and the Gentlemen of Bombay have written to Mr. Tayler, desiring him to obtain the Permission of the Council at Calcutta for this Purpose: This has conveyed to me the greatest Satisfaction. I remain at the Kella of Dummen in Expectation of an Answer. It is incumbent on you, and the Gentlemen of the Council in Calcutta, to afford me Support, conformably to the Orders of the Company; and signify your Permission to the Gentlemen of Bombay for the Continuation of the War, for the rainy Season is now expiring: You will thence evince the Uniformity of the Acts of the Nation, and your fraternal Connection, and it will add Vigour to our Friendship.

I repeatedly address you on the Subject of my Concerns, but receive no Answer, at which I am surprized. I request that you will be prompted by Friendship to favour me with a Reply.

I have written other Particulars to Wunkut Row, my Vackeel, who will explain them to you. I cheerfully repose implicit Confidence in you.

Extract of Bengal Secret Consultations, the 30th September 1776.

PRESENT,

The Honourable Warren Hastings, Esq; Governor General, President,
Richard Barwell, } Esquires.
Philip Francis, }
General Clavering indisposed.

Received the following Letters from Lieutenant Colonel Upton:

Gentlemen,

I am honoured with your Letter of the 16th May, with the Copies of the Letters to the Honourable the President and Council of Bombay of the 16th and 20th May, and the Packet for that Board, which arrived at the same Time, and was immediately forwarded.

The Ministers express great Satisfaction at the Assurances you have given them regarding Ragonaut Row, and hope, in Consequence of them, soon to see their Country in perfect Tranquillity.

Another Competitor for Power in this Country has lately sprung up. The Account the Ministers give of this Man is as follows: That about Eight Years ago a Man was confined for calling himself Sedashee Row Bow, Son of Chamagee Ophah, who was the Brother of Bajee Row, Peshwa, Ragonaut Row's Father. He was then led through and about the City of Poona Four different Times, to see if any one could recollect in him Sedashee Row. As Nobody could, he was ordered into Confinement.

Sedashee Row was said to be killed in the Battle of Paneput against the Abdallahs Fifteen Years ago, but it seems his Body was never found. This Man, who has taken his Name, lately found Means to persuade the Killedar of the Fort where he was confined to release him; the Killedar is also in Rebellion. Sedashee Row, as he is called, (or more generally the Bow) has collected Eight or Ten Thousand Men, and has possessed himself of Part of the Cockun Country (which extends from Salsette almost to Surat) and is also in Possession of Three or Four Forts. The Ministers have sent an Army to dispossess him, &c. but they say the Rains are so heavy in that Part of the Country, that their Troops cannot possibly act until the rainy Season is over. They tell me they deputed about a Month ago Two Men, who knew Sedashee Row, to go to this Man's Camp, and see if he was really the Person he gave himself out to be; if so, these Men were authorized to assure him of the Friendship of the Ministers, and to offer him on their Part the Share in Government he required: But these Two Men, on their Arrival in the Bow's Camp, were immediately confined, and the Ministers have never been able to get any Reply from them.

The Ministers say now, that they are quite easy about Ragonaut Row; and as their whole Country will be fully assured of the Part the English have taken, they shall soon quiet this Rebellion: However if it should prove, as this Man asserts, that he is really the Son of Chamagee Ophah, they declare they will give him the First Office in the State.

I am able, Gentlemen, in this Business, to say little more than what the Ministers have related; I see very few People, and these are always on their Guard when with me; their Government is too absolute for much Freedom respecting it. The principal People amongst them seem to think this Man an Adventurer; the lower Class are assured of his being Sedashee Row, and wish to see him fortunate: At all Events, should he succeed to the governing Power of this Country, his confirming the late Treaty will be necessary, as the Peshwa is a Minor.

Ballajee

Ballajee Pundit requests you will be pleased to favour him with Passes, &c. for himself and Suite, of the same Kind and Extent as Siccaram Babou's; he intends taking the earliest Opportunity of going to pray at Benares, &c. Maduro Shedashew, the Minister's principal Agent in the late Negociation, makes the same Request.

Madurow Shedashew has repeatedly requested of me to advise you, Gentlemen, of a Perquisite always claimed by the Heads of particular Offices on the Conclusion of a Peace, and has related the many Instances where it has been complied with. I always answered, That the English had no such Customs; but even if we had, as we have given up a great deal more Country than we have received, we should claim from them this accustomed Perquisite. I told him of the Impossibility of my making an Application of such Sort; he has begged he might be permitted therefore to write to me on this Subject, and wished I would send the Letter to the Supreme Council. The enclosed is his Letter, and explains his Claim better than I can do. May I entreat you will be kind enough, Gentlemen, to furnish me with a Reply to his Request; he will then be satisfied.

I am in daily Expectation of hearing from Bombay, what Measures they have taken in Consequence of your Orders to them regarding Ragonaut Row. Lieutenant Paterson sailed from Bombay the 14th last Month. He had Charge of the Treaty, which I hope has been safely delivered.

I have, &c.
(Signed) J. Upton.

Poona,
19 July, 1776.

Gentlemen,

I am honoured with your Letter of the 20th June. A Packet which arrived at the same Time for the Honourable the Governor and Council of Bombay, was immediately forwarded.

The Proposal from the Nabob Fazil Beg Cawn was never intended to be put in Execution, unless it readily met with my Sanction: In this Case, the Business preparatory to it was to be forwarding, and the Approbation and Orders from the Supreme Council were to be waited for. I told the Nabob's Vackeel, that the Engagements now entered into by the English, would be most inviolably adhered to; that, as I had promised, so his Master's Proposal should be forwarded to Calcutta; but that the Nabob would easily conceive how such an Attempt on the Honour and good Faith of the English Nation would be received; and also assured the Vackeel, that if I heard of any Motions being made to forward the present Scheme against this Government, during my Residence at Poona, I would immediately advise the Peshwa's Ministers of their Danger; but if (as he had most solemnly promised me) the Nabob did not interfere or endeavour to counteract the Engagements entered into by the late Treaty, I would never take any further Notice about it. He departed, assuring me, that the Thought would be immediately dropped, on his delivering my Answer to the Nabob.

I have never corresponded with any foreign Power, but at the Request of the Ministers, since my Residence at Poona. The Jealousies of the Ministers towards me have been long since removed. Untoward Circumstances have been continually happening, but these on my Part have been so candidly accounted for, that the Ministers are perfectly satisfied of the good Faith of the Supreme Council, and that my Conduct has been strictly honourable.

I shall most attentively, Gentlemen, observe your Directions, and neither write, nor otherwise correspond, with any of the Country Powers, so as to occasion the least Jealousy to this Government. At present they rather betray Fears of our being too well acquainted with the distracted State of their Country, than Jealousies regarding their Contentions with Ragonaut Row.

Colonel Keating's Letter to me, of the 14th April last, was not in Reply to any Letter of mine; but, as the Colonel observes therein, at the Request of Ragonaut Bajerow. I enclose my Answer; also a Copy of the Ministers Denial of their ever having made such Proposals for Ragonaut Row as were set forth in that Letter; the Original (under the Seal of the Peshwa) is with me. I also forward a Letter from me to the Honourable the Governor and Council of Bombay, dated 21st May. I hope, Gentlemen, these will furnish every Particular you were desirous of knowing.

 There

There is little or no Change in the Affairs of Sedashew Row since I had the Honour to write last (19 July). He seems rather to be gaining Ground; and the People in general are more persuaded of his being really the Son of Chummagee Oppah. Neither Party can do any Thing until the Rains are over.

I am daily expecting Letters from Bombay; when these arrive, I hope to be able to advise of Ragonaut Row's having left Surat. I shall wait the Receipt of these Letters, and then close this. The accompanying Letters, dated the 13th and 24th July, and 7th August, will fully acquaint you, Gentlemen, with the Measures that have been pursued since the Receipt of your Letters; that to me, of the 16th May, and that to the Honourable the Governor and Council of Bombay, of the 20th May.

Gentlemen, August 26, 1776.

I have just received the Letter from the Honourable the President and Council of Bombay, which advises of Ragonaut Row's having left Surat. The following Extract is all therein that relates to Ragonaut Row's Departure.

Extract of a Letter from the Honourable the President and Council of Bombay to Lieutenant Colonel Upton, dated 19th August, 1776.

" We shall wave any further Reply to your Letter, as Ragoba has thought proper to " retire from Surat of his own Accord, which of Course will remove the Jealousy the " Ministers had conceived at his Residence there."

The Ministers had complained to me, Two Days before I received this Information from Bombay, that Ragonaut Row had been permitted to make his Escape from Surat, after having been covered and protected by the English for near Six Months (contrary to the true Intent and Meaning of the late Treaty they had entered into with us) which must occasion to their State further Troubles and great Expence.

I had been constantly requesting of the Ministers to agree to a Change of Abode for Ragonaut Row, and to take off the Troops allotted for his Service, which he looked upon in no other Light than as a Guard placed over him; and to increase his Stipend, so as to enable him to support his Rank. The Peshwa's Consent had been obtained and sent to Bombay the 22d Instant, for Ragonaut Row's residing at Benares, unattended by Troops; and an Allowance of Five Lacks of Rupees a Year, or a Jaghire to that Amount, fixed upon him in the Neighbourhood of Calpee.

Should this Indulgence of the Peshwa's reach Ragonaut Row, I am of Opinion he will not accept it, as his Vackeel, who resides at Bombay, wrote me a few Days ago in Terms, expecting his former Demands to be complied with.

I have, &c.
(Signed) J. Upton.

Gentlemen,

I had just closed the accompanying Letter, when I was honoured with your Letters of the 1st and 3d July; and about an Hour after the enclosed Letter and Extract from the Honourable the President and Select Committee of Bombay arrived. You will perceive, Gentlemen, by this Letter, the determined Part (at all Events) the Gentlemen at Bombay mean to take. This perplexes me exceedingly; for should I take my immediate Departure from this Place, and proceed to Bombay, no Arguments could ever induce the Ministers to believe otherwise than that this Determination of the Select Committee of Bombay was in Consequence of Orders from the Supreme Council, and that I must all along have been privy to these Intentions. I should find it very difficult to persuade the Ministers, by Letter from Bombay, that this Matter would be adjusted, when Replies to my Letters should arrive from Calcutta. As it will necessarily be some Time before either Jambooseer, or the Cession made by Futty Sing, will be restored to the Peshwa, there would be little to apprehend, until your positive Orders should arrive, unless the Resolves of the Committee of Bombay be made known; and in this Case I should imagine a Maratta War inevitable, unless by my being on the Spot they were satisfied that there must be some Mistake, and might perhaps be induced to wait its being adjusted. On the other Hand, should the Council of Bombay determine to prosecute the

the War, it would be no longer safe for me to remain another Hour at Poona, enraged as these People are at the Opposition they have already met with, in carrying into Execution the Part of the Treaty that relates to Ragonaut Row, and its Consequence, the Defection of many of their Chiefs, who by the Ministers Enemies have been made to believe that the War would be renewed when the Rains were over.

I shall immediately write to the Select Committee at Bombay, to keep their Resolves for the present profoundly secret; but I am afraid it will be impossible for me to wait at Poona, in Expectation of your further Orders to that Presidency, which I shall nevertheless endeavour to do, if the Risk does not become too great; for it plainly appears, by the determined Manner in which this Letter from Bombay is worded, that I can be of little Service there, in forwarding the Conditions of the Treaty. Another Letter from them may perhaps satisfy me, that they mean to go no greater Lengths than those already mentioned; if so, I hope all may yet end well.

Mr. Fowke has forwarded Passports from Cheyte Sing for Siccaram Pundit and Goupkaboy; as soon as those from Mr. Bristow arrive I will present them, and make the Professions of Friendship and Protection agreeable to your Directions.

I will take the earliest Opportunity of requesting the Ministers to settle a Provision for the Payment of the Twelve Lacks of Rupees as it becomes due to the Presidency of Bombay.

When I advised, that I imagined Morabah would succeed to the Vacancy that Sacaram Pundit might make in the Administration at Poona, it was from a natural Influence, as at that Time Ballajee Pundit was treating with him to engage him to come over to the Ministerial Party; and as I understand he receives Part of the Emoluments of Ballajee Pundit's Appointments, and it is said nominally to be joined with him in the Revenue Department, though he has for some Time declined acting, it never could have happened by the Inclination of Siccaram Pundit, as there is a Hatred between him and Morabah, amounting almost to a mortal Enmity. Perhaps the Bow may be brought in, who, if the real Person he gives himself out to be, has Claim to the first Appointment; and it is said Siccaram Pundit is not averse to it, though he will be strongly opposed by Ballajee Pundit and Morabah. How these contending Parties will adjust their Differences Time alone can discover; they stand in great Need of some one related to the Peshwa, or of more exalted Rank than the present People, at the Head of the Ministry.

It is currently reported here, that the Bow means to march to Poona immediately upon the Rains breaking up: The Ministers also acquainted me, that they heard of the Bow's having such Intention; that they much wished he would attempt putting it in Execution, as they only wanted to get him out of his strong Holds, to be insured of putting an immediate End to this Rebellion. The Ministers are daily augmenting the Force that is acting against the Bhow. It is said Ragonaut Row is on his March by the Sea Shore to join the Bhow.

I observed, in my Letter of the 19th July, that the Cokun Country extends from Salsette almost to Surat; I then meant, and should have said, it was the Part of the Country that was likely to be the Seat of War; for the entire Cokun Country extends from near to Surat almost to Mysore, the Capital of Hyder Ally's Country, and I now understand that Sedashee Row possesses the greatest Part of this Country.

I should imagine a few Days would make the travelling from Poona to Bombay impracticable, as the Pindarries (Free Booters) from the Two Armies are laying the Country Waste all round, and making Prisoners of all that fall in their Way.

I wrote last Night to Bombay, as there was no Time to be lost, and enclose a Copy of this Letter. The Reply will determine whether I must immediately proceed to Bombay, or remain some Time longer at Poona, though I think it very probable I shall be obliged to retire to Masulipatam, and there wait your further Orders; from whence, if Occasion should require, I can with Ease, in a Journey of about Thirty Days, reach Poona, and Letters pass in about Thirteen or Fourteen Days (less if necessary) from Poona to Masulipatam.

I shall do myself the Honour to write again as soon as I receive a Reply from Bombay.

In the present Uncertainty you will be pleased, Gentlemen, to forward my Letters by Way of Masulipatam. Should I go to Bombay, I shall advise the Chief of that Settlement, and my Letters will be safely conveyed to me.

General

General Carnac landed at Bombay on the 16th Instant; his Appointment is Second in Council, and to succeed to the Chair.

I am, &c.

Poona, (Signed) J. Upton.
28 August, 1776.

APPENDIX, N° 140.

IN Consequence of the Intelligence contained in Lieutenant Colonel Upton's Letters; it is resolved, that the following Letter be immediately written to Bombay:

Gentlemen,

We have just received Advices from Lieutenant Colonel Upton, dated the 28th Ultimo, with which he transmits us a Copy of your Letter to him of the 20th August, and of his Reply to it on the 27th.

We have read with great Surprize, the Resolution declared in your Letter to Colonel Upton, that "you were determined at all Events to keep Possession of such of the late "Cessions as are not yet relinquished:" And we are equally alarmed at the fatal Consequences which may attend such a notorious Breach of a public Treaty, and consequently, Violation of the national Faith. We hope however that the Arguments urged to you by Colonel Upton, and supported by our Resolutions, on Receipt of the Company's Orders respecting the Maratta War, which we communicated to you in a Letter of the 1st July, will have had sufficient Influence on your Conduct to prevent the Execution of the Measure you had resolved on, or at least to have suspended the Issue of any Orders in Consequence therefore until this may arrive.

We now desire you will call to Mind, that the Treaty with the Maratta State has been executed under the Sanction and by the Authority of an Act of Parliament; that therefore it is not only binding on all the Company's Settlements in India, but even on the Company themselves.

We claim and demand your Aid, in supporting and maintaining the Treaty which is now in Force; declaring at the same Time that we shall hold you responsible for all the Consequences which must follow a Breach of it on your Part.

But we see no Difficulty in reconciling the Conditions of the Treaty with the Object of the Company's Orders, although those Orders are manifestly framed without any Knowledge of the Part we had taken. The Interchange of Jambooseer, and the other Lands stipulated to be restored to the Marattas for the Country adjoining to Broach, which is specified in the 5th Article of the Treaty to be ceded on their Part to the Company, will leave the Company in Possession of a Territory obtained by peaceable Means from the Marattas, equally convenient in Point of Situation, and not much inferior in Value to that which the Company have impowered you to keep Possession of, though originally obtained, and still requiring to be preserved, by Force of Arms.

If our positive Injunction should effect no Change in the Resolutions you had agreed to, we desire you will reflect on the Means you are possessed of to carry on a War. You have represented to us, that the State of your Treasury is very low; yet your Supplies from this Presidency have been anticipated to a considerable Amount. The Returns of your Troops prove, that the Establishment of your Army is very deficient; and upon the Whole we think your actual Condition very far from being such as would in Prudence justify your exposing the Company's Possessions under your Government to the immediate Hazards of a War, admitting that no other Motives opposed your engaging in it.

We are, &c.

Agreed, That the following Reply be written to Colonel Upton.

Sir,

We have now before us your Letters of the 19th July, and 24th, 26th, and 28th August.

The

The Information contained in the Letter respecting the Resolution of the President and Council of Bombay, has greatly alarmed us; and we may very anxiously wait for the subsequent Advices which you have promised to transmit to us; yet we think it necessary to write immediately to Bombay, to prevent the Execution of a Measure, which may prove so fatal in its Consequences to the Interests of the Company.

We inclose a Copy of our Letter to that Presidency for your Information; and as we cannot foresee the Event which it may produce, we can prescribe no Line for your Conduct in case the Government of Bombay should still persist in their Determination: But we leave it entirely to your Direction, either to remain at Poona, to demand your Dismission, or to take any other Measures which present Circumstances shall point out to your Judgment as most conducive to the Good of the Company's Service, your own Safety, and that of the Party under your Command.

In your Letter of the 19th July, you say, "At all Events, should he (Sedashee Row) "succeed to the governing Power of this Country, his confirming the late Treaty will "be necessary, as the Peshwa is a Minor." We desire to know on what Ground or Information you have formed this alarming Conclusion: We on our Parts have always considered the Treaty as formed with, and binding on the Maratta State; without regarding in whose Hands the actual Power of the Government may now or at any Time hereafter be lodged.

We are, &c. &c.
(Signed) Warren Hastings,
J. Clavering,
Richard Barwell,
P. Francis.

APPENDIX, N° 141.

Extract of Bengal Secret Consultations, the 14th October, 1776.

PRESENT,

The Honourable Warren Hastings, Governor General, President,
Richard Barwell, } Esquires.
Philip Francis, }
General Clavering indisposed.

READ, and approved the Proceedings of the 10th Instant.

Received the following Letter from Lieutenant Colonel Upton;

Gentlemen,

I had the Honour to address you last on the 28th Ultimo.

It is with great Pleasure I forward the inclosed Letter, which I received last Night from the Select Committee of Bombay: I wish these Gentlemen had been a little more communicative; though I hope they now mean to do all in their Power to facilitate the carrying the few remaining Articles of the Treaty into Execution. The Ministers have still their Doubts from this Quarter; the accompanying Letter from the Peishwa, which I received Two Days ago (and forwarded to Bombay) will inform you, Gentlemen, of some recent Causes for these Doubts; which, added to the prevailing Report that Assistance will be given by the English to Ragonath Row after the Rains, must certainly occasion to the Ministers much Uneasiness; and this they shewed very strongly, when I desired them to appoint a Day for my taking Leave. They have assured me, that whatsoever Turn the Affairs of their Country may take, they are, and shall be thoroughly convinced of the honourable Part the Governor General and Council have taken; and that I may remain at Poona entirely secure of their best Opinion,

nion, and in the utmost Safety; I have accordingly consented to stay if (as I told them) it met with your Approbation, until the Treaty shall be accomplished, or nearly so, or until a Resident shall be sent from Bombay.

I believe all Thoughts of my going to Bombay must be given up, not only from the Jealousy it would occasion here, but from the Danger of the Attempt: May I be permitted to add, That I think every Inconvenience, without a single Advantage to the Business of the Treaty, might be apprehended, should I leave Poona and go to Bombay; as it remains entirely with the Ministers to carry into Execution the following Stipulations, which are all that are now left unaccomplished, viz. The making over the Country of Three Lacks near Broach; the producing the Proofs of the Paishwa's Right to the Guzerat Country entire; and making a Provision for the Payment of the Twelve Lacks. I have frequently represented to the Ministers how much we suffered by the dilatory Method of carrying on the Correspondence with Fort William, and have at last got their Promise, that they will immediately lay Dawks (I believe to Benares) by which Means the Letters will go from Poona to Calcutta in about 17 Days; this will give Spirit to the Business, and I should imagine Three Months might compleat it. Futty Sing is expected at Poona shortly: I have told the Ministers that I should refer the Matter in Dispute, respecting his Right to making Grants of any Part of the Guzerat Country, and receive your Orders concerning it; as I did not conceive, now the Treaty was ratified, the Power of determining this Business was vested in me. You will please, Gentlemen, to give me your particular Instructions regarding this.

You will also, Gentlemen, be pleased to instruct me how to proceed should the Bow be successful; though I see no great Reason to expect this, it is nevertheless necessary to be provided against such an Exigency. I hope, and think, I shall be able to remain at Poona till I have the Honour to receive a Reply to this Letter. Ragonath will not be able to occasion much Disturbance in so short a Time, and the Bow's Successes cannot affect me. You may depend, Gentlemen, on my giving the most early Advice, should we meet with any future Rebuffs in adjusting the Conditions of the Treaty, or should this Government undergo any Alteration, by Change of Ministers, &c.

I acquainted the Ministers in the Manner you directed, that the Peshwa's Vackeel would be properly received, &c. at Calcutta; and they have requested that he may accompany me on my Return to Bengal. From what I can learn, they have not yet been able to fix upon a Man in whose Abilities and Attachment they can sufficiently confide, otherwise I suppose they would send him away sooner, for they were much pleased to find their Desire of having a Person reside at Calcutta so favourably received.

The Passports from the Vizier are not yet arrived for Goupkaboy and Siccaram Pundit.

Poona, I have the Honour to be, &c.
9th September 1776. (Signed) J. Upton.

P. S. I believe the most favourable Reading may be given to the inclosed Letter from the Select Committee of Bombay. I have again wrote to these Gentlemen for a fuller Explanation, and herewith forward a Copy of this Letter.

Ordered, That the Enclosures be entered after the Consultation.

Resolved, That the following Reply be written to Lieutenant Colonel Upton:

To Lieutenant Colonel Upton.

Sir,

We have received your Letter of the 9th Ultimo.

We have already given it as our Opinion, that your longer Continuance at Poona is unnecessary; we see no Grounds to alter that Opinion, and cannot therefore consent to your Stay. We require you to demand your immediate Dismission from the Maratta Court, if this Letter should find you still at Poona. You will, however, take Care to do it in Terms of the greatest Delicacy, and with such Cautions that it may not have an abrupt or unfriendly Appearance.

We enclose a Letter from the Governor General to Siccaram Baboo, which you will deliver to him, and a Copy is herewith transmitted for your Perusal.

Notwithstanding

Notwithstanding any Revolutions that may happen in the Marratta State, we consider that State, as well as ourselves, equally bound to abide by the Treaty, and to maintain the Conditions of it, without any Regard to the Persons actually in Possession of the ruling Power, for the Government itself remains the same, whatever Change of Hands the Administration may fall into.

On these Principles you will see that we deem it totally unnecessary to open any fresh Negociation with Sudaba, in case that Chief should prevail; nor do we see any Subject which will remain for Negociation, unless some Conditions of the Treaty should be unaccomplished, and he, disclaiming the Treaty, refuse to execute them. Supposing the Party of Sudaba, or any other foreign Party, to be established in the Poona Government, you will call upon them to execute the Articles of the Treaty remaining to be performed on their Part, and you will take their Reply as an Acknowledgment or Disavowal of the Treaty; but you must be cautious to avoid expressing any Doubt of the Validity of the Treaty, or that the Force of it can be impaired by any internal Changes or Revolutions in the Government of Poona.

Fort William, the 14th October 1776. We are, &c.

Read the following Letters from Bombay:

Referred to in Appendix, No. 139.

Honourable Sir, and Sirs,

We have received your Letters, dated the 6th, 16th, and 20th May.

It is with much Pleasure we can assert, that none of the bad Consequences have ensued which you apprehended from our receiving Ragoba into Surat, and on which you ground your Directions for requiring him to withdraw from the Company's Settlements: The Treaty has not only been ratified and exchanged, and Orders given by the Ministers for the Communication being opened between the Company's Settlements and the Maratta Dominions; but we are not without Hopes that Colonel Upton will prevail with them to assign an Establishment for Ragoba, as he mentions, in his Letter dated the 13th June, that he would continue his Endeavours for that Purpose; and we have since again urged this Point to him, but have not received his Reply. Circumstances therefore being thus altered, and the above Conduct of the Ministers implying an Acquiescence on their Part to Ragoba continuing under the Company's Protection, we have not signified to him the Directions you have thought proper to give respecting him.

When the Peace was proclaimed at this Presidency, the whole Extract, as transmitted by Colonel Upton, was read verbatim to the Garrison, and we therefore suppose any further Publication to be unnecessary.

We have ordered Copies to be made of the several Treaties you desire, which shall be transmitted to you when finished. The Grenville was dispatched to England on the 27th Ultimo, with Directions to the Commander to touch at Fort Saint George.

We are, &c.

Bombay Castle, 7th August 1776. (Signed) William Hornby, &c. Council.

Honourable Sir, and Gentlemen,

Our last Letter was dated the 7th Instant, of which a Duplicate is enclosed; and we have since received your Letters, dated the 20th and 27th June.

The Vessels taken by the Maratta Fleet have not yet been restored, though the Owners went down to receive them, with the Orders from the Ministers, which were entirely disregarded.

The Aurora, an English Merchant Ship, was wrecked in the Month of June last on the Maratta Coast near Rutneah Gherry. The greatest Part of the Cargo was landed; and as it is stipulated in the late Treaty, that the Whole of what may be saved from English Vessels wrecked on any Part of the Maratta Coast shall be restored, we have sent the necessary Information to Colonel Upton, that he may demand full Restitution;

tution; we also enclose for your Notice Copy of a Letter from the Supercargo, giving a particular Account of this Accident, and of the Treatment he received from the Marattas.

We consider ourselves as bound by the late Act of Parliament to transmit you every Proposal or political Information, which in its Consequence may affect the Company's Interest, and we were therefore surprized at the Wish you expressed in your Letter of the 30th June. We had no other Concern in Ragoba's Proposal respecting the Nizam than merely transmitting to your Honour, &c. a Copy of the Letter we received from him on the Subject, which had we suppressed, might have made us liable to your Censure, and we do not see how this Transaction, of which the Ministers were totally ignorant, could create in them any Jealousy or Distrust.

We have, from Time to Time given you an Account of Sudaba's Proceedings, as they have come to our Knowledge; and as the Event of his Operations is likely to become of much Importance to the Honourable Company, we wished to be assured of his true Situation, as well as the Identity of his Person; and for this Purpose Abdul Gunny was sent down to Rutna Gurry, on the Pretence of making Enquiries respecting the Aurora's Cargo: This Man having been frequently employed on Government Business at Poona, while Sudaba was in Power there, was perfectly acquainted with his Person; and from his Report, and from every other Circumstance, there remains not a Doubt with us, that the Person now in Arms in Opposition to the Ministers, is the real Sudaba; he is encamped for the Rains Two Days March from Fort Victoria, with an Army of about Thirty thousand Men, and expects to be joined by a considerable Body of Horse from the Ranne. It is thought he will march this Way before he proceeds to Poona to take in Bassein, the Killadar of which Place was put in by his Father, and we hear is ready to admit him.

We enclose Copies of a Message from Sudaba, brought us by Abdul Gunny, and of a Letter since received, in which he explains his Designs, and expresses a strong Desire of being joined by Ragoba.

From the present Appearance of Affairs, there is every Reason to expect that Sudaba will very shortly become Master of Poona, and that the Ministers will not be able to maintain their Government; and we therefore esteem it our Duty to request your immediate Directions for our Conduct upon this Event: He totally disallows any Right in the Ministers to conclude a Treaty in Behalf of the Maratta State; and we apprehend it is highly necessary we should be early furnished with Powers to enter into a Negociation with him or Ragoba, or both jointly, which we beg you will furnish us with. Our affording Protection to Ragoba may be considered as a most fortunate Circumstance, as we still hope to be able to secure the Advantages for the Company stipulated in the Treaty of Surat, which we should have forfeited all Pretentions to, had we denied him an Asylum in his Distress.

The President has received Advice from the Chief of Surat, that Ragoba, on the 9th Instant, had suddenly retired from that Place entirely of his own Accord. The enclosed Extract from the Chief's Letter will acquaint you with the Apprehensions which led this unfortunate Man to this precipitate Step, and we can give you no further Information of his future Intentions than is therein contained.

We enclose a Continuation of our Correspondence with Colonel Upton. The Latham arrived here from Great Britain on the 17th Instant, and we now transmit an Extract from the Commands of the Honourable the Court of Directors, received by that Ship. With these special Orders before us, we cannot think of relinquishing Jambooseer, or any other of the Possessions which are not yet restored; and we have therefore, in Obedience thereto, determined at all Events to retain them, which we shall signify to Colonel Upton, that he may regulate his Conduct accordingly.

We have the Honour to be, &c.

Bombay Castle, (Signed) William Hornby, &c. Council.
20th August 1776.

Ordered, That the Enclosures be entered after the Consultation; and
Agreed, That the following Letter be written to Bombay:

To the Honourable William Hornby, Esquire, President, &c. Council at Bombay

Gentlemen,

We have received your Letters of the 7th and 20th August; which have been in a great Measure replied to by ours of the 30th Ultimo.

We

We are pleased however to find, by a Letter just received from Colonel Upton, dated the 9th September, that your Resolution to maintain Possession of the conquered Countries on the Continent from the Marattas had not been divulged, and that you had thought proper to countermand the Orders given on that Occasion. We hope that you will not have taken any subsequent Measures to preclude you from carrying the Injunctions contained in our Letter of the 30th Ultimo implicitly into Execution; and we again repeat the same, requiring your strict Obedience thereto.

We have directed Colonel Upton, in case the Party of Sudaba, or any other Party, should have prevailed in the Government of Poona, to demand the Performance of any Conditions of the Treaty which may still remain to be executed on the Part of the Marattas, and to receive their Answer as an Acknowledgment or Disavowal of the Treaty; but not to enter into any fresh Negociations with them. We consider the Maratta State to be bound by the Treaty; and that the Engagements formed by it continue in Force as long as the State itself subsists, notwithstanding any internal Revolutions in the Government, or any Change of Persons in the actual Administration.

We have further ordered Colonel Upton to demand his immediate Dismission from the Court of Poona, to return to Bengal. If he should leave any Articles of the Treaty unaccomplished at his Departure, as the Case of carrying it into compleat Effect will of course devolve to you, we recommend for this Purpose, as well as to maintain a continued amicable Intercourse with the Maratta State, that you appoint an Agent to reside at Poona; and we request that you will be pleased to advise us of the Person whom you may nominate to that Station.

We are, &c.

Fort William,
14th October 1776.

P. S. We have this Instant received your Letter of the 14th September, with the several Papers inclosed in it. We are very happy to see it thus confirmed to us, that you had anticipated our Instructions of the 30th September, by repealing the Orders which you had issued on the 20th August last.

Extract of Bengal Secret Consultations, 14th October 1776.

ENCLOSURES.

To Colonel Upton.

Sir,

We have received your Letter dated the 27th Ultimo.

The utmost Secresy has been observed, with respect to the Measures we had resolved to pursue, in Consequence of the Honourable Company's Commands, communicated to you in our Letter of the 20th; and we have now to acquaint you, that from some Circumstances which have since happened, we have thought proper to countermand the Orders we had given on this Occasion.

We are, &c.

Bombay Castle,
4th September 1776.

(Signed) William Hornby,
John Carnac,
Robert Gordon,
D. Draper,
T. Mostyn,
N. Stakhouse,
Robert Garden,
Andrew Ramsay.

Extract of Bengal Secret Consultations, 21st October 1776.

PRESENT,

The Honourable Warren Hastings, Governor General, President,
Richard Barwell, and Philip Francis, Esquires.
Lieutenant General John Clavering indisposed.

Read, a Letter from Bombay as follows:

Honourable Sir, and Gentlemen,

Agreeable to what we mentioned in our Letter, dated the 24th April, we now dispatch the Eagle, one of the Company's Cruizers, commanded by Captain John Hall, to receive on board whatever Treasure you may think proper to send round in Part of the Year's Supply, and likewise to afford you an Opportunity of conveying any Sums of Money you may have taken up as Loans for this Presidency in Consequence of our Letter dated the 30th of June.

Our last Address, dated the 20th Ultimo, was forwarded in Duplicate by the Ships St. Helena and Resolution; and we have since received your Letters, dated the 1st, 3d, and 4th July.

We felt the utmost Concern upon receiving from you Orders so very different in their Tenor from those of the Honourable the Court of Directors, in Obedience to which we had formed the Resolution communicated to you in our last Letter. From the high Respect we entertain for both Authorities, and the present critical Situation of Affairs, these very opposite Orders occasioned us much Embarrassment; though we think it incumbent on us to declare to you our Opinion, that the Orders of the Court of Directors should supersede every other, and that we should never hesitate a Moment which to prefer, if we are so circumstanced as to have an Option, unless our Obedience might tend to the manifest Injury and Danger of the Company's Affairs. With these Sentiments, and a strong Persuasion that the Conduct we had adopted would prove favourable to their Interest, we do yet find ourselves under a Necessity of deviating from their Orders, and of revoking our first Resolution, from an Apprehension of the bad Consequences which must ensue should your Honour, &c. persist in the new Alliance, and withhold from us all further Supplies, as from the peremptory Manner in which your Orders are conveyed we had every Reason to expect. We have therefore countermanded the Orders we had issued to the Chiefs of Surat and Broach for retaining Jamboosseer, &c. of which we also gave immediate Advice to Colonel Upton.

Mr. Draper having differed in Opinion from us respecting the Construction of the Company's Orders, and dissented from our Resolution in Consequence, we at his Request transmit you a Copy of the Dissent he delivered on the Occasion. Brigadier General Gordon likewise concurred with Mr. Draper in both Points, and delivered a Minute, of which the enclosed is a Copy; and the other Members thinking it necessary to explain their Sentiments on the Subject, we have the Honour to transmit Copies of the Minutes made by the President, and Messrs. Carnac, Mostyn, Stackhouse, Garden, and Ramsay. Ragoba, after quitting Surat, proceeded to the Southward, and has already collected Two or Three thousand Followers: He is now at a Fort which surrendered to him, a small Distance from Damaun, and we hear is negociating with the Portugueze for their Assistance. We cannot yet judge what Probability there is of an Alliance taking Place between them; but this leads us again to lament that more Attention was not shewn to Ragoba in the late Treaty. We foresaw this Event, with all its bad Consequences, if satisfactory Terms were not settled for him, and urged this Point to Colonel Upton in the most forcible Manner, in our Letter dated the 18th January. This Gentleman has since acknowledged, in his Letter dated the 7th Ultimo, that had Ragoba sent a Vackeel to him at Poona, the Conditions might perhaps have been made more agreeable to him; and we are sorry that any supposed Failure of Ceremony on the Part of Ragoba should have had any Consideration in a Point wherein the Honour and Interest of the Company were so much concerned.

Twelve

Twelve or Thirteen Days after Ragoba had quitted Surat, the Ministers made Colonel Upton the Proposal mentioned in his Letter dated the 22d Ultimo, respecting an Increase of his Stipend, and a Change of Abode. The Distance between Surat and Poona is not so considerable that they could possibly be ignorant of this Circumstance when they made the Proposal, of which we have further incontestable Proof, by a Body of Three or Four thousand of their Horse marching suddenly from the Gauts to within a small Distance from Surat, on the 20th Ultimo, with a View, no Doubt, to intercept him, whereas the above Proposal was made to Colonel Upton, at Poona, on the 21st. This sufficiently evinces the Artifice of the Ministers, and that Colonel Upton can receive no Intelligence at Poona but such as is agreeable to them.

We observed, with the utmost Surprize, your Intention of recalling Colonel Upton from Poona, to carry on his Negociation from this Presidency. His Interference in political Matters in the immediate Seat of our Government, would be contrary to every Rule of the Service, and would sensibly affect that Consequence and Importance which is so necessary to be preserved to the Members thereof. You will permit us to remark, that your ordering him to Bombay upon any such Purpose, implies a Want of Confidence in us, which we are not conscious of having merited, and is not warranted by any Necessity, as no Part of the Treaty remains unaccomplished on our Side.

We have Advices from Broach, so late as the 31st Ultimo, when the Maratta Agents for settling the Country of Three Lacks were not arrived, though the Purgunnahs lately subject to that Chiefship have been relinquished so long ago as the 18th June. The Company must suffer considerably by the dilatory Manner in which the Ministers perform their Engagements, as the Season is too far advanced to take the proper Measures for the Improvement of the Revenues for this Year.

Your Honour, &c. are pleased to acquaint us in your Letter, dated the 3d July, that you had directed Colonel Upton to settle for the Payment of the 12 Lacks at this Presidency; but though the Time fixed for the First Payment is already considerably elapsed, we have not yet received a Rupee on this Account; and Colonel Upton has proposed to us to send a Gentleman to Poona for this Business, which does not appear to be agreeable to your Intentions.

Sudaba continues moving to the Northward, and, as we at first understood, with an Intention of joining Ragoba, but we know not as yet what Effect the latter's Negociation with the Portugueze may have on his Conduct. On his passing Fort Victoria he paid a Visit to our Resident, and with Professions of much Friendship to the Honourable Company, he offered a Grant of Two Villages contiguous to that Settlement, which we however have directed our Resident to decline. We are persuaded you will see the Propriety and Necessity of furnishing us with immediate Instructions and Powers for negociating with Sudaba, as recommended in our last Letter, for upon his becoming possessed of Poona, which in all human Probability will be the Case in a few Months, the Ministers will not be in a Condition to comply with the Treaty made by Colonel Upton, nor will the Company have any Right to the Possessions ceded by Ragoba.

The enclosed Copy of the sailing Orders will apprize you of the Instructions given to the Commander of the Eagle.

Since writing thus far, we have received a Letter from Ragonath Row, as per Copy enclosed, which confirms our Intelligence of his having commenced a Negociation with the Portugueze. He however promises to return to us in case we will give him Assurances of effectual Assistance.

We have the Honour, &c. &c.

Bombay Castle, (Signed) Wm. Hornby, &c. Council.
14th September 1776.

The above Letter having been acknowledged in a Postscript to the Letter written to Bombay on the 14th Instant; Ordered, That Duplicates of that Letter be prepared and dispatched.

Enclosures

APPENDIX, N° 141.

Enclosures in the Letter from Bombay.

The President's Opinion.

The President with much Reluctance agrees to countermand the Orders sent under the 20th August, to the Chiefs of Surat and Broach, for keeping Possession of such of the Purgunnahs, &c. as had not already been delivered to the Agents of the Poona Government, as it is contrary to the express Orders of the Court of Directors. For that he has every Reason to expect no Assistance from the Governor General and Council of Calcutta, or that they could permit the Governor and Council of Madras to do it, who are much better situated to assist us with Troops, as they are soon got over to this Coast; at the same Time it gives him real Concern to think, that we are necessitated to give up in a Manner all the Advantages we had acquired for the Honourable Company (and which they had been long so much in Want of on this Coast) and at a Time he believes, were we to espouse Ragoba's Cause, he might be fixed in Poona, without any or very little Opposition: At this Time there is the greatest Likelihood, that Sudaba will not be many Months before he gets thither, when the Treaty that has been made by the present Ministers at Poona will be void and of no Value, and of Ragoba's likewise; nor are we entitled to any Thing from it, if he should be seated without our Assistance.

A true Copy.
(Signed) Edward Ravenscroft, Sec.

Mr. Carnac's Opinion.

Whatever may be my Sentiments as to the Propriety of the Treaty with Ragonath Row, or of the Measures for the Requisition of Salsette and its Dependencies, it is not my Inclination, nor perhaps would it become me, to pass a retrospective Opinion upon Matters for which I have no Degree of Responsibility, and which have been subjected to the Verdict of the Court of Directors. My Duty only calls upon me to give my most strenuous Assistance with the other Members of Council, that the present Views and Orders of our Honourable Employers may be complied with to the fullest Extent that our Means and Circumstances will admit of. It is not to be wondered at, that the Court of Directors should have so long and so earnestly had at Heart the obtaining of Salsette, with the adjacent Islands; being from every local Advantage, its Vicinity to Bombay, its Compactness, the Facility of its being administered under the immediate Eye of the Presidency, a Treasure for which they can have no Equivalent; and that being possessed of it, and therewith, as they had Reason to suppose, of the important Fort and Districts of Bassein, they should be so earnest for the Preservation of them. Indeed their Orders on this Head seem so explicit as to leave no Plea or Evasion, unless under the Conviction of the Impossibility of their being executed, or that our Obedience may tend to the manifest Injury and Danger of the Company's Affairs; as for Instance, the involving ourselves in a War, which the low State of our Finances, and the considerable Diminution of our European Force, render us very ill able to support; and we are got into an unhappy Dilemma, from the clashing of the Orders received from Home with those received from the Supreme Council, which is to me a Matter of the most serious Concern, as I have the highest Veneration for the Authority by which it is constituted, and a singular Respect for the Gentlemen who compose it, from a Persuasion that they have the most honourable Intentions towards the Public, and a zealous Regard for the Interests of the Company. Into this Dilemma we would not have been brought, had our Army proceeded to Poona the last Campaign, agreeable to the main Object of our Treaty with Ragonath Row, and which was pointedly recommended in your Instructions to the Officer commanding that Army. Had this been done, it is more than probable that Ragonath Row would have been securely seated in the Peshwary; that the Ministerial Confederacy would have been crushed; and that there would have been no Competitor, with whom to enter into new Engagements. There appeared to be but one Opinion at the first Committee held after the Receipt of the General Letter per Latham; but Mr. Draper has since entered a Dissent, in which the most weighty Reason

Reason offered for deviating from the Orders of our Honourable Masters, arises from an Apprehension, that we may draw upon ourselves a Maratta War: But it is now become problematical at least, whether an Adherence to the former Treaty would not be the most likely Means of avoiding it; for, if your Intelligence of Subadah is to be relied upon, and that he really means, as is said, to co-operate with Ragonath Row, we have Cause to expect, that so soon as the Season for Action commences, the Face of Things in the Maratta Empire will be changed, the Ministers will be reduced to the same deplorable State Ragonath Row has been in, and he in his Turn will be triumphant. There is indeed an Objection almost unsurmountable against our continuing firm to Ragonath Row, though but slightly touched on by Mr. Draper; namely, That if the Gentlemen of the Supreme Council persist in the new Alliance, we may and probably shall have our Resources from Bengal cut off, without which we are in no Condition to give him that effectual Assistance as he may think sufficient to merit the Confirmation of the Concession stipulated in the Treaty of Surat.

(Signed) John Carnac.

Bombay,
Aug. 30th, 1776.

A true Copy.
(Signed) Edward Ravenscroft, Esquire,
Secretary.

Minute made by Briadier General Gordon.

The Brigadier General continues of the same Opinion he has ever been, that the Conditions of the last Treaty with the Maratta Government, so solemnly ratified and confirmed by the Supreme Council, should be strictly complied with and adhered to on our Parts, unless it should be broke through by the Maratta Government. The Court of Directors could not know of Peace being concluded, nor the Circumstances that attended it, when their last General Letter by the Latham was wrote. The Countries ceded by Ragoba were all conditional of his being made Peshwa, and of his being re-established by us in the Government of Poona, which on our Part was never done or attempted, as the Troops never marched that Way, until after the Cessation of Arms was declared. Should this present Treaty of Peace, concluded between the Maratta Government and the Supreme Council, be broke through, under Pretence of other Orders from the Court of Directors, no Country Powers would trust us in future, as they would then have experienced the Supreme Council having overturned the Treaty made between Ragoba and this Presidency, and now the Court of Directors had overturned the succeeding Treaty of Peace, concluded between the Supreme Council and the Maratta Government.

A true Copy.
(Signed) Edw. Ravenscroft, Secretary.

To the Honourable Wm. Hornby, Esquire, President and Governor, &c. Council, Bombay.

Honourable Sir, and Sirs,

On recovering from my late Indisposition, I observed, from the Minutes of Council and Correspondence during that Interval, that your Honour, &c. had on the 20th Instant resolved that the 38th, 39th, and 40th Paragraphs of the Honourable the Court of Directors their Commands, dated the 5th April last, received by the Latham, contained special Orders for keeping Possession of all such Territories ceded by Ragoba, as were not then relinquished, notwithstanding the late Treaty of Peace concluded by Colonel Upton with the Maratta State; and that you had dispatched positive Orders to the Chiefs of Surat and Broach, on no Account whatever to deliver up Jamboseer, and such other Cessions as then remained in our Hands, and were to be relinquished agreeable to the Treaty; also that you had wrote, conformably to the above-mentioned Resolution, to the Governor General and Council, and to Colonel Upton. The first Notice of your Honour, &c. having taken such Measures, affected me very sensibly, as I had perused the aforementioned Commands, without perceiving that they ought to be construed in that Manner; and the more I have considered the Subject, the more necessary it has appeared to me to differ in Opinion with your Honour, &c. for my Justification with the Honourable the Court of Directors, and the Governor General and Council.

I conclude

I conclude your Honours, &c. have been influenced in the above Resolution, by knowing that the Court of Directors had received Intelligence by the Northumberland, that the Governor General and Council had appointed a Cessation of Arms, and that Colonel Upton had proceeded from Calcutta, with full Powers to conclude a Peace at Poorunder; also, that you think a particular Stress should be laid on the Words, "under all Circumstances," contained in the 39th Paragraph; but it appears to me, that the Honourable Court by no Means intended those Paragraphs to convey special Orders, to counteract any Thing Colonel Upton might have done; not choosing to take it for granted that he would be able to conclude a Peace, as had very near proved the Case, but rather, according to our Advices, to consider us in a State of War, and enjoin us to attend to the Security and Preservation of the Cessions we were entitled to by the Treaty with Ragoba; the Directors well knowing, that if Colonel Upton should conclude a Treaty, it will operate according to the late Act of Parliament, till they could be informed of the Conditions, and give their definitive Orders thereon.

I allow that the above quoted Words "under every Circumstance," are very comprehensive; but I can by no Means concur with your Honour, &c. that they relate to our present peaceable Situation; I am rather induced to think that they are expressive of the Directors Approval of the several Stipulations contained in the Treaty with Ragoba, and that when they become acquainted with our present Circumstances, they will be sorry to find that your Honour, &c. have construed those Words in the Manner you have done, and in Support of my Opinion, that they meant only in a general Way to reply to our Advices then before them; considering us in a State of War, without superseding and unhinging every Thing established by the Treaty, I beg Leave to refer your Honour, &c. to the several Expressions contained in these Three Paragraphs relative to the Security and Preservation of the Cessions made by Ragoba, on a Supposition that we enjoyed them by that Tenure only; for, as above observed, they well know that we must submit to the controlling Power of the Governor General and Council as to War and Negociation, till their definitive Orders might be received.

The Expressions alluded to above, for my believing that the Honourable Court chose to confine their Orders, as considering us in a State of War instead of Peace, as is now the Case, are the lasting Security and Preservation of the Possessions acquired from Ragoba, mentioned in the 38th Paragraph; their Approval of keeping them, and Directions to the Governor General and Council, and Governor and Council of Fort Saint George, for adopting Measures most proper for the Preservation of those Territories according to Exigencies, as comprehended in the 39th Paragraph; and requesting Countenance and Support from the King's Ships, for the Security of those Possessions, as noticed in the 40th Paragraph, which surely are not at all applicable to a State of Peace and Tranquillity.

Having thus fully stated to your Honour, &c. the Reasons which have induced me to differ in Opinion with you regarding the Honourable Court's Paragraphs, I am now particularly to assign the Reasons for my dissenting to the Resolution you took the 20th Instant, and all Consequences which may result therefrom, viz.

First. Because, in my Opinion, your Honour, &c. Resolution is a direct and manifest Infringement of the Treaty concluded by Colonel Upton, as well as of the strict Orders lately given by the Governor General and Council, for avoiding every Measure which might even give the Marattas Distrust or Jealousy.

Because, in our Situation, considering the Advantages reaped and to be reaped by the Treaty, the Resolution is both unreasonable and impolitic; unreasonable considering the Advantages of the Treaty, and impolitic on the Two following Accounts.

Because, I take it for granted, we shall forfeit the Receipt of the 12 Lacks of Rupees stipulated to be paid; Six Lacks of which would have been due the First of next Month.

Because, the Cession of the Country of Three Lacks per Annum, contiguous to Broach, will of course likewise be forfeited; the peaceable Enjoyment of which would in my Opinion be far preferable to the Purgunnah of Jambooseer, the only one we shall probably retain in Consequence of the Resolution, though estimated at Five Lacks per Annum; as I am of Opinion more than the Difference will be absorbed by maintaining it by Force of Arms; and your Honour, &c. well know that Jambooseer has been continued with us merely as a Security for the Country of Three Lacks, without being allowed to collect the Revenues.

Because, I think we ought religiously to have proceeded in the Execution of the Treaty, or at least to have temporized till we could hear further from the Court of Directors,

rectors, or the Governor General and Council, but I should have preferred the former Conduct.

Because, we are at this Place about 29 Lacks of Rupees in Debt, accumulating at an Interest of ½ per Cent. per Month; also because the Governor General and Council furnishing us with sufficient Supplies of Money, in case of the Peace being disturbed by the above Resolution, I think very uncertain.

Because, on the 31st Ultimo, the Company's Remains of Europe Goods amounted to about Ten Lacks, to the Amount of Three Lacks have since been received by the Latham, and the Purchasers Remains under the 31st Ultimo amounted to nearly Eight Lacks; the realizing of which I apprehend will be much obstructed, and that the Trade of private Mercants will equally suffer.

Because, the Number of European Troops since the Attack of Tannah is reduced from 1996 to 1416.

Because, the State of public Affairs at Home prevented any Number of Recruits being sent this Season, and the same Reason may unfortunately subsist the next Year.

I beg that a Copy of this my Dissent may be transmitted to the Governor General and Council by the First Opportunity; and am very respectfully, &c.

(Signed) Daniel Draper.

Bombay,
28 August 1776.

A true Copy.
(Signed) Edw. Ravenscroft, Secretary.

Messrs. Mostyn, Stackhouse, and Garden, join in Opinion with Mr. Draper, that temporizing Measures, as far as Prudence will admit, should be observed, and every Means used to avoid a War; and were we convinced that the Persons with whom Mr. Upton has concluded a Treaty could possibly support themselves in the Government, we should be also of his Opinion in every other Point: But we firmly believe the Ministers will not be able to continue in Poona many Months longer, for there remains not a Doubt with us but Sudaba will, as soon as the Season opens, get Possession of the Government, more especially as there is a Prospect that Ragoba means to join them by coming to the Southward; and should this be the Case, we apprehend they will not want our Assistance, consequently we can have no Right to the Possessions granted by the Treaty made with Ragoba, nor can the Ministers comply with theirs. Thus situated, and the Company's express Orders by the Latham before us, we cannot help thinking the Resolution of the Board last Council Day the properest Measure we can adopt in the present unsettled Situation of Affairs; though, for the Reasons given in the General Minute, we are obliged to deviate from the Company's Orders.

A true Copy.
(Signed) Edw. Ravenscroft, Secretary.

Mr. Ramsay's Minute.

If the Maratta Empire was now in the same settled State it was in before the Death of Narron Row, and the present Government at Poona in a Condition to fulfil the Treaty concluded by Colonel Upton, however inadequate in some Respects that Treaty may be, Mr. Ramsay would entirely concur with Mr. Draper, that the unanimous Resolution of the Board at their last Meeting, for retaining Jamboseer, and such other Territory as has not yet been restored to the Marattas in Consequence of that Treaty, would be impolitic and unreasonable, and the Reasons Mr. Draper has brought in Support of that Opinion, would in that Case weigh most forcibly; but circumstanced as we now are, Mr. Ramsay cannot hesitate a Moment in declaring it as his Opinion, that we ought to retain every Possession we possibly can, consistent with the Orders of our Employers, who, though they knew of Colonel Upton's Mission, and must suppose it probable, from the Tenor of his Instructions, he would conclude some decisive Terms with the Poona Government, are notwithstanding pleased to approve, *under every Circumstance*, of our keeping Possession of the Territories ceded to them by the Treaty with Ragoba. A pacific System Mr. Ramsay will ever hold to be most for the Company's real Interest, and would therefore wish to avoid every Measure which would tend to involve them in War; but in the present Situation of Affairs it seems next to a Certainty, that the present ruling Government at Poona cannot long exist. Sudabah is said to be at the Head of a very formidable Force, and ready to support our late Ally Ragoba in his Pretensions to the Peshwaship: This latter, it is further said, is negociating with the Portugueze for Assistance; which should they grant, and he succeed in establishing himself at Poona without our Aid, we cannot have the least Shadow of Right to withhold from him the Cessions made by the Treaty of Surat. In short, from the present distracted State of the Maratta Empire, it can scarcely admit of a Doubt, that in order to secure the Possessions we already hold, as well as to preserve the Company's Influence in these Parts, we shall necessarily be obliged to take an active Part in the Troubles which are likely to ensue; in which Case the ill Consequences which Mr. Draper apprehends from keeping Possession of Jambouseer, &c. can have no Weight. As to our infringing Colonel Upton's Treaty, it is notorious, and will fully appear by our Records, that every Thing has been done on our Part to carry it into Execution in the fullest Extent, while no one Step appears to have been taken for that Purpose on the Part of the Poona Government: On the contrary, our Vessels have been insulted, the Communication still continues shut, all Intercourse of Trade and Correspondence is still stopped, and we suffer every Inconvenience attending an actual State of War; to which if we add, their having made over Countries not their own, which may probably hereafter involve us in Troubles with the Guicawar Family, sufficient Grounds are not wanting to invalidate the Poona Treaty without hurting the National Faith. If the Governor General and Council should judge it eligible to take Advantage of the present Crisis, those Gentlemen have already been fully advised of every Thing that has passed in our Neighbourhood, and we may therefore hope shortly to receive their Orders what Conduct we are to pursue; but as the Season for Action is now approaching, and we may be under an indispensable Necessity of taking some Steps for the Company's Interest, Mr. Ramsay thinks their speedy and express Orders should be again requested, and a Letter in Duplicate immediately dispatched to them for that Purpose, although he much fears the Distance is so great as to render it impossible to give Orders with that Precision which the Nature of Affairs may require; which makes it much to be wished that the Governor General and Council would have sufficient Confidence in this Board to give us a Latitude to act as from Circumstances may be deemed most for the Company's Interest; having Regard at the same Time, as far as the Situation of Affairs will possibly admit, to the general Views and Orders of the Governor General and Council.

A true Copy.
(Signed) Edw. Ravenscroft, Secretary.

APPENDIX, N° 142.

To Siccaram Pundit: Written 14th October 1776.

I HAVE received your Letter, wherein you advise me, that the Consideration of my Authority over the other Settlements had induced you to assent to some of Colonel Upton's Proposals, and refer others to my Justice, and desire that I will forbid every Englishman to support Ragonaut Row, or to interfere in the Concerns of the Family, or obstruct the Collection of the Chout; and that I will order Shasty to be delivered up; you also advise me, that with a View to the Preservation of Friendship you accepted the Copy of the Treaty, which was executed in Calcutta, and delivered a Counterpart to Colonel Upton; and that you are assured that you shall obtain Salsette and the small Islands: These, and all the other Particulars, I very clearly understand.

When a Treaty has been agreed to, and executed on both Sides, I am surprized that you should still dispute the Points which have been decided by the Treaty. The English have performed no Act, whether in their Conduct towards Ragonaut Row, or in any other Instance, which is not strictly conformable to it, nor shall it ever in any Respect be violated on our Part; but near a Twelvemonth has elapsed since Colonel Upton has arrived with you, and the Treaty has long since been executed by both Parties. Nothing now remains but the Performance, which will depend on you and the Governor of Bombay, who is connected more particularly than the English in any other Settlement

tlement with the Maratta Government. Strict Orders have been written to him on this Subject, and the Authority of this Government has been exercised to command a rigid Observance of every Stipulation. The Presence therefore of Colonel Upton can be no longer necessary. Indeed it is improper, as it conveys the Appearance of a doubtful Friendship, and that the Object of this Negociation is not completed. Conformably therefore to the Orders which he has received, I conclude that he will before this Time have taken his Leave and departed: I have now written to him, that in case he shall still be with you, he do immediately, having received his Dismission, return to Bengal; and I request that there may be no Delay in giving him his Dismission, that the Mouths of false and designing Men may be stopt; and that the World may see that every Difference which formerly subsisted between your Government and the English is totally effaced, and a firm Friendship established for ever. This is my Wish, as it is also my firm and unalterable Resolution to maintain the Treaty, in every Article of it, inviolate; nor shall any Change in the Affairs of that Quarter, of which there are many Rumours, influence me to depart from this Resolution: And relying on your Honour and Friendship, and on the good Faith of the Maratta Government, I am assured that it has received a Sanction which will constitute the Observance a sacred Obligation on you and your Nation for ever.

APPENDIX, N° 143.

Extract of Bengal Secret Consultations, the 9th December 1776.

READ the following Letter from Lieutenant Colonel Upton:

Gentlemen,

I now inclose what Correspondence I have had with the Select Committee of Bombay, since I had the Honour to write last on the 10th September, also Copies of Two Letters I received from the Paishwa; these will inform regularly of the Measures that have been taken since that Time to fulfill the Obligations of the late Treaty; and I have added, for further Information, Remarks on the Letter from the Select Committee of the 21st September.

I have at last the great Satisfaction to advise of my having brought the Treaty nearly to a happy Conclusion. The Peshwa has consented to make over the Purgunnahs of Hansood, Occlaseer, and Desbora, for the Country of Three Lacks. His Ministers say the annual Amount of the Revenues of the Districts exceeds Three Lacks, but a fresh Estimation is to be made, as shall be agreed upon between the Commissaries on each Side; and the Surplus (if any) taken off any Parts of these Districts, as our Commissaries shall name. I hope, therefore, this Business will readily be adjusted, as I cannot myself see a single Difficulty. Objections cannot well be made by the Gentlemen of Bombay to these Purgunnahs, because they before proposed receiving those of Hansood, and Occlaseer; and in observing the Value set upon Desbora by our Commissaries, I made a Point with the Ministers of its being added. It was impossible to get either Ahmood or Jamboseer, they both belong to Siccaram Bappoo, and I am told, should he be divested of these, he would have very little landed Property left; besides, Jamboseer is worth upwards of Four Lacks and a Half per Annum, according to their Revenue Books.

From the Ministers declaring, that their late large Disbursements had almost exhausted their Treasury, and desiring some longer Time might be allowed for the Payment of the first stipulated Six Lacks, and also finding that I might importune long before this Money would be paid, I proposed their making over the Collections of Jamboseer for the Payment of the whole Twelve Lacks, and their leaving Jamboseer in our Possession for the Security until this Money should be paid. To this they have consented, and for the more speedy Payment have added their annual Collections in and about Surat. Upon the Sum of Twelve Lacks being paid, either by the Collections on Jamboseer, &c. or otherwise, we were immediately to restore that Purgunnah. This was agreed upon

until

until the Pleasure of the Superior Council should be known; and I have accordingly advised the Select Committee of Bombay, and have also informed them of what Purgunnahs the Peshwa is willing, and has given his Orders to his Commissaries, to make over for the Country of Three Lacks.

This Letter goes by Cassids, laid every Fifteen or Twenty Coss, to Benares, and I imagine will reach Calcutta in about Eighteen Days.

I shall endeavour to wait for further Instructions at Poona; but if I find this impracticable, I will stay at Auringabad, distant about Seventy or Eighty Coss; through which Place the Cossids pass.

The Peshwa writes to you, Gentlemen, to assist him with Two Battalions of Sepoys, and promises in return to send at any Time, on Demand of the Superior Council, a Body of Cavalry, to act as the English may require. He has been induced to make this Request of Two Battalions of Sepoys, from the friendly Professions you have been pleased to make, and because his Enemies have been enabled to head against him, from Ragonaut Row's having been so long supported by the Presidency of Bombay, after the Treaty was concluded. The Ministers say if their Request is complied with, It will be every where known the Part the English take, and their Disputes soon end; this Request was intended to have been made Two Months ago, when Ragonaut Row first made his Escape from Surat; their Reasons might be somewhat stronger then for asking this Aid; I observed this to the Ministers, but they insisted on sending their Letter, and desired me to write to endeavour to enforce their Request.

Neither Vackeel or Letter has arrived from Futty Sing, except what has been already forwarded. I imagine the Man keeps back until he sees which Party will get the better; though the Ministers will not acknowledge this, they excuse his Delays from his being kept at Home and constantly employed defending his Country against his Brother. As before, I have again assured the Ministers, that the Proofs respecting the Paishwa's having the sole Right to the Guzerat Country, must be found satisfactory by you, Gentlemen, before the Cessions made by Futty Sing can be restored.

It is now Six Weeks and upwards since Sedashew Row has been in Possession of almost the whole Country between Bombay and Poona: An advanced Party of his was for several Days within Five Coss of Poona; Sedashew Row has never himself been nearer than about Eighteen Coss. Skirmishes are happening daily between the Two Armies; the Peshwa's Troops are said in these generally to have been victorious. Orders are sent to the Peshwa's Army, to march to where the Bow's grand Army is posted, and make a general Assault. The Ministers expect this will take Place in Three or Four Days; they are to make several Attacks, and to endeavour to cut off a Retreat to the Bow. Sinda and Tucojee, who had been some Time at Poorunder, are to command these Attacks. Imrut Row, Ragonaut Row's adopted Son, is with the Bow. Ragonaut Row is said to be near the Portugueze Settlement of Daman.

Moribah left Poona, and went to a Fort of his own, about Twenty Coss distant, Fourteen Days ago. I cannot learn what his Intentions are, though it is generally thought he will either join Ragonaut Row or the Bow; the Two latter have not yet met: I should think it impossible, having nearly the same Object in View, that they can act in Concert. I had written thus far, when the Ministers sent to desire me to defer writing to Calcutta for Three or Four Days, as they would re-consider the Subject of their Letter, before they sent it off. I therefore dispatch this by Way of Masulipatam, as, upon a Revisal, I think it the more proper Route; besides, these People have already so long delayed writing, that it is not impossible their Letter may not be ready yet these Six or Eight Days; and I wish to advise immediately of what has been already done towards carrying the Treaty into Execution.

I hope I shall receive a Reply from Bombay, to my Letter of the 19th, soon enough to send off with the Paishwa's Letter.

The Passports from the Vizier have arrived for Goukaboy and Siccaram Bappoo; and have been presented, together with those from Chete Sing, to Siccaram Bappoo, who expressed his warmest Acknowledgments for this Favour.

I have been honoured, Gentlemen, with your Letter of the 24th of July, and am greatly obliged by the Indulgence, in permitting me to chuse my Route on my Return to Bengal, which I suppose shall be by Hyderabad and Masulipatam.

I have, &c.
(Signed) J. Upton.

Poorunder,
26th October 1776.

Ordered,

Ordered, That the Inclosures be inserted after the Consultation.
Agreed, That the following Letter be written to Lieutenant Colonel Upton:

Sir,

We have received your Letter of the 26th October, with its sundry Inclosures.

We have only to acquaint you, that we have approved the Accommodation which you have made with the Ministers, for the Mortgage of the Territory of Jamboosеer, and the Paishwa's Collections in and about Surat, for the Payment of the Twelve Lacks of Rupees, stipulated by the 6th Article of the Treaty to be paid by the Maratta Government to the Company.

We are, &c.

Resolved, That the following Letter be written to Bombay:

Gentlemen,

Since the Date of our last Letter to you from this Department, we have received Advices from Lieutenant Colonel Upton, dated 26th October, wherein he acquaints us, That he had obtained from the Maratta Government a Cession of the Purgunnahs of Hansood, Occlaseer, and Desbora, as the Territory of Three Lacks, stipulated by the 5th Article of the Treaty, to be yielded to the Company; and that he had made an Accommodation with that Government, by which the Country of Jamboosеer, together with the Maratta Collections in and about Surat, have been mortgaged for the Payment of the Twelve Lacks of Rupees, agreeable to the Condition of the 6th Article. We cannot but approve of this Mortgage, as it affords a good Security for the Discharge of the Sum to be paid by the Paishwa, and is less liable to cause Disputes with his Government than any other Mode he could have proposed. As Colonel Upton will most probably have left Poona, on his Return to Bengal, before the Arrival of this Letter, we think it proper to repeat our Recommendation, that you will appoint some Person to reside at the Paishwa's Court after his Departure, with Instructions to correspond with us on any material Occurrences which may come to his Knowledge.

We are, &c.

APPENDIX, N° 144.

[*Extract Bengal Secret Consultations, 23d December 1776.*

Letter from Colonel Upton.

Gentlemen,

I HAD the Honour of addressing you last on the 26th October.

The Ministers have at length got their Letter ready; they have declined asking the Assistance of Troops, as now their intestine Disturbances are nearly at an End. There is some Excuse for the Delay of this Letter; the Information from their different Sirdars in the Cokun Country, which are arriving daily, kept them from closing it, as they wished to advise fully, and with Certainty.

The Paishwa is very desirous of a Resident being sent to Poona.

They now see the Reason why the Council of Bombay decline sending one. The Ministers desired me to be very particular in making this Request.

Sidashu Row was totally defeated on the 27th Ultimo; he was taken Prisoner by one of their Sirdars, Ragoojee Angria, who commands a Fort on the Sea Shore, just as he had put off to have escaped, as is said, to Bombay. The inclosed Letters will inform so very particularly of every Transaction since I had the Honour to write last, that little is left for me to say.

I have not yet received an Answer from Bombay, to my Letter of the 19th Ultimo, which was sent by Way of Surat; but that no Time might be lost, I dispatched Extracts

of

of such Parts of this Letter as related to the Cession of the Country of Three Lacks, and of the Manner proposed by the Paishwa for Payment of the Twelve Lacks, by the direct Road to Bombay. I shall do myself the Honour, Gentlemen, to write immediately on the Adjustment of these Particulars.

As there is every Appearance of Hostilities soon commencing between the Presidency of Bombay and this State, I shall endeavour to convince the Ministers to how little Purpose I now remain at Poona, and that my Services may be more effectually employed in their Behalf at Calcutta. That I cannot render them any here, is certain; therefore I imagine they will consent to my Departure. I have convinced the Ministers, that the Government of Bombay will soon receive such Orders as will put an entire Stop to all Acts of Hostility; and that they might be assured, in the mean Time, no Assistance would be afforded them from any of the other Presidencies.

The Ministers are sensible they can sustain no other Injury than that of the immense Expence incurred by keeping up a large inactive Army, before the Orders will arrive; but they observe, as these Gentlemen have thought proper to disobey the Orders that have been heretofore sent, and disregard such solemn Engagements as the Treaties now subsisting between the Two Nations, they shall have still every Thing to apprehend that can be effected by their Intrigues; their Arms they seem to disregard.

The Peshwa has ordered Sadashu Row to be brought to Poona. I hear they again intend shewing him to the People.

Rogonaut Row is still in the Neighbourhood of the Portugueze Settlement, Daman. He has wrote to the Ministers lately, and proposed accepting a Jaghire, either in the Candeish Country, or near Jansi; as the Ministers will agree to this, they expect soon to see him settled. He has at present very few People with him, and is almost surrounded by about Fifteen Thousand of the Peshwa's Troops.

In a few Days the Peshwa intends sending an Army of Forty or Fifty Thousand Men, under Hurry Pundit and the Prerinctly, against Hyder Ally.

As I expect to leave Poona very shortly, I have to request you will be pleased, Gentlemen, to order my Letter to be forwarded by Way of Masulipatam.

Poona, 13th November 1776. — I have, &c. (Signed) J. Upton.

Translation of a Letter from Mhada Row Peshwa, to Lieutenant Colonel Upton; received 8th November 1776.

A seditious Man, who assumed the Name of Sedashu Row, assembled an Army, plundered the whole Cokun Country, and brought the War to the very Environs of Poona. But Madajee Sindia and Banrow Panue, Two of the Officers of the Government's Army, after repeated Defeats, plundered his Army, and pursued him to the Sea. He attempted an Escape with some of his Party in a Boat; but Ragjee Angria, one of our chief Officers, being informed of it, followed, and at length seized him, and was bringing him to the Capital. While he was prosecuting this Design, he received a Letter from the Governor of Bombay, in the following Terms.—" He (Sedasheerow) was on his " Way to Bombay, and you have carried him with you. Our Charge is now in your " Hands. Send him, and give him Liberty to see us."

This Circumstance has affected us with the greatest Surprize; for it is engaged, both in the former Treaties, and in the late Treaty concluded between the Maratta Government and the English, that neither of the contracting Parties shall harbour or aid the Rebels of the other; and that the Deserters shall be mutually delivered up. What Relation does the Governor of Bombay bear to that seditious Man, which should incite him to desire to see him; and what does he mean by writing such a Letter?

Another Matter of Complaint is as follows: About a Thousand of his Adherents, after the Defeat, crossed a Branch of the Sea near Salsette, and placed themselves and the Elephants, Horses, and Baggage of their Leader, under the Protection of the Fort of Salsette; when Bheim Row arrived in Pursuit of them, as far as the hithermost Shore, Mr. Halsey, the Chief of Salsette, wrote Two or Three Letters to the Commanders of our Army, one of which I enclose. I request that you will do me the Favour to transmit a Copy of this Letter, with a Letter from yourself, containing a circumstantial Relation of all these Facts to the Governor and Council of Bombay, that they may deliver up to our Officers all the Rebels, who are now harboured by the English, either in Bombay or Salsette,

sette, or other Places; and forego their Desire of seeing the Rebel, as well as refrain from every Act which may be inconsistent with the Treaties, or injurious to the good Understanding which subsists between the two States. By this Means the Friendship will be established on a firmer Basis. Inclosed is a Letter which I have written to the Governor of Bombay, on the Subject of those Proceedings. You will forward it to Bombay, and desire a compliant Answer immediately, for had any Deserter from the English entered my Country, and you required him, I would have him delivered up. A Copy of the Letter addressed to the Governor of Bombay, is enclosed for your Inspection.

Translation of a Letter from the Peshwa to the Honourable the Governor of Bombay.

(The Words used in the preceding Letter, from the Beginning to " one of which I enclose," are repeated here; the first Person in what respects the Governor of Bombay being substituted for the Third.) Brimrow having charged Mr. Halsey, the Chief of Salsette, with the Elephants, Horses, and Baggage belonging to the Rebel, went away to perform other Business for the Government. You are required to deliver up the Rebels who are harboured by the English in Bombay, Salsette, &c. to our Officers, and refrain from such Acts which are inconsistent with the Treaty, and injurious to the good Understanding which subsists between the two States, by which means Friendship will be established on a firmer Basis.

P. S. Dispatch an Answer complying with the Contents of this Letter speedily, or should you have other Intentions, inform me that I may write accordingly to the Supreme Council in Calcutta.

Translation of a Letter from John Halsey, Esquire, Chief of Salsette, to the Commander of the Peshwa's Army.

The Village of Calvan is situated within the Range of the Salsette Guns, I cannot therefore permit you to carry on a War there, but request that you will neither send your Men into it, nor attack it with Fire Arms; should you do so, we shall be under the Necessity of firing from the Fort. On this we have resolved; be it your Part to preserve the Friendship.

Dated 19th Ranzaun, 1190 Higera.

Letter from the same to Bhuns Row Bhauree.

I have received Two Letters from you; I before wrote to desire that you would not make War, and desired in the same Manner of the Men who were near Calvan, that they would not make War with you; they came of their own Accord into our Dependencies, and I cannot deliver them up to you; some of your Chiefs and Bramins, through Fear of Serrimunt Rajesherry Bhow Sudabah, came into this Place for a short Time; we likewise gave them Protection. Those Men were demanded on the Part of the Aumildars of Sudabah, and we refused to give them up to them. What shall I write more? Let Friendship ever subsist.

Lieutenant Colonel Upton's Letter having arrived in Time to be forwarded to the Court of Directors by the Shrewsbury, a Copy of it was sent a Number in that Ship's Packet.

APPENDIX, N° 145.

Extract of Bengal Secret Consultations, dated 30th December 1776.

Col. Upton. RECEIVED the following Letter from Lieutenant Colonel Upton.

Gentlemen,

I trouble you with this, purposely to acquaint you that Ragonath Row went to and was received at Bombay, about Twelve Days ago, to the very great Surprise and Concern of the Paishwa's Ministers, who at the very Time thought their domestic Disturbances quite at an End, by having agreed to fix on Ragonath Row the Jaghier he had requested.

I have wrote to the Select Committee of Bombay, to know the Particulars of this extraordinary Event, and am expecting their Reply daily, but would not defer advising you, Gentlemen, for One Day, of so material a Circumstance as this, of Ragonath Row's being received into Bombay so obviously in Breach of the late Treaty.

Sida Shu Row is on his Way to Poona, escorted by Sindia; he is permitted to travel with his customary Retinue, as the Ministers declare he shall suffer no Indignities till they and the Public shall be satisfied that he is not the Person he has given himself out to be.

The Paragraph in my Letter of the 19th July, where I mentioned the Necessity of confirming, &c. was altogether meant on the Part of this Country, to restore Peace and Tranquillity to it, and to accelerate the Accomplishment of the Treaty. Residing as a Minister at this Court, when such Event should have taken Place, I should have conceived it necessary and usual, to have mentioned the Treaties subsisting between the Two Nations, and the making and receiving the customary Professions of Friendship.

I have been honoured by the Receipt of your Letter of the 30th September, with the Copy of a Letter of the same Date, to the Governor and Council of Bombay; my last to you, Gentlemen, was dated the 13th November.

This goes by the Peshwa's Dawk, and I hope will be in Calcutta in Twenty Days at farthest.

Poona, 24th November 1776.

I have the Honour to be, &c.
(Signed) J. Upton.

Read the following Letter from Bombay:

Honourable Sir, and Gentlemen,

Bombay, 24 April. We have received your Letter, dated the 30th December, and the enclosed Papers.

The Extracts we have now the Honour to transmit from our Secret Consultations, will place in their proper Light the Circumstances mentioned in your Letter, of our giving Protection to some of the defeated Adherents of Sudabah, our Interposition with Ragojee Angria in his Favour, and our receiving into Bombay the Person of Ragonaut Row. We are persuaded, that when you have given these Extracts a candid Perusal, the Impression made on your Minds by the Representation you have received from Poona on these Points will be entirely removed, and that you will no longer consider our preventing a Handful of wretched Sepoys from being slaughtered under the Walls of a British Fortress as repugnant to any Treaty, but as an Act dictated by Humanity, and warranted by the Law of Nations. We sent the Message mentioned in our Minutes to Ragojee Angria, after he had by Treachery got Sudabah into his Possession, because the latter had been promised our Protection, and we esteemed it our Duty to endeavour to save him from being murdered, which we concluded would be the Case if he was sent to Poona, by the perfidious Angria; but we disclaim any Declaration of War in case of his Refusal to deliver Sudabah up.

We

We beg Leave to observe, that we are not answerable for any Thing the Adherents of Sudabah may have thought proper to write to his Confederates.

Without entering into any Discussion of your Authority to give us an Order to expel Ragoba from Bombay, and putting out of the Question the Disgrace and bad Consequences which would have attended such a Measure, and every Consideration of Honour and Humanity by which we esteemed ourselves bound to protect him, it appeared to us quite unadvisable, and warranted by no political Necessity, to compel him to depart, as Colonel Upton had acquainted us, under the 12th December, that the Ministers seemed well pleased, and for the present satisfied with the Assurances he had made them at our Desire in Consequence of Ragoba's having taken Refuge here; and we had Reason to hope, from the Professions they made, that satisfactory Terms would soon be settled for him, Mr. Mostyn being then shortly to proceed to Poona, to whom this Point would be given in especial Charge. We therefore have not signified your Orders to Ragoba, and we flatter ourselves Mr. Mostyn will meet with Success, and that your Intentions will thereby be answered, as it is very pleasing to us whenever we can promote the Execution of them. Mr. Mostyn set off for Poona the 14th Ultimo, and arrived there the 29th: He had not then had an Audience from the Paishwa, but was to proceed to Poorunder in Two Days for that Purpose. He advises the Death of Ram Rajah on the 24th Ultimo, which may probably occasion some Alteration in the Poona Government. We enclose Copy of his Instructions, which we hope you will approve, and that they will convince you of our Disposition to preserve a good Understanding with the Maratta State.

Much has passed between us and Colonel Upton on the Subject of the evasive Conduct of the Ministers in complying with the 5th Article of the Treaty. In the Beginning of December last he advised, that he had settled with them that the Purgunnahs of Ahmood, Hansood, and Desbora, should be made over to the Company, and that if the Revenues of these Places amounted to more than Three Lacks, the Excess should be deducted from Amoor or Hansood; on the contrary, if there was any Deficiency, it was to be made up by Grants of Villages from the Purgunnah of Occlaseer. This was a very fair, equitable Agreement, and we then hoped the Business was entirely concluded in an advantageous Manner to the Company; but owing to some Collusion between the Poona Agents at Broach and their Principals, the Country is not to this Hour made over to the Company. That you may have full Information of our Proceedings, and be better able to judge what Measures to pursue, we now transmit Copies of all the Papers on this Subject since the Settlement made by Colonel Upton, and the Letters from Messrs. Carnac, Boddam, and Ramsay, now at Broach, and hope that our Conduct will be satisfactory to you.

In the above Papers you will observe the Demand made by the Ministers for the Possession of Jamboseer, which is equally opposite to the Agreement made with Colonel Upton, and if complied with, would leave the Company without any Security for the Twelve Lacks on the Country ceded by the 5th Article.

Since writing the above, we have been honoured with your Letter, dated the 27th January.

What we have already wrote, and the Extracts above referred to, will in a great Measure serve as a Reply to one of them; and we can only further observe, that we ever understood it to be the Custom of all Nations, and we think it inconsistent with Reason and Common Sense, not to permit of Hostilities being committed within the Reach of the Guns of a Fortification, which induced us to give the Orders we did to the Chief and Council at Tannah, and not any Intention of invading the Territorial Rights of the Marattas.

By the Extracts of our Minutes, it will appear that Ragonaut Row escaped from the Fort of Tinapore, where he was besieged by his Enemies on Board an English Vessel, and came in Person to Bombay, to solicit our Protection, without any Encouragement or Invitation from us. The Fort soon afterwards was taken by the Poona Forces.

In Deference, Gentlemen, to the Sentiments you have been pleased to express of the late Revolution at Madras, we will in future address our Letters for that Presidency "To the Honourable the President and Council of Madras," instead of the Address we have hitherto continued, declaring however, that we still retain the Opinion of that Transaction expressed in our Letter of the 17th November.

Mr. Draper having differed from us on this Point, we, at his Request, transmit Copy of his Dissent, and acquaint you, that he still continues of the same Opinion.

The Extracts you have requested in your Letter of the 30th December, being exceedingly long, and having very few Assistants in our public Offices, it is out of our

 Power

Power to comply at present with your Desire, but we now transmit a Copy of the Treaty now in Force between this Presidency and Hyder Ally, the others having been already sent to you at different Times.

We have, &c.

Bombay Castle, 14th April, 1774. (Signed) Wm Hornby, President and Council.

APPENDIX, N° 146.

Extract Bengal Secret Consultations, 30th November, 1776.

Reply to Lieutenant Colonel Upton.

Sir,

WE have received your Letters of the 13th and 24th Ultimo.

It is with much Surprize we read the Information contained in them, respecting the Conduct of Mr. Halsey, Chief of Salsette, in threatening to fire on the Peshwa's Forces, if they should continue their Operations against Calvan; and of the Governor of Bombay, in sending Deputies to Ragojie Angria, one of the Maratta Chiefs, to demand the Person of Sudaba. These Facts are so contrary to that repeated Injunction to the President and Council of Bombay, and to their Assurances in Reply, that we cannot give Credit to the Reports which have been made to you, until we are furnished with the Explanation of them, which we have required from the Presidency.

We have also given positive Orders to the President and Council, to require and compel Ragoba to quit Bombay, or any of its Dependencies that he may be in, at the Receipt of our Letter.

We must observe, that the Letters written by the Ministers since the Conclusion of the Treaty, are filled with Reproaches against the Government of Bombay, for Acts committed by them previous to the Date of it; all which ought to have been cancelled by the Treaty. They likewise put the most unfavourable Constructions on every Report which is made to them, concerning the Conduct of the English. These Circumstances mark a Disposition to Enmity in the Ministers, which is the more obvious to us, from your Assertion, that you will endeavour to convince the Ministers to how little Purpose you now remain at Poona: "That it is certain, that you cannot render them any Service there, and you therefore imagine they will consent to your Departure;" and from their Declaration, "That the Reason you have not left Poona, is, that no other Person has been sent from Bombay to reside there." What can we conclude from these Expressions, but that you are detained there by Compulsion? We hope this is not the Case; but on the Supposition that it is, a Letter has been written to the Paishwa, requiring your immediate Dismission: And we hereby positively order and command you, if you shall be at Poona on the Receipt hereof, to take your Leave immediately of the Maratta Court, and return to this Presidency.

Fort William, 30th December, 1776.

We are, &c.

Resolved, That a Letter be written to Bombay, as follows:

Gentlemen,

We have been informed, by a Letter from Colonel Upton, dated the 13th November, and by Letters from the Paishwa and his Ministers, which were received at the same Time, that Mr. Halsey, the Chief at Salsette, had threatened to fire on the Paishwa's Forces, if they attempted to carry on their Operations against the Village of Calvan; that he had given Shelter to about a Thousand of the Adherents of Sudabah in Salsette, whom he refused to deliver up, on the Requisition of the Paishwa's Officers; and that

Two

Two Deputies on the Part of your Government had arrived with Ragojee Angria, and demanded the Person of Sudabah in his Name; making a Declaration of War in case of Refusal.

By a Letter just received from Colonel Upton, of the 24th November, we are further informed, that Ragonaut Row had taken Refuge in the Island of Bombay, Twelve Days previous to that Date; and that he had actually been admitted there.

These Acts, if they have really passed, are so repugnant to the repeated Injunctions we have given you, to your repeated Assurances in Consequence of them, to the Treaties of Peace concluded with the Maratta State, and to the Powers which are vested in this Government by Parliament, that we cannot give entire Credit to the Report of them, however good the Authority may appear to be from which they are received; but we consider these Subjects of too much Importance to withhold the immediate Communication of them from you: And for your better Information, we enclose Copies of the several Papers alluded to; among these you will perceive the Translation of an intercepted Letter, said to have been written from one of the Adherents of Sudaba, residing at Bombay, to his Confederates, encouraging them with Assurances of Support from your Government.

We desire that you will inform us very minutely of the real Circumstances to which all these Representations refer; and in the mean Time we think it necessary to repeat our most earnest and positive Injunctions, that you abstain not only from every Act of Hostility against the Maratta State, but from every Occasion which may tend to renew the former Breach between us, except in the Case of your being actually attacked by them.

If it be true, that Ragonaut Row has received the Protection of your Government, and shall be at Bombay, or in any of its Dependencies, when you receive this Letter, we peremptorily order and insist, that you immediately require and compel him to depart therefrom. It is our fixed Determination, that the Peace which has been established shall not be broken by any Act of us, or our Dependants. We expect that you will join heartily with us in this Resolution, and that your Endeavours be united to ours, in preserving a good Understanding with the Maratta Government.

We request that you will furnish us with Extracts from your Consultations of all your Minutes, Debates, and Resolutions, upon the Subject of your Transactions with the Marattas, since the Commencement of your first Correspondence with Ragoba; but as we deem it of Consequence, that we should be immediately apprised of the Circumstances which have a Relation to the Facts alluded to in the Beginning of this Letter, you will be pleased to transmit to us, as soon as possible, exact Copies of all your Proceedings upon those Subjects; particularly specifying the Names of the Members present at each Consultation, and their several Opinions.

We are, &c.

Fort William,
30th December 1776.

To Sicearam Pundit: Written 6th January 1777.

I have received your Letter, wherein you inform me that Salsette was perfidiously seized by the English of Bombay, in Violation of the Peace which subsisted between the Two States; that they then gave their Aid to Serrimunt Ragonaut Row; in Consequence of which Disturbances ensued, and that by Means of Colonel Upton, whom I had deputed for that Purpose, a Peace was concluded; that the English did not observe the Treaty in withdrawing themselves from Ragonaut Row, but carried him near the Fort of Surat, where he remained with his Army for Three Months and Twenty Days after the Conclusion of the Peace; that his Army was afterwards disbanded, but he was sheltered under the English Protection during the Time that your Army continued in those Parts; and that when the rainy Season arrived, and that your Army was withdrawn, they in Consequence of my peremptory Injunctions dismissed Ragonaut Row, but gave no Intimation of it to you. You add, that this can by no Means be considered as an Act of Friendship, but on the contrary, that it astonished you. You also advise me, that a Victory has been obtained by the Peshwa's Forces over a seditious Man, who had assumed the Name of Sedashew Row, and created Disturbances in the Cucun Country; and that this Man, after his Defeat, had been taken Prisoner by Ragojee Angria, one of your Chiefs; but that about a Thousand of his Adherents had taken Refuge in Salsette, whom Mr. Halsey, the Chief of that Place, had refused to deliver up; and that he had moreover threatened to fire on the Peshwa's Troops, if they persisted on carrying their Operations so near as Calvan.

 You

You inform me, in a Postscript of the same Letter, that Ragojee Angria had advised you of the Arrival of Two Deputies with him from the Governor of Bombay, to demand the Person of Sedashew Row, who had declared that the Consequence of not sending him immediately would be War.

I rejoice to hear of the Success of the Peishwa's Arms, and of the Restoration of Peace to the Maratta Dominions; and I congratulate you with Pleasure on both these Events, but my Joy is considerably damped by the unexpected Reports above-mentioned.

The Conduct of Mr. Halsey in threatening to fire on your Army, and of the Government of Bombay, in sending Persons to demand the Person of Sedashew Row, if true, are both Acts inconsistent with the Treaty, and with the Friendship which now subsists between us; but they are so contrary to the peremptory Injunctions which have been given, and to the repeated Assurances received from that Government, that I do not know how to give Credit to them till I hear from Bombay: I have written to the Governor there for an Explanation, and as it would be wrong to condemn him unheard, I must suspend my Determination till I am furnished with his Reply. In the mean Time, you may rest assured that I shall suffer no real Acts of Hostility or Violence to be committed against your Government by the English in any Quarter.

At such a Time as this, we must expect that false Reports will be made to us, either from Motives of Self-interest, Malice, or Distrust; and it is the Point equally of Friendship and of Prudence to be on our Guard, that we do not suffer such Representations to make any Impression on our Mind, unless they are supported by undoubted Authority.

This I have laid down as a Rule for myself, being in my Heart determined to maintain the Peace which has been established between us. It is with this View that I must express to you my Regret in observing Symptoms of a very different Disposition in you. It is one of the Duties of Friendship, and a Principle of good Policy, when Peace is concluded, to give the Causes of War to Oblivion, because the Remembrance of them cannot exist without a Desire of Revenge; yet every Letter that I have received from you since the Ratification of the Treaty has been filled with Epithets of Reproach, and exaggerated Enumerations of Injuries, which if received, that Treaty ought to have cancelled for ever. Not content with this, you raise up new Pretensions, which are equally opposite to good Faith and to Justice.

I too could recriminate, and on better Grounds, but I forbear, because my Eyes look only to Peace, and the Confirmation of it: I have repeatedly desired that you would grant Colonel Upton his Dismission; you now declare that the Reason of his Stay is, that the Governor and Council of Bombay may send a Deputy to Poona to satisfy you that Colonel Upton afterwards shall receive his Dismission, otherwise the Council of Bombay will soon break the Engagements subsisting between the Maratta State and the English.

What am I to understand by this, but that Colonel Upton is detained by Compulsion, and that under the specious Appellation of a Resident, you require a Hostage from Bombay in his Room? That I may not injure you by such a Conclusion, however justified by your own Declaration and too strong Appearances, I have now given peremptory Orders to Colonel Upton to return, and rely on your Honour that no Impediment or Objection will be made to it on your Part, but I have Hopes that he will already have received his Dismission from you, and that what I have written on the Subject is unnecessary.

I have taken Notice of your raising up new Pretences; the Instance which I shall allude to is this, you desire to be furnished with a Letter to the Governor and Council of Madras, ordering them in positive Terms, to see that Raja Tulkajee be firmly established in his Rajaship, and that Raminautpore be restored to him. Raja Tulkajee is a Subject of the Carnatic; the Company, out of Tenderness to him, were induced to give particular Orders for his being restored to the Possessions which he now holds—he has been accordingly restored to them. In all the Time of our Correspondence and Negociations, the Name of Tulkajee has not been mentioned. On what Grounds or what Purpose is this Subject now introduced? Though I do not hold myself accountable to any Power but the King of Great Britain, or the Company, whose Servant I immediately am, for any Conduct that may be observed to the Raja of Tanjore, either by the Soubah of the Carnatic, or by our Government, yet I make no scruple to assure you, that I shall ever conform to the Faith of Treaties, and to the Dictates of Justice in all my Dealings with the Raja, as well as in my Transactions with any other Powers; nor has he any Cause to complain of the Want of either.

To Ballajee Pundit.

Of the same Tenor and Date.

APPENDIX, N° 146.

Extract of the Secret Letter from Bengal; dated 6th January 1777.

Par. 4. You will observe by the Letter from Colonel Upton, dated 13th November, which arrived just in Time to be transmitted to you by the Shrewsbury, that the Ministers at Poona have charged the Chief of Salsette with threatening to fire at the Paishwa's Troops, if they persisted in carrying on their Operations so near as the Village of Calvan, which, though lying on the Continent, appears to be within Cannon Shot of the Fort; and with granting Protection to about a Thousand of Sudaba's Adherents, who had fled to Salsette after his Defeat; and that they also accuse the Governor of Bombay of having sent Two Deputies to demand the Person of Sudaba from Ragojee Angria, one of the Maratta Chiefs, who had taken him Prisoner, with a Menace of War in Case of Refusal. By a Letter since received from Colonel Upton, under Date the 24th November, we understand that Ragonaut Row had gone to Bombay, and actually been received into that Island.

5. These Facts in general, but particularly that respecting the Deputies, appear too extraordinary to gain any Credit from us; however we thought them of so much Consequence as to make an immediate Communication of them to the President and Council of Bombay, from whom we have required a full Explanation of the Circumstances to which they allude, and Extracts of all their Proceedings upon the Subject, specifying particularly the Names of the Members present each Consultation, and their several Opinions.

6. Whatever Grounds may have been afforded to the Ministers for Complaint in these Instances, we cannot but remark strong Symptoms of Indisposition on their Part, in the continual and exaggerated Repetition of former Injuries, the Remembrance of which ought to have been obliterated by the Treaty, in the Exceptions made by them to the Conditions of the Treaty itself, in the Introduction of new Pretensions, under Colour of a Family Connection with the Rajah of Tanjore, and in the too strong Reasons they have given us to suspect them of taking Advantage of our Confidence in their good Faith, to detain Colonel Upton by Compulsion, and under frivolous Pretences, notwithstanding our peremptory Orders for his Return. This last Conclusion we ground on the following Passages in the Letters last received from the Peshwa and Colonel Upton, which we cannot give any other Construction; viz.

Extract from the Peshwa's Letter.

" You have desired that I will give Colonel Upton his Dismission; the Reason of his " Stay is, that the Governor and Council of Bombay may send a Deputy here, person- " ally, to satisfy us. Colonel Upton shall afterwards receive his Dismission, otherwise " the Council of Bombay will soon break the Engagements subsisting between the Ma- " ratta State and the English."

Extract from Colonel Upton's Letter, dated 15th November.

" As there is every Appearance of Hostilities soon commencing between the Presi- " dency of Bombay and this State, I shall endeavour to convince the Ministers to how " little Purpose I now remain at Poona, and that my Services may be more effectually " employed in their Behalf at Calcutta; that I cannot render them any here is certain, " therefore I imagine they will consent to my Departure."

A Letter has been dispatched to the Peshwa, requiring the immediate Dismission of Colonel Upton; and another to Colonel Upton, ordering him to take his Leave of the Maratta Court without further Delay. To both these we beg Leave to refer you.

Extract

APPENDIX, Nº 146.

Extract of Bengal Secret Consultations, the 13th January 1777.

PRESENT,

The Honourable Warren Hastings, Esquire, Governor General, President,
Lieutenant General John Clavering,
Richard Barwell, } Esquires.
Philip Francis, }

General Clavering having objected to the Sixth Paragraph of the General Letter prepared for the Triton, the Secretary received the following Letter and Minute from him on that Occasion, and Copy of the Minute was sent a Number in the Packet.

To Mr. Auriol.

Sir,

I send you my Protest to the 6th Paragraph in the Letter to the Court of Directors, written in the Secret Department, and desire it may make a Number in the Packet.

I am, &c.
(Signed) J. Clavering.

I protest against the 6th Paragraph of the Letter going from the Secret Department to the Court of Directors by this Dispatch, because I conceive the Board is not warranted by any Act of the Government of Poona, or Declaration of their Ministers, to draw the Conclusions that are inferred, and even expressed in this Paragraph, that "we have "Reason to suspect they mean to take Advantage of our Confidence in their good Faith, "to detain Colonel Upton by Compulsion."

If we consider the Two Letters referred to, there is nothing that can imply the Construction that is given to them: The Word "dismiss" in the Peshwa's Letter, and "consent" in Colonel Upton's, import the same Meaning, which is no more than expressing the usual Ceremony in Indostan, of granting Dismission or Leave to go away to Inferiors by Superiors. If we refer to the public Conduct of the Maratta State, we have no Reason to complain of their Violation of Treaties, or their Breach of good Faith: They strictly observed the Suspension of Arms, though it was not maintained on the Part of the Presidency of Bombay: They have endeavoured to fulfil the Treaty concluded with Colonel Upton, though it has been all along evaded by the Government of Bombay; First, by giving Refuge to Ragoba at Surat; then secretly negociating with Sudabah, and protecting his Followers; and lastly, by affording an Asylum to Ragoba himself in Bombay. If after the Sacrifice of Salsette, the Territory near Broach, and what was still more degrading to them, the Offer to pay the Expences of the War, by giving up certain Territories till they were liquidated, nobody can blame the Peshwa for uttering Complaints, that he made all these Sacrifices without obtaining what he had a Right to expect, Peace. The Conclusions therefore drawn from any Expressions of Complaint in the Peshwa's Letters are ungenerous, and rather imply an Intention to quarrel with him than he with us.

(Signed) J. C.

APPEN-

APPENDIX, N° 147.

Extract of Bengal Secret Consultations, the 27th January 1777.

PRESENT,

The Honourable Warren Hastings, Esquire, Governor General, President,
Lieutenant General John Clavering,
Richard Barwell, } Esquires.
Philip Francis, }

READ, the following Letter from Lieutenant Colonel Upton:

Gentlemen,

I am honoured with your Letter of the 14th October; the Letter that accompanied it from the Governor General for Siccaram Bappoo, was received by that Minister, with warm Expressions of Satisfaction—You forgot, Gentlemen, to write to Ballajee Pundit; I made such necessary Observations as occurred on the Occasion, and left him very well pleased.—The Ministers residing generally Ten Coss distant from each other, in some Measure makes it necessary to write to them separately, but it is more particularly so from their esteeming themselves equal in Office, to avoid a Jealousy that a seeming Preference given to either would cause.

I wrote last on the 24th Ultimo, purposely to advise of Ragonath Row's being at Bombay; and I have received One Letter only since that Time from those Gentlemen, dated the 20th November.

The following is all therein that relates to Ragonath Row: "Ragoba has put him-"self under our Protection, and he now resides at Bombay."—I have now the Honour to inclose what Letters have passed since my Letter of the 13th November—these contain the Measures that have been pursued towards the Completion of the 5th Article of the Treaty, &c. &c.

The Ministers promise I shall take my Departure immediately on the Receipt of Replies to my Letters to Bombay, of the 17th and 19th November—The last contained the Peshwa's Representations of the active Part taken by the Presidency of Bombay, in the Contentions of their Country, and requiring their Reasons for such Conduct.—I am expecting these Replies daily, and shall be ready to depart immediately, after having acquainted the Ministers with the Sentiments and Intentions of the Government of Bombay towards them.

I hope it has not been forgot to name a Resident for Poona; the Council of Bombay decline sending One, without an Order from the Superior Council, and the Business of the Two Governments cannot well be transacted without One.

I am convinced the Ministers will have as little Connection as possible with Bombay, until their present Jealousies and Prejudices are removed; to effect this, will be full Employ for a Resident, I fear for many Months.

The Reply from the Governor of Bombay to the Peshwa's Letter has disgusted exceedingly; the Ministers think the Language very free for a public Letter between Nations at Peace with each other, and express the greatest Surprize that the Council of Bombay should assume to themselves the Right of Arbitration in the Disputes between the Peshwa and his Subjects; they say they see no End to the disaffected Subjects of the Peshwa flying to Bombay, and receiving Countenance and Protection.

Sedashee Row arrived at Poona a few Days ago—the Ministers intend enquiring into the Identity of his Person in a very public Manner, in Two or Three Days.

Since writing the above, I have received a Letter from the Select Committee of Bombay, dated the 30th November, a Copy of which I have the Honour to inclose.—I have again

again requested the Ministers to fix an early Day for my Departure, and I expect to be on my Journey in Five or Six Days from this Date.

I have, &c.
(Signed) J. Upton.

Poona,
5th December 1776.

Ordered, That the Enclosures in the above Letter be entered after the Consultation.
Resolved, That the following Letter be written to Bombay:

Gentlemen,

By a Letter dated 5th December from Colonel Upton, we have, to our great Regret, received a Confirmation of the Reports which he formerly communicated to us, and which we in Consequence intimated to you in our Letter of the 30th Ultimo. Colonel Upton having now transmitted to us Copies of the Correspondence which passed between you and him, and between your Presidency and the Maratta Government, we think these Documents too well authenticated to admit of our entertaining any Doubts of the Facts as they were before represented. We inclose a Translation of the Letter from Mr. Hornby to the Paishwa; but as we apprehend that the Sense of it may have suffered some Variation from the repeated Translations into different Languages which it has undergone, we request that you will furnish us with a Copy of the original Draft as it was written in the English.

In your Letter to Colonel Upton of the 20th November, we observe the following Passages:

1st. "Subada's People having fled for Protection immediately under the Guns of "Tanna Fort, you, as a Military Man, must very well know it would have been totally "inconsistent to have permitted them to be attacked in that Station."

2dly. "Ragoba has put himself under our Protection, and he now resides in "Bombay."

As the Assertion contained in the first of the above Quotations seems to imply a Claim which may produce future Disputes with the Maratta Government, similar to that which has lately happened, we request that you will inform us on what Principles you found such a Claim, as it appears to us to be an Invasion of their Territorial Rights.

Our Duty requiring us to foresee, and to prevent as much as lies in our Power, every Occasion of Difference between your Presidency and the Maratta State, we think it incumbent on us to demand this Information from you, that we may be able to lay down a certain Rule for your Guidance, by which the Peace of India may not be broken.

As the Propriety of your receiving Ragoba depends solely on the Necessity of the Circumstances which gave Occasion first, we desire that you will communicate to us, in the most explicit Manner, all the Transactions which led to this Measure, particularly whether Protection was granted to him at his own Solicitation, and in Consequence of his appearing in Person to claim it, or if he was encouraged or invited to come to Bombay by any Act of your Government.

ENCLOSURES.

To Lieutenant Colonel Upton.

Sir,

We received your Letters, dated the 19th and 20th Ultimo; the former did not reach us till the 6th Instant.

We enclose for your Notice a List of the several Districts contiguous to Broach, with their computed annual Revenue. This List was transmitted to us by our Commissioners, who have therein ranked the Districts agreeable to the Priority of Choice they give to each. The Revenue assigned to each of these Places is founded upon Experience of their real Value, whereas the Estimation formerly sent you was framed merely from the Information of Ragoba's Agents, before we were put in Possession, and accordingly, as you will observe, much exceeds what we have since found they will produce. However, we are willing to accept the Places offered, if the Ministers will make up the Deficiency by an Assignment of some other convenient Territory; and if, contrary to our Expectation, the annual Revenues of Oalaseer, Hansood and Dehbarah, should exceed Three Lacks, we we will, in like Manner, consent to restore the Difference. We have accordingly given the proper Instructions to our Commissioners.

The Method proposed by the Ministers for discharging the Twelve Lacks of Rupees, is satisfactory to us, and we shall give the necessary Orders for an exact Account being kept, of all Receipts from Jamboosier and the Surat Chowkies.

We shall make Enquiry respecting the Circumstances complained of by the Ministers, when we shall give you our Answer; but the last Article, immediately relating to ourselves, is without Foundation.

We are, &c.

Bombay Castle, (Signed) Wm. Hornby,
7th November, 1776. President, &c. Council.

List of Districts in the Neighbourhood of Broach, with their computed annual Value.

District		Value
The Eight Villages dismembered from the Broach Purgunnah by the Guicawars, and now in Possession of Futty Sing, computed together at	Rupees	40,000
Desborah		30,000
Ahmood		1,00,000
Coral		35,000
Sinore		80,000
Hansood, exclusive of its present Assignments and Tributes to Surat and Broach		70,000
Oulaseer, Do. Do.		75,000
Dubpay		1,30,000

N. B. Verseawaw is mentioned in the Map, but should not, on any Account, be accepted, as its Situation is bad, the Villages in the worst Condition, and the whole District poor and bare of Inhabitants; and it is moreover liable to continual Depredations from the Bhills, and Disputes with the Gracias and Rajah Pipliahs.

(Signed) Rt. Gambier,
Geo. Perrott,
Js. Cheape.

N. B. The above is a Copy of the List of Districts, mentioned in the Letter from the Select Committee of Bombay to Lieutenant Colonel Upton, dated 7th November 1776.

To the Honourable the President, &c. Members of the Select Committee, Bombay.

Gentlemen,

I have been honoured with your Letter of the 7th Instant, and have acquainted the Peshwa's Ministers, that " you are willing to accept the Places offered, provided the Ministers will make up the Deficiency by any Assignment of some other convenient Territory; and if the annual Revenues of Oulaseer, Hansood, and Desborah, should exceed Three Lacks, you will in like Manner consent to restore the Difference."—The Peshwa consents to this, and Instructions are accordingly sent to the Agents at Broach.

In the List of Districts that accompanied your Letter, Hansood and Oulaseer are estimated at One hundred and Forty-five thousand Rupees per Annum, exclusive of their present Assignments and Tributes to Surat and Broach. Not knowing on what Account there were Assignments or Tributes on these Places, I asked Information from the Ministers, and to what Amount Assignments, &c. on them were made? But they knew as little of this Matter as myself; however they have promised very particularly to examine Revenue Books: In the mean Time I have to request, Gentlemen, you will be pleased to favour me with such Particulars as have come to your Knowledge concerning these Assignments and Tributes.

Hanfood and Oulafeer are now valued at little more than Half their former Eſtimation, which you ſent me on the 18th of January, and then you had been in Poſſeſſion of theſe Places (from the preceding Month of April) Nine Months or upwards. The Miniſters, as well as myſelf, ſuppoſe this ſo very ſhort Valuation muſt be owing (for they eſtimate thoſe Places to the full as high as in your Liſt of the 18th January) to the Decreaſe of Inhabitants, or to other Cauſes incidental on War. They ſay the Inhabitants will of courſe ſoon return, and the Country as ſoon recover itſelf, when Peace and Tranquillity ſhall be reſtored to theſe Purgunnahs. They farther obſerve, and with great Juſtice, that were the Purgunnahs they cede, to be eſtimated by the Collections that were made there, during the late War, or even now in their ruined State, they might give Diſtricts to the real Value of Eight or Ten Lacks of Rupees, inſtead of Three Lacks, as ſtipulated. You will pleaſe to favour me, Gentlemen, with your Opinion on this Subject, that I may endeavour to form that of the Miniſters to it, or acquaint you in what they differ, that proper Directions may accordingly be ſent to the Commiſſioners. The Miniſters in this Buſineſs are very ready to meet half Way; I think we ſhould not be backward in giving them the Meeting, as the Advantages are all on our Side. A Report prevails here that Ragonaut Row is at Bombay; I am convinced of the almoſt Impoſſibility of its being true. The Miniſters told me two Days ago, that they had agreed to fix on Ragonaut Row, a Jaghire in the Canduh Country, or near to Janſi, that would be quite ſatisfactory to him; and that they expected this would be ſettled in Eight or Ten Days.

I now forward Two Packets that arrived laſt Night from Fort William. The Governor General and Council have ſent for my Peruſal a Copy of their Letter to you of the 30th September. The very powerful Arguments they make Uſe of, are now I hope no longer required; nevertheleſs I have taken the Liberty, in Addition to them, to acquaint you, Gentlemen, that the Commiſſion by Virtue of which I had the Honour to negociate with the Maratta Government, is given by the Superior Council, the Seal of the Company affixed thereto, and in it is inſerted expreſsly; "We the Governor General "and Council of Bengal, in Virtue of the Powers veſted in us by the Legiſlature of "Great Britain, &c. &c. have deputed you," &c. &c.

I have to requeſt, Gentlemen, you will honour me with a Reply to this Letter as ſoon as you can conveniently.

Poona, I am, &c.
17th November 1776. (Signed) J. Upton.

To the Honourable the Preſident, &c. Members of the Select Committee, Bombay.

Gentlemen,

In my Letter of the 17th Inſtant, I acquainted you that a Report prevailed here that Ragonaut Row was then at Bombay. I am exceedingly concerned to find this Report confirmed by a Letter I have juſt now received from the Peſhwa. He deſires you may be made acquainted with the Contents of this Letter, and that your Anſwer may be immediately procured; for theſe Purpoſes therefore, I have encloſed a Copy of the Peſhwa's Letter, and have to requeſt, Gentlemen, you will favour me, as expeditiouſly as poſſible, with the Reply to the Peſhwa's Accuſations; ſome of which are, admitting the Truth of them, but too obvious, in my Opinion, Infringements of the Treaty. The Peſhwa's Miniſters think them highly ſo, both of late and former Treaties, and complain accordingly.

Poona, I have, &c.
19th November, 1776. (Signed) J. Upton.

Tranſlation of a Letter from the Peſhwa Mhaderow to Lieutenant Colonel Upton; received the 19th November 1776.

I have juſt now heard that Ragonaut Row arrived at the Port of Bombay on the 28th of Ramzaun, and the Governor of that Place gave him an Aſylum in the ſaid Port. He alſo before gave Protection in the above Port and Salſette, to the Followers of the Seditious, with Elephants, Horſes, and Baggage, belonging to Sircar.

Theſe Actions are very foreign to the Meaning of the Treaty under the Company's Seal, concluded by you between the Sircar and all the Engliſh.

Prior

Prior to this I received Letters from the Superior Council of Calcutta, that "We will "not give Ragonaut Row a Residence in any of the Company's Settlements; and all "the Councils of the English Ports will act according to Treaty."

It is entered in the present and former Treaties, that the Rebels of each Side shall be delivered up to one another.

Notwithstanding of these Treaties, which are existing and present with the Sircar, the above Measures by the Governor of Bombay is Cause for Astonishment. What can be the Meaning of giving Habitations to the Enemies of the Sircar; causing the Ruin of the Sircar's Dominions; constantly raising new Seditions; and throwing my Business into Disorder? And what Connections has the Governor and Council of Bombay with this Business?

In order to remove the Disturbances which were between the Sircar and the Council of Bombay, you brought a credential Letter from the Superior Council of Calcutta; we placed an entire Dependence on it, and Peace and Friendship was established between the Sircar and all the English. Notwithstanding of this, the Governor and Council of Bombay are repeatedly acting in this Inconsistent Manner; then how can the Writings or Engagements of the English be depended upon?

You should in Friendship write distinctly the Purport of this to Bombay, and procure a clear Answer immediately, that Measures may be taken accordingly.

It has happened well, that during your Presence, breaking the Engagements appeared on the Part of the English of Bombay. To this Moment, on the Part of the Sircar, no Deviation from the Treaty has occurred; never was such improper Conduct as this heard or seen in Chiefs of high Rank.

Prior to this the Council of Bombay broke the Engagements of former Governors, took Possession of Salsette, &c. ruined the Guzerat Country and other Places belonging to the Sircar, and in Consequence of the Assistance they gave to Ragonaut Row, we sustained the Expence of Crores; but for the Satisfaction of the Superior Council of Calcutta it was dropped. Now the Council of Bombay are again in the same Manner beginning Mischief. If they will not immediately withdraw their Hands from all Actions that are contrary to Treaties, what Advantage is there in making a Treaty with the English?

Measures satisfactory to Ragonaut Row had nearly been concluded, and it was hoped that all the Family Disturbances would have been at an End, when Ragonaut Row, without Notice or Cause, took the Road to Bombay; it is most extraordinary!

We took so much Pains that he might be settled comfortably and satisfactorily; had we wished otherwise our Army was round him. Probably the Sircar's Enemies will say he went to Bombay, his Life being in Danger, but this was never the Case; and if any Person thinks so, it is without Foundation.

An Answer to this Letter is necessary. What more is to be wrote!

(Signed) All. Macpherson,
Pers. Interpret.

To Lieutenant Colonel Upton.

Sir,

We received your Letter, dated the 8th Instant, with the inclosed Papers.

Sudabah's People having fled for Protection immediately under the Guns of Tannah Fort, you, as a Military Man, must very well know it would have been totally inconsistent to have permitted them to be attacked in that Situation, or to suffer any Hostilities to be committed on either Side, and therefore on the Ministerial Forces drawing up near to Sudaba's, and preparing to attack them, the Chief of Salsette sent their Officer the Letter you forwarded us. The River between Tannah Fort and the Maratta Shore, which is stiled in the Paishwa's Letter a Branch of the Sea, is little more than Pistol Shot over, and the Ministerial Forces, as we have been assured by a Gentleman on the Spot, were drawn up within Cannon Shot from the Fort. We were induced by Humanity alone to receive the People of Sudabah into Salsette, to preserve their Lives from the Swords of their Enemies, and should have acted in like Manner to the Poona Forces, had they been reduced to the same Situation.

On the 30th Ultimo Sudabah, after his Defeat at Razimatchee, arrived in this Harbour from Bellpore, and requested Protection, which was promised; but the President being then absent at Salsette, he declined coming on Shore, and went to Mandieun, a Place at a small

small Distance from hence, intending to wait there till the President returned. Here he was invited on Shore to refresh himself by Ragojee Angria, with Professions of the utmost Friendship and Regard, and, as we are assured, under the most sacred Obligation not to molest him; which Ragojee Angria most treacherously violated when he got him in his Power, and after stripping him of Jewels to a great Amount, imprisoned him in his Fort of Colabba.—Immediately on receiving this Intelligence, a Message was sent to Ragojee Angria to demand his Release, as we were certainly bound in Honour to do, Sudabah being at that Time under the English Protection, which he had solicited, and we had promised him. Our Message however was not attended with Success, and we conclude that Ragojee will sell his Prisoner to the Ministers. Ragoba has put himself under our Protection, and now resides at Bombay.

Bombay Castle, We are, &c.
20th November, 1776. Wm. Hornby,
Presid. &c. Council.

Translation of a Letter from the Honourable William Hornby, Esquire, Governor of Bombay, to the Peshwa—Received 13th Shewal 1190.

After the usual Compliments:

The Letter which you sent is received. You write, that an Exciter of Commotions had taken the Name of Sedashee Bowe; if you do not know that he is Sedashee Bowe, I now make it appear, that he is the true Sudaba, regard which I am perfectly satisfied, and this is sufficient for me. You also write that Ragojee Angria seized upon the Bowe in his Retreat: This is a Mistake, from this Reason, that he came to the Port of Bombay merely to meet me, but I was not at that Time in Bombay; on this Account he was going to stay at Undery till I should come to the Island of Bombay. On the Way to Undery, Ragojee Angria agreed to some friendly Proposals, and requested that he should come on Shore; after which Angria acted in a treacherous Manner; it is therefore reasonable that the above Angria should be reprimanded and punished. The said Bowe came to meet me, he was prevented by him. On receiving this Intelligence, I wrote to Angria that "I am expecting him, and give him Leave to come to "me;" but the said Angria did not permit him to come; therefore the Remembrance of this ill Behaviour from the above Angria, will be kept engraved upon my Mind.

I did not consider the Bowe as a seditious Man, I even knew him as a Friend to the Sircar, and he has met with very unmerciful Treatment from the Sircar.—You further write, that Protection has been given to some of the Bowe's People in Salsette; This that you say is true; and this is also true, that the People of your Sircar ran away from the Bowe, came, and Protection was given to them.—Mr. John Halsey acquainted me, that he wrote Letters under his own Signature to the Sircar's Chief, One according to that you sent, and Two others. Humanity always gives the Great a Desire that Persons who come in Affliction should meet with Protection. I have acted accordingly, and will also act in future. This is all to be said to you. You may write whatever you see best, and wherever you please. What more is to be wrote, &c.

This Letter dispatched the 10th Shewal.

N. B. The Governor's Letter to the Peshwa is wrote in the Maratta Language, a Persian Translation of it was sent by the Ministry to Lieutenant Colonel Upton.

(Signed) Allen Macpherson,
Persian Interpreter.

To the Honourable the President, &c. Members of the Select Committee, Bombay.

Gentlemen,

Since the Receipt of your Letter of the 7th Ultimo, I have been continually urging to the Ministers the Necessity of their naming some other Purgunnah, lest it should be found on a fresh Estimation, that the Purgunnahs already allotted for the Country of Three Lacks, should not yield sufficient Revenue.

Ahmood I requested particularly might be the additional Purgunnah. I observed, that our Motive for asking this preferably, was its Contiguity to Broach, and that I thought

thought they should be equally desirous that our Districts should intermix as little as possible: The Ministers therefore, at my repeated Solicitations, have consented that Desborah, Ahmood, and Hansood, shall be the ceded Purgunnahs; with this Reserve, that should the Revenue of these Three Purgunnahs exceed Three Lacks, Villages to the Amount of the Surplus will be withheld by the Sircar; on the other Hand, should there be a Deficiency of Revenue in these Purgunnahs, the Peshwa consents to make over Villages from the Purgunnah of Occlaseer to complete the Sum of Three Lacks.

I inclose the Copy of the Peshwa's Instructions on this Occasion to his Agents at Broach; also an Account of the Assignments or Tributes (as received from the Ministers) on Hansood and Occlaseer, in which is included the Yearly Revenue of the Purgunnahs of Desborah, Ahmood, Hansood, and Occlaseer, as collected by the Mahratta Government.

I now hope, Gentlemen, every Obstacle to the Completion of the 5th Article of the late Treaty is removed, and that the ceded Country of Three Lacks will be immediately made over to the Honourable Company.

My Continuance at Poona will be no longer than till I am honoured with your Replies to my Letters of the 17th and 19th of last Month, and an Acknowledgment of the Receipt of this Letter, which I have to intreat you will favour me with as soon as possible.

Poona, December 1st, 1776.

I have the Honour to be, &c.
(Signed) J. Upton.

An Account of the Yearly Revenues of the following Purgunnahs, as collected by the Maratta Government and the Mogul of Surat; sent by the Peshwa's Ministers from their Revenue Office to Lieutenant Colonel Upton, 1st December 1776.

Purgunnahs.	By the Maratta Government.	By the Mogul of Surat.	Total.
	Rupees.	Rupees.	Rupees.
Dahegebareh, belonging entire to the Sircar -	40,000	—	40,000
Ahmood, Ditto Ditto -	1,63,791	—	1,63,791
Hansood - - - -	1,19,159	8,000	1,27,809
Occlaseer - - -	1,67,401	12,600	1,80,001
- Total Rupees - -	4,90,351	21,250	5,11,601

(Signed) An. Macpherson,
Persian Interpreter.

Translation of Instructions from the Peshwa Madeurow to the Maratta Agents at Broach, for making over the Country of Three Lacks.

You were formerly dispatched to give the English Company a Country of Three Lacks of Rupees; I now write that the Purgunnahs of Ahmood, Hansood and Dehegebareh, are settled with Colonel John Upton to be given to the English Company. An Account of the full Revenues of them in former Years, is taken from the Sircar's Office, and sent you. In Conjunction with the English Agents, the Zemindars and Kanugows of the said Purgunnahs are to be called, and the above Account shewn; and you will also enquire particularly into their full Revenues in former Years according to their Papers.

If the full Revenues of the said Purgunnahs should exceed Three Lacks, you will retain Villages to that, Ahmood or Hansood for the Sircar. If the full Revenues of the Three Purgunnahs should happen to be something less, Villages to that Amonnt are to be given from the Purgunnah of Occlaseer.

If the English should wish to fix the Revenues according to the present Year, whereas hose Purgunnahs were laid Waste by the March o the Armies of Ragonath Row, the

Sircar

Sircar and the English, the present Collections are not equal to the Revenues of former Years, but their Collections will hereafter become as before.

It is entered in the Treaty, that Purgunnahs of a complete Revenue of Three Lacks shall be given to the English.

Colonel Upton has wrote to the Council of Bombay concerning this, and the Council of Bombay will write accordingly to the Chief of Broach.

You are, agreeable to the above, to deliver to the English of Broach, a Country of a complete Revenue of Three Lacks of Rupees, and take their Receipt in the Name of the Sircar, and come away.

(Signed) A. Macpherson,
Persian Interpreter.

To Lieutenant Colonel Upton.—Secret Department.

Sir,

We have already very fully explained our Motives for first affording Protection to Ragonath Row, and these still continuing to operate upon us with equal Force, we could not deny him an Asylum when he again solicited it.

We cannot suppose any Person who has been in the least conversant with the Natives of Asia, can be so totally unacquainted with their Genius and Disposition, as not to allow that Treachery and Perfidy are their peculiar Characteristics, and most particularly so of the Marattas, who are the most treacherous and perfidious of all Asiatics. No one possessed of this Knowledge can suppose for a Moment that Ragobah's Life would not be in Danger, were he to trust himself in the Power of the Ministers, his professed Enemies, who must dread even the Possibility of his future Elevation, and surrounded as he would be, by Persons entirely at their Devotion. Convinced by Experience of the Truth of these Sentiments, we could not hesitate in receiving a Person to whom we had once pledged the Faith of the Company, and who absolutely came himself to implore our Protection. We only mean to extend this Protection to his Security from personal Danger, until the Ministers can settle some Terms that are satisfactory to him; for you must be sensible it is far from our Desire that he should reside here, and we shall be very glad whenever he can be removed from the Company's Settlements with Safety to himself.

If therefore the Ministers will settle any Terms agreeable to Ragobah, it will afford us real Satisfaction, and we will with great Readiness not only communicate to him, but use our Influence to persuade him to accept any consistent Offers they may make him.

And as we are very desirous to give all possible Satisfaction to the Poona Government, and to remove, as far as we can, all Doubts the Ministers may entertain in Consequence of Ragoba's Residence at Bombay, we request you will assure them in our Name, that Ragoba only resides here as a private Person for the Security of his Person, and that we will not in any Shape countenance or promote any Schemes or Designs to their Prejudice, or in the least infringe the late Treaty; of which, as we have before said, we cannot allow our affording him mere personal Protection to be any Breach.

We will send you an accurate Account of all the Assignments or Tribute paid from Hansood and Occlaseer to Surat and Broach, as soon as we receive the necessary Information from these Places.

We esteem it worthy of Remark, and even of Ridicule, that the Letters you receive from the Poona Government are stiled the Peshwa's Letters, considering that the Person meant is only an Infant not Three Years of Age. Artful as the Ministers are, they may hereafter think it convenient to disavow these Letters; and it appears to us to be more proper and agreeable to the Form observed by all Governments, that Letters from the State should be wrote in the Name of the Regent, or the Persons who conduct the Administration during the Minority.

Bombay Castle,
30th November, 1776.

We are, &c.
(Signed) Will. Hornby,
and Council.

P. S. We have just received your Letter of the 27th Instant.

Extract

APPENDIX, N° 147.

Extract of Bengal Secret Consultations, the 26th February 1777.

PRESENT,

The Honourable Warren Hastings, Esquire, Governor General, President,
Lieutenant General John Clavering,
Richard Barwell, } Esquires.
Philip Francis, }

Received a Letter from Lieutenant Colonel Upton, as follows:

Gentlemen,

I had the Honour to address you last on the 5th December 1776.

I have the great Pleasure to acquaint you, Gentlemen, that I have taken my public Leave of this Court; but at the very repeated Entreaties of the Ministers, I am under the Necessity of waiting the Arrival here of Mr. Mostyn, who is appointed from Bombay, Resident at the Maratta Durbar. I expect he will be at Poorunder within Eight Days. I shall have the Honour to attend him once or twice to the Peshwah's Durbar, and then set out on my Return to Bengal.

You will perceive, Gentlemen, by the Correspondence I have had with the Select Committee of Bombay, how very fully I have been employed in reconciling the Differences subsisting between that Presidency and the Maratta Government, very particularly regarding the Reception of Mr. Mostyn, as Resident on the Part of the Honourable Company at this Durbar: The Peshwah's Ministers, however reluctantly, have at last consented to receive this Gentleman, being determined to convince that every Part of their Conduct shall tend to the Re-establishment of that Peace and good Friendship which heretofore subsisted between their State and the Presidency of Bombay. The Ministers say Mr. Mostyn's Continuance in a public Character at their Durbar, must depend on the Mode in which he conducts himself towards their State. As they have consented to receive him, and rested it in this Manner, I have no Doubt of his reconciling what little Jealousies or Differences there may be, which I hope are chiefly imaginary.

The Person who was called Sidashew Row, underwent a public Examination of Five or Six Days, and was sentenced to lose his Life, which was put in Execution on the 17th of last Month, and little more is now said of him here than had no such Person ever existed. As it may be satisfactory to you, Gentlemen, to know the Accusations brought against this Man, and what he had to urge in Vindication of himself, I enclose the First Day's Examination, as related by an intelligent Hircarrah, who was sent to observe in what Manner the Proceedings were conducted.

I have the Honour to be,
Gentlemen,
Your most obedient Servant,
J. Upton.

Poorunder,
22d January, 1777.

Ordered, That the Enclosures in the above Letter be entered after the Consultation.

Agreed, That Lieutenant Colonel Upton's Letter lie for Consideration.

Warren Hastings,
J. Clavering,
Rich. Barwell,
P. Francis.

ENCLO-

APPENDIX, N° 147.

ENCLOSURES.

To Lieutenant Colonel John Upton.

Sir,

We have just received your Letter, dated the 1st Instant, and shall immediately send the necessary Directions to our Commissioners at Broach. We hope with you, that no further Obstacle will now arise to the entire Completion of the 5th Article of the Treaty.

We are, &c.

Bombay Castle, the 6th December 1776.

(Signed) W. Hornby, &c. Council.

To Lieutenant Colonel John Upton.

Sir,

We have before repeatedly represented to you the little Effect that has attended the Orders the Ministers tell you they have issued, for restoring a free Communication of Trade and Intercourse with the Maratta Dominions; the entire Stoppage of which, notwithstanding these Orders, has been severely felt by the Honourable Company, and threatens Ruin to many Individuals.—The principal European and Country Merchants of this Settlement have represented to us, in the most strong Terms, the melancholy State to which the Trade of this Island is reduced, owing to the total Obstruction of our Trade with the Maratta Country; and we think it highly necessary to enclose for your Notice, a Copy of the Memorial they have delivered us on the Subject, in which we assure you the Facts are not in the least exaggerated; and our Regard for the Interest of the Company calls upon us to recommend to you, in the warmest Manner, to insist upon the Poona Government giving the most speedy and effectual Orders, without any Prevarication, for opening the Communication with the Maratta Country, in the same Manner as before the War commenced; and we must observe, that this Conduct is totally inconsistent with the Professions the Ministers so frequently make of Amity and good Inclination towards the English, and contrary to the Spirit and Meaning of the late Treaty.

We likewise enclose a Letter this Day delivered to us by the Agents for the concerned in the Ship Aurora, before mentioned to you. By the Defeat of Sudaba, the Ministers are deprived of the Plea they before made for evading Restitution; and we think the Honour of the Company is engaged to procure full Satisfaction for the Sufferers, agreeable to the express Tenor of the Treaty concluded by you; and we therefore think it highly proper you should exert your most strenuous Efforts in their Behalf. The List of the Aurora's Cargo was before forwarded to you.

The Chief and Council at Broach acquaint us, under the 29th Ultimo, that the Maratta Agents had not then received any Orders from Poona, in respect to the Cession of the Purgunnahs mentioned by you in your Letter of the 19th October; and the Gentlemen at Surat likewise acquaint us, in a Letter dated the 5th Instant, that the Maratta Amuldar had refused paying him the Collections from their Chowkies in that City, alledging, that he had received no Orders from the Principals. This is evasive, trifling Conduct; and we would advise you to require the Ministers to deliver to you the proper Orders for their Officers, and either to forward them yourself, or transmit them to us, for we are inclined to believe the Ministers have deceived you, and have never issued the Orders in Question, as the Maratta Pundits are urging with all possible Expedition the Recovery of the Revenue for this Season from the Purgunnahs intended to be ceded to the Company.

We hope the Ministers will make you some Proposals, respecting Ragonath Row that may be satisfactory to him. What can be their Objections to his residing in one of the Company's Settlements, and assigning to him a suitable Stipend there? If you would gain this Point, we think it would be rendering a most essential Service to the Honourable Company.

We are, &c.

Bombay Castle, 11th December, 1776.

(Signed) Wm. Hornby, &c. Council.

To

APPENDIX, N° 147.

To the Honourable the President, &c. Members of the Select Committee, Bombay.

Gentlemen,

I am honoured with your Letter of the 30th Ultimo. I have given, Gentlemen, in your own Words, the Professions you wished should be made to the Peshwa's Ministers, regarding Ragonath Row; with these they seem well pleased, and for the present satisfied.

The Peshwa's Ministers will order the Vackeel, now residing at Bombay on the Part of the Sircar, to lay before the Honourable the President and Council, Terms of Reconciliation between the Maratta Government and Ragonath Row. They will offer such Conditions as (they say) heretofore appeared acceptable to him, and to make them the more so, they now consent to his residing at Benares, and enjoying there the Jaghier, as full as they had lately proposed fixing on him, had he resided in the Maratta Dominions. The Ministers profess themselves much obliged, Gentlemen, by the Offer you have made of using your Influence with Ragonath Row to accept suitable Conditions towards an Accommodation. They hope these now given in Commission to the Vackeel, will prove satisfactory to him, and wish to be favoured with your Reply regarding them, as soon as convenient.

The Ministers wish and request, before I leave Poona, that I would fix with you, Gentlemen, the Method of Correspondence between your Presidency and this Government, in order that the late Treaty may be fully and expeditiously carried into Execution; and they now request a Letter, either to the Peshwa or his Ministers, to satisfy them that there will be no Delay in the Accomplishment of it, and expressive of your friendly Intentions towards this Government. The Letter from the Honourable the President to the Peshwa, dated the 10th of the Month Shewal (the 23d November) has occasioned a good deal of Uneasiness, which they much wish should be removed before my Departure. I have therefore to intreat, Gentlemen, you will signify to the Peshwa, or his Ministers, your Intentions of adhering strictly to the Treaty lately entered into with the Maratta State; and that you will propose to them, that a friendly Correspondence may be immediately opened for this Purpose. As I am very particularly requested by the Ministers to stay here until your Letter to them shall be received, I shall esteem myself much obliged by its being dispatched with all possible Expedition, and could wish to have it enclosed in the Reply to this Letter.

Mahadagel Ram Chunder is the Person appointed Agent on the Part of the Sircar, to reside at Jamboosee r. The Ministers requested Receipts may from Time to Time be given to him, of such Collections as may be made by the Honourable Company upon Jamboosee r; also for the Payments he may make from the Choukies in and about Surat.

Poona,
12th December 1776.

I have the Honour to be, &c.
(Signed) J. Upton.

To Lieutenant Colonel John Upton.

Sir,

We have received your Letter dated the 12th Instant.

The Maratta Vackeel has not yet laid before us any Proposals for an Accommodation between the Poona Government and Ragonath Row; when he does, we shall use our Influence with him to accede thereto, if we think them reasonable, and that he can accept them consistent with his personal Safety. Benares appears to be a very eligible Place for his Residence, if a Method can be settled for conducting him thither in Safety. He will be very apprehensive of undertaking the Journey over Land, and being a Brahmin, his religious Scruples will make him very averse to proceeding to Bengal by Sea.

It is our Wish and Desire to maintain the most friendly Intercourse and Correspondence with the Maratta State, of which the President now assures the Ministers, in a Letter, which agreeable to your Desire, is inclosed to you; and we shall expect the like friendly Conduct on their Part.

As a Proof of the Sincerity of our Intentions, we are ready to depute a Gentleman to reside at Poona, as heretofore, the Moment the Ministers express a Desire that we should, and provided they will give us Assurances that they will receive and treat him in a Manner suitable to the Character he will be invested with, of Representative for the Honourable Company.

We shall issue the necessary Orders for Receipts being given for all Collections received from Jamboseer and the Surat Chowkies.

We are, &c.

Bombay Castle, 18th December 1776. (Signed) Wm. Hornby, &c. Council.

To the Honourable the President, &c. Members of the Select Committee, Bombay.

Gentlemen,

I have been honoured with your Letters of the 11th and 18th Instant. My Letter of the 12th nearly replies to these, and I make no Doubt, on the Arrival of a Resident, every Thing relative to the Intercourse and Trade between the Two Governments, (which only remains unreplied to) will be adjusted to the Satisfaction of each; I promise no Endeavours of mine shall be wanting during my Stay here, to put these Objects in a Train of easy Adjustment to the Gentlemen who may be appointed to this Residence on the Part of the Honourable Company.

The Ministers, to convince of their friendly Intentions towards your Presidency, readily accept the Offer made, of deputing a Gentleman to reside at Poona as heretofore; and now write on the Part of the Circar, expressing their Desire that he should depart instantly, and that they will receive and treat him in a Manner suitable to the Character he will be invested with, of Representative for the Honourable Company.

If this Gentleman takes his Departure from Bombay agreeable to this Request and your Promise, I shall have the Honour to see him at Poorunder, as I have consented to continue here some Days longer for this Purpose, thinking, and indeed being persuaded, that it may be of mutual Advantage to the Two Governments; very particularly so, I hope, to our own.

I have to intreat, Gentlemen, you will be kind enough to meet immediately, if possible, on the Receipt of this Letter, to give the Resident his Dispatches, that I may not be deprived the Pleasure of giving him every Assistance in my Power on his Arrival at Poona.

The Ministers have given Orders for Bearers being laid from Panwelly to Poona, for the greater Ease and Dispatch of the Journey.

Poorunder, 29th December 1776. I have, &c. (Signed) Jno. Upton.

To Lieutenant Colonel John Upton.—Secret Department.

Sir,

This is purposely to inclose Copy of a Letter we have just received from the English Commissioners at Broach.

We shall wave remarking on the manifest Duplicity in the Conduct of the Ministers, at a Time when they are making such Professions of the most strong Desire to have every Article of the Treaty fully accomplished. We think it however proper to repeat the Recommendation in our Letter of the 11th Instant, to procure the proper Orders from the Ministers, and to forward them to us, that they may be transmitted to Broach by a Sea Conveyance, to prevent any Chance of their being intercepted, which might be the Case if sent over Land. The proper Sunnuds should be likewise sent us for the ceded Countries.

We request you will inform us from what Term the Collections of the Country of Three Lacks are to be considered the Property of the Honourable Company.

We are, &c.

Bombay Castle, 31st December 1776. (Signed) Wm. Hornby, &c. Council.

APPENDIX, N° 147.

To Lieutenant Colonel John Upton.

Sir,

We have been favoured with your Letter of the 29th Ultimo, and we at the same Time received a Letter from the Poona Government, requesting that a Gentleman might be sent to reside there as heretofore.

The Ministers have in their Letter expressed a Desire that Mr. Mostyn, our former Resident, might not be the Person appointed for this Charge. We are rather at a Loss to discover what Objections they can have to this Gentleman; but we are inclined to believe their Repugnance to him proceeds from a Suspicion that he was privy to the Attack on Salsette, or that it was concerted at his Instigation. This Idea, if entertained by them, is totally without Foundation. We do assure you, that this Scheme was not suggested by any Advices from him; that it was determined upon previous to his leaving Poona, by a Resolution of Council, to which he was an entire Stranger; and that he was only ordered from thence a few Days before the Attack commenced, without even any Intimation being given him of the Reason for his Recall. These Circumstances we request you will state to the Ministers, and we are persuaded they will entirely remove their Objections to Mr. Mostyn; and as the Honourable Company's Nomination, and his Knowledge and Experience of the Maratta Politics, point him out as the proper Person to reside at Poona, we have resolved to depute him thither, as Resident for the Honourable Company at the Maratta Durbar.

Even allowing the Ministers had Cause for Suspicion of Mr. Mostyn's proposing Schemes to the Prejudice of their Government, all former Animosities ought to be removed by the Treaty that has lately taken Place, and we cannot allow them to prescribe who we are to employ upon any Commission to the Poona Durbar.

Our Motive for the Attack upon Salsette was founded upon some Intelligence we had received from Goa, that the Portugueze were actually preparing an Armament to reduce it; and as we were then in Expectation of procuring the Cession of it by Treaty from Ragonaut Row, we took that Step to secure the Possession of it for the Honourable Company, which you may communicate to the Ministers, if you think necessary.

Mr. Mostyn will set out for Poona with all convenient Expedition after the proper Passports are received for him and his Attendants, which we request you will expedite. He will bring with him a Company of Sepoys.

We are, &c.

Bombay Castle. (Signed) Wm. Hornby,
3d January 1777. &c. Council.

To the Honourable the President, &c. Members of the Select Committee, Bombay.

Gentlemen,

I have been honoured with the Receipt of your Letters of the 31st December and 3d Instant.

I acquainted the Peshwa's Ministers with the Contents of the Commissioner's Letter: They assure me that the positive Orders they sent to their Agents for immediately making over the Purgunnahs, (as advised in my Letter of the 1st December) are carrying with all possible Expedition into Execution; and they have been informed by the Suba of Guzzerat, of the Receipt of these Orders by him, and that they shall be immediately complied with.

On the Arrival of the Resident at Poona, the Ministers will fix from what Time the ceded Districts are to be considered the Property of the Honourable Company; they never meant any Collections should be made by the Circar after the Ratification of the Treaty, on the Districts that were to be ceded, and declare their Ignorance of any having been made since that Time.

I have acquainted the Ministers, Gentlemen, with your Arguments in Favour of Mr. Mostyn's being received as Resident on the Part of the Honourable Company at the Maratta Durbar, and urged every Thing that occurred to me in Support of them. I am sorry to be obliged to inform you with the absolute Refusal of the Ministers to receive this Gentleman. I enclose the Copy of a Letter I received from the Peshwa last Night, by which you will observe how desirous they are of receiving any Gentleman as

Resident except Mr. Mostyn. I also enclose a proper Passport for the Gentleman (and his Attendants, &c.) who may be deputed.

I dispatch this Letter with all possible Expedition, and have to request you will favour me with an immediate Reply, as the Ministers are desirous of knowing who is to come Resident, and when his Departure from Bombay is to take Place, before I leave Poona, which is fixed for the 18th Instant.

Permit me, Gentlemen, to return many Thanks for the repeated Informations and Assistance you have honoured me with, during my Negociations at this Court. I have to beg you will be persuaded, that the utmost Deference and Attention has been paid by me to every Advice and Recommendation you were pleased from Time to Time to favour me with since my Arrival at Poona, and that I have suffered greatly whenever I was unable to effect your Wishes with the Maratta Government.

I make no Doubt, and most sincerely wish, that on the Arrival of a Resident at this Durbar from your Presidency, the free Intercourse and Harmony which heretofore subsisted between the Two Governments, may be again restored.

Poorunder, I have, &c.
9th January, 1777. (Signed) John Upton.

Translation of a Letter from the Peshwa Maderow to Lieutenant Colonel Upton—Received 8th January, 1777.

All the Particulars of the Letter from the Council of Bombay, in regard to sending Mr. Mostyn, and his Recommendations for the Circar's Durbar, are fully understood from you.

The Governor of Bombay has been wrote to by the Circar, not to send him. Let them send a trusty Person here on the Part of the Company; we do not fix upon him by Name; but, exclusive of Mr. Mostyn, every trusty Person that the Council of Bombay shall send here, will be treated as heretofore by the Circar, only Mr. Thomas Mostyn must never be sent, as he is not acceptable to the Circar. If the Council of Bombay are attentive to the Friendship on both Sides, they will, according to the above, dispatch another trusty Person immediately this Way.

A Letter is received from the Suba of Guzzerat regarding the Country of Three Lacks, that "agreeable to the Circar's Orders, I am now delivering the Purgunnahs "of Three Lacks to the Chief of Broach." This is wrote for your Information. What more is to be wrote?

A true Translation.
(Signed) An. Macpherson,
Persian Interpreter.

To Lieutenant Colonel John Upton.—Secret Department.

Sir,

We have received your Letter of the 9th Instant.

The Honourable Company's especial Appointment of Mr. Mostyn to reside at the Maratta Durbar; the Knowledge and Experience he has acquired of their Views and Interests during a long Intercourse with that Government; his personal Acquaintance with the Ministers and every other Person of Consequence in the Durbar, and with their Characters and Dispositions; are such forcible Reasons for supporting our Appointment of that Gentleman, that we cannot consent to set him aside from an Appointment which he has so long filled with Reputation to himself, and with the Approbation of our honourable Masters and this Presidency, even to the Satisfaction of the former Poona Government, upon so trivial a Foundation as the Letter to you from the Infant Peshwa, which only contains an Objection in general Terms to Mr. Mostyn, without a single Reason from what Cause it is derived. In the present Situation of Affairs it is particularly requisite that the Company's Resident at Poona should possess the most complete Knowledge of the Genius and Disposition of the Persons he has to negociate with; and we apprehend Mr. Mostyn's Qualifications for this Station, which induces us to appoint him to it, are very principal Reasons with the Ministers for objecting to him. We have resolved therefore to abide by our Appointment; and we should not think ourselves justified to our honourable Masters, were we to depute any other Person to Poona, unless

some

some specific Objections are made to him, that we can deem admissible. We also consider this Conduct of the Ministers, in refusing to receive a Member of our Administration, and pretending to make a Merit of not objecting to any other Person, as very unprecedented, and inconsistent with that Harmony they profess themselves so desirous should subsist between the Two Governments.

We wish you a most safe and pleasant Journey to Bengal; and remain,

Sir, &c. &c.

Bombay Castle, (Signed) Wm. Hornby,
13th January, 1777.

Extract of Bengal Secret Consultations, dated the 7th April, 1777.

PRESENT,

The Honourable Warren Hastings, Governor General, President,
Lieutenant General John Clavering,
Richard Barwell, } Esquires.
Philip Francis, }

Read the following Letter from Bombay:

Honourable Sir, and Sirs,

We have been honoured with your Letters, dated the 30th September, 14th October, and 9th December.

The sudden Depression of Sudaba's Party, and his subsequent Death, of which Colonel Upton would be enabled to advise you with more Certainty than you could have done, have added much Stability to the present Poona Government, and removed the Expectations we conceived from Sudaba's rapid Progress of a speedy Revolution taking Place therein.

Colonel Upton having intimated to us his Intention of quitting Poona, and the Ministers expressed a Desire that we should depute a Gentleman to reside there, we accordingly, in Conformity to your Recommendation, resolved again to fix a Resident at the Maratta Court, and appointed Mr. Mostyn, our former Resident, for this Service, of which we gave immediate Advice to Colonel Upton. We were not a little surprized at receiving soon afterwards Letters from the Poona Government, objecting in general Terms to Mr. Mostyn being the Person sent thither, but without assigning the smallest Reason for their Repugnance to receiving this Gentleman; we therefore thought we could not with Propriety set him aside from an Employment to which he was expressly appointed by the Honourable Company, and had long filled to their Approbation, and with Reputation to himself, unless the Ministers could point out some specific Objections to him, that we could deem admissible; neither could we with Credit permit the Ministers to refuse, in so unprecedented a Manner, to receive a Member of our Administration, without assigning some sufficient Cause. And judging that the Knowledge Mr. Mostyn acquired in his former Residence, which so peculiarly qualified him for his Commission, was a principal Reason with the Ministers, to wish some other Person might be deputed, we resolve to adhere to our Appointment; and we have now the Pleasure to advise that they have consented to receive him, and he will soon proceed, furnished with proper Instructions for his Conduct, of which we shall transmit you a Copy; and he will be particularly directed to correspond punctually with your Presidency.

We shall likewise direct Mr. Mostyn to do all in his Power to promote the most friendly Correspondence with the Poona Government; and we hope a suitable and permanent Accommodation will be effected between that State and Ragonaut Row, who still resides at Bombay, whereby all future Jealousies will be removed, and the Honourable Company relieved from the Expence incurred by his Residence.

We are, &c.

Bombay, (Signed) William Hornby, President,
7th February 1777. and Council.

Read

Read the following Letter from Lieutenant Colonel Upton:

Gentlemen,

I have been honoured with your Letters of the 9th and 30th December.

By the Papers that accompanied my Letters of the 5th December and 22d January, you will have been satisfied, Gentlemen, of the Truth of Reports that were heretofore made to me, regarding the demanding by the Governor of Bombay the Person of Sadashee Row from Raggujee Angria, and the Part taken by the Chief of Salsette in the Maratta Disputes.

I much fear the Order you have been pleased to send to the Presidency of Bombay respecting Ragonaut Row, has not been received, as the Council have as yet been silent on this Head. To prevent any bad Impression this may make on the Ministers, I shall this Day forward to Bombay the Paragraph of your Letter of the 30th December, that regards Ragonaut Row.

On the Receipt, Gentlemen, of your last Letter, I observed to the Ministers, as I had repeatedly done before, the Impropriety of their Censures on the Government of Bombay, for Acts committed before the Peace was concluded, all of which were of course cancelled by the Treaty. They acknowledge the Impropriety of this, and say they should not have been so frequent in their Reproaches, had not the Part taken by these Gentlemen, since the Conclusion of the Peace, been so very active against their Government; their Anger, they add, might have led them too far, but they hope there will be no Occasion to repeat their Grievances. This, Gentlemen, is the Purport of their Answer to me now, and was ever the same, when I before observed on the Unfitness of such Upbraidings.

I wish it may appear, by my Correspondence with the Select Committee of Bombay, (since my last Letter of the 22d January) that some Advantages have been derived to the Honourable Company, by my Continuance at Poona. A compleat Lack is gained by the Period fixed for commencing our Collections upon the ceded Country of Three Lacks; and in this a Matter is adjusted that might have been attended with some Difficulty.

I leave Poorunder To-morrow, on my Return to Bengal. Had I done this sooner it must have been without the Consent of this Government, which I conceive, Gentlemen, could not have met with your Approbation.

I am requested by the President and Council of Bombay, to forward the accompanying Packet.

Poorunder, 6 March 1777.

I have, &c.

(Signed) J. Upton.

To Lieutenant Colonel John Upton.

Sir,

Concluding you have not yet left Poona, we think it necessary to transmit to you a Copy of a Letter received by your President from the Peshwa, under the 19th Instant.

This Letter having been conveyed to us in a Manner so different from the former ones from the Poona Government, and the Purport thereof being directly contrary to the Advices from you, which mention that the Purgunnah of Jambooseer is to remain in our Possession until the Payment of the Twelve Lacks, we shall therefore pay no Attention to it until we hear again from you.

We have, &c.

Bombay Castle, 22d January 1777.

(Signed) W. Hornby, President, and Council.

To the Honourable the President, &c. Members of the Select Committee, Bombay.

Gentlemen,

My Desire of being at Poorunder on the Arrival of the Resident from Bombay, has till now detained me, and afforded me the Opportunity of receiving your Favour of the 22d of last Month.

I have

I have the Honour to inclose a Letter from the Peshwa to the Honourable the President, which assures, that the Maratta Government mean strictly to abide by the Agreement made regarding Jamboseer continuing in our Possession until the Twelve Lacks shall be paid, as expressed in the Peshwa's Letter to me, received the 18th of October last; a Copy of which accompanied my Letter of the 19th October.

It seems the Ministers were apprehensive that the Collections of Jamboseer might fall short, from a Conclusion that their Zemindars would take Advantage of the English Chiefs being unacquainted with the former Sums they were accustomed to pay, and take that Opportunity of reducing the annual Revenues of their respective Districts: To avoid this Inconvenience the Peshwa now writes, proposing Two Methods for making the Collections upon Jamboseer, and wishes, Gentlemen, to know to which you give the Preference.

In the accompanying Letter from the Peshwa to the Honourable the President, he agrees that we commence our Collections on the ceded Country of Three Lacks, from the first of the present Year, and that we are to account for no Collections made upon Jamboseer prior to that Date; which I conceive must be found very satisfactory.

I have received a Letter from the Honourable the Governor General and Council, in which they signify their Approbation of the Manner in which the Twelve Lacks are to be paid by the Maratta Government to the Honourable Company.

We have yet no Intelligence of Mr. Mostyn's being on his Journey; at this some Surprize is expressed by the Ministers. I purpose staying here Two Days, or Three if necessary, after this Gentleman's Arrival.

Poorunder, I have, &c.
5th February, 1777. (Signed) J. Upton.

To Lieutenant Colonel John Upton.

Sir,

The Peshwa, in his Letter to the President, having requested that a Duplicate of our Orders to the Chief at Broach, respecting the Country of Three Lacks, and the Purgunnah of Jamboseer, might be sent to him, we have complied with his Desire; and inclose likewise for your Notice, a Copy of the Orders we have given on the Occasion to Messrs. Carnac, Boddam, and Ramsey, who have now the sole Administration of the Honourable Company's Affairs at Broach and its Dependencies.

We are, &c.
Bombay Castle, (Signed) William Hornby, President,
13th February 1777. and Council.

Gentlemen,

I have been favoured with your Letters of the 12th and 13th Instant, with their several Inclosures.

I have the Honour to forward, under the Seals of this Government, a Copy of further Orders which the Peshwa is now sending to his Agents at Broach; these I hope will remove every Difficulty: The Peshwa's Ministers declare they have no other Wish than that the ceded Country of Three Lacks should be made over in the most equitable Manner; for which Purpose these further Orders will be dispatched to their Agents as expeditiously as possible.

You forgot, Gentlemen, to forward to the Peshwa a Duplicate of your Orders to Broach; I have however supplied the Omission, by giving a Copy of those you sent for my Information, and have wrote a few Lines myself to Messrs. Carnac, Boddam, and Ramsey, to be sent therewith.

I am greatly concerned to hear Mr. Mostyn has been so much indisposed as to disable him from travelling; it is Pity that the Expediency of sending Mr. Mostyn's Deputy to Poona with proper Powers, till Mr. Mostyn might have been in Condition to have come himself, should never have occured. From the strong Representations you so repeatedly made of the Necessity of a free Intercourse between your Presidency and Poona, the Removal of Jealousies, and the Re-establishment of Commerce with the Maratta Dominions, I should have conceived you would have readily embraced the first

first Opportunity that offered, to carry such very desirable Measures into Execution; but you are, Gentlemen, certainly the best Judges how to act in the immediate Concerns of your own Presidency. Much has been expected, and many Things have been recommended to me during the Correspondence I have had the Honour to hold with your Board; permit me now to recommend, that some Gentleman be deputed to Poona as soon as possible, until Mr. Mostyn can make the Journey himself; and I am convinced the good Effects of such Measure would be immediately felt. Whatever Jealousies there now may be between the Two Governments, would soon disappear. So long a Time having elapsed, and no Resident sent, occasions strange Surmises amongst the Marratta Chiefs.

I shall wait at Poorunder to be honoured, Gentlemen, with your Acknowledgment of the Receipt of this Letter, in which I have to intreat there may be no Delay; and you will be pleased to carry on your Correspondence in future as has been settled, either with the Peshwa or his Ministers, as my short Stay here will prevent my transacting any further Public Business.

Poorunder, 19th February 1777.

I have, &c.
(Signed) J. Upton.

Sir,

We have received your Letter of the 19th Instant, and as you have expressed your Desire that the Receipt thereof may be immediately acknowledged, we dispatch this Pattamar for no other Purpose, not having yet had Time to take your Letter into Consideration.

We repeat our Wishes that you have a pleasant and safe Journey to Bengal; and are, &c.

Bombay Castle, 25th February 1777.

(Signed) Wm. Hornby, President, and Council

Sir,

The inclosed Packet being of Importance, we request you will forward it, in the most expeditious Manner, to the Governor General and Council.

Mr. Mostyn is so far recovered from his Indisposition that he will be able to set off for Poona in a few Days.

We are, &c.

Bombay Castle, 26th February 1777.

(Signed) Wm. Hornby, President, and Council.

Extract of Bengal Secret Consultations, dated the 12th May, 1777.

PRESENT,

The Honourable Warren Hastings, Governor General, President,
Lieutenant General John Clavering,
Richard Barwell, Philip Francis, Esquires.

Read, and approved, the Proceedings of the 5th Instant.

Received the following Letter from Mr. Mostyn, at Poona:

Honourable Sir, and Gentlemen,

Agreeably to my Instructions from my Superiors at Bombay, I dispatch this purposely to inform you of my Arrival near Proondur Yesterday, and that I shall have my first Audience this Evening.

Enclosed I have the Honour to transmit you Copy of a Letter from the Committee at Broach, directed to Colonel Upton, or the English Resident at Proondur. You may depend on my utmost Endeavours being exerted for the settling this Business, as well as with respect to the District of Jambooseer, deposited with us for the Payment of Twelve Lacks of Rupees, conformable to what the Peshwa wrote to Colonel Upton under the 18th October last.

From

From what Intelligence I could get on the Road, I do not find that there is any Alteration in the State of Affairs at this Durbar since Colonel Upton left it, which was on the 7th Ultimo. I shall constantly keep you advised of all material Occurrences; and remain with Respect, &c.

Curreet, near Proonder, (Signed) T. Mostyn.
the 4th April 1777.

P. S. Should I have Occasion to address your Honour, &c. in Cypher, I shall make Use of the Honourable Company's great Cypher No. 1. Letter A.

To Lieutenant Colonel John Upton, or to the English Resident for the Time being at Poorunder.

Sir,

We have received your Favour of the 18th Ultimo, enclosing Copy of a Letter from Bombay Presidency to our Address, the Original whereof reached us some Time before.

In Obedience to their Orders, we have repeatedly assured the Maratta Agents that we are ready to conform to the Tenor of the Instructions communicated to them from the Peshwa, agreeable to the Copy transmitted by you to the Governor and Council, the 1st December last, viz. To accept the proposed Districts of Ahmood, Hansoot, and Desborah, and give and receive, according as they may exceed or fall short of the stipulated Amount of Three Lacks, which we proposed to have ascertained by the Average Produce of the Three ensuing Years; but the Agents insist on our abiding by their Estimate of Rs 3,33,000, and that there must be a Deduction from Ahmood, for the Surplus of Rs 33,000, and they will admit of no Alternative, although our Commissioners here, who have accurately inspected the Revenues for a Series of Years past, maintain they will not exceed Rs. 2,10,000.

We are sorry to observe, there must be some Collusion on the Part of the Ministers, as the Instructions conveyed directly to the Agents differ widely from the Copy transmitted by you, and seem to authorize their Servants in their obstinate Refusal to accede to our reasonable Proposals.

We have the Honour to be, &c.

Broach,
the 12th March 1777.

(Signed) John Carnac,
R. H. Boddam,
Andrew Ramsey.

APPENDIX, N° 148.

Extract of Bengal Secret Consultations, the 20th January 1777.

PRESENT,

The Honourable Warren Hastings, Governor General, President,
Richard Barwell, } Esquires.
Philip Francis, }

RECEIVED the following Letter from Fort St. George.

Honourable Sir, and Sirs,

We have the Honour to enclose you Intelligence received in a Letter from the Nabob, which, after giving an Account of the Situation of Affairs at Poona, represents Hyder Ally Cawn to be raising Troops and preparing for War, and that the Poligars and Zemindars were ordered to attend at the Passes towards the Panyinghaut: This, however, is in a great Degree weakened by Advices we have received through another Channel, Copy of which we enclose you, which represents Hyder's Preparations to be in Consequence of Apprehensions of the Marattas.

We also send you Copy of a Letter our President has received from the Rajah of Travencore, together with a Copy of his Answer. He is included in the Treaty with Hyder, as being dependent on the Carnatic.

We understand that the French have received at the Islands, Troops and Stores from France, and that Barracks are building at Pondicherry. They most probably look forward to dispute with us the Government of this Country, and considering their Views with those of Hyder Ally, who has reduced many of the petty Princes around him, we ought to prepare ourselves against the Designs of either. Were we able, when Necessity should require to take the Field, with a well-regulated and well-paid Army, with good Conduct, we might hope One vigorous Campaign would restore Peace to the Country. We are sensible of the Necessity of Peace, and every Endeavour shall be used towards a Continuance of it.

We have resolved on the Increase of the Number of our Battalions, by reducing the present Establishment of a thousand Men in each, to Seven hundred, which will enable us to garrison the Forts of the Nabob under our Charge, and to take the Field at a short Notice with Two Battalions of Europeans, Three Companies of Artillery, and Nine Battalions of Sepoys; and these joined by the Nabob's Cavalry, would, we think, be sufficient against any Forces that could be brought against us—but Troops cannot be maintained, Military Operations cannot be conducted without Money, and herein we fear we shall fail. The Balances due from the Nabob, the Rajah, and our Revenues, until September 1777, with the Amount of Bills to be drawn on the Company, amount to 28,34,000 Pagodas, and our Disbursements, in case of Peace, with the Amount of our Investment, would leave a Balance in our Hands not inconsiderable, were the Whole to be received; but the very great Scarcity of Specie, from the considerable Exports which have been made to China and Europe, fills us with Apprehension that our Receipts from the Nabob and from the Company's Lands will fall short of the estimated Sums. The very Report of a Force of 1,500 Europeans and 12,000 Black Troops assembled, with the Means of Payment in our Treasury, would command Respect from all, and would be likely to deter any from attempting to disturb the Carnatic. The Necessity of such a Fund has long appeared, and in our Letter of the 29th March last we had the Honour to write to you, how serviceable to us such Assistance might prove. We beg Leave to repeat the same Representation to you, and if the State of your Treasury can admit of your supplying us, we shall reserve it for the Support of an Army, in case we should be obliged to take the Field.

When we reflect on the Company's Situation here, we confess it is hard upon them to be at the Risque, and then to advance for the Defence of the Carnatic; but no Alternative occurs, for the Nabob's Resources being in his Lands when Troubles ensue, nothing considerable can be obtained from him, as we have often experienced. We have recommended to him the Reduction of every unnecessary Expence; he has dismissed Part of his Sepoys, and we understand he is making other Arrangements, which will greatly relieve his present Difficulties.

We shall only add, that had we not supplied Bombay and Bencoolen with the Sum of nearly Four Lacks of Pagodas during the Years 1774 and 1775, we should at this Time have had a considerable Sum in our Treasury.

Since writing the above, some Intelligence has come in, which we have now the Honour to enclose.

Fort St. George, We are, &c. &c.
4th December, 1776.

Ordered, That the Enclosures in the above Letter be entered after the Consultation.

ENCLOSURES.

From His Highness the Nabob to Governor Stratton.

2d November, 1776.

I have sent you enclosed a Copy of the News received from Syringapatam, by which you will discover the Intentions of Hyder Ally Khan.

What can I write more?

Copy

Copy of the News of Syringapatam.

News is arrived from Poona that Sukharam, Bapoo, Nana, Phaar Nueso, and other Chiefs, are in the Forts of Peorundhar and Poona. As yet no Preparations are made; they have raised a few Troops, but have not Money to pay them. Ragonaut Row has quitted the English at Surat, and intends coming here.

Sedaree Row has collected a numerous Force, and has taken the Country of Hookum, with all the Forts, &c. and is arrived near Poona. Tranquillity is therefore fled from that Quarter. From Madras we hear that the former Governor, Lord Pigot, is in Confinement, and is at Variance with the Nabob and the English; and also that the Nabob is greatly harrassed by his Creditors, and his Army, for their Money, which has very much rejoiced the Chief here; he is raising Cavalry and Infantry, and collected a large Quantity of Ammunition and Stores, and has sent Orders to all his People on the Borders, and at the Passes of the Payinghaut, to hold themselves in Readiness. After the Duwallee they are determined to march. An Express on a Camel was sent with Letters to the Chiefs of Cudapa, Chittaldorook, and Sanoor, and all the Zemindars and Poligars, to desire they would come immediately with all their Troops, Ammunition, Stores, &c. I am very certain their Designs are against the Carnatic; but Time will discover. They are here so particularly severe with the News-writers, that if it was known any one wrote ever so little, he would certainly suffer Death. Notwithstanding this I have wrote these Particulars: And if in future another Opportunity shall present itself, I will embrace, otherwise you will consider these Circumstances as true; and be upon your Guard.

A true Copy.
(Signed) D. Baine,
Dty My Sy.

Intelligence received from Hyder's Country; brought by Hircarrahs who left Syringapatam 17th October, and arrived at Madras 2d November 1776.

Hyder Ally and Teepoo Saib are at Syringapatam. When Hyder Ally was at Bunkaporam, he had News that his Brother-in-Law, named Small Cawn Saib, Morarow, and Kurtur (formerly the Head of the Mysore Country) having considered with each other; upon that Hyder Ally left about 5,000 Horse at Bunkaporum, and Darvady with 4,000 Horse, and 8,000 Sepoys at Paraguddy, which he gave to the Command of a Moorman. Hyder Ally then went to Syringapatam, and on his Arrival there, People say he killed the said Small Cawn Saib with his own Hands. This Man was Killedar of Syringapatam Fort. On a certain Day, when Hyder Ally went to Kurtur, as was his usual Custom, Kurtur asked him, Why do you keep me always in Confinement? If you will carry me along with you to Camp, I shall have an Opportunity of walking. Upon hearing this, Hyder Ally told him, very well; but after that Kurtur died in about 15 Days, whereupon Hyder Ally appointed a Boy of 8 Years of Age (a Cousin of Kurtur's) in Kurtur's Room; and lately being a Dossarah Feast (usually given to Boys) Hyder Ally sent for the Boy (now the Head or Master) and shewed him much Respect and Civility, after which he sent him to his House with great Pomp.

The Particulars of the Force that serves in Hyder Ally's Camp, are as follows, viz.

Horse, - - - -	15,000
Sepoys, - - - - -	20,000
Portugueze, - - - -	500
French Soldiers, - - -	150

The above Force is stationed in the following Places:

6000 Horse in Gungapellah, on the East Side of Syringapatam,
4000 Horse about the Villages,
8000 Sepoys at Syringapatam,
5000 Poligar Pions, Ditto,

And the rest of the Force in the Pavaguddy and Marwaddle. The whole of the Poligar's Army that serve him, will be about 20,000 Pions.

In this Year the strong Current of the Cavarce River carried away the Bridge of the small Fort of Syringapatam, and they are now repairing it.

Hyder Ally has given Orders to the Head Conicoplys of every Village, and the Managers, to settle all the Purgunnahs Accounts, and to collect all the Balances due from the Inhabitants of his Circar; which they are now doing; besides this, Hyder Ally has wrote to the different Polligars to pay him the following Sums due to him, or more properly that he obliges them to pay annually,

	Pagodas.
The Chittracuttoo Polligar, - -	200,000
The Roya Durgum Ditto, - - - -	100,000
The Jemindar of Ponganoer, - - -	23,000

He has also wrote to several other Polligars in the same Manner. He is making ready his Camp: The People say, that about 20,000 Maratta Horse had marched as far as the River Kistna, and which and Hyder Ally is making there Preparations, for it is said the Marattas will soon be in these Parts, that is the Syringapatam Country.

Note, Pavaguddy and Marwadne are distant about 120 Miles North of Syringapatam.

A true Copy from the Translation.

(Signed) D. Baine,
Depy My Sy,

APPENDIX, N° 149.

Copy of an Extract from an Arzdasht of Mahomed Bahadre, Naib of the Fort of Mullebharry; dated the 19th of Zekaida (31st December) and received the last of the same Month: Forwarded to Mr. Stratton in a Letter under Date the 12th of January 1777.

A Person of Credit in the Talook of Mullebharry lately sent some People of his own, accompanied by Two Hircarrahs on my Part, towards Ballagaut, to learn the real State of Hyder Ally's Affairs, and I also wrote a Letter for the same Purpose to Cunkunny Durkwalah. From his Answer, and the Accounts given by the Agents sent on this Business, I learn that Shasram, the Brother of Murrar Row, at the Head of 80,000 Maratta Horse, had entered Hyder Ally's Country by the Village of Adelly, situated on the Confines. In this Village Hyder Ally had a Garrison of 3000 Horse under the Command of Kishen Row, the Son of Ramajee Pundit: The Maratta Army surprized him in the Night, and got Possession of the Villages, together with Binkapore and Mullery.

Besides the 30,000 Men abovementioned, another Army of 60,000 Cavalry have entered the Country on the Side of Culkey.

As soon as Hyder received this Intelligence, he sent his numerous Army under the Command of his Son Tuppoo, and his Brother-in-Law Mukdoom Khan, to engage the Marattas, and is himself at Serringapatam to defend that Fort. This is undoubtedly Fact.

By the Blessing of God, and your Highness's auspicious Fortune, the Troubles which are now fallen on Hyder Ally Khan must put a Stop to the evil Designs he has formed.

Whatever further I am able to learn I shall transmit your Highness.

Extract of a Letter from Mr. Robert Adams to the Resident at Onore; dated Seringapatam, 20th September 1775, and received at Onore the 30th, per Anchers.

The Nabob Yesterday told Badjee Row in the Durbar, that his and his Brother's Wits were gone for taking Assistance from the English, a good-for-nothing deceitful People, who do not mind breaking any firm Agreement, and that their Assistance was of no Value; on which Badjee Row and Pursing Point told him, their Wits were not gone, unless it was because they had eaten the Rice and drank the Water of this Country, and that the English assisted Ragoba when he was deserted by his People, and no one else would assist either in Men or Money, but that the English had done both, and collected for him 50,000 Horse, and he hoped they would in a short Time be in Poona, and if he chose to march he might; if not, they, Badjee Row and his Brother, would go without him; on which the Nabob was silent, and promised he would march with them after the Dussora.

There is great Reason to suspect the Nabob is tampering with the Ministerial Party and the Nizam to our Prejudice; he has lately wrote to the latter, observing to him how the English took Bengal, Arcot, &c. therefore should they be suffered to place Ragobah in Poonah, the Riches of that Town must fall into their Hands; all the Powers and Countries from Calcutta to Cape Comorin must be subject to the English, therefore *now* is the Time to frustrate them; and that he may depend they will be on both the Nizam and himself in a short Time.

A true Copy.
(Signed) Edwd. Ravenscroft, Secy.

APPENDIX, N° 150.

Extract of Bengal Consultations, the 22 April, 1776.

PRESENT,

The Honourable Warren Hastings, Governor General, President,
Lieutenant General John Clavering,
The Honourable George Monson,
Richard Barwell, } Esquires.
Philip Francis, }

From Lord Pigot to the King of Tanjore.

THE English East India Company disapproving of the late Conduct of their Servants with Respect to Tanjore, have thought proper to direct me to replace you upon the Throne of your Ancestors, upon certain Terms and Conditions to be agreed upon for the Benefit of yourself and the English East India Company, without infringing the Rights of Mahomed Ally Khan, Nabob of the Carnatic.

I have, in Consequence of these Orders from my Masters, concerted Measures with the Nabob, so as to carry them properly into Effect; and Colonel Harper, who will deliver you this when he has relieved the Nabob's Troops, will appoint for your Protection such Guards as may be thought necessary.

I request of you to allow me a few Days after hearing that the English are in Possession of Tanjore before I say more to you, than to assure you I will study to do every Thing that is for the mutual Benefit of you and my Employers, and I hope you will permit the Nabob's Officers to continue in the Management of Affairs, until I have again the Honour to write to you.

A true Copy.
(Signed) R. J. Sulivan, Secy.

Fort St. George,
2d February, 1776.

To the Right Honourable Lord Pigot, President, and Governor, &c. &c.

My Lord,

The Letter which your Lordship has honoured me with, and which was delivered me by Colonel Harper, has given me a Joy which no Tongue is able to express.—Overwhelmed with a Transport of Joy, I am as one who is raised from the Dead. When I seemed to be cut off from all the cheering Hopes of seeing better Days, then it was that God, by his over-ruling Providence, turned my Sorrow into Joy. Your Lordship has been the happy Instrument Providence has made Use of to restore me to my former

Dignity

Dignity and the Throne of my Anceſtors. I ſhall therefore from henceforth look upon you as my Father, and venerate you under that moſt amiable Character as long as I have a Being.

Convinced that whatever your Lordſhip ſhall think proper to determine or regulate will be to my real Advantage, I ſhall cheerfully reſign my Concerns to your kind Hands, and willingly acquieſe in your Determinations.

As by your generous Regard for my Happineſs, your honourable Name muſt and will be had in the moſt grateful Remembrance by me and my Family; ſo I hope it will be celebrated over the World.

I remain, &c.

(Signed) [signature in Devanagari]

Tanjore, 13th February, 1776.

A true Copy. (Signed) R. J. Sullivan, Secry.

Letter to the Honourable the Court of Directors for Affairs of the Honourable the United Company of Merchants of England trading to the East Indies.

Honourable, Military Department.

1. We paid our Reſpects to you by the Ankerwyke and Hillſborough, under Date the 14th February, and then acquainted you that the Nabob had admitted your Troops into the Garriſon of Tanjore the 9th of that Month.

2. No Perſuaſions however could induce him to concur in reſtoring the Rajah. He ſaid he would not oppoſe the Execution of your Orders, but would never conſent to give up the Tanjore Country. So circumſtanced, we determined, in Conſequence of the Orders you had been pleaſed to ſend us by the Grenville, to reſtore the Rajah by your Authority; and we thought proper to entruſt the Execution of thoſe Orders to our Preſident. He ſet out the 30th March, and returned from Tanjore the 5th May; and we have now the Pleaſure to tell you that the Rajah is put into Poſſeſſion of the whole Country his Father held in 1762, when the Treaty was concluded with the Nabob.

3. His Fort is not only garriſoned by your Troops, but his Country protected by them alſo. He has on this Account engaged to pay into your Caſh 400,000 Pagodas annually, and will keep no other Troops himſelf but what are neceſſary for his Guards, the Number not to exceed 500. We have the greater Satisfaction in informing you of this, as every Meaſure we have taken has been at his Requeſt.

4. And the encloſed Copy of the Rajah's Letter will, we flatter ourſelves, give your Honours perfect Satisfaction. We did not think it right to accept any additional Country near Devy Cotah. We have complied with the Rajah's Requeſts in all other Reſpects; and our Preſident begs Leave to aſſure you, that he cannot expreſs how grateful the Rajah is for the Juſtice you have done him, nor how much he merits your Countenance and Protection.

Fort St. George,
14th May, 1776.

APPENDIX, N° 151.

Country Correſpondence, 1776.——Extract of Intelligence from the Decan, received 30 July, 1775.

THE Deſign of the Decan Sirdars now is, after croſſing the Nurbudder, to collect together all the Armies of the Decan, and being joined by Nizam Ally Khan to make one powerful Effort by a general Engagement with the European Army; and that the Struggle for the Chiefſhip of the Decan may be at once decided in Favour of him to whom the Almighty giveth the Victory.

Madhajee Sindha has reſolved to join whatever Party finally prevails.

Regonaut Row has laid Siege to Burrood a near Goujeraut, which Futty Sing Guickwar, who is in the Place, is prepared to defend. After the Rains, he propoſes to proceed into the

the Decan. Nizam Ally Khan is encamped near Ellichpore, and has put to Death Ishmael Khan, the Chief of that Place, as well as Rukkun-ul-Dowlah, his own Dewan. Madhajee Boosila, having visited Nizam Ally Khan, entered into a Friendship with him, which has been since broken, and their former Enmity renewed, by Nizam Ally's having assassinated Usoph Gardee, the Murderer of Narrain Row, who was an Associate of Madhajee Boosila. Nizam Ally Khan is now inclined to assist the Sirdars of the Decan, but is kept in Suspence through Fear of the Power of the Europeans.

Extract of Bengal Secret Consultations, the 17th July 1777.

PRESENT,

The Honourable Warren Hastings, Governor General, President,
Lieutenant General Sir John Clavering, K. B.
Richard Barwell, Philip Francis, } Esquires.

Secret Department, Thursday.

The Proceedings of the 14th Instant read, and approved.

Lieutenant Colonel Upton attending, according to the Order of the last Council Day, is called in, and delivers to the Board the following Paper:

Information, and Requests of the Nizam to the Honourable the Governor General and Council of the Superior Council, as delivered by himself to Lieutenant Colonel Upton, dated 13th April 1777.

The following Circumstances will shew our steady Attachment to the English.

Treaties of the strongest Nature were in Force between us and the Paishwa Maderow and Narrain Row. When the latter was murdered, Ragonaut Row wrote twice, acquainting us of what had happened, and declared in the most positive Manner, his Intentions were to abide strictly by the above Treaties; being therefore under no Apprehension from that Quarter, we sent our Army to settle some Disturbances in Berar, and remained at Hyderabad with the necessary Guards only, but what was our Surprize when we were informed that Ragonaut Row was on his March towards Buder with a large Army. We were consequently under the Necessity of withdrawing the Forces from Berar, and marching with all Expedition to Buder. On our Arrival there we sent a Vaqueel to Ragonaut Row, to know the Cause of such an extraordinary Measure, after his Letter to us, and to ask him if he was sure he had left all quiet at Poona, after what had happened so lately there? However, if this sudden Attack was in Expectation of finding us unprepared for War, he had better send a Person on whom he could fully depend, to look at our Troops and Artillery, by which he would be convinced that we were ready for the Field. He complied, and a Peace was concluded agreeable to the former Treaties; we returned to Hyderabad, and he marched towards the Kistna: But the very Day we parted he began to burn and lay Waste the Country on this Side the River, after which he crossed it, and had a Meeting with our Brother, whom he endeavoured to persuade to join him in Arms against us. Our Brother asked him what he could mean by making such strange Proposals to him, when he had but just concluded a Peace with the Circar? and answered him in every Respect becoming our Brother. The Maratta Ministers, Succaram Pundit and Ballajee Pundit, wrote us at the same Time of his extraordinary Conduct, and that they were determined to return to Poona, and wait with Patience till the Widow of Narrain Row, who was pregnant, should be delivered, and if the Child should prove a Boy, they begged for our Assistance to support him in preserving his Birthright. Seeing there was no Dependance to be placed on Ragonaut Row, as well as our Desire of placing the Son of Narrain Row on the Musnud, we sent an Army to join them, and Ragonaut Row was drove across the Nirbunda; however, he returned, and was again forced back, and his Followers dispersed, except the Guicawars, who found Means to carry him to Surat, where a Treaty of Alliance was concluded between him and the English, promising their Assistance to carry him to Poona.

Soon after this we received an Address from the French, requesting that we would, as in former Times, accept of their Services. We sent no written Reply to this Address, but desired the Vaqueel who brought it, to acquaint them, that there was a Treaty subsisting

subsisting between us and the English, declaring our Enemies their Enemies, their Enemies ours.

They answered, that the English had in some Degree infringed that Treaty, by joining Ragonaut Row, against whom the Sircar had an Army in the Field; but we declared that we would take no Steps which should appear contrary to the Treaty with the English, and particularly as we were about this Time informed that there was a Council superior to all the others arrived at Calcutta, whom we were persuaded would not deviate from former Treaties; we therefore determined to wait till we should fully learn their Intentions; at which the French were greatly disappointed.

Some Time after we were informed, that Proposals of Peace were made between the English at Surat and Hurry Pundit; and we received a Letter from Ragonaut Row, requesting we would send an Army to assist him, and that he would give us in Return a Country of Fifty Lacks, and several Forts. We replied, we would send no Army to join him, but if he chose it, we would use our Influence with the Ministers of the young Paishwa, to get a Jaghire settled upon him.

We ordered Ziffer ul Dowlah the Dhousu, with an Army to join Hurry Pundit, with strict Orders to prevent, as much as possible, any Battles or Skirmishes between the English and Maratta Armies, till we should fully understand the Disposition of the Superior Council, and upon no Account to join in the War without further Orders from us.

When we were informed that the Superior Council had deputed a Sirdar of high Rank to Poona, to negociate a Peace with the Ministers of the young Paishwa, we were convinced of the Justness of our former Conjectures, that they would not approve of the Treaty of Surat with Ragonaut Row; and sent Orders to Ziffir ul Dowlah to return with the Army under his Command.

After the Treaty was concluded, Ragonaut Row's being received into Surat gave the Ministers great Uneasiness, from which they were soon relieved by the Orders from Calcutta, and his having quitted that Place; but when he was received into Bombay, they began to think there was no End to their Troubles; and from the Two following Motives, sent to invite the French to enter into an Alliance with them; the First, that they might prepare against any future Attempts which the English of Bombay might make to assist Ragonaut Row; the Second, to join them in recovering what they considered their ancient Right, the Chout, from the Nabob of Arcot.

The French being disappointed in their Expectations from the Circar, promised to enter into an Alliance with the Marattas, particularly against the Nabob of Arcot, and consequently the English, provided they would act as follows, viz. That the Marattas should march an Army into the Carnatic, from which a large Detachment should be sent to the Neighbourhood of Pondicherry, which is to alarm the French, and they are immediately to send to the Officer commanding the Maratta Army, to know his Demands; he will reply, that he insists upon the French joining the Marattas against the Nabob of Arcot, to recover their Choute; the French will give out that they had nothing left but to comply, and will, under this Pretence of Necessity, send an Army to join the Marattas.

We have also been informed, that a Ship, with Five French Officers of Rank, arrived lately at a Maratta Island. The Inhabitants required their immediate Departure; but the French assured them that they had particular Business with the Peishwa's Ministers at Poona, and desired Notice might be sent with all Expedition of their Arrival; which the Chief of the Island did; and we have Intelligence that Elephants, Camels, &c. are now sent to the Sea Shore nearest the above Island, to carry the French Officers to Poona.

Our Attachment to the English has made us think of the following Plan to prevent the Marattas from attacking the Carnatic; viz. That Ragonaut Row shall be continued at Bombay, until the Poona Ministers agree to settle a reasonable Jaghire upon him, in the Kandee Country, which will be so near our Dominions that we can threaten to join Ragonaut Row with an Army the Moment they shew any Intention to march against the Nabob of Arcot, which will prevent their sending their Army from Home.

Another very material Circumstance which we suppose the English are not acquainted with, is, that Moodaje Bonsla, who claims a Right to the Choute of Bengal, is wishing for an Opportunity to march a large Army into that Province, which must greatly injure the English. However our real Desire of being upon the most friendly Terms with the English Nation has induced us to fall upon a Plan which will enable us to

thwart

thwart Moodajee's Intentions on Bengal, viz. Suckojee Boonsla, the Son of Rajajee Boonsla, claims a prior Right to the Chiefship of Napore, &c. This young Man was some Time ago under our Protection; but having concluded a Treaty of Peace with Moodajee, we sent him to Poona, to prevent Jealousies while the other continues quiet; but the Moment he attempts to distrust the English, we will acquaint him that our Intention is to place Suckojee on the Musnud, which will thoroughly prevent his Designs on Bengal, &c.

It is imagined the French are in Alliance with Hyder Ally to attack the Nabob of Arcot, and the English of Madras; and should Ragonaut Row be turned out of Bombay before the Ministers have made a proper Provision for him, he will certainly join Hyder Ally.

It is our particular Desire to transact all Business concerning the Sircar immediately with the Supreme Council, and that no other shall interfere.

In order to strengthen the Friendship subsisting between us and the English, we should be glad to have the following Article inserted in the Treaty, if agreeable to the Superior Council, viz.

Should the Sircar have any Service to perform in the Decan, the English are to join and assist the Sircar's Army, except against the Marattas; and should the Company have any Service in the Decan towards Arcot, the Sircar's Army will join to assist the English Army, except against the Marattas.

APPENDIX, N° 152.

Extract of Bengal Secret Consultations, the 17th October 1776.

PRESENT,

The Honourable Warren Hastings, Governor General, President,
Richard Barwell, Philip Francis, } Esquires.
Lieutenant General John Clavering indisposed.

READ, and approved, the Proceedings of the 14th Instant.

The Governor General lays before the Board the following Minute:

Many Ships have been wrecked on the Coast of Orissa, near Point Palmiras, which, from the Shoals and the Currents at certain Times of the Year, joined by the Violence and Artifices of the Inhabitants, is the most dangerous Part of the Navigation of the whole Coast: Several Instances of these Disasters come within our Knowledge, and as the Fact is notorious, I think it unnecessary at present to accompany the Proposal which I am going to make, with a List of the Ships that have thus unfortunately suffered, but will endeavour afterwards to furnish it.

I now submit to the Consideration of the Board, the Propriety of soliciting the Rajah of Berar to grant a Portion of Land adjoining to that Part of the Sea Coast, in Property to the Company, for the Establishment of a small Fort and Garrison for the Protection of Shipping, and for the Preservation of the Lives of the Seamen, and the Cargoes of the Vessels that may be wrecked upon it.

If the Board concur in Opinion with me, I think no Time should be lost in making the Application, in order to render it useful before the next Rains. The present Juncture also seems favourable; the Rajah of Berar has now a Vackeel here, and he himself is solicitous to cultivate the Friendship of this Government. Should he comply with our Request, the Advantages to Trade are obvious; should he refuse it, which I think is not unlikely, I shall never propose to make an Establishment in his Dominions, without his Consent; but it will, I am convinced, at least make him seek to palliate the Refusal by forming some Establishment of his own, to protect and prove an Asylum to our Shipping, which is the only Object I have in View.

I cannot pretend to ascertain exactly the Military Establishment which it may be necessary to keep up for the Protection of this Grant, in the Event of its being made to us; this will depend upon many local Circumstances which cannot be at this Time foreseen.

For the better Information of the Board, I deliver in a Map of the Coast in the Neighbourhood of Point Palmiras.

To Madhajee Bhoosela.

Many Ships have been cast away upon the Coast of Cannice and Boojing, their Cargoes plundered, and the Seamen and Passengers imprisoned and ill-treated by the Zemindars of those Parts, who appear to be a lawless and savage Race, neither acknowledging any Government, though nominally subject to your Authority, nor observing any Rule but the Gratification of their own Rapacity. Many Instances have happened within my Knowledge, of shipwrecked Persons who have suffered cruel Treatment and Imprisonment from the Zemindars of Cannice and Boojing, and in particular of one Captain of a Vessel, named Rogers, who with many of his People were basely murdered by the Rajah of Boojing, as appeared by the Testimony of the few Seamen who escaped, and who left the said Rogers and their Ship Mates in Confinement, and who have never since been heard of.

These are Actions which are a Disgrace to every civilized Government, and inconsistent with the Justice and Humanity which distinguish your Character; at the same Time I am convinced that it is not in your Power to apply the effectual Remedy to them, your Residence being too remote, and the Country uncultivated, and almost inaccessible but by Sea; I should long since have punished the Authors of these atrocious Crimes, but they call themselves your Subjects, and this Consideration has restrained me; besides, it is not Vengeance for the past that I want, but a Prevention of the like Evils for the future. For this Purpose I request that you will permit me to erect a proper Building for the Safeguard of the Coast, for the Directions of the Vessels in their Passage, and for the Protection of the Lives and Cargoes of such as may be wrecked in that Neighbourhood, and that you will grant to the Company a Sunnud for the perpetual Possession and Property of the Land which lies between the River of Banka and the Mahanudee, running in a Line with the Sea Coast above and below it. For this I will consent to pay you the same Rent which you now receive from the present Occupiers of it, or any other Rent or Equivalent which you shall judge reasonable; my Wish being to make you the Partaker with me of an Act of extensive Humanity and Hospitality, in which you may suffer no Loss, and in which I cannot derive any other Gain than in the Benefits of the Commerce, to protect which is the Object of this Proposal, as the rude State of the Country itself will render it totally useless and unprofitable, either as a Fund of Revenue or internal Traffic.

On this Subject Beneram Pundit will also address you, and can inform you of other Particulars from his own Knowledge and Enquiry.

The Board agree to the Governor General's Proposal.

From Moodhajee Bhoosila; received 28th March 1777.

What you write on the Subject of insuring the Security, Safety, and Protection of Merchants and Traders, from the Dangers of the Voyage, and from the Calamities of Pillage; and that the Zemindars of Coojung and Runka have seized and appropriated the Cargoes of such Ships as have been wrecked on the Sea Coast, and ill-treated and imprisoned the Crews and Passengers; that the Punishment of this Race of People, and affording Redress to the unfortunate Sufferers, has been delayed by Reason of the difficult Access of the Country, the Authority they have established in those Parts, and the Remoteness of my Residence, is, through the sincere Friendship and Attachment you bear me, expressed in so delicate a Manner, and with so much Attention to the Honour and Rights of my Government, as is highly pleasing and agreeable to me. Such Conduct is incumbent at all Times on the * Ornaments of the Musnud of Government.

As I delight in Justice, and am a Friend to the whole Race of Mankind, the Happiness and Prosperity of the People, and Security and Protection of the Human Race in general, whether Travellers or fixed Residents, are the Objects of my most earnest Desire and Attention. By the happy Influence of this good Disposition, notwithstanding

* Meaning, Rulers of a State.

the

the small Number of my Allies, and the great Number of my Enemies, Victory accompanies me every where, and Peace and Friendship court me on every Side.

When weighed in the Balance against the Heroes and Conquerors of the Decan, whose Horses make no more of a Journey of 1,000 Coss than if it were a Party of Pleasure of 100, what Power have the Zemindars of Coojung and Runka to breathe forth Sentiments of Enmity, to take any base or improper Step, or to plunder and murder any one?

Once before that evil-disposed Zemindar cloathed himself in Rebellion, and refused to submit his Neck to the Yoke of Obedience; but at last, by the Terror of the avenging Army, he was subdued and rooted out. Having found a favourable Opportunity, he again established himself there, and entered the Paths of Ill, which he still treads in.

On the first Intelligence of this, and on the Perusal of your friendly Letter, I dispatched the most express Orders to Madajee Hurry, Subadar of Orissa, to proceed without a Moment's Delay, at the Head of a powerful Army, to extirpate that foolish Rebel, the Author of all the Evil, and to afford Protection and Security to all Merchants and Traders, whether cast on Shore by Shipwreck, or passing backwards and forwards, and on no Account whatever to suffer them to be troubled or molested, but so to act as to give Satisfaction to them. The said Subahdar has lately written me, that conformable to my Orders he is set out to chastize and extirpate him; and that he shall very soon reduce him to Obedience, or shall entirely extirpate him. Probably this News has also been transmitted from those Parts to you; if not, it will be. You will set your Mind at perfect Rest on Account of the Merchants and Traders, as the Subahdar will exert himself with the utmost Industry.

As I am constantly desirous of the agreeable News of your Health and Welfare, the Receipt of your friendly Letters will relieve me from Anxiety, and afford me the greatest Pleasure.

From Moodhajee Bhoosila; received 28th March 1777.

Your very agreeable Letter, every Character of which conveyed to my Mind a pleasing Sense, and refreshed the Flower Garden of Friendship and Union, the Copiousness which the truest Friendship induced you to give to it; your Congratulations on the Marriage of the illustrious Youth, and on the Success of my Arms; your hearty Acceptance of my Presents, agreeable to the List which accompanied them; and after learning the Particulars entrusted to Beneram Pundit, assuring me under your Hand, that the Conviction of the Sincerity of my Friendship is firmly engraved on the Tablet of your Heart; and that you have therefore no other View but to cultivate and strengthen the Root of Friendship which has been planted; and that with respect to the Money, I shall receive an Answer through Beneram Pundit: This Letter, filled with such Expressions of Regard, arrived at a happy Period, and caused my Heart to overflow with Pleasure, encreasing my Friendship an Hundred-fold. At the Time of its Arrival I was diligently engaged, in Consequence of Intimation from Madhoo Row Pundit Purdhaun, in levying Forces, and preparing Store of Arms and Artillery for the Purpose of settling the Affairs of Mundellah, the Raja of which is lately dead without Children, and has left no legitimate Heir, either on the Father's or Mother's Side, nor any one fit to be placed on the Musnud. I have now raised near 15,000 expert Cavalry, and have dispatched an advanced Detachment, which I shall follow in Person in Three or Four Days. It has been also determined to send the auspicious Youth, Ragojee Bhoosila, with 5,000 Horse to Poona, to pay a Visit to Madhoo Row Pundit Purdhaun, a Measure which our long and steady Friendship renders absolutely necessary: He is already set off, and is advanced Twenty Coss on his Journey, and will proceed there by long Marches.

The Purport of a Precept which adds Lustre to the Principle of Friendship, is this, "Give Presents, and thereby encrease Friendship." This we have mutually performed; and it is known to the Nabob Nizam ul Dowlah, and to Madhoo Row Pundit Purdhaun, the Two most powerful Princes of the Decan, that such an Intercourse subsists—that Presents, such as Elephants, Jewels, Cloths, and Cheetas, mutually pass between us, and that our Friendship and Engagements are firmly established: And the said Nabob, when we sat together in Discourse, dwelt very long on this Sub-

 ject.

ject. He observed the excellent Disposition of the English Chiefs is highly pleasing and praise-worthy, in that, with whomsoever they form Friendship, or enter into Engagements, should the whole Course of Nature be changed, they would faithfully adhere to them.

In a Word, as our Friendship is arrived to such a Degree of Perfection, and the Fame of it is spread to all Ranks of People, it is equally necessary to us both, as well as for our mutual Interest, to preserve it inviolate. I am steadily fixed on every Occasion in this Path, and your good Faith, your Candour, and Uprightness, have been by the Contents of your Letter deeply engraved on my Mind, as on a Stone; our Friendship will daily take deeper Root. I am in Expectation of an Answer from the august King of England to a Letter expressed in Terms of Friendship, which was formerly dispatched: He will certainly send one, which will afford me the highest Degree of Pleasure.

APPENDIX, N° 153.

Extract of a Paper of Intelligence, dated the 21st of Moburrum; received the 28th March 1777.

THE Poona Sirdars are at Poorunder. It is said that Bysagee and Peetul Sahib * and Tocojee Holdcar, are appointed for the Invasion of Hindostan.

* Scidia.

APPENDIX, N° 154.

Extract of a Letter from the Governor and Council in Bengal, in their Secret Department, to the Court of Directors of the East-India Company, dated the 24th Feb. 1775.

Par. 2. WE then informed you of the declining State of the Vizier's Health, according to the Intelligence we received from Mr. Middleton; and that in his Opinion he could not survive long; on the 6th Instant, by Letters from Colonel Galliez, we were informed he was actually dead. The Colonel had previously apprized us of the imminent Danger in which the Vizier lay, and we had dispatched Instructions to him to support the Pretensions of Mirza Amanny, the Nabob's eldest and only legitimate Son in the Succession in Case of his Father's Death, and immediately to move the Brigade down to Fyzabad to prevent any Disturbance in the City on the Occasion; we at the same Time ordered the Third Brigade to march up from Barrampore to Dinapore, that it might be nearer to the Frontier in case any Service should be required.

Conf. 3 Feb.

Conf. 6 Feb. 3. We confirmed these Instructions after the News of that Event having actually taken Place, and further directed Colonel Galliez to continue his Negociations for the Payment of the Money due by the late Vizier; and also on this Occasion to keep a watchful Eye over the Foreigners who had been entertained in his Service, and to endeavour to engage the new Nabob to dismiss them totally; we have further enjoined him to discourage the Offer of any Present from the Nabob to the Army or to Individuals.

Ditto, ditto. 4. Just before the Vizier's Death, he wrote a Letter to the Governor General, which was afterwards transmitted to its Address by Mahomed Elich Khan, his Minister and favourite Servant, accompanied by one from himself. By these Letters it appears that Mirza Amanny, otherwise called Asoph ul Dowlah, had his Father's positive Nomination to the Succession; and though by all Accounts he possesses neither the

the Qualities of the Heart nor Head, equal to the Station to which he is thus called, we have not as yet any Reason to think that his Right will be disputed.

5. In Conformity to those Assurances which we gave in our last Letter to your Honourable Court, we have had in Deliberation the Line which on this important Event it may be most proper for us to pursue, for drawing from it the greatest possible Benefit to the Company's Affairs. We have already determined that
the specific Conditions of our former Alliances with the Vizier expired Conf. 13
with him; and that although we owe Friendship to the present Nabob, February.
as Heir to his Father, we are not bound to any special Services to him.
In this essential Point it is necessary to mention, that the Sentiments of the Board were not unanimous, as will appear upon the Proceedings: Our present Engagement goes no farther than to a simple Acknowledgment of his Title, and therefore should he apply to us for Assistance and effective Support, we mean to afford it only on such Terms and Stipulations as to us shall appear most advantageous to the Company, and honourable to the British Name. As this is a Subject of great Magnitude and Importance, we have chosen to enter upon it in Council, with all the Deliberation which it requires. The Ideas of the different Members will appear 14 February.
in the Consultation referred to in the Margin: They are not given in as conclusive Opinions, but as Sentiments subject to be canvassed, modified, and corrected, and tending only to throw Lights on the Subject before the final Determination of the Board; when that Determination takes Place, you shall be duly advised.

6. Mr. Bristow, who has set out for his Residency at the Court of the new Nabob, will be furnished with ample Instructions on these Heads; in the mean Time we have charged him particularly with the Business of settling the Payments of
the different Sums due by the late Vizier, and given him such further 3 February.
Directions for his general Conduct at the Nabob's Court as we thought
necessary. We also furnished him with Copy of a Report from Mr. Mid- 6 February.
dleton, of the Characters, Views, and Interests of the principal Persons there; which cannot fail of being useful to him on his first Arrival. Mr. Middleton arrived at the Presidency in the End of last Month, with the 15 Lacks
of Rupees, which we have formerly advised you he had received from 31 Jan.
the Vizier; this Money is in Part Payment of the 40 Lacks stipulated for our Assistance in the Rohilla War.

7. We have also Advice, that the Assignment of 5 Lacks of Rupees,
granted by the Vizier on Raja Cheit Sing, has been received on the Ditto.
Company's Account at Benares, and is on the Way down to the Presidency.

8. Colonel Galliez advises us of his having received Three Lacks of
Rupees from the late Vizier, in further Acquittal of his Engagements on 30 Jan.
Account of our Assistance in the late War.

9. Some Time before the Vizier's Death, he applied to Colonel Galliez
to know whether we would permit a Battalion or Two of Sepoys, or any 31 Ditto.
Body of the Company's Troops to return into the Rohilla Country, should he have Occasion to make such a Requisition.

11. Notwithstanding our Orders to Colonel Galliez were very precise to keep the Brigade together, we were sorry to find that he had, without Leave from
us, or even any previous Intimation of his Design, detached Two Bat- 9 Feb.
talions of Sepoys to Cawnpore, for the Purpose of aiding the Nabob to reduce the rebellious Zemindars in the Province of Corah, a Service we disapproved of much; and had also marched one Battalion to Fzzabad, and detained it there without any apparent Purpose. We thought this Disregard of our Orders
worthy of our particular Reprehension, and we wrote him accordingly, 11 Feb.
giving him at the same Time, a Caution to avoid such Detachments for the future, as by thus dividing his Strength, he might endanger the Safety of the whole Troops under his Command.

APPENDIX, N° 155.

Extract of Bengal Secret Consultations, the 6th June 1775.

Translation of the proposed Articles of the Treaty with the Nabob Asuf ut Dowlah.

THE Nabob Asuf ut Dowlah, Icayaa Cawn Behadre, Hozeblus Jung, on the one Part; and the Honourable Warren Hastings, Esquire, Governor General, and the Members of the Supreme Council of Fort William, for and in the Name of the English East-India Campany, on the other Part, agreeable to the following Articles.

First. That universal Peace, firm Friendship, and perfect Union, shall for ever be established between the Nabob Asuf ut Dowlah and the English East-India Company; the contracting Powers, with a View of maintaining a reciprocal Friendship in the future, shall not for any Cause, or under any Pretence, encourage the Reiats and the Inhabitants of their Soubahs in committing Hostilities and Disturbances, and every Thing shall be avoided by the said Powers which might occasion them. Their Friends and Enemies are mutual; and any Person who shall run away and take Refuge in the Country of one of the said Parties shall be given up to the other, and no Assistance afforded him.

Second. The aforesaid Nabob engages never to entertain or receive in his Dominions Cossim Ally Cawn, the former Soubahdar of Bengal, and Sumroo, the Murderer of the English; even in Case of his getting them into his Hands, he will out of Friendship make them Prisoners, and deliver them up to the English Company. He also engages, not for any Cause, or under any Pretence, to entertain Europeans of any Nation in his Service, without the Consent of the English Company: That he will prevent, oppose, and send back such as offer to come in, to pass through, or remain, or shall now be in his Dominions, without the Perwannah of the English Company. The Europeans of every Nation in the Service of the said Nabob are hereby dismissed; and now, and in the future, he engages never to entertain the said Europeans; and to deliver up to the English Company such of their Servants who have deserted or may desert, in Case of his apprehending them.

Third. If the King should write any Thing relative to the Affairs of the Nabob Asuf ut Dowlah to the English Serdars, they will attend to the Satisfaction, Advantage, and Inclination of the said Nabob, and not consent to what the King may say or write. In like Manner, if the King should write to the Nabob Asuf ut Dowlah, relative to the Affairs of the English Serdars, he will attend to their Satisfaction, Advantage, and Inclination, and not consent to what he may say or write.

Fourth. The Countries of Corah and Allahabad shall always, and for ever, remain in the Possession of the Nabob Asuf ut Dowlah, on the same Footing as the Subah of Owde; and they shall on no Account, in the future, be disturbed by the English; nor will they ever request a Dam or Derrum, or any Thing from the said Countries. The English Serdars engage to defend the Soubah of Owde at all Times, and Corah and Allahabad, until the Pleasure of the Court of Directors shall be known.

Fifth. The said Nabob, for the Defence of his Country, as above specified, declares that he has given up, of his own free Will and Accord, unto the English Company, all the Districts dependant on Rajah Chyte Sing, together with the Land and Water Duties, and the Sovereignty of the said Districts in Perpetuity. That the English Company shall, after One Month and a Half from the Date of this Treaty, take upon them the Sovereignty and Possession of the Districts under Rajah Chyte Sing, as hereunder specified, viz.

Sircar Benares,	The Districts of Juanpore,
Sircar Chumar,	Bighpore Bahdore,
Sukteslgun,	Mullbooz Kawss,

The Sircar Gawzypore,

The Purgunnahs of Seckunderpore, Jeride, Shaay, Abad, Toppa, Surchehur, &c. as formerly.

The Mint and Cutwally of Benares.

Sixth.

Sixth. The Nabob Asuf ut Dowlah, for the Aid and Assistance of the English Troops when stationed with him, shall pay Monthly from the Date of this Treaty, for the Charges of a Brigade, the Sum of Two Lacks Sixty thousand Owde Sicca Rupees, of the 16th Year, agreeable to the present Currency. If in future this Currency should be abolished, the Decrease or Increase of Batta shall be mutually given and received by the Parties. The Particulars of a Brigade are, viz.

Two Battalions or one Regiment of Europeans,
One Company of Artillery, and
Six Battalions of Sepoys.

The aforesaid Nabob shall, whenever the English Troops pass the Boundaries of the Company's Provinces, at his Request pay the stipulated Sum Monthly, from that Time until their Return to the abovesaid Boundaries.

Seventh. If the aforesaid Nabob shall ever require the Aid and Assistance of the English Company, for the Defence of any other of his Countries, besides those above specified, he will fix something for the Company proportioned to the Service.

The English Company, and all the English Serdars, engage to perform whatever Articles are now mutually settled, and in the future, during the Life of the Nabob Asuf ut Dowlah, they will never vary or depart from them. They will not, in any Respects or Manner, make Requests of any Thing now contrary to the Tenor of this Treaty.

The Parties mutually swear according to their respective Faiths, to abide by these Engagements. Dated the 20th of Rubby-ut-Euril, 1189 of the Hegira, or the 21st of May 1775.

A true Translation.
(Signed) John Bristow,
Rest. at the Court of the Nabob of Owde.

Compared with an attested Copy sent down by Mr. Bristow, and found to be an exact Traslation, except that the Word Bahdoer, in the List of Districts, was omitted, which I have inserted.

J. H. D'Oyley,
Actg. Persn. Tr.

Translation of an Agreement under the Seal of his Excellency the Nabob Ausuf-ut-Dowlah.

In Case of any Persons having Demands, or having received Tuncaws on Rajah Chyte Sing, or on the Districts under him, agreeable to my Orders, such Demands or Tuncaws do not depend on the said Rajah, or on the Districts, but are due from myself.

The Possession and Sovereignty in Perpetuity of the said Districts, under the said Rajah, without Incumbrances, Delay, Dues, Debts, Tuncaws, &c. I wholly give up to the English Company, at the Expiration of One Month and a Half.

Dated the 20th of Rubby-ut-Ewut, 1189 of the Hegira, or the 21st of May 1775.

A true Translation,
(Signed) John Bristow,
Rest. at the Court of the Nabob of Owde.

Compared with an attested Copy sent down by Mr. Bristow, and found to be an exact Translation.

(Signed) J. H. D'Oyley,
Pn. Tr.

Considered the proposed Articles for a Treaty of Alliance with the Nabob Asuf-ul-Dowlah. Treaties concluded.

Approved the 1st Article,
Do. the 2d,
Do. the 3d,
Do. the 4th,
Do. the 5th,
Do. the 6th,
Do. the 7th.

Ordered,

Ordered, That the Treaty be compared with the Persian Copy, and if it be found exact, that Two fair Copies be engrossed in Form, for the Seal of the Company and Signature of this Board, to be forwarded to Mr. Bristow, that he may obtain the same Testimonies on the Part of the Nabob, and return One of them.

APPENDIX, N° 156.

Extract of Bengal Secret Consultations, dated 7th December 1775.

PRESENT,

The Honourable Warren Hastings, Esq; Governor General, President,
Lieutenant General John Clavering,
The Honourable George Monson,
Richard Barwell, } Esquires.
Philip Francis, }

GENERAL CLAVERING, Colonel Monson, and Mr. Francis, also deliver in their separate Address to the Court of Directors, per Salisbury, as follows:

Minute from General Clavering, Colonel Monson, and Mr. Francis.

Fort William, 21 November 1775.

Since our Arrival in this Country, it has been one of our principal Objects to give the Honourable Court of Directors an Insight into the real State of their Affairs in every Branch and Department: We must now request their Attention to a short and general Review of our Conduct, the Effects it has produced, the Difficulties in which this Government is involved, and the State of the Country.

Notwithstanding the constant Opposition we have met with from the Governor General and Mr. Barwell, we believe it will appear that our Labours have not been useless to the Company: Some salutary Measures have been carried into Execution—some Abuses have been checked, or corrected—some important Advantages have been obtained—much more might undoubtedly have been done, if the System of Government in which we found Mr. Hastings involved, had permitted him to co-operate heartily with our Endeavours for the Public Service.

We are sensible that in the regular Course of Government the Measures of the Council should originate with the Governor; and that it is the Duty of his Colleagues to advise and assist him.

We came into this Country filled with the most favourable Impressions of his Conduct, and determined to support his Administration: The Records of the last Twelve Months will we hope justify our departing from this Resolution, and taking that Lead in the Conduct of Business, which naturally belongs to his Station. The Representations sent Home will give the Company but a faint Idea of the accumulated Difficulties with which we have been perplexed or opposed; we therefore hope that in reviewing our Measures, large Allowance will be made for the Disadvantages under which we have acted.

1st. We began with recalling the Company's Troops from a Service equally unjust, impolitic, and dishonourable. In this Instance the Approbation of our Conduct is anticipated, in Terms as strong and precise as we ourselves could have dictated, by the General Letter of the 7th of March last: No Condemnation can be more severe than that which the Court of Directors have passed on the Rohilla War, and on the Conduct of the late Administration, even on their own State of the Facts: What Judgment will the Company form of the Measure, and of the Persons who planned it, when they see our Representation of it?

2d. As soon as it was possible for us to obtain sufficient Lights into the Nature and Institution of the Bank, we resolved to abolish it. In Addition to the Arguments suggested to to us by the Court of Directors, we soon saw Reasons for taking that Step, which probably were not suspected at Home.

3d. We put an immediate Stop to an arbitrary Inquisition into the Titles, by which the Inhabitants of Dacca held their Lands in the City. We have Reason to believe that this Inquisition, which in Fact was undertaken by the sole Authority of Mr. Barwell, and without the Sanction of the late President and Council, would have depopulated Dacca, and spread a general Alarm, productive of the same Effect, thro' all the Provinces.

4th. In order to relieve the Company from the Burthen of their bonded Debt, we set out with a Plan of reducing the Interest upon the whole Debt, from Eight to Five per Cent. a considerable Portion of the Capital has also been discharged. Unless our expected Resources fail us, and setting aside the Case of a foreign War, which it shall be our Study to avoid, or of a domestic Calamity which we cannot foresee or prevent, we have great Hopes of being able to congratulate the Company in the Course of the ensuing Year, on the total Annihilation of their Bonds, or at least on the Acquittance of so considerable a Part of them, as to leave a Debt too trifling to deserve their Attention.

5th. We have enquired with unwearied Diligence into the Frauds and Corruptions almost universally practiced, and connived at under the late Administration. In this Branch of Duty the Governor General and Mr. Barwell were able to have given us the surest Lights, and the most effectual Assistance; in this Branch of Duty they have most strenuously thwarted and opposed us: We lament the Success of our Enquiries, they are invidious in their Nature, and cannot fail to load us with the Enmity of Individuals. If the Importance of a Service were to be measured by the Labour and Anxiety of the Persons who perform it, we should not scruple to say, that our Efforts in this Line of Duty, particularly entitle us to the Support and Approbation of the Company.

6th. The Board of Ordnance planned and recommended by the Commander in Chief, will, we believe, be found a beneficial Institution. Where considerable Savings are the Object, Regularity is the first Step to Oeconomy; the Operation of a Year or Two must be allowed to prove the Advantages of this Establishment; in the mean Time the Expence incurred by it is trifling.

We are happy to observe that our Opinion of the Impropriety of employing the Commissary General to furnish contingent Supplies to the Army, is confirmed by the strong Disapprobation which the Court of Directors have expressed of this Measure in the Case of Colonel Macleane: We have anticipated their Orders on this Head, by the Regulations under which the above Supplies are now furnished.

7th. The Principles on which we have condemned the War in which the Presidency of Bombay have engaged themselves with the Marattas, and the Steps we have taken to obtain a secure and honourable Peace, will, we doubt not, be honoured with the entire Approbation of the Court of Directors: They were founded on the Knowledge we had of their pacific System of Policy, and in Effect we have the Happiness to see them implicitly confirmed by the Sentence passed on the Rohilla War. On the same Principle we refused the alluring Offers made to us by the Subah of the Decan, to relinquish the Paishcush paid to him by the Presidency of Madras, and to give the Company his Aid for the Conquest of Cuttac.

8th. The Motives on which we have restored Mahomed Reza Cawn to the Office of Naib Subah, have been clearly explained. To recover the Country Government from the State of Feebleness and Insignificance to which it was Mr. Hastings's avowed Policy to reduce it, was no easy Task. According to the Governor General's Plan, we should have confined the only Man perhaps of real Abilities and extensive Knowledge in the Country, to the important Office of Steward to the Nabob's Houshold, at a Time when a Minister of the Government was wanted, and when the Administration of criminal Justice through the Country was at a Stand. The Measure seems to us indispensably necessary, and promises Success. In recommending Mahomed Reza Cawn to his present Post, we presume to think that we have rendered an essential Service to the Company.

9th. The permanent Advantages secured to the Company by our Treaty with the present Subahdar of Oude, are equally conspicuous and important; they have extorted an Acknowledgment from the Governor General, with which he has not been accustomed to honour any Measures but his own. In Return for an Acquisition of Twenty-two Lacks a Year for ever, with an Encrease of Fifty thousand Rupees to the Monthly Subsidy of the Brigade, besides many other Advantages and honourable Stipulations, hardly any Thing is granted on our Part, but a Personal Guarantee of the same Countries to the Son, which we were before bound to guarantee to the Father. The Frontier Country of Ghazipore must at any Rate have been defended by our Arms, in case of an Invasion, whether the Revenues of it had been ceded to the Company or not. These Revenues are in Effect a clear Gain to the Company, and a seasonable Relief to the declining Circulation of Bengal. The Measure is strictly and exclusively ours: The original Plan was opposed in every Step by the Governor General and Mr. Barwell. It gives us the highest Satisfaction to observe, that by the Terms of the Treaty, the Guarantee of the Nabob's Dominions, and the Service of the Company's Troops, were exactly confined within the same Limits which the Court of Directors, in their last Letter, have thought fit to prescribe to us, in our Engagements with the Vizier.

In spite of numberless Discouragements, our Endeavours to serve the Company have not entirely miscarried: If more shall be expected from us, the Power and the Means must be proportioned to the End. Considering the Resistance and Opposition we meet with from every Quarter, we are in Truth unable to determine, whether any and what Powers are left to this Government. If by our Authority as Duan, confirmed to us by Parliament, a Farmer be confined for Arrears of Rent, the Supreme Court of Judicature take the Cause out of our Hands, decide upon the Merits, and discharge the Prisoner: If we dismiss the Judge Advocate, he applies to the Supreme Court for a Mandamus to reinstate him in his Office: If we dismiss the Secretary of our own Board, we see him encouraged to bring an Action for his Salary against his Successor: If we order a British Subject to repair to the Presidency, he pleads the Protection of the Supreme Court of Judicature, and declines or refuses to obey us: If, for Reasons of the most serious political Importance, we endeavour to support the Authority of the Country Government, and the Sovereignty of the Soubah, we have not only the foreign Factories, but the Supreme Court of Judicature to contend with; they publicly deny the Existence of such a Government, and affectedly hold out the Person and Authority of the Prince to the Contempt of the World.

According to the Doctrines maintained by the Judges, there is scarce any Act of Government, however necessary or expedient, which, if it tends to controul the Actions or to thwart the Interest of Individuals, may not expose the Members of the Council to Actions in the Supreme Court. We even doubt whether we are authorized to prevent any Persons from quitting the Provinces and going up the Country, though we should be certain of their Intention to enter into the Service of a foreign Power; in these Circumstances many useful and obvious Regulations for the Benefit of the Country must necessarily be left unattempted. A general Re-coinage has been repeatedly recommended to us by the Court of Directors; such a Measure is without Doubt indispensably necessary; but it is of a Nature too delicate and important, and likely to be attended with too many Difficulties in the Execution, to be undertaken with Safety by a divided Government, with a hostile Court of Judicature.

We could point out a Number of other Objects, which would deserve our Attention, and of Abuses which call upon us for Redress; but this is not a Season for a mere Majority of a Council to undertake any Measure for the Public Service, in which the learned in the Laws of England can discover any Thing to cavil at.

While a Standard is publicly hoisted against our Authority, and every Individual in the Country invited to repair to it; while Protection is given to every Man who denies or resists the Authority of Government; and while the Governor General takes a willing and decided Part in every Measure that tends to degrade the Council, and to disarm us of our lawful Powers, we are not sanguine enough to expect that any Efforts of ours should be equal to the Execution of the Trust reposed in us: We cannot answer for the Collection of the Revenues; we cannot answer for the internal Government of the Country, nor for the Safety of the State. Our utmost Endeavours shall still be exerted to preserve the Peace, and to promote the Welfare of the Country, until the Necessity or Expediency of a new Arrangement shall be determined at Home. But, divested as we are of all Power, we owe it to our Safety and Character to discharge ourselves in the most solemn Manner from all Responsibility.

(Signed) J. Clavering,
Geo. Monson,
P. Francis.

Warren Hastings,
J. Clavering,
George Monson,
Richard Barwell,
P. Francis.

APPENDIX, N° 157.

Extract Bengal Secret Consultations, 29th February 1776.

THE Governor General delivers in his Minutes sent to the Honourable the Court of Directors, by the Hillsborough.

To the Honourable the Court of Directors, &c.

Honourable Sirs,

Enclosed I have the Honour to send separate Observations on Three Minutes of General Clavering, Colonel Monson, and Mr. Francis; One belonging to the General, and Two to the Revenue Department; and all bearing Date the 21st November 1775.

I have the Honour to be,
Honourable Sirs,
Your most obedient and
faithful humble Servant,
(Signed) Warren Hastings.

Fort William,
the 20th January 1776.

Observations on the Minute of General Clavering, Colonel Monson, and Mr. Francis, dated the 21st November 1775.

Hitherto the Letters and Minutes of the Gentlemen of the Majority addressed to the Court of Directors have been confined to one unvaried Theme, the Condemnation of my Conduct, and of the Measures of the last Administration. They have now changed the Subject to the Enumeration of their own Services; but even in this they have not lost Sight of their original Object; as the Sum of their Merits on which they lay Claim to the Applause of the Court of Directors, amounts to little more than a Disavowal of the Principles, and a Subversion of the Measures of the late Government.

They begin with asserting generally, that "Some salutary Measures have been carried "into Execution; some Abuses have been checked or corrected; some important Ad"vantages have been obtained." These general Positions are afterwards particularized in the following Instances:

1st. The Recall of the Troops from the Rohilla War.

2d. The Abolition of the Bank.

3d. The Stop put to the Inquisition into the Titles by which the Inhabitants of Dacca held their Lands in that City.

4th. The Reduction of the Interest on the bonded Debt, from 8 to 5 per Cent. and the Payment of Part of the Capital.

5th. The Inquisition into the Frauds and Corruptions, almost universally practised and connived at under the late Administration.

6th. The Board of Ordnance.

7th. The Condemnation of the War in which the Presidency of Bombay had engaged with the Marattas.

8th. The Appointment of Mahomed Reza Cawn to the Office of Naib Subah, and the Restoration of the Powers of the Nizamut.

9th. The Treaty with the Nabob of Oude.

When this List shall be read by those whose Wisdom planned the System established by Parliament for the controlling Government of India, and compared with the Expectations which they must have naturally formed from so great and extensive a Design, they may be led to think very differently from the Gentlemen of the Majority, of such Services; and be disappointed to find, that instead of converting the great Powers granted to the Governor General and Council to the Confirmation of the British Dominion, and the Improvement

provement

provement of the British Property in India, their Time and Attention in a long Period of 13 Months have been occupied on no greater Objects than negative Measures; the temporary Adjustment of the Right of Property in a Heap of old Ruins; the Substitution of a new Treaty, in Violation of former Engagements; and Attempts to usurp or depreciate the Merits of their Predecessors.

To shew that these are the Amount of the Services which have been so pompously displayed, I shall take the Liberty to examine them in their Order.

1st. The Majority improperly claim a Merit in having withdrawn the Troops which were employed in the Rohilla War, before that Service was accomplished. It was imprudent in every Sense; it was highly prejudicial to the Company's Interests, if that Service was undertaken on expedient and allowable Grounds. It was unjust if that Government was bound by previous Engagements to prosecute it to a Conclusion; and yet more unjust if it has since exacted the Sum stipulated as a Part of these Engagements.

I cannot admit either the Justice or Decency of binding the Court of Directors to the Interpretation which the Majority have been pleased to force on their Orders. I understand the Paragraph of the General Letter of the 3d March, to be an Approbation of the Rohilla War. I understand the Disapprobation expressed in their Letter of the 7th of March, to apply to a Subject totally different from it, to a Supposition that the Troops which were employed in the Rohilla War had quitted the Country which was the Seat of it, and had crossed the Ganges, to engage in an indefinite Service beyond the prescribed Line of their Operations. These Censures arose from a Misinformation, or from a Misconception of the Words of a Letter from the late Select Committee; and I presume, that the Explanation given them in my Letter of the 25th November, which went by the last Ship, will have totally removed all their Displeasure upon this Head.

2d. The Answer from the Provincial Councils to the Queries stated to them, proved that some Advantages had been produced from the Institution of the Bank; and that it was not attended with any Inconveniencies to justify the Majority's hasty Abolition of it.

3d. This hardly merits a Comment: The Council at Dacca had ordered an Enquiry to be made into the Titles by which the Inhabitants of the City of Dacca held the Lands occupied by them. Mr. Francis warmly espoused the Cause of the Occupants. The Board ordered the Enquiry to be suspended, and this very important Act of the Governor General and Council, which probably was never heard of Ten Miles from the Spot which was the Object of it, is blown up into Magnitude, and is held up as a Measure which by the critical Interposition of the first Powers of Government rescued the City of Dacca, and all the Provinces, from Depopulation.

4th. This is an Usurpation of the Merits of the late Administration. The Reduction of the Interest of the Bonded Debt was unnecessary. The Payment of the Principal was effected by the Treaty of Benares; by the Rohilla War; by the Savings made by the former Board of Inspection in the Civil and Military Expences; by the Reduction of the Nabob's Stipend; by the Suspension of the King's Tribute; and by the other œconomical Regulations of the late President and Council. I again defy the Gentlemen of the Majority to produce a single Instance in all their Measures by which a Rupee was gained to the Company, or a Rupee saved to them. I beg Leave to refer to the Consultations of the 10th of February, 3d of March, and 26th of July 1774, which successively ordered, that the Bonds of 1769, 1770, and 1771, including all of prior Dates, amounting altogether to 38,16,933. 10. 9. should be discharged; and to my Minute, which was entered in Consultation of the 26th January 1775, recommending the Discharge of the Whole, by Means which the different Balances of the Treasuries since that Date have proved to have been effective. But my Recommendation was rejected, and the Proposal of General Clavering, which was delivered to the Board on the same Day, for paying off Part of the Debt by new Loans of a reduced Interest of 5 instead of 8 per Cent. was adopted. In the Prosecution of this Plan, the Debt on the 31st December last was reduced to 62,51,280. 0. 3. bearing 5 per Cent. Interest; and it is certain, that had mine been followed none would have remained, since the Balance of Cash in all the Treasuries on that Day amounted to Rupees 97,97,199. 8. 17. 2.

My Proposition for liquidating the bonded Debt was founded on an Estimate of Receipts and Disbursements drawn out by the Accomptants General: which stated the probable Balances in the Company's Treasuries on 31st Dec. last, at Rupees 18,71,365. 5. 11. after cancelling the Debt, and providing for every Expence. Many Flaws in the Estimate were pointed out; and the Company were warned against giving Credit to the flattering

tering Account of their Affairs which I had laid before them. I endeavoured to support the Probability of the Estimate by Arguments, and the Gentlemen of the Majority to controvert the Principles upon which it was formed. What was then a Subject of Debate may now be precisely ascertained; and the Court of Directors will please to observe, by the accompanying State No. 1, that although the Salt, and several other Branches of Revenue, failed in yielding those Funds which were expected, the Estimate was formed with so much Moderation, that the Surplus Balances in the Company's Treasuries on the 31st December turned out actually to be near Fifteen Lacks of Rupees more favourable to the Company than what I had supposed it. While I congratulate the Company upon this prosperous Situation of their Affairs, I have only to regret, that they should have continued so long to be burthened with a Debt at Interest, which the State of their Finances could long ere now have cancelled.

5th. I cannot but allow that the Labours of the Majority to obtain Accusations against the former Agents of the Company, have been carried on with unremitted Attention. For this grand Object the Management of the current Business, and the Administration of Justice throughout the Provinces, have been neglected.

I do not admit that "the Importance of a Service is to be measured by the Labour and "Anxiety of the Persons who performed it," but by the Utility which may be derived from it. Let it be shewn by what Obligation, either of Office or Necessity, the Gentlemen of the Majority were pressed into so regretted a Service; let it be shewn how it has operated either in its immediate Effect on the present Interests of the Company, or tends to influence the future; and that the same Zeal which has animated them in their Search of past Abuses, hath equally incited them to attend to the Discharge of the Trusts which have been directly committed to them. That the Revenue has been improved; that new Sources of Profit have been discovered; that inordinate Expences have been reduced; that the Dispatch of current Business has been promoted; that Justice has been administered; that the Discipline of the Army has been attended to; in a Word, that any One important Object of Government has been vigorously pursued; but if these Duties are neglected by the Rulers of a Country, it will avail them little to plead in Excuse, that busied in arraigning the Conduct of their Predecessors, they were unable to attend to their own.

6th. I should be sorry to object to any Measure of the Gentlemen of the Majority that appears to have Oeconomy or real Business for its Object. I shall not now offer any Judgment of the Utility of this Institution; this can only be proved from the Savings which it may produce; and as the Operation of a Year or two is required for this Effect, I am diffident in forming Conjectures at so distant a Period, when I reflect with Regret on the many Plans from which I myself expected to have derived Credit, but which have been blasted while I was rearing them to Maturity.

The Remarks repeated under this Head, upon the Impropriety of employing the Commissary General to furnish contingent Supplies to the Army, appear to me as much out of Place as unluckily applied to an Encomium on the Board of Ordnance, which is liable to the very same Objection as the Members who compose it, excepting those of the Superior Council, consisting of the Heads of those Offices which are placed under its immediate Controul and Superintendency.

I shall avail myself however of this Occasion to vindicate both the late President and Council, and Colonel Macleane, from the Censures to which this Appointment has given Occasion, by requesting that the Honourable Court of Directors will be pleased to read the Letter of Colonel Dow upon this Subject, addressed to the Board of Inspection on the 23d May last, of which I have annexed an Extract, No. 2; and I will venture hardily to pronounce upon the Strength of it, that whatever Reductions may hereafter take Effect in this hitherto unbounded Stream of Military Expence, they will derive their Origin from the Grant of the contingent Supplies to Colonel Macleane, and to his Integrity in the Provision of them, notwithstanding the Severity with which the Conduct of the Board in this Instance has been condemned.

7th. The Honourable Court of Directors will be the best Judges of the Merits of the Gentlemen of the Majority, in the Steps they have taken to degrade the Presidency of Bombay in the Eyes of the Marattas, and to deprive the Company of the Advantages which might have been secured to them, even with an honourable Peace, which there is every Reason to believe might have been much sooner obtained by more vigorous Measures.

8th. I do not think that the uncontrolled Administration of criminal Justice ought to be entrusted to any Native; if it should, Mahomed Reza Cawn may be as fit for it as any other.

other. As to the Country Government, it must ever, in my Opinion, continue feeble and insignificant while the real Power is in our Hands, and the nominal Authority is vested in a Person who receives his Salary from us, and is removeable at our Pleasure.

9th. The new Treaty with Asof o Dowla is certainly advantageous to the Company, if the Conditions of it can be fulfilled; but of this I ever did, and do still, entertain a Doubt, notwithstanding the Acknowledgments which it is said to have extorted from me, but which I do not remember to have expressed, and now disclaim; for I cannot deem it honourable to have extorted from the Nabob, Concessions inconsistent with our former Treaties, to which the Necessity of his Situation alone obliged him, however unwillingly, to submit. The fairest Opinion which I could now give of those Concessions, would be to repeat the Substance of my Minutes, entered on our Proceedings of the 13th of February and 3d of March. To those I refer as prophetic (if I may so express myself) of the Effects which have been since experienced from the Conditions of that Treaty.

The Remainder of the Minute to which this is a Reply, consists of little more than a Repetition of the Complaints which have been before repeatedly made against the Supreme Court of Judicature; yet I may not pass them without Reply; but I shall make it as brief as possible, placing it in opposite Columns to the Cases which are stated in the Minute.

If by our Authority as Duan, confirmed to us by Parliament, a Farmer be confined for Arrears of Rent, the Supreme Court of Judicature take the Cause out of our Hands, decide upon the Merits, and discharge the Prisoner.	This I suppose alludes to the Case of Comaul o Dean Cawn. He appealed to the Court against an Act of Oppression, and was a proper Object of their Jurisdiction.
If we dismiss the Judge Advocate, he applies to the Supreme Court for a Mandamus, to reinstate him in his Office.	Which the Court refused to grant.
If we dismiss the Secretary of our own Board, we see him encouraged to bring an Action for his Salary against his Successor.	I know not who encouraged Mr. Stewart. His Friends I believe have attempted to dissuade him from bringing his Action into the Court, thinking it imprudent and likely to prove hurtful to his Interest. But it was not in the Power of the Court to prevent it.
If we order a British Subject to repair to the Presidency, he pleads the Protection of the Supreme Court of Judicature, and declines or refuses to obey us.	Not knowing to whom or to what Fact this Sentence alludes, I cannot reply to it.
If for Reasons of the most serious political Importance, we endeavour to support the Authority of the Country Government and the Sovereignty of the Soubah, we have not only the Foreign Factories, but the Supreme Court of Judicature to contend with. They publicly deny the Existence of such a Government, and affectedly hold out the Person and Authority of the Prince to the Contempt of the World.	The Person and Authority of the Nabob (I know not who made him a Prince) ought to be held out to the Contempt of the World, if these are employed like a Sanctuary to protect Debtors from their Creditors, and Criminals from the Pursuits of Justice. I know no other Uses the Nabob's Name and Authority can be applied to.
According to the Doctrines maintained by the Judges, there is scarce any Act of Government, however necessary and expedient, which if it tends to controul the Actions or to thwart the Interest of Individuals, may not expose the Members of the Council to Actions in the Supreme Court.	I do not believe that any Doctrines have been delivered in the Supreme Court to warrant this Conclusion of the Majority, nor do I apprehend that the Members of the Board are liable to any ill Consequences from the Decrees of the Court upon any such of their Acts as, although not strictly legal, shall have arisen merely from Error in Judgment, and do not evidently tend to Purposes of Oppression, since there is always an Appeal to a Superior Tribunal.
We even doubt whether we are authorized to prevent any Persons from quitting the	The Right of preventing Europeans from passing through these Provinces to enter into

the Provinces and going up the Country, though we should be certain of their Intention to enter into the Service of a Foreign Power.

into the Service of any Foreign Powers, has not been yet before the Court, but I do not conceive it to be a Matter of Difficulty. The Opinion of the Chief Justice delivered in the Case of Pavesey, applies only to the Right of our Government, to expel unlicensed vagabond Foreigners from the Country. I cannot let this Occasion pass without remarking, that the Conduct of the Judges in the Case just referred to, manifests in the most striking Manner the Candour and Temper with which they examine the Acts of this Government, and their Endeavours to support its Authority.

In these Circumstances many useful and obvious Regulations for the Benefit of the Country, necessarily must be left unattempted.

This will appear from the Attorney's Report, entered in the Consultation of the 23d December, in the Secret Department.

A general Re-coinage has been repeatedly recommended to us by the Court of Directors. Such a Measure is without Doubt indispensably necessary; but it is of a Nature too delicate and important, and likely to be attended with too many Difficulties in the Execution, to be undertaken with Safety by a divided Government, with a hostile Court of Judicature.

It will require Leisure and Attention to carry into Execution the Orders of the Court of Directors for the Improvement of the Coinage of this Country; but no Doubt with respect to the probable Interference of the Court in the Execution of such a Measure either has proved or can prove an Impediment to it.

The Remainder of their Minute is pure Declamation, and of a Kind which I find it difficult to answer, in the want of determinate Facts, which might serve as a Colour for their Allusions. Where is a Standard hoisted against their Authority? and by whom have the People been invited to repair to it? Who affords Protection to Persons denying or resisting the Authority of Government? What are the Proofs that the Governor General has taken "a willing and decided Part in every Measure that tends to degrade "the Council, and to disarm them of their lawful Power?"

They form an invariable and decided Majority at the Board, and arrogate to themselves the whole Authority of the State, to the utter Exclusion of Mr. Barwell and myself. The Collection of the Revenues, the internal Government of the Country, and every political Arrangement, are at their absolute Disposal; and every Measure they have adopted has operated in its fullest Extent. It will avail them but little with their Employers and the Public, to declare that they discharge themselves from all Responsibility, when it is as manifest as the Light of the Sun, that they act as they please, without any present Power to controul or oppose them.

(Signed) Warren Hastings.

APPENDIX, N° 158.

Extract of Bengal Secret Consultations, the 19th February, 1776.

PRESENT,

The Honourable Warren Hastings, Governor General, President,
Lieutenant General John Clavering,
The Honourable George Monson,
Richard Barwell, } Esquires.
Philip Francis, }

Honourable Sirs,

I THINK it my Duty to inform you, that the Intelligence which I have received for some Days past, from Delhi, Akburabad, Dige, &c. seems to confirm a Report, that the Marattas are assembling in large Bodies to the Southward, with an Intention of moving towards these Parts. It is said that a Body of 25,000 Horse have already arrived at Jainnigur, under the Command of Beher Jee Sydeah, Son-in-Law to Maddo Jee Sydeah, and that they have exacted large Contributions from Pretta Sing, the Rajah of that District: Another Body is said to be advanced on this Side of Jainnigur, within Twenty or Thirty Coss of Dige; that these Bodies have been invited by Ringut Sing, the Chief of the Jauts, besieged in the Fort of Dige by Nijif Cawn, to come to its Relief, and that their Design is to give the Army of Nijif Cawn Battle. Several Bodies are likewise reported to be advancing towards Jaanse, that some small Parties are arrived in that Neighbourhood, and at Calpee, and that they are become very troublesome to the Nabob's Troops under the Command of the Gossaine Rajah, Himmit Behader, now lying before Jaansee. It is also said that Vackeels are arrived in the Nabob's Camp at Etawa, demanding the Cheut for the Provinces of Korah, and the Doab, &c. But as Mr. Bristow is on the Spot, and in the Way of more Information than what I am, I must beg Leave to refer you to his Correspondence for this Particular, as well as for such other private Matters relative to these Advices, which at this Distance may not have come to my Knowledge.

I have, &c.

Camp near Belgram, (Signed) G. Stibbert.
3d February, 1776.

Resolved, That the following Reply be written to Colonel Stibbert.

Sir,

We have received your Letters of the 14th Ultimo, and 3d Instant. We approve of your having complied with the Requisition of Mr. Bristow, for Two Companies of Sepoys to be detached to Pertagur, to assist the Aumil of that Place in securing the Receipt of the Collections, to enable him to discharge the Nabob's Tuncaws in favour of the Company; and we leave it to your Discretion to grant Aid to Mr. Bristow on all future Occasions of a similar Nature, so far as it may be consistent with the Safety of the Troops under your Command. This is the more necessary as it is to obtain the Pay of the Troops from the Lands assigned for that Purpose.

We are, &c. &c.

Extract

APPENDIX, N°. 158.

Extract of Bengal Secret Consultations, the 26th February, 1776.

PRESENT,

The Honourable Warren Hastings, Governor General, President,
Lieutenant General John Clavering,
The Honourable George Monson,
Richard Barwell, and Philip Francis, Esquires.

Read, and approved, the Consultation of the 19th Instant.
Received the following Letter from Colonel Stibbert.

Honourable Sir, and Sirs,

The following is the Continuance of the Maratta Intelligence which I had the Honour to transmit to your Honourable Board, in my Letter of the 3d Instant.

They have made no great Advances this Way since their Arrival at Sainagur, and which I before had the Honour of acquainting you with. Their Design seems to be to give Assistance to Rigeet Sing, besieged by Nizzif Khan in Dege, and to relieve the Fort of Jaansee, belonging to them, besieged by the Troops of the Nabob, under the Command of the Gussain Rajah: In an Assault made by Nizzif Khan on the Out-works of the Fort at Dege, he effected a Lodgement near the Kumehir Gate, and took Four Pieces of Cannon from the Jauts; but in a Sally which was soon after made by Ringeet Sing, at the Head of a Body of his Garrison, Nizzif Khan's Troops were repulsed, and the Out-works retaken, notwithstanding his coming up with a fresh Body to their Assistance, when an obstinate Engagement ensued, with an immediate Loss to Nizzif Khan of Five hundred Men and upwards, and near One Thousand of Ringeet Sing's. Juswant Sing is the only Maratta Chief, by these Accounts, who has as yet joined the Jauts; but on the Arrival and joining of the other Chiefs moving towards Dege, I think it is most likely that Nuzzif Khan will be obliged to raise the Siege. With respect to the Fort of Jaansee, I do not yet hear of any considerable Bodies being arrived in that District, but should the Force, which it is said is moving towards its Relief, join, I think it is probable the Nabob's Troops will be under a Necessity to retire. This, Sirs, is the whole Intelligence worthy your Perusal, which has come to Hand since I had the Honour to address you last.

I have the Honour, &c.

Camp, near Belgram, February 11th 1776. (Signed) G. Stibbert.

Honourable Sir, and Sirs,

In my Address of the 26th Ultimo, I mentioned Nudjif Cawn's having returned to the Siege of Dike, the Success of which is at present doubtful, as the Jauts make a brave Defence. The enclosed Copy of a Letter of Intelligence will, I hope, give the Honourable Board an Idea of the Spirit with which it is conducted on both Sides.

By this Day's News I understand a Mine has been sprung by Nudjif Cawn to little Effect. He purposes to work another, and the Jauts to countermine it. Myrza Hellyle is again returned to this Camp, with a Request to the Nabob for Assistance; but he has as yet had only a complimentary Audience, in which no Business has been canvassed. It is very surprizing that the War between Nudjif Cawn and the Jauts is supported thus long, as both are exceedingly distressed for Money, and hardly ever have any Supplies beyond the Day. Nudjif Cawn has above Thirty-five Thousand Horse and Foot before Dike; the Jauts near Thirty Thousand to defend it, and the Fort is so extensive that Provisions are introduced without the least Difficulty. Nudjif Cawn points his Artillery chiefly against Gopall Gur, which is situated on an Eminence, and when once taken, he thinks he shall easily command the rest of the Works.

Sabiter Cawn is treating with the Sikes for the Cession of Part of his Country, upon the Condition of their entering into an Alliance with him. He has lately quarrelled with Abdul Ahul Cawn, in Consequence of which he has solicited a Reconciliation with Nudjif Cawn, and wants to induce him and the Sikes to join him to invade Rohilcund, in

 the

the Hope of recovering the Dominions taken from him by the late Vizier; but I fancy his Negociations will avail little.

The Nabob, although I have repeatedly urged him upon the Subject of Bolow Row's Letter to me, a Copy of which I forwarded in my Address of the 26th Ultimo, yet he has hitherto come to no Determination. I humbly conceive his Excellency cannot have a better Opportunity to make an honourable Peace than the present, that the Marattas themselves solicit for it.

I have however not neglected my Negociation with Bolow Row, but requested him to point out the Terms on which he wishes for Peace: His Answer I hourly expect.

I have the Honour, &c.

(Signed) John Bristow,
Resident at the Court of Oude.

Read the following Letter from Mr. Bristow.

Camp near Etawa, Feb. 25, 1776.

To the Honourable Warren Hastings, Esq; Governor General, and the Members of the Honourable Supreme Council at Fort William.

Honourable Sir, and Sirs,

I addressed the Honourable Board on the 19th Instant, and am sorry to mention a disagreeable Event which occurred Yesterday.

The Nabob had dismissed Meer Afzul's Corps, which had been stationed on the other Side the Jumna for some Time past with the Gossanes. There were Five Months Arrears of Pay due to them, which his Excellency engaged they should have in Fifteen Days; the Men considered this Delay an Artifice to deprive them of their Right, refused to admit of it, and Four Thousand of them marched from their Station to within Six Coss of our Camp. The Day after their Arrival, the Nabob went in Person amongst them, and thought he had settled the whole Affair for only a Part of the Pay, on the Receipt of which they were to give up their Cannon and Arms, and to disperse. The Persons employed by his Excellency in conducting the Negociation, had carried false Messages; and when the Nabob found the next Day that the Matchlock Men would not give up their Arms, he resolved on cutting them all to Pieces. I heard of this by Chance, at Ten o'Clock at Night, and immediately waited on him to dissuade him from it, as it was an Act that could not do him any Credit. He urged their Disobedience of Orders, in leaving their Stations contrary to his Injunctions; and that if after he had settled the Matter once, and they refused to abide by what they had agreed to, and he suffered their Conduct to pass unnoticed, his Army would be constantly in actual Mutiny. I answered, he must expect it unless he paid them; and represented, in the strongest Terms I could, that his cutting them to Pieces would disaffect his Troops in general, and that I thought it probable they would not fight in such a Cause, as they might naturally say, the same would be their Situation another Time. I observed, on these Occasions there were a few who spirited the rest; and recommended to his Excellency to pick out those Men and punish them, but to pay and dismiss all those who had no other Hand in the Mutiny, than being led into it by Persuasion, and Ignorance of the Consequences. I sat with his Excellency till One o'Clock in the Morning, without being able to dissuade him from his Resolution; he therefore ordered the Minister to march against them early the next Morning, with about 15,000 Men, with Directions, that if they gave up their Arms and accepted of about Twenty Thousand Rupees, he would suffer them to go away unmolested, otherwise there should not be a Man of them left alive. The Matchlockmen would gladly have compounded for a Part of their Pay; but when about Two Lacks were due to them, and they even doubted their obtaining the small Sum that was offered after they had once grounded their Arms, they were therefore rendered desperate; all treating was at an End, and they resolved on meeting their Fate. Out of Four Thousand, Fifteen Hundred refused to fight, and left the Camp; so that the Engagement was supported by Two Thousand Five Hundred, who did every Thing that Men in their deplorable State could. They had been for some Days past reduced to the greatest Distress for the Necessaries of Life, were weak, and terrified by the Numbers they had to oppose.

Notwithstanding all the Disadvantages they laboured under, the Nabob got the Victory by a Chance. He was repeatedly repulsed, some Guns were even taken from him, and his

his Army put to the Route; when a Tumbril blew up, and threw the Matchlockmen into Confusion, upon which his Excellency's Troops broke in upon them, and carried the Day.

The Nabob had about Three Hundred Men killed; of the Matchlockmen there were Six Hundred, many wounded, 800 were taken Prisoners, and released To-day, the rest escaped; as his Excellency's Troops fought with Ill-will, and suffered them to get away, otherwise a Man could not have been saved.

The Eleven old Battalions, that is, those under Jaoo Loll and Bussant, who are formed into Two Brigades, were not in the Engagement, but drew out when the News of the Nabob's Troops having given Way reached them. The Men in general declared it was not to attack the Matchlockmen, they only meant to defend the Camp. Upon the whole, this Act, as might be expected, has given great Discontent amongst the Troops, and it is the general Cry, that they are never to expect their Pay, but when they can exact it. It is well known I advised the Nabob against the Measure, and I flatter myself the Credit of the British Nation was never at a higher Pitch in this Country than now. The Nabob's Behaviour at Mindijhaut is a striking Contrast to that on the present Occasion.

On my Return from the Nabob the Night before the Affair, a Deputation of Five of the Matchlockmen presented me a Petition just as I entered my Tents, which I refused to receive; but understood from them that it contained a Request for me to get them their Pay. After what had passed I could not interfere further. I told them they were the Nabob's Servants, and that the Company had nothing to do with them.

I have the Honour to be, &c.

John Bristow,

Resident at the Court of the Nabob of Oude.

APPENDIX, Nº 159.

Extract of Bengal Secret Consultations, the 8th January, 1776.

PRESENT,

The Honourable Warren Hastings, Governor General, President,
Lieutenant General John Clavering,
The Honourable George Monson,
Richard Barwell, Philip Francis, } Esquires.

Honourable Sir, and Sirs,

I ADDRESSED the Honourable Board on the 6th Instant.

In my Letter of the 11th October I particularly explained the State of Foreign Affairs at this Juncture; the Attention of the disaffected Persons to the Nabob's Government and the neighbouring Powers is much raised, owing to our March. Nudjiff Cawn has, principally from this Cause, discontinued his Attacks against Dike, and arrived at Santrush Fort, Ten Coss Distance from it: On hearing of the Nabob's Intentions to march to Cole, he dispatched a Vackeel to him, a Person much in his Confidence, to enquire what he purposed by it, as he had to expect no Foreign Enemy in that or any other Part; that his own Aumils were, if any Persons, ill-disposed towards him; but they were to be found in other Quarters of his Dominions: He expressed his Desire of preserving his Friendship with him, but should the Nabob Asoph ul Dowla break through it, he was ready to do the same, and meet him in the Field. His Excellency has not returned any Answer, though I believe he does not now intend to march to Cole, at least he may avoid doing it without any Reflection on his Character, by its being said that he is terrified into the Measure by Nudjif Cawn. It seems Cossim Ally Cawn is come to Delhi, at his Majesty's Summons, by the Instigation of Abdul Ahut Cawn. His Excellency consi-

 dering

dering his strict Alliance with the Company, thought it inconsistent to have an Interview with the King, whilst Cossim Ally Khan followed the Court; he therefore gave it as a Reason for his purposing to march to Etawa, and also for countermanding Nyaz Ally Cawn, who he has directed to join him: His Presence in that Part of the Country will tend much more to establish his Affairs, than the effecting of an Interview with the King at Cole, which would be his Design, as well as to lay Plans of possessing himself of Part of Nudjiff Cawn's Country in that Neighbourhood. Abdul Ahut Cawn might apparently agree in any Proposal of the Nabob's; but it would be with a Design of ingratiating himself into his Favour, in Order to obtain the Management of his Affairs; he is artful and insinuating, and an Interview with the King, when this Man is to conduct it, will always be productive of much Intrigue.

The Nabob, by marching to Etawa, will subside the Jealousy of Nudjif Cawn, with whom he may accommodate all Differences, and have the Opportunity of restoring his Authority in the Doab: Whereas, though Nudjif Cawn may want Money, yet his Reputation, and the constant War his Troops have been engaged in, will, when joined with the Rebels, give at least an Equality, if not a Superiority against the Nabob. I believe that Nudjif Cawn himself would be glad of the Opportunity to settle his own Country; but Abdul Ahut Cawn has constantly corresponded with the Nabob and Murtezzah Cawn, and I am apt to think he has encreased their Jealousy of Nudjif Cawn, by insinuating he entertained Designs, which have never once occurred to him. It is certain the granting Refuge to Elich Cawn and Basheer Cawn, and his corresponding with the Gosseines, might have given some Grounds. The Nabob has nevertheless on his Side acted the ame Part in receiving many of Nudjif Cawn's disaffected Servants.

In regard to Cossim Ally Cawn, I imagine he will not be of much Service to any Party, for by the best Intelligence I can obtain, he must have very little Money left. It is true he has offered his Majesty Twenty Lacks in Jewels, which I rather consider a Boast to serve a temporary Purpose, than what he will be able to supply. I herewith enclose Copies of Letters which have passed between his Excellency and the King relative to him. They ought to have been forwarded some Days ago, but were neglected to be given me by the Nabob's Moonshy. I thought it unnecessary to trouble the Honourable Board with Murtezza Cawn's Correspondence, which is just in the same Style.

By marching immediately to Etawa, the Nabob will awe the Gosseines, and in case Syndea has really Intentions of joining them, he will at least secure the Rents of the Lands on this Side the Jumna. The Gosseines wish it to be believed that Sindea will invade the Country, and have even proceeded so far as to have their Vackeel propose to the Nabob to put him in Possession of the Districts of Kalpy, upon the Pretences of attaching him to his Excellency's Interest, and that he is entitled to them, from the Three Maratta Chiefs, Tocojy Holker, Bysagg, and the said Sindea, having divided them amongst themselves on their Invasion of Hindostan; admitting that the Nabob was to equal his most sanguine Expectations, and at present obtain the peaceable Possession of the Countries on the other Side the Jumna, the having extended his Dominions to that Distance, will prove an Inducement to him to involve himself in Schemes of Conquest, in which it is probable, unless supported by the English, that he will fail of Success. The Honourable Board will be better able to judge of this Matter on recurring to Events since his Excellency's Succession, for although the Example at Myadv Gaut had every Effect that could be wished, to subject his Troops, yet he himself neglects the Opportunity he now has of putting them under some Kind of Discipline, which makes it that they have no Confidence in him, and the People whom he will have to deal with well know it. It also happens to be his Excellency's Misfortune, that in Camp there is not a Man capable of commanding the Army. Bussaunt Ally Cawn appears to be the fittest Person, but by the Opinion of most Military Gentlemen with whom I have conversed, he can hardly have sufficient Experience for such a Trust.

The State of the Country on the other Side the Jumma, is as follows: The Gosseines have made an Acquisition of what yielded the Marattas Twenty-five Lacks of Rupees a Year, and taken Moat, an exceeding strong Fort, their Birth Place, and was possessed by Ender Gyr, the Man who adopted them as his Sons: They are laying in a Store of Provisions and Ammunition in it; and though they have offered to attend on the Nabob, yet their Conduct is as independent as ever: They were much pressed by the Marattas at the beginning of the Campaign, but they have latterly defeated several Parties. Anoop Gyr is now at Moat, and Amrow Gyr is gone towards Shahabad, on the Frontiers of Nudjif Cawn's Dominions, upon the Pretence of making the Settlement of that Country.

Country. Mahood Ally Cawn, the Nabob of Corah, is suspected by many People to be disaffected to the Nabob. His Excellency himself and the Ministers say they can depend upon his Attachment; but he entertains a constant Correspondence with the Gosseines, and Bundlecund Raja talks of crossing the River instead of meeting the Nabob, and is fortifying a Place in his District, strong by Situation, called Behaadeh. His Troops are attached to him, and know, in a Mutiny that happened at Rajgyr Gaut, that he underhand encouraged the Ringleaders, and was indirectly accessary to the Entrance of the Pay of the Matchlock Men.

The Possessions of the Rajas of Bundlecund are to the Southward of the Districts of Kalpy. The Ancestor of the present Incumbents was Raja Chutter Saul, who had Two Sons named Kyrdasaw, who held Sixty Lacks of the Country, and Puggut Raja, who held Fifty D°,

Lacks 110.

Mahomed Cawn Bungush, the Father of Ahmud Cawn Bungush, the Nabob of Ferokabad, attacked these Rajahs, who called upon the Marattas to assist them, which they did, and overcame him, but they seized a Third Part of the Country, and then there remained nearly as follows:

To Kyrdasaw	—	—	42 Lacks,
Juggut Raja	—	—	32 D°
			74 Lacks.

Hindoput is the Grandson of Kyrdasaw, and had Two Brothers, one named Aumaun Sing; he killed the other: Keit Sing is now in Confinement. Hindoput's Residence is at Punna, and in his Dominions is the famous Fortress of Callinger: He at first held per Annum, — — — Lacks 42

	He has since possessed himself of Part of the Countries of the undermentioned Rajas, Gomaun Sing and Comaun Sing, and of the Raja of Dattya — —	18
These two Rajas are the Sons of Kyrut Sing by diff. Mothers, & Grandsons of Juggut Rajah.	Gomaun Sing possesses Bander and Ajihgur per Annum, Lacks — — —	12
	Comaun Sing possesses Chicarry Fort and Districts, amounting to Lacks per Annum — —	10
The Sons of Paher Sing, Brother of Kyrut Sing.	Gudji Sing possesses Jytepore — —	6
	Maun Sing Collipehar — —	3
	Lacks per Annum —	91

The above Rajahs entertain an Enmity to one another, and are all equally solicitous of obtaining the Nabob's Countenance and Protection. The Ranna of Goad possesses the same Sentiments; he now holds a Country of about Seven Lacks of Rupees a Year; he had more formerly, as well as a large Sum of ready Money, both of which he has lost and spent.

The above Circumstances, together with the Facts I have stated in my former Addresses, will I hope fully explain the Nabob's Situation. The Minister, on mature Consideration, is I believe fully convinced his Excellency would do better to settle his Affairs by Negociation, than by himself taking the Field against an Enemy. This Reason has principally induced him to form the following Plan:

To place the Country on the other Side the Jumna, in the Hands of the Ranna of Goad, or of one of the Bundlecund Rajas, upon a Lease for Life, of a fixed Rent per Annum; whatever Surplus may accrue to be his Emolument, and all Charges to rest with him; the Nabob to take upon him the Guarantee of the Country against a foreign Enemy. If upon the Whole, the Rent pays the Expence of the Troops kept to defend it, it is all that can be wished; and I do not despair (if this Plan be executed) of seeing it one Time or other save his Excellency's Country from being the Seat of War. The Determination regarding the properest Person, is to be deferred until the Nabob shall reach Etawa; the only Proposal yet made is Twelve Lacks a Year, by Gomaun Sing.

With

With Nudjif Cawn the Minister purposes to advise his Excellency to preserve a good Understanding, which he may very easily do; in respect to other Powers there is apparently little to be apprehended from their Intentions.

The Intelligence of an Invasion by Timur Shaw is premature; and it is unlikely the Sykes will not attack the Nabob.

His Excellency's Stay at this Place will I expect be very short.

I have the Honour, &c. &c.

Camp, near Ferokabad, December 13th 1775.

(Signed) John Bristow,
Resident at the Court of N. of Oude.

Honourable Sir, and Sirs,

In my Address of Yesterday's Date, I informed the Honourable Board of the Embassy Nudjif Cawn had sent to the Nabob: The Conclusions of his Negociations will in a great Measure depend on the Sentiments of the Honourable Board, and I shall therefore submit what has passed to their Consideration.

Myrza Hellile, the Ambassador, was charged with Powers to settle an Interview between the Nabob and Nudjif Cawn, but as these Two Princes entertained great Doubts of each other, they would not either of them venture into the Dominions of the other, without a positive Assurance of personal Safety. Unless the Company should be the Guarantees of any Engagements to be entered into on this Head, it appeared impossible to come into Terms. Myrza Hellile therefore expressed his Master's Commands to apply to me for this Assurance, and Yesterday Night waited upon me in Form. The Nabob, accompanied by his Minister, did me the Honour to meet him; when he explained his Master's Readiness to set aside the Jealousy and Distrust which for some Time appeared to have lost him the Friendship of the Nabob Asoph ul Dowla, although Variances might occur on trifling Matters, yet in any Thing material he wished to preserve a good Understanding: He assured it to be both his Master's and his Excellency's Interest, for that the Marattas, from whom we might expect an Invasion whenever their Affairs would admit, were their mutual Enemies.

Myrza Hellile afterwards addressed me; said, his Master was the Well-wisher of the English, to whom he considered himself much obliged; to be sure his Jaghier had been withheld from him, and there was a Coolness in the Treatment his Master had met with, which he thought he did not deserve by his Conduct, and that if he failed in any Point it was unintentional, as he entertained the highest Respect for the English.

The Nabob took upon him to answer Myrza Hellile: He urged in regard to his own Connection with Nudjif Cawn, that he was really injured by him in receiving his rebellious Subjects, particularly Basheer Cawn, and Elich Cawn, who had embezzled large Sums, and whom he had placed so high in his Confidence as to grant to the latter the Government of Pydeabad, and to the former that of Rotuck, &c. He then expressed himself in very warm Terms of his Alliance with the English, whom he supposed were offended with Nudjif Cawn because he had treated him ill. Myrza Hellile, and the Nabob, after this entered very warmly into the Argument, when his Excellency abruptly took his Leave, desiring me to write a Letter of Assurance of personal Safety to Nudjif Cawn, and that he would agree to the Company's being the Guarantees, for although he had a Reason sufficient to complain of Nudjif Cawn, yet he still wished to be upon good Terms with him; other Particulars, such as the Place of holding their Interview, and the Mode, he left to be decided by himself, Mirza Hellile, and Murtezza Cawn.

After his Excellency left us, we entered more coolly into the Discussion of the Subject. For my Part I acknowledged the strict Alliance that the Company had formed with the Nabob, which exceeded the Limits it had borne with the late Vizier; still, I said this Alliance was no Bar to their Friendship for other Princes, to whom they entertained favourable Sentiments, so long as no Cause was given to alter them.

In regard to the particular Business with which Mirza Hellile was entrusted, the English were ready to enter into any Measure that might tend to Nudjif Cawn's or the Nabob's Advantage, or the Peace of Indostan in general; but I could not upon any verbal Message write a Letter of Assurance of personal Safety to the Nabob Nudjif Cawn, unless the Terms of the Interview were previously requested of me directly from him, as well as concluded and assented to in Writing. I desired him to observe I did not say this with a View of offending him, for though he had brought no Letter of Introduction to me, me, yet I could have no Doubt of his Character, and Weight and Consequence with Nudjif Cawn, at least the Nabob Asoph ul Dowlah's acknowledging him as his Ambassador was alone sufficient to me for paying him every Attention; I therefore recommended it to him to express my Sentiments in these Terms to his Master.

I further proposed to Murtezza Cawn, and Mirza Hellile, to have Etawa fixed upon for the Place for the Interview, and that the latter should set off as this Morning, there being no Time to lose, especially as the Nabob had many Affairs to settle, and the sooner they were commenced upon the better.

My Proposals were agreed to without any Objection, and the rest of the Conversation passed upon general Subjects. Mirza Hellile set off as had been settled.

I beg to be favoured with the Commands of the Honourable Board, regarding my Conduct between the Nabob and Nudjif Cawn. Possibly they may apply to the Company to be the Guarantees of any Treaty of Alliance they may enter into together; but I will avoid it if I can; and in case I should consent to such a Proposal, it shall be only conditional until the Pleasure of the Honourable Board be known.

The Assurance of personal Safety, should it take Place, will I hope be approved of; at least the Nabob could hardly acquiesce in the Company's being the Guarantees, unless he means strictly to abide by any Promise he may make on this Head.

I have the Honour, &c. &c.

Camp near Ferokabad, (Signed) John Bristow,
the 14th December 1775. Resid. at the Court of the Nb. of Oude.

P. S. Should Nudjif Cawn come to Etawa under the Sanction of the English, he will have a very few Attendants; in such case I humbly submit it to the Consideration of the Honourable Board, whether he ought to have a Guard for his Person from the Brigade.

(Signed) John Bristow.

Ordered, That the Enclosures in the Letter dated the 6th of December, be entered after the Consultation.

Agreed, That the following Reply be sent to Mr. Bristow.

Sir,

We have received your Letters of the 6th, 13th, and 14th Ultimo; and shall now give you Directions with respect to the Case stated in the latter, which we desire you will consider as a general Rule for your Conduct on all such Occasions.

We approve of your being present at the Meeting of the Nabob and Nudjif Cawn; and we desire you will interpose all the good Offices in your Power, to create as good Understanding and Friendship between them; but we forbid your engaging the Company in any new Treaty whatsoever with foreign Powers, or in the Guarantee of any Treaty which they may enter into among themselves, without obtaining the express Orders of the Board for that Purpose.

Extract of Bengal Secret Consultations, the 8th April 1776.

PRESENT,

The Honourable Warren Hastings, Governor General, President,
Lieutenant General John Clavering,
The Honourable George Monson,
Richard Barwell, } Esquires.
Philip Francis, }

Honourable Sir, and Sirs,

I wrote last on the 11th Instant. I have to acknowledge the Honourable Board's Letter of the 26th Ultimo. I hope to be very shortly able to transmit a Statement of the Nabob's Revenues.

Mirza Hillile, Nudjif Cawn's Ambassador, continues to urge me very strongly to obtain the Company's Guarantee to a Treaty of Alliance between his Master and the Nabob

bob Asup ul Dowlah, which I have constantly declined in Terms to avoid disgusting him as much as possible. He now openly avows his Master's Want of Confidence in the Nabob, on whom he lays no Sort of Dependance in any Engagements he may enter into.

The Minister seems at present to think that it is good Policy to support Nudjif Cawn, in order to attach him to the Nabob's Interest. The Reason on which he grounds this Opinion is, that he is, by late Intelligence, likely to take Dike, as the Jauts have had some Convoys of Provisions intercepted, and the Soldiers desert the Garrison in great Numbers. As to the Impression made on the Fort by the Mine Nudjif Cawn was conducting, or by his Artillery, all Attempts by these Means have failed; by what I understand the Event is still doubted; but Appearances are more favourable to him than to the Jauts.

In my Address of the 1st Instant, I informed the Honourable Board of the Junction of Sabiter Cawn and the Sikes, and that Abdul Cossim, Abdul Ahut Cawn's Brother, had marched to oppose them. The Event has been very fatal to the King. The Account of the Battle which has happened, is so fully expressed in the enclosed Paper of Intelligence, No. 1, that I refer the Honourable Board to it for Particulars; I must observe, in regard to the Nabob, that prior to this Event he had ordered Lettafut to march to Delhy, in Hopes of obtaining the Vizarut, and to comply with the King's Solicitation to send him a Body of Troops; I did not know of the Step until it had taken Place; otherwise I could have persuaded his Excellency against it, or advised him to assist Abdul Cossim; for he has now, by not co-operating heartily with the King, suffered the worst Consequences to ensue. I think it not improbable that Sabiter may be tempted to invade Rohilchund. His Fortune is desperate, and the Recovery of his lost Dominions an Object he has much at Heart; besides, he seems to think that the Nabob has taken Part against him, and therefore he shall be justified in commencing Hostilities: Whenever he does it, probably a Number of the Rohillas will join him. I before informed the Honourable Board, that in Consequence of the Breach between Abdul Ahut Cawn and Sabiter Cawn, the latter was reconciled to Nudjif Cawn. Now the Nabob is apprehensive that in case Dike shall be taken, Nudjif Cawn will be able to attend to Enterprizes against him, and perhaps join Sabiter Cawn. The sending of Lettafut to Delhy is in Fact in Support of Abdul Ahut Cawn's Measures, and therefore disgusting to Nudjif Cawn; but there appears in the Nabob's Conduct, in this whole Affair, an Obscurity which I cannot understand; and I suspect there was some other Motive for it than the avowed one. There is a great Contradiction I know in the Observations on it on both Sides. Mirza Hillile mentions it as a Step highly detrimental to his Master, as giving Assistance to his declared Enemy; and that he solicited the Nabob to send Lettafut to Dike: His Excellency, on the contrary, says, Nudjif Cawn wrote to him to let him go to Delhi; whichever may be true I shall not pretend to decide, but the Duplicity of their Conduct discovers the great Jealousy subsisting between them, in which I shall not interfere further than to prevent them from coming to Hostilities. Upon considering the March of Lettafut, in my humble Opinion, it was in every respect an injudicious Step.

The Reconciliation of Nudjif Cawn with Sabiter Cawn, and the Probability there is of his succeeding against Dike, alarm the Nabob, and he himself now wishes the Company would become Guarantees of the Treaty betwixt them. The Minister requested of me to promise it, but I declined, saying, it was a Matter of that Importance, that I must have Instructions previously from the Honourable Board. I further observed it was a most delicate Point for the Company to be the Guarantee of a Treaty between Two of the greatest Princes in Hindostan, and should not be hastily entered into before the Parties were firmly resolved on conforming to it. Upon the Whole, the Negociation is in such a Situation, that if the Honourable Board are still resolved on not interfering, I believe, from the present State of Affairs, that I can evade doing it without any great Detriment to the Nabob.

I have the Pleasure to enclose a Paper of Intelligence relative to the Marattas, No. 2. The Chief, Jesswent Row, whose Troops plunder about Joynagur, is the same Person who was united with the Rajepoots against Nudjif Cawn. Jesswent Row pretends that he has no Command over his Men; but it is suspected they have his secret Instructions to act in this Manner, in order to exact Money; he himself is with Hashhally Ram Bohra, the Rajpoot General.

I enclosed the Copy of a Letter I this Day wrote Colonel Stibbert on the Arrival of the Brigade,

Brigade, or a Detachment at Putahgur, as Colonel Stibbert shall judge necessary. I hope the Rebels will soon be dispersed.

I have, &c.
(Signed) John Bristow,
Resid. at Owde.

Camp near Etawa,
19th March 1776.

Honourable Sir, and Sirs,

I have the Pleasure to inform the Honourable Board, that the Rebels at Pertabgen are dispersed without the March of the Brigade, and that his Excellency has in Consequence desired of the Commanding Officer to countermand it.

I have, &c.
(Signed) John Bristow.

Camp near Etawa,
21st March, 1776.

Exract of Bengal Secret Consultations, the 15th April 1776.

Received the following Letter from Mr. Bristow.

Honourable Sir, and Sirs,

I had the Pleasure to address the Honourable Board on the 21st Ultimo, since when the Nabob resolved on immediately putting under the Command of British Officers altogether Seven of his established Battalions of Sepoys. In Consequence of this Resolution, Captain Erskine Yesterday had his Corps completely delivered over to him, and Captain Hoggan received one Battalion; the other he will have in Rohilchund, where it is now stationed, to which Country both he and Captain Erskine will march, as a Force of at least Two Regiments is necessary to awe the Sikes and Sabiter Cawn from attempting an Invasion.

The very large Funds which will be required to raise and support so considerable a Body of Cavalry as Six Regiments, are much beyond the Nabob's Ability to undertake at the present Juncture. He has therefore directed only Two Regiments to be immediately formed, and whenever his Finances will admit of it, he proposes to raise additional ones. In the Interim, that the Services of the British Officers may not be lost, the Minister wishes to have Battalions of Sepoys put under the Command of the Supernumeraries, and to effect this Point, recommended it to the Nabob to have them all recalled from the recruiting Stations to Head Quarters. A Measure that I hope will meet the Approbation of the Honourable Board, as I humbly conceive, if these Officers are employed to effect the Nabob's Service, it matters little whether in the Cavalry or Infantry; the introducing of them into the latter is hardly any additional Expence, at the same Time that it establishes the Discipline of his Excellency's Army, and strengthens his Government; some of the Cavalry Officers also express an Inclination to change into the Infantry, in whose Room his Excellency may, whenever it will be necessary, apply for others. The Honourable Board having offered to lend him other Officers on applying for them, I thought myself authorized to assure the Minister they would be granted.

The Establishment of the Artillery Corps on the most formidable Footing, being of the greatest Consequence, Captain Hill was consulted on the Plan; I have the Pleasure herewith to enclose it, his Excellency having signed and approved of it; I humbly submit it to the Consideration of the Honourable Board; the Golundar Company being to supply the Place of Europeans, I hope the Pay allotted them upon the Footing of Sepoys will be admitted. This Subahdar is thought a necessary Officer, because a very considerable Charge will always rest with him, and in Time of actual Service, as there is only One European Officer, his being of some Weight and Consequence in the Corps will be absolutely necessary. This Establishment is founded nearly upon a Proportion with that of the Brigades; One of the Nabob's Companies of Artillery being about a Third of One of ours.

The Men put under the Command of the Officers seem so well satisfied, that I have little Doubt of their being very obedient. I am apprehensive of the bad State of the Arms of the Nabob's Battalions, excepting those taken from the Mutineers at Mindy Gaut, which are also old and nearly unserviceable; the Whole were made at the late Vizier's Foundery at Fuzabad, when the French Men who had the Charge of it, either from the Want of proper Artificers, or the Impossibility of preparing the Metals properly, never did bring them to any Perfection. The Country-made Muskets, I am told, hardly ever last any Time, and the Metal is so bad that the greater Part burst if fired a Number of Times successively: A Survey is not yet completed of the Arms of the Battalions delivered over to Captains Erskine and Huggan, but I fear they must be detained a few Days to have them repaired and exchanged, so as to be serviceable. His Excellency has ordered all his Muskets from Fyzabad (about Four Thousand) to be immediately sent him, though I do not suppose there will be much above Two Thousand Stand out of them good for any Thing. The Artillery attached to these Two Regiments will go away compleat, as to the Number of Guns, and I hope it will be possible to get the Weight of Metal, agreeable to the Establishment. I expect to have to write to the Honourable Board more fully on these Heads in a short Time; I have secured a Tuncaw of Rs. 260,000 on the Naib of Rohilcund, which will suffice for the Detachment to that Province, for I hope at least Five Months, especially as the Battalion stationed there, which is to be put under Captain Huggan, has already Assignments made for it.

The First Battalion delivered over to Captain Webber has been since put under Lieutenant Connellan for the Body Guard, which makes now altogether Five Battalions with British Officers.

I have, &c.

Camp near Etawa, (Signed) John Bristow,
2d April 1776. President at Owde.

Agreed, That Mr. Bristow be replied to as follows:

Sir,

We have received your Letter of the 2d Instant.

Having already written to you fully on the Subject of the Establishments proposed for the Nabob's Troops, we shall not take Notice of the Statement you have transmitted to us.

We acquiesce in the Nabob's Intention to employ a Part of the Cavalry Officers in the Command of his Infantry, until it may suit him to furnish them with Horse, provided he adopts the Plan for appointing them, which we have already laid down for those recommended to Sepoy Commands; and as you have promised that when he shall raise the Cavalry he may have other Officers to command it, in Lieu of such as may prefer to remain in the Infantry, we assent to this also.

We are very desirous to see a State of the Nabob's Account with the Company, and we therefore desire you will immediately prepare and transmit it to us adjusted to the latest Period; we further direct that you forward to us, as soon as possible, a compleat Account of the Subsidy; that you continue regularly to furnish us with monthly Accounts of the same, and in future every Quarter, with a regular Account Current.

We are, &c. &c.

Extract of Bengal Secret Consultations, 13th May 1776.

Extract of a Letter to Mr. Bristow.

With respect to the Negociation you have entered into on Behalf of the Vizier with the Marattas, we can give you no particular Instructions, as we are yet unacquainted with the Objects of Contention, and the Nature of the Transactions which have hitherto passed between them: But we advise you on the Whole, to endeavour to accommodate Matters between them on the most secure and honourable Terms that you may be able to obtain for the Vizier, without engaging the Company in any Guarantee, or risking an Interruption of the Peace lately concluded at Poona.

We are, &c.

Fort William, Warren Hastings,
13th May 1776. J. Clavering,
Richard Barwell,
Philip Francis.

APPENDIX, N° 160.

Shajehanabad; dated the 24th of Rubbee ul Aweel, (25th of May) received 15th June, 1775.

RAM NARAIN, the Vackeel of the Nabob Nizam Ally Khan, who resides at Shajehanabad, is negociating with the Nabob Abdul Aid Khan, to procure the Vizarut for his Master, offering to pay down a Sum of Money as Peiscush: His Majesty has in Consequence sent a Shukka Khas to the Nabob Nizam Ally, desiring him either to attend personally at Court, or to send some Sirdar on his Part there, that being thus made acquainted with his Views, he may negociate this Affair with him. There has been a Battle between the Nabob Nijiff Khan and Nole Sing, in which the latter was defeated, and fled.

Extract of Intelligence; dated 1st of Rubbee Assance, or June, received 21st June, 1775.

Neaz Ally Khan, who is arrived at the Presence on the Part of Murtezzur Khan, to negociate the Terms of Khellats of Investiture of the Vizarut, &c. has proposed to pay one Lack of Rupees Peiscush immediately, and 9 Lacks in future Payments. His Majesty expressed his Displeasure at this Proposal, saying, that Mahomed Ellich Khan had agreed to the immediate Payment of 10 Lacks, and that he would treat with him. His Majesty wrote to the Nabob Bhigum, desiring that all Affairs might be negociated through Mahomed Ellich Khan, by whom they would be settled in the most satisfactory Manner, and not through Meer Murtezzur Khan.

APPENDIX, N° 161.

Extract of Bengal Secret Consultations, the 29th April, 1776.

PRESENT,

The Honourable Warren Hastings, Governor General, President,
Lieutenant General John Clavering,
The Honourable George Monson,
Philip Francis, Esquire.

Mr. Barwell indisposed.

READ, and approved, the Consultation of the 25th Instant.

Received the following Letter from Mr. Bristow.

Honourable Sir, and Sirs,

I addressed the Honourable Board on the 9th Instant; and this Day had the Pleasure to attend his Excellency Three Miles out of Camp, to meet the Kelaat of the Vizarut, with which he was cloathed on the Spot, in a Tent pitched for that Purpose. The Vizier expressed more Satisfaction on the Occasion than ever I yet saw him. He had the Ceremony conducted with great State, and on receiving the Kelaat, fired a Royal Salute.

In my last Address I mentioned the Plan intended to be pursued for the Defence of this Country, and the Prosecution of the War with the Marattas, in case they would not listen to the Vizier's Proposals for Peace. On maturely considering the Force to be put under British Officers, Four Battalions of Infantry were deemed inadequate to the Ser-

 vice,

vice, for which Reason Seven more of those under Bussant were recommended by the Minister to be delivered over to their Charge, and it has been accordingly done, including the Body Guard; there are now altogether Twelve Battalions under British Officers.

The Marattas express an Inclination for Peace; it is however judged necessary to guard against the worst, and therefore Muhboob has been ordered to march to Kalpy, there to remain till further Orders; and for the Defence of Cora, as was before planned, the Nabob has requested of Colonel Stibbert to order Two Battalions to that Province. The principal Reason for urging the Vizier to act with Vigour and Spirit at the present Juncture, is the Approach of the Rains, at which Season the Marattas cannot act, and it is probable they will be glad to conclude a Peace.

The Disposition of the Officers is not yet compleatly made by the Vizier, so that it is impossible for the Adjutant General to furnish a general Return. No Time will be lost in doing this, but I believe I may inform the Honourable Board, that there will not remain above Two or Three of the Officers unprovided for.

I have, &c.

Camp, near Etawa, 16th April 1776. (Signed) John Bristow, Resident at Oude.

Extract of a Letter from Mr. Bristow to the Governor General and Council; dated Camp, near Etawa, 9th April 1776.

The King's Affairs are reduced to the lowest Ebb; for besides the near Prospect of losing the small Extent of Country which he possessed, he will have every Thing to fear from his discontented Troops, who have now Six Months Arrears due to them, which his Majesty has no apparent Means of being able to discharge. The only Security he has left for the Safety of his Person and the City, is the Presence of Lettaupick with him, which may prove a Check to the mutinous Spirit of his Troops, and prevent it from breaking out into any open Acts of Violence. The Rage of the Soldiery is supposed to be chiefly directed against Abdulabad Cawn, as to him they impute the ill, unprovided State, in which they were sent against the Enemy, and consequently consider him as the Author of their late Disgrace. The withholding of their Pay they likewise suppose to be owing to the same Person. The Sikes and Sabiter Cawn have already sent Agents into some of the King's and Nudjif Cawn's Districts adjacent to where the Body of their Army at present is, an Aumil on the Part of Sabiter Cawn, and a Mutusuddee on that Part of the Sikes act jointly in each District, but the Shares to accrue to the several Parties have not yet been finally settled between them. At one Time it was agreed to by the Parties, that Sabitur Cawn's Share should be Ten Sixteenths, and that of the Sikes the remaining Six. The latter, however, whose Numbers are increased within these few Days, now refuse to abide by that Division, so that the Matter remains undetermined, and it appears not improbable may occasion such a Misunderstanding as may terminate in an absolute Rupture of the Two allied Powers. This Point Abdulahed Cawn is labouring with all his Might to bring about, and exerting every Artifice to excite and foment mutual Jealousies to that End; it is said that his Artifices have had their Effect with the Sikes already. Of this People there may be now collected together about Ten Thousand, and more it is reported will join them shortly: They are all irregular Cavalry, but the best mounted of any Troops in Hindostan. Sabiter Cawn may have about Twenty Thousand Foot and Horse, ill accoutred, worse disciplined, ill provided with Arms and Ammunition, and many Months in Arrears. The Defeat of the King's Troops does not appear to have been in any Respect owing to their Want of Conduct or Courage, but to their being ill provided, and also overpowered by Numbers. The Body of the united Army of the Sikes and Sabiter Cawn is marching towards Sarranpore, a Part of the King's Territories distant about Eighteen Coss from the Nabob Ausuf ul Dowla's Frontiers; small Parties of them have even come on this Side, One in particular plundered a Village near Sutulgor, whereupon One of the Battalions which Captain Hoggar is to command, and a Body of Horse, were detached by Soorut Sing to defend that Part of the Country. I understand the Enemy have since withdrawn these Detachments, and I hope the Force under Captain Erskine will put an effectual Stop to any further Attempts. Mulla Reim Daad Cawn has collected near Twenty Thousand of his Countrymen, and is seizing Hansey Hassar, a District belonging to Nudjif Cawn, to the South West of Delhi. Bushen Cawn being totally unable to stand his Ground, has joined Nudjif Cawn. The Apprehensions the King

King himself entertains from his Situation, the Honourable Board will be apprized of from the inclosed Papers, viz.

No. 1. Copy of Three of His Majesty Shokas to the Nabob and Moktar ul Dowla.
2. Copy of a Shoka to the Resident, with the Nabob Asuf ul Dowla; as also a Letter from Abdulahed Cawn to the same.

N. B. These Papers are not to be found.

The Grant of the Vizaerat upon the Terms specified in one of the above Shokas, was by no Means his Majesty's Free Gift, but entirely owing to his distressed Situation. He entertains great Hopes of Assistance from the Nabob, which it appears to me his Excellency can hardly, with Prudence and Safety to himself, afford his Majesty; a considerable Part of his Troops having been reformed, his Country being still in an unsettled State, and his Finances low. The Defence of his own Dominions will indubitably be the first Consideration; and in Rohilchund, exclusive of the Force under Captain Erskine, he will scarcely have Twelve Thousand Men to collect the Revenues and defend the Province.

APPENDIX, N° 162.

Extract of Bengal Secret Consultations, 2d May 1776.

Extract of a Letter from Colonel Stibbert.

SINCE I had the Pleasure of addressing you last, on the Subject of Maratta Intelligence, &c. nothing has occurred so particular as to require the immediate Attention of the Honourable Board. Their internal Divisions seem to prevent those Bodies that were moving this Way, from making further Advances; Biher Jee, with about 25,000 Men, is said to be encamped at Toodah, which is about 40 Coss from Dege.

Ringeit Sing continues to importune them to come to his Assistance at Dege, which Muzzif Khan still lies before with his Army; and it is reported that the Garrison is greatly distressed for Provisions. With respect to Jaamee, besieged by the Gossaines, a large Body of Marattas are said to be advanced within some few Coss of it, which is the last Intelligence I received from thence.

The Chastisement given by the Nabob to the Nuzzif Pultan, which you have been fully acquainted of from Mr. Bristow, has been productive of Circumstances favourable to the Plan of his receiving our Officers, and also towards restoring Order and Regularity among his Troops. Every Thing in his Camp since that Time has been perfectly quiet. I have the Honour to be, with profound Respect, &c.

(Signed) Giles Stibbert.

Honourable Sir, and Sirs,

I addressed the Honourable Board the 17th Instant, and enclosed them the Copy of a Letter I had received from the Nabob, on the Subject of a Detachment which he requested might be made from the Army for the Defence of the Cora Province, together with a Translation thereof, and my Answer accompanying. I do myself the Honour of transmitting you the Copies of Two Letters I received Yesterday from Mr. Bristow, the one in the Morning, dated the 16th Instant, enclosing to me a Second Letter from the Nabob during the March of the above Detachment; the other of the 17th, by an express Dawk at 11 o'Clock at Night, informing me of the Assassination of Muctar ul Dowlah, his Excellency's Minister.

By the private Intelligence which I have received this Morning, he had been invited to an Entertainment at the House of Bussunt Ally Khan, the 17th Instant, in the Morning,

Morning, when intending to depart after the Repast at Noon, Bussunt and his Friends prevailed upon him to repose himself in his Tiah Connah, (a Room built under Ground to retire to in the Heat of the Day) when he and some others soon after followed him, who immediately plunged their Daggers into his Belly, and killed him on the Spot. Bussunt, after the Murder had been committed, about 3 o'Clock went to the Nabob, who had just before been informed of the Assassination of his Minister, who asked him how he dared to come into his Presence? and ordered his Attendants to draw their Swords, and put him to Death, which was immediately executed. About this Time Intelligence was received, that the Battalions of Sepoys were in Motion, and advancing, upon which his Excellency set out immediately to meet them; and on enquiring from the Commandants the Occasion of their being under Arms, they replied, for his Safety; which, after having assured them was unnecessary, he ordered to return to their Encampment, which they without Hesitation complied with. His Excellency on his Return, sent for Saidit Ally, his next Brother, whom he was informed had fled to Fayzabad; on which he dispatched a Party of Horse to bring him back; but whether they overtook him or not, is not mentioned; neither is it said, what were his Motives for taking this Step, but I should rather apprehend it was from a Fear of his Person in the general Confusion.

In Consequence of these Tumults, and not knowing what further Designs might be intended, I shall not think it prudent to send off from the Army the aforementioned Detachment required by the Nabob, till I am assured of every Thing being restored to its former Tranquillity; in the mean Time I have wrote Mr. Bristow, advising him, in Case of his Excellency being under any Apprehensions for his own Safety, to recommend to him to retire to this Camp, from whence I shall take Care to send a sufficient Escort to meet and conduct him here, on his acquainting me of such his Intentions.

I have the Honour to subscribe myself, with the utmost Respect, &c.

Camp, Belgram, (Signed) Giles Stibbert.
April 19, 1776.

Resolved, That the following Reply be written to Colonel Stibbert:

To Colonel Giles Stibbert, commanding in the Field.

Sir,

We have received your Letters of the 6th March and 19th Ultimo; but that of the 17th, to which you refer in the last, is not come to Hand.

We do not approve of Detachments of more than 500 Men being sent from the Camp on any Occasion, except it may be found necessary for the Protection of the Camp itself, or to provide Subsistence for the Army. We therefore positively forbid your granting any Detachments for other Services. On the present Occasion we believe it will be totally unnecessary, as we have directed that the whole Brigade should march, if the Nabob has no Objection, to Allahabad; which Place is contiguous to the Province of Corah, where he wanted to station the Two Battalions, for which he had applied to you.

We are, &c.

Fort William,
2d May, 1776.

Received the following Letter from Mr. Bristow.

Honourable Sir, and Sirs,

I did myself the Pleasure to address the Honourable Board on the 17th Instant; since that I have made the strictest Enquiry into every Circumstance of the Assassination of Muctar ul Dowlah, in order if possible to ascertain the Authors and Motives of it, as well as the Extent it was meant to be carried to. So uncertain however must be the Result of all Enquiries in Affairs of this dark Nature, where the Secret could have been trusted but to a few, who would be afraid to divulge, nay, would certainly attempt to misrepresent, and where Reports also might be spread, by the Designs or idle Suspicions of others, which might be divulged as authentic Facts; I shall not therefore pre-

sum-

sume to decide, but submit the Whole to the Judgment of the Honourable Board. The following previous Circumstances come within my own Knowledge:

On Javo Loll's Disgrace, Bussunt having obtained his Officers, became a formidable Opponent of the Ministers, and they mutually endeavoured to overset each other. Bussunt joined himself with Tipper Chund, the Treasurer Amrd Gyr, and the Telinga Rajas. These People used every Argument they could think of with the Vizier, to induce him to disgrace the Minister; particularly they urged to him, that instead of having established his Government upon a permanent Footing, Muctar ul Dowlah had embroiled him with all the old and confidential Servants of his late Father, and that relying on his Connection with the English, and the Security he might derive therefrom, his Views of Influence, and Independance of his Master, knew no Bounds.—The Vizier was so much affected by these Suggestions, that he resolved on displacing the Minister, but first did me the Honour of asking my Advice as to the Propriety of the Step: I replied, that if the Minister had failed in his Duty, the Measure would certainly be right. I observed, that he had had many Difficulties to contend with, particularly the Suggestions of ill-affected People about his Excellency's Person, who were continually counteracting every Advice and Measure he recommended. I particularly quoted the Instance of the Gossayne, whom he had continued a long Time in Office, to the great Loss of his Excellency in his Revenue, and probably might prove the Cause of some Difficulty and Trouble in settling Matters with the Marattas, from whom, by prudent Measures, he might ere this have had it in his Power to have exacted a Peace on his own Terms. I asked his Excellency what particular Offences his Minister had been guilty of? To this he replied, None; but that he was disgusted with, and determined on removing him. I took the Liberty to observe, in a respectful Manner, that I had always found Muctar ul Dowlah ready in forwarding the Company's Business, and hoped that as his Excellency did not alledge his having committed any Crime, he would assure me his Life at least should be safe, and, if possible, an honourable Provision made for his Subsistence: That otherwise, Persons who could not know the real Motives for his Excellency's Conduct, might impute his Minister's Disgrace to his Attachment to the English. Both the Vizier and the Minister entered into a very warm Dispute before me, and I with very much Difficulty effected a Reconciliation. All this happened a very few Days before the Assassination. During the Altercation, Muctar ul Dowlah repeatedly mentioned his Apprehensions of losing his Life by Bussunt, who he said had offered to break into his House with Two Companies of Sepoys, and kill him, and that whenever he had lately gone out, he always feared to be taken off. The Vizier told him he was totally ignorant of any Offer of the Kind, and that it must be all false, and insisted on his being reconciled with Bussunt, which was apparently effected, for Bussunt afterwards spent Three or Four Hours every Day at his House.

The Minister nevertheless resolved on having Bussunt dismissed from all his Offices, as, after what had happened, he could not think himself safe with such a Person about the Vizier; Bussunt, apprized of his Intentions, determined to take the first Stroke, and perpetrated the Assassination.

From the late Rupture between his Excellency and the Minister, I own I was led to conclude that the former must at least have intimated to Bussunt, that his Assassination would be agreeable to him, and that without such an Intimation, and even Assurances of his Pardon and Favour, he would not have dared to attempt it; but I own I am at present at a Loss what to think, and the more I reflect on the Circumstances following the Murder, the more I find the Matter involved in Obscurity.

Immediately on the Fact being committed, it is certain that Bussunt went to the Nab.b's, came out immediately after having seen him, and got the Artillery and Troops under his Command in Readiness. It is said that when in the Nabob's Presence, the Nabob abused him for the Crime he had committed, and dismissed him in the most opprobrious Manner. Bussunt alledged to him, that others, and not himself, had committed the Murder. After getting the Troops ready, Bussunt returned to the Nabob, with his Uncle and Five or Six of his Companions, entering the Presence with a naked Sword in his Hand. The Nabob then asked him, If he intended to murder him too? to which he replied, No; and gave away his Sword to his Uncle standing by him. The Nabob immediately ordered his People in waiting to put Bussunt to instant Death, which was not executed without one of the Nabob's People being wounded in the Scuffle by Bussunt's Uncle and his Comrades, who were suffered to escape. I should

have

have mentioned, that previous to Buffunt's entering a Second Time into the Presence, and immediately on his going out, the Nabob gave Orders for his Guards to be at their several Posts and in Readiness.

Mirza Saadat Ally, as he himself writes me, went, on the first News of Mucktar ul Dowla's being killed, to the Nabob's, and being refused Admittance, turned back.

The Nabob himself asserts, that he was not refused Admittance, and that he sent a very urgent Message to him to come. It was told me as a Fact by some People, that he did not hear of Buffunt's Death until he had entered the Court Yard, and that this News occasioned his returning; however, he instantly fled, and though the Nabob, in an Hour or two afterwards, desired me to write to him, persuading his Return, with Assurances of kind Treatment, and also to send Mr. Grant to escort him, no Intelligence could be positively got of his Route till late last Night, when I received a Letter from him, informing me of his Arrival at Gaulier, a Place in the Possession of the Marattas, about Thirty-four Coss from hence. Another Circumstance I have heard was, that the Assassins of Mucktar ul Dowlah, immediately after having committed the Act, went to Saadat Ally. Some say, as they mounted their Horses, which had been previously saddled, they talked "of having the Business of Two or Three other People to "do," but this I cannot positively assert to be a Fact.

The Opinions as to the Authors and Abettors of the late Assassination, have been various, but the principal ones are the Three following, namely, that the Nabob himself either gave the Orders to Buffunt, or intimated that it would not be disagreeable to him; led to this Step by the evil Suggestions of some near his Person, by the Quarrel he had lately had with the Minister, and the latter's haughty Conduct. Another Opinion given is, that Mirza Saadat Ally was the Author of the Whole, and made Use of Buffunt to cut off Mucktar ul Dowlah, only as a previous Step to the taking off the Nabob himself. To support this, they alledge that Buffunt, the Night before the Fact was committed, went in the Dress of a Knotch Girl to Saadat Ally's House, and that there had been a close, though most private Correspondence, between them for some Time; they also insist on his Flight, which they assert was on hearing of Buffunt's Death, as a strong Proof of his Guilt; lastly, there are some who suppose that both the Nabob and Saadat Ally were concerned; that the Nabob, urged by Resentment against the Minister, and Fear of Buffunt, ordered the Murder; that Buffunt thinking himself secure so far from all instant ill Consequences, had betrayed the Design to Saadat Ally, with whom he had concerted also to take off the Nabob when he should have got the Troops ready, which he imagined the Nabob would not hinder his doing, under Pretence of preventing Disturbances from Mucktar ul Dowlah's Soldiery. There are scarcely any that suppose Buffunt was led solely by Motives of Revenge, for the Mortifications and Disgraces he had suffered from Mucktar ul Dowlah. Perhaps the Prevalence of this Opinion may be partly owing to the bad Constructions the ill-natured Part of the World are apt to put on all Transactions which cannot be clearly ascertained, but are of this dark Nature; and therefore suppose Plots and Machinations, much deeper than ever really existed.

His Excellency did me the Honour to consult me on the Measures to be taken after Mucktar ul Dowlah's Death. I suggested to him the Propriety of dividing the consequential Offices amongst different People, and not suffering so uncontollable a Power as the late Minister's to be lodged in the Hands of any one Man; I also advised the Nabob not to give the Command of his Battalions to One Man, but to keep them under his different Commandants. I am in great Hopes that the Battalions put under English Officers, will soon be accustomed to their Command, and prove obedient Troops. This I think will take Place with very little Difficulty, as I recommended to his Excellency to put the Pay of the native Officers on the same Footing with the Company's, as they before receives less; his Excellency has accordingly consented, and it is a Measure that will attach the Troops much to our Officers for their Subsistence. Assignments have been granted me on the Douaul Country, where they will be stationed.

Letters, the Evening of the Assassination, were sent to the different Aumils, confirming them in their Offices. This Country, and the Army, are at present in Peace and Quietness.

The Vizier consulted me on the Conduct he should observe to Saadat Ally; he made Two Proposals, either for him to reside at Fyzabad, in which Case he should insist on his being confined to his House, or to retire into the Company's Territories. It was observed, that after what had happened, his being about the Vizier's Person would be the

the Occasion of eternal Jealousies; and his Excellency very candidly confessed to me, that he could not be at Ease in his Mind, if he should remain with him. I thought for Saadat Ally to be at Fyzabad, would be equally dangerous, as there are always a numerous Body of Troops, and many of the principal People of the Country at that Place; Circumstances which would open a Channel for Intrigue and Suspicions; it was therefore determined to make him the Offer of retiring into the Company's Territory, and I am authorized by the Vizier to propose it to him, and tell him a Jaghire of One Lack of Rupees a Year, and his travelling Charges to his intended Place of Residence, will be allowed him. I hope this Arrangement will meet with the Approbation of the Honourable Board; I humbly conceive it a political one, that will for ever secure the Vizier's Alliance to the Company; I shall To-day write to Saadat Ally, and beg to know what Place in the Provinces the Honourable Board deem fittest for his Residence, in case of his returning at my Instance.

The Vizier having attended to my Advice, has in all Offices disposed of since the Death of his Minister, distributed them amongst his late Father's Adherents. For Instance, the Duan Khana, a principal Office, from the Head of it attending constantly about him, has been given to Hussun Reza Cawn. By what I could ever see of this Man, he bears the Appearance of Attachment to the Family, and even Uniformity in his Conduct. The late Minister, on his First Admission into Office, used every Means to induce this Man to join his Party, by the Dread of his Power, or the Hopes of Emolument to himself. He positively refused, but has throughout conducted himself with Respect to the Vizier, and not intrigued, as others have done, to overset his Government.

The Artillery remains in the Hands of a separate Daroga; and Tipperchund, the Treasurer and Paymaster, having lost his Places for his Intrigues against the Minister, is put in again.

These Measures seem all to have a good Tendency, and the Vizier has himself attended to Business since the Minister's Death. But I know well his Disposition, that this can be considered only a temporary Effort; and unless there are One or Two capable Men about him, Affairs will revert to their late State of Anarchy and Confusion. Hussein Reza Cawn will find sufficient Employment in his Attendance on the Vizier; and I conceive it out of his Line to regulate the Finance and Military Departments; the latter, Tipper Chund has been long accustomed to, and is very capable of conducting; but for the Finance it will be a very difficult Point to fix it on a regular System. The Duan Surat Sing, in the late Vizier's Time, had much Authority in this Branch; having the Controul of all Accounts, and being well versed in all the Usages from long Experience, he was exceedingly useful. But this Man having acquitted himself well in the Government of Rohilchund, to withdraw him from thence would, in my humble Opinion, especially at this Season of the Collections, be an unadvisable Measure; I think the more so, as his Place may be supplied by his Son in Law, who has been educated under him in Office, and equally capable with Soorut Sing.

There are no Adawlects in this Country, but the Execution of Justice rests with the Aumil and Cutwal. There is generally a Cutwal in each Town, or any Village of Consequence; he is totally subordinate to the Aumil, and I am sorry to say, in the Execution of Justice there is hardly any Decision made but what is biassed by Money.

Upon a Review of the Offices through which the Business was transacted at the Presence in the late Vizier's Time, the principal ones were the Dewanny and Treasury, but a Check upon these being necessary, the Vizier did think proper, before I left him, to establish the Office of Amanut: The Duties of which will be to see that no Innovations are made in the fixed Establishment, either Military or Civil; and that no final Adjustments of Accounts should be considered legal, without the Superintendant's Signature.

I humbly conceive it to be in every Respect the Plan to support the Heads of Office in their several Departments, and to keep every Man solely in his own Line, not to suffer him to interfere in Business in general, as has been too much the Case, and one Cause of the Confusion that reigned. As a Mode of obviating any Inconvenience from the Want of proper Persons for the executive Part of the Business, there ought to be One or Two able Men about the Nabob's Person, without any ostensible Offices; to receive and present Petitions, settle all Contracts, conclude all Agreements for Farms, judge of the proper Persons for Aumils, and other Departments of Government; to see that the Business of each Office is regularly conducted, and report the State of them, are Duties it would be impossible for the Heads of Offices themselves to do, as taking up too much of their Time, which should be usefully employed in the Minutiæ of their own Departments. I think it would be improper, for whoever were about the Vizier in these Capacities, to have a decisive Authority, which was the great Evil in Mucktar ul Dowlah's Administration. They should positively not have the adjusting of a single Point, without the Nabob's Sanction. The great Labour in all Business is to collect Materials, which, when once done, it is easy to decide on; and I should imagine this would not be an Undertaking beyond the Reach of his Excellency's Industry or Inclinations. The late Vizier observed this Plan in his Conduct, and the Persons whom he entrusted were Elich Cawn, and Basheer Cawn. The Day after the Death of the Minister, when the fittest Person to transact the executive Part of the Government was considered upon, Nobody was thought so capable as Elijé Cawn; he is the likeliest Man to reconcile the Parties at Court; a Man of unwearied Application, and well known. Besides this, it might be further expected by his Means to effect a Reconciliation with the Begum, a very material Object, and I believe what his Excellency has much at Heart. Mucktar ul Dowlah being out of the Way, it was generally supposed he would return; he was in consequence wrote to by his Agent, and has consented; but I look upon it to be a doubtful Matter. In regard to the Part I ought to take in this Negociation in the Name of the Honourable Board, I am much at a Loss, as Elijé Cawn paid great Inattention to the Protection before granted him; but in this Case there is great Allowance to be made for Circumstances, particularly the Nabob's Inclinations, and the Advantages to be reaped by the Public.——I hope to meet with Excuse for the Freedom with which I have expressed my Sentiments; but I consider the Company's Interest so closely connected with this Government, that I could not avoid being thus particular in so material a Point.

Mr. Chandler has attended the Vizier, and the Intent of the Nabob's leaving me here, is to mediate the Peace with the Marattas; the only Nation from which I think the Nabob has now Reason to apprehend any Attacks. From these I think there can be no real Danger, as the very formidable Force of Eight Battalions of Sepoys, under British Officers, with a proportionable Artillery, is surely sufficient to defend this Country. Relative to Military Matters I shall write the Honourable Board very fully before I leave this, as it has been an Object of my Stay to settle the Accounts, and have the necessary Arrangements to take Place.

Whilst I shall remain here his Excellency has thought proper to direct all Orders from me to be obeyed by the Army.

I have the Honour to be, with the greatest Respect,
Honourable Sir, and Sirs,
Your most obedient, humble Servant,

Camp, near Etawa, the 24th April, 1776.

(Signed) John Bristow,
Resident at the Court of the Vizier.

Extract of Bengal Secret Consultations, dated 15th May, 1776.

PRESENT,

The Honourable Warren Hastings, Governor General, President,
Lieutenant General John Clavering,
The Honourable George Monson,
Richard Barwell, } Esquires.
Philip Francis, }

Read, the following Letters from Colonel Stibbert:

Honourable Sir, and Sirs,

In Consequence of the Defection of the Gasseins, the March of Hemet Bahader with his Troops towards Agra, who has since joined Nudjiff Cawn at Dege, and their abandoning to the Marattas the Districts on the other Side the Jumna, that were entrusted by the Nabob to their Government; and also on Account of fresh Bodies of Marattas arriving from the Southward, I beg Leave to inform you that I have been applied to by his Excellency for Two or Three Battalions of Sepoys, to march into the Corah

Corah Province for the Protection and Defence thereof, whilst he is employing his own Troops in opposing the Enemy, and recovering his Authority in the aforesaid Districts; a Copy of which Application I herewith do myself the Honour of transmitting to the Honourable Board, together with a Translation thereof, and my Answer; which I hope will meet with their Approbation.

Proposals of Peace having however been since offered, and a Negociation set on Foot between his Excellency and the Maratta Chiefs, he has on this Account desired that the Movement of the above Detachment may be deferred, till he makes his further Request for their so doing. What those Proposals are, the Honourable Board will learn from Mr. Bristow. The Plan proposed by his Excellency for prosecuting the War, should a Peace be not brought about, is so fully explained in his Excellency's Letter, that I shall not trouble the Honourable Board concerning it. In this Case, I beg Leave to assure them, that I shall take the most particular Care, that no Infringement or Violation may be made of the Peace lately concluded between the Company and the Maratta Power, and that their Troops are no further employed than in Defence of the guaranteed Provinces.

I have the Honour to be, with great Respect, &c.

Camp at Belgram,
April 17, 1776.

(Signed) G. Stibbert.

Honourable Sir, and Sirs,

I did myself the Honour of addressing the Supreme Board, on the 19th Instant, informing them of the Assassination of the Vizier's Minister, and the Disturbances which have lately happened at the Durbar. I then acquainted them, that every Thing at that Time had the Appearance of being restored to Tranquillity, which I now have to confirm, from the accompanying Letters received this Day from the Nabob and the Resident, as well as from my own private Intelligence.

In Consequence of which I have ordered the Detachment of Two Battalions of Sepoys, which his Excellency has requested for the Defence of the Korah Province, to march the Day after To-morrow under the Command of Lieutenant Colonel Parker, to whom I have given the accompanying Instructions, which I hope will meet with your Approbation.

I have had no further Intelligence concerning the Treaty on Foot with the Marattas, than what Mr. Bristow has informed me in his enclosed Letter. My Intelligence from Calpee and Jahause say, they are daily establishing themselves in the Districts on the Side the Jumna, and that a smart Action has lately happened between the Deteah Raja and Luckman Row Pundit, in which many Men were killed on both Sides. His Excellency marched with Part of his Army for his Capital at Lucknow, the 23d Instant, and has ordered Boats to be got ready for his crossing the Ganges at Manamow, about 8 Coss from hence, where I am informed he proposes making some little Stay. Sadit Ally, whom you have been acquainted of, went off on the Report of the Minister's Death; I have received an Account this Morning, arrived the 20th Instant at Futtyabad, within 7 Coss from Agra, and that Elize Cawn on hearing of it, sent Tents and People out to meet him; but whether he mistrusted Elize Cawn, or for what Cause, it is said he took another Route, and it is supposed has proceeded on to Nezib Khan at Dege.

Camp near Belgram,
April 25th, 1776.

I have the Honour to be, &c.
(Signed) G. Stibbert.

Resolved, That the following Reply be written to Colonel Stibbert.

To Colonel Stibbert, commanding the Forces in the Field.

Sir,

We have received your Letters of the 18th and 25th April. By the last we perceive that you had ordered the Two Battalions of Sepoys to march to Korah, in Consequence of the Nabob's Desire. This Step being directly contrary to our positive Orders, notified originally to Colonel Galliez, under Date the 10th February 1775, and delivered ever to you with the general Instructions which you received from your Predecessor in that Command, we cannot refrain from testifying our Displeasure, and censuring your Conduct for this Disobedience. We must inform you, that whenever our Orders are peremptory, we expect they shall be implicitly obeyed. We are the more surprized at your Conduct on this Occasion, because it appears by your Letter of the 14th January, that you were thoroughly apprized of the full Force of these Orders. We hope that the Battalions which have marched, did not go without the Boundaries of the guaranteed Provinces, in their Way across the Country from Belgram to Corah, and desire you will acquaint us with the Route they took.

We are, &c.

Translation of a Letter from his Excellency the Nawab Asoph ul Dowlah.

You are well acquainted with the Account of the Marattas having come to the other Side of the Jumna, in Consequence of the Ingratitude of the Gusain. If now we should be negligent, they will gain Opportunity and Leisure, and collect together a considerable Force. Now is the Time to repulse and repel them, when the Pleasure of God to oppose and chastise them is no difficult Task; the Plan that I have been considering on I will here communicate to you. To detach from hence Four Battalions, together with a proper Train of Artillery, to the other Side of the Jumna, and to send also Four more Battalions and 1000 Horse from Korah, which are under the Command of Mehboob Ali Khan; besides which, having an Intention of resigning the Country on the other Side of the Jumna to the Rana Zemindar of Gohud, with whom I am on friendly Terms, he will be present, and ready with some Thousands of Horse, and if it be necessary I myself will also march.

The fighting Army of the Marattas amounts to 5 or 7000, besides Ten or Twelve thousand Pindarahs, in the Whole about 17 or 18,000 Men, so that I am on no Account apprehensive of their coming. Mihboob Ali Khan brings 4 Battalions from Corah, and leaves only One there; there will not remain an Army sufficient for the Defence of that Place. On this Account therefore do I trouble you to desire that you will send Two or Three Battalions from the English Camp for the Protection of Korah, I myself at present not having any other Troops to replace Mihboob Ally Khan's Battalions, the March of which is absolutely necessary, since otherwise my Affairs must go to Ruin; and God forbid that the Marattas conquering in that Quarter, they should afterwards (as certainly would be the Case) form the Design of invading this Country also, and spreading wide Trouble and Disturbance, and in the End seizing upon the Soubahs.

Translation of a Letter to his Excellency the Nawab Asoph ul Dowlah.

Your Favour, intimating the Ingratitude and Treachery of the Gussain Unoap Gir (Rajah Himut Behadur) and the Disturbances created on the other Side the Jumna by the Marattas, as also your Design of sending an Army from your Camp, and Mihboob Alli Khan with Four Battalions and some Horse from Korah, shewed its Face in the Midst of Expectation.

Learning of the Troubles excited by the Marattas, I was much affected; I ever implore the Almighty for *your* Safety and the Destruction of *your* Enemies; and God forbid that any Disturbance be in the Subahs; I should be unmindful of the Friendship that subsists between you and the English Nation; in Consequence, therefore, of your demanding Two Battalions to march to Korah, in order to maintain Peace and Order in that Quarter, I shall direct the required Force to be in Readiness to repair thither; and I am in all Respect the Obeyer of your noble Pleasure, &c.

Translation of a Letter from his Excellency the Nawab Asoph ul Dowla Wuzier ul Mamalik.

I fully comprehend what you say, with respect to your having before this put Two Battalions in Orders to proceed to Korah, agreeable to my Desire, for the Protection of that Place; but that hearing of the Martyrdom of Moackter ul Dowlah, which much troubled

troubled and afflicted you, you have delayed their March, and wait for a Letter from me on the Subject. The detaching of the Battalions is extremely necessary and advisable, for as much as I have positively ordered Mihboob Alli Khan to march with Expedition to Calpee, and I have furthermore empowered Mr. Bristow, who for this Purpose remains behind me, to treat the Marattas either with Peace or War, as he shall think proper. Hence it is not fitting that the March of the Battalions be any longer deferred.

I esteem your desiring me to reside in the English Camp till all Disturbances be quelled, as the Result of hearty Kindness and Friendship. Through the Favour of God no Troubles now subsist. Whatever was decreed has happened; the rest is Happiness and Welfare.

I have now (April 23) marched from Etawa towards Lucknow, in order to settle all my Affairs and properly regulate my Subahs. I have left behind me in the Doab, &c. a considerable Force, and expect, through the Favour of God, that every Thing will turn out well.

To Colonel Stibbert, commanding the Army in the Field.

Sir,

I have been favoured with your Letter of the 19th Instant, and have the Pleasure to inform you, that Appearances at present, both in the Nabob's Troops and those under the English Officers, promise the utmost Tranquillity. His Excellency wishes you to dispatch the Two Battalions to Corah as soon as possible; he sets off for Lucknow by the Manamon Road To-morrow Morning, and has promised to write to you before he sets out, in Answer to your Letter which I delivered. There is as yet no certain Intelligence arrived where Saadit Alli is fled to. The present tranquil Appearances render it (I should suppose) unnecessary to send any Force as an Escort to his Excellency. I shall stay here for some Days, in order if possible to adjust Matters with the Marrattas. Mr. Chandler has been directed to attend the Nabob on his Journey; if therefore you should have any Business relative to my Department, to transact with his Excellency, be kind enough to make Mr. Chandler acquainted therewith, who has my Directions to expedite every Matter of that Kind to the utmost of his Power.

I am, &c.
(Signed) John Bristow,
Resident at the Court of the Nabob of Oude.

Camp, near Etawa,
April 22d 1776.

Lieutenant Colonel Parker.

Camp Belgram,
April 25th 1776.

Sir,

You will please to proceed with the 15th and 16th Battalions of Sepoys, directed to march, and cross the Ganges the 27th Instant in the Morning, under your Command, to Korah, where on your Arrival you will encamp your Detachment in any of the Topes you may find most commodious and convenient for this Purpose, adjacent to, or within Two or Three Coss of that Town.

His Excellency the Vizier having ordered his Troops from Corah under the Command of Mahboob Alli Khan, to march to Calpee, and attack the Marattas on that Side, who have lately seized upon the Districts belonging to his Excellency on the other Side of the Jumna, while a Detachment of his Army marches against them from Etawa, in Conjunction with the Rana of Gohud; in Case a Peace should not be concluded between them, (a Treaty being now on Foot for adjusting Matters between the Vizier and them) the Service to be performed by your Detachment is to be an Awe upon, and to prevent any Insurrections arising among the Zemindars in the Korah Province, and also defend the same, should it be attacked by any Enemy during the Absence of Phousdar Mahamed Aly Khan and his Forces.

You are on no Account whatever to cross yourself, or suffer any Parties from your Detachment to cross the Jumna, or march out of the Korah Provinces, and to avoid as much as possible dividing your Force; should it at any Time be necessary so to do, you are immediately to inform me thereof, also by a regular Correspondence of all Occurrences that may from Time to Time fall out and happen during your Command.

—I am

—I am to recommend to you, in the strongest Manner, to pay the strictest Attention to the Discipline and Conduct of your Men, and that no Irregularities or Oppressions are committed by them, or Subjects of Complaint of any Sort given to the Inhabitants or Country People.

I am, Sir,
Your most obedient, and most humble Servant,
(Signed) Giles Stibbert, Colonel,
Commanding the Army.

Extract of Bengal Secret Consultations, dated the 12th August, 1776.

Read the following Letter from Mr. John Bristow:

Honourable Sir, and Sirs,

The Vizier's real Resources (if properly managed) are so much superior to those of any foreign Power, that I entertain little Doubt of his withstanding any Attacks that might be made on him; notwithstanding which, the present reduced State of his Army gives an Opening which may never happen again, and if it were seized, might be productive of much Loss and Trouble to him, both in Rohilcund and the Doab; the Forces now stationed there are inadequate to their Defence, and the Rains alone I believe, prevent his Excellency's Enemies from invading of those Provinces. To some of Nudjif Cawn's Troops, Six; to others, Eleven Months Arrears were due, only a small Proportion of which he has been able to pay; and as for these Three Months to come, he cannot possibly expect any considerable Collections, I humbly conceive it to be very possible that, rendered desperate by Distresses, he might be induced to undertake Operations against the Vizier. His Troops, though mutinous, laying at Dikes as they now are, without even the Prospect of a Subsistance, would, in all Likelihood, follow his Standard with Alacrity, on any new Enterprize, in Hopes of Plunder. Their Situation cannot be well worse than it is, and it appears to me, that it must be indifferent both to them and to Nudjif Cawn himself, what Service they undertake, so that it even only has the Shadow of Success. Runjut Sing has been soliciting at Onpine for Assistance, and it is said Mahajy Syndea promises him Twenty-five Thousand Men, and that they are really marched, with an Intention to come straight to Dike. I remember, on many former Occasions, the Jauts have propagated Reports of expected Succours from the Marattas, when they were never really meant to be sent; such I conceive to be the present Case. The Marattas rarely move, without some Prospect of the Payment of their Troops; the Jauts have absolutely no Money for them, and at this Season of the Year for the Marattas to march to their Assistance, in Hopes of drawing their Subsistence from the Country, (which has been a long Time the Seat of War) it is very improbable they would think of doing it. These Reasons, and the Divisions which I understand subsist in the Administration at Poona, make me rather discredit the Reports of Mehajy Sindea's Succours. If though there be any Truth in his March, I think there must be more intended than the avowed Cause of Assistance to the Jauts, from whom he cannot expect any Advantages adequate to the Expence of the Enterprize. I look upon it, that this must be a Cloak to his invading the Vizier's Territories, by which he might gain his Ends, and revenge the Disgrace thrown on the Arms of the Marattas, by the Loss of the Doab. I know they ill brook this, and whatever Willingness they may profess to conclude a Treaty of Amity with his Excellency, I believe they are in this only awed by his Alliance with the Company.

Admitting Nudjiff Cawn to be free from Danger from other Quarters, there are People about him personally inveterate against the Vizier, whose Fortunes are desperate, and will lose no Opportunity of raising his Jealousy. The Gossayne Basheer Cawn, and all the Vizier's Subjects, who have left his Service in Disgust, may be reckoned amongst this Number; and if he be deprived of all Hopes of a Provision from this Qnarter, I look upon it Saudit Ally might, from his Rank and Abilities, become really formidable; he at present is greatly distressed, and I am convinced would be happy to return. His Agent has repeatedly urged me to remit him Fifty Thousand Rupees, to bear his Expences to the Company's Territories; I have not yet been able to obtain any honourable Terms for him from the Vizier, but his remaining with Nudjif Cawn, with whom his only Object can be to interrupt the Peace of his Brother's Government,

Government, is a Matter of that great Consequence, that I humbly submit it to the Consideration of the Honourable Board. I am convinced in my own Mind, Nudjiff Cawn would be glad to be at Variance with the Vizier, as he has given a very strong Proof of it in the late Negociation of the Niabut of the Vizarut. His Ambassador, Mirza Hellyle, solicited for this Appointment in the most urgent Style, whilst we were at Etawa. The Vizier for some Time refused it him, until the King's Approbation was previously obtained; but Mirza Hellyle got over this Difficulty, and received the Kelaat the Day before his Excellency left that Place. The Mutiny in the Army a short Time after broke out in the Doab, and the Vizier's Affairs had an unfavourable Appearance, upon which Nudjif Cawn refused to put it on, nor did he do it until very lately.

His Majesty, according to his last Year's Plan, has fixed on a Day to take the Field the 14th of the Lunar Month. It is said the Sikes are collecting a numerous Army, with which they have agreed to join him; that they had previously refused to attack Nudjif Cawn, but offered readily to undertake any Enterprize against the Vizier. Fyzulla Cawn has for some Time been treating with them, and is suspected of having encouraged them with Hopes of entering into their Views of invading Rohilchund; and in order to cloak his raising a large Body of Troops, he does not himself entertain above the Number of Five Thousand, stipulated by the Treaty with Sujah ul Dowlah, but he authorizes his Zemindars and Servants to do it in their Names. It is further said that Sabiter Cawn is invited to join the Confederacy; what Dependence is to be laid on this Intelligence, I cannot say, but it appears to me absolutely necessary that the Vizier should lose no Time in putting his Army, especially that Part under British Officers, on the most respectable Footing; for, in less than Two Months, the Rains will subside, and the Country be open to the Attacks of his Enemies.

I have the Honour, &c.

Lucknow,
July 29th, 1776.

APPENDIX, N° 163.

Extract of Bengal Secret Consultations, the 28th August 1776.

PRESENT,

The Honourable Warren Hastings, Governor General, President,
Lieutenant General John Clavering,
Richard Barwell, Philip Francis, } Esquires.
Colonel Monson, indisposed.

READ, and approved, the Proceedings of the 26th Instant.

Received the following Letter from Lieutenant Colonel Goddard.

Gentlemen,

I have the Honour to acquaint you, that from Accounts received of the Junction of a Body of Seiks, with Zabta Chawn's Army, and of their united Forces having moved to Sucker Taal, on the Banks of the Ganges, there is Reason to apprehend he is meditating an Attempt to invade Rohilcund, and it is reported he has already seized upon a great Number of Boats for the Purpose of crossing his Army: I do not however think he will carry his Designs into Execution till after the Rains, a Passage being at this Season extremely hazardous, and indeed almost impracticable.

His Excellency the Vizier has in consequence of the above Intelligence directed me to proceed to Daranagur, with the Body-Guard under the Command of Lieutenant Connellan, tellan, and Lieutenant Clarke's Battalion of Sepoys, which is all the Force I can at present possibly collect, the Five new-raised Battalions still continuing under the Command of Colonel Stibbert: I am hopeful the Board will see the Expediency of ordering that Part of the Vizier's Army to be delivered over to me, particularly as there is a Prospect of their Services being soon required, and I could wish to accustom them early to that Mode of Discipline and Subordination I intend they shall hereafter continue to practise. I need not urge any Thing further on this Subject, as I flatter myself the Board will have acquiesced with my former Address concerning it.

I expect the Two Battalions above-mentioned will reach Furruckabad about the 20th Instant, by which Time I shall be able to judge with more Precision of the Designs of Zabta Chawn, and shall endeavour to inform myself of every material Circumstance, which shall be faithfully transmitted to you. From the present Appearance of Affairs, I am firmly of Opinion his Intentions are fixed on recovering the former Possessions of his Nation from the Vizier, and from every Account I am inclined to believe Fyzoolah Cawn will join him in the Attempt. Should that really be the Case, with the Addition of Captain Erskine's Regiment now at Daranagur, and Captain Hoggan's also stationed in that Quarter, joined to the Two Battalions already with me, I shall be of Force sufficient not only to prevent their effecting a Passage over the Ganges, but to oppose them fairly in the Field.

I beg Leave to inform you, that in Obedience to your Instructions, I have done all in my Power to controul the enormous Expences of the Army, and shall continue to pay the strictest Attention to that Task, and your future Directions respecting it.

I take the Liberty to submit to your Consideration, how far it would be conducive to the Settlement and Regularity of the Troops, after their late distracted and dispersed State, the assembling them in one Place for the present; and having modelled and disciplined them, I would propose that the Infantry might be divided into Two Bodies, one to be stationed for the Protection of Rohilcund, and the other in the Doab, where they would be separately powerful enough to repel any Invasion; or, should Occasion require, might easily move to the Assistance of each other.

I take the Liberty to point out to you, the immense Expence arising from the Number of Staff Appointments in the Army, and to submit to your Decision, how much it would contribute to diminish the Expence, the annulling the Post of Adjutant and Quarter Masters to each Battalion of Infantry, a Measure which will not, I am convinced, be attended with any Injury to the Discipline of the Troops, and must be of manifest Advantage, by curtailing the very heavy Charges now incurred on Account of their great Allowances and Contingencies.

I also beg Leave to represent to you, the Service it would be of to the Artillery, to have an Officer of approved Skill and Experience, appointed to command that Corps. As it is a Body on which the chief Dependance is to be placed, and which may be said to constitute our greatest Superiority over the Country Arms, I am exceedingly anxious for its Improvement, and conceive the enlarging that Establishment, and augmenting the Number of Artillery Officers, would be a Measure highly beneficial to the Service.

I have the Honour, &c.

Belgram, (Signed) Thomas Goddard.
August 12th 1776.

Resolved, That the following Reply be written to Lieutenant Colonel Goddard:

To Lieutenant Colonel Goddard.

Sir,

We have received your Letter of the 12th Instant. In ours of the 29th Ultimo, we informed you of the Orders we had given to Colonel Stibbert, to deliver over the new-raised Battalions to your Charge and Command, though we have no Doubt that these Orders would arrive in due Time; yet to guard against the Possibility of any Accident, we now enclose a Duplicate of our Letter to you, and have also sent a Duplicate of that to Colonel Stibbert.

We very much commend the Attention you have shewn already to controul the contingent Expences of the Nabob's Army under your Command, and you may rest assured of our firmest Support in the Prosecution of so necessary a Service.

The

The Offices of Adjutant and Quarter-master, are considered in every well-regulated Army so essential to the Discipline and Accommodation of the Men, and to the Preservation and Arrangement of the Stores, that we cannot judge of the Propriety of abolishing them on the sole Ground of Oeconomy, but we rely entirely on your Prudence and Discretion in forming and regulating the Vizier's disciplined Troops; we therefore leave it to you to reduce those Appointments, if upon more mature Deliberation you shall think it advisable.

We cannot possibly spare more Artillery Officers at this Time from our own Service; you will therefore use your Discretion, in distributing Commands in the Nabob's Artillery in such Manner as may best supply the Want of a Commandant, or a greater Number of Subaltern Officers, until it may be in our Power, should it hereafter be deemed necessary, to encrease their Number.

By Colonel Stibbert's Return, transmitted to the Commander in Chief, we are sorry to observe the slow Progress made in raising the Recruits of the new Regiments, especially of that under the Command of Captain Home, which is deficient 1011 Men. We need not mention the Necessity to recommend to you the greatest Diligence and Expedition in compleating these Corps, as so little Time will be left to discipline them before it is likely they may be wanted for Service.

As we think it probable that many of the Officers of the Battalions lately disbanded, may apply to be admitted into the Service of the new Establishment, we recommend it to you to be particularly attentive to the Characters of the Officers whom you may appoint to Commands in them; and if you shall find that any Persons who have received Commissions had formerly distinguished themselves in the late Seditions, you will remove them immediately, and dismiss them from the Service, lest their Example and Influence should introduce the same Spirit of Mutiny among the Sepoys under your Command, which has before been carried to such Lengths in the Nabob's Army, and which has too frequently been experienced in his disciplined Corps, even during the Government of the late Vizier.

We are, &c.
(Signed)

Fort William,
28th August, 1776.

The Governor General delivers in the following Minute:

From the repeated Accounts which have been received of a Combination formed by the King, the Marattas, the Seiks, and the Rohillas, to invade the Dominions of the Vizier after the Conclusion of the Rains, and from the too great Notoriety of his Inability to oppose an Invasion by any Force of his own, the Probability of such a Design is at least so apparent as to merit the Attention of this Board to the Means of guarding against it; for this Purpose I submit to their Consideration the Expediency of engaging the Nabob Nudjiff Cawn in the Interests of the Company and of the Vizier, and of concerting with him a Plan for our common Benefit and Safety. The First Step to this Object would be obviously the Confirmation of his Pension, and the Payment of the Arrears which are due of it, both as the Means of fixing his Attachment and enabling him to make it serviceable to the common Cause; but I think it would be improper to make further Advances on this Point until his Answer shall be received to the Letter which was written to him on the 13th June last. As there is no Time to be lost, and as the Accomplishment of any Alliance with Nudjif Cawn, which can be converted to Purposes of solid Utility, must depend upon the previous Arrangement of many Points which can only be settled in a Personal Negociation with him, I recommend that a Person be deputed for this Purpose to Nudjiff Cawn, who may learn and report to the Board his Situation and Views, and those of the other Powers in his Neighbourhood, and who may treat with him upon the Conditions of his Alliance, and the Measures to be adopted in Consequence of it; I do not think it necessary or proper to appoint a public Commission for this Business, but recommend that it be privately entrusted to some English Gentleman in the Service of the Company, who may be previously known to Nudjif Cawn, and with whom he may treat with Confidence.—I will take the Liberty to remark, that I should have considered it as falling within the ordinary Powers and Duties of my Station, to have formed all the preparatory Lines of a Measure of this Nature, by my own Authority, for the Sake of Secrecy and Dispatch, and to have reported my Proceedings to the Board, with all the Materials which I had collected, when they were ripe for Execution; but in the present Constitution of this Government such a Power may be deemed improper; I therefore only recommend the Measure for the Approbation of the Board, and will name the Person whom I would wish to propose for the Service, when I know whether the Measure itself shall be approved.

(Signed) Warren Hastings.

Ordered that the above Minute lie for Consideration until To-morrow.

Warren Hastings,
J. Clavering.
Richard Barwell,
P. Francis.

APPENDIX, Nº 164.

Extract of Bengal Secret Consultation, the 29th August 1776.

RE-CONSIDERED the Governor General's Minute, delivered in to the Board Yesterday.

Mr. Francis—By a Resolution of this Board, in which I did not concur, it has been already determined to restore Nudjiff Cawn's Pension, on the Condition of his dismissing from his Service certain Persons justly obnoxious to this Government. I still think that this alone is not sufficient to entitle him to such a Mark of our Favour, and that further Measures will be necessary to secure the Attachment of a Man of his Qualifications, and to make him really serviceable to us and our Ally, the Nabob of Oude. I do not therefore object to the proposed Deputation in itself, but reserve any farther Opinion of it until I understand on what Plan, and under what Instructions, the Person deputed is to act; I cannot assent to any which may have a Tendency to engage the Company's Troops beyond the Line of our present Guarantee.

Mr. Barwell—I approve of the Governor's Proposal, to depute an English Gentleman to learn and report Nudjiff Cawn's Views and Situation, and to treat with him on the Condition of his Alliance, and the Measures to be adopted in Consequence of it.—In this I do no more than adopt the Sentiments of the Company, who have particularly directed this Government to use its Endeavours to benefit the general Cause by the Abilities of Nudjiff Cawn. I concur with the Governor General, that we cannot order the Payment of the Arrears of Nudjif Cawn's Salary, nor proceed a Step further in that Particular, before we receive his Answer to our Letter of the 13th June.

General Clavering—The Combinations which the Governor General mentions to be forming by the King, the Marattas, the Seicks, and the Rohillas, to invade the Dominions of the Vizier after the Conclusion of the Rains, I do not find to be yet so well established as to be admitted as a Truth on which we can depend. In a Letter which I beg Leave to deliver in, from Colonel Stibbert to Colonel Goddard, the Invasion of the Vizier's Dominions is treated as very problematical. Whether the Intention of invading the Country be real or not, I do not think that we can place any Dependance on the Attachment of Nudjif Cawn, whilst he entertains Two such implacable Enemies of this Government near his Person, as Sumroo the Assassin, and Mador the Deserter; till he shall therefore have performed his Promise of dismissing from his Confidence those Two Persons, I cannot agree to maintain any Intercourse whatever with him.

The Governor General—I have always understood, and I believe it to be certain, that Nudjiff Cawn has been compelled, by an unavoidable Necessity, to retain Sumroo in his Service; that the First Motive of his receiving him, was to prevent his Enemy Abdul Ahed Cawn, who was then in Treaty with Sumroo, from employing him in his Service,

vice, of which Nudjif Cawn apprehended that his Death or Ruin were the sole Objects; and that the long War in which he has since been engaged with the Jauts, and his own internal Weakness from Want of Money, have put it out of his Power to comply with the urgent Requisitions which this Government has made to him for the Dismission of Sumroo, who has been principally, if not, as I am informed, always employed in remote Services, and now maintains himself in a Degree of Independency, but never possessed any Share in his Master's Confidence, nor even the public Appearance of it; but I agree nevertheless with the other Members of the Board, in requiring this as a preliminary and indispensible Condition of our further Alliance with him. The specific Advantages which I expect may be derived from the proposed Deputation, will best appear in the following rough Draft of the Instructions which I have prepared for the Purpose. I must add in this Place, that although I cannot expect the Board should place implicit Confidence in the Reports which I have mentioned, of the Junction of the King, the Marattas, the Scicks, and the Rhohillas, yet I have received Reports through various Channels, in Confirmation of this Intelligence, contained in the Letter from Colonel Goddard, recorded Yesterday, which leave me without a Doubt of the Formation of such a Confederacy.

Read, the rough Draft of the Instructions proposed by the Governor General.

Ordered, That they be copied fair, and sent round for the further Consideration of the Board: And

Agreed, that an English Gentleman may be deputed to treat with Nudjif Cawn, on the several Points expressed in the Governor General's Minute of Yesterday.

Governor General—I beg Leave to recommend Major Hannay for this Service, as a Person well informed of the political State of Affairs in that Part of India, personally known to Nudjif Cawn, and in every Respect well qualified to answer the Purposes of such a Commission.

Mr. Francis—I have no Objections to Major Hannay.

Mr. Barwell—I acquiesce in the Governor's Nomination.

General Clavering—I should have no Objection to Major Hannay's going there, or any where else, where it might be thought his Services could be usefully employed, if it was not for the Reason I have already given, from holding any Communication with Nudjiff Cawn, whilst Sumroo is his Chief Confidant. Under these Circumstances, I think it an Indignity to the Company to depute an Officer to Nudjif Cawn, and a Degradation of the Officer himself, to be admitted into Nudjiff Cawn's Presence under the Auspices of an Assassin.

Resolved, That Major Hannay be appointed to proceed on the Deputation abovementioned.

Mr. Francis—I understood the previous Dismission of Sumroo and Mador to be the Basis of the Proposition; without which I could certainly have no Thoughts of treating with Nudjif Cawn.

Governor General—The General's Objection supposes me to have proposed what is the most foreign from my Intentions. I should hold it, equally with him, a Disgrace to this Government, and an Indignity to its Representative, to employ any Officer, or other Servant of the Company, in a personal Negociation with Nudjif Cawn, were Sumroo at the same Time admitted into his Presence; but to put this Point beyond a Doubt, I would propose that the Dismission of Sumroo be formally required by Major Hannay, before he pass the Boundaries of our own Dominions; and that in Default of his Compliance, Major Hannay be forbidden to proceed. I cannot extend this Proposition to Mador, and the other Europeans in the Service of Nudjif Cawn, because I doubt whether it may be in his Power to dismiss them until he shall have acquired that Addition of Strength and Authority which may be expected from the Renewal of his Connection with the English, and from the Credit which it will give him with the other Powers of Hindostan.

The Governor General's Motion is agreed to by Mr. Francis and Mr. Barwell.

General Clavering—I object to it, because I think the same End may be answered, by writing from hence, without exposing the Honour of this Government to be affected by the Return of a Deputation which all Hindostan will know was expresly sent to invite Nudjif Cawn to an Alliance, on Conditions which we would not accept.

Governor General—I had already proposed, that this Commission should not be of a public Nature; and however the Existence or Object of it may be suspected, it can never injure the Credit of this Government, that an Individual, not charged with any declared Authority, shall have proceeded to the Frontier of our own Dominions, for Purposes which the World cannot be informed of, even though he should be obliged to return from thence, without having accomplished the real End of his Mission. Were there Time for it, I should be equally inclined to write to Nudjif Cawn, and to wait for his Answer to the Proposition of receiving a Minister from this Government, and to the preliminary Condition of any future Treaty which may take Place between us; but such a Delay would frustrate the Design of the Measure, nor have I the least Apprehension that Nudjif Cawn will not thankfully agree to receive Major Hannay, or that he will refuse to dismiss Sumroo so soon as it shall be required of him, as the Conditions of their Meeting.

Resolved, that the Dismission of Sumroo be formally required by Major Hannay, before he pass the Boundaries of the Company's Dominions, and that in Default of Nudjif Cawn's Compliance with this Requisition, Major Hannay be forbidden to proceed any further.

General Clavering—If so public a Measure as the Appointment the Board is now making, could be considered even in Calcutta, the Letter which Major Hannay is directed to write to Nudjif Cawn, and which as usual will be read in his public Durbar, must infallibly pronounce the Intentions of this Government, and must expose it to the Contempt of all India, in case Nudjif Cawn should refuse to send away both Sumroo and Mador, as he himself engaged to do by his former Letter; besides, I foresee that the King, whose Servant Nudjif Cawn is, will be justly incensed at so partial a Distinction in Favour of him, whilst he himself is intirely neglected by us. I still consider the King as much the natural Head of the Empire of Hindostan, as the Emperor of Germany is of the German Empire; Princes who are more potent than him, may neglect his Orders, but all of them seek, on one Occasion or another, to obtain his Favour, and the Honour which he has to bestow.

Governor General—I am far from expecting that Major Hannay's Deputation shall be concealed in absolute Secrecy, and upon this Occasion I cannot help lamenting the unhappy State of this Government, which binds the Hands of the first and executive Member of it from employing such preparatory Means for the Advancement of its Interests, or its immediate Security, as in the Nature of them require to be conducted with the strictest Secrecy; but in my Opinion it will be sufficient that Major Hannay's Deputation be not publicly made known before it shall have taken effect; neither will it be necessary for Major Hannay, in notifying his Approach to Nudjif Cawn, to say that he comes with a public Commission; this will be sufficient to guard it against any Disgrace on the Failure of it. I for my own Part will never join in any Act which shall give just Cause of Offence to the King Shaw Allum, and while I persist in those Sentiments, I shall little regard the impotent Resentment of a Man to whom I owe no Allegiance, and shall be always ready to support the Engagements of the Company, even with those whom he may call his Subjects, and even against his Person, if by an Opposition to these Engagements, he shall oblige this Government personally to oppose him. I should be lost in so wide a Field as I should be led into by the Discussion of the King's Rights, and the Obligations on this Government to maintain them; but with respect to the different Treatment which is due from us to him and Nudjif Cawn, a very few Words will suffice. The King separated himself from his Connections with the English, in Opposition to the strongest Remonstrances which were made to him on their Part; Nudjif Cawn refused even to accompany the King, or to separate himself from the English, until urged by them to both, as a Measure which the King's Safety, under the Circumstances of such a Resolution, rendered indispensably necessary, and which their Interests did not oppose.—I move that a Letter be written to Mr. Bristow, to inform him of the Design of Major Hannay's Commission, so far as it respects the Nabob of Oude, and to direct him to correspond with Major Hannay, and to concert with him the Means of rendering it effectual; but to conceal the Contents of this Information until it shall be necessary to reveal them.

Mr. Francis and Mr. Barwell agree to the Governor General's Motion.

General Clavering disapproves of every Step that may be taken in Consequence of the Appointment that has been made this Day.

Agreed,

APPENDIX, Nº 164.

Agreed, That the following Letter be written to Mr. Bristow, for the Purpose mentioned in the above Motion.

Sir,

Having thought proper to appoint Major Alexander Hannay, to proceed on a Deputation to the Nabob Nudjif Cawn, in order to treat with him on sundry Matters, we direct that you correspond with Major Hannay, and use your Endeavours to concert Means to render his Negociation effectual: For this End, we transmit you a Copy of his Instructions, as far as they relate to the Nabob of Oude; but we desire you will conceal the Contents of this Information, and the Nature of Major Hannay's Appointment, until it be found necessary to reveal them, or at least until he shall arrive at the Court of Nudjif Cawn.

We are, &c. &c.

The Instructions proposed for Major Hannay having been circulated agreeable to the Orders of the Board, after the breaking up of this Day's Council, they were received back, with the Remarks hereafter entered; and being agreed to by a Majority of the Board, were written fair, and delivered to Major Hannay.

Sir,

The Board having nominated you their Deputy to the Nabob Nudjif Cawn, you will wait upon the Governor General for your Credentials, and repair with all possible Expedition to the Court of that Prince.

We recommend your strictest Attention, and the utmost Exertion of your Zeal and Abilities, to obtain the following Points, the Objects of your Deputation:

1st. You will give the Nabob the strongest Assurances, in the Name of this Government, of their earnest Desire to renew the Friendship and Alliance which formerly subsisted between him and the Company, and of cementing and increasing both, on Conditions of mutual Support and Advantage.

2d. You will require of him to disband all his European Forces, and particularly to dismiss from his Service the Assassin Sumroo; you will acquaint the Nabob, that we consider his Compliance with these two Requisitions, as preliminary and indispensable to any Treaty which may hereafter be concluded with him, since no Degree of good Faith can subsist between us, whilst he employs the Subjects of Nations at Enmity with the English; and gives Protection to a Man, whose Name is held in such just and universal Detestation by them.

With respect to Sumroo, we cannot consent even to your proceeding on the proposed Negociation, whilst that Man is retained in his Service: We therefore direct that you previously direct a Letter to the Nabob, informing him of your Intention to visit him, without formally notifying the Authority with which you are invested; but to acquaint him, that you are precluded, by the positive Orders of this Government, from entering his Territories, until he shall have first dismissed Sumroo from his Service. And you will wait until you receive his Reply, and an Assurance of his having complied with your Requisition.

3d. You will represent to the Nabob, that we have observed with much Concern a Coolness and Distrust prevail between him and the Government of Oude, since the Period of the Nabob Asoph ul Dowlah's Succession; and as nothing can so effectually contribute to the Security and Advantage of his own and the Vizier's Dominions, as a close Union, and unreserved Confidence, and a mutual Participation of Benefits, you will tender your good Offices for accomplishing so desirable an End, either by offering our Mediation, or by concerting with our Resident at the Court of the Vizier, the Means of effecting an immediate Reconciliation; and for this End you will make exact and regular Communications with our Resident at that Court, of all your Proceedings upon such Points as have a Tendency to establish a Coalition, which we so ardently wish to effect, between the Vizier and Nudjif Cawn.

4th. You will obtain from Nudjif Cawn, as early as possible, the ultimate Conditions on which he is willing to form a lasting Alliance with the Company. As he may previosly demand the Confirmation and Arrears of his Pension, you will acquaint him, that our Determination thereon, by the Instructions of the Court of Directors, necessarily depends on his Answer to the last Letter written to him by the Governor General

General; and you will observe to him, that as Treaties of Alliance between different States can have no other solid Basis nor Security for becoming permanent, than that of mutual Advantage, we shall expect in Return for the pecuniary Benefits he may derive from the Company, the most effectual Support he can afford to the Security of their Dominions; on which, in Fact, that of his own must essentially depend, by contributing, with his whole Force, where it may be practicable, to repel the hostile Designs of the Marattas, or any other Power who may rise in Arms against them.

5th. You will concert with the Nabob Nudjif Cawn, the best probable Plan of defensive Operations for opposing any Invasion of the Marattas, or other Powers in the ensuing Campaign; but you must guard against his entertaining any Expectation of actual Aid from us, by informing him, that we are not permitted, on any Account whatever, to carry the Arms of the Company beyond the Limits of the Nabob Asoph ul Dowlah's Dominions of Oud, Corah, and Allahabad.

6th. You will use your utmost Endeavours to gain and transmit to us, from Time to Time, the most exact Information of the natural Strength, Situation, Forces, and Revenues, and the Characters, Interests, Connections, and Designs, of the Princes who respectively govern the Countries in the Neighbourhood of Nudjif Cawn, and particularly of such whose immediate Vicinity, or other Circumstances, may involve them in the Transactions of his Government.

The following Paragraph is added in consequence of Mr. Francis's Minute, and the Assents thereto hereafter entered.

The Intent of your Deputation being merely to concert Measures of a defensive Nature with Nudjif Cawn, we positively restrain you from listening to any Proposals which may be made to you of a different Tendency.

We are, &c. &c.

Mr. Francis—I consider the proposed Deputation to have no Object but *defensive* Measures only; I shall never *concur* in any other; I think that an Article should be inserted in these Instructions, positively restraining Major Hannay from listening to any Proposals whatsoever of a different Nature.

(Signed) P. F.
R. B.

I readily agree to the Clause proposed by Mr. Francis, although I think the Substance is clearly and fully expressed in the concluding Sentence of the 5th Article of the Instructions.

(Signed) W. H.

I have already entered my Objections so fully to the Measures to be pursued in Consequence of these Instructions, that it remains only for me to repeat my Dissent and Protest to any new Treaty with Nudjif Cawn; the Object and Extent of such new Engagements having not yet been communicated to us. Nudjif Cawn is an Adventurer, who has made his Fortune on the Ruin of the Jauts, a People like the Rohillas, who have never given us any Offence, whose State was a Barrier to Bengal, but whose total Ruin seems to be determined in order to form a large Establishment for Nudjif Cawn.

(Signed) J. C.

Warren Hastings,
J. Clavering,
Richard Barwell,
P. Francis.

APPENDIX, Nº 164.

Extract of Bengal Secret Consultations, the 23d September, 1776.

P R E S E N T,

The Honourable Warren Hastings, Governor General, President,
Richard Barwell, } Esquires.
Philip Francis, }
General Clavering indisposed.

The General Letter in this Department having been revised and approved by the Members present, it was ordered to be sent to General Clavering; and having been communicated to him, he declared his Dissent to the 13th, 14th, and 15th Paragraphs respecting Nudjif Cawn; and afterwards delivered in the following Minute, a Copy of which was sent a Number in the Packet with the General Letter.

I object to the 13th, 14th, and 15th Paragraphs of the Letter in the Secret Department to the Court of Directors. My Objection to the First is, that it is not conformable to the Resolutions of the Board: To the Second, that it contains Facts not authenticated: To the Third, that it seems calculated to induce the Court of Directors to believe that Bengal requires the Alliance of Nudjif Cawn, to protect it against the Marattas, or some other Power which may rise up against it.

Explanation 1st. On the 10th June it was resolved to restore Nudjif Cawn his Pension, on Two Conditions: The First, That he should send away all the Europeans who are so offensive to the English: The Second, That he should dismiss Saudit Ally Cawn from his Camp: Although the 13th Paragraph refers to the Consultation of the 10th June, the last Condition is totally omitted. It has been in like Manner excluded from the Instructions of Major Hannay.

Explanation 2d. The Confederacy said to be in Agitation against the Nabob's Dominions, has been mentioned by Mr. Bristow and Colonel Goddard, but it has been as much slighted by Colonel Stibbert. It consists, according to the Governor General's Minute, entered on the Consultations of the 29th August, of the King, the Marattas, the Seiks, and the Rohillas. After having seen, on so many Occasions, the King's Power and Authority vilified by the late Administration, I was not a little surprized to see his Name mentioned as a dangerous Power in this formidable Alliance. I as little expected to see the Name of the Marattas introduced, because we have lately concluded a Treaty with them; and according to all Appearances, they are more desirous of our Friendship than we can be of theirs. The Seiks are so far from wishing to quarrel with us, that they are disposed to court our Alliance; and with regard to the Remains of the Rohillas, although they have no Reason to respect our good Faith, or to admire our Justice, yet I believe they are not so formidable as to become the Objects of an Embassy and a public Treaty.

Explanation 3d. If I have well comprehended the Instructions, the Treaty which is to be made with Nudjif Cawn is to be formed on the Basis of mutual Interests; namely, That we are to give him Money, and he is to give us Assistance in case Bengal be attacked by the Marattas, or any other Power who may rise up in Arms against us. Whether the Money we are to pay him is to be limited to Two Lacks, or to be encreased, is not expressly said; but I should conjecture, from the Tenor of the First and Fourth Articles, that the latter is intended; and indeed when one considers that by the Treaty of Illiabad in the Year 1765, he was already entitled to receive the Sum of Two Lacks, and that this Sum had been repeatedly offered to him, no other Inference can be drawn but that more is intended to be given him by the new Treaty. The Words I refer to in the First Article, are " the cementing and increasing the Friendship and Alliance " which formerly subsisted between the Company and him, on Conditions of mutual " Support and Advantage." The Fourth Article is more explanatory, and therefore it shall be inserted entire."

Explanation 4th. " You will obtain from Nudjif Cawn, as early as possible, the " ultimate Conditions on which he is willing to form a lasting Alliance with the Com- " pany. As he may previously demand the Confirmation and Arrears of his Pension, " you will acquaint him that our Determination thereon, by the Instructions of the " Court of Directors, necessarily depends on his Answer to the last Letter written to

" him

" him by the Governor General; and you will observe to him, that as Treaties of " Alliance between different States can have no other solid Basis nor Security for be- " coming permanent than those of mutual Advantage, we shall expect, in Return for " the pecuniary Benefits he may derive from the Company, the most effectual Support " he can afford to the Security of their Dominions, on which, in Fact, that of his own " must essentially depend, by contributing with his whole Force, where it may be " practicable, to repel the hostile Designs of the Marattas, or any other Power who " may rise in Arms against them."

Understanding therefore that by the new Treaty, he is to have an additional Subsidy, and in return he is to give us the Assistance of his whole Force, when required, for the Defence of these Provinces, it seems to me natural to suppose, that the Gentlemen who formed and agreed to these Instructions, do suppose that the formidable Confederacy which is to be counteracted by this Treaty, is rather directed against the Province of Bengal, than against our Ally the Vizier; who is only held forth as the Object of it in the Governor General's Minute, entered in Consultations the 29th August.

These are the Reasons on which I have objected to the Three Paragraphs in the General Letter.

With respect to the Propriety of making even a defensive Treaty with Nudjiff Cawn; as a public Measure, it cannot avoid being condemned; it does not appear prudent to confide on the Fidelity of a Man who openly appeared in Arms against the English Camp in the Year 1772, who still detains in his Army Sumroo, the Assassin of the English at Patna, together with Madoc and the other English Deserters. Would his dismissing them now be any Proof of his Attachment to us? Could it be thought safe to bring into these Provinces for their Protection, an Army of Banditti, who are daily mutinying for their Pay, and living by Rapine? If there was a Necessity of introducing Foreign Troops into these Provinces, every Reason requires that we should give a Preference to those commanded by British Officers in the Service of our Ally the Vizier; they could give us no Umbrage. Our being able to avail ourselves of their Assistance, in case of an Exigency, was not one of the least of the Advantages which we ourselves proposed in forming those Corps, and which have so happily coincided with the Views of the Court of Directors, in their Orders to us received in this Season, directing us to " re- " commend to the Nabob of Oude, to permit some Part of his Cavalry to be com- " manded by Officers of the Company."

Hitherto I have only considered the intended Treaty as a Measure burthensome to the Company, but eventually dangerous, on a Supposition that Nudjif Cawn's Troops were permitted to enter into Bengal. I will now take a Review of it as it may affect the Company, indeed more remotely, but still not with less Danger.

In the Year 1773, Nudjif Cawn was yet no more than an Adventurer, not possessing a Foot of Land. At the fatal Congress at Benares was laid the Foundation of his Power, on the Ruin of the Jauts; as was likewise that of the Vizier by the Destruction of the Rohillas. In the Year 1774, while the English Troops were marching to extirpate one Nation, Nudjif Cawn's Army besieged and took the strong Fort of Agra, belonging to the Jauts, aided by some Troops of the Vizier, and assisted by Major Polier, with the Approbation of the Governor General.

In the following Season he pursued his Advantage, and took from the Jauts another strong Fort called Deig. It ought not to appear surprizing, that those People who were formerly considered as the Allies of the English, but now abandoned by them, should, as the last Resort of Despair, apply to the Marattas for their Assistance.

That very different Sentiments from those which have been lately adopted in Bengal, were entertained formerly by Lord Clive, who I believe understood the Politics of India better than any Englishman who has ever been in the Country, will appear by a Letter from the Select Committee to the Court of Directors, dated 8th September, 1768.

During Lord Clive's Residence in the Bahar Province, " a Congress was held at " Chupra, at which his Lordship, General Carnac, Suja Dowlah, and the King's Mi- " nisters, assisted. Here was laid the Foundation of a Treaty between the Company, " the Vizier, and the Jaut, and Rohilla Chiefs, for their mutual Defence and Security " against all Attempts of the Marattas to invade their several Dominions; but his " Lordship and General Carnac, from Consideration of the little Advantage the Com- " pany would deduce from such distant Allies in case of an Invasion, chose to leave this " Matter unfinished, and to entrust Sujah Dowlah with the Management of such " Treaties as he might think convenient for his own and the Company's Welfare;

" but

"but he is not to conclude any Thing, nor to enter into any absolute Engagements,
"without having previously acquainted the President of every Proposal, and obtained
"his Approbation."

Lord Clive's Views are clear: He wished to preserve the independant Nations of the Jauts and Rohillas, as Allies of the English, and to put them under their Protection, but avoided making any specific Treaty with them, because he knew, that from their great Distance they never could be of Use for the Protection of Bengal. After having raised the Power of Nudjif Cawn to such an Height as to become formidable both to the Vizier and to ourselves, it is at last judged adviseable to make the most indecent Advances to him; I call them indecent, because he has not made any Reply to the Letter that was written to him on the 10th of June; because we are uninformed whether he will send away Sumroo, Mader, and the other Europeans, or dismiss Saudit Ally Cawn from his Durbar; and because Nudjif Cawn, though now an independant Chief, is still in the Service of the King, by whom it will be considered as the highest Indignity to see an Officer of high Rank deputed to his Servant, while he himself is neglected: The King will naturally say, "What has Nudjif Cawn done for the Company? He did "not grant the Dewannee of Bengal to them, or give them Sunnuds for the Five "Circars."

To the Objection of Sumrooo and Mader remaining with Nudjiff Cawn, the Gentlemen who have planned this Deputation will reply, that they have provided against the Disgrace and Dishonour that would ensue from an English Officer being introduced to that Chief, in the Presence of those Persons, by directing that Major Hannay shall not proceed further than Chunar until he hears of their Dismission.

At all Events we have committed our Honour into the Hands of Nudjiff Cawn, and it now remains with him not to disgrace us, and to give Sumroo the Triumph of setting our Power at Defiance.

Whatever ostensible Motives have been assigned for this Embassy in the Governor General's Minute of the 29th August, and have been introduced in the General Letter to prepare the Court of Directors for it, I cannot help suspecting, that much more is intended than what has been discovered either to them or to us.

I form my Conjectures from Two Circumstances: First from the Precipitation with which the Design of this Embassy was opened and carried into Execution: The Second by the Omission of Saudit Ally Cawn's Name in the Instructions. On the 28th August the Governor General shewed me his Minute, which was to introduce this Business, and told me he intended to bring it before the Board the next Day; accordingly it no sooner appeared, than the Proposal contained in it was agreed to by One Resolve, the Nomination of Major Hannay by a Second, and the Instructions by a Third.

I could do no more than protest against them all severally. I had already represented to the Governor General, that he was rescinding a former Resolution of a full Board during the Absence of Colonel Monson, which was not to enter into any further Correspondence with Nudjiff Cawn till he had complied with Two Conditions stipulated on the Consultations of the 10th June, namely, his sending away the obnoxious Europeans, and dismissing Saudit Alli from his Durbar. As the gaining this last Point from Nudjiff Cawn had been the chief Inducement of the Board to make him any Proposals what ever on the 10th June, it must appear to every one very remarkable, that this particular Condition should be omitted in the Instructions.

When the Terms of the Letter which was written to Nudjiff Cawn on that Occasion by the Governor General, are examined, my Suspicions that something more is intended by permitting Saudit Alli to remain with Nudjiff than what we have been allowed to know, will not appear ill-founded.

"It is for this Reason that nothing may remain to cast even a Shadow of Doubt be-
"tween us, that I earnestly recommend to you to prevail upon Mirza Saudit Ally
"Cawn, either to return to his Obedience, and to the Presence of his Brother Asoph ul
"Dowlah Behader, or to accept of the Asylum which has been offered him in the Pro-
"vince of Bengal, but on no Account let him remain with you, for although those
"who know you, and knew him, will entertain no Suspicions of your Intentions, the
"uninformed Part of the World will attribute such Appearances to hostile Designs
"in both, and that Opinion may be in the End productive of real Misunderstandings."

I will now leave the Court of Directors to draw their own Conclusions, whether my Suspicions on the above Circumstances be well or ill founded.

(Signed) J. Clavering.

The 16th September, 1776.

APPENDIX, N° 165.

Bengal Secret Consultations, 23d September, 1776.

RECEIVED the following Letters from Mr. Bristow:

Honourable Sir, and Sirs,

I addressed the Honourable Board the 9th, 10th, and 11th Instant, and am now to acknowledge their Letter of the 22d Ultimo.

In going to Fyzabad to procure an Interview with the Begum, I had no Intention to interfere between her and the Vizier; I only went to be present when any Settlement might take Place, without which the Begum never would have been satisfied, as she looked upon the Guarantee of the Company as her Security. My Rule of Conduct at Fyzabad not having exceeded this Line, and as the Five Lacks were on the Company's Account, I hope the Honourable Board will for these Reasons approve the Event of this Negociation.

The King has dismissed the Two Battalions which were formerly under the Command of Captains Brooke and Stuart, and given the Two Commandants Recommendatory Letters to the Vizier, to whom I introduced them. They urged that General Barker promised, that (should they behave well) they should be re-admitted into the Company's Service whenever they chose to leave his Majesty's; and Colonel Goddard had already addressed the Honourable Board on this Subject, but as the Vizier desired on my introducing them, he has written to the Governor General for Permission to entertain them. I do not well see how his Excellency can raise any Battalions, as I believe he will find some Difficulty in paying the Army he has already on Foot.

I have, &c. &c.

Lucknow, 18th August, 1776. (Signed) John Bristow, Resident at the Vizier's Court.

Honourable Sir, and Sirs,

I had the Honour to write on the 18th Instant.

In my Letter of the April last, I informed the Honourable Board of the Flight of Hemmut Bahadre with his Troops to Agra, and as he had placed Aumils of his own in the Vizier's conquered Countries to the South West of the Jumna, the Government on that Event fell into Disorder; the Vizier wished to have retained the Country, but his Army was at that Time so mutinous, and the principal Persons of his Court disaffected, that he really had not, though there were above Thirty thousand Men upon the Spot, a Force that he could entrust the Undertaking to. The Marattas benefited themselves by this; they in the Course of Twenty Days retook the Fort of Moat, and all that had been conquered on the other Side of the Jumna, excepting a small District adjacent to Etawa, which they were prevented doing, wholly from its peculiar Situation, surrounded and defended by Creeks and Nullas which fall into the Jumna; the Vizier can hardly be said to govern it; he has, 'tis true, an Aumil in the District, to whom the Zemindars pay no Rents, and in Defiance of his Authority retain Two Forts, called Cammeté and Sassaon: It was to reduce these Forts that Captain Stuart crossed the Jumna.

The Vizier's Loss of the conquered Countries, and the Cessation of Arms entered into with the Marattas, set aside the Scheme planned with the Rana of Goad. The Rana however considers himself a Dependant of the Vizier's, and in case of the Marattas attempting to invade these Countries, he might be made a very useful Ally.

I have, since I last wrote the Honourable Board relative to the Negociations of Raja Punsibur Pundit, the Maratta Vackeel, had repeated Conversations with him on the Subject of a Treaty with the Vizier, on the Terms of which I cannot bring him to any reasonable Determination. He always enlarges upon the Friendship which the Peshwa wishes to preserve with this Court, and his Willingness to enter into a Treaty with Amity,

Amity, but he cannot think of entering into one, ceding the Province of the Doab. He says, it is a small Extent of Country, and no Object for the Vizier to retain, and thereby disgust a Nation which can bring into the Field an Army of One hundred thousand Men; I urged to him, an Examination into past Proceedings is not the Way for him to establish a Friendship between the Vizier and his Master, as both would be equally solicitous to shew the good Grounds on which they had intended to act; that for my Part I was persuaded the English were anxious to see their Differences ended to their mutual Satisfaction; the best Way to do which, in my Opinion, was to look to what appeared adviseable at the present Juncture. His Master could hardly expect that Asuph ul Dowlah should cede Countries he was in actual Possession of, whilst he had a Force to defend them; and that he had done a great deal in giving up all Thoughts of the Country, on the other Side the Jumna, which I recommend as the Boundary to both their Dominions. The Districts in which the Forts of Cammeté and Sassoan are, I particularly excepted, and stipulated to be the Vizier's, being in his Possession.

This passed in a Conversation I had with him Yesterday; and he observed upon it, that he had received his Instructions, and if these were intended to be the Terms for the Treaty, he begged Permission to return to Poona, from whence every Article might be settled; but he had not Powers to do it. In my several Interviews with him, he has often proposed for the English and the Marattas to act in Conjunction, and make joint Conquests up to Lahere. It appears to me, that the Marattas do not wish to make any Treaty with the Vizier, but to leave the Matters in Dispute between them in the present State, until such Time as their own Affairs will admit of their making a vigorous Attack. By the general Purport of the Intelligence we got from the Decan, I can hardly think any Thing of the Kind is likely to happen this Year. The most the Marattas have hitherto done, was to promise the Jauts the Assistance of Fifteen thousand Men, who were magnified to Twenty-five thousand, and said to have marched from Ougywe, whereas, I do not really understand if any have marched, that their Numbers exceed Four or Five thousand. At any rate at present it is only Mehajy Sindea who has entered into this Undertaking. In regard to the Insinuations of the Maratta Vackeel, who would have it be thought that his Master would go any Lengths sooner than give up the Doab, I sincerely believe, that if the Vizier was unconnected with the Company, their Aumil Bolow Row would at this Time send Detachments into that Province. But the Awe in which Foreign Powers are held by our Troops, is the sole Cause of the Vizier's Security, otherwise there is a general League already formed against him, and the Execution of it would be at a short Period. The Copy of the Treaty proposed by Punsibun Pundit, I do myself the Pleasure to inclose.

Nudjiff Cawn is at Dike, endeavouring to satisfy his Troops, without Effect. I believe as he has not yet met with any Treasures in the Fort, he declares his Intention of going shortly to Delhi, accompanied by Saudit Ally, to pay his Respects to the King. It is the common Conversation at his Durbar, that the Intent of this Journey is, in Conjunction with Zabita Cawn, to form a Plan of Operations against the Vizier's Dominions. Appearances are preserved with Nudjiff Cawn at this Court, but Zabita Cawn threw off the Mask in consequence of a Negociation that had been for a long Time carrying on with him through Littaput, to conclude a Treaty of Amity, which he positively refuses, unless Nudjiff Abad shall be given up to him. He has dispatched a Vackeel, to offer Three Lacks to the Sikes, on their joining him; but it is not thought that he will succeed in getting any considerable Body, as they have Divisions amongst themselves. Fyzoola Cawn was wrote to by Somet Sing, and charged with entering into the Views of Zabita Cawn; he was likewise made acquainted, that Captain Erskine had stopt a Hircarrah, who took upon him his Name, was entrusted with Letters from one of his Dependants to the Sike Chiefs, and that he himself had directed this Hiccarrah to assure them verbally of his Friendship: In Answer to this, he asserts that he does not ever correspond with any Body but the Vizier and the English; however, he sent a particular Justification of his Conduct through his Vackeel at this Court; to the inclosed Copy of which, No. 2, I beg Leave to refer the Honourable Board. I likewise inclose Copies of Lettafut's Letters to the Vizier, inclosing one from Zabita Cawn, which amounts to little less than a Declaration of War. I suppose Zabita Cawn may be able to collect Thirty thousand Men, but they are not subject to any Subordination, ill armed, and ill provided with Ammunition; and he himself is esteemed a Man of less military Genius than any Prince of Hindostan; but his Uncle who is with him is a very able Officer.

 Upon

Upon a Review of the Situations of the Vizier's Enemies, I cannot entertain the least Apprehensions of any real Danger to his Dominions, particularly as there is now no Doubt but that Subordination and Discipline will be introduced amongst the Troops under the Command of the British Officers. They are every where put upon the same Footing with regard to Pay, as in the Company's Service; their submitting to the Reduction of it, is I think a strong Instance that the Spirit of Mutiny is entirely broke through. The Troops being thus brought into a State to be serviceable to the Vizier, he wishes much to collect a formidable Force in the Doab and Rohilcund. His Enemies are numerous, and if their Declarations are to be credited, inclined to attack him; and if those Provinces should long remain in their present defenceless State, it will be a Temptation to them to make Attempts; whereas by a judicious Disposition at this early Period, every bad Consequence may be avoided. The Plan approved by the Vizier, is to form Two regular Brigades, consisting of a Park of Artillery, Six Battalions of Sepoys, and One Regiment of Cavalry, in each of the Frontier Provinces, to be commanded by the British Officers; but the raising of Five Battalions having been given over by the Honourable Board's Advice to Colonel Stibbert, the Vizier cannot dispose of them until they be delivered up to him by Colonel Stibbert, for which he is very anxious, and wrote some Days ago to the Governor General on the Subject. By his own Desire, I also trouble the Honourable Board with a Repetition of his Request; and further, that he hopes Orders may be sent to Colonel Stibbert to deliver them over.

I have, &c.

Lucknow, 22d August 1776. (Signed) John Bristow, Resident at the Vizier's Court.

P. S. I forgot to mention to the Honourable Board, that in Consequence of Zabita Cawn's Declarations, and the Inclination all Foreign Powers shew to attack the Vizier; he has been pleased to authorize Colonel Goddard to assemble and dispose of his Troops in Rohilcund, as well those under British Officers as not, in case of an Invasion being attempted.

(Signed) J. Bristow.

APPENDIX, N° 166.

Extract of Bengal Secret Consultations, the 24th October, 1776.

PRESENT,

The Honourable Warren Hastings, Governor General, President,
Richard Barwell, } Esquires.
Philip Francis, }
General John Clavering indisposed.

See Appendix, No. 46.

READ a Letter from the Nabob Nudjiff Cawn, received the 22d Instant, and recorded No. 242, in the Book of Persian Correspondence.

The Governor General lays before the Board the following Minute:

Although I have been some Time since informed of the Circumstance mentioned in Nudjif Cawn's Letter, respecting the Request made by the Nabob Usoph ul Dowla to him, for the Protection of Saadut Ally, (and the Members of the Board will probably recollect my having verbally intimated the same,) yet as the Nabob Asoph ul Dowla has since represented Saadut Ally as an Object of Jealousy, and complained of the Protection granted to him by Nudjif Cawn, I move that a Letter be written to Major Hannay, containing an additional Instruction to him, to urge Nudjif Cawn to use every Means to prevail upon Saadut Ally to leave this Court and withdraw from his Dominions, offering him an Asylum in ours, if he shall have any Objection to return

to

to those of his Brother; but that Major Hannay be cautioned not to see Saadut Ally, or to hold any private or direct Communication or Correspondence with him; also that a Letter be written to the same Effect to Nudjif Cawn.

Agreed to the Governor General's Proposal.

Resolved, That the following Letter be written to Major Hannay, and that the Governor General be requested to write to Nudjif Cawn.

To Major Alexander Hannay.

Sir,

In Addition to the Instructions we have given you for conducting the Negociation with which you are entrusted, we direct that you urge Nudjif Cawn, by every Means that may occur to you, to use his Endeavours to prevail on Mirza Saadut Ally to withdraw from his Dominions, and to return to the Court of his Brother the Nabob of Oude; authorizing him, if Saadut Ally should, from any Apprehension of Danger to his Person, object to trust himself within his Brother's Territories, to offer him an Asylum within the Company's Possessions: But we desire that you will neither see Saadut Ally, nor hold any Communication or Correspondence with him directly or indirectly.

We are, &c.

Extract of Bengal Secret Consultations, the 30th October 1776.

PRESENT,

The Honourable Warren Hastings, Governor General, President,
Richard Barwell, Philip Francis, } Esquires.

General Clavering indisposed.

General Clavering sends in the following Minute relative to Nudjif Cawn:

General Clavering—The Letter which has been lately received from Nudjiff Cawn, and read the 24th Instant, is an Answer to the Letter written to him on the 10th June last, in which the Board offered him his Pension on Two Conditions, namely, the sending away the offensive Europeans, and the Dismission of Saudit Ally from his Court. In his Answer he has positively refused complying with either of the Conditions. The Offer of those Conditions was the Result of an unanimous Resolution of the Board, Colonel Monson being then present; which Resolution not having yet been rescinded by any other Resolution, the Orders now given for treating with Nudjiff Cawn, before he has complied with them, are not only informal with respect to the Propriety of the Board's Proceedings, but are more, a high Indignity to the Government itself. It appears to me, that the formal Manner of proceeding should have been to have moved the Board, that notwithstanding the direct Refusal that Nudjiff Cawn had given to the Two Conditions which had been proposed to him on the 10th June last, Major Hannay should still pursue his Negociation with Nudjiff Cawn; this Method of proceeding would have brought the Matter fairly before the Board, to have learnt from the Governor General his Reasons for prosecuting a Negociation so apparently derogatory to the Dignity of Government. The public Reasons assigned by the Governor General in his Minute of the 28th August, are founded on the Apprehensions which he then entertained of formidable Alliances, that were contracting by the Seiks, by Zabita Cawn and the King, against the Dominions of our Ally Asoph ul Dowlah; although I myself was convinced at the Time, from the Correspondence of Colonel Stibbert, that no Danger was to be apprehended from the neighbouring Powers, to disturb the Peace of Asoph ul Dowlah's Dominions, yet I was very much pleased to find that Opinion confirmed by the last Letter received from Colonel Goddard, and read on the 24th October last, wherein he mentions, that the Nabob has so little to apprehend an Attack from any of his Neighbours, that he recommends to this Government that the Nabob should be advised to lend his Assistance to the Ranna of Goad, now attacked by the Marattas. If this be the real Situation of Affairs in that Country, and that the Maratta Empire be so distracted with intestine Divisions as to be incapable of invading Bengal; I confess I cannot perceive what public

Reasons

Reasons can be offered for persevering in a Design of forming an Alliance with a Man who so openly set our Friendship at Defiance, by entertaining in his Service every Enemy to this Government, and to procure whose Assistance, in Case of an Invasion of Bengal by the Marattas, is the Object of the Treaty proposed to be formed with him. If nothing more however is meant than to procure a lucrative Commission for Major Hannay, I should imagine that other Means might be devised for that Purpose, without sacrificing the Honour and Reputation of this Government. To that End, as Doubts are entertained that the Nabob Asoph ul Dowlah has himself authorized Nudjiff Cawn to afford his Brother Saudit Ally his Protection, I beg Leave to recommend that a Letter be written to Mr. Bristow, to communicate to him the Suggestions of Nudjiff Cawn, and to know whether in Fact the Nabob has authorized him to grant his Protection to his Brother; because were that to be the Case, I should no longer be so strenuous as I am for his Removal from Nudjiff Cawn's Camp; in my own Opinion he only remains there in order to be near at Hand, to foment Divisions in the Government of Asoph ul Dowla, and perhaps to attempt something more, should a favourable Occasion offer.

Governor General—I object to the Proposals made by the General, to communicate to the Nabob Asoph ul Dowlah the Assertion made by Nudjiff Cawn, that the Protection granted by him to Saudit Ally was at the Nabob's own Instance, because it can serve no Purpose but to create an Animosity between them; but I shall approve of Mr. Bristow's being directed to enquire into the Truth of the Assertion, as he may obtain it by other Means, and if he can, to obtain and send us a Copy of the Letter alluded to by Nudjiff Cawn, if any such was ever written.

Agreed, That the following Letter be written to Mr. Bristow.

To Mr. Bristow.

Sir,

In a Letter which we have lately received from Nudjiff Cawn, he informs us that the Protection which he still continues to afford to Mirza Saudit Ally, is in Compliance with the Solicitations of the Nabob Asoph ul Dowlah, who has written to him on the Subject, and desired him to keep Saudit Ally from forming other Connections. As this is a Circumstance with which we could wish to be more particularly acquainted, we desire you will enquire into the Truth of it; and endeavour to obtain and transmit to us, without making any direct Application to the Nabob himself, a Copy of the Letter alluded to by Nudjiff Cawn, if any such was ever written.

We are, &c.

Extract of Bengal Secret Consultations, the 30th December, 1776.

Honourable Sir, and Sirs,

Agreeable to the Orders contained in the Honourable Board's Letter of the 30th Ultimo, I have enquired into the Truth of Nudjiff Cawn's having been solicited by the Vizier to grant his Protection to Sadut Ally, and prevent him from forming other Connections; and I find it very true, that his Excellency did write in this Stile to Nudjiff Cawn. In my humble Opinion the View he had in it was merely to keep up Appearances, for in case he had requested that Sadut Ally might either have been delivered up, or not received by Nudjiff Cawn, he was convinced his Request would not have been complied with. When the Gossagne and Dushein Cawn fled, Nudjiff Cawn pretended to receive them out of Regard to the Vizier; and the Vizier on his Part again has in some Instances received Nudjiff Cawn's rebellious Subjects in the same Way. They both of them in their Correspondence acknowledge these Acts as reciprocal Favours, but they have nevertheless been the Cause of increasing their Jealousy and Distrust of each other. For the Information of the Honourable Board relative to Sardat Ally's Reception by Nudjiff Cawn, I have procured Copies of the following Letters, which I do myself the Honour to inclose, viz.

One from the Nudjiff Cawn to the Vizier.
From Mirza Khalyle ditto.
The Vizier's Answer to the above.

In

APPENDIX, N° 166.

In procuring the Copies of these Letters, I have used the necessary Precautions to prevent his Excellency from being informed of it.

I have the Honour to be,
Lucknow, 18th Nov. (Signed) John Bristow,
Resident at the Vizier's Court.

Honourable Sir, and Gentlemen,

I am happy to inform the Honourable Board that on a Review of the State of Foreign Affairs there is a great Prospect of Security to his Excellency; but as many Circumstances have occurred of which it may be necessary to give particular Information, I shall endeavour to explain the Vizier's present Situation in the fullest Manner.

Notwithstanding the Appearances kept up between his Excellency and Nudjiff Cawn, I have great Reason to think they still entertain the same Jealousy of each other as formerly. In regard to the Vizier, I do not see any Cause that he has to be apprehensive of Nudjiff Cawn, as he still continues in great Distress for Money, and has been compelled to give a certain Extent of Country to the Sikes, to prevent their joining Zabiter Cawn; the Circumstances relative to which are as follows:

In the Month of August last, I informed the Honourable Board of the Conduct observed by Zabiter Cawn in respect to the Vizier. He did certainly endeavour to form Alliances with the View of invading Rohilcund; but the Awe with which the Name of the British Officers commanding so considerable a Body of his Excellency's Troops struck all Foreign Powers, together with the low State of Zabiter Cawn's own Affairs, entirely overset it. Upon this his old Enmity to Nudjiff Cawn revived, and he exerted his utmost Abilities to attach the Sikes to him, in order to invade and dispossess Nudjiff Cawn of his Dominions. Abdul Ahud Cawn increases their Animosities all in his Power, by writing inflammatory Letters against Nudjiff Cawn, both to the Sikes and Zabiter Cawn. The Scheme seemed to have succeeded, for the Sikes, in Conjunction with Zabiter Cawn, entered Hansey, Nudjiff Cawn dispatched Nudjiff Cooley Cawn from Dike (where he himself then was) with a considerable Part of his Army to oppose them.

The League appeared so formidable, that Nudjiff Cawn even proposed to march in Person, and had really moved his Encampment Three Coss out of Dike with this Intent, when he received Intelligence that Nudjiff Coolly Cawn had concluded a Peace with the Sikes on the 18th Instant, granting Gohana and Hansay Districts, yielding about Eleven Lacks Revenue, as Jaghires to their Two principal Chiefs, Gudge Sing and Hummer Sing, in Consequence of which they had renounced their Alliance with Zabiter Cawn.

I should imagine Zabiter Cawn will hardly be able to extricate himself from his present Difficulties, for Abdul Ahud Cawn has it not in his Power to assist him, and his own Army is very unequal to Nudjiff Cawn's; it is however impossible to speak with Precision of the Turn Affairs are likely to take, from the little Dependence to be placed on the Sikes, who, should they find it their Advantage, would in all Probability reunite with Zabiter Cawn, especially as I understand their Negociations with Nudjiff Cawn are not finally adjusted. Besides Gohana and Hansay as Jaghires, they are in Treaty for Hissar and Rotue, as Farms; a Compliance with this may perhaps determine them to abide by the Peace. Nudjiff Cawn has for some Time declared his Intentions of going to Delhi to pay his Respects to the King; at which Abdul Ahud Cawn expresses great Apprehensions lest it should be with a Design against his Life, or to displace him from about his Majesty's Person. I am however of Opinion, that he will not go, at least for the present, as the unsettled State of his Country, and the War with Zabiter Cawn, require his Presence elsewhere.

The Sikes on concluding the Peace, sent Nudjiff Cawn all the original Letters which they had received against him from Oboul Ahud Cawn, and thus encreased the Breach between them.

Saadut Ally still continues with Nudjiff Cawn, but is extremely dissatisfied with his Situation. Some short Time after his Arrival, he obtained for his own Support and that of the Two Battalions which deserted to him from Etaya, the District of Byana, yielding a nominal Revenue of Nine Lacks of Rupees a Year. Nudjiff Cawn now wants him to give it up, and promises him Mecret in Lieu of it, as a Jaghire. The Fact is, that he wishes to be rid of him, for Mecret is a District in Zabiter Cawn's Possession,

ſeſſion, which muſt be conquered before it can be diſpoſed of to him. I have every Reaſon to believe that he would be happy to return, but am ſorry to obſerve that the Vizier is ſtill as much averſe to it as ever.

On this Subject however I mean to make an ultimate and full Repreſentation to his Excellency, and then forward his Reaſons at large for refuſing to conſent.

The low State of Nudjiff Cawn's Treaſury has compelled him to reduce his Army very conſiderably indeed; a great Number of his People have deſerted him, in particular Madoc, who is now in the Service of the Rhana of Ghode.

In regard to the Sikes, they make Profeſſions to the Vizier, of preferring his Alliance to that of all other Princes, and propoſed a Treaty with him, in which he did not acquieſce; he approved of their Profeſſions of Attachment, and ſaid, he ever wiſhed to continue upon the beſt Underſtanding with them, and ſo long as they did not interrupt the Peace of his Dominions, he ſhould not form any Deſigns againſt them. Soorut Sing conducted this Negociation, and it was particularly given him as a Reaſon for rejecting a Treaty that it was unbecoming the Dignity of the Vizier, the whole Body of the Sikes hardly amounting to Seven thouſand Men, their Chiefs numerous, and none of them of the leaſt Conſequence.

It is aſſerted, and the Vizier himſelf gives Credit to it, that Fyzulla Cawn entertains a Correſpondence with all Foreign Powers, in order to form an Alliance againſt him: In my humble Opinion it appears to want Foundation. Fyzulla Cawn is certainly in a better Situation than he ever was before the War with Sujah ul Dowlah, and I cannot ſee what Inducement he can have for Defection. Before the War, he had, I underſtand, a Country of about Six Lacks; laſt Year he collected from his preſent Dominions about Sixteen Lacks; and this Year he has laid an Increaſe of Two Annas in the Rupee, which I am informed he will be able to realize without diſtreſſing the Country. He is eſteemed a Man of great Abilities as a Financier, and he does not ſeem to want them in any other Branch of Government; it is therefore impoſſible he ſhould be ſo weak as to forfeit the Vizier's Friendſhip, on which his Exiſtence depends. He has however been made to believe, that the Vizier wiſhes to deprive him of his Territories; and it is by ſome imagined, that conſidering this as a Fact, he is ſeeking Alliance to guard againſt it.

In the Intelligence of Timur Shah, he is ſaid to have ſent an Ambaſſador to that Court with a particular Commiſſion, inviting him to invade Indoſtan, and offering to join and pay him a Lack of Rupees a Day after he ſhall have reached Lahore. But admitting Timur Shah to be ever ſo well inclined to this Expedition, the Seiks would oppoſe his Paſſage through their Country; Timur Shah is himſelf now in Cabul.

I am very happy to inform the Honourable Board, that there is not any Appearance of the Marattas being this Year able to create the leaſt Diſturbances to the Vizier, as the preſent Diviſions in their own Government will employ their whole Attention; the Rhana of Ghode laid Siege to the Fort of Goalier, which is in their Poſſeſſion, and was obliged by Baboo Holcar to raiſe it; but after Madoc joined him, became too ſtrong for Baboo Holcar, whom he had compelled to retreat, and in a Skirmiſh he had with him, the Rhana took Five Guns and Two Elephants, and ſome Horſes; a Negociation was afterwards propoſed for a Treaty of Peace, to ſettle the Terms of which the Rhana deputed a Perſon of his Confidence to the Maratta Camp; but by this Day's Intelligence I learn that they treacherouſly Way-laid him, and I ſuppoſe the War will now be continued. The Rhana has made repeated Applications to the Vizier for the Aſſiſtance of Two Battalions of Sepoys, which his Excellency refuſed to grant; his principal Reaſons were the Lowneſs of his Treaſury, and the very weak State of his own Government in all Parts, but in the Daub particularly, owing to the refractory Behaviour of the Zemindars, who, under the Protection of their Forts, have hitherto kept that Country in a conſtant State of Warfare againſt the Aumil. The Rhana poſſeſſes a very ſtrong Attachment to the Vizier, whoſe Intereſt it might be to ſupport him in caſe his own Affairs would admit of it; but no poſitive Engagements had been made to him to give him Reaſon to expect Aſſiſtance. As the Vizier aſked my Advice on this Subject, I perfectly agreed with him in Regard to making the Settlement of his own Government the firſt Object of his Attention, and I thought it the more adviſeable to confirm him in his Reſolution, as the Honourable Board had directed me to recommend it to his Excellency, not to employ the Troops under Britiſh Officers on any Service but the Defence of his own Dominions, and he had no other to ſend upon this Expedition. I did not know likewiſe whether a Britiſh Officer, commanding a Detachment

tachment against the Marattas, might not be considered as improper, after the Treaty concluded at Poona.

From the above Relation of Facts, the Honourable Board will, I hope, be satisfied of the little Cause the Vizier has to fear the Attacks of any foreign Enemies. The Situation of his own Court is much the same as it was, for his Favourites have so much Influence in the Government, that the same Abuses still exist, and it will be extremely difficult to convince him of the Inconveniencies and Loss which result from them. The Measures of the Ministers perpetually clash with the Interests of the Favourites, who oppose every Thing they propose to the Vizier. I shall in a few Days write the Honourable Board fully on the State of this Government, and have for that Purpose procured a complete Statement of the Receipts and Disbursements which I am transcribing into English, and to which I must refer for Particulars.

It is with much Concern I observe the Want of Discipline, which still reigns in that Part of the Vizier's Army, not under British Officers; Two Battalions marched a short Time ago from their Stations to this Place, and demanded their Pay, which if they were not granted, they threatened to plunder the Town. The Vizier was obliged to comply with their Demands, and when he wanted to dismiss them for their mutinous Behaviour, they refused to give up their Arms, unless his Excellency would promise through me not to use any Violence towards them. The Night of the Mutiny I was sent for at Ten o'Clock by the Vizier, to be the Arbitrator between him and the Mutineers, which Office I however unwillingly took upon me, in order to prevent a Disturbance at Fyzabad; the Troops have gone to great Extremities, and compelled the Begum to pay them a considerable Sum of Money. The Particulars of this Disturbance the Honourable Board will understand from her Letter to me on this Subject, Copies of which I have herewith the Honour to enclose, No. 1. The Vizier, the Night before last, received Intelligence, that after the Mutineers dispersed, the Begum had thought proper to put her own People into all the Offices in the Town, and displaced his: That she had confined a Soubadar and some Sepoys, who were Guards in the Store Houses, seized the Gates, and published to the World, that she had bought the Town for the Money the Troops had exacted from her. The Vizier was extremely mortified at this Intelligence, and sent at past 11 o'Clock at Night to let me know that he had some very particular Business to speak to me about, and before I could return him an Answer to his Message, he did me the Honour to call on me. He complained heavily of the Begum's Behaviour, and declared, that if it was not for the Treaty he had made with her through the English, he would immediately order her Two principal Eunuchs to be capitally punished; he at first determined to send the Body Guard to Fyzabad, and retake Possession of the Town, but changed his Mind on my asking him, whether there was a Probability of any farther Disturbance; he answered there was not the least, as the Troops concerned in the Mutiny were all dispersed, and another Battalion had been ordered to Fyzabad, which would be arrived there by that Time. After many Propositions, he at last resolved on sending the Minister Hussein Reza Cawn, to which I advised him, knowing the Begum was well affected towards him, and that he would act with Moderation. The Vizier insisted on my immediately writing her a Letter, that Hussein Reza Cawn might set off with it before Day-break. I inclose a Copy of it, No. 2. I am inclined to think the Begum's Conduct has been exaggerated, in order to cause Ill-will between her and his Excellency; but I hope the Honourable Board will approve the Part I was obliged to take to moderate Matters.

I have the Honour, &c.

Lucknow, (Signed) John Bristow,
25th November, 1776. Resident at the Vizier's Court.

APPENDIX, N° 167.

Extract of Bengal Secret Consultations, the 4th November, 1776.

P R E S E N T,

The Honourable Warren Hastings, Governor General, President,
Richard Barwell, } Esquires.
Philip Francis, }
Lieutenant General John Clavering, indisposed.

READ, the following Letter from Major Hannay:

Honourable Sir, and Sirs,

I beg Leave to acquaint you that I arrived here last Night, and that by this Morning's Dawk I received the Nawab Nidjiff Khan's Reply to my Address of the 1st Ultimo; a Copy of which I have the Honour to inclose for your Perusal. It is so fully descriptive of his Situation, the Difficulties with which he is surrounded, and how he is circumstanced with regard to Sumroo, that it requires no Comment. His ready Compliance with the Pleasure of the Board, in the Dismission of Maddox, and the French in his Service, I humbly apprehend to be a favourable Indication of his Disposition to conform to that Mode of political Conduct which Administration may be pleased to recommend as most agreeable to the Interests of the Company; and I do not entertain a Doubt but he will fulfil his Promises with respect to the Fate of Sumroo as soon as the Necessity of his Affairs will admit. Nidjiff Kooly Khan, who is his principal Military Officer, is now detached against a numerous Army of the Sieks, who are assembled in the Neighbourhood of Delhi; and Sumroo's Troops compose a very considerable Part of the Corps which is under his Orders. Sumroo is in Person present with his Troops; and under these Circumstances, I beg Leave to submit to your Wisdom, how far it is in Nidjiff Khan's Power, at this Juncture, which has every Appearance of being so very critical to his Fortunes, and even Existence, to dismiss Sumroo, or bring him to the just Punishment of his Enormities.

I have acknowledged the Receipt of Nidjiff Khan's Letter, and acquainted him with my having transmitted a Copy of it to your Honourable Board, but that the Obedience I owe your positive Commands precludes my proceeding further.

I shall remain here until I have the Honour to receive your further Orders, and if they are not to proceed, I beg Leave to offer my most earnest Assurances that my utmost Zeal and Abilities shall be exerted to bring the Business of my Commission to a happy Issue.

I have the Honour to be, &c.

Chunargur, (Signed) Alex. Hannay.
October 19th, 1776.

Copy of a Letter from the Nabob Nudjiff Khan to Major Hannay; dated 22d Shawbaun, 18th Year of the King's Reign.

I have received your Letter, advising me that you have taken Leave of the Gentlemen of the Council, having their Permission to pay me a Visit; and that you will set out in Two or Three Days. You have written that the Entertainment of Sumroo is a Breach of Friendship with the English, and that while he remains with me you cannot carry into Execution your Design of paying me a Visit. You well know that the Entertainment of Sumroo was a Breach of Friendship in the ruling Powers of Hindostan [here follows an exact Copy of Extract from the Letter to the Governor General, entered in Persian Corespondence, No. 242, from "whence I took my Leave," &c. to "unsatisfactory Service."] I will also expel Sumroo in Time, but he is not at present in my Army.

Army. Proceed therefore on your Journey, and afford the Satisfaction of an Interview. Impart to me your Sentiments and Purposes, and observe the true State of Affairs here; and having satisfied yourself beyond all Doubt, inform the Gentlemen of the Council whether I am sincere, or whether you discover an Appearance of Deceit. I am faithful and true in my Friendship and Attachment: But should I immediately break with those Men, the Good which I have effected by my Efforts and Labour in a Course of Years, would at once be annihilated; and my Enemies, who are now in Ambush, would excite more Trouble than before. It is therefore necessary that I should consult Expedience, by preventing the Flames from blazing, and the Mischief from ensuing. I have already accomplished One Object, and will in Time accomplish the Second, be assured of it: And until I have the Pleasure of seeing you, favour me with your kind Letters.

The Secretary lays before the Board the following Note and Minute from General Clavering:

Sir,

The State of my Health not permitting me to come to the Board as I intended To-day, I desire you will lay the inclosed Minute before the Governor General and Council, for their Consideration.

I am, &c.

Calcutta, Nov. 4th, 1776. (Signed) J. Clavering.

The Disapprobation that I have on all Occasions shewn to the Measures of deputing an Officer of high Rank to Nudjiff Cawn, before an Answer could be received from him whether he would accept the Conditions proposed to him in Consequence of an unanimous Resolution of the Board on the 10th of June last, so fully evinces the Propriety of my Opposition to the Resolution taken by the Board to send Major Hannay on that Commission, that I need not add any further Arguments to justify it. The Answer received from Nudjiff Cawn, addressed to the Governor General and Major Hannay, are precisely what I expected, that he would not dismiss either Sumroo the Assassin, or Maddoc, or Saadut Ally Cawn; I must therefore beg Leave to propose that a Question be submitted to the Determination of the Board, whether the unanimous Resolution taken on the 10th June shall be rescinded, or not.

The Board must remember, that the only Reason assigned by the Governor General in his Minute of August, for proposing that a Treaty should be entered into with Nudjiff Cawn, was a supposed League forming by the King, the Seiks, and the Rohillas, to attack the Dominions of our Ally the Vizier. If the Board will take the Trouble of reading the last Letter received from Colonel Goddard, they will see, that so far is he from apprehending any Danger to the Vizier's Dominions from any of the neighbouring Powers, that he has proposed that the Board would advise the Vizier to march his Army to the Assistance of the Rana of Goad, attacked by the Marattas. He is besides confident that the Troops commanded by British Officers in the Vizier's Service, are fully sufficient to secure the Tranquillity of the Nabob's Country against the Ambition of any of his Neighbours.

In this State of Affairs, therefore, the Expediency of a subsidiary Treaty with Nudjiff Cawn seems to be entirely unnecessary, either for the Protection of the Nabob's Dominions, or those of the Company, the Object of the proposed Treaty.

If the Board shall be of Opinion, that the Resolution of the 10th of June should be rescinded, and that Major Hannay should proceed to the Presence of Nudjiff Cawn, I beg Leave to recommend that they would fix his Appointments, in order that the Court of Directors may know by the First Ship the Expence of this Deputation, as well as the new Grounds on which the Treaty is to be formed.

(Signed) J. Clavering.

The Governor General—I object to rescinding the Resolution, because it remains as it originally stood unchanged by the Objects of Major Hannay's Appointment. The Letter from Nudjiff Cawn is by no Means a Proof either of his Disaffection to us, or of his

 Disinclination

Disinclination to comply with our Requisitions. It appears from the Words of his Letter, that he has actually dismissed Maddoc, and the other Frenchmen, who were in his Service: I am informed by other Channels, that he has dismissed them; and I knew and foresaw that the Removal of Sumroo could not be effected without much Difficulty and Danger, yet I shall not propose any Deviation from Major Hannay's original Instructions, nor shall I recommend or consent that he proceed to the Court of Nudjiff Cawn while Sumroo remains in his Service. As the General has desired that Major Hannay's Allowances may be fixed, I recommend that his present Allowances be confined to the established Batta of his Rank, and Rupees 100 for a Moonshy, and from the Time of his passing the Boundary of the Company's Possessions, that his Allowances be fixed by those allowed to Colonel Upton, in the Proportion of their respective Ranks; I would further recommend, as it appears that the Account of Major Hannay's Expences is to be referred to the Court of Directors, that the Paymaster General be directed to draw out an Account of the Expences incurred by Colonel Upton's Deputation from the Day of his Departure, that they may be the better enabled to judge of the Propriety of the Expence incurred by Major Hannay, by a Comparison with those.

Agreed, That the Resolution of the 29th August be not rescinded.
Resolved, That the following Letter be written to Major Hannay.

To Major Alexander Hannay.

Sir,

We have received your Letter of the 19th of October, inclosing a Copy of Nudjiff Cawn's Reply to your First Address.

We are still of Opinion, that it would be highly improper for you to proceed to the Court of Nudjiff Cawn whilst Sumroo remains in his Service; we do not think fit therefore to make any Alteration in your original Instructions.

As long as you continue on your present Service at Chunar, you will only draw the established Pay and Allowances of your Rank, and 100 Rupees for a Moonshy; but we shall augment them from the Time of your passing the Caromnassa, if future Circumstances should admit of your proceeding to Nudjiff Cawn, in Proportion to those which were fixed for Colonel Upton.

We are, &c,

4th November, 1776.

Extract of Bengal Secret Consultations, 2d December 1776.

PRESENT,

The Honourable Warren Hastings, Governor General, President,
General John Clavering,
Richard Barwell, and Philip Francis, Esquires.

Read, and approved, the Proceedings of the 11th Ultimo,

General Clavering having sent in the following Minute before the Dispatch of the Nassau, a Copy of it is sent by a Number in the Packet by that Ship.

General Clavering's Minute in Answer to the Governor General's of November 4th Instant.

The Governor General objects to the rescinding the Resolution of the 10th June, "because, (he says) it remains as it originally stood, unchanged by Major Hannay's Appointment", viz. That till the Persons who are so obnoxious to the English, namely, Sumroo and Madoc, as also Syded Ally Khan, were removed from Nudjiff Khan, no Treaty of Alliance should be entered into with him. The Governor General must excuse me if I take the Liberty of contradicting him, and declaring, that by the Omission of Syded Ally in the Instructions to Major Hannay, the Resolution does not now remain as it originally stood, and therefore it ought either to be rescinded or enforced; if rescinded, then the Exception in Major Hannay's Instructions would only include Sumroo and Madoc,

doc, and not Syded Ally; if enforced, the latter would be included in the Exception with the former. The Governor General further says, that Nudjiff Cawn's Letter is by no Means a Proof of Disaffection to the Company, or his Disinclination to comply with our Requisitions; I cannot conceive what Idea the Governor General can form of Affection or complying with our Requisitions, when he will not allow that Nudjiff Cawn entertaining Sumroo in his Service, a Man who was a Murderer of the English at Patna, is not Disaffection, or his evading to send him away is not a Refusal of our Requisition. In regard to Madoc, and the other Frenchmen in his Service, I think the Words of Nudjiff Cawn's Letter are very equivocal; but I have written to Colonel Stibbert to be informed precisely of the Fact, whether they be sent away or not.

If the Governor General foresaw, as he declares, the Difficulty of removing Sumroo from Nudjiff Cawn, why, it may be asked, was he in such a Hurry to send the Deputation to him, particularly as he does not mean to recommend or to consent that Major Hannay shall proceed to the Court of Nudjiff Khan whilst Sumroo remains there? Had he thought proper to have retarded the Major's Departure till that Information could have been received, he would at least have saved the Difference between Half and Double full Batta of a Major, which is 22 and 10 Rupees per Day, that Major Hannay will draw more at Chunagur than if he had remained at the Presidency; the Governor General may think such a Sum trifling, as 8,000 or 9,000 Rupees per Annum, but it was Inattention to these and smaller Sums that occasioned the immoderate Expence of the Military Establishment before.

The Design of giving Major Hannay the same Appointments when he passes the Company's Territories that Colonel Upton has, is certainly just, as the Governor General must deem the Journey to Agra equal in Length and Difficulty to that to Poona, and the Majesty of Nudjiff Cawn equivalent to that of the Maratta State. But supposing even that Sumroo, and every other Impediment, were actually removed to the Major's Access to this powerful Prince, it is proper that the Company should have the Satisfaction of knowing what the new Motive for the Treaty is to be.

When the Governor General introduced to the Board, the Proposition of sending the Deputation to Nudjiff Khan, the formidable Alliance of the Seiks, of the King, and of the Rohillas, were alledged as the Motive. Whilst the Rains last, such a Bugbear might be held out, as it could not be contradicted; but at present, that we know from Nudjiff Cawn himself, that he is marching against the Seikes, to exterminate them as he had done before the Jauts, and that we are informed from Colonel Goddard, that the Nabob's Dominions are likely to remain in profound Peace, some other Motive should be assigned for the proposed Treaty, instead of the Reason which was given Two Months ago: I call therefore on the Governor General once more, before the Departure of the Ship under Dispatch, to declare his public Reasons for wishing to pursue this Treaty; a Treaty, if it is ever to have any Effect, it must be by affording Nudjiff Cawn the Means with the Company's Money of oppressing his Neighbours, or of invading Bengal with his Banditti, under the Pretence of defending it.

This is the only Light I can see it in; but if the Governor General has better Reasons to assign, it is proper that he should declare them, in order that the Company may judge, on the fullest Information, whether they will chuse to ratify it or not. I have been all along singular in my Opinion in the Council on this Business; but the full Conviction I have of the Rectitude and Propriety of it, persuades me, that the Company will not disapprove the different Steps I have taken to avert the pernicious Effects this Treaty must produce.

I desire that this Minute may be sent a Number in the Packet, accompanied with any Answer that the Governor General may please to give to it.

(Signed) J. Clavering.

The Secretary having waited on General Clavering with a Draft of the General Letter for his Approval, was desired by him to add the following Information, in the Paragraph which treats of the Nabob Asoph ul Dowlah; viz.

"Indeed Colonel Goddard informs us, that the Seiks have not come to any Agreement with Zabiter Cawn, and that he now apprehends no Danger from that Quarter; he therefore the more strongly recommends, that the Nabob be advised to grant Assistance to the Rhana of Gohud, who has been attacked by the Marattas."

Which having done, the Secretary again shewed the Letter to the Governor General, who made a further Addition to the same Paragraph, viz.

"Although

" Although the distracted Condition of the Vizier's Government, the reduced State " of the Finances, and his extreme and known Weakness of Mind, will still afford too " much Encouragement for the Attempt."

The Paragraph, as above collected, was circulated for the Approbation of the other Members of the Board, and the following Minutes were received upon it.

General Clavering—I object to the Part introduced by the Governor General, as it seems only introduced to deceive the Court of Directors, without any Authority from Mr. Bristow's Letters, in order to justify the proposed Treaty with Nudjiff Cawn.

(Signed) J. Clavering.

Mr. Barwell—I acquiesce to the Governor General's Addition.

(Signed) R. Barwell.

Mr. Francis—I am by no Means satisfied that the Dominions of the Nabob of Oude are in a State of Security, or that Nudjiff Cawn might not be usefully engaged in the Service of our Ally. If he will not previously dismiss Madoc and Sumroo, of course there can be no Negociation of any Kind with him. If he complies with the preliminary Demand, I then think that we ought to avail ourselves in some Shape or the other, of the Renewal of his Pension, (against which I stood singular in Council) and not give it him for nothing.—This was the Ground of my Assent to Major Hannay's Appointment; and I adhere to my Opinion.

(Signed) P. Francis.

Approved. (Signed) R. Barwell.

Extract of Bengal Secret Consultations, 2d December 1776.

The Governor General delivered to the Secretary the following Minute, with Directions that it should make a Number in the Nassau's Packet; which, after having been circulated for the Information of the other Members of the Board, was accordingly done.

Governor General—I hope it will not be expected from me, that I should give up my Time to a minute Discussion of all the Arguments, or to refute all the personal Insinuations which occur in the numerous Minutes, Dissents, and Protests of General Clavering, which have been entered in the Consultations, of the Public, Secret, and Revenue Departments, in the Course of the last Two Months.

Though the Measures of the Board have been chiefly confined in that Period to the Dispatch of current Business, yet in the daily Progress of it they have been opposed by the General with a Vehemency, suitable only to Measures in which the vital Interests of the Company were at their last Hazard.

The Appointment of Major Hannay to negociate the Terms of an Alliance with Nudjiff Cawn, though the inevitable Consequence of my own Recommendations made to the Court of Directors so long ago as the Year 1773, and approved by them, is ascribed to the Design of procuring a lucrative Commission for Major Hannay. To this End I am charged with sacrificing the Honour and Reputation of this Government; of loading the Company with an unprofitable Expence; and devoting Nations to Destruction; to those Reflections I shall not reply. While I remain in Charge of the Company's Interests, I shall endeavour to secure them by the closest Engagements that can be formed with Nudjiff Cawn, as the only Resource, besides our own Army in that Quarter, which can guard our Ally the Nabob of Owde, where Alliance is become both an Embarrassment, and a Danger to us; and eventually the political Interests of the Company, which are unfortunately connected with him. I regret that it is not in my Power to complete the political Barrier to this Country; my Influence and Authority are too circumscribed.

Whether a Zeal for the Interests of the Company, or a Desire to obstruct and embarrass those Operations of Government which he can no longer direct, is the Motive which actuates the General in his Opposition to every Measure which has been adopted since his Absence from the Council, I leave to the Judgment of my Superiors.

The Death of Colonel Monson, whose Memory I respect for the Military Talents which he possessed, and the Services which he formerly rendered to the Company, and whose

whose good Will, amidst the unfortunate Disagreements which subsisted between us, I studiously endeavoured to conciliate, having placed the superior Weight of Authority in that Scale which should constitutionally preponderate, but clogged with such Disadvantages of Instability and Opposition, as to render the Responsibility annexed to it peculiarly difficult and hazardous, I had determined to avoid all Kind of Innovation, and to confine the Influence which had thus unexpectedly devolved upon me, to the current and ordinary Occurrences of Government, and to such extraneous Objects as might eventually arise and occupy our Deliberations. I flattered myself, that the only Instance in which I should be obliged to depart from this Resolution, was in the Revenue, which the approaching Period for forming the new Settlement, and the Time required for the necessary Preparations of it, made unavoidable, and as a Decision must arise before this can be effected, and the Measures dependant on it carried into Execution, no possible ill Consequences can be apprehended from it. But the studied and vehement Opposition of the General upon every Occasion, as it encreases the Responsibility with which I am charged, must force me, in many Instances, to pursue a more decisive Conduct, and to act where I might otherwise only deliberate. Drawn into this Situation, I shall no longer think myself bound to observe that regular Attention which I have hitherto paid to every Minute of Controversy, but reserving to myself the Privilege of replying only to such as I may judge important enough to merit it, I shall pass the rest in Silence.

I expect to meet with Opposition and Obstruction in every Step that I take. It will therefore be the more incumbent on me to shun every Occasion which may divert me from my immediate Duty, by a Waste of Time in useless Disputation.

It is now the Third Year that I have endured a State of the most mortifying and unmerited Humiliation; my Conduct arraigned, my Character aspersed, and my Authority annihilated.

Impressed with the deepest Sense of Obligation to the Company, whom I have progressively served during a Series of Twenty-six Years in the most important Stations; to the Parliament, which invested me with the distinguished Office which had been assigned me, and to my Sovereign who nominated me to it, I resolved, though with inexpressible Reluctance, to sacrifice my Repose, and expose myself to that Persecution and unavailing Toil which I saw prepared for me, and which has continued, without the smallest Remission, from the Arrival of my Colleagues in Administration till the present Hour; persuading myself that the first Reference of Disputes of so alarming a Nature, would produce a final Decision, and if not determine the Victory in my Favour, at least relieve me from a Situation equally painful and degrading. The Disappointment of this Hope has been deeply aggravated by the Harshness of the Censures which have been conveyed through the General Letters of the Court of Directors in Terms of Severity, greatly exceeding those which have been experienced by any, even the most obnoxious of my Predecessors; how merited, it does not become me to say, nor will the Respect and Submission which I owe to their Decrees, permit me either to examine the Facts or Principles upon which their Reproaches are founded.

I can safely aver, that I have prosecuted the Company's Interests with the most ardent and disinterested Zeal, and with an unremitted Labour. If this be Profession, let my Administration be judged by its Effects. In what Period of the Company's Existence have they experienced a State of Prosperity, I will not say superior, but equal to that in which I had their Affairs in Charge?

Notwithstanding the Discouragements I labour under, and the Difficulties I must still expect to encounter, I will adhere to my former Declaration, of remaining in the Government, *until I shall be removed from it by Authority*, which I confess I shall regard as a more desirable Event than to continue under the present Circumstances of a feeble and disputed Influence.

With the Assistance of Mr. Barwell, on whose Support I most confidentlally rely, and I will hope for that of Mr. Francis, I shall endeavour to discharge the Responsibility so pointedly thrown upon me, so as to promote the necessary Dispatch of current Business, and least to embarrass those into whose Hands the Administration may be hereafter committed; wholly regardless of personal Consequences, and assured of leaving this Country, whenever I leave it, with the good Wishes of its Inhabitants, and meeting the just Applause of my Constituents, and of every discerning and impartial Man in the whole Country.

Fort William,
25th November, 1776.

APPEN-

APPENDIX, N° 168.

Extract of Bengal Secret Consultations, the 3d February 1777.

PRESENT,

The Honourable Warren Hastings, Esquire, Governor General, President.
Richard Barwell, Philip Francis, } Esquires.
General Clavering, indisposed.

Honourable Sir, and Sirs,

IN my Address of the 25th of November last, I expressed my Opinion of the Security of his Excellency's Dominions from Foreign Attacks, and I really thought, that however well inclined Nudjiff Cawn might be to come to a Breach with the Vizier, the distressed State of his Affairs, and the Conviction of the Inferiority of his Troops to the Vizier's, would deter him from such an Attempt. There is however no positively speaking on a Point of this Nature, as Nudjiff Cawn's People did, within these few Days, commit Depredations on the Vizier's Territories. The Circumstances were, that Nudjiff Cawn had besieged the Fort of Marsaan, the Possessor of which made his Escape, and some Marattas in Nudjiff Cawn's Service pursued him to Sasty, which is in the Vizier's Dominions, and they plundered the Country; but Colonel Goddard, through whom the Information of the Circumstances came, imputes this to the Licentiousness of the Troops, and not to Nudjiff Cawn himself. The Colonel has wrote to Nudjiff Cawn that he was convinced the Depredations were committed without his Knowledge, and therefore requested Restitution, and the Offenders to be punished. A Copy of the Instructions his Excellency was pleased to issue on this Occasion to Colonel Goddard, I have herewith the Honour to inclose.

In my Address of the 25th of November, I mentioned to the Honourable Board my Opinion of the Probability, that the Sikes would not abide by the Peace they had made with Nudjiff Cawn; but I now understand it is most likely to last, as the Chiefs, Gudjeput Sing and Ummer Sing, despair of any Reinforcements from their own Countrymen, and they consider Nudjiff Cawn's Force superior to their own and Sabiter Cawn's united. Nudjiff Cawn still declares his Intention of proceeding to the Presence, and afterwards to bring his whole Force against Sabiter Cawn. He purposes to solicit his Majesty to dispossess Sabiter Cawn of the Office of Myr Buxshy, and grant it to Saadit Ally, to whom he now professes the strongest Attachment. In Lieu of wanting him to give up Byaana, he has promised to grant him Futty-abad, and the Districts assigned to Sumroo for the Support of his Party; but this only appears a Pretence, for it is a doubtful Case if he will be able to dispossess Sumroo.

In regard to Saadit Ally's Return, the Vizier is still extremely averse to it, and I am afraid my Hopes of getting the better of his Excellency's Objections will not be accomplished; however, I shall refer Mr. Middleton to the Instructions the Honourable Board were pleased to give me on this Head. His Excellency excuses himself principally on account of his Inability to grant a Jaghier suitable to Saadit Ally's Rank, and that from the Situation of Affairs, he has nothing to apprehend from any Foreign Enemies. His Arguments may in some Measure be just; he however might with greater Propriety bestow a Jaghier on Saadit Ally than many others who possess them; and although there is nothing to apprehend at present, still this Tranquillity may not last; and whenever it should be interrupted, Saadit Ally will always be a Tool in the Hands of the Vizier's Enemies. In my humble Opinion, both for Saadit Ally's own Security, and the Interests of the Company, he could not be better situated than to reside under the Protection of the English, where, in Case of Accidents, the Government would also without Difficulty be able to conclude their own Terms with him, and he be convinced of the Propriety of them; but in the present Situation of Affairs, the Succession not being positively determined, and Saadit Ally considering himself independant, it might cost some Trouble to induce him to comply with the Company's Interests in the Manner he ought. I doubt if now Saadit Ally would wish to return without at least a Jaghier of Three

Lacks

Lacks of Rupees; however, I have endeavoured to ascertain this Point by getting his Vackeel to write to know his real Sentiments upon it.

The Power of the Jauts appears now to be on the Eve of being entirely extirpated, as Runjeet Sing remains in the Possession of the Fort of Commene alone, and he cannot make the least Head against Mahomed Beg Hammadapy, Nudjiff Cawn's Officer in that Part of the Country; and it seems he also despairs of obtaining any Assistance from the Marattas. The Rana of Ghode is likewise in a very bad Situation: He had but a short Triumph; for the Marattas have at length fallen upon the most effectual Means for ruining him. They have carefully avoided coming to Action, turning all their Views to plundering the Country and cutting off his Supplies, in which they have succeeded so well, that a few Days ago they carried off from Two considerable Towns, Money and Effects to the Amount of Three Lacks of Rupees; and Flour sells in his Camp for Two Seers a Rupee.

Raja Hindooput having died some Time since, his eldest Son, Sunnud Sing, succeeded to Nine Lacks of his Dominions, and his Second Son, Unrud Sing, to the Remainder, without any Disturbance or material Occurrence.

I have the Honour, &c.

(Signed) John Bristow.

Lucknow,
January 19th 1777.

Extract of Bengal Secret Consultations, dated the 21st April 1777.

PRESENT,

The Honourable Warren Hastings, Governor General, President,
Lieutenant General John Clavering,
Richard Barwell, Philip Francis, } Esquires.

Honourable Sir, and Sirs,

Since I last addressed the Honourable Board, I have received Intelligence, the Authenticity of which there is no Reason to doubt, that Saadut Allee, who was besieging Beeh, in the Beaunah Province, with an Army of about Three thousand Men, having attempted to storm the Place, was repulsed with great Loss, and after his Repulse surrounded by a Party of Marattas, brought by the Rana Kishoorey to the Assistance of the Jauts, and a Detachment of Pertaut Sing's Troops. After a short and most unequal Conflict, Saadut Allee's Forces were totally defeated, and he, with his People, obliged to retreat precipitately towards Deig, leaving most, if not all his Artillery, Ammunition, and Baggage behind him; he has reached a Place called Candoo, a few Coss distant from Deig, where it appears he means to wait until he receives a Reinforcement from Nudjiff Cawn's Army.

By the Public Accounts it appears, that Saadut Ally has lost upwards of a Thousand Men in the Repulse at Beeh, and subsequent Attack, in which are numbered many of his Sirdars and principal Officers, but as the Intelligence was sent off immediately after the Action, it may in this Particular be defective.

I shall do myself the Pleasure to address the Honourable Board To-morrow, on the Subject of my Negociations with Zyne-ul-ab-deen Cawn.

Lucknow,
20th March, 1777.

I am, &c.
(Signed) Nath. Middleton,
Resident Vizier's Court.

Honourable Sir, and Sirs,

I acquainted the Honourable Board, in my Letter of the 20th Instant, of the Arrival of Zyne-ul-ab-deen Cawn, Naib of the Doab; and I was in Hopes I should have been able, long before this, to have informed them, that some satisfactory Adjustment had been effected with him, by which I might hope to relieve the large Balance due from him, and secure the punctual Payment of his future Kists; to this End I proposed to him the raising a Sum of Money on Loan among the Merchants of this Place, at a moderate Interest, and making over a certain Proportion of his Revenue, to be appropriated in monthly Kists, to the Liquidation of this Debt; to which he was very willing to consent: But his Credit among the Merchants, and Men of Property, was so low, that even with the Security offered them, none would listen to his Proposals, unless I would become a Party in the Agreement, and pledge the Faith of the Honourable Company for the ultimate Security of the Debt; this was an Expedient I could by no Means agree to, for besides the Risk there might be in taking any Degree of Responsibility on myself, and the Impropriety of engaging the Honourable Company in any private Engagements of this Nature, it might possibly be supposed to invalidate their Claim upon the Vizier, to whom, as the Tuncaws he has given I presume can only be considered as collateral Security, we must ultimately resort for any Balances arising upon them. Upon the Failure of the Expedient I proposed, I could think of no better Method of guarding against the fatal Consequences of Zyne-ul-ab-deen Cawn's Mismanagement, than endeavouring to get from him Jaydaards to the Amount of the Balance now due upon my Tuncaw, and obliging him to enter into an Obligation with me, that the Revenue of the Districts thus assigned over shall be solely and entirely appropriated to the Payment of my Tuncaw; which he, after much Altercation, consented to; and I have the Pleasure to inclose the Honourable Board a Copy of his written Obligation to that Effect, marked No. 1. In order that I may have a sufficient Check upon him to prevent any Deviation on his Part, from the Terms of the Obligation he has entered into, I have appointed a Sezanwul over each of the Naibs on whom the Assignments are given, who, with the Consent of Zyne-ul-ab-deen Cawn, is invested with Authority to call upon the Naib for an Account Wasil Bakee of his District, to require regular Information of the daily Receipts of Revenue from every Purgunnah, and to take effectual Care that no Part of it is appropriated to other Uses. For the more particular Information of the Honourable Board, I beg Leave to inclose a Copy of my Instructions to the Sezanwuls, No. 2, which I flatter myself will evince to them that I have omitted no Precaution whatever, which could tend to the Security of the very heavy Demand I have upon Zyne-ul-ab-deen Cawn. The People I have sent in the Capacity of Sezanwuls are all Men of Credit and Ability, and as they will by their Stations gain a local Knowledge of the present State and Capacity of the Doab, I apprehend they will be the properest Men to succeed Zyne-ul-ab-deen Cawn, should it hereafter be found necessary to dismiss him his Aumildary; which I am of Opinion must be the Case, as he appears to possess neither Integrity or Ability equal to so important a Charge, nor has he been able to account, in any satisfactory Manner, for the Appropriation of the Money he appears to have collected; but an Investigation into this Matter would have taken up many Days, and have kept him from his Business at a most critical Period; and whatever Proofs of Delinquency might appear against him in the Course of such an Investigation, it would still be impossible to dismiss him from his Office, without risking the most mischievous Consequences: for at this Season of the Year no Men of Credit or Responsibility would take the Country but upon the most advantageous Terms to Government; I therefore thought it most prudent to appear satisfied myself, and to advise the Ministers to content themselves with taking every Means in their Power for the Security of the future Collections, suspending an Enquiry into Zyne-ul-ab-deen Cawn's past Conduct until a more favourable Opportunity. —I beg Leave to inclose the Honourable Board a List of the Districts which have been assigned over to me in Jaydaad, No. 3.—I have to remark, that I have made Choice of those Purgunnahs which have been represented to me as the most flourishing and the most likely to yield the Revenue at which they are estimated; but until the Sezanwuls arrive in the Districts, I cannot positively ascertain how far my Hopes may be realized, as I have little more than Zyne-ul-ab-deen Cawn's own Report to form my Judgment upon. If however, upon a local Investigation, it should appear that these Districts have been overrated, I will insist on their being exchanged, or having the Revenue of others assigned over to me to make good the Deficiency. As the Mode of taking separate Jaydaards seems best calculated to obviate large Balances upon my Tuncaws, I have adopted it in every District where I thought it likely the Collections would fall short, which I am sorry to say comprehends almost every one upon which I have any Demand, and the Description, with a very few Exceptions, might justly be extended to every District in the Vizier's Dominions. It is with Concern I exhibit to the Honourable Board so unfavourable a Picture of his Excellency's Affairs, but I should ill acquit myself of the Duty I owe my Employers, were I to conceal my Sentiments upon a Matter which appears of such serious Consequence to this Government. By the Accounts and Statements which Mr. Bristow transmitted the Honourable Board a few Days after my Arrival, they would perceive that the Nabob's Disbursements, at the Rate he is now going on, exceed his annual

nual Income many Lacks; but if those Statements are just, which from the best Information I have been able to obtain, I have no Reason to doubt, the Deficiency will be far more considerable than Mr. Bristow has supposed, he having formed his Estimate upon the Jummabundy of the Country without making any Allowance for Balances, which I believe I may venture to affirm will, at the Close of the Year, be little short of One Fifth of the whole estimated Revenue at the Time; as I have already observed, there is scarcely a District throughout the Nabob's Dominions that is not considerably in Balance. In this and the ensuing Month, 'tis true large Collections will be made, and the Arrears to that Time probably nearly paid up; but it is also equally true, that after that Period the Collections will bear no Proportion to the Kists. In this Situation I submit it to the Consideration of the Honourable Board, how far it may be proper to interfere in pressing the Nabob to regulate his Expences, either by a Reform in his military Establishment, or a Retrenchment in his civil Disbursements, so as to bring them more upon a Footing with the probable Income.

I have, &c.
(Signed) Nathaniel Middleton,
Resident Vizier's Court.

Lucknow,
21st March 1777.

Honourable Sir, and Sirs,

Accompanying I have the Honour to transmit you my Cash Account for the Month of February last. I have not yet received from Mr. Herbert his Receipts for the Two Sums specified to be paid him on Account of the Troops in the Field, but have wrote to that Gentleman for, and shall forward them as soon as they come to Hand.

I am, &c.
(Signed) Nathaniel Middleton,
Resident Vizier's Court.

Lucknow,
20th March 1777.

Honourable Sir, and Sirs,

Enclosed I have the Honour to forward you the Paymaster of the 3d Brigade's Receipts for the Two last Remittances made him, as charged in my Cash Account for February, transmitted the Honourable Board with my Address, under Date the 20th Instant.

I am, &c.
(Signed) Nathaniel Middleton,
Resident Vizier's Court.

Lucknow,
24th March 1777.

Honourable Sir, and Sirs,

I have just received Intelligence through an authentic Channel, that the Jauts under Runjeet Sing, reinforced by the Body of Marattas which lately defeated Saadut's Ally's Party, have pursued their Conquest to the Walls of Deek, and were actually preparing to besiege that Place. Nudjiff Cawn, some Days ago, detached Mahommed Beg Amdany with Three Battalions and some Irregulars, to succour Saidut Allee, but this Force is by no Means equal to the united Army of the Jauts and Marattas now assembled at Dick; and it is supposed, that he himself will be obliged to march immediately with the greatest Part of his Army, to maintain his Possessions in that Quarter.

Nudjiff Cawn is using all his Influence to persuade the King to accompany him to Dick, but his Endeavours have hitherto proved ineffectual, and all Accounts seem to agree his Majesty will shortly return to his Residence in the Capital, being wearied with fruitless Negociations, and more distressed than ever by the Cabals and opposite Interests and Views of his Ministers and Nudjiff Cawn. His Majesty's Expectations were raised to the highest Pitch by the flattering Assurances of Nudjiff Cawn, on his Arrival at Court; and the Extremity of his Distresses would probably have induced him to sacrifice the Cause of his favourite Minister to any Means of immediate Relief, but he soon discovered that Nudjiff Cawn had not the Power, nor, as he suspected, the Inclination, to afford him effectual Support; and being taught to suppose, that his Views were directed to an arbitrary and independent Controul over every Department, he chose rather to confide in the Attachment of his old Minister, than to throw himself at once into the Hands of one who he suspected

suspected would assume the entire Reins of Government, and leave him not even the Shadow of Majesty.

These are the Principles on which the King professes to have supposed the Influence of Nudjiff Cawn, but I apprehend he has suffered his Suspicions to counteract what would appear to be his true Interest; for however Nudjiff Cawn may in his present Situation be unable to assist his Majesty, he is certainly the only Person he can ultimately look to for Support.

I have, &c.

Lucknow, 29th March 1777. (Signed) Nathaniel Middleton, Resident Vizier's Court.

Extract of the Secret Letter from Bengal, dated 25th November 1776.

2. At the Period we wrote that Letter, we had received News of the Death of Elich Cawn, the Nabob of Oude's Chief Minister. Sorut Sing, the Naib of Rohilcund, was the Person designed by the Nabob to succeed to the vacant Appointment, but he declined that Trust, and it has since been conferred upon Hussen Reza Cawn, a Man who Mr. Bristow assures us is well inclined to promote the Interests of the Company, and to cement the Friendship which subsists between them and the Nabob's Government.

3. The Regulation of the Nabob's domestic Affairs appears to be the chief Object at present which requires the Attention of the new Minister, as the late Apprehensions of Danger suggested to us from that Quarter, on Account of Combinations said to be forming between the different Powers whose Territories lie adjacent to those of the Nabob's, have not been mentioned in the Letters we have received from thence since the Conclusion of the Rains. The low Situation of the Nabob's Treasury, the Dissensions in his Army, the subsequent Reduction of his Forces, and the Animosities which at that Time subsisted in his Court, no Doubt combined to raise the Expectations of the Enemies of his Government, and to cause in some Measure his own Alarms on the smallest Appearance of Warlike Preparations, or secret Negociations among the States in his Neighbourhood.

Cons. 24 Oct. 4. The fair Season being advanced without any Attack on the Nabob's Dominions, or any immediate Probability of such an Event, we hope it will not happen; indeed Colonel Goddard informs us, that the Seiks have not come to any Agreement with Zabita Cawn, and that he now apprehends no Danger from that Quarter; he therefore the more strongly recommends, that the Nabob should be advised to grant Assistance to the Rana of Gohud, who has been attacked by the Marattas. Colonel Goddard's Attention is taken up with training the Nabob's Army under his Command to Military Discipline, and establishing the different Corps after the Plan of the Company's Service, which will soon give them Consequence in the Eyes of the Country Powers, and consequently make an Attack on his Territories the more difficult, although the distracted Condition of the Vizier's Government, the reduced State of his Finances, and his extreme and known Weakness of Mind, will still afford too much Encouragement for the Attempt.

5. We have recommended to Colonel Goddard to be particularly careful that the Pay of the Troops under his Command be regularly issued and paid to them without any Stoppages or Deductions. We have also forbid the Officers in the Nabob's Service from taking any Concern in the Collections of his Revenues, under Colour of the Nabob's Tuncaws, or otherwise, from lending Money to any of the Nabob's Subjects, and from dealing in any pecuniary or mercantile Transaction with them.

6. Colonel Goddard has made an Application to us for an Officer to be appointed to the Chief Command of the Nabob's Artillery; but the Establishment of our own Corps of Artillery being too small to admit of our sparing any more Officers from it to the Nabob's Service, we were under the Necessity of refusing our Compliance. The Nabob also desired an Officer to hold the Post of Quarter-Master General to his Troops; and Colonel Goddard having mentioned this Application in one of his Letters, the Commander in Chief proposed Captain Primrose Thomson, whom you had recommended to his Notice, for the Appointment; but as we are not yet convinced of the Necessity for such an Appointment in the Nabob's Service, Colonel Goddard not having recommended it, and the Nabob who applied for it not being, in our Opinion, a competent Judge of the

the Propriety of it, we have for the present agreed that his Request shall remain suspended for further Consideration.

8. Major Hannay, who is now at Chunar, and has written to Nudjif Cawn from that Place on the preliminary Conditions of his proposed Deputation to him, will wait there till he obtains a final Answer respecting the Dismission of Sumroo. We have also directed Major Hannay to urge to Nudjiff Cawn, in the strongest Terms, the Necessity of his prevailing on Saudit Ally to quit his Court.

10. The Persian Correspondence sent Home by the Syren, will have furnished you with Copies of an extraordinary and peremptory Requisition from Shaw Allum, for the Amount of his Tribute on the Dewanny Lands. Our Reply, which first imparted to him your Sentiments on this Subject, was founded on your Letter of the 3d April 1775, directing the Suspension of all Payments on this Account till further Orders. Mudjeed O'Dowla, the King's Prime Minister, has lately renewed his Application in a Letter to the Governor General, in which he also desires an Interview at Benares, promises that he will perform the Journey himself, to accomplish it, on the Condition of our remitting 15 Lacks of Rupees in Part to the Presence, and he endeavours to make this Proposal as specious as possible by Assurances that "if we will attend to his Councils for the Space of One Year, "the Affairs of all Indostan should be disposed of so properly, that the Company will reap "Two-fold the Advantages they now receive."

APPENDIX, N° 169.

Extract of a Letter from Lieutenant Colonel Goddard.

Gentlemen,

IN a former Letter I had the Honour to address you, I mentioned the Situation of the Ranna of Gohud, and how much he appeared to me an Object worthy the Attention of this Government. I again request to recommend this Matter to your Consideration: The Marattas have entered his Country, and threaten to make themselves Masters of it, which they will easily be able to effect if the Ranna is left to himself. He has implored Assistance from the Vizier, and as his Country is so situated as to form a Barrier betwixt the Marattas and the Nawab's Dominions, it must surely be Policy to assist a Man whose Interest will always prompt him to be faithful to the Power that supports him.

The Intelligence from Delhi mentioned, that the King, disappointed in his Wishes of Protection and Countenance from the English, proposes throwing himself into the Arms of the Seiks, who have never yet come into any actual Agreement with Zabita Cawn, as he cannot comply with their Demands of a Sum of Money, the Payment of which they insist upon as a preliminary Article. Indeed there now appears no Grounds to apprehend the Vizier's Dominions will be attacked from that Quarter; and I am led to mention this as a further Inducement why Protection should be given to the Gohud Ranna, in which his Excellency will only act as an Auxiliary, and by a timely Interposition most probably prevent his becoming a Principal on some future Occasion, when the Marattas having conquered Gohud, shall find themselves powerful enough to make Incursions into the Vizier's Dominions.

I also beg Leave to represent to you the present State of the Nawab's Troops, which I can with Satisfaction affirm, from their Subordination and Obedience to their Officers, as well as the Degree of Discipline they have obtained, to be capable of executing every Service that may be required from them with Spirit and Fidelity. That Part of the Army in Rohilcund was the last which submitted properly to Authority, nor was it till after the Dismission of one of Captain Hoggan's Battalions that the Remainder stationed in that Quarter, intimidated by such an Example, made those Professions of Attachment and Submission mentioned in Captain Erskine's Letter to the Commander in Chief; and it is even since that Period, that they have consented to receive their Pay by the Calendar Month, to a Reduction of it, to Stoppages for Cloathing, &c. and to some other Regulations I thought it necessary to make on my first Arrival, putting them upon a Level with the Sepoys in the Company's Service.

Camp at Ferochabad,
October 8, 1776.

Thomas Goddard.

Extract

A P P E N D I X, N° 169.

Extract of Bengal Secret Consultations, dated the 5th May, 1777.

P R E S E N T,

The Honourable Warren Hastings, Governor General, President,
Lieutenant General John Clavering,
Richard Barwell, } Esquires.
Philip Francis, }

Read the following Letter from Mr. Middleton:

Honourable Sir, and Sirs,

By Intelligence just received from the Westward, I understand that the Rana of Goad has concluded a Peace with the Marattas; in Consequence of which he has restored to them all the Countries, Elephants, Guns, &c. which he had taken from them in the Course of the Campaign. It does not appear from the Accounts transmitted me, what are the Conditions of the Peace, or whether any Compensations have been made the Rana for the Advantage he has relinquished; it is certain, however, although he has supported himself with great Credit and Success against the Marattas during the whole Campaign, he has long wished for Peace, and probably was glad to purchase it on any Terms, more especially as a Detachment of Ten Thousand Men, with Twelve Guns, were on their Way from the Decan to reinforce Baboo Hulcar, at the Time the Peace was concluded, and have since actually joined him. This Army will now probably be turned against Nudjiff Cawn in the Jaut Country, with which View it is supposed the Peace was so hastily concluded with the Rana of Goad. Mahomed Beg Amdarny, who was some Time since sent with a Detachment against the Jauts and Marattas in the Neighbourhood of Dick, has had several Skirmishes with different Bodies of them, and been tolerably successful; but Two other of Nudjiff Cawn's Battalions, which were employed separately upon the same Service, have been defeated, with a considerable Loss of Blood, and the Whole of their Cannon, which they were obliged to leave behind them in their precipitate Retreat.

In my Address to the Honourable Board of the 6th Instant, I mentioned the Improbability of Zabita Cawn's obeying the King's Summons; but it seems likely that he will soon make his Appearance at Court; a Deputation having been appointed by the King to meet and escort him to the Presence. Lettafut Ally Cawn, from whom I derive my Information, is one of the Deputies.

I have, &c.

Lucknow, (Signed) Nath. Middleton,
16th April, 1777. Resident, Vizier's Court.

To the Honourable the Court of Directors for Affairs of the Honourable United Company of Merchants of England trading to the East Indies.

Honourable Sirs,

1. Our last Address from this Department, under Date the 27th March, was dispatched to you by the Ashburnham; we have now an Opportunity of forwarding a Duplicate of it by the Hector from Madras.

2. We had just received the News of Colonel Goddard's having subdued the Fort of Minpory in Time to communicate this Event to you by our last Dispatch. Although the Nabob's Troops had hitherto been successful in their Operations against the refractory Jemindars in the Doab, yet it was not without Loss on both Sides; and we considered that such violent Measures might tend to alienate the Affections of the Nabob's new Subjects from his Government, and at the same Time affect the Credit of the English Name; we therefore recommended it to him to try the Effects of more lenient and conciliatory Proceedings. We have, however, the Pleasure to observe, that the Reduction of the abovementioned Fortress has put an End to the Campaign, and that all the remaining Zemindars have come to an amicable Adjustment with the Nabob's Aumils.

3. We

3. We are informed that a Peace has been concluded between the Rana of Goad and the Marattas, by which the former has engaged to restore all the Countries which he has taken from the Marattas since the Commencement of their late Differences. Mr. Middleton supposes, in Consequence of this Pacification, that the Marattas will turn their Arms against Nudjiff Cawn in Support of the Iauts, who had renewed the War with him, and gained some Advantages over a Part of his Army in the Neighbourhood of Deig.

4. The last Advices which we received from Major Hannay were dated at Lucknow, to which Place he had gone for the Sake of a more ready Communication with Nudjiff Cawn on the preliminary Articles of his Deputation; and because Mirza Kaleel, a Person high in the Confidence of that Chief, resided there in the Capacity of his Vackeel at the Vizier's Court, and might be useful in promoting the Success of the Negociation. On Receipt of this Information we debated on the Propriety of Major Hannay's Conduct in quitting Chunar, and we beg Leave to transmit you a Copy of our Minutes on this Occasion.

5. The Governor General has laid before us a Plan for the Regulation of the Nabob's Troops commanded by British Officers, which is now under our Consideration; we beg Leave to send a Copy of it for your Information.

6. Mr. Bristow having brought down to the Presidency a Parcel of Jewels, invoiced at 2,35,451 Rupees, which remained of a Quantity received of the Nabob on Account of the Company, we have ordered them to be sold at public Auction on the 15th Instant, and should give the Nabob Credit for the Amount of their Produce, according to an Agreement made by Mr. Bristow with him for that Purpose.

7. We understand from private Advices, that Colonel Upton left Poona on the 7th March, on his Way back to Bengal, and that he was at Hydrabad on the 5th Ultimo.

We have the Honour to be,
Honourable Sirs,
Your most faithful humble Servants,

Fort William,
the 9th May 1777.

Warren Hastings,
J. Clavering,
Richard Barwell.